What They Wished For

What They Wished For

American Catholics and American Presidents, 1960–2004

Lawrence J. McAndrews

The University of Georgia Press
Athens

Parts of this book originally appeared in different form in the following publications: "Agents of Change: Lyndon Johnson, Catholics, and Civil Rights," in *Politics and the Religious Imagination*, ed. John H. A. Dyck, Paul S. Rowe, and Jens Zimmermann (London: Routledge, 2010); "Catholic Cacophony: Richard Nixon, Catholics, and Welfare Reform," *Catholic Historical Review* 98, no. 1 (January 2012): 41–66; "Lonesome Dove: The Pope, the President, the Church, and Vietnam, 1963–1969," in *Presidents and War*, ed. Anthony J. Eksterowicz and Glenn P. Hastedt (Hauppauge, N.Y.: Nova Science Publishers, 2010); and "Parallel Paths," *American Catholic Studies* 119, no. 1 (Spring 2008): 1–28.

Paperback edition, 2018
© 2014 by the University of Georgia Press
Athens, Georgia 30602
www.ugapress.org
All rights reserved
Set in Adobe Garamond Pro by Graphic Composition, Inc.

Most University of Georgia Press titles are
available from popular e-book vendors.

Printed digitally

The Library of Congress has cataloged the
hardcover edition of this book as follows:
McAndrews, Lawrence J. (Lawrence John), author.
What they wished for : American Catholics and American
presidents, 1960–2004 / Lawrence J. McAndrews.
xi, 503 pages ; 24 cm
Includes bibliographical references (pages 383–483) and index.
ISBN 978-0-8203-4683-0 (hardcover) — ISBN 0-8203-4683-7 (hardcover)
1. Catholics—Political activity—United States.
2. Catholics—United States—History.
3. Presidents—United States—History. I. Title.
BX1407.P63 M433 2014
261.7088'28273—dc23

2014932369

Paperback ISBN 978-0-8203-5386-9

To Nelly

CONTENTS

Acknowledgments ix

Abbreviations xi

Introduction 1

ONE Catholics and John Kennedy (1961–1963) 15

TWO Catholics and Lyndon Johnson (1963–1969) 51

THREE Catholics and Richard Nixon (1969–1974) 94

FOUR Catholics and Gerald Ford (1974–1977) 133

FIVE Catholics and Jimmy Carter (1977–1981) 169

SIX Catholics and Ronald Reagan (1981–1989) 198

SEVEN Catholics and George H. W. Bush (1989–1993) 249

EIGHT Catholics and Bill Clinton (1993–2001) 293

NINE Catholics and George W. Bush (2001–2004) 335

Conclusion 377

Notes 383

Index 485

ACKNOWLEDGMENTS

I am grateful to Scott Appleby, Kory Baker, Shannon Fasola, Kailin Olejniczak, Paul Schlegel, Merryl Sloane, and all of the archivists who helped me in researching and preparing this manuscript. Thank you to the St. Norbert College Faculty Personnel and Faculty Development Committees for helping to fund this project. Special thanks go to the readers of my manuscript, as well as to Beth Snead and Mick Gusinde-Duffy, who recommended it for publication by the University of Georgia Press.

LIST OF ABBREVIATIONS

AID	Agency for International Development
CAIP	Catholic Association for International Peace
CARE	Charity, Aid, Recovery, and Empowerment Act
CHA	Catholic Health Association
FAP	Family Assistance Plan
FY	fiscal year
HEW	Department of Health, Education, and Welfare
HHS	Department of Health and Human Services
HUD	Department of Housing and Urban Development
IDE	intact dilation and evacuation
INF	intermediate nuclear forces
LCWR	Leadership Conference of Women Religious
MX	missile experimental
NATO	North Atlantic Treaty Organization
NCC	National Council of Churches
NCCB	National Conference of Catholic Bishops
NCCIJ	National Catholic Conference for Interracial Justice
NCCW	National Council of Catholic Women
NCRR	National Conference on Religion and Race
NCWC	National Catholic Welfare Conference
NIH	National Institutes of Health
NOW	National Organization for Women
OEO	Office of Economic Opportunity
SALT	Strategic Arms Limitation Treaty
SDI	Strategic Defense Initiative
START	Strategic Arms Reduction Talks
UN	United Nations
USCC	United States Catholic Conference
USCCB	United States Conference of Catholic Bishops
WMD	weapons of mass destruction

What They Wished For

Introduction

THE REMARKABLE ODYSSEY of American Catholics has been one of triumph and trial. If Catholic presidential candidate John Kennedy's victory in 1960 marked the coming of age of the United States' largest religious denomination, the road leading to Catholic presidential candidate John Kerry's defeat in 2004 bespoke an arduous adulthood. Armed with a powerful message and represented by capable messengers, the American Catholic people have struggled to influence the greater society and the presidents who govern it. But rather than surrender to history, American Catholics continue to shape it. Though their country's reality has often fallen short of their church's expectations, the words and actions of American Catholics have dramatically helped to narrow the gap between the two.

The American Catholic People

The Catholics who first invaded America were the ultimate outsiders. One year after the first of Christopher Columbus's four voyages, Pope Alexander VI's 1493 bull *Inter Caetera* ("Among Other") conferred upon the Spanish monarchy the sole right to evangelize in the Americas. By 1565, Spanish Catholics had colonized Florida; by 1610 they had established New Mexico. In less than a century, they had launched a chain of missions along the California coast.[1]

These Catholics not only carried the cross; they wielded the sword. In California alone, within sixty-five years they converted over fifty thousand natives to Catholicism. But through high infant mortality, rampant disease, and hard labor, they killed at least as many. While other European-Americans would later mythologize their "settlement" of this "New World," Hispanic and Native Americans knew better. To victors as well as vanquished, it was, plain and simple, a "conquest."[2]

Tales of the conquistadores reached the "Old World," and French Catholics sailed first to Canada, then down the Mississippi River in search of souls and furs. British explorers followed, populating much of the northern and eastern reaches of the continent. Between the establishment of Jamestown in 1607 and the defeat of the French in 1763, British Protestants instituted traditions and passed laws that kept Catholics on the lower rungs of their nascent societies. In 1634 Catholics founded Maryland as a haven from persecution by the Church of England, but by the end of the seventeenth century, their tormentors had followed them there.

The American Revolution of 1775–1783 would greatly improve the fortunes of the 25,000 Catholics, mostly in Maryland and Pennsylvania, who survived the war. In 1789 the new nation's 22 priests elected their first bishop, John Carroll of Baltimore. Within two decades New York, Philadelphia, Boston, and Bardstown, Kentucky, had bishops too. By 1820 there were 122 priests, 9 bishops, and 124 churches for the 160,000 Catholics in the United States.[3]

From 1820 to 1920, over thirty million immigrants flooded the country, most of them from Europe and many of them Catholic. Irish, Germans, Italians, Poles, and French Canadians flocked to American shores, only to encounter nativism and neglect. Protestants burned Catholic churches in Philadelphia in 1844 to keep the Douay Bible out of the city's public schools, formed the Know-Nothing Party in 1850 to keep Catholics from holding public office, and founded the Ku Klux Klan in 1866 to terrorize anyone who was not like them. When the United States won its war with Mexico in 1848 and annexed one-third of Mexico's territory, the descendants of the Spanish conquerors became the second-class citizens of California and the American Southwest.[4]

Feeling under siege, American Catholic immigrants separated themselves not just from the mainstream Protestant culture, but from each other. They clustered in neighborhoods with others who shared their languages and cultures. They attended "national parishes," where only their kind were welcome. They sent their children to schools where they could learn their religion in their native tongues. In 1884 the American Catholic bishops sanctioned this segregation by ordering the construction of a parochial school for every church.[5]

Yet even as they shielded themselves from the worst aspects of the mainstream culture, they were benefiting from the best. The second and third generations of German, Polish, Italian, and French-Canadian immigrant families, beneficiaries of the work ethic that their ancestors instilled and the opportunities that their ancestors ensured, climbed the ladder to the middle class. And Irish-Americans complemented their own considerable economic progress by assuming disproportionate influence in the hierarchy of their church and the governments of their cities. In 1900, almost two-thirds of the Catholic bishops in the United States were of Irish descent. In 1928, so too was the Democratic Party's presidential candidate, New York's Catholic governor, Al Smith.[6]

By that time, the federal government, responding to a post–World War I outbreak of nativism rivaling its nineteenth-century antecedent, had imposed immigration quotas, which would largely remain in place until 1965. But while the numbers of the nation's foreign-born Catholics were descending, the fortunes of the nation's native-born Catholics were ascending. The Catholic population of the United States doubled between 1928 and 1960, exceeding the birthrate of non-Catholics. By 1960, thanks in large measure to the G.I. Bill for World War II veterans and the unprecedented prosperity that the war unleashed, American Catholics under the age of forty had reached a "rough economic parity" with their Protestant counterparts.[7]

Virtually every aspect of American life—economic, social, cultural, and political—was now accessible to Catholics. All, it seemed, except the White House.

The American Catholic Messengers

While the Americanization of Catholics in the United States in many ways undermined their allegiance to their church, it could not erase it. In an egalitarian society infatuated with change, many American Catholics found comfort in a hierarchical Church imbued with continuity. So even as governors, congressional representatives, and presidents were collecting votes, nuns, priests, and bishops were taking vows.

At the top of the American Catholic hierarchy was the United States Conference of Catholic Bishops. In August 1917, 115 delegates from sixty-eight dioceses and twenty-eight national organizations met at Catholic University in Washington, D.C., "to devise a plan of organization throughout the United States to promote the spiritual and material welfare of the United States troops at home and abroad and to study, coordinate, unify, and put into operation all Catholic activities incidental to the war."[8] In November this organization became the National Catholic War Council.

Two years later, World War I had ended, but the work of the council had not. The bishops renamed the organization the National Catholic Welfare Council, which included a seven-member Administrative Committee chosen by the bishops and a general secretary picked by the Administrative Committee. They also established the Executive and Legal Departments and the Departments of Education, Social Action, and Lay Organizations, each to be chaired by a member of the Administrative Committee.[9] In 1922, the Holy See approved the council, which then became the National Catholic Welfare Conference. In 1966 the NCWC split into the National Conference of Catholic Bishops, in charge of canonical matters, and the United States Catholic Conference, dealing with civil issues. In 2001 the two entities became one, the United States Conference of Catholic Bishops.[10]

By 1960, as Catholics became more American and politics became more national, the bishops had become more visible. Along with the popes in Rome, the bishops in the United States would therefore play a prominent role not only in the narrative of their church, but in the direction of their country. Within the next four decades, their conference would grow to represent almost seventy million Catholics in 195 sees through thirty-four standing, fifteen ad hoc, and five executive committees with a budget of $130 million and branches in all fifty states. Their effectiveness in leading the Church would help determine their success in affecting the nation. And the American people, inside and outside of the Church, would be the final arbiters of both.[11]

The American Catholic Message

The word "catholic" means "universal," so the teachings of the Church honor no specific time or place. Yet on the issues of war and peace, social justice, and life and death, which have been central to papal encyclicals and episcopal pastorals, they have proven especially relevant to the politics and policies of U.S. presidents since 1960.

The fundamental tenet of the Roman Catholic Church on matters of war and peace is the "just-war" doctrine. The doctrine traces its roots to the early fifth century, when St. Augustine of Hippo reacted to the Christian sacking of pagan Rome by defending violence only as a last resort. At the height of the Crusades in the thirteenth century, St. Thomas Aquinas justified war by Christians against infidels, but only when living alongside them became untenable.[12] Building upon the foundations of Augustine and Aquinas, just-war theory came to encompass the right to wage war (*jus ad bellum*), the manner of waging war (*jus in bello*), and the manner of making peace (*jus post bellum*).

Jus ad bellum must incorporate the following:

(a) the cause is just;
(b) the justice of the cause is sufficiently great as to warrant warfare and does not negate countervailing values of equal or greater weight;
(c) on the basis of available knowledge and a reasonable assessment of the situation, one must be as confident as one reasonably can be of achieving one's just objective without yielding longer-term consequences that are worse than the status quo;
(d) warfare is genuinely a last resort: all peaceful alternatives that may also secure justice to a reasonable and sufficient degree have been exhausted;
(e) one's own moral standing is not decisively compromised with respect to the waging of war in this instance;

(f) even if the cause is just, the resort to war is actually motivated by that cause and not some other (hidden) reason;

(g) one has a legitimate, duly constituted authority with respect to the waging of war: one has the right to wage it; and

(h) one must publicly declare war and publicly defend that declaration on the basis of items (a)–(g), and subsequently be prepared to be politically accountable for the conduct and aftermath of the war, based on the criteria of *jus in bello* and *jus post bellum*.

Jus in bello must include:

(i) discrimination in the selection of targets: avoiding the direct targeting of those not directly participating in the immediate conduct of war, and taking all reasonable measures possible to avoid casualties among such non-participants;

(j) the doctrine of double effect: the foreseeable deaths of "innocents" do not render a war unjust so long as they are not directly intended as the object of policy but are the unavoidable side effect of a use of force justified by the other criteria of the theory;

(k) proportionality in the use of force required to secure the just objectives;

(l) just treatment of all noncombatants, including prisoners of war and noncombatants in the wider arena of the war; and

(m) one must observe all national and international laws governing the conduct of war that do not fundamentally conflict with the theory's often moral requirements.

Jus post bellum must include:

(n) helping to establish peace terms that are proportionately determined to make the peace just and stable as well as to redress the injustices that prompted the conflict;

(o) taking full responsibility for one's fair share of the material burdens of the conflict's aftermath in constructing a just and stable peace; and

(p) taking a full and proactive part in the processes of forgiveness and reconciliation, which are central to the constructing of a just and stable peace.

Just-war theory also allows for a "supreme emergency exemption." In such a contingency, a combatant may suspend the criteria of discrimination.[13]

Accepting defensive war, however, did not mean condoning all war. According to the Second Vatican Council's *Pastoral Constitution on the Church in the Modern World* (1965), total war "aimed at the destruction of entire cities or extensive areas along with their populations is a crime against man and God himself," which "merits unequivocal and unhesitating condemnation."[14] And nuclear war promised nothing short of complete annihilation. Thus did the American Catholic bishops construct their 1983 pastoral, "The Challenge of Peace," to all but forswear any use of nuclear weapons. In 1990 *La Civilta Cattolica*, the Rome-based Jesuit periodical that speaks unofficially for the pope, added that even a non-nuclear war, because it renders obsolete the criterion of noncombatant immunity, is "morally unacceptable, whatever the reasons given for its justification," except in the most extreme case of "defending oneself from a grave aggression."[15]

The threat of terrorists acquiring weapons of mass destruction, awakened by Al Qaeda's September 11, 2001, attacks on the United States, provoked the bishops to issue their November 2001 pastoral, "Living with Faith and Hope after September 11," in which they invoked the just-war criteria to support the American invasion of Afghanistan while urging the United States to accelerate its efforts to "reverse the spread of nuclear, chemical, and biological weapons." By challenging the *jus ad bellum* prerequisites of necessity and last resort as well as the *jus in bello* requirements of proportionality and discrimination, President George W. Bush's 2002 doctrine of preemptive war failed to persuade the bishops.[16]

In the area of social justice, the Church has a long history of repudiating the excesses of the Right and the Left. Even before the birth of modern ideologies like capitalism and communism, St. Thomas Aquinas was defining "general justice" as the pursuit of the "common good." To this first principle he would add "distributive justice," which dictated the "subsidiarity" of society, and "commutative justice," which required the "solidarity" of society in the quest for the common good.[17]

Pope Leo XIII tailored these themes to the modern age in his 1893 encyclical, *Rerum Novarum* ("Of New Things"), in which he defended collective bargaining and private property, while condemning the extremes of socialism and unchecked capitalism. Though the American Catholic bishops were slow to embrace the encyclical, a quarter century later they transcended it with a resounding proclamation of their own. Authored by the progressive intellectual Rev. John Ryan, the 1919 "Bishops' Program of Social Reconstruction" espoused a minimum wage, collective bargaining, and old-age and disability insurance more than a decade before Franklin Roosevelt's New Deal legislated these ideas into the American social fabric.[18]

In his 1931 encyclical, *Quadragesimo Anno* ("The Fortieth Year"), Pope Pius XI expanded upon *Rerum Novarum* as the Church became even less enamored of the employer and more empathetic toward the employee. "Every effort, therefore," Pius XI wrote, "must be made that at least in [the] future only a fair share of the fruits of the production be permitted to accumulate in the hands of the wealthy, and that an ample sufficiency be supplied to the working men." Pope John XXIII's encyclical *Mater et Magistra* ("Mother and Teacher") in 1961 further aligned the Church with the mission of the modern welfare state. "What could be clearer," Protestant theologian Reinhold Niebuhr commented on the encyclical, "than that the path from the Thomistic theory of a just price based upon labor value, to the theory of Adam Smith, guaranteeing social justice by the automatic balances of a free market, descends steeply from the heights of justice to the morass of private greed?"[19]

In the eyes of the American Catholic bishops, this descent became a free fall in the 1980s, as the twice-elected president Ronald Reagan proclaimed that "government is the problem," and the fictional Wall Street tycoon Gordon Gecko declared that "greed is good." The bishops thus issued the countercultural 1986 pastoral "Economic Justice for All," whose scathing critique of Reaganomics aimed to stir the consciences of Catholic managers just as Popes Leo, Pius, and John had raised the hopes of Catholic workers. By this time, the bishops' message was a familiar refrain. Of their almost two hundred statements and pastorals from 1966 to 1988, over half discussed questions of social justice.[20]

Among matters of life and death, the Church had long objected to artificial contraception and abortion. Pope Pius IX condemned abortion in 1864, and by 1869 the Church was excommunicating Catholic physicians who performed abortions. Over the next century in the United States, despite little pressure from Catholic outsiders, the federal government banned the distribution of contraceptive materials through the mail, and many states restricted abortion. Pope Pius XI's 1930 encyclical, *Casti Connubi* ("Of Chaste Marriage"), rejected unnatural means of birth control. In 1951 Pope Pius XII endorsed the "rhythm method" by which Catholic couples could limit childbearing by restricting sex to the woman's sterile period.[21] That same year, the National Catholic Welfare Conference established its Family Life Bureau, which coupled support for a "family living wage" with opposition to artificial contraception. The American Catholic bishops' 1959 statement rejected any public assistance that promoted birth control or abortion. In 1966, the bishops formed the National Right to Life Committee, headed by Rev. James McHugh. The committee would remain in the NCWC for seven years before declaring its independence, though remaining predominantly Catholic.[22]

In his 1968 encyclical, *Humanae Vitae* ("Of Human Life"), Pope Paul VI asserted that the only morally acceptable means of birth control was the natural cycle of fertility. The American Catholic bishops upheld the ban on artificial contraception, while also proscribing abortion, in their 1968 pastoral, "Human

Life in Our Day." When the Supreme Court in *Roe v. Wade* in 1973 overturned state laws outlawing abortion in the first six months of pregnancy, the bishops inaugurated the Committee for Pro-Life Activities and opened pro-life offices in almost every diocese. In numerous subsequent statements, they established the abolition of abortion as their primary political priority. By 1984 they had adopted the formulation of Joseph Cardinal Bernardin of Chicago that the Church adhered to a "consistent ethic of life," which portrayed opposition to abortion, euthanasia, and capital punishment as threads in a "seamless garment."[23]

In 2004 the Vatican's Pontifical Council for Justice and Peace systematized the Church's teachings in the *Compendium of the Social Doctrine of the Church*. Thus did the Church apply the Catholic messages on war and peace, social justice, and life and death to the modern era. It remained, however, for that message to reach beyond the pulpits and the pastorals, from houses of worship all the way to the White House.

American Catholics and the Presidents

In 1960 Catholic Democratic senator John Kennedy of Massachusetts won the presidential election with the votes of over three-quarters of the electorate from his church. In 2004, however, Catholic Democratic senator John Kerry of Massachusetts lost the presidential election with fewer than half of the ballots from his church. In a little over four decades, most American Catholics had gone from celebrating to repudiating one of their own, authoring a story that historians have yet to tell.

James Hennesey's *American Catholics* (1981), Lawrence Cunningham's *The Catholic Heritage* (1983), Jay Dolan's *The American Catholic Experience* (1992) and *In Search of an American Catholicism* (2002), Charles Morris's *American Catholic* (1997), Mark Massa's *Catholics and American Culture* (1999), John McGreevy's *Catholicism and American Freedom* (2003), Patrick Carey's *Catholics in America* (2004), and James Fisher's *Communion of Immigrants* (2008) have all told the narrative of the Catholic rise from European rags to American riches. These are general surveys of the socioeconomic and cultural trajectory of American Catholics from their roots in the Spanish conquest of the sixteenth century to their role in the Mexican migration of the twenty-first.[24]

Others have acknowledged the importance of Catholics in the election of American presidents. Mary Hanna's *Catholics and American Politics* (1979), George Gallup and Jim Castelli's *The American Catholic People* (1987), William Prendergast's *The Catholic Voter in American Politics* (1999), Margaret O'Brien Steinfels's *American Catholics, American Culture* (2004), Kristin Heyer, Mark

Rozell, and Michael Genovese's *Catholics and Politics* (2008), and Deal Hudson's *Onward, Christian Soldiers* (2008) have examined the considerable, and complex, impact of the "Catholic vote." Timothy Byrnes's *Catholic Bishops in American Politics* (1991), Thomas Reese's *A Flock of Shepherds* (1992), Michael Warner's *Changing Witness* (1995), and Hugh Heclo and Wilfred McClay's *Religion Returns to the Public Square* (2003) have explored the role of the American Catholic bishops in shaping the nation's political dialogue before, during, and after presidential campaigns.[25]

Catholics also figure prominently in studies of specific issues and events, such as George Weigel and James Turner Johnson's *Just War and the Gulf War* (1991), John McGreevy's *Parish Boundaries: The Catholic Encounter with Race in the Twentieth Century Urban North* (1996), Donald Critchlow's *Intended Consequences: Birth Control, Abortion, and the Federal Government in Modern America* (1999), Leslie Tentler's *Catholics and Contraception* (2004), David Settje's *Faith and War* (2011), and my *Broken Ground: John F. Kennedy and the Politics of Education* (1991) and *The Era of Education: The Presidents and the Schools, 1965–2001* (2006). A single article, Thomas Carty's "White House Outreach to Catholics," offers a broad overview of relations between American Catholics and American presidents from Franklin Roosevelt to George W. Bush.[26]

This book is the first study to examine the political ascendancy of American Catholics between Kennedy's victory and Kerry's defeat. In arguing that American Catholics have had much to say about the leadership of their country during this era, I challenge the conventional narrative of the increasingly secular decades of the 1960s and 1970s, as reflected by the Supreme Court's outlawing of school prayer and legalization of abortion, followed by the inevitable backlash of the 1980s and 1990s, as demonstrated by the rise of evangelical Protestants and the election of a Republican Congress. Throughout these tumultuous times, many American Catholics warily yet wisely negotiated the political landscape by taking on the courts, playing off the political parties, fending off other churches, and fighting off the critics within their own ranks. The more their adversaries told them to stay out of politics, the further these Catholics, led by their popes and bishops, waded in. Although Catholics never found shelter from the prevailing political winds of this era, they often were effective in steering those currents in the direction of the Church.

Each of the administrations from Kennedy's to Kerry's opponent, Methodist George W. Bush's, marked setbacks as well as successes for American Catholics on matters of war and peace, social justice, and life and death. During the presidency of John Kennedy (1961–1963), the predominant concern of war and peace was the Cold War between the United States and the Soviet Union. Like Kennedy, his church grappled with the nuclear arms race, which invited the Cuban missile crisis of October 1962 and the nuclear test ban that followed it. The primary issue of social justice was civil rights. Like Kennedy, American Catholics found themselves at various times on all sides of the issue—effecting yet postponing change, moving with courage yet caution. The major subject related to life and death was artificial contraception. Like Kennedy, American Catholics were torn between the population boom in emerging countries, about which their government and the Church were apprehensive, and the means of addressing it, which their president approved but their pope did not.

The dominant issue of war and peace during the Lyndon Johnson presidency (1963–1969) was the Vietnam War. Like his administration, American Catholics began Johnson's presidency largely endorsing the escalation of the conflict in the name of Cold War containment, yet ended it plagued by doubt and division. On the preeminent social justice concern of the day, civil rights, Johnson produced the legislation that Kennedy had only been able to propose. And American Catholics again contributed to both sides of the country's racial divide: participating in the revolution of the Civil Rights Act of 1964, the Voting Rights Act of 1965, and the Fair Housing Act of 1968, as well as in the counterrevolution of white backlash and white flight that these landmark laws unwittingly evoked. The ferment of the anti–Vietnam War and civil rights movements helped fuel a rejection of all forms of authority, which ushered in the counterculture, cost Johnson his job, and, along with the dramatic changes at the Second Vatican Council (1962–1965), turned most American Catholics against their church on the life-and-death matter of birth control. While Pope Paul VI's *Humanae Vitae* (1968) was proscribing artificial contraception, Sargent Shriver, the Catholic architect of Johnson's War on Poverty, was prescribing it as part of a solution to the nation's urban crisis.

Richard Nixon's presidency (1969–1974) was at once the continuation and the circumscription of the Johnson administration. In the realm of war and peace, Nixon's gradual end to the Vietnam conflict and expansion of its boundaries into Cambodia incited the Catholic Left and alienated the Catholic hierarchy. In the area of social justice, Nixon's Family Assistance Plan welfare reform proposal attracted liberals with its minimum income guarantee, conservatives with its work requirement, and many American Catholics with its combination of both, only to die on Capitol Hill. Abortion entered the life-and-death arena like a lamb on January 22, 1973, with the Supreme Court's *Roe v. Wade* decision, which was overshadowed by Lyndon Johnson's death on the same day. It would soon become a lion, however, as Nixon was only the first in a long line of presidents who would hear from the U.S. Catholic bishops about their principal preoccupation.

When Watergate sank Nixon, Gerald Ford took his abbreviated turn in the

White House (1974–1977). As the Vietnam civil war ended with the president and the Congress blaming each other for the communists' victory, many American Catholics joined the administration in turning their attention from war to peace, and to the question of resettling Indochinese refugees. On the overriding social justice issue of world hunger, Ford shared the concern of many American Catholics, if not their price tag, for feeding the hungry abroad during a recession at home. And as the first post–*Roe v. Wade* election neared, Ford and his opponent, Jimmy Carter, clashed over the life-and-death repercussions of abortion, foreshadowing the hardening of the Republicans' "pro-life" and the Democrats' "pro-choice" positions four years later.

With Vietnam a painful memory, Jimmy Carter's presidency (1977–1981) focused in the area of war and peace on continuing the détente of the Nixon and Ford years, recognizing China and signing the Strategic Arms Limitation Treaty II with the Soviet Union in 1979. The Soviets' invasion of Afghanistan later that same year scuttled the best-laid plans of Carter and many American Catholics, led by University of Notre Dame president Rev. Theodore Hesburgh, to obtain Senate ratification of the treaty. In the realm of social justice, Carter's attempt at national health insurance attracted considerable Catholic support, but fell to interest group and congressional resistance as well as his own fiscal reservations. While abortion continued to raise its profile as a life-and-death issue, many American Catholics reluctantly accepted Carter's studied ambiguity—personally opposed to abortion, against federal funding, and yet effectively pro-choice in his policies.

Ronald Reagan's presidency (1981–1989) endeared itself to many Americans, including a majority of Catholics, by offering the certainty that had eluded Carter. But for some Catholics, Reagan was *too* sure of himself. On war and peace, Reagan's increases in defense spending and combative rhetoric toward the Soviets led the bishops to write "The Challenge of Peace," which advocated their version of a nuclear freeze. In the name of social justice, the bishops penned "Economic Justice for All," a pastoral highly critical of Reagan's reductions in taxes on the rich and in expenditures for the poor. On abortion, however, the bishops remained in Reagan's corner, arguing that on this life-and-death issue, Reagan's politics, if not all of his policies, were a marked improvement over his predecessor's.

The presidency of George H. W. Bush (1989–1993), though sometimes called Reagan's third term, in other ways echoed Carter's zigs and zags. On matters of war and peace, Bush finished what Reagan and Pope John Paul II had begun—the ending of the Cold War, which liberated the long-suffering Catholics of Eastern Europe and the pontiff's native Poland—but he opened the Persian Gulf to an American war, which severed the Catholic faithful, who applauded it, from the hierarchy, who questioned it. After daring his audience to "read my lips" as he denounced tax increases, he signed one, discouraging Reagan Catholics but encouraging the bishops, who welcomed more federal spending for the nation's decaying cities in the name of social justice and in the wake of the 1992 Los Angeles riots. The Supreme Court's *Webster v. Reproductive Health Services* (1989) and *Planned Parenthood v. Casey* (1992) verdicts were in some ways the perfect metaphors for the Bush era on matters of life and death—restricting *Roe v. Wade* by permitting parental consent and a waiting period before abortions, yet upholding *Roe v. Wade* as the law of the land. Bush, like many American Catholics, had wanted the Court to overturn *Roe*, but neither he nor they put up much of a fight when it didn't.

Bill Clinton (1993–2001) became the first Democratic president to be elected twice since Franklin Roosevelt and became the first impeached president since Andrew Johnson. On war and peace, Clinton sent U.S. warplanes and peacekeepers into the former Yugoslavia, prompting many American Catholics to invoke the just-war doctrine against the Serbs of Slobodan Milošević, whose "ethnic cleansing" of Croats, Bosnian Muslims, and Kosovar Albanians seemed to offer a textbook case. In the area of social justice, Clinton resurrected Carter's health care reform effort, dividing Catholics in the process. As with Carter, even a Congress controlled by the president's party could not enact his plan. On the life-and-death issue of abortion, Clinton outraged the Church hierarchy by reversing the policies of his Republican predecessor, and he antagonized the rank and file by twice vetoing bans on "partial-birth" abortion.

With the first term of the George W. Bush presidency (2001–2004), Americans ushered in a new century and a new era. In regard to war and peace, they witnessed the first attack on American soil since Pearl Harbor. Pope John Paul II and the U.S. Catholic bishops joined most Americans in backing the retributive invasion of Afghanistan in the aftermath of 9/11, but they considered the preemptive strike on Iraq an "unjust" war. Bush's perceived "toughness" against terrorism nonetheless helped him win most Catholic votes in his victory over Kerry in 2004. Bush also heartened most of the Catholic clergy and laity with his "faith-based" social justice initiative, by which the federal government would subsidize church-related programs at historic levels, even though the Congress of his own party refused to give him most of what he requested. Bush enlisted the support of most Americans of whatever faith by signing the "partial-birth" abortion ban that Clinton had vetoed, though he disappointed many Catholics in the realm of life and death by compromising on embryonic stem cell research and capitulating on *Roe v. Wade*.

In radically different ways, the election of the first Catholic president and the rejection of his first successor as a major party nominee testified to the substantial moral and spiritual influence of the Church on the nation's political affairs. Kennedy's triumph in a campaign that had much to do with his religion helped to ensure that Kerry's loss would have little to do with his religion. In 1960, widespread religious prejudice, especially in the South, forced Catholic voters and the Catholic candidate onto the defensive. Seizing the historical moment, many Catholic voters put their religion before their politics, while the Catholic candidate put his politics before his religion. By 2004, however, Catholics had become so politically significant, and anti-Catholicism had so greatly diminished, that this time most of them put their politics before their religion, not only voting for a southern Protestant, but voting against a Catholic Democrat. More affluent and less aggrieved than the Catholics of 1960, Kennedy's offspring became Kerry's orphans.[27]

In the intervening forty-four years, however, American Catholics, who had overcome their working-class origins to become arguably the most prosperous and prominent of the country's churches, could not always buttress their socioeconomic and cultural elevation with political clout. Kennedy and Johnson defied the Church hierarchy with their funding of artificial contraception. Nixon and Ford disappointed the Church leadership and divided the rank and file by prolonging the Vietnam War and evading the abortion issue. Carter gave up on arms control and universal health care before the bishops did. Reagan persisted in flouting the prelates on the economy and procrastinated in following them on abortion. The elder Bush decided for a war, the pope decided against it, and the bishops couldn't decide at all. In the eyes of the pope and the bishops, Clinton did too much promoting of abortion, while the younger Bush did too much fighting against Iraq and too little fighting against abortion. For many American Catholics, if the Kennedy victory seemed the fulfillment of what they wished for, the Kerry defeat seemed the confirmation of the admonition to be careful.

Overall, American Catholics, though often fractious and at times feeble, contributed mightily to the nation's political history as the twentieth century gave way to the twenty-first. Catholics, led by the pope and/or the bishops, accelerated Kennedy's pursuit of arms control and civil rights. They helped fuel Johnson's sure footing on civil rights and his equivocation on Vietnam. They helped prod Nixon first to propose welfare reform, then to postpone it. They helped persuade Ford to save the war's refugees and to feed the world's hungry. They helped effect Carter's moderation on abortion and Reagan's reversal on arms reduction. They helped focus the elder Bush's attention on the urban crisis and the abortion issue. They helped move Clinton to prevent genocide in the Balkans. They helped furnish the rubrics for Clinton's health care plan and the younger Bush's faith-based initiative in the White House—and the rationales for derailing them on Capitol Hill. American Catholics opened the door to the White House in 1960. And in the face of constitutional challenges, political objections, religious resentments, internal squabbles, and a whole lot of history, they have kept it wide open ever since.

CHAPTER ONE

Catholics and John Kennedy
(1961–1963)

ALL EYES WERE ON THE NATION'S first Catholic president as he took the oath of office in January 1961. Those non-Catholics who feared that John Kennedy would be a captive of his church awaited his first theocratic tendencies. Those Catholics who worried that he would capitulate to the skeptics anticipated his first secular signals. Both would be disappointed. Kennedy would seldom speak of his faith. But he would often practice it. Kennedy's turns from confrontation to negotiation with the Soviet Union and from political caution to personal courage on civil rights were in large part responses to pressure from his church. And his change from aversion to adherence to federal funding of artificial contraception was in large part a rebuke to pressure from his church.

War and Peace: Nuclear War

John F. Kennedy's presidency began famously with his stirring inaugural address, in which he pledged to "pay any price" to prevent the spread of Soviet communism around the globe. By promising to outdo his predecessor, Republican Dwight Eisenhower, in his commitment to Cold War containment, the Catholic entering the White House was professing the ardent anticommunism not only of his party, but of his church.[1] Yet within two and a half years, Kennedy told an American University audience in June 1963 that the United States must peacefully coexist with the Soviet Union in a world made "safe for diversity." Once again, the president was speaking not only for his party, but for his church.[2]

Two months later, the United States, the Soviet Union, and Great Britain signed the Limited Test Ban Treaty, which ushered in an era of détente between the superpowers by outlawing nuclear-weapons testing in the atmosphere, underwater, and in outer space. In their apparent metamorphoses from hawks to doves on the issue of nuclear war, the U.S. government and the Roman Catholic Church traveled parallel paths from 1961 to 1963. In their dramatic coalescence behind the slowing of the arms race, however, neither the president nor his church forgot whence they came.

Hawks of a Feather

Kennedy's inaugural address earned rave reviews in many quarters, including American Catholic ones. As if agreeing with Kennedy, Pope John XXIII in his 1961 Easter message interrupted an otherwise apolitical statement to convey his "anxiety and deep distress" over "the terrifying actions of a great number of men" who threaten "those who love justice, liberty, and a life that is laborious, honored, beneficent, and tranquil"—a thinly veiled assault on the Soviet bloc.[3]

Emboldened by the American failure in Cuba at the Bay of Pigs in April 1961 and his perceived mastery over Kennedy in their first summit meeting in Vienna in June, Soviet premier Nikita Khrushchev warned the United States to remove its troops from West Berlin. Kennedy responded forcefully, vowing never to abandon the western zone until the entire city was free, and calling up twenty-five thousand reserves to prepare for the Cold War's worst-case scenario. "We are now engaged in a struggle for survival against the greatest enemy that ever threatened world civilization," said Boston's Richard Cardinal Cushing, Kennedy's closest friend in the U.S. hierarchy.[4]

Pope John XXIII also weighed in on the side of the Americans, and against naïve diplomacy. Repeating his earlier repudiation of "godless" communism, the pontiff in his July 1961 encyclical, *Mater et Magistra* ("Mother and Teacher"), admonished that East-West summitry could not bridge "different or radically opposed concepts of life" without the reciprocal trust conspicuously absent in the Berlin crisis.[5]

Khrushchev indeed relented over Berlin, but not before he had authorized the construction of the wall that would divide the city and define the Cold War for almost three decades more. Though chastened over Berlin, Khrushchev renewed the nuclear arms race, ordering eighteen atomic tests in five weeks in the fall of 1961, as the Soviets and the Americans entered the sixteenth consecutive month without disarmament negotiations. Kennedy condemned the blasts, vowing to build fallout shelters "for every American as rapidly as possible." On November 4, Pope John marked his eightieth birthday and the third anniversary of his coronation by denouncing the Soviet tests, and his Christmas message lamented that "mutual distrust is making conditions progressively worse" in the Cold War.[6]

At the annual "Red Mass" at St. Patrick's Cathedral in New York City in October, the homily by liberal Jesuit Rev. Robert Drinan called for more religion in government so "we can triumph over the threatening forces behind the Brandenburg Gate." The U.S. Catholic bishops at their annual fall meeting in November implored, "Because we have so often faltered in our course, and because the Communist nations have profited by our mistakes to inspire false ideals and to awaken glittering yet barren hopes," their fellow American Catholics "must not be discouraged. The hour of greatest opportunity is striking now, as the forces of freedom and tyranny gird for a decision."[7]

In its first annual foreign policy review, the Kennedy administration boasted of a 14 percent increase over the last of President Eisenhower's budgets and warned of the "drive to subject another 300 million to Communist domination" under way in the Far East. The editors of the liberal Catholic journal *Commonweal* sounded a similarly hawkish tone as the Catholic president completed his inaugural year. "Continued reliance on the nuclear threat will almost certainly end in the unimaginable horror of nuclear war," they wrote in January 1962. "But unilaterally abandoning our deterrent will even more certainly end in victory for the Communist system and the defeat of all we believe in."[8]

As his second year commenced, the president clung to his rigid anti-communism. In March 1962, while Kennedy publicly expressed hope that the resumption of long-stalled arms control talks in Geneva would produce meaningful progress, administration officials privately dismissed such optimism, and the president announced the resumption of American nuclear testing. The United States would conduct twenty-four nuclear tests between April and November 1962.[9]

Many prominent American Catholics also held to their hard line. By January 1962 Cardinal Cushing had authored three anti-communist articles, "Education on Communism—What Kind," "Flag Pledge Girds U.S. to Thwart Reds," and "Reds Plot War Despite Peace Cries." In March, Rev. John Cronin, assistant director of the Social Action Department of the bishops' National Catholic Welfare Conference and confidant of the staunchly anti-communist former vice president Richard Nixon, published a booklet entitled "Communism: A Threat to Freedom." On March 25 *St. Joseph Magazine*, published by the Benedictine monks, commemorated the twenty-fifth anniversary of Pope Pius XI's *Encyclical on Atheistic Communism* with a series of articles on the theme "Why We Have Failed to Stem the Tide of Communism." A confidential April memo from the bishops' National Catholic Welfare Conference Office for UN Affairs expressed fear that the Soviets were successfully pressuring Secretary General U Thant for greater communist representation in the world body.[10]

Similar concern about communist infiltration at the UN was the subject of letters to the NCWC's National Council of Catholic Women about the Institution of Peace and Progress, which was founded upon the principles of Pope

John's *Mater et Magistra* and met at the UN in April. "It seems clear," wrote Msgr. Paul Tanner, general secretary of the NCWC in May, "that no immediate changes will be made in the United States delegation [at the UN] but perhaps our reservations may influence succeeding choices."[11]

In the wake of Fidel Castro's May offer to free the prisoners captured in the Bay of Pigs invasion in return for $63 million of tractors, Eileen Egan, project director of the NCWC's Catholic Relief Services, proposed that the progressive Catholic Association for International Peace (a "semi-official" foreign policy arm of the bishops) recommend instead that $63 million of food be sent to Cuba to address famine-like conditions there. William O'Brien, president of the CAIP, rejected the "proposition that the United States has a moral responsibility to the Cubans *because* it supported the invasion." The tractor deal collapsed, O'Brien argued, "despite great and well-intentioned efforts by prominent Americans, with the support of the Administration . . . because of Castro's lack of cooperation."[12]

In May, Msgr. Francis Lally, editor of Boston's archdiocesan newspaper the *Pilot*, counseled Cardinal Cushing to reply to a question about the pacifist Committee for a Sane Nuclear Policy with a description of the group as "men of goodwill who have very little understanding of the reality of the world in which we find ourselves in 1962." In July Cushing told Concepcion Nodarse, whose brother was captured in the Bay of Pigs invasion, that he would do "the best I can" to raise money to free him.[13]

Doves of a Feather

October 1962 would become much better known for the bombs that did not explode in the thirteen-day standoff between Kennedy and Khrushchev over the placement of Soviet missiles in Cuba. The Cuban missile crisis ignited the new attitudes on both sides of the iron curtain that would lead directly to Kennedy's American University speech in June 1963.

On the night of October 21, 1962, minutes before Kennedy announced a blockade of Cuba to force the Soviets to remove their missiles, a conference between Americans and Soviets convened in Andover, Massachusetts, to explore possible avenues of cooperation between the superpowers. Among the attendees was Rev. Felix Morlion, president of Pro Deo University in Rome. At the encouragement of his fellow conferees, Father Morlion telephoned Pope John XXIII and urged him to intervene in the Cuban crisis. The pope proposed to Father Morlion that the United States lift its blockade in return for a Soviet pledge to stop sending warships to the island.[14] Members of the Soviet delegation at the Andover conference relayed the pope's proposal to the Kremlin while *Saturday Review* editor Norman Cousins, one of the American representatives, notified the White House. Khrushchev accepted, but Kennedy refused, explaining that the pope's plan left the missiles intact.[15]

On October 25 the pope publicly addressed the crisis without directly mentioning his proposal, Khrushchev, Kennedy, or even Cuba. "While the Second Vatican Council has just been opened amidst the joy and hopes of all men of good will," said the pontiff, alluding to the launch of Vatican II on October 11, "threatening clouds now come to darken again the international horizon and to sow fears in millions of families." The U.S. Catholic bishops, "in view of the present world crisis," proclaimed Sunday, October 27, to be a day of prayer for President Kennedy and his government.[16]

On October 28, for the third time in five days, the pope referred to the crisis, asking God to "dispel the ill omened clouds from the horizon of international coexistence." On the same day, the pope's prayers finally received an answer. In return for Kennedy's public promise that the United States would never invade Cuba and his private assurance that American nuclear missiles would soon depart Turkey, Khrushchev removed the Soviet missiles from Cuba.[17]

With the crisis defused, Norman Cousins seized the opportunity presented at Andover to try to prevent a recurrence of this most frightening episode of the Cold War. On December 4 he and Father Morlion met with Kennedy at the White House to propose that Cousins be the Vatican's first emissary to the Soviet Union in an effort to open a direct line of communication between the White House and the Kremlin. Cousins found the president to be "superbly tanned, [in] good health and sprits," and resolute to change his bellicose ways. "I don't think there's any man in American politics," Kennedy told Cousins, "who's more eager than I am to put Cold War animosities behind and get down to the hard business of building friendly relations." The president had been scared onto a new course.[18]

So had Khrushchev. In a letter to Kennedy on December 19, Khrushchev proposed a nuclear test ban treaty. "Mr. President, conditions are ripe," Khrushchev wrote, "for finalizing a treaty on cessation of tests of nuclear weapons in three environments" (in the atmosphere, underwater, and in outer space).[19] The Church agreed. "I am not religious but I can tell you I have a great liking for Pope John," Khrushchev told Cousins in Moscow in December. "His goal . . . is peace. . . . If we don't have peace and the nuclear bombs start to fall, what difference will it make whether we are Catholics or capitalists or Russians or Americans?"[20] For Khrushchev, "During that week of the Cuban crisis, the Pope's appeal was a ray of light. I was grateful for it. Believe me, this was a dangerous time. I hope no one will have to live through it again."[21]

Cousins went to Rome from Moscow to brief Pope John on his meeting with Khrushchev. "The Russian people [are] a very wonderful people," said the pope. "We must not give up on them because we do not like their political system." As Cousins was leaving, the ailing pontiff added, "World peace is mankind's greatest need. I am old, but I will do what I can in the time I have."[22]

Indeed he would. Nuclear test ban talks between the United States, the Soviet Union, and Great Britain began in New York in January 1963, only to founder over the question of inspections. Three months later, in the eighth and final encyclical of his papacy, *Pacem in Terris* ("Peace on Earth"), Pope John condemned the nuclear arms race, calling upon the world's leaders to reduce the "enormous stocks of armaments that have been and still are being made in more economically developed countries." In an unprecedented appeal beyond the Catholic community to "all men of goodwill," Pope John proposed the creation of an international authority to keep peace.[23]

Without waiting for permission from Moscow, the major communist parties in Western Europe praised the pope's message. A month later Pope John dispatched Franziskus Cardinal König, archbishop of Vienna, to Hungary and Poland to improve relations between the Vatican and the Soviet bloc. Khrushchev's son-in-law, Alexei I. Adzhubei, editor of the official Soviet newspaper *Izvestia*, became the first communist to have a papal audience.[24]

In what State Department spokesman Lincoln White called the first such official response to a papal encyclical, the Kennedy administration welcomed the pope's words as expressing what "should be the aspirations of all governments to make possible the attainment of the encyclical's central goal: peace." The next week at Boston College, Kennedy himself applauded the encyclical's "penetrating analysis of today's great problems of social welfare and human rights, of disarmament and international order and peace." In words that he seldom uttered, Kennedy announced, "As a Catholic, I am proud of it," while adding, "As an American, I have learned from it."[25]

Kennedy was speaking for many Catholics, and many Americans, in his preference for diplomatic over military solutions to Cold War conflicts. Writing in *Catholic World*, Victor Ferkiss and William Purdy lauded the pope's "opening to the left," which, in Ferkiss's words, "may do much to lower the temperature of the Cold War." *Commonweal* viewed the encyclical's unambiguous rejection of "a holy war against communism" as nothing short of "revolutionary."[26]

On May 4, Kennedy sent his congratulations to Pope John for his being awarded the Balzan Peace Prize, established in 1957 in memory of Italian publisher Eugenio Balzan and bestowed by a committee representing twenty-one countries. Two weeks later, the White House announced that on his upcoming visit to Italy, Kennedy would become only the third American president (after Woodrow Wilson and Dwight Eisenhower) to meet with a pope. For the first time, the world's two most famous Roman Catholics would discuss their mutual passion for peace.[27]

Within two weeks Pope John XXIII was dead. "The ennobling precepts of his encyclicals and his actions," said the president as he mourned the pope on June 3, "drew on the accumulated wisdom of an ancient faith for guidance in the most complex and troublesome problems of the modern age." TASS, the official Soviet news agency, remembered Pope John's "fruitful activity for the sake of consolidating peace and peaceful cooperation among nations."[28] President Kennedy's American University speech a week later seemed a fitting eulogy of Pope John XXIII. Echoing the pope's conversation with Norman Cousins, the president distinguished between the Soviet government and the Soviet people, noting that "no system is so evil that its people can be seen as lacking in virtue." In calling for a "strategy of peace," Kennedy announced a suspension of nuclear tests and a resumption of the stalled test-ban negotiations.[29]

The Kennedy speech led to an interfaith meeting in New York on June 19, called by Curtis Roosevelt, executive director of the United States Committee for the United Nations. The purpose of the gathering, according to one of the attendees, Catherine Schaefer of the NCWC's Office of UN Affairs, was "to strengthen the president's hand in test-ban negotiations and in general relaxing of tensions with Russia." Father Morlion, whom Schaefer identified as the "sparkplug" for the meeting, urged American religious leaders to assure the Soviets of the peaceful intentions of the U.S. government through letters to the White House, interdenominational days of prayer, and an ecumenical seminar on religion and peace.[30]

The president would meet the pope, but it would be John's successor, Paul VI. The forty-minute encounter in the immediate aftermath of his installation received as much attention for what the Catholic U.S. head of state did not do—kneel and kiss the pope's ring—as for what he did: discuss what the pontiff called "the peace of the world." After the meeting, Kennedy visited the Pontifical North American Ecclesial College, where Cardinal Cushing, in town for the Second Vatican Council, presented his old friend with the present that Pope John XXIII had intended to give him. Kennedy was visibly moved by the gift—one of three autographed copies of *Pacem in Terris*.[31]

Within a month, the "peace of the world" was on more secure footing, as the Americans, Soviets, and British agreed to a limited nuclear test ban. Kennedy signed what he called "an important first step—a step toward peace, a step toward reason, a step away from war." As Father Morlion had hoped, many notable Catholics lined up behind the president. Pope Paul VI proclaimed, "We welcome these events with the hope that they are really sincere and successful and that they may prepare the way for others, for the tranquility, order, and peace of the world."³²

The test-ban treaty sailed through the Senate, 80–19, on September 24. The fiercely anti-communist Cardinal Cushing saluted Kennedy for "proving to friend and foe alike the suicidal futility of nuclear war and the possibilities of eliminating the expenditure of world wealth for the production of atomic weapons that could destroy civilization." The leader who had brought the world to the brink was now talking the world off the ledge. And with few exceptions his church was with him every step of the way.³³

Conclusions on War and Peace

Arms control efforts by Kennedy and other Catholics preceded the Cuban missile crisis. And Cold War containment, in Vietnam and elsewhere, proceeded after it. But the tremors of those thirteen days steered the president, the pope, and many members of their church onto a seemingly irreversible course. If John F. Kennedy changed with his church on matters of war and peace, did his church change him? Most of the evidence shows that it did. But the president, for the most part, wasn't telling. Though the president was "faithful" and "churchgoing," the University of Notre Dame's president, Rev. Theodore Hesburgh, would remember that Kennedy "tried not to be too Catholic." Of Kennedy's top appointees, only 15 percent were Catholic, a number that Protestants and Other Americans United for Separation of Church and State applauded and some Italian-Americans decried. In August 1962 Kennedy reversed a directive from the Agency for International Development permitting religious organizations such as the NCWC's Catholic Relief Services to participate in the agency's programs after what Catholic Relief Services' executive director Edward Swanstrom called a "hue and cry" from Baptists.³⁴

On a political level, the first Catholic president, however lightly and privately he wore his faith, had to tread carefully on church-state questions. When Amleto Cardinal Cicognani, the Vatican's secretary of state and a former apostolic delegate to the United States, came calling on the White House in November 1961, he reportedly had to stay in town an extra day just for a twenty-minute unofficial meeting, sans photographer—a stark contrast, according to columnist Drew Pearson, to the very public "red carpet" treatment accorded by Kennedy to the Protestant evangelist Dr. Billy Graham. "For understandable political reasons, Mr. Kennedy has not been inclined to parade or in any way make much of his Irish or Catholic background," *America*'s editors concluded at the end of Kennedy's first year in office. "Catholic prelates and Catholic clergymen pay few if any calls these days at the White House."³⁵

"I agree completely with you and the president that he must in no way be connected to or identified with the communications between the Holy See and Moscow," wrote Norman Cousins to Ralph Dungan, requesting a meeting with Kennedy following his discussions with Pope John and Khrushchev, "but I have received two inquiries from Rome about the reactions in our headquarters to specific points of exchange." Dungan counseled Kennedy, "It would not be a useful conversation," and Cousins would have to wait three months to see the president.[36]

If Kennedy was reticent to advertise his Catholicism, his church's American hierarchy was reluctant to reveal its anti-nuclearism. "During his campaign, our enemies alleged that the hierarchy would pressure for control of government" under a Catholic president, warned the NCWC's Education Department (Archbishop Karl Alter of Cincinnati, Bishop Lawrence Shehan of Bridgeport, Msgr. Paul Tanner, Msgr. Frederick Hochwalt, Msgr. Francis Hurley, William Consedine, and George Reed) in February 1961.[37]

The bishops' ill-fated preoccupation with federal aid to Catholic schools throughout the Kennedy presidency relegated even nuclear war to the background. It would remain there not only because of the inevitable liberal-conservative split within the hierarchy (which mirrored divisions among all American Catholics), but because Pope John's apostolic delegate to the United States, Egidio Vagnozzi, did little to heal the rift. Rather than do the pope's bidding, Vagnozzi, a "very strong conservative," according to a White House memo, was "critical of Pope John—rather imprudently in private conversation, more circumspectly in public."[38]

Wary of public scrutiny and lacking a unifying force, the bishops remained largely silent on the paramount issue of their time. When Father Cronin released his pamphlet in March 1962, Milwaukee archbishop William Cousins issued a statement on behalf of the NCWC, distancing the bishops from Cronin's conclusions. The bishops' response to *Pacem in Terris* at their spring meeting in April 1963 was to mask their differences through an amorphous annual statement, "Bonds of Union," to be drafted by the conservative Auxiliary Bishop Philip Hannan of Washington, D.C. The document would be "positive in tone, in keeping with the recent Encyclicals of Pope John XXIII and would include many of the other subjects proposed by different Bishops." The editors of *Commonweal* lamented in May, "For once it seems impossible to find any significant support [among American Catholics] for an important part of a major encyclical. . . . No major Church spokesman or theologian has espoused the idea, so clear in the encyclical, that the times may require a different approach to Communism."[39]

In June 1963, in the wake of Kennedy's civil rights message, Msgr. George Higgins, the liberal director of the NCWC's Social Action Department, wrote that "while . . . some sort of interfaith conference on international peace is needed at the present time . . . we are literally swamped these days with the interfaith commitments in the field of race relations." Indeed, the first item on the agenda of the special meeting of the NCWC's administrative board in August was a pastoral message on "racial equality under the law," and there was no mention of *Pacem in Terris* beyond the completion of Hannan's annual statement.[40]

Neither Kennedy's nor the hierarchy's hesitation to acknowledge the religious contours of nuclear détente, however, could completely obscure the strides that each was taking toward the other. Kennedy's letter to Pope John at the outset of Vatican II, his unprecedented statement on *Pacem in Terris*, his Boston College speech, his emotional display in Rome, and his historic appearances before record audiences in Ireland in June 1963 displayed a public embrace of his private religion. "One of the things that disturbed some of our Catholic friends is the fact that he would not give more express credit to the greater influence that his religion . . . would have on his decisions," Kennedy campaign advisor James Wine would recall of the 1960 presidential effort. "Yet I had many people say to me in writing or orally within a period of two years after 1962, 'I can see now that I was wrong'": Kennedy had often acted like a Catholic even if he had not often talked like one.[41]

Cardinal Cushing would remember that Kennedy became a more prayerful man during his presidency. Despite his "desire to never exploit religion," Kennedy aide Brooks Hays would recall, the president was "in the finest sense of the term a devout man." Attorney General Robert Kennedy challenged the press reports: not only did Kennedy treat Cardinal Cicognani with the proper respect, but the Vatican secretary of state's visit was "the first time in the history of the United States that a ranking dignitary of the Catholic Church was received in the White House."[42]

Similarly, the American bishops' participation in the historic Second Vatican Council marked the acceptance—by most conservatives and liberals alike—of a changing church in a changing world. If Kennedy's ecumenical presidency was not always to the liking of American Catholics, it was often in harmony with the spirit of Pope John XXIII. Though neither would live to see the results of the meeting in Rome, both Johns, in their cautious evocation of *aggiornamento* (modernization) inside and outside their church, were "post–Vatican II" Catholics.[43]

In his sermon on the first anniversary of Kennedy's death, Cardinal Cushing couldn't help but see the resemblance: "Like all of us, he had his faults and failings, but he was nevertheless a precursor of another John, the lovable and loving Pope John XXIII, who during his brief Pontificate became the great

Bridge Builder between people of all Faiths." The Gallup Poll in April 1963, five months after the Cuban missile crisis and on the eve of *Pacem in Terris*, reported that Kennedy's "sharpest gains since the 1960 vote have come among Protestants," up 20 percent. And despite the uneasy silence among the bishops, American Catholics (who had a shorter distance than Protestants to travel) said they were 8 percent more likely to vote for Kennedy than they had been in 1960.[44]

Thus did Americans, led by their president, and Catholics, led by their pope, move from a fear of inevitable war to a hope of incremental peace. Though neither was inclined to admit it, the president and the pope also led each other on this dramatic, yet durable quest. On matters of war and peace, Kennedy made history not only as a president who happened to be Catholic, but as a Catholic who happened to be president.

Social Justice: Civil Rights

Compromise is at once the bedrock and the bane of American representative democracy. Quick to deplore obstinate partisanship, many Americans are equally apt to extol principled statesmanship. But there are some issues, it seems, that compromise demeans rather than decides. The scourge of slavery and the march of fascism could only ultimately end when their enemies forsook bargains for battles.

By the time of President John Kennedy's election in 1960, Jim Crow segregation had acquired a stigma throughout much of the United States. Yet the liberal Massachusetts Democrat spent most of the first two and a half years of his presidency compromising with it. Wary of more violence and fewer votes, Kennedy staked out a cautious middle ground, until events began to overwhelm him and his conscience began to unsettle him. And his fellow American Catholics began to prod him. The same church that wandered on matters of war and peace, and worried over the drift of population control, stood resolute in the face of racial discrimination. In this arena, for much of the Kennedy era, the Church would lead and the president would follow.

The Church Leading

"There are no schools for Negroes. There are no schools for whites. There are only schools for all children." So said New York's Francis Cardinal Spellman in 1939, five years after Rev. John LaFarge founded the first Catholic Interracial Council in that city. Archbishop Joseph Ritter desegregated Catholic elementary and secondary schools in St. Louis in 1947; Archbishop Patrick O'Boyle did the same in Washington, D.C., beginning in 1948, six years before the Supreme Court's historic *Brown v. Board of Education* decision called for the end of segregated public education in the South.[45]

In 1958 the U.S. Catholic bishops issued a pastoral letter, "Discrimination and the Christian Conscience," written by Rev. John Cronin of the National Catholic Welfare Conference's Social Action Department. They advocated the end of legal segregation of the races because it "imposes a stigma of inferiority upon the segregated people" and produces "oppressive conditions and the denial of basic human rights." The next year over four hundred Catholic clergy and laypeople combined the forty-three local interracial councils into a national organization, the National Catholic Conference for Interracial Justice, dedicated to the execution of the bishops' mandate.[46]

As the Kennedy era dawned, the Church continued to lead on civil rights. On January 29, 1961, the National Catholic Conference for Interracial Justice condemned the intransigence of Louisiana public school officials toward desegregation. The NCCIJ called upon the administration to "move forward along the whole frontier of just human relations." A week later at its meeting in Chicago, the NCCIJ urged the new president to act aggressively in safeguarding civil rights. Chicago's Albert Cardinal Meyer encouraged the integration of African-Americans into "the complete life of the Church." The cardinal explained, "We are not restricting our attention to our schools. We are thinking of accepted and wholehearted membership in the entire life of the parish, in our fraternal and parish organizations, in our hospitals."[47]

In a February 1961 pastoral letter, Bishop Paul Hallinan of Charleston, South Carolina, joined Bishops Timothy McDonough of Savannah, Georgia, and Francis Hyland of Atlanta in reiterating the bishops' 1958 statement and pledging, "Catholic pupils, regardless of color, will be admitted to Catholic schools as soon as this can be done with safety to the children and the schools." They continued, "Certainly this will be done not later than the public schools are opening to all pupils."[48]

Not all Catholics heard the bishops' plea, however. In New Orleans, the largest parochial school system in the former Confederacy remained largely segregated despite six years of promises by Archbishop Joseph Rummel to end this "morally wrong," "unjust," and "sinful" practice. Even after his own survey showed that most Catholic school principals and parents would accept desegregation, and after the first two public schools in the city admitted African-Americans in the face of citywide violence in the fall of 1960, Rummel had again bowed to the opposition of white Catholics, led by Leander Perez, Jackson Ricau, and B. J. Gaillot. The parochial schools, the archbishop now said, would remain segregated until "public school integration had been effectively carried out."[49]

The National Catholic Conference for Interracial Justice's executive director, Mathew Ahmann, lamented the annual postponement of Archbishop Rummel's 1955 desegregation decree. "On my most recent trip to New Orleans," Ahmann wrote, "every respectable person I spoke with felt the Catholic schools could be successfully desegregated." Ahmann urged the Washington, D.C., archbishop, Patrick O'Boyle, to fill the void caused when Rummel became ill. O'Boyle then dispatched Auxiliary Bishop Philip Hannan to meet with Rummel under the guise of seeking advice on how to desegregate the parochial schools of the Maryland suburbs of Washington, D.C. Rummel counseled O'Boyle to "listen." Hannan would later relate to Rummel's auxiliary bishop, Joseph Vath, that O'Boyle took Rummel's advice, listening for four hours in a Maryland town to virulent opposition to his desegregation plan. And then, Vath remembered, "they integrated before we did."[50]

The President Following

Just as Ahmann looked to the nation's capital for leadership on civil rights, so did many other Americans, anxious to witness the fulfillment of President John Kennedy's campaign promises to provide such guidance. After one general sentence in his first State of the Union address and an offhand allusion at his first press conference, however, it took the new president almost three weeks to utter what the *New York Times*'s Anthony Lewis called his "first substantial comment" on the subject. Kennedy vowed to "attempt to use the moral authority of the presidency" to enforce the court order in New Orleans, where white students were boycotting or avoiding classes in two newly desegregated public schools.[51]

In the ensuing weeks Kennedy issued an executive order banning racial discrimination in federal employment and in companies doing business with the federal government, created the President's Committee on Equal Employment Opportunity, to be chaired by Vice President Lyndon Johnson, and directed Attorney General Robert Kennedy to initiate litigation against voting discrimination in Louisiana and Mississippi. With white southerners controlling ten of the twenty standing committees in the House of Representatives and nine of the sixteen in the Senate, while comprising 101 of the 261 Democrats in the new Congress, Kennedy adopted an extralegislative strategy that appeared to acknowledge political reality without abandoning his idealistic vision.

Then the Freedom Riders, led by James Farmer, president of the Congress of Racial Equality, commenced their troubled quest to compel the enforcement of the Supreme Court's 1960 *Boynton v. Virginia* decision, which outlawed racial segregation in interstate transportation. The Freedom Riders, and Kennedy's wish that they would just disappear, revealed the limits of his extralegislative strategy. At an April meeting of the White House Subcabinet Group, White House aide Frederick Dutton relayed the conviction of John Hannah, chairman of the United States Civil Rights Commission (created by the Civil Rights Act of 1957), that desegregation was moving to "the basement of the White House." Kennedy's Catholic assistant attorney general for civil rights, Harris Wofford, urged Kennedy in May to exhibit "moral leadership . . . during an occasion of moral crisis." In October Hannah's commission took the administration to task for not doing enough to further the cause of civil rights.[52] Though *America* blamed "public opinion" for deterring a "determined president" from fulfilling the commission's recommendations, other Catholic voices were not so forgiving. Civil Rights Commission member Rev. Theodore Hesburgh, president of the University of Notre Dame, would later lament that "the Kennedys put [the commission reports] in the drawer; civil rights imposed itself on the Kennedys, not the other way around."[53]

After the president had written Ahmann, praising the NCCIJ's "commendable efforts to promote greater understanding between people of different classes, creeds, and colors," Ahmann wrote Kennedy, pressing him to sign a public housing desegregation order. "The recommendations of the Civil Rights Commission are currently being reviewed by the Administration, and you may be assured that your recommendation will be taken into account," assistant special counsel Lee White replied to Ahmann in December. But Ahmann and the commission would have to wait almost another year.[54]

The year 1962 opened with Catholics continuing to lead and Kennedy continuing to follow on civil rights. In January Rev. John Cronin of the Social Action Department of the bishops' National Catholic Welfare Conference testified on Capitol Hill in favor of a congressional equal opportunity bill. Two months later, Archbishop Rummel finally desegregated New Orleans' parochial schools. When Catholic segregationists Jackson Ricau of the Citizens Council of South Louisiana, Leander Perez of the Plaquemines Parish Council, and B. J. Gaillot of Save Our Nation loudly protested the decision, Rummel did something he had never done in his twenty-seven-year tenure: he excommunicated them.[55]

Robert Kennedy's administrative assistant John Siegenthaler offered "assistance . . . at any time" in the New Orleans controversy to Henry Cabirac, the NCCIJ's director of the Southern Field Service, and in April Cabirac accepted. He requested that the assistant attorney general for civil rights, Burke Marshall, help the NCCIJ by "keeping [Leander] Perez busy by defending himself" in his attacks on Rummel's endorsement of school desegregation. After Marshall threatened Perez and other Louisiana officials with contempt-of-court sentences if they did not release state desegregation funds, Cabirac thanked the assistant attorney general.[56] When Marshall appeared on television to urge the nation's churches to do even more to confront racial injustice, Ahmann commended him for his forward-looking message. Marshall, in turn, praised the leadership of Rummel's co-adjutor archbishop, John Cody of New Orleans, in helping to quell the crisis there.[57]

In October Cabirac encouraged Marshall to enforce the desegregation of public schools in Georgia and South Carolina as a way of expediting the opening of integrated Catholic schools in those states. Cabirac informed Marshall that he had assured the bishops of the Dioceses of Savannah and Charlotte that "you have cooperated with us and that when they decide to move . . . this could be coordinated with you as much as possible."[58]

By the end of 1962 the administration was trumpeting several civil rights achievements: the housing order, a significant increase in all levels of black employment in the federal government, prosecution of several voting rights cases by the Justice Department, the elimination of racially segregated interstate transportation, and the intervention at the University of Mississippi to admit James Meredith as its first black student. Yet Congress remained largely immobile, prompting John McDermott, executive director of the Catholic Interracial Council, to write Kennedy aide Ralph Dungan, urging "dramatic personal action" as "the only way to move Congress along." Among McDermott's suggestions was "that [Kennedy's daughter] Caroline have a Negro playmate."[59]

As 1963 began, American Catholics raised their profile while increasing the pressure on the Kennedy administration. In January 1963, the black presence in the world Catholic hierarchy included one cardinal, thirteen archbishops, twenty-eight bishops, and seventeen auxiliary bishops. From January 14 to 17 in Chicago, the Social Action Department of the National Catholic Welfare Conference joined the Department of Racial and Cultural Relations of the National Council of Churches of Christ and the Social Action Commission of the Synagogue Council of America in sponsoring the first National Conference on Religion and Race. Twenty-four Catholic bishops, including four archbishops, were among the almost seven hundred delegates and five hundred observers who formed thirty working groups to discuss case histories of race relations in every aspect of organized religion. The delegates unanimously adopted an "Appeal to the Conscience of the American People," which held that "racism is our most serious domestic evil. We must eradicate it with all diligence and speed." NBC television asked the group to serve as a consultant to a series of educational programs on race planned for 1963. The NCCIJ's Mathew Ahmann, who helped organize the meeting, would remember that the conference "provided a vehicle for interreligious fraternity which, for the first time, capitalized on the growing earnestness in the relationships between our various religious groups."[60]

President Kennedy declined an invitation to address the conference, but his "Special Message" to the Congress the following month echoed the conference's conclusions. Sounding like many of his fellow American Catholics, Kennedy concluded of racial discrimination, "Above all, it is wrong."[61]

Kennedy called for an expansion of his former nemesis, the Civil Rights Commission, into a clearinghouse for information and assistance to local communities. He advocated technical and economic aid to local communities to facilitate school desegregation. He reiterated his demand for the end of literacy tests for those with at least a sixth-grade education. He pressed for faster voter registration in the South. Special counsel to the president Theodore Sorensen would recall that the speech "signaled a shift in [Kennedy's] thinking about civil rights legislation." The president now believed that Congress was finally ready to accept its responsibility in the civil rights crusade.[62]

He was wrong. In 1961, 63 percent of Americans had opposed the Freedom Riders. Now, 63 percent of Americans embraced school desegregation. Yet Congress showed little inclination to represent its constituents.[63]

"When Negroes attempting to register to vote in LeFlore County, Mississippi face violence and are even harassed by policemen and their dogs," *America* editorialized in April 1963, "we begin to ask what century this is, and what country." In the same month, Baltimore's archbishop, Lawrence Shehan, issued a pastoral letter calling for an end to racial discrimination in Catholic schools, hospitals, and organizations and in "all the circumstances of everyday life," while Bishop Victor Reed of Oklahoma City–Tulsa endorsed a state bill outlawing racial discrimination in employment.[64]

In May a national television audience watched police dogs and fire hoses scatter peaceful black demonstrators protesting racial segregation in the public facilities of Birmingham, Alabama. As the Birmingham crisis was unfolding, Washington, D.C., archbishop Patrick O'Boyle was excoriating racial discrimination in a speech before the National Urban League. St. Louis was hosting its own Conference on Religion and Race, again co-sponsored by the National Catholic Welfare Conference, the National Council of Churches, and the Synagogue Council of America. The city's archbishop, Joseph Cardinal Ritter, told the conference that racial segregation "can be every bit as cruel as gas chambers and concentration camps," and labeled the doctrine of racial superiority "insane." The conference defused a threatened boycott by a local group of black ministers and laypeople who accused the organizers of ignoring the "viewpoint of the Negroes in St. Louis" by adding more black representation at the conference.

One of the African-American additions to the program, Rev. Amos Ryce, pastor of St. Louis's Lane Tabernacle Church, criticized white Catholic flight from the city, which "has left a number of blacks presided over by white priests, . . . predominantly white nuns, and other white hierarchy."[65] The diocesan newspaper, the *St. Louis Review*, while acknowledging that racism remained alive and well in many local Catholic quarters, nonetheless confronted critics like Rev. Ryce. "If it is real religion for a Negro to hold a white child in her arms in Birmingham," the *Review* editorialized, "is it any less real religion for white priests and sisters to 'hold the fort' and staff and teach in parishes that have been abandoned by whites and occupied by Negroes?"[66]

Msgr. Daniel Cantwell, chaplain of the Catholic Interracial Council of Chicago, perhaps best summed up the challenge facing the Church, and the nation, as American Catholics increased their visibility in the civil rights struggle. "It takes courage to take positions now," said Cantwell at the end of May 1963, "that everyone will be taking in fifteen years."[67]

Leading Together

If President Kennedy were to accept Cantwell's challenge, *Commonweal* asserted, "a speech to the mayors will not do, nor will a message to Congress. But a nationally televised address . . . would help." But when the president suggested such a message to his inner circle, all spoke in opposition except Robert Kennedy. Yet even the attorney general believed that his brother's proposed civil rights legislation was "maybe going to be his swan song."[68]

He did it anyway. "I want to pay tribute to these citizens North and South who have been working in their communities to make life better for all," President Kennedy told a nationwide audience on June 11, acknowledging the efforts of, among others, the religious groups that had framed civil rights in the moral context to which the president had mostly paid lip service. This time, however, Kennedy's voice was firm and his resolve was steady: "We face a moral crisis as a country and as a people. . . . It is a time to act in the Congress, in your State and local legislative body, and, above all, in all your daily lives." The president announced his support for pending fair employment legislation, advocated federal litigation and the withholding of federal aid in order to accelerate school desegregation, and offered legislation to prohibit racial segregation in public accommodations.[69]

The Catholic president, previously reluctant to talk about religion, also decided to open the front door of the White House to representatives of several denominations and to form his own advisory committee on religion and race to help sell his civil rights bill. In preparing Kennedy for the meeting, the White House Catholic liaison, Ralph Dungan, urged the president to emphasize the moral aspect of civil rights while beseeching the religious leaders to establish biracial committees so as to promote equal employment opportunity, fair housing, and quality education. "It will be important for you to stress the important work which has already been undertaken by the three major faiths in the United States, particularly the Conference on Religion and Race which was held in Chicago recently, and the work which has stemmed from it," Dungan counseled Kennedy. "You might make some reference to the Declaration of Conscience which came out of that meeting."[70]

Only six days after his civil rights message, Kennedy greeted 250 religious leaders, including 35 Catholic bishops from North and South, and representatives from several Catholic interracial councils. Washington archbishop Patrick O'Boyle was the first to speak, and according to fellow participant Rev. John LaFarge, "His remarks and those of the main speakers who followed him revealed strong, almost unanimous support for the president's aim to enforce strong desegregation legislation enforceable by the federal government."[71]

If the guests remembered their lines, however, the host appeared to have forgotten his. Despite Dungan's instructions, Kennedy failed to recognize the religious groundwork that had been laid for the meeting. "I am sorry to be so long in acknowledging the report of the National Conference on Religion and Race you were kind enough to send," White House special counsel Lee White would reply to Ahmann seven months after the conference. "Much of the work which you suggested the religious groups could do in the field of civil rights has been recently undertaken by the continuing committee of the National Conference on Religion and Race," Irwin Miller, president of the National Council of Churches of Christ, would remind the president a month after the meeting. "I'm glad to receive your letter reporting steps being undertaken by the religious groups in the cause of racial justice," Kennedy replied to Miller, asking him to chair the advisory committee.[72]

Despite these missteps, Kennedy continued to make up for lost time in embracing the religious commitment to civil rights. On June 18 he approved a proposal by Time-Life that leaders in religion, civil rights, sports, entertainment, and labor join the president in a series of television spots to promote the civil rights legislation. Among those to be featured were Richard Cardinal Cushing of Boston, Francis Cardinal Spellman and Auxiliary Bishop Fulton Sheen of New York, and Frank Heller, president of the NCWC's National Council of Catholic Men. The next day the NCWC's Msgr. Francis Hurley was among a group of education leaders who met with Kennedy at the White House to discuss school desegregation.[73]

On June 20 Irwin Miller, in his new capacity as special counsel to the president, met at the White House with Dungan, White, and special assistant to the president Louis Oberdorfer to define the responsibilities of Miller's committee. They decided that the committee would establish biracial groups of clergy and laypeople to attack racial discrimination in local communities. It would work with churches, schools, businesses, and local governments to promote the civil rights bill. It would seek to enlist the support of the media in confronting racism. It would help the administration identify potential trouble spots and prevent racial crises. It would address the racial problems of the North as well as the South. In other words, Miller's committee would do much of what the National Conference on Religion and Race had been doing all year. So it would have the title Continuing Committee of the National Conference on Religion and Race.[74]

Msgr. George Higgins of the NCWC's Social Action Department was among twenty-nine opinion leaders who met with President Kennedy, Vice President Johnson, Attorney General Kennedy, and Secretary of Labor Arthur Goldberg at the White House on June 22 to discuss civil rights legislation. About fifteen members of the group, including Higgins, then had lunch with Walter Reuther, head of the American Federation of Labor–Congress of Industrial Organizations, who lent his support to the Kennedy bill while registering his opposition to a proposed civil rights march on Washington.[75]

The Kennedy-Catholic civil rights offensive gathered strength in July. Seventeen members of the NCWC's National Council of Catholic Women were among three hundred female leaders who heard Kennedy at the White House request their support for his civil rights proposals. The NCCW then launched a campaign among its membership to write members of Congress, urging their endorsement of the Kennedy bill. Peggy Roach of the NCCW and the NCCIJ attended a meeting of about thirty organizations called by the Leadership Conference on Civil Rights to promote the civil rights bill. "Time and again," Roach recounted, "it was stated that religious groups ... could make a difference in passage of this legislation." The NCWC's Rev. Cronin joined Dr. Eugene Blake of the NCC and Rabbi Irwin Blank of the Synagogue Council of America in testifying before the House Judiciary Committee in favor of the Kennedy bill.[76]

Although the efforts of the Conference on Religion and Race were continuing, obstacles remained in its path. Henry Cabirac informed Galen Weaver, executive director of the conference, of the persistence of Leander Perez, "the most diabolical baptized Catholic in the country," in opposing Archbishop Cody's efforts to desegregate New Orleans' Catholic hospitals, retreat houses, and employment contracts. Yet not all the news from Cabirac was bad: he reported that Bishop Thomas Toolen of the Mobile-Birmingham Diocese had relinquished his segregationist stand and desegregated Pensacola, Florida, parochial schools, earning the moniker "Nigger Bishop" from segregationists in his diocese.⁷⁷

At the request of its chairman, Archbishop O'Boyle, the administrative board of the National Catholic Welfare Conference, at a special meeting in Chicago on August 6–7, devised a pastoral letter, "On Racial Harmony," again written by Father Cronin. In their strongest statement yet, and the first since 1958, the bishops called upon their fellow Catholics to "do our part to see that voting, jobs, housing, education, and public facilities are freely available to every American." The bishops would release the statement on August 25 and, in O'Boyle's words, "set a proper and peaceful tone" for the March on Washington for Jobs and Freedom scheduled for three days later.⁷⁸

By August 1963 the number of interfaith, interracial house visits, begun by Chicago's Friendship House in 1955, passed forty and included the South for the first time. When asked about the project, President Kennedy had responded, "I think it would be very helpful, and you can start right here in Washington, where this is greatly needed."⁷⁹ The president thus added his support to that of the NCCIJ, which concluded an all-day emergency meeting of its fifty-seven councils in Chicago on July 27 by announcing its endorsement of the Kennedy civil rights bill, advocacy of peaceful civil rights protests, and participation in the August 28 March on Washington. New York's Cardinal Spellman and Washington's Archbishop O'Boyle were among other prominent Catholics backing the march. "Catholics, Negro and white, will turn out in support of this noble cause," *America*'s editors wrote. "In all probability the president will dignify the occasion by receiving the parade and even speaking to the demonstrators."⁸⁰

The president would do neither. "Aware of the hard political fact that a crowd of 230,000 is capable of many reactions," wrote Kennedy speechwriter Theodore Sorensen, the president would sit home on August 28. O'Boyle, slated to give the invocation at the march, threatened to do the same after reading the proposed speech by John Lewis, president of the Student Nonviolent Coordinating Committee, the day before the demonstration. "We will march through the South, through the heart of Dixie, like Sherman did. We shall pursue our own scorched-earth policy and burn Jim Crow to the ground non-violently," Lewis planned to say. O'Boyle considered such language "quite incendiary . . . and nothing less than rabble-rousing incitements to violence."⁸¹

Kennedy, unhappy about another line in the Lewis speech—"We cannot support the Administration's civil rights bill, for it is too little and too late"—dispatched Burke Marshall to join civil rights leaders A. Philip Randolph and Martin Luther King Jr. in pressuring Lewis to change the text. The morning of the march, with the president himself doing the editing, Lewis agreed to excise the Shermanesque language and revise the expression of his opinion on the civil rights bill to "support with great reservations." While Lewis was agreeing to the revisions, Bayard Rustin, one of the organizers of the march, persuaded O'Boyle to give the invocation by assuring him that he would see a copy of the final text in time to walk off the stage, a move that, although the archbishop considered Lewis's final version "still radical," proved unnecessary.[82]

The march, best remembered for King's soaring "I Have a Dream" speech, fulfilled none of Kennedy's worst fears. There were no arrests related to the march, and the crowd chanted, "Pass the bill, pass the bill," in support of Kennedy's civil rights legislation.[83]

No one knew, of course, that Kennedy had fewer than three months remaining to lead. His fellow Catholics would have to press the fight beyond November 22. By that time, the Vatican newspaper had called the death of four black girls in the September 15 bombing of Birmingham's Sixteenth Street Baptist Church a "massacre of the innocents." The NCWC's National Council of Catholic Men had sent a statement to Congress urging a vote for "meaningful civil rights legislation" and pledging to "do everything possible" to help achieve it. The NCCIJ had met in Washington to press the "necessity for supporting strong civil rights legislation in the Congress."[84]

The first Student Leadership Conference on Religion and Race, which included Catholic and non-Catholic students from eighty-six campuses, convened in the nation's capital and devoted "considerable time and attention . . . to the Civil Rights Bill in the Congress and what students might do to enlist support for the passage of strong legislation." The National Conference on Religion and Race spread to forty-six cities, with "significant programs of action" undertaken in nineteen. The U.S. Catholic bishops issued "Bonds of Union," a statement calling for the completion of the "unfinished business of the Emancipation Proclamation by full recognition of all their rights for millions of our fellow citizens of the Negro race." The NCCIJ praised the bishops' "massive drive to eliminate racism from the nation," lauded the National Federation of Catholic College Students, the National Federation of Sodality, and the National Councils of Catholic Men and Women for their "forthright" defense of desegregation, and pledged to seek the repeal of laws in nineteen states banning interracial marriage. Having largely started without the president, many Catholics devoted to civil rights would have to finish without him as well.[85]

Conclusions on Social Justice

The remarkable marriage of the Catholic president and his church before the altar of civil rights was a triumph in the American quest for racial justice. But it was not an unmitigated one. For every hopeful sign, there was a warning; for every forward step, a retreat.

The first, and most stubborn, barrier that Kennedy and his fellow Catholics had to confront was the historic chasm between black and white. The burgeoning Catholic interracial councils, the proliferating Conference on Religion and Race, the growing National Catholic Conference for Interracial Justice, and the myriad white Catholic clergy and laypeople at the March on Washington seemed the embodiment of Dr. King's dream. Two days after Kennedy's death, thirty thousand people and a CBS television crew turned out for a demonstration against job discrimination called by the St. Louis Conference on Religion and Race, held at the courthouse where Missouri slave Dred Scott had unsuccessfully sued for his freedom over a century earlier.[86]

But white Catholics remained on both sides of the racial divide, hindering as well as hastening the long-overdue reconciliation. "The scandal which is created by anti-Negro demonstrators in large urban and suburban areas against Negro house-buyers, or against the extension of courteous service to Negro patrons in business houses and places of public services is irreparable," the NCCIJ argued in St. Louis. "Catholics are often conspicuous by their religious emblems, miraculous medals, school insignias on clothing, or class uniforms in these demonstrations." Not only were there few black Catholics, but within the Church "religious orders have themselves developed on the basis of race so that we have 'colored' orders distinct from other orders—and missionary orders of priests and sisters devoted exclusively to the care of persons of color to make up for the limitations suffered within the Church itself."[87] Rev. John Wagner of the NCWC's Committee for the Spanish-Speaking reminded Msgr. Tanner in September 1963 that although most were Catholic, the Church required Latinos to "become middle-class and sacrifice all . . . cultural traits and religious motivations." Hispanics thus remained an "almost totally unrecognized minority in the United States."[88]

The bishops assigned Father Cronin to poll the country's Catholic dioceses on race relations at the end of 1963. Ninety-four of 143 dioceses and archdioceses responded, with 51 reporting "substantial race problems," 62 noting the existence of "interreligious, interfaith" civil rights programs, and only 34 acknowledging "concrete plans for interracial activities."[89]

The second hurdle that Kennedy and the Church faced was the gap between Catholics and non-Catholics. During the 1960 presidential campaign, John Kennedy had phoned a pregnant Coretta Scott King to comfort her while her husband, Martin Luther King Jr., was in jail, and Robert Kennedy called a Georgia judge to help free King. King's father, Martin Luther King Sr., also a Baptist minister, announced that although he thought he would never vote for a Catholic, the Kennedys' actions had changed his mind. "Imagine Martin Luther King having a bigot for a father," John Kennedy marveled.[90]

Kennedy's own experience with religious prejudice before and during the campaign helped him empathize with the struggle of African-Americans, even if he was slow to address it. Kennedy biographer James Giglio discerned a parallel between candidate Kennedy's statement on religious intolerance in the 1960 West Virginia primary—"Nobody asked me if I was a Catholic when I joined the U.S. Navy. Nobody asked my brother [Joseph Jr.] if he was Catholic or Protestant when he climbed into an American bomber plane to fly his last mission"—with President Kennedy's statement on racial intolerance in his June 11, 1963, civil rights address: "No one has been barred on account of his race from fighting or dying for America—there are no 'white' or 'colored' signs on the foxholes or graveyards of battle."[91]

By the time of his June 1963 speech Kennedy had erased the misgivings of many non-Catholics about his presidency. His confrontation with his church over federal aid to non-public education in the early days of his administration and his careful public distance from his fellow Catholics ever since had made the interfaith cooperation that he sought to pass his civil rights bill politically safe, in a way it would not have been two years earlier. In addition, the political liberalism of Pope John XXIII's encyclicals *Mater et Magistra* (1961) and *Pacem in Terris* (1963), as well as the ecumenical spirit of the Second Vatican Council, launched in 1962 with Protestant observers in attendance, went a long way toward heralding a new day in interfaith relations throughout the world.

Msgr. George Higgins, director of the NCWC's Social Action Department, declared that *Mater et Magistra* had put the Church "decidedly on the liberal side," helping to soften the image of an archaic, inflexible institution that was anathema to the dynamic American Protestant culture. As Vatican II opened in Rome in October 1962, Robert Tracy of Baton Rouge successfully urged his fellow bishops to add racial discrimination to the proposed statement condemning bigotry based on gender and national origin, eliciting applause from the rest of the 178 American bishops assembled in St. Peter's basilica, where such ovations were forbidden. "In the United States, before the present Ecumenical Council, the record of interreligious cooperation has been spotty," wrote Father Cronin after the first National Conference on Religion and Race in January 1963. "By contrast, the Chicago meeting was a gathering of long-separated relatives." In *Pacem in Terris* in April 1963, Pope John XXIII said that "racial discrimination can in no way be justified." If Pope John helped move Catholics toward Protestants, Kennedy helped move Protestants toward Catholics.[92]

Yet neither president nor pope could undo centuries of history. There were still too many non-Catholics, especially in the South, growing up with attitudes similar to those of King Sr. Taylor Branch, a biographer of Martin Luther King Jr., relayed the conviction among some non-Catholics that heavy Catholic participation in the National Conference on Religion and Race in 1963 was part of a campaign to draw African-Americans from racially insensitive Protestant denominations. Indeed, Ellis Henican, president of New Orleans' Catholic Council on Human Relations, had told Archbishop Rummel in November 1961 that "by not desegregating our schools right now, we'll look worse than the Protestants."[93]

Mathew Ahmann of the NCCIJ noted in October 1963, "There is special need for a coordinated interreligious approach to Southern communities. . . . While a variety of religious leaders in the South are becoming involved in new biracial communities, there is little specific interreligious leadership launching programs." Historian James Findlay argued that although church lobbying for civil rights was "always couched in ecumenical terms," the NCC's own Commission on Religion and Race was first among equals.[94]

There were also still too many Catholics with the pre–Vatican II belief that God does not save non-Catholics, helping to foster another kind of segregation. "Where there are large concentrations of Catholics in major cities and urban areas, the extensive system of Catholic education, originated for the purpose of protecting and transmitting the teachings of our faith," the NCCIJ addressed the American bishops at Vatican II, "has at the same time been a factor in maintaining a separateness in educational institutions on both religious and racial lines." In other words, it was hard to wage two revolutions at once.[95]

A third challenge posed by the Kennedy-Catholic alliance on civil rights was the gulf between North and South, which a civil war had not healed. Kennedy's choice of Texan Lyndon Johnson as his running mate, the extralegislative strategy that dominated his first two years in office, and the hawkish foreign policy that largely preceded the Cuban missile crisis won Kennedy points in the South, and the Republican Party had not yet adopted a southern strategy. In the midterm elections in November 1962, the Democrats gained four senators and lost only four representatives, an unusually good performance for the party in power in an off-year election.[96]

Just as Kennedy was not hurting himself too badly in the South, so Catholic civil rights efforts achieved some success there. Archbishops Rummel, Cody, and Toolen eventually stood up to racism in New Orleans and Pensacola, and as of August 1963 only four of the twenty-five Catholic dioceses in the eleven states of the former Confederacy had either not announced a policy of parochial school desegregation or did not have one well under way. The National Conference on Religion and Race had opened chapters in Little Rock, Birmingham, Houston, New Orleans, and cities in North Carolina and Oklahoma by November 1963.[97]

Yet Kennedy's church displayed the same geographical limitations as the president had. A 1963 Gallup Poll found that Kennedy's approval rating in the South had dropped from 60 percent in March to 40 percent in September, and even Johnson's presence in the administration had not forestalled the erosion of support in Texas that prompted Kennedy's fateful trip to Dallas. Many northern bishops remained reluctant to permit their priests to demonstrate in the South for fear of antagonizing their southern colleagues. When not condemning racial discrimination in Rome, Bishop Robert Tracy was postponing the desegregation of Baton Rouge's parochial schools because his diocese was "still in the early stages of organizing . . . its Catholic school system." Of the forty-six chapters of the National Conference on Religion and Race when Kennedy died, forty were outside the Deep South.[98]

A fourth roadblock to racial progress was the division between the national and the local. Like many presidents, Kennedy preferred foreign to domestic policy because it avoided the middle man, such as a governor or mayor. Part of the goal of Kennedy's extralegislative civil rights strategy, therefore, was not only to circumvent Congress but to supersede state and local governments. Kennedy's Catholic assistant attorney general for civil rights, Harris Wofford, exploited this preference by arguing in May 1961 that a presidential statement against racial discrimination in interstate travel "should have a good effect abroad."[99]

Similarly, the Catholic hierarchy benefited from the centralizing tendencies of the Church. Historian John McGreevy praised Chicago's Archbishop Meyer, Washington's Archbishop O'Boyle, Baltimore's Archbishop Shehan, and Detroit's Archbishop John Dearden for their leadership in desegregating Catholic parishes. Reinhold Niebuhr, the prominent Protestant theologian and editor of *Christian Century*, confessed to a bit of envy when examining the Catholic hierarchy's role in civil rights. "Of course, I don't prefer an authoritarian Church to a democratic one," said Niebuhr, but he conceded "a measure of respect for what they're doing."[100]

There nonetheless were limits to the nationalizing of civil rights by the president and the bishops. After over two years of local, state, and even federal foot dragging, the administration issued yet another summary of its civil rights achievements to counter the widespread impression that Kennedy's "interest in civil rights . . . commenced with the Birmingham demonstrations." When Henry Cabirac appealed to the bishops for a statement repudiating the potential use of violence by Governor George Wallace in Birmingham, Father

Cronin replied that "our bishops rarely respond to pleas of this nature.... They usually would consider a national statement on a local situation as an intrusion on the authority of the local bishop." And absent aggressive action by the bishops, local religious organizations could only do so much. A June 1962 memo on the preparations for the first National Conference on Religion and Race professed a "definite awareness that the committee members cannot speak with the full authority of the Church." Cronin rejected calls for the dissolution of the national office of the NCRR in April 1963 with the observation that "it is almost impossible for voluntary committees, composed of delegates with full-time jobs, to coordinate activities and work on programs."[101]

A fifth obstacle before Kennedy and American Catholics was the tension between fast and slow. Kennedy in many ways appeared to have expertly calibrated the speed of his civil rights policies. Eighty-nine percent of African-Americans—those with the most at stake in the civil rights campaign—approved of the Kennedy presidency in September 1963. "I think we are going at about the right tempo," Kennedy opined at his September 12 press conference. The bishops were also attuned to the importance of moving at a reasonable pace. "We may well deplore a gradualism that is merely a cloak for inaction," they had said in their 1958 statement, "but we equally deplore rash impetuosity that would sacrifice the achievements of decades in ill-timed and ill-considered ventures."[102]

For some, however, the president and many other Catholics were moving too quickly. Fifty percent of whites—and 70 percent of southern whites—believed in September 1963 that Kennedy was pushing integration too rapidly. In the same spirit, the bishops had rejected Ahmann's plea for an "Interracial Sunday" throughout the nation's parishes in November 1961. Two months later, Alba Zizzamia of the NCWC's Catholic Association for International Peace rejected a proposal for a CAIP "open letter to fellow Catholics" on race relations because "rehashing our sins and more public breast-beating are not going to help anyone."[103]

To others, Kennedy and his fellow Catholics were not moving fast enough. The NCCIJ wrote the bishops at Vatican II in the fall of 1962, citing the example of nuns on picket lines in Chicago as "the most effective instrument in the twenty-five-year endeavor to permit Catholic Negro membership in the Catholic Women's Club." Such "direct action" techniques, the NCCIJ argued, "become necessary when peaceful negotiations fail. The old adage that 'actions speak louder than words' has never been more true than in this era of race relations." Yet *Time* found that the January 1963 National Conference on Religion and Race had produced fewer actions than words, leading the Catholic Interracial Council founder Rev. John LaFarge, who attended the meeting, to write an angry letter to the editor. By October, *Time* would judge most of the NCRR's follow-up efforts in fifteen cities as "unimpressive." A few delegates at the group's November 1963 conference similarly told the *Washington Post* that the bishops' concurrent "Bonds of Union" statement was longer on words than actions, prompting the NCCIJ executive director, Mathew Ahmann, and the Catholic Interracial Council of Washington, D.C., president, Joseph Neusse, to pen their own letters to the editor, disavowing the dissidents' comments. Biographer David Southern judged the civil rights commitment of LaFarge, who was active until his death (at age eighty-three) two days after Kennedy's, as "primarily doctrinal and intellectual," citing the conclusion of black Catholic historian Cyprian Davis that LaFarge believed that "good manners and reasonableness" could overcome racism.[104]

A sixth rift that Kennedy and his fellow Catholics faced was between conservatives and liberals. Kennedy effectively appeased both wings of his party by charting a centrist course on civil rights for most of his presidency. "Kennedy had intended to effect racial advances gradually, smoothly, and with a minimum of conflict," wrote historian James Giglio.[105] Many American Catholics similarly found a comfortable middle ground on volatile questions of race. "My conviction is that a large number of our bishops will be glad to support civil rights legislation," Cronin wrote in October 1963. "Even the more conservative among them might feel that this will remove the incentive for direct action programs that can lead to racial turmoil."[106]

There is no absolute middle, however, and both Kennedy and the Catholic community at times widened the conservative-liberal split. By warily navigating between black militancy and white resistance, Kennedy biographer Thomas Reeves argued, Kennedy inadvertently encouraged both. The progressive pastoral letters of the bishops, like the decisions of the courts, were only as good as their enforcement. "The Church is not and should not be a power bloc, capable of compliance with directions of its leadership," the otherwise liberal Cardinal Ritter of St. Louis argued in May 1963. "Rather, it is for the Church to enunciate principles and their application to modern problems clearly and without equivocation, leaving it to men of the Church as free citizens to devise the most effective means of applying them to concrete situations." *Time* noted that the archbishop of Los Angeles, James Cardinal McIntyre, discouraged clergy from active roles in civil rights efforts.[107]

Commitment, of course, is often in the eye of the beholder, and perhaps no other people in American history evinced the degree of commitment as did those who spoke, wrote, walked, went to jail, and even died in the cause of civil rights. Meanwhile, the Catholic in the White House and the Catholics in the streets had to traverse a final schism: their country's historic separation of church and state. In the same year that the Supreme Court banned Bible reading in the public schools, Irwin Miller, Ralph Dungan, Louis Oberdorfer, and Lee White nevertheless agreed to mount "an active joint program of regular speaking and counseling worked out by religious leaders and school authorities" to press the cause of civil rights. That American Catholics, led by the president, had so much to do with this union of church and state testified to how far they had come in a country that had long considered them not much different from the African-Americans with whom and for whom they were demonstrating.[108]

Yet the willingness of largely secular liberals, led again by the president, to march alongside them, even though it meant an uncomfortable merger of church and state, often proved too good to be true. The Josephite Order foreshadowed such tension when it forbade Rev. Philip Berrigan and another priest from arranging their own arrests during the Freedom Rides in August 1961, and there were few Catholic Freedom Riders that summer. "It is not wrong for the president to ask religious leaders to pronounce on civic morality and to ask the president to uphold basic human rights," Cronin wrote Cabirac two weeks before Kennedy's meeting with religious leaders in June 1963. "But I have heard reports that some religious leaders are concerned that any contacts with the White House, in the current situation, be clearly defined."[109]

After two Washington priests were arrested during the July 4, 1963, civil rights protest in Baltimore, Archbishop O'Boyle directed the priests of the archdiocese not to violate any trespassing laws for fear of violence. The NCWC's Msgr. Francis Hurley warned the National Council of Catholic Women's Peggy Roach after her July 17 meeting with the Leadership Conference on Civil Rights that "there can be no affiliation" between the LCCR's special office, which would organize civic and religious groups to lobby for the civil rights bill, and the NCWC. Hurley boycotted a September 18, 1963, meeting of Kennedy's advisory committee, called by chairman Irwin Miller to rally support for the civil rights bill in the wake of the Birmingham church bombing, because "it was our understanding at NCWC that the advisory group to the president was not going to be a lobbying group."[110]

In the end, however, the persistence of these racial, religious, jurisdictional, attitudinal, political, and historical obstacles could not undermine the equally tenacious leadership of many American Catholics on civil rights. In his famous appearance before the Greater Houston Ministerial Association in September 1960, candidate John Kennedy had promised that if any conflict should arise during his presidency between his religious beliefs and the U.S. Constitution, he would opt for the latter. "No Catholic prelate," Kennedy assured the ministers, "would tell the president how to act." In his June 11, 1963, civil rights speech, however, President John Kennedy cited both. By the time he said, "We are confronted with a moral issue . . . as old as the scriptures and . . . as clear as the American Constitution," Catholic prelates had been telling him that for two and a half years.[111]

Life and Death: Birth Control

In 1959 President Dwight Eisenhower appointed General William Draper to study whether population control assistance should become part of the foreign aid program of the United States. When the Draper Report answered affirmatively, the U.S. Catholic bishops reacted forcefully, expressing the Church's opposition to "any public assistance, either at home or abroad, to promote artificial birth prevention, abortion, or sterilization, whether through direct aid or by means of international organizations."[112] Eisenhower agreed with the bishops and renounced his own administration's study. "I cannot imagine anything more emphatically a subject that is not a proper political or governmental activity or function or responsibility," said the president. "This government has not, and will not . . . as long as I'm here, have a positive political doctrine in its program that has to do with this problem of birth control. That's not our business."[113]

"As long as I'm here" was Eisenhower's acknowledgment that with a new administration might come a new policy. Sure enough, under John Kennedy, the federal government, in the words of special counsel to the president Theodore Sorensen, "quietly but extensively increased its activities in the area of birth and population control," in defiance of the policies of his predecessor and the teachings of his church. The first Catholic in the White House thus became the first president to place the federal government firmly on the side of birth control. On this volatile issue, Kennedy recognized that the nation and the world were changing even if his church was not.[114]

Kennedy Acts

In the 1960 presidential campaign, John Kennedy had supported the Eisenhower policy forbidding population control assistance to other countries. At his July 19, 1961, press conference, the president reiterated his campaign position, asserting that population control "is a personal decision and a national decision which these [developing] nations must make."[115]

Despite these assertions, however, the Kennedy Administration would break with the past. Upon taking office, Kennedy commissioned a study by the State Department to devise administration policy toward the "population explosion," which was attracting considerable attention throughout the world. In a secret memorandum to Kennedy in June 1961, the National Institutes of Health recommended six courses of action subsequently taken by the president: (1) appoint an assistant (Robert Barnett, a career diplomat) to the undersecretary of state to collaborate with public and private agencies on population issues, (2) reverse the Eisenhower policy rendering such matters off-limits, (3) provide population information through the Census Bureau and the Agency for International Development to countries requesting it, (4) encourage other countries and the United Nations to expand assistance to countries with population problems, (5) undertake a modest public relations effort to apprise the American public of the population problem, and (6) direct the National Institutes of Health to expand its research on population problems.[116]

In September the NIH concluded its own review, noting that the $5.7 million of public and private funds then being expended on human fertility research, $1.3 million of which came from the NIH, was gravely inadequate. The report recommended a five-year, $90 million program of "research, testing, and field trials of family planning techniques, construction, and operation of research facilities, and training of scientists." In the next seven months, however, the administration removed the price tag and kept the report secret.[117]

In December 1961 the American delegation to the United Nations General Assembly voted to put on the agenda a six-nation resolution inviting countries with population problems to request "technical assistance" from the UN. A month later former Eisenhower science advisor George Kistiakowsky asked for and received permission from the State Department to hold a symposium on population issues that, according to a department memorandum, "would in no way be sponsored by the government, would not involve government financing, and that a State Department interest in and approval of the meeting would not be given publicity."[118]

A year later the United States endorsed an eleven-nation proposal to inaugurate birth control assistance to other nations through the UN. In announcing the policy shift, Richard Gardner, the deputy assistant secretary of state for international organization affairs, stressed that while each country would make its own decision whether to seek such technical assistance, "obstacles should not be placed in the way of other governments which, in the light of their own economic needs and cultural values, seek solutions to their population problems." Though the resolution itself would pass in a diluted form, which recognized the problem while withholding the assistance, *Science* magazine hailed Gardner's statement as nothing short of a "landmark in U.S. policy toward population problems."[119]

As if to reinforce this sentiment, Kennedy himself finally acknowledged publicly what his administration had been doing privately for two years. In replying to an April 24, 1963, press conference question about the recent recommendations of both the National Academy of Sciences and Catholic professor John Rock of Harvard University that the federal government should "participate actively in an attack on uncontrolled population growth," the president characterized ongoing federal "research in the whole area of fertility, biological studies, and all the rest," financed by "several millions of dollars of federal funds," as "very useful." Three weeks later, the Kennedy administration contributed $500,000 to the World Health Organization for research on human reproduction. In December 1963, shortly after Kennedy's death, both houses of Congress passed a foreign aid bill that earmarked funds "to conduct research into problems of population growth of underdeveloped countries," but the legislation died in the House-Senate conference committee.[120]

The Church Reacts

In his address to the Association of Large Families in Rome and Italy on January 20, 1958, Pope Pius XII said, "Overpopulation is not a valid reason for spreading birth control practices. It is simply a pretext used by those who would justify avarice and selfishness." Exactly three years later, President John Kennedy was sworn into office and undertook to challenge that position.[121]

In response, the U.S. Catholic bishops challenged Kennedy. Two days before Kennedy took office, Catherine Schaefer, director of the bishops' National Catholic Welfare Conference Office of United Nations Affairs, noted "considerable pressure on the birth control issue here and in Washington." In September 1961 Harmon Burns of the NCWC met with Richard Gardner to discuss his pending vote on the Swedish proposal for UN population assistance. Burns warned Gardner that "any undertaking by the U.N. of an affirmative birth control program, in the common understanding of the term . . . would have adverse repercussions among United States Catholics," since "our Bishops are clearly on record that we will not support any public assistance program, directly or through international organizations, which is designed to promote artificial birth prevention." Gardner assured Burns that while the United States would vote for discussion of the proposal, it would oppose the proposal itself.[122]

On November 30–December 1 representatives of the bishops expressed their views on population issues at a workshop sponsored by the influential, nongovernmental National Conference on Economic and Social Development, composed of farm, labor, educational, cooperative, civic, and religious organizations. State Department and AID officials represented the Kennedy administration at the meeting.[123]

Kennedy's liaison to Catholics, Ralph Dungan, in July 1962 sent the NCWC's

Msgr. Francis Hurley a copy of the recent State Department memorandum authorizing changes in U.S. population policy. Hurley identified three major parts of the report: (1) the identification of research projects carried on by both the government and private agencies, (2) a memorandum of legal opinions and statements by religious groups about birth control and population control, and (3) suggestions for the allocation of funds for future projects by the NIH. Hurley assessed the first part as "fairly objective," but found the others "objectionable" because "number two used the quotations inaccurately, apparently in an attempt to imply little opposition to birth control," and "number three suggested birth control projects."[124] Later that month, Schaefer responded to a newspaper advertising appeal by Hugh Moore and Margaret Sanger for Kennedy's support of population control assistance to foreign countries. Schaefer wrote the president that "a country's population policy is the responsibility of its people."[125]

In November Burns met again with Gardner about the latest version of the Swedish proposal advocating "technical assistance" to address population growth. Gardner reassured Burns that while the Kennedy administration supported "research and study" of population problems, it opposed "technical assistance." When the vote came in December, however, Gardner merely abstained from the inclusion of the resolution's sixth paragraph, which the NCWC opposed as "suggesting technical assistance for controlling population." Hurley concluded that Gardner's vote for the resolution put the administration "on the side of the planned parenthood people" and in favor of contraception.[126]

Conclusions on Life and Death

In the realm of birth control, President John Kennedy moved while his church stood still. Whether Kennedy changed his position on birth control, however, was less significant than how and why he was able to change with seemingly so little effort and even less attention.

The first reason the Kennedy administration was able to reverse the Eisenhower precedent was the exceptional media glare trained on the so-called population explosion, which was predicted to increase the world's population to six billion by 2000; there had been a tripling in the previous eighty years and there would be a doubling in forty. "That a president who is a Roman Catholic should be the first to advocate such a [fertility research] program," wrote the editors of the Protestant *Christian Century*, "is evidence that population control is, as the National Academy [of Sciences] statement said, 'an international problem from which no one can escape.'"[127]

A second reason for Kennedy's effectiveness in the face of Church opposition was that many prominent Catholics were at least acknowledging the population problem, and some were urging the Church, if not the federal government, to address it. "Catholic scholars today realize the need to explore the population problem," *America* editorialized in May 1961, "and contribute to its solution." In October, *Commonweal* criticized the Church for its "sporadic and scattered response" to population problems.[128]

In November 1962 the Associated Press reported that a "number" of bishops at the Second Vatican Council in Rome were preparing a petition urging the Church to study population issues. In March 1963, *America* announced that Georgetown University had received a $150,000 Ford Foundation grant to conduct research on population issues, including an examination of possible improvements in the rhythm method. In April came the release of Dr. John Rock's book, *The Time Has Come: A Catholic Doctor's Proposals to End the Battle over Birth Control*, in which he advocated a "crash program" of fertility research by the NIH to devise birth control methods "which all religious groups can accept." Boston's Richard Cardinal Cushing, while criticizing parts of Rock's work, nonetheless concluded, "In this book, there is much that is good."[129]

If Catholics split over the ends of the Kennedy population policies, they also divided over the means, leading to a third reason for the administration's success. There was enough careful ambiguity in the administration's sales pitch to confuse its Catholic adversaries, who relentlessly sought silver linings amid gathering clouds. Schaefer asserted hopefully at the outset of the Kennedy presidency, "It seems assured that this year more [population] studies will be undertaken and no definitive action taken." At its July 19, 1961, meeting the NCWC's Committee on International Affairs agreed to take a "positive approach" to population issues. "In this way," the committee optimistically contended, "birth control issues could be considered only as one aspect of an extensive field."[130]

Schaefer reported on an October 18 briefing for American nongovernmental organizations, including the NCWC's Office for United Nations Affairs, at which Philip Klutznick, speaking for the Kennedy administration, predicted that although there would be "a bit of acrimony" on population issues, the resolution of these matters "won't present too great a problem to anyone." Klutznick explained that "most delegates [at the UN] were anxious to avoid the moral and theological aspects of the question." In planning the National Conference on Economic and Social Development in November 1961, Rev. James Vizzard of the NCWC boasted that "our constructive contributions have been effective in shifting the former view of the discussion from 'population control' to 'population and resources.' In addition we have won broad agreement on our insistence that doctrinaire birth controllers must be kept off the panel and denied the floor during the discussion."[131]

Hope persisted in the second year of the Kennedy presidency. After Chester Bowles, Kennedy's special advisor on African, Asian, and Latin affairs, told the Michigan Council of Churches to "leave [population] decisions to the people in the country involved," *America* wistfully wondered, "Is the pressure to make artificial birth control an arm of U.S. foreign policy proving an embarrassment to the State Department?" In December Hurley applauded the input of the NCWC's Rev. John Knott on the NIH's Survey of Research on Population Control for helping to produce a "much better presentation, more objective and less inflammatory." A week later, Hurley begrudgingly acknowledged that Gardner's "fuzzy" explanation of his vote at the UN was "an attempt to forestall criticisms from Catholics."[132]

This effort appeared to be working. In a February 1963 briefing to American nongovernmental organizations, Leighton Van Nort of the State Department's Bureau of International Organization Affairs noted that the title of the Associated Press story on the Gardner vote was "U.S. Supports Birth Control Policy," while United Press International led with "U.S. Opposes Birth Control Policy." In reality, Van Nort paradoxically claimed, "The U.S. took a clear stand which cannot be described as either pro– or anti–birth control."[133]

When asked directly at his April press conference to endorse birth control aid for other nations, Kennedy ducked the question, and Catholics largely heard what they wanted to hear. *Science* had opined on the eve of the UN vote that while the Church opposed birth control assistance, "in much of Church thinking on the subject, there has been a warm spot for research." *America* editorialized in the aftermath of the press conference that the Kennedy policy hardly constituted an "about-face" from the Eisenhower years. "If we understand the President's words correctly," wrote the editors, "he said that the United States should continue and even expand the basic research it is doing in the field of human fertility. . . . To that proposition, there will be little objection and certainly none from us." When *Science* marked the end of 1963 by contending that "the efforts of population-planning organizations and the enormity of the population problem overwhelmed long-established and tenaciously-held ideological positions," Catholic pollster Thomas Benham of Opinion Research Corporation decried the editorial's "tone of jubilation."[134]

If the birth control proponents at *Science* magazine were making a lot of noise, the administration and the Church were mostly keeping quiet, creating a fourth reason for the relative ease with which Kennedy changed course. Both seemed to have learned from the very public quarrel over federal aid to nonpublic education that had pitted Kennedy against the U.S. Catholic hierarchy at the outset of his administration. In April 1962 Kennedy assigned most population concerns to the Agency for International Development, which, in Ralph Dungan's words, "would stimulate in a discreet way" discussion of such issues. In July, after AID and the United States Information Agency proposed a poll of Latin American governments about the "desirability of birth control," Donald Wilson, the agency's acting director, warned that any publication of the survey results would spell domestic political "trouble." *Science* noted in November, in the wake of the State Department's secret study and secret symposium, as well as the NIH's secret memorandum and secret report, that the Kennedy administration was "operating under the assumption that if it bears a birth control label, hide it." The following June the same magazine reported that AID "has quietly advised its foreign missions that the U.S. government is now receptive to requests for certain types of assistance in population planning."[135]

The Church's opposition to Kennedy was equally circumspect. "Widespread distribution of contraceptive devices to both unmarried and married persons at public expense was recommended here today by a population control assembly which included members of the Catholic faith," began a front-page story in the November 18, 1963, *Washington Post* by Eve Edstrom on a conference sponsored by George Washington University and the American Assembly. "On only one occasion, and with the support of the majority of the delegates who represented all the states and a wide variety of private and public occupations," Edstrom continued, "did a Catholic spokesman, the Rev. Theodore McCarrick, speak against a suggested change in a recommendation" to support abortion. Two days later, the *Post* editorialized that the conference showed a "softening of the Church's opposition to publicly-funded birth control which is indeed comforting."[136]

McCarrick, the director of development at Catholic University, privately protested Edstrom's "implication that we approved the conference proposals in toto." McCarrick insisted to the NCWC's Msgr. Tanner and New York auxiliary bishop John McGuire that the 24 Catholics among the 120 conference delegates were simply unwilling to "impose our views on the majority." Yet McCarrick found the *Post* editorial "somewhat less disturbing," and he authored neither an op-ed piece nor even a letter to the editor to set the record straight.[137]

"Once again, ears were tuned for reaction from the Catholic hierarchy" to the foreign aid bill, which passed Congress, wrote the editors of *Science* in December 1963, "but none of any significance was forthcoming." Largely because of the bishops' reticence, *Science* concluded that on the subject of birth control, "the electricity has gone out of the issue."[138]

A fifth explanation for the smooth transition from Eisenhower's birth control policy to Kennedy's was the ineffectiveness of the bishops on Capitol Hill. A February 1962 *Redbook* survey asked members of Congress to rate twenty-eight interest groups according to their impact on legislation. Only the American Federation of Labor–Congress of Industrial Organizations received a "high influence" ranking, while sixteen organizations earned a "low influence" designation. The bishops' National Catholic Welfare Conference was one of eleven groups, and the only religious organization, credited with "moderate influence." The article accompanying the poll noted, however, that the NCWC had directed virtually all of its congressional lobbying efforts in the first year of the Kennedy presidency toward its unsuccessful quest for federal aid to parochial schools. "I don't know whether we have a 'Cary' [sic] available to bottle it up or not," Msgr. Tanner wrote Msgr. Hurley as the foreign aid bill worked its way through Congress in October, alluding to New York's Catholic Democratic congressman, Hugh Carey, an NCWC ally in the school aid wars. They didn't.[139]

The final factor that facilitated Kennedy's shift was that it aligned him with his true beliefs. According to Sorensen, Kennedy interpreted the timing of the bishops' 1959 statement as a thinly veiled rejection of his presidential candidacy. Only a few days later, Kennedy voiced his opposition to any reduction of foreign aid to a country because it directed the funds toward birth control. "You know, just because Jack and I are Catholics," First Lady Jacqueline Kennedy would tell Kitty Galbraith, the wife of Kennedy's ambassador to India, "don't think we don't believe in birth control."[140] Even so, Kennedy confidant Richard Cardinal Cushing would defend his fellow Catholic in the White House. "On the question of birth control," Cushing would recall, "a Catholic president would necessarily obey his oath of office. Every state in the Union [had] legalized in some form or another the authority of doctors and others to recommend birth control in various forms permitted by their respective laws."[141]

If American Catholics largely surrendered to the Kennedy administration on birth control, however, they would live to fight another day. "This is going to be a long battle," wrote Msgr. Hurley as 1963 drew to a close. On that, at least, everyone could agree.[142]

By the time John Kennedy's life ended too soon in November 1963, he had assumed the mantles of a crusader for peace, a champion of civil rights, and a defender of artificial contraception. But he reached those positions only after protracted struggles with and against his church. Because he was one of them, many Catholics pressed Kennedy especially hard on arms control and civil rights. And because he was one of them, they were relatively soft on Kennedy on birth control. Whether elements of the Catholic hierarchy were winning on matters of war and peace and social justice or losing on issues of life and death, Kennedy's historic presidency could not escape the long shadow of his church.

CHAPTER TWO

Catholics and Lyndon Johnson
(1963–1969)

MANY HAVE CALLED the American presidency the "loneliest job in the world," and photographs of Lyndon Johnson's furrowed visage during the depths of the Vietnam War provide ample evidence. But the papacy could also be a lonely place during the Johnson years. No matter how hard he tried, Pope Paul VI could not convince the president to stop waging his war in Southeast Asia, or to wage his War on Poverty without artificial contraception. And he could not coax enough of the American Catholic episcopate toward the former or enough of their congregants toward the latter. So the soaring success that the pope, the bishops, and the faithful enjoyed in helping to enact and implement Johnson's civil rights and anti-poverty legislation could not obscure the searing schism that undermined the Church's efforts to shape his policies on Vietnam and birth control.

War and Peace: The Vietnam War

With his imposing stature and outsize arrogance, Lyndon Johnson seemed eager to take on the world as he ascended to the presidency in November 1963. And soon he would have to. Questions of war and peace, especially in Vietnam, would obsess and ultimately overwhelm the president and the nation, as American unilateralism earned international enmity and presaged national humiliation.

Nobody tried harder than Johnson to achieve a durable peace in Vietnam and a meaningful respite from the Cold War. Nobody, except perhaps Pope Paul VI. Just as Johnson often invoked John F. Kennedy in his determination to contain communism yet deepen détente, so too did Pope Paul build on the considerable foundations laid by Pope John XXIII. Pope Paul VI's tireless pursuit of peace prodded the American president, encouraged many American Catholics, and often embarrassed much of the American Catholic hierarchy, to whom the world remained, even in the wake of the historic Second Vatican Council, less modern than Manichaean. As a result, the American Catholic

Church that so enthusiastically welcomed change in other areas seemed terribly frightened by it in this one.

It is perhaps unsurprising, then, that when a president uncomfortable with nuance sought refuge from a world grown too complex, he would often find sanctuary in a Catholic church, where the uncertainties of his own faith would give way to the sturdy predictability of another. Yet ultimately neither Johnson nor the American Catholic bishops could escape the challenges to his foreign policy that undid his presidency and unsettled their church.[1]

The Pope and the President

In February 1965, two months after Johnson's landslide victory over Arizona Republican senator Barry Goldwater, a Viet Cong assault on an American air force base in Pleiku, South Vietnam, killed eight and wounded over one hundred. Over the lone dissent of Catholic Senate majority leader Mike Mansfield, Democrat of Montana, Johnson followed the advice of his National Security Council and congressional leaders and ordered the selective American bombing of North Vietnam.[2]

Pope Paul VI responded to the American escalation of the Vietnam War first by endorsing a suggestion by French president Charles de Gaulle that the United Nations mediate the conflict. Then the pope sent a letter to South Vietnam's Catholic bishops, urging their efforts to prevent "the horrors of a prolonged and extensive commitment of arms."[3]

The pope's pleas fell on deaf ears. In March, Johnson dispatched the first American combat troops to join the thousands of advisors already training South Vietnamese forces in the fight against the communists. "I thought you would like to see some of the support we are getting from some of the more level-headed clergy on Vietnam," White House press secretary Bill Moyers wrote Johnson in April, after receiving a copy of a pro-war column by the director of the American bishops' National Catholic Welfare Conference Social Action Department, Msgr. George Higgins, which was to appear in twenty-five diocesan newspapers throughout the country.[4]

The Catholic bishops of South Vietnam similarly were more concerned about defeating the communists than accommodating them. White House aide Jack Valenti briefed Johnson before the president's February meeting with the pope's apostolic delegate to the United States, Rev. Egidio Vagnozzi, by noting that "communists have infiltrated the Buddhist movement in South Vietnam," and that Rev. Patrick O'Connor of the National Catholic News Service "has been in Vietnam for over fifteen years [and] . . . could be useful" to the administration. Following a meeting with Prime Minister Phan Huy Quat, the South Vietnamese bishops accused their government of failing to forestall a Buddhist-led purge of Catholic military commanders. Rev. Hoang Quynh, a spokesman for the nine hundred thousand Catholic refugees who had fled the communist North, was heading an effort in 116 parishes in the vicinity of Saigon, the southern capital, to arm young Catholic men with knives and sticks to defend their communities. Not only were South Vietnam's Catholic leaders ignoring the pope's entreaties for peace, but some of them had even intimated that the Johnson administration was behind the purge as a step toward a negotiated settlement of the war.[5]

Even a papal encyclical could not deter the South Vietnamese church. In *Mense Maio* ("In the Month of May"), Paul VI implored the world's governments to "continue at all times to foster and encourage conversations and negotiations at all levels" and to "condemn acts of guerilla war and of terrorism, the practices of holding hostages and of taking repeated reprisals against unarmed civilians." The South Vietnamese hierarchy's reply was to tacitly approve the formation of the Greater Unity Force, a Catholic political organization devoted to "invading and holding" North Vietnam "to deliver our compatriots from the yoke of Communist dictatorship." A month later, the Quat regime fell to a military coup, with Catholic major general Nguyen Van Thieu in charge of the new government.[6]

The pope did influence the president, however, as Johnson asserted his willingness to negotiate with the enemy in Vietnam. Then he prepared to sit down with Paul himself. "It is of great importance to impress the Pope with our passion for peace in Vietnam," Secretary of State Dean Rusk counseled Johnson, while conceding "faint indications that not all Vatican circles are persuaded on this point."[7]

After publicly urging the United Nations in October to commit itself to "never again war," Paul VI privately pressed Johnson toward that lofty goal. "The entire world is indebted to His Holiness, as I said to him in our private conversation," Johnson told the press, "for the sacrifices he has made in coming on this long trip across the water to provide leadership in the world's quest for peace. His Holiness and I discussed ways and means of advancing that cause."[8]

Yet Pope Paul and President Johnson did not engage in specifics about Vietnam, where the U.S. military presence continued to grow and American peace efforts continued to founder. Majority leader Mansfield returned in December with four other senators from a fact-finding mission in Vietnam with a report so pessimistic that Johnson ordered a bombing pause in hopes of igniting peace talks.[9]

Without naming either side or even the conflict itself, the pope's Christmas message pointed out the "limits of self-interest or one's own ambitions" as "obstacles to peace," and called instead for "just and sincere negotiation to restore order and friendship." No sooner had the pontiff sent a message to the governments of North Vietnam, South Vietnam, and the United States praising a thirty-hour holiday truce, however, than the fighting resumed.[10]

Having failed to reconcile the competing factions in Vietnam, the pope turned to neutral parties, futilely advocating an international peace conference convened by the United Nations and conducted by governments with no direct stake in the outcome. After his latest endeavor produced only six months of inaction, Pope Paul VI acknowledged that "our sincere and disinterested efforts failed to come to fruition," and warned of the "possible extension of the conflict" in Southeast Asia. Johnson conceded as much in a letter to Mansfield. "We can get out of Viet Nam. We can get out next week or next month," Johnson wrote the Catholic senator. "But what happens then? . . . We know what would then happen to the Catholics, Buddhists, and every other non-Communist group, because we saw it happen in 1954–56."[11]

In July, Johnson's top commander in Vietnam, Gen. William Westmoreland, accepted the Honor et Veritas Award, the Catholic War Veterans U.S.A.'s highest honor, given in appreciation of the U.S. bombing of North Vietnamese military targets in Hanoi and Haiphong. In a letter to Johnson, the organization's leader, Martin Riley, expressed the wish for a "speedy and just victory in Viet Nam."[12]

In his strongest language yet, Pope Paul VI's September encyclical *Christi Matri* ("To the Mother of Christ") urged "with piercing cry and with tears" an end to the "bloody and difficult war . . . in areas of East Asia." White House aide Tom Johnson informed the president that the pope's pleas for peace were winning "considerable sympathy" among the American people. The U.S. ambassador to the United Nations, Arthur Goldberg, followed the encyclical with an offer that the world body mediate a settlement predicated upon a U.S. bombing halt, North Vietnamese and U.S. withdrawal from the South, and peace talks that would include the Viet Cong. Though Goldberg's "major policy speech to the [General] Assembly did not mention the Encyclical," the U.S. Catholic bishops' Office of United Nations Affairs observed, "the Encyclical assured discussion of the question [of Vietnam] within the context of international responsibility."[13]

Pope Paul VI sent a special envoy, Most Rev. Sergio Pignedoli, the titular archbishop of Iconio and the apostolic delegate to Canada, on an October peace mission to Saigon. Then he commemorated the first anniversary of his UN speech by exhorting 150,000 Catholics in St. Peter's Square in Rome with words grown tragically ironic over the preceding twelve months: "Never again war." President Johnson also remembered the occasion by attending a special Washington Peace Mass at St. Matthew's Cathedral, where he heard Archbishop Patrick O'Boyle blame the enemy for failing to respond to the president's repeated peace overtures. As Christmas approached, Paul VI reiterated his previous year's hope that a holiday truce would unlock a lasting peace. From Austin, President Johnson promised "sympathetic consideration" of the pontiff's latest plea but from Saigon, Secretary of State Rusk conveyed serious doubts.[14]

Almost a year after greeting Foreign Minister Andrei Gromyko, the first Soviet official to enter Vatican City, Pope Paul VI hosted Soviet premier Nikolai Podgorny in January 1967. A week later he appealed to Presidents Johnson, Ho Chi Minh of North Vietnam, and Nguyen Van Thieu of South Vietnam to extend their ninety-six-hour truce in observance of Tet, the lunar new year. Podgorny told Paul VI that his country would never abandon its North Vietnamese ally, and he rebuffed the pontiff's call for direct Soviet-U.S. negotiations on the war. Johnson reiterated his desire to negotiate "at any time and place, in any forum," while adding that surely the pope "would not expect us to reduce military action unless the other side is willing to do likewise." Condemning the "U.S. imperialists [who] have sent to South Vietnam half a million U.S. and satellite troops and used more than 600,000 puppet troops to wage a war against our people," Ho Chi Minh encouraged Paul VI to "use his high influence to urge that the U.S. government respect the national rights of the Vietnamese people." Thieu joined the Catholic hierarchy in South Vietnam in implicitly supporting a Saigon street protest organized by a Catholic group, the Committee for a Just and Legitimate Peace, in opposition to any peace efforts that would "sell out" South Vietnam to the communists.[15]

The pope pressed on nonetheless. An April meeting with U Thant in Rome preceded the opening of the Pacem in Terris Institute in New York, where the secretary-general admiringly described the pontiff as "obsessed with peace." A month later, Paul VI observed the fiftieth anniversary of the appearance of the Virgin Mary to three shepherd children in Fatima, Portugal, with a call for a U.S. bombing halt and an end to North Vietnamese infiltration of the South. Yet in August, when celebrating the feast of the assumption of the Virgin Mary, the pope lamented the absence of "the force and coherence and constancy" necessary to achieve those goals.[16]

The Johnson administration persisted in welcoming the Holy Father's peace efforts without changing its course in Vietnam. The president also met again with the pope. This time, unlike in their meeting two years earlier, the two leaders were quite specific in their discussion of the Vietnam War. "You went to South Vietnam to protect your good intentions and your good hopes," Paul VI reassured Johnson in December in Rome. "But you must understand that I can never agree to war." The pope then encouraged the president to end the bombing of the North. "We have stopped bombing five times, but this only increases the murder," Johnson replied. "Archbishop [Robert] Lucey [of San Antonio] went to South Vietnam as one of my observers during the [September] election. He told me that every time we quietened [sic] down they increase[d] their pressure. In the thirty-seven-day bombing pause [of 1965–1966], they built up a seven-months' supply."

Charging that "Hanoi is ignoring and violating the Geneva Convention prisoner rules," Johnson urged the pope to send a representative to visit the prisoners on both sides. He then proposed that the pontiff press South Vietnam and the National Liberation Front, the political wing of the Viet Cong, to engage in informal peace talks in Saigon, without their North Vietnamese and American sponsors. "Thieu is a good man—honest—and a Catholic," Johnson assured the Holy Father. "As you know, the Catholics are in a minority in South Vietnam. In the recent election, a new Senate was voted in, and a Catholic was elected as President of the Senate. . . . I hope the Pope will encourage them to talk." Johnson smiled broadly: "Just as the Pope encouraged me to pass my education bills. We are now spending nine billion dollars more on education. And the Pope can claim some responsibility for this." Paul VI returned the smile, and, reaching out his hands toward the president, promised to try to investigate the treatment of POWs as well as attempt to bring the South Vietnamese government and the National Liberation Front together: "I will do whatever is possible. I will study the prisoner situation and see what contacts can be made. This is a cause which is close to my heart."

The pope then inquired, "Is it possible that the truce at Christmas could be extended a day or two? Could you not show the world that on the day of peace January 1 you will also make this a day of truce?"

"My problem is this," Johnson responded. "My military leaders tell me that the North Vietnamese have trucks lined up bumper to bumper, and as soon as the truce begins they start them moving, and those supplies and those men kill our soldiers." Having been refused yet again in his desperate quest for an end to the Vietnam War, the pontiff relented. "We shall pray for you," he told the president. "And we shall pray for your efforts for peace."[17]

Subsequent events would vindicate both pope and president. For the first time, the Catholic hierarchy of South Vietnam criticized its government, not for being "soft" on communism, but for standing in the way of peace. The seventeen bishops representing South Vietnam's two million Catholics finally fell in line with the Holy Father in calling for an end to U.S. bombing and North Vietnamese aggression. "How can there be peace when those in responsible places mask their false promises behind rhetoric?" the bishops demanded of the Thieu government. "How can there be peace if laziness, hypocrisy, and corruption prevail everywhere in society?"[18]

But for the umpteenth time, the North Vietnamese and Viet Cong violated a truce, with a massive assault on some thirty major cities in South Vietnam, including Saigon, during the Tet cease-fire at the end of January. The ferocity of an enemy thought to be on its last legs horrified the millions of Americans witnessing the offensive on their television screens. In February's New Hampshire Democratic presidential primary, Johnson barely defeated antiwar Catholic senator Eugene McCarthy of Minnesota. So, following two days of meetings with his foreign policy team, Johnson announced to the nation that he would stop most of the bombing of the North, commence serious peace talks, and, to the amazement of even his closest aides, not seek reelection. The United States would not surrender to North Vietnam and the Viet Cong for another seven years. But on the last day of March in 1968, the president surrendered to the pope.[19]

The Bishops and the President

But many American Catholic bishops kept fighting. Their staunch anticommunism and empathy for the Catholic minority in South Vietnam had long evoked a sympathetic stance toward the war by most members of the hierarchy. In July 1964 Harmon Burns of the bishops' National Catholic Welfare Conference Legal Department met with Michael Forrestal, Johnson's assistant secretary of state for Vietnamese affairs, to demand that the South Vietnamese government release Major Dang Sy, a prominent Catholic prisoner. The bishops considered Dang Sy a victim of religious discrimination by a pro-Buddhist regime that blamed him for suppressing the Buddhist riots that helped ensure President Ngo Dinh Diem's ouster in November 1963. Forrestal assured Burns that although the United States would not request the major's release for fear of bloody protests by Buddhists in the northern part of South Vietnam, Johnson's ambassador to South Vietnam, Maxwell Taylor, had secured from Prime Minister Nguyen Khanh pledges of a reduction of his life sentence and eventual permission for him to leave the country.[20] The bishops' attention to the Dang Sy case stood in marked contrast to Pope Paul VI's view of the internal divisions in South Vietnam. At the end of August, *L'Osservatore Romano*, the Vatican newspaper, denied that South Vietnamese street clashes that had led to the killing of a Catholic youth by a Buddhist mob were signs of a religious conflict.[21]

In May 1965 Higgins blasted an antiwar vigil at the Pentagon organized by national clergy, which "almost inevitably took on the character of an anti-

Administration gathering." Lyndon Johnson's favorite Catholic prelate, Archbishop Robert Lucey of San Antonio, assured Catholic White House aide Jack Valenti that "the situation in Vietnam has . . . made a turn for the better." The Catholic Association for International Peace's World Order Committee issued a July 1965 statement staunchly defending the new U.S. combat role in Vietnam. But quoting Pope John XXIII in *Pacem in Terris*, committee chairman Charles O'Donnell expressed the hope "that by meeting and negotiating, men may come to discover better the bonds that unite them."[22]

UN ambassador Arthur Goldberg echoed this mixed message when he addressed the CAIP's annual convention in December. Citing Paul VI, he said that though "the tragedy of our times may be that the Pontiff's cry of 'war never again' may be the one condition of survival in our atomic age," he also lamented that quite possibly "men and nations are too wrapped up in the habits of the past to recognize it."[23]

So, perhaps, were the bishops themselves. A group of fifty college students picketed outside the chancery of New York's archbishop, Francis Cardinal Spellman, in a December 1965 protest of Spellman's "silencing" of antiwar Jesuits Revs. Daniel Berrigan, Daniel Kilfoyle, and Frank Keating. Three weeks later Spellman arrived in Saigon for a Christmas visit with U.S. troops. When asked, "What do you think about what America is doing in Vietnam?" the cardinal replied, "I fully support everything it does."[24]

In March 1966, the *National Catholic Reporter* distributed a questionnaire on the war to the nation's 225 Catholic bishops. After five weeks, only six had replied, with half expressing support and the other half evading the issue. Rev. John Bennett, the president of Union Theological Seminary and a leader of Protestant-Catholic ecumenical dialogue, marked the October anniversary of Pope Paul VI's United Nations speech by recalling that although "the Pope did all in his power . . . he had no leverage with the North Vietnamese, and apparently not much either with the Roman Catholic hierarchy of the United States on the question of peace."[25]

The bishops strove to reconcile their own backing of the war with the pope's search for peace. Baltimore archbishop Lawrence Cardinal Shehan's June pastoral, "Peace and Patriotism," while stopping short of criticizing the administration, nonetheless reminded Catholics of the wartime imperatives of the Second Vatican Council's *Pastoral Constitution on the Church in the Modern World* to "exert whatever moral and civic influences seem dictated by . . . conscience." The bishops' November pastoral toed the same wobbly line. "It is reasonable to argue that our presence in Vietnam is justified," they wrote. "But we cannot stop here. . . . It is the duty of everyone to keep looking for other alternatives."[26]

As evidence of how short a distance the bishops had traveled, the statement passed 169–5. "Your support for the war is accompanied by qualifications," a group of antiwar Catholics addressed the bishops from the nation's capital, "but you have so underemphasized these qualifications that they are being forgotten." The critics then cast their lot with Pope Paul VI, whose *Christi Matri* ("To the Mother of Christ") had summoned both sides in the war to "stop—even at the expense of some inconvenience or loss." They cast their lot against Cardinal Spellman, whose Christmas Eve address to the American troops in Saigon calling for victory in Vietnam provoked unofficial angst in Vatican City, official repudiation in Moscow and Peking, and unusual vitriol from California Episcopal bishop Kilmer Myers. "I can find no evidence that the Pope's stirring plea has ruffled the surface of American Catholic life," Rev. John Sheerin, the editor of *Catholic World*, lamented. "Who speaks for the Church on Vietnam?"[27]

In March 1967 Auxiliary Bishop James Shannon of Minneapolis–St. Paul joined ten presidents of Catholic colleges in denouncing the indiscriminate bombing of civilians in Vietnam, but they neglected to address the overriding issue of the war itself. "Though the American people are divided on the Vietnamese War," Daniel Callahan wrote in the April *Atlantic Monthly*, for tactical or strategic reasons, "not one bishop has opposed it."[28]

The following year would expose a few cracks in the bishops' façade, however. In July, Rochester bishop Fulton Sheen became the first Catholic prelate to advocate immediate U.S. withdrawal from Vietnam. Though still refusing to break with the administration, Atlanta archbishop Paul Hallinan, Minneapolis–St. Paul auxiliary bishop James Shannon, Oklahoma City–Tulsa bishop Victor Reed, and Newark auxiliary bishop John Dougherty lent their support in August to the Negotiation Now movement, which called for an end to U.S. bombing, a beginning of peace talks, and an enormous economic aid package under UN auspices as steps toward an end to the war. Without parting with the administration, Catholic Association for International Peace president William O'Brien decried the resumption of U.S. bombing near North Vietnamese cities, singling out an August 11 bombardment of Long Bien bridge less than two miles from downtown Hanoi. "No one who takes seriously the social teaching of the Catholic Church on the moral limits of defensive warfare," O'Brien maintained, "can countenance counter-city warfare in North Vietnam."[29]

In November the bishops promulgated a new "Resolution on Peace," which continued to back "the repeated efforts of our government to negotiate a termination to conflict" while rejecting "peace at any price." The statement nevertheless urged "even greater determination and action in the cause of negotiation" by the Johnson administration. The following April, in the wake of the Tet offensive, the bishops applauded Johnson's moves to restrict the bombing and pursue a diplomatic solution to the war, but confessed a "growing anxiety for peace." They formed a Secretariat for World Justice and Peace to better articulate their position on the war.[30] But the administration did not feel threatened by these gathering clouds. "Not all churchmen are by any means opposed to what we are doing in Vietnam," said press secretary Bill Moyers in reaction to the World Council of Churches' December 1965 resolution against the war.[31]

White House aide Joseph Califano shared with Johnson the September 1967 assessment of his fellow Catholic, the Democratic Speaker of the House of Representatives, John McCormack of Massachusetts, that "most Catholic clergy" were still "with you on Viet Nam." The president acknowledged Cardinal Spellman's death in December by foreshadowing "the first Christmas in many years when our men in uniform will not share the comfort of his presence." And three days before Johnson shocked the world by announcing that he would not seek reelection, Cardinal Cushing advised him that he should. "He said to look out for the Kennedys," Eugene Rostow relayed to fellow White House aide Marvin Watson. "He said he predicted to President Kennedy before he was killed that he would lose the election in 1964." Rostow recounted his conversation with the former president's favorite Catholic prelate: "Bobby had made many enemies for President Kennedy, and the Cardinal didn't think those enemies had forgotten." Though Johnson would not run in 1968, Catholic New York senator Robert Kennedy would, as an antiwar candidate, but his campaign ended with an assassin's bullet in June.[32]

The Church and the President

"We must keep the world from being devoured by the Communists," *Commonweal* editor James O'Gara wrote in July 1965, "but we also must keep it from destroying itself." Such was the dilemma that American Catholics faced between the often conflicting aims of President Lyndon Johnson and Pope Paul VI on matters of war and peace. The result was an unsteady wavering between right and left, opposition and obedience.[33]

To assist conscientious objectors and to register his opposition to the Vietnam War, Rev. Daniel Berrigan joined James Forest of the Catholic Worker movement and James Douglass, a theology student in Rome, in forming the Catholic Peace Fellowship in the summer of 1964. When poet Daniel Berrigan and professor Philip Berrigan joined five hundred others in signing a March 1965 "Declaration of Conscience" against U.S. policy in Vietnam, they became the first priests publicly to protest the war. The statement urged Americans to avoid the draft, refuse to participate in the manufacture or transportation of weapons, and obstruct the mobilization of U.S. troops.[34]

They were not the only Catholics to take such a stand. In November Catholic Worker Roger LaPorte immolated himself in front of the United Nations building. After Rev. Daniel Berrigan eulogized LaPorte, his Jesuit superior exiled him to Mexico. In December, the Catholic Peace Fellowship placed two-page ads in the *National Catholic Reporter, Commonweal*, and *Ave Maria*, urging Catholics to refuse service in the "unjust" Vietnam War. Rev. John Sheerin marveled in *Catholic World* in March 1966, "Is it not strange that so many of our clergy who have no hesitation about making positive moral judgments week after week in confession have no opinions on the great moral problem of our generation?"[35]

Catholic laypeople rushed to fill this void. Father Daniel Berrigan was among over one hundred clergy from many faiths who inaugurated the National Emergency Committee of Clergy Concerned about Vietnam (later, Clergy and Laymen Concerned about Vietnam) in January 1966. By the end of the year, the group was advocating a negotiated peace in Vietnam and had grown to sixty-eight chapters. By mid-1966, James Forest, co-chairman of the Catholic Peace Fellowship, an antiwar organization with headquarters in New York, had published a booklet, "Catholics and Conscientious Objection," and his group was counseling up to fifty Catholics per week about whether and how to seek this option to military service. *Commonweal* ended the year by advocating an immediate, unconditional withdrawal of U.S. forces from the "unjust" war in Southeast Asia.[36]

Rev. Philip Berrigan of Baltimore was the only Catholic among twelve clergy who criticized the war in an open letter to President Johnson in December 1966. Rev. James Drane of Little Rock, Arkansas, engaged in a shouting match in the Washington office of his state's pro-war Democratic senator, John McClellan, then returned home to lead a three-day fast by clergy and students, which prompted Democratic state senator Dan Sprick to label the young priest a "communist."[37]

But the Left remained largely left out of the American Catholic consensus on Vietnam. From the right, William Roberts, the director of Catholic University's Institute of International Law and Relations, took on Rev. Philip Berrigan in a December 1965 debate in which Roberts declared Vietnam a "just war" in defense of "human rights." The *National Review*'s Anthony Bouscaren in March 1966 attacked the Berrigan brothers and Catholic Worker founder Dorothy Day for being soft on communism.[38]

Most American Catholics planted themselves firmly in the middle of the Vietnam debate. Rev. Andrew Greeley, a sociologist, took issue in June 1965 with those "peaceniks" who equated the escalating resistance to the Vietnam War with the increasing mobilization against racial segregation.[39]

Conclusions on War and Peace

An "argument without end" is how Lyndon Johnson's secretary of defense, Robert McNamara, would characterize the debate over the Vietnam War three decades after its conclusion. Since the United States was losing in Vietnam, the conventional wisdom has come to hold, the Johnson administration was losing the argument that had put Americans there. The commander in chief explained the rationale for U.S. military involvement in Vietnam in April 1965: to the communists, "we must say in Southeast Asia—as we did in Europe—in the words of the Bible, 'Hitherto shalt thou come but no further.'" The American Catholic shepherds and much of their flock, who unabashedly or tacitly accepted this argument even at the risk of offending Pope Paul VI, therefore appeared complicit in this national tragedy.[40] After all, a Gallup Poll in late 1966 found far more Catholics than Protestants and Jews on Johnson's side in the Vietnam conflict. At the same time, a survey conducted by *World Campus*, a Maryknoll Fathers magazine, showed one-third of American Catholic college students in favor of U.S. policy in Vietnam, and over half supporting more bombing of North Vietnam while opposing demonstrations against the war. Two years later, American Catholics gave 59 percent of their votes to Johnson's vice president, Hubert Humphrey, who essentially vowed to continue the administration's military and diplomatic initiatives in Vietnam.[41]

In reassuring their president, the American Catholic majority was largely rebuking their pope. The pontiff himself seemed to recognize the limits of his effectiveness as the Church's and arguably the world's spiritual leader. In his September 1966 encyclical, *Christi Matri*, Paul VI acknowledged that the acceleration of his petitions for peace had begotten only escalation on the battlefield. "What is the use of it?" he asked plaintively, answering that despite his many setbacks, he remained convinced that "to pray is not in vain."[42]

But American Catholics were not always on the "wrong" side of the argument over Vietnam. *Commonweal*'s verdict that President Johnson's mantra of "we cannot just get out" was "not a suitable substitute for a war policy" arrived as early as August 1965, almost eight years before the remaining U.S. troops just got out. The same month, *Life* published a picture of Catholic Worker Christopher Kearns burning his draft card. By the end of August Congress had passed a law prohibiting such actions, and Catholic Worker David Miller would become the first person to go to prison for breaking it. In May 1968 the

Berrigan brothers and six other Catholics raided the office of the Catonsville, Maryland, draft board and burned the records with napalm.[43]

Though most American Catholics repudiated such radical activities, a July 1967 Harris Poll showed that they had become more dovish on the war than their Protestant counterparts, with one-quarter of American Catholics now in opposition. Even the bishops finally showed substantial movement in that direction. At their November 1968 annual meeting, the bishops issued a pastoral, "Human Life in Our Day." While expressing the hope that the Johnson administration's bombing halt and peace negotiations would soon bear fruit, the bishops nonetheless wondered, "How much more of our resources in men and money should we commit to this struggle?" And they emerged from their anti-nuclear shell to advocate early Senate ratification of the administration's August 1968 Nuclear Nonproliferation Treaty with the Soviet Union and sixty other nations.[44]

Lest they be charged with undermining their pope, the bishops voted 121–64 that their pastoral apply the principles of the Vatican II *Pastoral Constitution on the Church in the Modern World* to the Vietnam War and 142–51 to the question of selective conscientious objection. They also voted 153–44 that the pastoral explicitly define the role of conscience during wartime. The results were the document's taut embrace of "Pope Paul's positive, dynamic concept of peace" and advocacy of a new law permitting conscientious objection to a particular war.[45]

More important than whether American Catholics were winning or losing the argument on Vietnam during the Johnson era, however, was the reality that the argument, like the war that it spawned, was not yet over. The bishops' statements and their followers' responses to them reflected the extant mysteries of an arduous work in progress. "A careful reading" of the bishops' November 1966 pastoral, war critic Rev. John Sheerin opined in *Catholic World* in January 1967, "reveals that their assent to the policy is so provisioned as to be lacking in any enthusiasm."[46]

Though the Vietnam War was fast becoming the paramount moral issue of the day, the question of whether and how American churches should address it remained as inconclusive as the war itself. Somewhere between President Lyndon Johnson's appeal to Americans' "Christian duty" to "help our neighbors" in Vietnam, and Rev. Martin Luther King Jr.'s antiwar jeremiad from the pulpit of New York's Riverside Baptist Church, lay a religious no-man's land that only true believers on either side dared to enter. Dr. Carl Henry, the editor of *Christianity Today*, the world's most widely read interdenominational religious periodical, told the *New York Times* in March 1965 that his fellow clergy possessed "neither a divine mandate . . . nor special competence" to address the nation's burning political issues. "It's a terrible thing," Episcopal priest G. R. Wheatcroft of Houston told *Newsweek* in July 1967, but on the Vietnam War, "we don't know what to say."[47]

So civil rights champion Patrick Cardinal O'Boyle's instructions to the priests of the Archdiocese of Washington, D.C., that Vietnam not be a subject of their Sunday homilies or the admission by an official in civil rights opponent James Cardinal McIntyre's Archdiocese of Los Angeles that the war "is not a topic of debate in any of our churches" in many ways fell comfortably within the mainstream of American organized religion. And Auxiliary Bishop James Shannon of Minneapolis–St. Paul, himself growing more dovish by the day, could at once lament that his fellow bishops "obviously aren't getting the Pope's message" while at the same time attacking the non-bishops who said essentially the same thing. After Stanford University theologian Robert McAfee Brown deplored the bishops' absence at the January 1967 Clergy and Laymen Concerned about Vietnam event, Shannon questioned Brown's authority to do so, though he did not frame his dispute with Brown as being about Vietnam, but about the hierarchical nature of his church. "Dr. Brown's style of protest," Shannon succinctly summarized, "is simply not the style of the Catholic bishops."[48]

"We are having an argument within the family," an antiwar Chicago priest explained in December 1965. Many American Catholics would have preferred that it remain there. But a war that would fail to contain communism had shaken a church that would fail to contain dissent. In this way the American Catholic bishops had more in common with Lyndon Johnson than they realized.[49]

Social Justice: Civil Rights

Upon his death on November 22, 1963, John Kennedy became a transitional rather than a transformational president. His New Frontier opened the way for Lyndon Johnson's Great Society, as Johnson fulfilled Kennedy's objectives in passing federal aid to education and enacting health care for the elderly and underprivileged. Most significantly, Johnson signed the civil rights legislation that Kennedy had proposed. To Johnson's credit, he gratefully acknowledged the debt he owed his predecessor for preparing the ground for the Civil Rights Act of 1964, the Voting Rights Act of 1965, and the Fair Housing Act of 1968.

Like Kennedy, Johnson also recognized the contributions of religious groups, including Roman Catholics, in helping to pass these landmark laws. Unlike Kennedy, however, Johnson entered office without the religious qualms that had accompanied his predecessor's historic selection. "Will you join in the battle to give every citizen the full equality which God enjoins and the law requires," the new president asked at the University of Michigan in May 1964, "whatever his belief, or race, or the color of his skin?"[50]

But Johnson himself was the first to concede that "rights are not enough." He faced the new challenges that accompanied the implementation of his legislation—black riots, white resentment, and the stubborn persistence of a racially polarized society. If American Catholics were present at the creation of the civil rights revolution, they were also there for the emerging counterrevolution. During the Lyndon Johnson presidency, many Catholics helped change America, but America could not change all of them.[51]

The Revolution

Only five days after Kennedy's assassination, President Johnson addressed a joint session of Congress to urge action on Kennedy's civil rights measure. "No memorial or eulogy could more eloquently honor President Kennedy's memory than the earliest possible passage of the civil rights bill for which he fought so long," said the new chief executive.[52]

Just as Johnson pledged to continue Kennedy's civil rights efforts, so too did many Catholics. On December 22, the last day of official mourning for President Kennedy, Washington, D.C., archbishop Patrick O'Boyle's Interreligious Committee on Race Relations held a memorial service at the Lincoln Memorial, with President Johnson as the primary speaker. The next month, O'Boyle, speaking in New York to 4,800 Catholic school teachers and administrators, said that although Catholics were "involved as never before" in the civil rights struggle, more needed to take up the fight. At the same time in Washington, Rev. John Cronin, assistant director of the Social Action Department of the bishops' National Catholic Welfare Conference, was among a group of religious leaders who met with Senate majority leader Everett Dirksen, Republican of Illinois, to enlist his support for the Kennedy civil rights bill. "To our surprise," Cronin would report, "the Senator had only mild objections."[53]

The bill passed the House, 290–130, on February 10, with church groups receiving credit for easing its passage. Dirksen's crucial support for the legislation, however, could not prevent a plan to filibuster the measure by a group of southern Democratic senators. A *New York Times* editorial encouraged the churches to oppose such a filibuster. "There is one imponderable . . . that could change almost total defeat for the Southerners," E. W. Kenworthy wrote in

February 1964. "This is the unknown impact on Senators in an election year of the church-affiliated groups that, for the first time, are throwing their weight behind a civil rights bill."⁵⁴

The National Council of Churches and the Synagogue Council of America then wrote O'Boyle, in his capacity as chairman of the NCWC's administrative board, requesting the bishops' participation in a convocation of religious leaders in the nation's capital to speak out against the potential filibuster. Over the objections of James Cardinal McIntyre of Los Angeles that such a meeting would constitute "the introduction of religion into a political situation," and the reservations of Albert Cardinal Meyer of Chicago (who otherwise supported the idea) that the timing of the gathering would risk immersing the bishops in partisan politics, the proposal passed.⁵⁵

At the beginning of March twenty-five priests from across the country met at O'Hare Airport outside Chicago to urge greater Catholic participation in southern civil rights protests. Father Cronin, who attended the gathering, also participated in the following week's meeting of the administrative board of the National Catholic Conference for Interracial Justice, which agreed to dispatch a representative to local communities to spur passage of the civil rights bill, and to send letters of commendation to groups furthering the cause of civil rights. By the end of the month, all the major religions were sending large groups to Washington to lobby for the civil rights bill. Throughout the country, according to historian John McGreevy, Catholic clerical and lay participation in civil rights demonstrations had become "routine."⁵⁶

In April in the nation's capital, while Catholic, Protestant, and Jewish seminary students were conducting a round-the-clock vigil near the Lincoln Memorial to promote passage of the civil rights bill, Mathew Ahmann, the executive director of the National Catholic Conference for Interracial Justice, was meeting with Attorney General Robert Kennedy. At the end of the month, the interreligious convocation proposed two months earlier occurred at Georgetown University. An overflow audience of 6,500 heard O'Boyle and Baltimore archbishop Lawrence Shehan urge an end to the filibuster of the civil rights bill well under way in the Senate. "Not since Prohibition," the *New York Times* quoted Church spokesmen as saying, had religion so "roused itself to political action for good or ill."⁵⁷ The next day on the Senate floor, on the twenty-seventh day of debate on the bill, New York Republican Kenneth Keating praised the gathering he had attended, and entered O'Boyle's remarks at the convocation into the *Congressional Record*. Minnesota Democrat Hubert Humphrey similarly lauded the meeting, submitting Shehan's remarks, which cited Pope John XXIII's condemnation of racism in his April 1963 encyclical, *Pacem in Terris*.⁵⁸

The same day, upon the recommendation of his Catholic liaison, Ralph Dungan, that he could not ignore "such a large and important meeting" as the Georgetown convocation, President Johnson met with 150 of the attendees at the White House. The NCWC Social Action Department, National Council of Catholic Men, National Council of Catholic Women, National Newman Club Federation, National Federation of Catholic College Students, Christian Family Movement, National Catholic Conference for Interracial Justice, and Third Order of St. Francis, along with 120 Catholic rural-life directors, over 200 directors of Catholic charities, editors of diocesan newspapers, and diocesan social action and rural action directors joined in a massive letter-writing offensive to persuade senators to back the civil rights legislation.[59]

The Catholic full-court press paid dividends on June 10, when, for the first time ever on a civil rights bill, the Senate overcame a filibuster, 71–29, and by 73–27 passed the measure, which outlawed racial discrimination in education, employment, and public accommodations. On June 19, the Paulist Fathers ended their general chapter meeting with a pledge of even more participation in ecumenical civil rights endeavors.[60]

The day after the Senate passage, Father Cronin attended an interfaith prayer service in the nation's capital, where he thanked Congress for its "patience and wisdom" and thanked God for delivering a bill that reflected the nation's "moral greatness." Though there was plenty of credit to go around, Catholics deserved much of it. Msgr. George Higgins, director of the NCWC's Social Action Department, would claim a decade later that, due largely to the efforts of Father Cronin, the NCWC had "lobbied more consistently and more effectively in favor of the landmark 1964 civil rights bill than it has ever lobbied before or since on any single issue."[61]

President Johnson, who signed the Civil Rights Act of 1964 on July 2, concurred. "A critical factor in holding the campaign [for the civil rights bill] together was the pressure applied by the major citizens' groups behind the bill," Johnson would recall, with "the religious groups" topping his list. Segregationist Democratic senator Herman Talmadge of Georgia was more succinct: "The goddamned preachers beat us."[62]

Catholics gave 76 percent of their votes to Johnson in November in his landslide victory over Republican senator Barry Goldwater. Johnson won 61 percent of the popular vote and majorities in all but six states, five in the Deep South and Goldwater's native Arizona. His coattails brought a 295–140 House majority and a 68–32 Senate advantage for the Democratic Party. The assistant attorney general for civil rights, Burke Marshall, thanked Mathew Ahmann for the NCCIJ's "significant contribution in gaining a national consensus on the race question," which helped to elect Johnson.[63]

Three days after the election, Martin Luther King Jr., who had already won the Nobel Peace Prize, received the Catholic Interracial Council of Chicago's John F. Kennedy Award for furtherance of race relations. But King was far from finished. Having secured the end of legal segregation in schools, workplaces, and public facilities, he turned his attention to voting.[64]

On March 7, 1965, King began a march from Selma to Montgomery, Alabama, to dramatize the need for legislation to enforce the Fifteenth and Nineteenth Amendments in the South. The marchers received brutal beatings by state police and sheriffs' deputies, as witnessed by a national television audience. King vowed to repeat the march, inviting the nation's religious leaders to join him. Aware of the bishops' reluctance to allow their priests and nuns to demonstrate, King asked few Catholics to participate.[65] But the Catholic Interracial Council of Washington, D.C., claiming approval from Archbishop O'Boyle, mobilized Catholics around the country to go to Selma and to the White House for an all-night vigil in support of the marchers. In reality, O'Boyle had officially dispatched only four priests to Selma, and then only in full clerical garb and if the bishop there, Rev. Thomas Toolen, approved—a near-impossibility given Toolen's conviction that such "outsiders" were better off "at home, doing God's work." Unofficially, O'Boyle effectively looked the other way, allowing even his top aide, Rev. Geno Baroni, to join the march. O'Boyle "told me that I had been in all the papers with King marching arm-in-arm without a hat on, that this kind of action was not priestly, and that he would not tolerate this any longer," Baroni would recall. "I asked what he was going to do, and he said, 'Geno, next time, wear a hat.'"[66]

In all, priests from fifty dioceses, nuns, and laypeople comprised a substantial Catholic contingent in Selma. King aide Rev. Ralph Abernathy lauded the large Catholic presence, quipping that "the only ones they hate more than Negroes down here are Roman Catholics, especially monsignors."[67]

At the White House, the week-long vigil in support of the Selma demonstration was under way. On the vigil's fifth day, Msgr. George Higgins of the NCWC's Social Action Department was among a group of clergy who met with President Johnson in an effort to defuse the crisis.[68]

By March 13, as many as 1,500 people at the vigil were praying, singing, and shouting that Johnson should act forcefully to protect the Alabama demonstrators. That afternoon, after a three-and-a-half-hour meeting with Alabama governor George Wallace, Johnson told a press conference that "people should have the right to peacefully assemble, to picket, to demonstrate their views, and to do anything they can to bring those views to the attention of people provided they do not violate laws themselves and provided they conduct themselves as they should." Higgins defended the president, whose "commitment to the cause of civil rights is just as sincere as that of any priest, minister, or rabbi—or any seminarian or nun—in the United States."[69]

In the end, Johnson heeded the picketers' counsel. On March 15, the president told a prime-time, nationally televised joint session of Congress, "I will send to Congress a law designed to eliminate illegal barriers to the right to vote." When Johnson quoted the anthem of the Selma marchers and the civil rights movement, "We Shall Overcome," King, watching on television in Alabama, began to cry. With Governor Wallace's tacit approval, Johnson sent Federal Bureau of Investigation agents, U.S. marshals, and two army military police battalions to Selma and federalized the Alabama National Guard. On March 21, 3,200 marchers departed from Selma. Four days and fifty miles later, 25,000 marchers, including many Catholics, arrived in Montgomery.[70]

When the pope's apostolic delegate, Rev. Egidio Vagnozzi, complained of Catholic clerical participation in the march, Archbishop O'Boyle replied that while nuns should not march, male religious could. Francis Cardinal Spellman of New York said that all clergy should be free to demonstrate. The NCWC administrative board implicitly defended O'Boyle and Spellman, leaving such decisions to individual bishops.[71]

The day that the marchers reached Montgomery, Father Cronin testified for the NCWC Social Action Department in favor of Johnson's voting rights legislation before the House Judiciary Committee. He quoted from the bishops' August 1963 "On Racial Harmony" statement that "no Catholic with a good Christian conscience can fail to recognize the rights of all citizens to vote." Two weeks later, Cronin told the National Conference on Religion and Race, "Catholics should be in the forefront of demonstrations to show our support for the civil rights movement."[72]

As the focus of the civil rights campaign turned to voting rights, the National Catholic Conference for Interracial Justice reminded the nation of the promises of the previous year's civil rights law. In May 1965 the Archdioceses of Detroit and St. Louis inaugurated Project Equality, by which Catholic (and eventually non-Catholic) churches would use their power of the purse to promote fair employment. Under the program, churches would only purchase products and services from businesses committed to equal employment opportunity.[73]

In July, as the voting rights bill worked its way through Congress, Cronin represented the NCWC at the Interreligious Clearinghouse Meeting in New York, where the delegates complained not that the Johnson administration had consulted them too little, but that it was calling upon them too much. On a more positive note, Ahmann told the conference that Project Equality was showing early signs of progress in Detroit and St. Louis.[74]

The conference report on the bill passed the House, 328–74, on August 3, and the Senate, 79–18, the next day. On August 9 Johnson signed the Voting Rights Act, which ended literacy tests and other voter qualification ploys while authorizing federal examiners to ensure the registration of African-Americans in states that failed to meet a minimal threshold of black participation. Because of this long-overdue legislation, Father Cronin observed, "our democracy will become total for the first time in our history."[75]

With civil rights retrieved and voting rights restored, the Johnson administration turned its attention to the barrier at the root of the racial divide: residential segregation. Housing discrimination had threatened to be the deal-breaker for the Civil Rights Act of 1964, when the fictional "Mrs. Murphy" became almost as famous as the civil rights leaders themselves. Testifying before the Senate Commerce Committee in favor of the civil rights bill in July 1963, Father Cronin had maintained that a female homeowner renting five or fewer rooms "has every right to insist that people who come into her private home are well-dressed, well-behaved, mannerly, the type of person that she would like to associate with. But I cannot morally accept the decision that color is the basis of discrimination." The otherwise sympathetic Democratic senator John Pastore of Rhode Island replied, "Nobody wants to, Father. This is a question that has been tossed around quite a bit, about 'Mrs. Murphy's' exception."[76]

Although Cronin had conceded no distinction between public and private facilities, the Civil Rights Act of 1964 would, leaving the question of private housing discrimination for another day. In November 1964 at the Catholic Interracial Council dinner in Chicago, Martin Luther King Jr. had challenged his audience to "dare to live in racially integrated neighborhoods." The following July, when King returned to Chicago to address the council again, he praised a group of nuns for their arrests in demonstrations against public school segregation rooted in residential patterns.[77]

Washington, D.C.'s archbishop, Patrick O'Boyle, opened 1966 with a series of seminars on housing issues for all archdiocesan priests. In May he proclaimed "Fair Housing Sunday," contending that to deny a house, an education, or a job to an African-American "is in effect denying that right to Christ himself." The same month Father Cronin again joined representatives of the National Council of Churches and the Synagogue Council of America, as he had for the civil rights and voting rights legislation, in testifying on behalf of the bishops before the House Judiciary Committee.[78]

In June, James Meredith, who had become the first African-American student at the University of Mississippi four years earlier, provoked a federal investigation when he took a bullet in the back as he began a projected 220-mile march for voting rights from Memphis, Tennessee, to Jackson, Mississippi. James McGuire, the associate director of the National Catholic Conference for Interracial Justice, thanked Johnson's assistant attorney general for civil rights, John Doar, for helping to resolve the crisis. Doar agreed that "there is a need for mediators, both public and private, not only in crisis situations" but, more important, "during the quiet periods." The federal government thus envisioned a role for a Catholic agency to help prevent and solve crises, even in Mississippi.[79]

And even in Chicago, where Dr. King returned in July to speak at a rally sponsored by his Southern Christian Leadership Conference, launching a campaign against residential segregation there. Archbishop John Cody, recently arrived from New Orleans, issued a statement in support of the rally, to be read in all the city's Catholic parishes. King then inaugurated a series of marches in Gage Park, a heavily Catholic, heavily segregated neighborhood, which led to a city-wide open housing agreement that Cody helped negotiate.[80]

As 1966 came to a close, Johnson's fair housing legislation fell to a month-long filibuster, and Johnson's party lost forty-seven House seats and three Senate seats in the midterm elections. The bishops, meeting in Washington in November, urged their fellow Catholics not to give up the fight for civil rights. In their third statement on the subject in eight years, again written by Father Cronin, the bishops, like the president, linked racism with poverty. The statement, "On Race Relations and Poverty," won the unanimous endorsement of the bishops and the enthusiastic approval of the Johnson administration. Robert Weaver, the secretary of the new Department of Housing and Urban Development and the first African-American Cabinet member in the nation's history, called the pastoral "perhaps the most sensitive and understanding statement of the present crisis in American domestic affairs that it has been my privilege to see." He promised "the closest cooperation of this Department in all local or national efforts by the Catholic clergy and laity to implement your call to give all Americans the opportunity to live a decent life."[81]

As 1967 began, Johnson tried again with a fair housing law, and prominent Catholics pressed the fight. In July, in his first official statement as a cardinal, Rev. Patrick O'Boyle advocated an open housing ordinance for Montgomery County, Maryland, as "morally right and just" as well as "sound public policy."[82]

In August, Thomas Hinton testified for the NCWC (now the United States Catholic Conference) Social Action Department alongside representatives of the National Council of Churches and the Synagogue Council of America in favor of the Johnson fair housing bill before the Senate Subcommittee on Housing and Urban Affairs of the Committee on Banking and Currency.

Cardinal O'Boyle sent supplies to Resurrection City, the makeshift village constructed by the Poor People's Campaign on the Mall in Washington to dramatize the need for affordable housing. He joined the National Council of Churches and the American Federation of Labor–Congress of Industrial Organizations in forming the Urban Coalition, which earmarked $2 million in private funds for housing development. On President Johnson's "National Day of Prayer," August 5, the cardinal issued a pastoral letter calling upon Congress to fund low-income housing for the District of Columbia. Johnson telephoned O'Boyle to applaud the statement's "great contribution to civil rights."[83]

As 1968 dawned, Johnson tried a third time for fair housing legislation. An intense lobbying effort by the administration and its allies, including the National Catholic Conference for Interracial Justice, National Council of Catholic Men, National Council of Catholic Women, National Federation of College Students, and the USCC Social Action Department, targeted Catholic Democrats Ray Madden of Indiana and James Delaney of New York, whose House Rules Committee votes had helped to prevent previous housing legislation. The NCCW's Peggy Roach appealed to Delaney's pastor, Rev. Kevin Kelly of St. Thomas the Apostle Church, and his bishop, Rev. Terence Cooke. The bill passed the Senate, 71–20, on March 11, and the House, 250–172, on April 10.[84]

Johnson signed the Fair Housing Act on April 11, 1968. The law would by 1970 "prohibit discrimination based on race, creed, or color in the sale, rental, and financing of housing" in all cases except for the facilities of religious organizations, private clubs, and "dwellings of four or fewer units where the owner occupies the units." In other words, the act would cover 80 percent of the nation's dwellings, but would exempt, among others, the churches and that notorious Irish Catholic, "Mrs. Murphy."[85]

Following this long-awaited enactment of a national housing law, the bishops at their April meeting in St. Louis commemorated the tenth anniversary of their 1958 declaration on race with a new pastoral, "Statement on the National Race Crisis." Having staunchly supported Johnson's legislative push for civil rights, the bishops now were moving beyond it. Like Johnson, for the first time they declared "war on poverty." Unlike Johnson, they embraced the Commission on Civil Disturbances' March 1968 indictment of white racism as the primary culprit for the nation's racial maladies. An extensive effort, they acknowledged, must begin in their own communities, in Catholic parishes, schools, hospitals, and nursing homes. "Let us act," the bishops ominously admonished, "while there is still time for collaborative peaceful solutions."[86]

By the time of the passage of the Fair Housing Act in April 1968, however, the civil rights movement and the president who endorsed it seemed exhausted. With Martin Luther King Jr.'s recent assassination and Lyndon Johnson's impending retirement, the movement was suddenly without a leader. Catholic assistant to the president Joseph Califano reminded Johnson that he had promised before the April 1968 riots to give a nationally televised civil rights address, and that a failure to deliver would "give militants a chance to say 'whitey will promise anything to cool it, but never delivers when the heat is off.'" Johnson replied, "I promised nothing. I stated my intention only, since changed by [the] riots."[87]

Cardinal O'Boyle also received a suggestion that he go on television in the wake of the King assassination on April 4. Washington, D.C., Democratic mayor Walter Washington appealed to the cardinal to join other area religious leaders in a plea for calm as federal troops patrolled the city to prevent more violence. O'Boyle aide Msgr. Geno Baroni dissuaded him. "The rioters aren't watching TV," Baroni told O'Boyle. "They're *stealing* TVs." So neither Johnson nor O'Boyle appeared on television, and order eventually returned to the nation's capital—but only after the president, the cardinal, and many American Catholics had moved on to other things.[88]

Conclusions on Social Justice

The historian's task ultimately is to judge the past through the prism of the present. He can neither apologize for the limitations of the time of which he writes nor proselytize the accepted wisdom of the time in which he writes. This challenge becomes all the more difficult when the content of his subject is profoundly moral.

There is certainly much evidence to indict American Catholics for not doing enough to advance the cause of civil rights in the United States during the Johnson administration. From New Orleans in March 1964, Archbishop John Cody wrote National Catholic Welfare Conference legal counsel William Consedine that since "the Governor-Elect [Democrat John McKeithan] has announced publicly . . . that he would fight integration, I believe it all the more important not to agitate at the beginning of his reign a question that could throw all the segregationists in direct objection to the Church." Three years later, with only 17 percent of the nonwhite children in the parochial school system attending integrated schools, Herbert Kane, the regional director of the Office of Economic Opportunity, told superintendent Henry Bezou that the archbishop of New Orleans was not in compliance with the Civil Rights Act of 1964.[89]

In Detroit in 1965, Archbishop John Dearden launched Project Commitment, a program intended to "create in each parish a committed core of Catholics informed and active in human relations, particularly in racial matters, who will work within their own parishes and in the community." The project began auspiciously, but after the city's 1967 riots, it sparked considerable resentment. "My husband and I have worked on Project Commitment since last September," one woman wrote. "After speaking with people that have attended at least one of the three series our parish has held, I feel we have lost almost all we worked for as far as neighborhood integration goes, as far as communication, or person-to-person relationships." In Cleveland following its 1966 riots, the National Catholic Conference for Interracial Justice and the American Council for Nationalities Service founded Project Bridge, designed to train "priests, teachers, youth leaders, neighborhood-level and city-wide ethnic group leaders in an attempt to build solid bridges on common projects between the Negro community and much of white Cleveland." Almost from the start, the endeavor foundered amid charges of outside, even communist, influence.[90]

American Catholics seemed to be coming up short on the national level as well. In February 1964, the National Catholic Conference for Interracial Justice's Mathew Ahmann lamented the absence of an organized Catholic lobbying effort for the civil rights bill. In April the NCWC dissolved the secretariat of the National Conference on Religion and Race after barely a year, according to historian David Southern, because of a lack of funding and attention.[91] In November 1964, John Kenna of the NCWC's Family Life Bureau called for the closing of the NCCIJ's Southern Field Office in New Orleans because it was "lily white." Following Johnson's election, the NCWC's Father Cronin and Msgr. Hurley rejected a call for a meeting with the president. "I consider such a meeting unnecessary and one that could have some bad effects," wrote Hurley. "I think the President is quite aware of the continuing concern of religious groups for racial justice, and any reminder of this might be considered in bad taste." A March 1965 *Newsweek* article quoted a "Chicago Catholic civil rights leader" as labeling the NCWC "totally irrelevant and totally ignorant of racial matters."[92]

White Catholic reservations about civil rights extended to the movement's most prominent figure, Rev. Martin Luther King Jr., whose Southern Christian Leadership Conference was under surveillance by the Federal Bureau of Investigation for suspected communist sympathies. When the suggestion of a testimonial dinner for Dr. King arose in the NCWC's Social Action Department in February 1965, the reception was less than enthusiastic. "Whatever our views may be of Rev. Mr. King," Father Cronin advised Msgr. Tanner, "I think we will have to go along with this. After all, he had a private audience with the Pope and won the Nobel Peace Prize, so I do not see how we can avoid going along with the accepted image of the man."[93]

King's "accepted image" was quite different in many parts of the South. Bishop Thomas Toolen of Mobile-Birmingham forbade the priests and nuns of his diocese from participating in the Selma-to-Montgomery march. "A great injustice is being done to Alabama" by such protests, Toolen posited, adding that Dr. King is "hurting the cause of the Negro rather than helping it." When Congressman William Dickinson of Alabama cited a booklet, *The True Selma Story*, which accused the leaders of the march of immorality and communist leanings, apostolic delegate Egidio Vagnozzi solicited Msgr. Hurley's response. There was no credible evidence of immorality during the march, Hurley replied. As for "allegations of personal immorality on the part of certain civil rights leaders," Hurley concluded, "we are not surprised." And although Hurley said flatly that King was not a communist and had purged the Southern Christian Leadership Conference leadership of communists, he asserted that there were communists at the lower levels of groups like the Student Nonviolent Coordinating Committee and the Committee of Federated Organizations.[94]

Johnson's Catholic assistant secretary of labor, Daniel Patrick Moynihan, unwittingly contributed to the white backlash against the civil rights movement with his report, *The Negro Family: The Case for National Action*, which he completed in early 1965. Moynihan largely blamed black poverty on the preponderance of female-headed, single-parent families, rooted in the destabilizing legacy of slavery, and the inability of government programs to address this growing problem. Johnson presented Moynihan's findings in a speech at predominantly black Howard University in June. Msgr. Tanner wrote Archbishop O'Boyle that the Moynihan-Johnson critique "has a special and tragic relevance for the Archdiocese of Washington."[95]

The prevailing sentiment at the National Catholic Social Action Conference in Washington a year later was one of "Catholic indifference to social problems." *Ave Maria* editorialized in the wake of the conference that despite all of the Catholic efforts of recent years, "the 'idea' of Catholic social action—notwithstanding the cogent and magnificent documents of Pope John and the [Second Vatican] Council—simply has not yet arrived." A March 1967 *Newsweek* survey found that only 21 percent of American Catholics felt bound by a priest's call to integrate their neighborhoods, and 46 percent saw no sin in refusing to receive communion from a black priest.[96]

Though many Catholic clergy and laypeople did choose to disregard or confront the hierarchy on issues of race, enough of them heeded their bishops to effect historic change. The criticism of the bishops falters when one analyzes the voting patterns of American Catholics, as political scientist Seymour Martin Lipset did in the wake of the 1964 election. Far from ignoring or rebuking their bishops, Lipset found, American Catholics voted much as their bishops intimated that they should. "Voting studies have shown that when socioeconomic or class factors are held constant, Catholics are not only more Democratic, they are also much more likely to favor trade unions and welfare measures than are socioeconomically comparable Protestants," Lipset concluded. "Even Republican Catholics have been found to be on the average more favorable to welfare state or New Deal measures than their Protestant co-partisans."[97]

So in addition to helping to elect the liberals in the White House and the congressional majority, Catholics were following the liberals who headed most of their dioceses. If many of them followed the lead of a virtually all-white episcopate from the comforts of virtually all-white neighborhoods with virtually all-white churches, schools, and workplaces, they were unable or unwilling to see the contradiction. Lyndon Johnson promised a great society but failed to deliver; the U.S. Catholic bishops hoped for a great church but fell far short. Yet by January 1969 the president and the bishops, despite the almost inevitable counterrevolution against both, had left the country's race relations far better than they had found them when Johnson took office in November 1963.

Life and Death: Birth Control

"No other Great Society bills," wrote historian Paul Conkin, "had the focus, the clear goals, and the unambiguous results of the civil rights acts." As for President Lyndon Johnson's assault on poverty, however, "nothing is very clear." When one adds the complexity of the U.S. Catholic bishops' stance toward Johnson's labyrinthine anti-poverty legislation, one can see why this component of the Great Society became so controversial. While Johnson notoriously divided his attention between the war on communism in Southeast Asia and the war on poverty in the United States, to the detriment of both, the bishops allied themselves with the president in the anti-poverty offensive while rejecting the inclusion of family planning in his arsenal.[98]

In the process, the imposing alliance that helped enact the historic civil rights laws slowly unraveled, as church confronted state and the Catholic hierarchy took on its rank and file. The "church in the modern world," as the newly minted Second Vatican Council boldly marketed it, gave way to the reappearance of age-old tensions between reason and faith, science and religion, American and Catholic. Lyndon Johnson, who had appeared above the fray just a short time earlier, now seemed too Protestant to the American Catholic prelates with whom he had collaborated so successfully. In a war that seemed doomed from the start, unity with and among American Catholics was one of the casualties.⁹⁹

Not So Fast

Having failed to preclude "research into problems of population growth" from becoming part of the Kennedy administration's foreign policy, many American Catholics looked homeward, hoping to prevent anti-poverty funds from including family planning assistance. "Whether Americans are to be denied access to contraceptive information and devices is almost a dead issue in the United States today," *America* editorialized in February 1964. "The real issue is whether government agencies are to persuade people to practice contraception."[100]

And whether American Catholics could stop them. In his 1930 encyclical, *Casti Connubi* ("Of Chaste Marriage"), Pope Pius XI had said, "Any use of matrimony whatsoever in the exercise of which the act is deprived, by human interference, of its natural power to procreate life, is an offense against the law of God and of nature." The U.S. Catholic bishops in 1959 had therefore opposed "any public assistance either at home or abroad to promote artificial birth prevention, abortion, or sterilization, whether through direct aid or by means of international organizations."[101]

Yet the *Washington Post* reported in April 1964 that the Agency for International Development was preparing guidelines to implement the Fulbright Amendment to the 1963 foreign aid bill, which had authorized the dispensing of birth control information to foreign countries that requested it. In December 1964 the American Medical Association, representing most of the nation's 289,000 practicing physicians, for the first time advocated the public dissemination of birth control information. Although a majority of states still restricted or prohibited the sale of contraceptives and distribution of birth control information, only heavily Catholic Massachusetts and Connecticut were enforcing such statutes. A challenge to the Connecticut law had reached the U.S. Supreme Court, which struck it down in *Griswold v. Connecticut* in June 1965 as an invasion of privacy, protected by the First, Third, Fourth, Ninth, and Fourteenth Amendments. "There is probably no subject," *America* had posited, "on which the Catholic Church and the majority of non-Catholic Americans disagree more sharply today than the morality of contraception."[102]

Though *America*'s editors quipped that observers of the Second Vatican Council had translated *aggiornamento* as "the Italian word for contraception," even the open discussion of the subject in Rome had not produced any revision of doctrine. The pope's apostolic delegate to the United States, Rev. Egidio Vagnozzi, asked the general secretary of the National Catholic Welfare

Conference, Msgr. Paul Tanner, to poll the American bishops on five questions in February 1964: "1) the status of the problem of birth control in this country, 2) the general conduct . . . of Catholics . . . in the matter of conjugal morality, 3) the legislative and political attitudes and practices of civil authority in this regard, 4) the doctrinal and pastoral tendencies in this country, and 5) the viewpoint of the bishops on the whole question." While acknowledging that "some Catholic individuals through public statements, magazine articles, and the like have succeeded in creating the impression . . . that the Church . . . has modified her position on birth control," Vagnozzi instructed Tanner to "kindly see to it that the government is informed of the fact that the views of the Holy See and of the hierarchy of this country remain unchanged on the subject."[103]

Tanner assured Vagnozzi that although birth control proposals had appeared in congressional committees and at the United Nations, the Johnson administration had not proposed any such legislation and had consistently rejected UN attempts to provide family planning assistance to other nations. After William Rogers, the deputy director of the Agency for International Development, told NCWC legal counsel Harmon Burns in March that, notwithstanding the *Washington Post* story, his agency was conducting demographic research, not spreading birth control information, Burns concluded, "We have no present problems with AID programs." Catherine Schaefer of the NCWC's Office for United Nations Affairs reported in the same month that "although there is growing acceptance of a government role in population control" by the UN, "there remained the respect for individual, family, and cultural choices" supported by the United States.[104]

Two months later the Washington, D.C., archbishop, Patrick O'Boyle, sent to Vagnozzi the answers to his five questions from the 105 bishops who responded. Quoting Rev. John Ford, O'Boyle summarized the responses as demonstrating the uncertainty of "a great many Catholics, both priests and people," about "the Church's teaching and their own obligations" regarding birth control. Ninety-seven of the respondents agreed with Ford on the need for a "solemn declaration from the Holy See" on the subject.[105]

The Holy See remained silent, but the Johnson administration did not. In December 1964, the Office of Economic Opportunity announced that it would provide birth control services in anti-poverty programs if requested by local communities. The next month, Dr. Murray Grant, the public health director of the District of Columbia, informed the New York Academy of Medicine that the Children's Bureau of the Department of Health, Education, and Welfare had recently dispersed over $5 million to clinics in New York City; Baltimore; Detroit; Philadelphia; Augusta, Georgia; Portland, Oregon; San

Juan and Ponce, Puerto Rico; and West Virginia. If Dr. Grant had not mentioned it, few would have known of this new allowance for birth control assistance within the United States. "The official U.S. government policy on birth control used to be say nothing about it and do less," *Time* observed. "Last week it became clear that the Government has a new policy of say as little as possible, but do quite a lot."[106]

In his January 1965 State of the Union address, President Johnson would say very little about birth control, promising only to explore new methods "to help deal with the explosion of world population," but the local, state, and federal governments would begin to do a lot. According to the *Wall Street Journal*, by February 1965 cities and counties in twenty-one states were operating over 680 public birth control clinics aimed mainly at low-income families, up from 470 clinics in eleven states only a year earlier. Maryland, Michigan, New York, and the city of Chicago began referring unmarried as well as married welfare recipients to clinics to receive contraceptive counseling and devices. The Agency for International Development announced a new policy of contraceptive devices or funds for such devices to foreign countries, and would increase expenditures for research, information, and technical assistance for population control. The National Catholic Welfare Conference's Family Life Bureau director, Msgr. John Knott, insisted that "despite popular opinion to the contrary, the attitude of the Catholic Church toward contraception . . . has not changed." Yet his colleague Catherine Schaefer of the NCWC's Office of United Nations Affairs noted in April that the pro–birth control majority on the UN Population Commission had received encouragement not only from Johnson's State of the Union address, but from the winds of change blowing at Vatican II.[107]

To slow this momentum, the American Catholic bishops asked the Johnson administration to devise specific guidelines regarding the public role in family planning. In March, the Office of Economic Opportunity complied with "Special Conditions Applicable to the Use of OEO Grant Funds for Family Planning Programs." The regulations stipulated that participation in family planning must be voluntary; such participation could not be a prerequisite for enrollment in any other OEO program; the available birth control information must respect the religious beliefs of the recipients; the family planning methods must meet accepted medical standards; birth control materials must not promote one method over another; the funds could not be used to advertise the programs through the media; the funds could not be used for sterilization or abortion; the funds could not provide services for unmarried women or married women not living with their husbands, unless legally divorced or widowed; the funds would not go to a married woman beyond one year and above twelve dollars; the funds could not serve recipients outside of the community action program; and the family planning program must not conflict with state or local law.¹⁰⁸

The Office of Economic Opportunity director, Sargent Shriver, sent copies of its new guidelines to every American Catholic archbishop, requesting feedback. Only eight replied, with two wishing that the federal government would stay on the sidelines and six considering the guidelines "adequate" though not endorsing them. The NCWC's Catholic Charities also characterized the regulations as "adequate." Boston's Richard Cardinal Cushing wrote Shriver, "It is clear that we cannot exclude family planning and birth control activities from the Poverty Program, and I think the next best thing is to regulate them in a realistic fashion, safeguarding as much as we can of family and human values."¹⁰⁹

After prominent Catholic sociologist Joseph Neusse joined *Ave Maria* and the Indianapolis diocesan newspaper, the *Criterion*, in criticizing Msgr. John Knott's intemperate response to Johnson's State of the Union remarks on population control, an ad hoc committee at the National Catholic Welfare Conference began drafting a statement to clarify the bishops' position on the issue. The result was that a statement designed to eliminate ambiguity only sowed more, so the NCWC administrative board rejected it at its April meeting.¹¹⁰

No sooner had the bishops opposed one statement than they proposed another. In it, the bishops sought to answer, in Msgr. Francis Hurley's words, three questions about the War on Poverty: "1) Is it legitimate for the government to enter into the field of family planning? 2) If government involvement in family planning is legitimate, to what extent and under what conditions, and 3) What should the general approach of the NCWC be?"¹¹¹

As the bishops struggled to answer those questions, their adversaries on both ends of Pennsylvania Avenue accelerated the pace of federal involvement in birth control issues. When Johnson commemorated the twentieth anniversary of the United Nations in June by positing that "five dollars invested in population control is worth a hundred dollars invested in relief," Hurley wrote to White House aide Bill Moyers to protest. Ten birth control bills appeared in the Eighty-Ninth Congress, most notably Alaska Democratic senator Ernest Greuning's proposal to create offices on population problems in the Departments of State and Health, Education, and Welfare, where Greuning claimed fewer than twenty people were working on these issues.¹¹²

The bishops decided that, pending the completion of their statement, they would not testify on Capitol Hill for fear of giving Greuning and his fellow legislators the confrontation that they wanted to elevate the profile of their obscure legislation. Instead, the NCWC would continue to work behind the scenes to influence the Johnson administration's birth control policies. In August, Hurley and NCWC legal counsel William Consedine reminded Wilbur Cohen, Dr. Edward Deprey, and Dr. Philip Lee of the Department of Health, Education, and Welfare that while the bishops supported federal family planning research, they opposed "government advocacy of birth control, provision of devices, and training of personnel." Hurley telephoned Shriver to convey the bishops' concern over the addition of the term "family planning" to the services provided in the Senate version of the Office of Economic Opportunity's budget extension. Shriver assured Hurley that the administration position remained that it would supply family planning funds only at the request of local communities.[113]

The bishops' best-laid plans went awry, however, when Dr. Murray Grant, the health director of the District of Columbia, testified on Capitol Hill in August in favor of the Greuning bill. Dr. Grant claimed that although the Archdiocese of Washington had opposed public funding of artificial contraception, it had not objected to the dispensation of birth control information by the D.C. government. Washington's archbishop, Patrick O'Boyle, felt compelled, over Hurley's objections, to give a sermon to correct the record. O'Boyle also acted, as chairman of the National Catholic Welfare Conference administrative board but without the formal approval of his fellow bishops, to grant the imprimatur of the NCWC to the testimony of William Ball, the general counsel of the Pennsylvania Catholic Committee, against the Greuning bill. So when Ball provocatively claimed that the measure would "limit the production of Negro offspring," he was speaking for the U.S. Catholic bishops.[114]

Just as the bishops were breaking their silence on birth control, the pope also ended his. In October Paul VI entreated the United Nations to devote its efforts to feeding, rather than limiting, the world's population. So when the Office of Economic Opportunity's Joseph Kershaw privately floated a proposal to revise the agency's birth control guidelines to include married women not living with their husbands and to raise the maximum annual funds per participant to twenty dollars, the OEO's Donald Baker warned Shriver that such a move would incur Catholic wrath. Marveling at the OEO's "Never-Never Committee on Family Planning," Baker called for the acceptance of political reality. "I have been making discreet inquiries in NCWC and elsewhere," he wrote in October. "I am told there is a definite change in attitude, . . . a veering away from . . . silence on the part of the hierarchy, and mounting criticism." In anticipation of "a report within a month . . . as to what the Church's position . . . will be," he recommended that "our best position is to maintain the posture we have assumed heretofore, that is, one of complete neutrality."[115]

Baker's analysis of the bishops' "change of attitude" was astute. A November National Catholic Welfare Conference memorandum admitted that "we are not being completely honest in our approach" by obliquely defending "privacy" rather than explicitly opposing birth control. "A simple test of our motivation," the memo continued, "can be had if we ask ourselves whether we would be as deeply concerned over questions of law and public policy if the Church sanctioned artificial methods of contraception." The memo recommended that the bishops establish two task forces—one "negatively" opposing birth control on legal, social, and administrative grounds, and the other "positively" exploring creative and effective alternatives to artificial contraception.[116]

The bishops then began to pursue the "negative" track. A follow-up memo outlined three options for the bishops on the burgeoning issue of publicly funded birth control. The first was "peaceful coexistence" with the Johnson administration in the interests of ecumenism, civil peace, and the War on Poverty. The second was "limited opposition," resisting birth control programs unless and until the federal government precluded coercion, safeguarded privacy, forswore sterilization and abortion, and excluded unmarried persons. The third was "full opposition," a massive legal and public relations effort at the federal, state, and local levels to forestall further public inroads on birth control. The document recommended the third approach, arguing that "if the public 'case' of our opposition is well-presented, only the biased or irrational will assert that the Church is arbitrarily attempting to exercise a veto over other groups in our pluralist society." The bishops, meeting in Rome during the Second Vatican Council, opted for this course, commissioning William Ball to write a legal memorandum challenging federal authority to fund birth control.[117]

Baker's espousal of government "neutrality" was futile. In November, Johnson signed the Food for Peace bill, which allowed the use of U.S.-owned foreign currencies to promote activities "related to population growth" in countries requesting such assistance. At November's White House Conference on Health, Dr. Leslie Corsa of the University of Michigan contended that "federal initiative on family planning has been strikingly absent." The conference report recommended that the federal government offer birth control devices to all American families, especially the poor. The NCWC's Msgr. Knott decried not only the report, but the input of only one Catholic in writing it.[118]

The next month Shriver rejected a request by NCWC legal counsels William Ball and William Consedine that he declare a moratorium on pending applications for OEO birth control funds while Ball prepared his brief challenging such expenditures. Baker, who wrote the 1964 Senate report on the Economic Opportunity Act and wrote much of the draft of the 1965 report, argued that these documents left no doubt that the senators had intended to include family planning in the community action programs. "In parting," Ball reported, "Shriver warned that the more the Church excites the birth control issue, the more will other groups work against including her agencies in anti-poverty projects."[119]

A December 1965 *Washington Post* column by Rowland Evans and Robert Novak assailed Johnson's "pitifully cautious" approach to birth control. They attributed this "supercaution" to a "highly combustible mixture of two elements: conservative Catholic dogma against birth control and—surprisingly—fear of alienating Negro racists" convinced of a white conspiracy to limit black births. They blamed Johnson's then-secretary of Health, Education, and Welfare, Anthony Celebrezze, for successfully arguing for diluted OEO guidelines to avoid offending his fellow Catholics, a major Democratic Party constituency.[120] The column incensed Shriver, who prepared a response to Evans and Novak. The director asserted that far from taking "a pitifully cautious approach," OEO "is the first agency of the Federal Government in history to give money for private birth control clinics. We're still the only agency of the United States government to do so."[121]

As Shriver was defending the federal role in family planning, the Johnson administration was expanding it. When Secretary John Gardner, Undersecretary Wilbur Cohen, and Dr. Philip Lee confirmed to the NCWC's Msgr. Francis Hurley in January 1966 that their department was preparing no new birth control legislation, Hurley felt less than reassured. "Their definition of neutrality . . . is different from the NCWC definition of neutrality," Hurley concluded. "It is quite clear from the discussion that there are [already] many laws which will permit the funding of birth control services with federal money." At his third meeting with administration officials within two weeks, Hurley heard Cohen reveal that he was about to issue a memorandum to state and local public health officers permitting the use of federal funds to finance state birth control programs. When Cohen and Lee promised not to publicize the memorandum, Hurley again was skeptical. "It is almost certain," he replied, "that some columnist will pick it up and publicize it," placing the administration in "a direct confrontation with the NCWC."[122]

As if the confrontation wasn't already there. In January, Gardner announced that revised OEO guidelines would permit unmarried as well as married women to receive birth control information and devices. As Hurley had feared, "some columnist"—John Richmond of the archdiocesan *St. Louis Review*—publicized in March Cohen's directive releasing federal birth control funds to any states and localities requesting them, and Cohen himself quoted from it in a speech to Planned Parenthood–World Populace in May. And the

OEO director was spending all the family planning money he could. "As far as I know," said Shriver in July, "I have signed every such grant which has come to my desk."[123]

Persuaded, in Msgr. Tanner's words, that "one reason for the expanding role of government" in family planning "is the silence of the United States bishops," the National Catholic Welfare Conference acted on a suggestion by Bishop Walter Curtis of Bridgeport, Connecticut, to prepare a statement on birth control. So as not to upstage the pope's advisory commission, the bishops would seek permission from the Holy Father before issuing their message.[124]

While the bishops drafted their statement, they raised their profile in Washington. When the Agency for International Development administrator, David Bell, cited a clause in section 211 of the Foreign Assistance Act to justify his agency's family planning activities, Catholic Democrat and NCWC ally Clement Zablocki of Wisconsin told his House colleagues in March 1966, "It seems an utterly cynical interpretation of the phrase 'development of human resources' to promote the prevention of human beings." Msgr. Tanner blasted the new OEO guidelines for abandoning "government neutrality" by openly promoting birth control without congressional authorization. The NCWC Family Life Bureau sent a request to Senator Greuning to testify against his bill, only to be told that he had to rush home to resolve a crisis caused by wild moose rampaging through local communities. Since it was a violation of federal law to kill a moose in Alaska, population control was not an option for the senator.[125]

In September the NCWC's Consedine and Rev. James McHugh complained to the Department of Health, Education, and Welfare's Cohen, Lee, and Dr. Milo Leavitt about newspaper accounts of regional HEW officials advocating birth control. Cohen, Lee, and Leavitt promised to invite NCWC spokespersons to future regional HEW meetings. In October Msgr. Tanner sent a letter to committee chairman Harley Staggers, Democrat of West Virginia, unsuccessfully advocating the deletion of family planning from the comprehensive health planning bill. Cohen warned Johnson aide Douglass Cater, "Until the Pope restates a new policy, I think we can expect the National Catholic Welfare Conference to send such a letter to the Congress on any pending legislation that involves family planning."[126]

The next week, with Pope Paul VI's blessing, the bishops released the statement "On the Government and Birth Control," which the Office of Economic Opportunity's Donald Baker had predicted a year earlier. The bishops recalled, "On previous occasions we have warned of the dangers to the right of privacy posed by government birth control programs; we have urged upon government a role of neutrality whereby it neither penalizes nor promotes birth control." They added that "recent developments, however, show government rapidly abandoning any such role." As a result, "We call upon all—and especially Catholics—to oppose vigorously and by every democratic means, those campaigns already underway in some states and at the national level toward the active promotion, by tax-supported agencies, of birth prevention as a public policy, above all in connection with welfare benefit programs."[127]

The bishops' message, reported in a front-page story in the *New York Times*, unleashed an acrimonious exchange with the Johnson administration. HEW's Dr. Lee publicly denied that the U.S. policy was coercive. Leading birth control proponents General William Draper and John D. Rockefeller privately complained to White House aide Douglass Cater about the "cantankerous spirit" with which the bishops transmitted their message. White House aide Joseph Califano wrote the president, "I told Father Hurley that you were very disappointed that they felt they again had to go to the newspapers without any prior consultation with us." Califano conveyed his sense of betrayal: "I told Father Hurley that I had several months ago told him, as the representative of the American bishops, that if they ever had a problem all they had to do was pick up the phone . . . and I would be willing to see them at any time and would pass along whatever message they wanted to the president immediately." Johnson scribbled "terrible" at the bottom of Califano's memo, then gave his Catholic assistant a piece of his mind. "The first thing the Pope said to me [when they met in New York in October 1965] was that I was a doer, not a talker," Johnson told Califano, instructing him to tell the bishops that "the president is entitled to better treatment" and "please don't attack the administration that's helped you so much."[128]

Hurley responded that he had sent Shriver a memorandum warning of the bishops' statement, but the director had not replied. "The vast majority of the American bishops," Hurley explained, "felt they had to issue a public statement to answer all the public statements made by OEO and HEW officials." Hurley specifically mentioned remarks by Katherine Oettinger, the chief of the Department of Health, Education, and Welfare's Children's Bureau, in which she declared family planning a "right" that federal, state, and local governments should make available "on a universal basis." Hurley concluded with a peace offering, noting that the bishops' upcoming statements on civil rights and Vietnam would basically support the administration.[129]

Johnson remained unsatisfied by Hurley's justification, wrongly suspecting that because the bishops omitted specific mention of Shriver and the Office of Economic Opportunity, the statement must have come from Cardinal Cushing and one of Shriver's in-laws, probably Senator Robert Kennedy. The president vowed not to "deny contraceptives to any poor person who wanted them" nor to "piss away foreign aid in nations where they refused to deal with their own population problems." He nevertheless accepted Hurley's olive branch, because it was "important to make peace with the Catholic bishops because before long they may be the only allies we have on Negro rights and the poverty program."[130] So the administration made peace. Draper and Rockefeller now decided, in Cater's words, that the bishops' declaration had constituted "a step forward [that] tacitly accept[ed] family planning services provided by the government as long as they are not 'coercive.'" HEW undersecretary Wilbur Cohen admitted that Oettinger's comments "did go too far," and, according to Califano, Cohen had "taken care of this."[131]

The administration did not surrender, however. At Johnson's urging, Shriver countered the bishops' statement with one of his own, denying any coercion in the OEO's administration of birth control services, and assuring the public that he would act promptly if such involuntary planning should occur. Over Califano's objections, HEW secretary Gardner told the press that he had asked the bishops to provide evidence of such "coercion," but had received no reply. (The bishops claimed that it served no purpose to get specific.) And Johnson elicited an endorsement from Dwight Eisenhower, who as president had called federally funded birth control "not our business," but now vowed to "support all programs, public or private," that provided family planning assistance.[132]

The president and his team were not the only ones unsettled by the bishops' proclamation. Many Catholics were upset with the manner as well as the message of the bishops. The NCWC press chairman, Archbishop Philip Hannan of New Orleans, originally proclaimed the vote for the statement "unanimous," then he said it passed "without dissent," and finally he acknowledged dissent from the floor "mostly on the timing of the statement." Colman McCarthy, writing in *Christian Century*, called Hannan's version of events a "tall tale" concocted by "a few bishops with a bugaboo about the government family planning programs," who "by the time of the meeting had enough power to push their statement through." According to McCarthy, "No one could imagine pop-off bishops like [Paul] Hallinan of Atlanta, [Ernest] Primeau of New Hampshire, or [Victor] Reed of Oklahoma sitting mum, let alone giving their approval, to a charge as rank as it was rash."[133] Indeed, the minutes of the meeting show that when Bishop Primeau twice objected to the "hurried manner" of the meeting and moved that the bishops postpone issuance of the message until the last day of the meeting, Joseph Cardinal Ritter of St. Louis and Auxiliary Bishop John Dougherty of Newark, New Jersey, seconded the motions. Archbishop Hallinan was among eight prelates who discussed the Primeau motions before their defeat.[134]

Perhaps emboldened by the controversy surrounding the bishops' proclamation, Johnson pressed forward on family planning. In a November 1966 memorandum to Shriver, OEO counsel Donald Baker responded to the release of NCWC legal counsel William Ball's brief challenging federal birth control policies. To Ball's assertion that such policies broke with the past, Baker noted that "funds have been available for family planning activities from the Children's Bureau of the Department of Health, Education, and Welfare since 1963, and from the Public Health Service before that."[135] By the end of 1966, Shriver's Office of Economic Opportunity was funding family planning in seventy-five cities. In what the Vatican City newspaper *Osservatore Della Domenica* called "one of the most outspoken Vatican criticisms of a U.S. president in recent decades," Pope Paul VI said that Johnson's support for birth control posed "serious problems of a moral nature."[136]

Yet the pope could not deter the president. The 1967 Social Security Amendments required states to offer birth control on a voluntary basis to all welfare recipients, and budgeted 6 percent of all maternal and child health funds for family planning. In testimony before the House Foreign Affairs Committee on Johnson's foreign aid budget, the Agency for International Development's administrator, William Gaud, announced that his agency would double its family planning budget to $20 million in FY 1968 and, for the first time, would supply contraceptives to foreign countries. Johnson would proudly remember the change as a "giant" step toward world population control. At a September 1967 White House dinner party with Democratic senators George Smathers of Florida and Frank Church of Idaho and their wives, Lady Bird Johnson recounted in her diary, "The population explosion and birth control occupied much of the conversation for the evening."[137]

Johnson's FY 1969 budget would authorize "the OEO to provide . . . comprehensive family health care services for the poor through nearly fifty neighborhood health centers." In February 1968 Johnson established the Presidential Commission for the Study of Population Control, to be co-chaired by John D. Rockefeller and HEW undersecretary Wilbur Cohen. At the urging of the bishops, Johnson appointed Dr. Andres Hellegers, a member of Pope Paul VI's advisory commission on birth control, to the panel.[138]

As the Johnson administration planned to spend more money to limit births, Pope Paul VI was preparing to defy his advisory commission's recommendation favoring the incorporation of artificial contraception into Church doctrine. "To Rulers who are principally responsible for the common good, and who can do so much to safeguard customs," the pope entreated in his encyclical *Humanae Vitae* ("Of Human Life") in July 1968, "do not allow the morality of your peoples to be degraded; do not permit that by legal means practices contrary to the natural and divine law be introduced into that fundamental cell, the family."[139]

Though 17 percent of them told Rev. Andrew Greeley's researchers that they parted with at least some of the encyclical, the bishops had little choice but to obey it, some more vehemently than others. "When there is a question of theological dissent from non-fallible doctrine, we must recall there is always a presumption in favor of the magisterium," the bishops reminded American Catholics in their pastoral "Human Life in Our Day" in November 1968. "Even responsible dissent does not excuse one from faithful presentation of the authentic doctrine of the Church when one is performing a pastoral ministry in Her Name."[140]

While the pope had largely ignored his birth control commission, the president would embrace his. Despite Dr. Hellegers's repeated insistence at the Rockefeller Commission meetings that "the restricting of population growth should not be considered as a substitute for other kinds of development," the panel's final report said as much. Delivered to Johnson shortly before he left office, the report, as the president interpreted it, "urged that the United States enlarge its world-wide assistance in population control" and called for "an expansion of the federal government's role in family planning so that information and services would be available by 1973 to all women who desired but could not afford these services." Thus did the Johnson administration come to an end: the presidency that had started with the promise to provide jobs to all Americans finished with the promise to give them contraceptives.[141]

Conclusions on Life and Death

It's easy to say that the U.S. Catholic bishops were ultimately losers in the War on Poverty. Over their considerable opposition, the Johnson administration and Congress kept upping the ante in the birth control fight, from implicit to explicit authority, from private to public endorsement, from few to many federal dollars, from providing information to distributing devices. But the War on Poverty was not a completely empty exercise for American Catholics.

There was considerable evidence, of course, of the bishops' failure. "I was breaking sharply with presidential tradition," Johnson would recall of his 1965 State of the Union address. "Population control was not considered a fit subject for the federal government or a president to approach. I was constantly warned that I was dealing with the delicacies of the home and the dogma of the church." Yet between that speech and the bishops' November 1966 pronouncement, Johnson would, by Califano's count, twenty-three times "declare himself forcefully in favor of government promotion of birth control at home and abroad"—many more occasions than Johnson uttered the phrase "War on Poverty." From his first year in office through his last, Johnson increased federal spending on population control from $6 million to $115 million.¹⁴²

The National Catholic Welfare Conference (later, the United States Catholic Conference) responded to the Johnson administration's steady march with uncertainty and inconsistency. "One comment we hear all the time," Msgr. Hurley complained to Msgr. Tanner in October 1965, "is there is so much confusion." At the bishops' November 1965 meeting, bishop-elect Tanner relayed the frustration of "some Catholics" who wondered "now that the Church has said how *not* to solve the population crisis, how *not* to help the poor and the Negroes, what is the Church *for*?" His fellow bishops applauded, but Tanner ended his remarks not with a solution, but with a question, "What should NCWC do?"¹⁴³

The answer came in a public relations campaign to, in Hurley's words, "adopt a positive rather than an 'anti' position on the issue of family planning." Part of the campaign would be William Ball's February 1966 brief clarifying the bishops' stance toward the role of family planning in federal legislation. Yet the bishops concluded that the Ball memorandum "does not come to grips with the tactical political problem: is it better to oppose the government outright or is it better to try to *condition* present and future government birth control programs?"¹⁴⁴

Despite the front-page press treatment, which was reminiscent of their education confrontation with President Kennedy, the bishops essentially opted for the latter approach in their long-awaited, oft-postponed November 1966 statement. Yet their advocacy of government "neutrality" on the birth control issue neither significantly slowed the proliferation of federal pronouncements, policies, and payments furthering family planning nor removed the confusion that had plagued the bishops' lobbying efforts. Even the pope, who had authorized the bishops' declaration, undermined it in his March 1967 encyclical, *Populorum Progressio* ("The Progress of People"). "It is certain that public authorities can intervene, within the limit of their competence, by favoring the availability of appropriate information and by adopting suitable measures," said the pontiff, "provided that these be in conformity with the moral law and that they respect the rightful freedom of married couples." Paul VI went on to support "needed programs in the field of population consistent with the economic, social, religious, spiritual, and cultural circumstances of the respective countries."¹⁴⁵

Pope Paul VI appeared to be siding with President Lyndon Johnson against the U.S. Catholic bishops. So the Holy See, through its apostolic delegate to the United States, Egidio Vagnozzi, instructed the bishops that they, in order to clarify any doubts and to prevent erroneous interpretations regarding the teachings of the Church, could declare the following:

1) Because the problem of overpopulation brings with it important social, political, and economic aspects, the Church recognizes the competence of the state in these areas;
2) the moral order, the rights of the individual, and the consciences of spouses nevertheless establish certain limits that the state is not permitted to transgress; and
3) if the intervention of the state should be in conflict with the moral order based on the divine law and interpreted by the authentic magisterium of the Church, or if it should constitute a pressure that would violate the rights of the individual and the consciences of spouses, then such individuals should be condemned.[146]

If the pope at times seemed to be taking on the bishops, the bishops also appeared to be battling themselves. In August 1967 HEW's Dr. Philip Lee telephoned Msgr. Hurley's office to arrange a meeting to discuss the social security amendments dealing with birth control then working their way through Congress. Lee's concerns, according to a United States Catholic Conference memo, were that "there is always the danger of a *de facto* coercion and that the mandatory character of these family planning programs might in itself suggest coercion in one form or another." In a bizarre case of role reversal, a member of Hurley's staff assured the good doctor that "the acceptance of family planning services on the part of the welfare recipient remains voluntary."[147]

Johnson's War on Poverty nevertheless was not a complete defeat for American Catholics. The war had commenced by enlisting the support of the American Catholic hierarchy. Johnson said it was "no accident" that he picked a Catholic to lead the campaign, and Shriver said it was no accident that his religion led him to the position. Shriver viewed the War on Poverty as a natural response to Catholic social teaching, and the logical culmination of his own efforts to embody it.[148] The assistant secretary of labor, Daniel Patrick Moynihan, told Msgr. Hurley after briefing him on the proposed Economic Opportunity Act in February 1964, "It is absolutely necessary to keep the Church in the War on Poverty." He added, "The only agencies that are really committed to such a program are the churches."[149]

Though the marriage of the president and the Church would end in divorce, the Johnson administration went to extraordinary lengths to court the bishops in the fight against poverty at home and abroad. In July 1964 the deputy secretary of state for international organization affairs, Richard Gardner, invited the input of the National Catholic Welfare Conference in the selection of the American representatives to the upcoming Second World Conference on Population. At the Society for International Development Conference the next month, the University of Notre Dame sociologist and Catholic population expert Donald Barrett reported to the NCWC that despite Johnson's State of the Union address opening the door even wider for family planning assistance to other nations, "several State Department officers felt compelled to . . . assure me that President Johnson is not advocating birth control as government policy (perhaps at this time—the words may be a trial balloon)."[150]

When political scientist Leo Pfeffer wrote to the *New York Times* in June 1965 to complain that religious involvement in the War on Poverty threatened to turn public responsibility into private charity, OEO assistant director Hyman Bookbinder drafted a response. Quoting the bishops' 1964 pastoral "On Church and Poverty," Bookbinder replied that "the best form of help . . . is to help people help themselves." Bookbinder asked Pfeffer and his fellow separationists, "Have churches and synagogues been bombed and have religious leaders been killed in recent civil rights struggles because they were dispensing 'charity' in the traditional sense of the word?"[151]

Meanwhile, Shriver was testifying before the Greuning Subcommittee in the House of Representatives, sounding very Catholic in his outlook on the world population problem. "While expanded efforts in the area of population control are necessary," the director asserted, "one thing that disturbs me in all the talk about the 'population explosion' and the need for birth control is to look only to total population figures and to consider the problem only at a general level." Contending that family planning is an individual and family, not a national, decision, Shriver added, "I firmly believe that every couple should have as many children as they wish." He finished his testimony with the NCWC mantra that birth control research and information must become available "without coercion."[152]

Msgr. Hurley emerged from an August 1965 meeting with Cohen, Deprey, and Lee of HEW with the conviction that they were "eager to consult with Catholic specialists during the next few months." If the bishops "cannot stop them" from implementing birth control policies, at least they could "condition the policies and practices of the government." A November 1965 White House meeting among the NCWC's Considine, Knott, and Hurley and the administration's Califano and Cater led to a dialogue between NCWC representatives and HEW secretary Gardner, helping ensure that Gardner's 1966 directive guaranteed "freedom from coercion" in his department's family planning programs.[153]

Even Shriver's draft reply to Evans and Novak's column in December 1965 bespoke the Catholic influence he was seeking to dispel. Shriver concluded his original response with a "summary," in which he contended, "No highly educated people in the world suffers from overpopulation.... If the time and energy spent on 'yac yac' about birth control were given over to the provision of decent housing, better education, more jobs, etc., we wouldn't have the problem among the poor any more than among the rich." When Shriver sent the memo for vetting by the Office of Economic Opportunity's Bernard Boutin, Donald Baker, and Herbert Kramer, it returned with the summary crossed out. In the margin was the explanation: "I would drop or completely rewrite the summary. This is a little 'holier than thou.' . . . This is awfully close to a paraphrase of Pope Paul in New York."[154]

Shriver continued to sound "more Catholic than the Pope." In December 1966 he wrote in *Christian Century* that the "War on Poverty must be fought not only politically but morally." He defined the "test of twentieth-century Christianity" as "not how much the poor enter into the life of the church, but how much the church enters into the life of the poor." Thanking Vatican II for lifting "the theological cataracts from our eyes," Shriver concluded that "the great truth of our era is that God cannot be honored unless mankind is served."[155]

The bishops' endorsement of the War on Poverty, of course, contained a significant disclaimer—"except for family planning." So while the Johnson administration had begun by enlisting the Catholic hierarchy, it ended by empowering the rank and file, many of whom were loyal soldiers in the War on Poverty but powerful dissidents in the campaign against birth control. Writing in December 1964, Rev. Andrew Greeley observed that for young Catholics, "devoting a year or two of one's life to volunteer work has become so popular that it is now being said that such service is a big advantage on anyone's record when he is looking for a job." A 1965 Gallup Poll found 81 percent of Catholics, but only 67 percent of Americans, approving of Lyndon Johnson's job performance.[156]

Many of the same Catholics who were obeying their bishops' call to service were defying their bishops' call to abstinence. By better than 3–2, a 1964 Harris Poll reported, American Catholics believed that their church should permit them to use artificial contraceptives, and those numbers steadily climbed throughout the Johnson era.[157]

In May 1968, the newly formed National Committee on Catholic Concerns, a cross section of priests, sisters, brothers, seminarians, and laity, was in St. Louis, where the bishops' spring convocation was ending. The new organization drafted a "consensus statement," which asserted that "teaching, governing, and sanctifying need new contemporary forms." The editors of *America* wondered, "Do the St. Louis discussants represent a solid majority in the

American Church?" They did not make the same query about the other group meeting in St. Louis. On the question of support for the entire War on Poverty, birth control and all, they didn't have to.[158]

The Roman Catholic Church is not a democracy, as its leaders constantly have emphasized. But its followers comprise the Church, as the Second Vatican Council established. One lesson of the Lyndon Johnson presidency, therefore, was that the dictates of bishops, and even the pope, were only as effective as their reception by the people in the pews. When enough of the American Catholic masses followed the hierarchy in pressing the Johnson administration on civil rights, the result was a victory for both. But when too few congregants joined too few bishops in following the pope's lead and rejecting the administration's Vietnam policy, the Church merely intensified the president's and the country's indecision. And when American Catholics became defiant toward the pope and the bishops on birth control, the hierarchy's successes in abetting Johnson's War on Poverty ceded to failure in the struggle against Johnson's funding of artificial contraception. American Catholics won more than they lost in the Johnson years, but their worst enemies were often themselves.

CHAPTER THREE

Catholics and Richard Nixon
(1969–1974)

MOST AMERICAN CATHOLICS had long been Democrats, wedded to the party of immigration, organized labor, and the welfare state. Republican president Richard Nixon sought to change that. He granted uncommon access to the American Catholic hierarchy and paid unusual attention to the rank and file. It was not surprising, therefore, that when most Catholic leaders and followers tired of the Vietnam War, lost interest in welfare reform, and opposed abortion, so did Nixon. And when he ran for reelection, most Catholics rewarded him with their votes.

War and Peace: Vietnam

When Richard Nixon, who lost to President John Kennedy in 1960 and California governor Edmund Brown in 1962, narrowly defeated Hubert Humphrey in the 1968 presidential race, it was a remarkable comeback. He promised that his country, divided by racial resentments, disillusioned by a cultural crisis, and mired in an unpopular war, would do the same. The new president buoyantly recalled a handmade sign he had encountered on the campaign trail, imploring him simply to "bring us together."

So he tried. At times a hawk and at times a dove, Nixon orchestrated a foreign policy that sought to conquer yet coexist with Soviet and Chinese communism. For a time, he stilled the restless tides that had engulfed Lyndon Johnson. And he enlisted many Catholics along the way. Nixon's self-made story and patriotic pitch endeared him to the entrenched Catholic working class, while his traditional Republicanism won over the emerging Catholic middle and upper classes. But Vietnam would chase Nixon long before Watergate caught him. And though he increased his support among Catholics for most of his presidency, the war ultimately separated the president from much of the Church hierarchy he worked so hard to persuade.

Richard Nixon, like Lyndon Johnson, would have to prosecute the Vietnam War over the vociferous objections of the Catholic Left. But unlike Johnson, he would also face opposition from the Catholic bishops with whom he agreed on other important issues, and to whom many of Nixon's "silent majority" would turn. In large part because of the war, the marriage of the Nixon administration and most American Catholics nearly ended. In large part because of American Catholics, the war was finally ending instead.

Vietnamizing the War

The strategy Nixon would employ to end the war—dubbed "Vietnamization" by Secretary of Defense Melvin Laird—was essentially the policy he had inherited from his disgraced predecessor. The United States would gradually withdraw its troops, aggressively retrain South Vietnamese forces to take over the fighting, and urgently press the peace negotiations in Paris. Such was the plan hatched by Johnson's assistant secretary of defense for international affairs, Paul Warnke, in 1968, and Nixon would have no more success with it than Johnson had. American combat troops, albeit fewer and fewer of them, would remain in Southeast Asia longer under Nixon than they had under Johnson. And public opinion would largely follow the same trajectory, from support to opposition to exhaustion.[1]

Though the antiwar movement would not go away, most of the American people initially gave Nixon the benefit of the doubt on Vietnam. During the 1968 campaign, twice as many Americans believed in Nixon's capacity to end the war as they did in Humphrey's. "The President's Inaugural Address," noted William Pfaff of the antiwar *Commonweal* in February 1969, "spoke only of peace."[2] Pfaff's publication was optimistic enough to launch the second month of the Nixon presidency by proclaiming that "the peace movement is in shambles," and wondering, "After Vietnam, What?" When Pope Paul VI met with Nixon in March, he encouraged the president, "May you in your administration experience the deep satisfaction of making a real contribution to the total cessation of those conflicts now unfortunately in progress." The pontiff delivered parts of his April Easter message in several languages, including Vietnamese, but omitted mention of the war he had so ardently condemned throughout the Johnson years.[3]

The new administration gratefully acknowledged the honeymoon. White House aide Patrick Buchanan, a Catholic, reported to Nixon on his April meeting with cardinal-elect Terence Cooke, the archbishop of New York, at which Buchanan suggested to Cooke that "he might convey to the Pope the President's appreciation over the moratorium of Pope, Church press, and American bishops on criticism over Vietnam, while the President tries to work this difficult problem out." Cooke assured Buchanan that he stood with his fellow bishops in believing that "a precipitate withdrawal would bring about the loss of Southeast Asia."[4]

The nation received Nixon's May proposal of mutual withdrawal and internationally supervised South Vietnamese elections, in *Commonweal*'s words, "as little children might the assurances of a parent concerning difficulties in which the country was long mired." A leading Catholic war critic, Senate majority leader Mike Mansfield, Democrat of Montana, introduced an innocuous bill to prevent the United States from "backing into other Vietnams." In September, lamenting that "all political and moral arguments have been spent, . . . protesters languish in county jails, . . . and deserters are powerless in exile," *Commonweal* sarcastically asked about Vietnam, "*What* war?"[5] The next month *Commonweal*, while criticizing administration policy, nonetheless conceded that "Mr. Nixon sincerely wants to end the war." Catholic liberal Michael Novak admitted that "the political settlement of the war . . . now seems inevitable."[6]

The October moratorium on the war did not shake the president. "The hope of its sponsors," *America*'s sympathetic Mary McGrory opined, "was that the country would rise up in such overwhelming numbers that the president would be forced to see that majority opinion favors immediate withdrawal." But the opposite occurred: a poll taken ten days before the moratorium found 52 percent of Americans backing Nixon's Vietnam policy; a survey a day after the protest discovered 68 percent support. Rev. William Tobin, although representing Cardinal Cooke at New York's moratorium, nonetheless declared his personal opposition to the demonstration and refused to address the cardinal's position.[7]

After Nixon revealed in a November 3 speech that his early peace efforts even included a personal letter to North Vietnamese leader Ho Chi Minh, *America* praised the "sincerity of Mr. Nixon's desire for peace." Two weeks later Pope Paul VI told five American governors in Rome that he shared the determination "of your illustrious president" to reach a speedy conclusion to the Vietnam conflict. White House aide Alexander Butterfield sought "additional ways and means" in which the pope's endorsement "might be circulated to good advantage." The result was a campaign led by the Catholic head of the Veterans Administration, Donald Johnson, using personal contacts with priests and Catholic laypeople to publicize the pope's words.[8]

More than 250,000 protesters participated in the November 15 march on Washington, but "few in the multitude," Mary McGrory lamented, "thought it would have any effect on the Chief Executive." Charles Palmer, the president of the National Students Association, which helped organize the demonstration, conceded that "we could have shown up with one million people, and it wouldn't have made any difference." Indeed, the demonstrators outside his window did not deter the president from turning on a football game.[9]

An ecumenical Lenten and Passover fast by clergy and laypeople outside the White House from February through April 1970 was deliberately understated. "We have no illusions about the possibility of peace being declared because of our actions," the sponsors admitted. The announcement of the National Students Association's proposed April 15 strike at high schools and colleges was equally pessimistic. "People are just down," Palmer explained. "You go five years without a victory, you lose and you lose and you lose."[10] And this air of resignation transcended the boundaries of the United States. About seventy participants from thirty-eight countries, including the Rev. Patrick McDermott of the United States Catholic Conference, attended the Consultation on Christian Concern for Peace in Baden bei Wien, Austria, in April. "Surprisingly, but by tacit agreement," according to the minutes of the meeting, "there was little or no discussion of Vietnam as the prime current case of the use of violence in the North-South dimension." Back home in the United States, the bishops again sidestepped the war at their spring meeting.[11]

Vietnamization may have co-opted much of the opposition to the war, but it could not eliminate it. William O'Brien, the president of the bishops' Catholic Association for International Peace, announced in May 1969 that his organization was folding after forty-one years. While primarily due to the bishops' formation of their Division of World Justice and Peace, O'Brien attributed the group's demise in part to the defection of antiwar liberals for whom "even our moderate stands in recent years have been hard . . . to swallow." *Commonweal* not only expressed its preference for the Viet Cong's peace proposals to Nixon's, but approvingly quoted the Soviet newspaper *Izvestia* in doing so.[12]

In May 1969 fifteen protesters, including a Jesuit seminarian from Detroit named Joseph Mulligan, burglarized Selective Service offices in Chicago. In June the radical Chicago Eight attorney William Kunstler announced that his client Rev. Francis Buckley, a Connecticut priest removed from his parish for his antiwar sermons, would be suing the Church to preserve freedom of speech for all priests. In August three Catholic priests were among eight persons who called a press conference to boast of vandalizing Selective Service offices in the Bronx and Queens, New York.[13] *Commonweal* gave up early on the Nixon administration. "When will Vietnam end?" the journal inquired in September. "Assuming the prolongation of Hanoi's heroic resistance, never." Declaring Nixon's Vietnam strategy a "dead end," *Commonweal* announced that its offices would close to observe the October 15 moratorium.[14]

Rev. Christopher Mooney, the president of the Jesuit seminary Woodstock College, was among the religious leaders endorsing the New York moratorium. Rev. Theodore Hesburgh, the president of the University of Notre Dame, joined other college presidents in signing a letter in the wake of the protest, calling for a quick withdrawal from Vietnam. The liberal Catholic magazine *Ramparts* lauded the moratorium's "unprecedented broadening of anti-war protest."[15]

The *Catholic World* editor, Rev. John Sheerin, proposed a Vietnam ceasefire. Rev. Robert Drinan, the Jesuit vice president and provost of Boston College, ran for Congress on an antiwar platform. Richard Robbins, a Catholic sociologist from nearby University of Massachusetts, Boston, asked, "Will the 221 Bishops who met in Washington the very week of the ... March [on Washington] condemn the massacre of South Vietnamese villagers by American soldiers as strongly as they condemned the massacre of Catholic and other Vietnamese by the government of North Vietnam?"[16]

They would not. The bishops' November 14 pastoral praised the U.S. government's treatment of prisoners of war, if not the war itself. But even the hierarchy was approaching the point of exhaustion on the war. Cardinal Cooke, who inherited the late Cardinal Spellman's mantle as the Roman Catholic military vicar of the U.S. armed forces, was among the minority who dissented from the December 1969 report of the President's Commission on the Causes and Prevention of Violence, which denounced massive civil disobedience, even when nonviolent and a matter of conscience. Cooke asserted that such protests might be the only way to effect the change of unjust laws. Or, he might have added, unjust wars.[17]

Cambodianizing the War

On the evening of April 30, 1970, President Nixon told a national television audience that he was sending U.S. troops into ostensibly neutral Cambodia to destroy the enemy operation there. Nixon hoped to, as he put it, "buy time" for Vietnamization by distracting and disrupting the North Vietnamese and Viet Cong designs.[18] Some Americans accepted the Nixon argument. The day after his speech, the president met with James Dunn of the Association of Student Governments, Morton Blackwell of the Washington Campus News Service, Randall Teague of the Young Americans for Freedom, John Gray of the Air Force Association, Robert Cocklin of the Association of the United States Army, Robert Nolan of the Fleet Reserve Association, and Leno Delmolino of the Catholic War Veterans. All concurred with Delmolino's conclusion that the Nixon address was a "fine speech" that "hit home."[19]

The next day Delmolino's organization unanimously endorsed the Cambodian incursion. Two weeks later, Delmolino wrote several antiwar senators—

Democrats Frank Church of Idaho, Mike Mansfield of Montana, Clinton Anderson of New Mexico, and John Pastore of Rhode Island and Republicans Charles Percy of Illinois, Edward Brooke of Massachusetts, Peter Dominick of Colorado, and Winston Prouty of Vermont—that "Catholic War Veterans support our men in Cambodia and deplores [sic] action stabbing them in the back."[20] Delmolino spoke for many of his fellow white ethnics, according to Rev. Andrew Greeley of the National Opinion Research Center, who estimated that the radical peace movement had "turned off somewhere between sixty and ninety percent of the American people." White ethnics particularly objected to what he termed the "changing of the rules" from rallying behind American troops in World War II and Korea to castigating them in Vietnam.[21]

This sentiment was behind the tabling of a resolution at a meeting of the Conference of Major Superiors of Men, representing thirty-five thousand Catholic priests and brothers, to "encourage" the administration to take "even greater steps" to expedite the total withdrawal of American forces from Vietnam, progress at the Paris peace talks, and a reemphasis on domestic matters. It was also behind the studied ambivalence toward the Cambodian invasion in a May statement by the USCC's International Affairs Committee. After enumerating the bases of just-war theory, the committee asked, "Have we already reached, or passed the point, where the principle of proportionality becomes decisive?" Yet it also wondered, "Would not an untimely withdrawal be equally disastrous?" Professing "no special competence in making economic, political, or military judgments," the committee avoided answering either question. The lack of such competence did not prevent an Irish-American Jesuit from Providence, Rev. John McLaughlin, from defying his bishop in announcing his candidacy for the U.S. Senate from Rhode Island as a pro-war Republican. He would not become a senator, but he would join the Nixon administration as an advisor.[22]

As the president was moving away from democracy in Vietnam, the pope was moving toward it. In an apostolic letter in May 1971, Paul VI condemned unchecked liberalism, but he also excoriated Marxism for begetting violence and totalitarianism. At their September administrative board meeting, in light of the "ongoing and rapid withdrawal of troops from Vietnam," the bishops rejected a request to join the National Council of Churches in convening an ecumenical conference on the moral implications of the war, preferring to focus on the future, "rather than the all too tragic past," by aiding the people in that war-torn region.[23] "Try asking the American Catholic bishops how the abundant Catholic teaching on the moral theology of war applies to the American involvement in Vietnam," wrote a flustered Robert Hoyt, the founding editor of the antiwar *National Catholic Reporter*, in October 1971. "Is this a 'just war'? They won't say; in fact, they don't know and, over the past five years, they have not given visible priority to the job of making up their minds."²⁴

Having jettisoned the Catholic Association for International Peace, the bishops' next target was the USCC Division for United Nations Affairs, the first religious group with a full-time headquarters at the UN, which was to be closed at the end of the year. The bishops did not seem to appreciate "the cavern that would be left if the Catholic presence were removed even temporarily," protested Rosemary Cass of the World Federation of Catholic Youth, Irene Dalgiewicz of the International Catholic Migration Commission, Eileen Egan of Pax Romana, Rev. Edward Rooney of the International Catholic Education Association, and Miriam Rooney of the World Union of Catholic Women's Organizations in November 1971.²⁵

In January 1972 New York's Terence Cardinal Cooke, having just returned from his fourth consecutive Christmas trip to Vietnam, assured the president that U.S. troop morale was not only better than the media was depicting it, but better than a year ago. He also praised the relief efforts of American public and private agencies working with Vietnamese refugees. "This is something that you and the United States should press more," the cardinal told the president. "We're doing more than the rest of the world combined," Nixon replied.²⁶

For many Americans, including American Catholics, the Cambodian incursion nevertheless became Nixon's Tet, the watershed that ended his honeymoon. At the University of Notre Dame, Father Hesburgh helped defuse a week-long protest by joining the students in sending an impassioned plea for an end to the war to President Nixon.²⁷

In May 1970, after the bishops' Committee for International Affairs raised questions about the justness of the Vietnam War, its director, Rev. Marvin Bordelon, had proceeded to answer them, in a way that indicted his government. "The war, to be just, must be waged by a public authority," said Bordelon. "The war must have a just cause. . . . A compelling answer to the very question of why we are fighting in Southeast Asia at all is long overdue. . . . The war must be fought with right intentions. . . . Appeals to American prestige or the fact that the United States has never lost a war provide dubious grounds for escalation of military activity." Bordelon concluded, "The war must have proportionality. . . . The U.S. Bishops raised serious questions about the proportionality of U.S. involvement in Vietnam even eighteen months ago. Nothing that has happened in the last year-and-a-half has served to answer those questions."²⁸

The Berrigan brothers resurfaced just as their words, if not their actions, were winning vindication. At the end of June 1970 U.S. troops left Cambodia only two months after they had entered. In July, Rev. Philip Berrigan, serving a six-year sentence for the May 1968 destruction of draft files in Catonsville, Maryland, complained of unfair treatment at the federal penitentiary in Lewisburg, Pennsylvania. In August, the four-month fugitive status of Rev. Daniel Berrigan, who had sought to avoid a prison term for the same crime, ended when Federal Bureau of Investigation agents tracked him down on Block Island off the Rhode Island coast. Marshals brought him to the federal prison in Danbury, Connecticut, where he began serving his sentence.[29]

While the Berrigans remained in jail, another Catholic war critic was staying out. Defended by priests Rev. Robert Drinan of Boston College, Rev. James Cavanaugh of Northeastern University, Rev. James Rafferty of Framingham State College, and Rev. Edward Hoffler of the Ecumenical Center in Morgantown, West Virginia, First Lieutenant John Forrest in August became the first member of the U.S. military to earn an honorable discharge on the basis of Catholic theology. Though Forrest admitted that his church did not oppose all war, he cited documents from the Second Vatican Council and the World Conference of Bishops that allowed for abstention from fighting if a Catholic deemed a modern war to be unjust. At the September meeting of the United States Catholic Conference's administrative board, the bishops commissioned legal counsel William Consedine to determine whether they should file an amicus brief in two cases of selective conscientious objection that might reach the Supreme Court. Consedine recommended that they take up one of the cases. Msgr. Bordelon went even further, urging the bishops to advocate an end to the draft.[30]

Pope Paul VI joined the antiwar chorus in September, when he met with Nixon in Rome. "Recent happenings have shown what special need there is at this moment to work for peace," the pope told the president, in an apparent allusion to Cambodia. "Our anxiety is now increased by the danger of such a conflict involving more and more countries." An uncharacteristically sheepish Nixon responded by thanking the pope for his advocacy on behalf of American prisoners of war, a subject that should "be separated from the other political issues that may be involved in the very difficult war in Vietnam."[31]

"Once again, we're getting clobbered by the way-out Catholics," Robert Odle wrote to fellow White House aide Charles Colson in March 1971, noting a planned antiwar protest led by the auxiliary bishop of Rhode Island, Bernard Kelly, at the Newport naval base that President Nixon would be visiting the next day. "Coming on the heels of Drinan going to Congress and the Berrigans going to jail, we should be doing whatever we can to offset the idea that the Catholics oppose the president."[32]

Commonweal's Peter Steinfels was among a group of antiwar Catholics who prayed, sang, and read scripture outside the White House in April in order to force arrests and thus spend Holy Week in jail. On April 22 John Kerry, representing Vietnam Veterans against the War, issued an eloquent plea for an end to the war in testimony before the Senate Foreign Relations Committee, which he would later chair as a Democratic senator from Massachusetts. "We wish that a merciful God could wipe away our own memories of that service as easily as this administration has wiped away their memories of us," the Catholic former naval lieutenant testified.[33]

Two days later hundreds of thousands of antiwar protesters descended on Washington, D.C., prompting *America* reluctantly to acknowledge what Americans already knew: the demonstrators now represented a plurality of the country. According to a Gallup Poll, 46 percent of Americans disapproved of the president's conduct of the war, 41 percent approved, and 13 percent somehow had no opinion. In June, the National Association of Laymen, composed of twelve thousand Catholics, urged New York's Cardinal Cooke, the military vicar for Catholics in the armed forces, to remove Catholic priests from the military "in view of the repeated instances of silence on the part of the Catholic chaplains in the face of moral atrocities" in Vietnam. The army's chief of chaplains, Maj. Gen. Francis Sampson, also a Catholic, responded that "the man who doesn't resist the violent man becomes culpable," while Cardinal Cooke refused comment. Thomas Cornell, co-chair of the leftist Catholic Peace Fellowship, returned from a cross-country trip in July encouraged by the "respectful hearing" he received in "even the most conservative places."[34]

Such as the Catholic hierarchy. In their November 1971 "Resolution on Southeast Asia," the American bishops finally broke with the president, concluding that "whatever good we hope to achieve through continued involvement in the war is now outweighed by the destruction of human life and of moral values which it inflicts." For the first time, the bishops called for "the speedy ending of this war" as a "moral imperative of the highest priority." The pope followed suit, at least indirectly, by proclaiming January 1, 1972, to be a Day of Peace, one rooted in justice, not dictated by force. The pontiff's apostolic delegate to the United States, Archbishop Luigi Raimondi, hand-delivered the papal proclamation and its thinly veiled condemnation of the combatants in Vietnam to the White House two days later. Staggered by the one-two punch administered by the bishops and the pope, Nixon pointedly reminded Raimondi, in the words of White House aide Peter Flanigan, that while he "recognized the Holy Father was working for peace in the spiritual sense," the administration was "working for peace in the more immediate sense."[35]

Two weeks later an interfaith conference of 650 clergy organized by the National Council of Churches and called Ecumenical Witness gathered in Kansas City to denounce the war as immoral because it "forces Asian people to be our proxy army dying in our places for our supposed interests." Though the USCC had declined the NCC's invitation to attend, about two hundred Catholics, including seven bishops, went anyway to what *New York Times* religion writer Edward Fiske described as "the most comprehensive religious gathering ever assembled in the United States over the peace issue."[36]

Four days later Nixon marked the beginning of the fourth year of his presidency by welcoming Cardinal Cooke to the White House. Though Cooke continued to support the president, he betrayed his war-weariness when he urged Nixon to replace the term "Vietnamization" with "development" to, as Catholic White House aides Peter Flanigan and Brigadier General Alexander Haig related, "connote the winding down of the conflict and the concentration toward peaceful developments in South Vietnam."[37]

Ending the War

By March 1972 Richard Nixon realized, despite private denials and public invocations of his now-mythical "silent majority," that most of the country (and most Catholics) had turned against him on Vietnam. As the presidential primary season began in New Hampshire, Nixon recognized the political imperative to conclude the conflict that four years earlier he had promised to resolve. Nixon thus decided to pursue "peace with honor" with a vengeance. When North Vietnam launched a major offensive, the American commander in chief responded in kind, with saturation bombing, the mining of harbors, and a naval blockade.

Sixty percent of Americans approved of the heightened air war, which helped produce a breakthrough in the almost five-year-old Paris peace talks. Not all American Catholics, however, celebrated the war's latest escalation. In March 1972, just as the president was renewing the air campaign, the National Federation of Priests' Councils, meeting in Denver and representing about half the nation's Catholic priests, passed a resolution in support of the Harrisburg Seven, composed of Rev. Philip Berrigan and six others who were on trial for conspiring to bomb heating tunnels in the nation's capital and to kidnap national security advisor Henry Kissinger. The priests also urged the bishops to address the "immorality of the automated air war" at their April meeting.[38]

Nixon had other ideas. "Get [the] Pope, Cook [*sic*], and Krol on base re bombing of N[orth] Vietnam," he instructed White House chief of staff H. R. Haldeman in April. "Don't let them get on the wrong wicket." The president would get part of his wish. At the bishops' meeting later in the month, over the objections of a group of liberal colleagues, Archbishop Krol issued a statement in support of the bombing effort. Nixon then rewarded Krol by inviting him to the White House before the president's trip to Poland. White House aide Charles Colson reminded Nixon before the get-together to thank Krol "for his tremendous support on behalf of the United States Catholic bishops in supporting your decision on the war."[39]

Krol's statement incurred the wrath of twelve nuns and one laywoman, who lay down in the aisles of St. Patrick's Cathedral in New York City in the presence of Cardinal Cooke, chanting, "One more dead in Indochina." Police arrested seven nuns and the laywoman, hustling them off to the nearest police station while the other five remained on the floor. "Cardinal Cooke says he is against war," said Sister Patricia Harding from her East Fifty-First Street jail cell. "If he is, he should resign as Military Vicar to the Armed Forces." Cardinal Cooke would not resign, although three weeks later he not only urged a "speedy end to the war," but, a year after the bishops had dissolved their UN office, he suggested that the world body should intervene to make peace.[40]

Father Daniel Berrigan was not impressed. On parole after serving eighteen months of his three-year term, Berrigan walked out of a June Mass for Peace at St. Patrick's when Msgr. James Rigney, the administrator of the cathedral and chief celebrant of the Mass, did not permit Berrigan to give the homily. In what he called a "grave misunderstanding" but what Berrigan disciple Sister Judy Peluso called "a lot of hogwash," Rigney had scheduled another antiwar Jesuit, Rev. David Bowman, to preach the sermon. So Berrigan took his message, and about 250 followers, outside to the church's northeast porch, where he challenged Cardinal Cooke (who was not present) to denounce the U.S. bombing of North Vietnam and resign his post as military vicar.[41]

Before meeting with U.S. secretary of state William Rogers at the Vatican in July, Pope Paul VI made his strongest denunciation of the "intolerable" Vietnam conflict, beseeching all sides to "give proof of wisdom and magnanimity capable of putting human life and dignity above any other interest." The pontiff expressed the hope that the peace talks would become "speedy, loyal, and conclusive."[42]

The latest American aerial assault helped bring North Vietnam back to the peace table in January. The resulting Treaty of Paris authorized the withdrawal of all remaining U. S. forces, an internationally supervised cease-fire, free elections in South Vietnam, and the release and accounting of all prisoners of war and those missing in action.

Conclusions on War and Peace

Like Richard Nixon's trip to China in 1972, the U.S. Catholic bishops' reversal on Vietnam the previous year carried considerable clout if for no other reason than their impeccable anti-communist credentials. When one adds Nixon's demonstrated eagerness to please American Catholics on the eve of an election year in the midst of an unpopular war, one can see why the bishops' pastoral was so influential.

The U.S. Catholic bishops' decision on Vietnam nevertheless raises two questions. Since neither Tet nor Cambodia had turned them against the American conduct of the war, what took them so long? And why did they ultimately change their minds?

The answer to the first question commences with the American Catholic Church's historic resistance to communism and solidarity with the Catholic minority in South Vietnam. In the debate over the November 1971 statement, Archbishop Philip Hannan of New Orleans criticized its anti-American tone. John Cardinal Carberry of St. Louis worried about "the future of the South Vietnamese who would be abandoned."[43] Even the Catholic Left recognized the potency of the anti-communist cause in the United States and South Vietnam. "Will the American bishops at their forthcoming meeting speak out without equivocation or evasion?" Peter Steinfels asked in April 1971, in the wake of Lt. William Calley's conviction on twenty-two counts of premeditated murder at My Lai. Michael Novak then answered Steinfels's question in the negative, noting that "the support for Calley [as unwitting scapegoat] is localized in the most hawkish parts of the country. These parts happen to coincide with the Bible Belt, and with large Catholic populations."[44]

David and Joanne O'Brien, who accompanied over forty other American laypeople and clergy to the Assembly of Christians in Solidarity with the Peoples of Vietnam, Laos, and Cambodia in Southeast Asia in May 1971, blamed the reluctance of the American bishops to criticize the war on the disproportionate number of Catholics in the South Vietnamese government and the "truly despotic role" of the country's fervently anti-communist Catholic hierarchy. Rev. Richard Griffin of the Harvard-Radcliffe Catholic Student Center returned from the conference with the realization that "religious leaders are not allowed to stand in opposition to government policies" in North Vietnam. The Catholic chaplain of the University of Minnesota, Rev. Harry Bury, who along with fellow priests Rev. John Dee and Rev. Robert Willis chained himself to a fence at the American embassy in Saigon in June 1972 to protest the war, learned that "the majority of Catholics in the South are great supporters of the Saigon government and of the American presence in Vietnam."[45]

If the Catholic Left concurred with the bishops on the impact of the Cold War on church and state in both countries, they agreed on little else, furnishing a second explanation for the hierarchy's slow response on Vietnam. Though the Berrigans' end—the withdrawal of U.S. forces from Vietnam—

was becoming increasingly popular, their means (breaking and entering, destroying property, kidnapping) were not. Although the brothers won many adherents among their fellow Catholics, polls showed that their tactics were hurting their cause. A *Newsweek* survey a month before the bishops' decision showed that only 16 percent of adult American Catholics believed that Catholics who raided draft boards to protest the war were "acting as responsible Christians," while only 31 percent believed that "the Church should take a public stand" against the war. Though the bishops were reluctant to address the radical peace movement, Catholic pollster Rev. Andrew Greeley was not. "The truth is that the Catholic 'radicals' don't make any difference at all," said Greeley. "On the contrary, all the available data suggest that Berrigan-style protests are counterproductive for the causes they support." If the intent was to stir the bishops to action, the Catholic Left's tactics often had the opposite effect.[46]

A third ingredient in the bishops' reticence was the reality that they had other fish to fry. Prior to cardinal-elect Cooke's meeting with Nixon in April 1969, White House aide Patrick Buchanan informed the president that the "main concern" of the Catholic vicar of the armed forces of the United States was "the acute crisis in Catholic Education." When Nixon again met with Cooke upon the cardinal's return from Vietnam in January 1972, the first thing they discussed was the financial condition of Catholic schools. When Father Berrigan gave his impromptu homily on the steps of St. Patrick's in April 1972, Cooke was, in the derisive words of *Commonweal*'s editors, "too busy flexing the Church's political muscles in Albany brandishing a warm letter from Nixon defending the lives of the unborn." White House aide Charles Colson prepared Nixon for his May 1972 meeting with Cardinal Krol by noting that Krol had been "extremely helpful in supporting your positions on aid to non-public schools [and] anti-abortion" as well as the war.[47]

A fourth stimulus for the bishops' delay was that, in their minds, their statement would not really be all that new. Rather than a dramatic departure, the prelates preferred to depict their November 1971 pastoral as a natural culmination. Thus they cited their 1968 statement, "Human Life in Our Day," in which they had asked a series of "basic moral questions" about the war; the words of Vatican II's *Pastoral Constitution on the Church in the Modern World*, which called for "an evaluation of war with an entirely new attitude" and observed that "peace is not merely the absence of war, but an enterprise of justice"; and the statements of Pope Pius XII that "nothing is lost by peace, everything may be lost by war," Pope John XXIII that "in this age of ours which prides itself on atomic power it is irrational to believe that war is still an apt means of vindicating violated rights," and Paul VI urging "no more war, war never again." When the liberal Gordon Zahn challenged the bishops' view of history in a January 1972 article in *Commonweal*, Russell Shaw, the director of the bishops' National Catholic Office of Information, wrote a letter to the editor attacking Zahn's propagation of the "myth . . . that the U.S. bishops, with a handful of exceptions, had never taken any position on the war except one of explicit or implicit support."[48]

Indeed, fourteen New England Catholic bishops had enraged the conservative Catholic professor Jeffrey Hart of Dartmouth College with their May 1971 statement advocating American withdrawal from Vietnam. Hart conceded that the document "has the look of something hammered together to reconcile widely divergent viewpoints" and that its recommendation of "the most rapid possible termination of the war and establishment of a just peace" could be "heartily endorsed by President Nixon." He nonetheless indicted these bishops for not considering the impact of a communist victory on the Catholic population of South Vietnam. Two months later Detroit's auxiliary bishop, Thomas Gumbleton, was less ambiguous in an op-ed piece in the *New York Times* in which he branded U.S. involvement in Vietnam "immoral."[49]

If the dovish Gumbleton, who would later endorse George McGovern for president, appeared to be the exception who proved the rule of the bishops' conservatism on the war, there was evidence from less likely sources that the bishops' statement had built on earlier foundations. Belying their image as aloof authoritarians, the bishops in 1971 conducted eleven regional meetings to gauge the sentiments of American Catholics on a host of issues. Three regions appealed to them to be more forthcoming in addressing the moral questions of the Vietnam War. A few weeks before the November statement, the conservative Polish-American cardinal Krol spoke for the American delegation to the Synod of Bishops in Rome when he said, "Peace cannot be built or maintained by violence or terror." Only two months after the bishops' statement and four months before Cardinal Cooke's individual public break with the president on the war, national security advisor Henry Kissinger and White House aide Peter Flanigan prepared Nixon for his meeting with the cardinal. Their memorandum noted that "the Cardinal tends to have a dovish attitude on Vietnam issues." Whether correcting the record or engaging in wishful thinking, the president crossed out that sentence.[50]

A fifth cause of the bishops' procrastination was the consensus model that governs the adoption of their pastorals. American Catholics and their superiors were not immune to the polarization that characterized the country's attitudes about Vietnam. So the search for consensus on Vietnam, which the bishops found before the country did, was an arduous one.

Quoting the New England bishops who had criticized the war, Archbishop

Humberto Medeiros of Boston introduced the November 1971 statement with the admonition that "we must not allow complexity to deter us from addressing ourselves, as shepherds of the flock, to this grave national crisis nor, in the light of our ethical tradition and teachings, can we be deterred from attempting to provide guidance for the formation of the conscience of our people." In the debate that followed, the liberal Bishop Gumbleton quoted the conservative Cardinal Krol.[51] The first vote on the statement, which included the sentence "It is our firm conviction, therefore, that further prosecution of the war cannot be justified by traditional moral norms," passed 158–36. A second version, which substituted the language, "It is our firm conviction, therefore, that the speedy ending of this war is a moral imperative of the highest priority," passed almost unanimously by voice vote.[52]

The contentious epilogue to the bishops' vote underscored the magnitude of their achievement. John Cardinal Carberry charged that someone had deviously reinserted the offending phrase "cannot be justified by traditional moral norms"; Auxiliary Bishop John Dougherty of Newark blamed a wayward typist. The dovish Bishop Gumbleton claimed the revised statement precluded Catholic participation in the war. The hawkish Archbishop Hannan replied that it said no such thing. Yet the statement belonged to all of them, and it pitted them firmly, for now anyway, against a war and a president they had long refused to oppose.[53]

So why now? The first reasons that the bishops acted when they did were the rumblings of détente that punctuated the Nixon presidency. At their April 1970 spring meeting, the bishops lauded the Nixon administration's strides toward "workable relations" with China's communist government, with which the United States had conducted no formal diplomacy for two decades. The bishops placed Nixon's outreach toward China under the same broad rubric that he did, world peace, in an equally clumsy and ultimately doomed attempt to deflect attention from the war that the United States was fighting and China was funding. Yet the American hierarchy's juggling act was not nearly as awkward as the pope's, as he closed a November 1970 conference of over 150 Asian bishops in Manila with a two-thousand-word address that somehow condemned "militant atheism" without once mentioning the word "communism." Some of the Asian bishops, who included the word in their own statement, attributed the pontiff's glaring omission to his desire for a rapprochement between China and the Church.[54]

In March 1972, a month after Nixon's unprecedented visit to Beijing to defrost U.S. relations with the communist giant, the president prepared for his equally historic May trip to Moscow to sign the first Strategic Arms Limitation Treaty (SALT I) with the Soviet Union. In words that revealed the tragic asymmetry of American Cold War foreign policy, Charles Colson advised the president that "leaving aside Vietnam," Nixon's travel would "build on progress already achieved with the Soviets in such areas as SALT." Nixon reinforced this ill-fated dichotomy when he telephoned Cardinal Krol upon his return. "The only thing I regret is that there's not some way we can break them off," the president said of the Soviet satellite Poland, which he had also visited. Nixon added prophetically, "The Russians cannot depend on those Polish divisions."[55]

And the president and the bishops could not depend on the divisions within American, and American Catholic, public opinion to sustain their two-track policy of victory over the communists in Southeast Asia, but acceptance of them just about everywhere else. Even the more conservative *U.S. Catholic*, published by the Claretian Fathers; *Catholic World*, issued by the Paulist Fathers; and *Catholic Digest*, the mouthpiece of the Catholic Publishing Center of the College of St. Thomas, generally joined *Commonweal* in abandoning containment and embracing détente. The administration that demanded "linkage" between the pronouncements and practices of its Chinese and Soviet adversaries would ultimately have to hold itself to the same standard. The bishops recognized this reality about a year before the president did.[56]

A second factor in the bishops' transformation was the impact of the Catholic Left. "Anti-war protests, draft evasion, and desertion" by Catholics, political scientist Mary Hanna concluded, "influenced Church leadership activity in their support and probably helped in influencing general, public, and Congressional reaction against the war" in Vietnam. "Another thing that influenced me, and I think influenced the others," Gumbleton told the *National Catholic Reporter* after the vote, was the "activity of people like Dan and Phil Berrigan. . . . Well, when men are doing things like this, and these are serious men, . . . I have to face the question that they faced: Is the war moral or immoral?" Worcester archbishop Bernard Flanagan concurred. "I personally reflected on the Berrigans and asked myself what message . . . should be coming through to me if these men are prophetic witnesses in the Church today," he would remember. "I thought maybe these people are not so far off as prophetic witnesses—they certainly are willing to put their lives on the line—and therefore I think we should reflect."[57]

A third spark that ignited the bishops' decision was the realization that, in many ways, their other fish to fry had proven less appetizing than the Vietnam issue. Cardinal Cooke's preoccupation with the fate of Catholic schools seemed futile: as Nixon entered his fourth year in office, parochial schools were closing at the rate of one per day. Cardinal Krol's apprehension about abortion was prescient: the Supreme Court would reject the Church's position in January 1973. And the tumult within the Church unleashed by the internal dynamics of Vatican II and the external pressures of the cultural upheaval in American society was overwhelming: 3,413 men resigned from the priesthood from 1966 to 1969, and regular church attendance fell from 71 percent to 50 percent between 1963 and 1974. Next to these other concerns, the most divisive war in American history seemed the easy one.[58]

A fourth catalyst for the bishops' pastoral was that, despite the precedents they cited, it embodied more change than continuity. Though they would not admit it, the bishops, like the Supreme Court for Thomas Nast's fictional Mr. Dooley almost a century earlier, showed that they too "follow the election returns." Though not immediately receptive to the swings in public opinion after Tet and Cambodia, the gradual revision of the attitudes of many of the people in the pews facilitated their own conversion. As related by the *New York Times*, "authoritative Vatican sources" attributed Pope Paul VI's June 1971 declaration before the College of Cardinals that "we shall not cease . . . to support every favorable occasion for the restoration of peace, freedom, concord, and a new prosperity" in Vietnam to the "changing attitude in the United States toward the war." The pope's speech preceded the Synod of Bishops in Rome, whose denunciation of war became a major impetus for the bishops' stand, according to Boston's Archbishop Medeiros, chairman of the committee that drafted the statement.[59]

The war of attrition in Vietnam had spawned a campaign of attrition in public perceptions at home, and the Nixon administration was losing both by November 1971. According to an internal analysis by the administration, more than half of the nation's Catholics expressed "concern" over the war, a greater percentage than Americans as a whole. Lawrence Cardinal Shehan of Baltimore said in the debate over the pastoral that he "felt very deeply that it would be imprudent for the body of bishops to leave their general meeting without issuing a statement." Shehan explained that "there had been a ten-year undeclared war with great loss of life, and the bishops . . . were bound to address the many problems of conscience that had been created during that time."[60]

Yet despite the grassroots origins of Catholic repudiation of the war, change predictably came from the top, furnishing the final piece to the bishops' puzzle. The elusive consensus that the bishops finally attained in November 1971 owed a great debt to John Cardinal Dearden, the archbishop of Detroit and the first elected president of the United States Catholic Conference/National Conference of Catholic Bishops. A captive of neither extreme, Dearden was, in the words of *Christian Century*'s Alexander Sigur, "very patient, fatherly, and understanding with those who have sought to leave the active ministry and equally understanding and kindly toward the traditional right-wingers who desire the 'old days.'" *Newsweek* concluded that "under Dearden's leadership, the minority of about ninety moderately liberal prelates have sought compromises with the conservative majority to achieve limited progress." To Sigur, "Cardinal Dearden's greatest attribute probably is his ability to change," a quality improbably attached to his fellow bishops when Dearden completed his five-year presidency in November 1971.[61]

To an East-West proxy war in a time of détente and a polarizing president on the way to a landslide reelection, one could add still another paradox: staunchly anti-communist bishops urging total American withdrawal from Vietnam. So when a majority of American Catholics cast their ballots for a Republican presidential candidate for the first time in 1972, they were not just voting to coexist with atheistic communism in China, the Soviet Union, and North Vietnam. On this issue at least, they were on the same side as their bishops.[62]

Social Justice: Welfare Reform

Though attention to the "Catholic vote" was not new in 1969, the degree to which the president courted it was. The arguments of journalists Kevin Phillips, Richard Scammon, and Ben Wattenberg—that an electoral realignment of working-class white ethnics from Democrats to Republicans could occur if only the new president transmitted the proper political signals—fascinated Richard Nixon. Prominent among these potential Republicans were Catholics, and prominent among these political signals was welfare reform.[63]

Nixon's urban affairs advisor, Daniel Patrick Moynihan, the product of the Irish-Catholic working class of New York, would recall the president's interest in a *New Yorker* piece. Moynihan quoted an article by Pete Hamill, "The Revolt of the White Lower Middle Class," and described the resentments of the hard-working blue-collar class in New York, too poor to live in the suburbs and too proud to accept charity. By encouraging dependency and discouraging work, "welfare," Moynihan related, "was the supercharged object of their fury."[64]

Welfare reform therefore offered Nixon a way of confronting New Deal and Great Society liberalism while converting many disaffected liberals. If politics came to overshadow the principle behind Nixon's noble effort to employ the able and to insure the unable, so be it. After all, it wasn't as if Nixon didn't believe in what he was doing. If it wasn't for the transparent politics of wooing Catholic voters, the Quaker president privately allowed, he might even join their church.[65]

Nixon would not become a Catholic, and welfare reform would not become law. But the political and policy considerations by which American Catholics helped shape and sink his Family Assistance Plan helped to forge a legacy from which the country would not turn back.

The Proposal

Richard Nixon's welfare reform proposal was a repudiation of Lyndon Johnson's Great Society. Yet it originated with Johnson appointees, evolving from a task force recommendation by Richard Nathan of the Brookings Institution.[66]

The so-called Family Security System, endorsed by Moynihan and Health, Education, and Welfare secretary Robert Finch, included a negative income tax of $1,500 a year for a family of four, which would increase by $450 for each additional adult and $300 for each additional child up to a family of seven, which would receive $2,400. When family members found employment, payment would decline fifty cents for every dollar earned, until it eventually disappeared. If enacted, the system could end 60 percent of the nation's poverty. "That afternoon," Moynihan would recall of the presentation of the report to Nixon in March 1969, "the President was talking about a Family Security System."[67]

The next day, many Catholics were talking about their church's inadequate response to the urban crisis facing the country. Speaking at the first meeting of the House of Delegates of the National Federation of Priests' Councils, Msgr. John Egan, chairman of the bishops' Subcommittee on Pastoral Ministry, criticized the Church for refusing to "get its hands dirty" to allay the nation's urban ills. Three weeks later, at their April meeting, the bishops responded to this criticism by voting to augment the staff and budget of their Social Action Department and inaugurate an Urban Affairs Task Force. Patrick Cardinal O'Boyle of Washington, D.C., insisted that the bishops be spokesmen "for the principles of social justice."[68] The chairman of the Social Action Department, Bishop John Wright of Pittsburgh, worried, however, that his colleagues might go too far in addressing the needs of African-Americans at the expense of the white majority. Bishop Joseph Brunini of Natchez-Jackson, Mississippi, tried to unite the two camps represented by O'Boyle and Wright by suggesting that "many who are relatively unconcerned about social justice will respond if it is presented to them in terms of establishing a state of social peace within the [urban] community."[69]

The same debate was under way in the White House. Nixon quietly assigned domestic affairs advisor John Ehrlichman to revise his welfare reform proposal. The plan that Ehrlichman submitted to Nixon on July 10 established a national income floor, to be supplemented by the states, of $1,600 (to grow to $2,500 by 1971) for a family of four. All able-bodied heads of households except mothers with preschool children would "accept work or training" or lose their guaranteed income. All children, regardless of their parents' employment status, would receive a guaranteed income. Though eleven of his fifteen Cabinet members opposed it, Nixon, who had chaired six of the first eight meetings on welfare reform and had solicited input from inside and outside the administration, was ready to act.[70] He presented the Ehrlichman proposal (renamed the "Family Assistance Plan" by Secretary of Defense Melvin Laird) to Congress on August 8. "We cannot simply ignore the failures of welfare or expect them to go away," said the president, noting that three million more people had joined the welfare rolls in the previous eight years. In a nod toward conservatives, Nixon rejected a "guaranteed income" for parents. In an appeal to liberals, he spoke only of an "incentive to work."[71]

Sixty-five percent of those who had heard of the Family Assistance Plan approved of it. Eighty-one percent of the communications to the White House on FAP were positive. Ninety-four percent of editorials supported it. "President Nixon's message on welfare reform is a realistic attempt to move the country toward the adoption of a more comprehensive family-centered policy responding to the needs of low-income families," Rev. James McHugh, the director of the U.S. Catholic bishops' Family Life Division, responded. "If there is one thing that just about every citizen of this country agrees upon, it is this," *America* editorialized after the speech. "The present welfare system has to go."[72]

When the Family Assistance Plan arrived on Capitol Hill in October 1969, so too did an invitation from the administration to the United States Catholic Conference to testify on its behalf. Msgr. Aloysius Welsh, the staff director of the USCC Task Force on Urban Problems, recommended an affirmative reply. "The basic question to me is the opportunity presented to go from the traditional Catholic teaching on the need for economic recognition of the *family* structure (*family wage, family income*) to support of the Administration's initiative in offering it legal and political support," Welsh argued. Although "the latest statement of the Church's position in the bishops' pastoral of November 1968 ["Human Life in Our Day"] is somewhat ambiguous, calling for a 'family allowance,'" Welsh continued, "it does affirm the traditional family, and inasmuch as the administration bill includes it for the first time, the bill should first be commended for its intent before being analyzed for specific defects."[73]

The bishops accepted Msgr. Welsh's counsel. On November 12, John Cosgrove, the director of the USCC Department of Social Development, testified before the House Ways and Means Committee in favor of the Family Assistance Plan. Quoting from "Human Life in Our Day," Cosgrove lamented the "family instability in the urban areas of the country" due in part to "our national failure to adopt comprehensive and realistic family-centered policies during the course of this century." He praised FAP as "a new and realistic attempt to provide a basic income for poor families," which "merits our endorsement and support." Siding with liberal critics, however, Cosgrove criticized the $1,600 minimum income as "far too low," worried that the "proposed training program is curiously isolated from any job creation program," and proposed that no one be forced to take a sub–minimum wage job and that no mother of a school-age child be compelled to work.[74]

The bishops agreed, endorsing the entire Cosgrove testimony at their February 1970 administrative board meeting. Despite the bishops' problems with the legislation, the USCC's James Robinson assured Thomas Cosgrove (no relation) of the Office of Economic Opportunity that, in Cosgrove's words, he "would be glad to do anything to help" in enlisting other churches in support of the bill. The president was more than happy to accept the offer.[75]

On March 11 the House Ways and Means Committee reported the Nixon proposal, co-sponsored by committee chair Wilbur Mills, Democrat of Arkansas, and ranking minority member John Byrnes, Republican of Wisconsin, without any major changes. Two days later, Rev. James McHugh, director of the United States Catholic Conference's Family Life Division, circulated the "Special Memorandum on Family Assistance Plan," which reiterated the bishops' endorsement of the bill while continuing to press for amendments. Prophesying that the bill would pass the House but struggle in the Senate, the memo called for a massive lobbying campaign in which Catholic, interfaith, and government agencies would flood the media and contact senators via the mail, on the telephone, or in person.[76]

Moynihan encouraged the administration to "let the USCC know how much we appreciate all this." Nixon expressed his appreciation at a Catholic Mass at the White House on April 5. The USCC reciprocated the same day, when its general secretary, Bishop Joseph Bernardin of Cincinnati, joined Dr. R. H. Espy, the general secretary of the National Council of Churches, and Rabbi Harry Siegman, the executive vice president of the Synagogue Council of America, in writing all members of Congress to urge their votes for FAP.[77]

The Family Assistance Plan passed the House on April 16, 243–155, with 102 Republicans and 141 Democrats in the majority. The next week at their spring meeting, the bishops urged "prompt enactment of the Family Assistance Act or some similar family assistance program," while repeating their preference for "suitable" job training and a higher minimum income. They accepted a proposal by the Interreligious Committee against Poverty for a June 5–7 Welfare Reform Weekend, consisting of "sermons, adult education, youth group discussions, parish bulletins, newsletters, meetings of men's and women's groups, and [publicity] through the religious press" to push for enactment of FAP or a reasonable facsimile. Calling FAP "one of the most important and urgent issues to come before the Congress in recent years," the bishops pledged an all-out effort to secure its passage.[78]

Moynihan continued to salute the bishops' commitment. He sent the USCC a copy of his April 22 speech before the American Newspaper Publishers Association, in which he thanked "the major religious organizations of the nation," which "without exception came together in an alliance at once singular and spectacularly effective in helping to see that what needed doing [to pass FAP] was done." In July Moynihan passed on to Nixon a pamphlet from the bishops' National Conference of Catholic Charities on FAP, which "chides the bill just a bit for requiring mothers to register for work but then comes down hard for this 'landmark in social legislation'—support the bill, contact your Congressman." Noting that "no group has shown anything like the energy—devotion—to your proposal," Moynihan suggested that "if FAP passes—when it passes—I would hope you might invite a few of the bishops in for a cup of coffee." Nixon heartily concurred, scribbling on the Moynihan memo, "I think we ought to have them in anyway."[79]

So he did. Cosgrove, Bernardin, Msgr. George Higgins of the Social Action Department, Rev. Charles Burns of the Task Force Administration, Rev. David Finks of the Division on Urban Life, Rev. Geno Baroni of the Task Force on Urban Problems, and Russell Shaw of the Office of Information represented the United States Catholic Conference at the White House on August 17. But while the bishops and the president were discussing FAP, the Senate was refusing to vote on it.[80]

Unbowed by two years of failure on FAP, President Nixon vowed to try again in his January 1971 State of the Union address, in which he listed six legislative priorities for the new session of Congress, of which the "most important" was welfare reform. The National Conference of Catholic Charities was among a broad coalition of organizations that began weekly meetings with HEW assistant secretary John Montgomery to devise a winning strategy for FAP in 1971.[81]

The House Ways and Means Committee attempted to meet the objections that had defeated the previous year's bill, raising the minimum income from $1,600 to $2,400 by including the value of food stamps and inserting special provisions for families headed by women with children three years or younger, who were not required to work, and for the working poor or unemployed yet able-bodied poor, who were. The new bill provided federal benefit levels that were higher than the current levels in twenty-two states, but unlike the previous measure, it did not require those states with benefit levels higher than the federal minimum to maintain them.[82]

The committee's changes gave the bishops considerable pause. Though still in favor of the concept of welfare reform, they remained silent as the committee did its tinkering. In April the USCC legislative liaison, James Robinson, recommended that the bishops "stand on the statements issued on this subject last year and the testimony submitted to the House Ways and Means Committee and the Senate Finance Committee last year." The bishops thus refused to join the National Council of Churches and the Synagogue Council of America in the "Tri-Faith Statement on Welfare Reform," which advocated a minimum national income "not less than the current OEO/HEW poverty line ($3720)," the provision of "suitable" employment (defined as a job paying at least the minimum wage), a federal job creation program, and the exemption from the work requirement of mothers of school-age children and the adult guardians of ill or disabled family members.[83] Robinson preferred that the bishops follow the same route they had pursued the previous year, pressing for hearings before the committees to try to shape the bill to their liking. Robinson argued that although the bishops substantively agreed with the tri-faith statement, signing it would be tactically counterproductive. So it remained a bi-faith statement.[84]

Cosgrove proposed that the bishops author a proclamation of their own, to be sent to the House Ways and Means Committee, state Catholic conferences, and diocesan social action directors with a corresponding call for contacting one's congressional representative. Cosgrove's declaration, approved by the bishops after minor revisions, called for a minimum national income "approaching" the official poverty level with a timetable for reaching it, while otherwise mirroring the tri-faith proposal's minimum wage requirement and work exemptions.[85]

The new FAP passed the House Ways and Means Committee in May and reached the House floor in June. In a letter to Speaker of the House Carl Albert, Democrat of Oklahoma, President Nixon urged passage of the bill, which he called "the most important social legislation in thirty-five years." The next day the House obliged, 288–132. A majority of Republicans and Democrats sent the new bill to the old Senate Finance Committee.[86]

Rev. Robert Kennedy, the director of the bishops' National Conference on Catholic Charities, criticized the bill's failure to require a wealthier state to continue to provide welfare benefits above the $2,400 minimum, while offering an employer no incentive to pay adequate wages to the working poor and penalizing a mother for having children over age three by forcing her to work. The bishops regretted that "the Administration and the House-passed bill would not include payment of the federal minimum wage . . . , the earlier bad provision that mothers who are heads of families would have mandatory referral to jobs or training if they had children six years of age or older has worsened . . . to three years of age or older . . . , [and] there are no provisions to guarantee that the States' contribution to the program could not be decreased."[87]

The Defeat

With the Family Assistance Plan under consideration by the Senate Finance Committee, Nixon announced in August that he was postponing his campaign for welfare reform for another year in order to concentrate on a new anti-inflation economic package. "The President's decision to sacrifice this measure to his business-oriented plan for economic recovery is tragic," *Commonweal* editorialized in the wake of the Nixon announcement.[88]

The administration returned FAP to Capitol Hill in January 1972. Cosgrove again testified for the bishops, repeating their support for the bill yet insisting on a higher income floor, a wider range of recipients, a uniform national standard for eligibility, and a work incentive rather than a requirement. The Senate Finance Committee in September reported an alternative to FAP sponsored by its chair, Democrat Russell Long of Louisiana.[89]

The full Senate accepted the Long proposal, but only on a two- to four-year pilot basis, alongside the House-passed administration bill and a proposal by Democrat Abraham Ribicoff of Connecticut, which would raise the minimum income to $2,600. With only ten days remaining in the congressional session, the House and Senate bills went to conference, where they died a quick death.[90]

Though members of his Cabinet and staff did not abandon welfare reform, Nixon did, not mentioning it again publicly until his January 1974 State of the Union address. So too did the American Catholic bishops, whose next pastoral on the subject would not come until February 1977, at the outset of the Jimmy Carter administration. "The crisis atmosphere which surrounded welfare at the end of the 1960s has now pretty much vanished," Moynihan admitted to domestic affairs advisor Melvin Laird, who had replaced John Ehrlichman in April 1973. Indeed, a lot had changed since those heady days in 1969 when Moynihan championed the Family Assistance Plan and Ehrlichman drew up the blueprint for it. The advocate was now serving as ambassador to India. The architect was now serving time.[91]

Conclusions on Social Justice

As always, assigning blame for not passing legislation was much easier than passing it. In their diminishing enthusiasm for a proposal they had once heartily championed, many American Catholics, led by their bishops, had a hand in the death of the Family Assistance Plan. And they could only blame themselves.

Inside the Church, FAP was in part a victim of the residual backlash by the rank and file against Lyndon Johnson's War on Poverty. At the bishops' November 1969 meeting two weeks after Nixon coined the phrase "silent majority," Rev. Geno Baroni, the executive director of the Washington Archdiocese's Office of Urban Affairs, reported that "little attention has been given to the anguish of the socially and politically alienated 'middle American'—the second and third generation, almost poor, descendant of the largely Catholic immigrant, a major source of vocations and traditional backbone of the Church." Baroni's diagnosis that the New Deal coalition of white ethnics and minorities was falling apart earned him a promotion to director of program development for the bishops' Task Force on Urban Problems.[92]

At the same meeting, seven regional discussion groups arrived at similar conclusions. Contending that "the white majority in America . . . is largely united in its opposition to blacks," region I lamented that "while many resist integration, 'ethnic groups' tend to resist it more." Region II attributed the "ignorance" of the white majority to its "responsibility toward the majority, vested interests and the fact that adequate financial and professed service for the poor will mean an increase in taxes." Region III called for "tours of poverty areas for white suburban parishes." Region IV suggested that "polarization between blacks and whites can be avoided if efforts are made to bring the groups together in attacking their common problems." Region V posited that white-black conflict "very often reflects a lack of understanding on the part of those who live in suburban areas of the problems of those living in the cities." Region VI concluded that "white-black polarization has increased or decreased in different areas of the country." Region VII urged "collaboration with government programs for the unemployed."[93]

All seven groups agreed on the "recognized necessity . . . for the education of the total Catholic community in terms of a more generous, sympathetic, and Christ-like attitude toward the poor and minority groups." The bishops then voted to create a National Central Office for Black Catholics and to launch a National Crusade against Poverty, speaking about and raising $50 million "over the next several years" to combat the scourge that afflicted the "twenty-two million people certified as poor." They noted that "sixty-six percent of these poor people are white," while acknowledging "the intricate forces which lead to group conflict."[94]

The administration heard the rumblings at the bishops' meeting. White House aide John Brown argued in December 1969 that Nixon should intensify his outreach to "'gut,' conservative, predominantly Catholic Silent Majority Democrats." Observing that "our Catholic division, set up last spring, consists today of one girl—full time, as compared with the [Republican National Committee's] permanent black auxiliary," Brown contended that "Southern Protestants and Northern Catholics, predominantly white, are the missing elements in the Nixon Majority, waiting to join."[95] The president concurred, responding that, as Brown recounted, "the [Republican] National Committee always puts too much emphasis on guys we can't get." Nixon thus instructed aide Harry Dent "by the early fall of 1970 . . . to have clearly identified all the national Catholic press; expanded contacts in the Catholic communications world; and know[n] every district and every state where a hard-sell Catholic approach can win over the swing votes."[96]

In April 1970 a memorandum by Jerome Rosow, the assistant secretary for policy, evaluation, and research, reached the desk of Secretary of Labor George Shultz. Titled "The Problem of the Blue-Collar Worker," the memo warned that FAP would not help the "lower-income mothers who seek work and are outside the welfare system" because, unlike welfare mothers, they would not "receive subsidized child care to facilitate their move from welfare to work." Rosow lamented that these blue-collar voters, "many of whom are immigrants or sons of immigrants," had become "'forgotten people'—those for whom the government and the society have limited if any direct concern and little visible action." He urged Shultz to create a White House working group to address the problems of this increasingly neglected stratum.[97]

While the White House deliberated, the bishops acted. Under the leadership of Msgr. Baroni, the United States Catholic Conference convened the Workshop on Urban Ethnic Community Development in June 1970. "The largest single group of whites remaining in our large industrial and manufacturing towns and cities happen to be white working-class ethnics who for the large part are Roman Catholics [and] . . . who now feel trapped between Blacks on one side and middle-class suburbia on the other," Baroni explained the need for the conference.[98]

The bishops reached out to the administration during and after the gathering. Among the speakers at the workshop were Robert Podesta, the assistant secretary for economic development at the Department of Commerce, and Lawrence Brekka, the education director of the White House's National Goals Research Staff. Baroni wrote to Nixon requesting that he appoint a "special inter-departmental task force to review what assistance can come" to blue-collar workers "from present programs in OEO, HEW, HUD [Housing and Urban Development], DOT [Department of Transportation] and the Departments of Commerce and Labor and other agencies." Baroni also implored

Congress "to introduce and treat favorably legislation that is designed to promote the hopes of ethnic people as well as to alleviate their fears."[99]

Although Baroni was not "a heavy hitter, either in the hierarchy or intellectually," White House Catholic liaison Peter Flanigan allowed that "this area might be of some value to us from a political point of view." So Baroni was among those from the USCC who visited the White House in August. Observing that Baroni's workshop "covered much the same ground" as Rosow's memorandum, White House aide Charles Colson prepped Nixon for the meeting with the observation that "Baroni has attracted considerable publicity and has become a public symbol for forty million lower-middle-class white workers." Although "the Family Assistance Plan will be an important step in helping to create more work incentive in the black community and therefore partially dissipate" the rancor of white blue-collar workers toward African-Americans, Colson recommended that the president encourage the bishops to "provide the spiritual and moral leadership to help the white communities overcome this fear and suspicion." In response to Baroni's suggestion of an interagency task force, the president should assure him that, like the Rosow recommendations, this matter was under consideration.[100]

The bishops directed their Labor Day statement two weeks later toward "one of the most neglected segments in America society—the so-called white ethnic working class." They lamented that "public and private agencies devoted to the restoration of urban America have largely ignored working-class whites in designing programs to eliminate poverty, substandard housing, racial discord, declining schools, and physical decay." They therefore applauded the "renewed interest" in the plight of the blue-collar class by "the academic community, the mass media, the foundations, and a growing number of people in official Washington."[101]

After the November midterm elections brought one Irish Catholic Republican, Thomas Meskill, to the governorship of Connecticut and another, James Buckley, to the U.S. Senate from New York, Colson suggested that the administration "cultivate the right Catholic leaders in several key Northeastern states." Colson viewed the election results as the harbinger of a potentially historic shift: "The Democrats have always built their powerful machines around prominent Irish Catholic political bosses (occasionally Italian). Their Catholic leaders are now becoming much less important while ours are gaining in prominence." With an eye to Nixon's upcoming reelection campaign, Colson concluded, "Work should be started on this now—not in 1972."[102]

So the work began. Roy Morey of Nixon's Domestic Council conducted an internal analysis of the "Catholic vote." By September 1971, he had reached the conclusion that for white ethnic Catholics, their ethnicity was far more important than their religion, so "there are definite risks in attempting to woo Catholics as Catholics."¹⁰³ The Morey study provoked an angry response from Irish-Catholic White House aide Patrick Buchanan, who indelicately described it as "remorseless nonsense." While Buchanan conceded that ethnicity meant more to most American Catholics than religion did, he strongly disagreed with Morey's conclusion that courting the Catholic vote was fraught with danger. Instead, Buchanan ardently encouraged such an effort, as long as the administration pursued the right Catholics—not the "Catholic liberals, who ape the WASP Upper East Side liberals"—but the Catholics on the Right.¹⁰⁴ "There is a potential, latent majority out there, available to the President, which he has failed to put together," Buchanan argued. "It consists of the President's WASP and white-collar conservative base—added to it Southern Protestants and Northern, Midwestern, and Western Catholics."¹⁰⁵

Buchanan then sent Colson an analysis of the Catholic vote by Thomas Melady of the Business Council for International Understanding. Praising Cardinals Cooke, Krol, and Wright and "almost 150 weekly Catholic newspapers [that] have since 1968 been giving very good coverage to the Nixon Administration," Melady asserted that "anti-Nixon sentiment exists only in the 'Catholic left wing–underground' group which represents no more than ten to twelve percent of the Catholic community (as reflected in 'Commonweal' and the 'National Catholic Reporter')."¹⁰⁶

Despite their rift over the wisdom of attracting Catholic voters, Morey and Buchanan could agree that FAP, with its minimum income, meager work provisions, and high price tag, was not a way to most Catholic hearts. Morey responded to Buchanan's rant with poll data compiled by demographic specialist Arthur Finkelstein of the Committee for the Reelection of the President. Although Finkelstein concluded that "consistently [on most issues], Catholics give the President a better rating than the public at large," Nixon did not command majority support from Catholics on welfare reform. Only 45 percent of Catholics and 39 percent of all Americans believed that the president was "trying as hard as anyone else would" to "improve the welfare system." When asked to rank ten problems from most to least important, Catholics, like other Americans, put inflation first and welfare last.¹⁰⁷

To Nixon's liberal urban affairs advisor, Daniel Patrick Moynihan, therefore, the argument for FAP "appealing to a new majority," as historian Robert Mason put it, "was not robust." The problems addressed by FAP ultimately "were not of direct relevance to potential Nixon voters. The area of [their] concern was the perceived welfare crisis and an impatience with the apparently undeserving welfare recipients described by Hamill and others. The direct beneficiaries of FAP were the poor, most unlikely to support Nixon."¹⁰⁸

To Nixon's conservative speechwriter William Safire, FAP's moment had come and gone. "For years, during the liberal emphasis on welfare reform, the conservatives within the Administration were told that the Nixon followers on the far right would have to hold still and stick with RN because 'they would have no place to go,'" Safire would recall. Thus, he concluded, "Nixon . . . heard Buchanan loud and clear . . . and regardless of party turned more and more toward the people with whom he could feel congenial politically: in domestic affairs, people who resented the 'welfare bums.'"[109]

Yet just as the president was turning toward the Catholic Right, the bishops were turning away. Over the objections of Msgr. Baroni, who viewed the decision as a personal as well as a political affront, Bishop Bernardin announced in November 1970 that the USCC was disbanding its Task Force on Urban Problems. Bernardin explained that the mission of the task force had always been limited in scope and direction and that other USCC agencies would continue its work.[110] But the portly son of an Italian coal miner had an ace up his sleeve. The bishops begrudgingly announced in January 1971 a one-year, $163,831 Ford Foundation grant to start the Center for Urban Ethnic Affairs at the USCC. The Workshop on Urban Ethnic Community Development in June would be one of the center's major accomplishments.[111]

Baroni's grant expired within a year, however, and by that time the bishops' affinity for his message had diminished as well. With their growing desire for a higher minimum payment and deepening disdain for a work requirement in FAP, the bishops had drifted further from the more conservative majority and closer to the "liberal ten to twelve percent" of American Catholics identified by Melady. Among the casualties of the bishops' left turn were the white ethnics, to whom they had paid little more than lip service, and welfare reform, for which they were losing their enthusiasm. In April 1971, as the Senate Finance Committee kept maneuvering the legislation to the right even as the bishops tried to steer it to the left, the USCC legislative liaison, James Robinson, averred that "it is quite possible" that the "USCC made a mistake" in supporting FAP the previous year. By 1972, the bishops had withdrawn their endorsement. "The composition of the Senate Finance Committee is such that, given its overwhelmingly conservative majority and leadership and given the lack of practical and serious support from the White House, the only bill reported would have been repressive and damaging to family life," the USCC Division of Urban Affairs reported to the bishops in November. "In the circumstances, it is better that no legislation resulted."[112]

The bishops, and the president, had moved on to other things. In August 1971 Nixon became the first president to address the Knights of Columbus, just the kind of white ethnic Catholics Buchanan had targeted. But he made no mention of FAP. Cardinal Cooke's meeting with Secretary of the Treasury John Connally in January 1972 and Nixon's speech to the National Catholic Education Association in April focused on parochial school aid, an issue whose salience even Buchanan questioned. Melady's June blueprint for the reelection campaign's outreach to Catholics featured "abortion on demand, pornography for children, and drugs for children" on the list of Catholic concerns, but not welfare reform. When Nixon's appointee to chair the U.S. Civil Rights Commission, Rev. Theodore Hesburgh, issued a report criticizing Nixon's rightward lunge, Nixon fired him, and Hesburgh became, in his word, a "hero" to the Left.[113]

It is ironic that the Democrat Baroni, whose first parish assignment had been a black church and who would work for President Jimmy Carter, and the Republican Buchanan, who extolled his Confederate ancestors and who would work for President Ronald Reagan, were on the same side in their advocacy of a louder national political voice for white ethnic American Catholics. Baroni's popularity and Buchanan's pugnacity helped to overcome the liberals in the American Catholic hierarchy and the administration, as the more conservative Cardinal Krol won election in November 1971 and a more conservative Richard Nixon won reelection with majority Catholic support in November 1972.[114]

"Krol has an unbending manner which most of us simply can't hack," a liberal prelate complained after the cardinal's ascension. "But his election as president just might turn out to be a blessing for the American church. The illusion of unity would disappear." He could have said the same thing about Nixon. The illusion of unity on welfare reform, in the nation and the Church, had long since disappeared. So to the newly conservative president and the newly liberal bishops, the failure of FAP would turn out to be a blessing.[115]

Life and Death: Abortion

Presidents are not prophets. In the 1968 presidential campaign, neither Democrat Hubert Humphrey nor Republican Richard Nixon even mentioned abortion, and in 1972 Humphrey's attack on primary opponent George McGovern as the candidate of abortion put the South Dakota senator on the defensive all the way to his landslide defeat in the general election. Meanwhile, President Nixon opposed abortion only when he had to, whether to make policy or to play politics.[116]

Yet on January 22, 1973, in a majority opinion authored by Nixon appointee Harry Blackmun, the Supreme Court ruled in the *Roe v. Wade* and *Doe v. Bolton* cases that abortion is a constitutionally protected privacy right upon which state legislatures cannot infringe, almost without exception, in the first six months of a woman's pregnancy. Thus did Richard Nixon unwittingly become the gatekeeper of a new era in U.S. politics, in which abortion would occupy the forefront of the debate over American values, as the proponents of "life" confronted the defenders of "liberty."

If Nixon was less than steadfast in his position on abortion, many American Catholics stood firm. Legal abortion provided a rallying point around which their hierarchy led and, for a change, most of the rank and file followed. The abortion issue appeared too late to invigorate the Church, which was hemorrhaging its clergy and alienating its laity. But it did arrive in time to remind Americans that, unlike their president, Catholics as a moral, spiritual, and political force were not going away anytime soon.

Abortion after Roe

The Supreme Court had made sure of that. Thanks to the Court, on the same day that Lyndon Johnson died, so too did the "local option," which had often kept abortion in the back alleys and off the front pages.[117]

The timing of the *Roe v. Wade* decision, if not the content, caught the bishops off guard. John Cardinal Krol of Philadelphia, the president of the United States Catholic Conference, was unavailable, and Rev. James McHugh, the director of the USCC Family Life Division, was out of town. So New York's Terence Cardinal Cooke, who chaired the USCC's Ad Hoc Committee for Respect Life Week, prepared a response. Soon, all three would speak to the historic ruling.[118] Cardinal Cooke, referring to a North Dakota referendum and a similar anti-abortion vote in Michigan, claimed that this "horrifying decision" vitiated "the will of the American people who spoke their minds in favor of life as recently as last November." Cardinal Krol called the decision "an unspeakable tragedy for the nation." He said that "the child in the womb has the right to life, to the life he already possesses, and this is a right no court has the authority to deny." Father McHugh labeled the verdict "a terrifying use of judicial power," adding that "unborn children—and the nation—are victims of this judgment." McHugh predicted that "the Court action will energize the pro-life movement rather than destroy it."[119]

He was right. But where should the bishops direct their energy? Russell Shaw, the director of the USCC Office of Information, argued that the *Roe* decision had virtually precluded successful legislation and litigation to modify existing state and federal laws regarding abortion. He contended that given the absence of a broad national consensus against abortion, a constitutional amendment to overturn the Court's ruling would likely fail as well. Rather than relying solely on "pastoral letters, statements, resolutions, etc.," whose value is "limited at best," the bishops should conduct a campaign of "educating and motivating individual people against abortion" and toward morally acceptable forms of family planning. Shaw offered three principal audiences for such an endeavor: doctors, women, and young people.[120]

The next week the USCC Social Development director, John Cosgrove, agreed with Shaw on the need for education on, and alternatives to, abortion, while disagreeing that a constitutional amendment to reverse *Roe* was not feasible. Father McHugh also supported such an amendment, but only as one among many strategies, because "too much overt endorsement" by the bishops "may well impede passage because it will be called a 'Catholic Amendment.'"[121]

Shaw's skepticism notwithstanding, the bishops continued to make abortion pronouncements from on high. Their Administrative Committee issued a February 13 pastoral denouncing the Supreme Court's decision. The committee condoned civil disobedience to the new law of the land, instructing that Catholics "must oppose abortion as an immoral act." Lest there be any confusion, Chicago's John Cardinal Cody explained at a news conference the next day that the penalty for Catholics who underwent or performed abortions was excommunication.[122]

The bishops also backed a constitutional amendment. But which one? No fewer than twelve anti-abortion additions in the House of Representatives and two in the Senate, most of them authored by Catholics, had emerged in *Roe*'s wake. The most prominent was the "Human Life Amendment" sponsored by Catholic Democratic representative Lawrence Hogan of Maryland, which would prevent state and federal governments from depriving "any human being, from the moment of conception, of life without due process of law." The bishops' Ad Hoc Committee on Population and Pro-Life Affairs proposed an amendment protecting the rights of the unborn, while their Committee on Law and Public Policy suggested a "fallback position" of an amendment leaving abortion to the states if such a pro-life amendment could not pass.[123]

"If there is a more unspeakable crime than abortion itself," Cardinal Krol spoke for the bishops' Executive Committee after their April meeting, "it is using the victims of abortion as living, human guinea pigs for medical research." The Ad Hoc Committee on Population and Pro-Life Affairs stated, "Human life is a sacred value, which should be preserved and maintained even in the prematurely born or intentionally aborted fetus. It is no more justifiable to experiment with a fetus than to experiment with the life of the sick or terminally ill patient." Krol wrote a letter to President Nixon protesting reports that the National Institutes of Health was considering such a practice. The NIH's deputy director for science, Dr. Robert Berliner, replied that fetal research was not under consideration by his agency.[124]

With that matter out of the way, for now, the bishops could return to the question of a constitutional amendment. In June the USCC Administrative Committee, citing the endorsement of such an approach at their April regional meetings, unanimously chose a human life over a states' rights amendment. There were limits, however, to how aggressively they would promote it. With the Hogan amendment going nowhere in Congress, they refused to endorse any specific legislation. Echoing Russell Shaw, Bishop Walter Curtis of Bridgeport, Connecticut, representing Cardinal Cody's Ad Hoc Committee on Pro-Life Activities, ascribed the role of "motivational leadership" to the bishops to secure adoption of an amendment. Curtis explained, "It is not the proper task of this Conference to lead a lobbying effort."[125] Bishop Curtis's disclaimer not only denied the past, it clouded the future. "The statement of Bishop Curtis raises some very serious questions in my mind," attorney William Ball of the Committee on Law and Public Policy, wrote to the bishops. "I fear that, relatively soon, the most pro-life people in the country are going to be asking why it is that the Bishops cannot make up their minds to back an amendment."[126]

So the bishops dropped the façade, and prepared what Father McHugh called a "public affairs [i.e., lobbying] program" intended to convey the bishops' position "in a friendly yet strong and persuasive manner" to members of Congress. Though still undecided on the wording, they launched the effort in September, beckoning Congress to conduct early hearings on a human life amendment. At their November meeting the bishops created a new office to press for the passage of a pro-life amendment without jeopardizing the USCC's tax-exempt status. "By making use of the proposed office," Cardinal Krol explained, "it will be possible to avoid labeling the Conference's language as a 'Catholic amendment.'"[127]

That is, if the conference ever could agree on the language of an amendment. By February 1974 the bishops were considering six human life amendments, those proposed in Congress by Rep. Hogan and Catholic Republican senator James Buckley of New York as well as four internal USCC proposals. Meanwhile, Ball gave up on the idea altogether. He preferred the bishops' backup plan, a states' rights amendment.[128]

When Cardinals Krol, Cody, Timothy Manning of Los Angeles, and Humberto Medeiros of Boston testified before the Subcommittee on Constitutional Amendments of the Senate Committee on the Judiciary in March 1974, they still hadn't decided on the language of their amendment. But they were sure that they wanted one. And they were also certain that they did not want the kind of states' rights initiative backed by Ball. They insisted that such an addition would not be a purely Catholic product. "We do not ask the civil law to take up our responsibility of teaching morality," the cardinals intoned. "We do ask the government and the law to be faithful to its own principle—that the right to life is an inalienable right given to everyone by the Creator."[129] The cardinals' testimony proved futile, however, as pro-life proposals continued to founder on Capitol Hill. Robert Lynch, the president of the bishops' National Committee for a Human Life Amendment, told the USCC Administrative Committee in June 1974 that "there is little likelihood of any substantial action on the part of the House of Representatives toward a human life amendment in this Congress." The Administrative Committee complied with Lynch's recommendation of even more study before adopting specific wording for a pro-life amendment.[130]

If the bishops were raising the white flag now, the president had surrendered long ago in the battle against abortion. With his reelection in the increasingly distant past and his resignation in the all too imminent future, Nixon's ardor for the pro-life cause had dimmed considerably. "Philosophically, the president felt that unrestricted abortion was further evidence of a society granting approval to irresponsibility," Nixon speechwriter William Safire would recount, but "when the Supreme Court struck down abortion restrictions in 1973, the President shook his head and prepared to answer any questions with a grim support of the law." But there were no questions about abortion at his first post-*Roe* press conference. Later in the year, he signed the Health Care Extension Act, which contained a conscience clause protecting Catholic hospitals and health care workers from having to engage in sterilizations or abortions, and the reauthorization of the Family Planning Services and Population Research Act, which prevented federal funding of abortion as a form of birth control. But he did so with little fanfare.[131]

So when the suggestion came that Nixon meet with the four cardinals before their March 1974 testimony on Capitol Hill, White House aide David Parker, recalling Nixon's intercession in the New York legislature fight over abortion three years earlier, noted that "the President has gone with Buchanan on this sort of thing in the past." Parker's opinion, however, was that "I wouldn't touch this one with a ten-foot pole." Neither, it turned out, would the president.[132]

Conclusions on Life and Death

The first presidency of the *Roe v. Wade* era was a horrible time for pro-life Catholics. As if the Supreme Court ruling in favor of abortion was not bad enough, the pro-life president seemed largely unmoved by their efforts to repeal it. And the inherent risks of mounting a campaign against the decision threatened to outweigh the potential rewards.

In some ways, *Roe v. Wade* nonetheless benefited the American Catholic hierarchy. First, it changed the subject. *Humanae Vitae* seemed to many American Catholics a step back to the authoritarian, regressive tradition they thought they had left behind in Rome in 1965. By 1970, 78 percent of twenty- to twenty-four-year-old American Catholic married women were using forms of birth control other than abstinence or rhythm. As if to acknowledge this uncomfortable reality, Father McHugh argued in September 1970, "In all discussions and proposals in regard to family planning, we must separate abortion, sterilization, and birth control. Our greatest opposition must be against abortion."[133]

Second, the abortion issue promoted uncommon unity from top to bottom among American Catholics. The conservative National Wanderer Forum spent much of its June 1971 conference deploring the "timidity" of the bishops toward birth control issues. The liberal editors of *Commonweal* concluded after the bishops' November 1972 meeting that the hierarchy's "reluctance to do anything of note" about contraception "is becoming painfully obvious." But when the bishops' Administrative Committee commissioned its study of an anti-abortion constitutional amendment in June 1974, there were no dissenters.[134]

Many wayward clergy, disillusioned by the Church's stance on birth control, similarly returned to the fold. On the same day in April 1971 that the Vatican sided with Cardinal O'Boyle in his dispute with some Washington, D.C., priests over *Humanae Vitae*, the bishops at their spring meeting had released their own study showing that two-thirds of the nation's priests opposed the encyclical. "There is a sense in which the Church has truly been in crisis," Cardinal Dearden admitted in his November 1971 valedictory as president of the bishops' conference. In the wake of *Roe v. Wade*, however, the USCC's Russell Shaw noted the bishops' support from a "united front" of clergy, including the sixty *Humanae Vitae* dissenters in O'Boyle's archdiocese. The liberal priest and congressman Rev. Robert Drinan's otherwise temperate response to *Roe* ended with a clarion call to "those who believe that the inviolability of all human life, fetal or not, is the centerpiece of our civilization" not to be "silent about their convictions." Drinan posited that "there is some evidence to suggest that their new role may in the end be more successful."[135]

Or at least more popular. A year after *Roe v. Wade*, a Gallup Poll found that 47 percent of Americans favored the decision, with 44 percent opposed and 9 percent having no opinion. Among Catholics, however, only 32 percent approved, 61 percent disapproved, and 7 percent had no opinion—almost the exact inverse of American Catholic views toward *Humanae Vitae*. Rev. Luigi Raimondi, the apostolic delegate sent to the United States by the pope responsible for that divisive encyclical, thus assessed the Supreme Court's verdict as a "clear-cut rallying ground for polarized Catholics."[136]

Third, the bishops' identification with abortion provided the singular focus lacking in their birth control campaign. The bishops' on-again, off-again support for federal family planning services—as long as those services met their ever-changing specifications—sowed confusion in the Church as well as in the government. When the USCC legislative liaison, James Robinson, told New Jersey Democratic senator Harrison Williams in May 1972 that the bishops did not object to increased funding for an extended Family Planning Services and Population Research Act, Edward Hanify, chairman of the board of the USCC Human Life Foundation, complained that "most of the agencies receiving the funds would consider themselves to be ethically disabled from participation under the Act."[137]

But the abortion issue augured clarity in place of chaos. "Those who feel that the Church itself will gradually come around to a tacit, if not open, acceptance of abortion, just as it has on birth control," Paul Weber wrote in *Catholic World* in November 1970, "do not realize the basic difference between the two issues." Sister Jo Dunne, the education coordinator of the bishops' Campaign for Human Development, looked forward in March 1973 to the consistent, unifying message that abortion persuasively promised but birth control sorely lacked.[138]

Despite these potential rewards, however, the bishops' shift to the abortion issue carried several risks. First, the change of subject from contraception to abortion could not obscure the most visible link between the two: both involved debates by men over the bodies of women. "On its deepest level, I think the issue [of abortion] is not as different from the issue of birth control as many, particularly liberal Catholics, would make it appear. There are deep questions involved which touch the very meaning of human existence," Catholic feminist theologian Mary Daly of Boston College argued, so the "declaration of war between the women's movement and the official church should come as no surprise." Noting that in their post-*Roe* press conference the USCC's male panelists addressed the male reporters as "Mister" but the female journalists by their first names, the USCC's Shaw called for a USCC position paper on "abortion and women's rights" to address those women "increasingly alienated by having male celibates preach to them about abortion."[139]

And those male celibates had linked birth control and abortion before they belatedly and uncomfortably attempted to disconnect them. Norman Miller reported in the *Wall Street Journal* in August 1970 that "the Church is now trying to rouse its members against a large-scale federal birth control program by arguing that such relatively uncontroversial activity would pave the way for abortion-on-demand laws." So when the Supreme Court effectively legalized abortion, Shaw worried that "the tendency to disregard the moral teaching of the magisterium which received such impetus from the birth control controversy has spread to other areas and issues," such as abortion.[140] In other words, Shaw feared that Catholic women might follow their consciences, just as the bishops had been prodding them to do in defiance of government family planning programs. "To safeguard the right to privacy and freedom from coercion of mind and conscience—especially among the poor who are often the target of population control—there must be preserved a clear and unqualified separation of welfare assistance from birth control considerations," Father McHugh had objected to California Democratic senator Alan Cranston's zero population growth proposal in Congress in November 1971. Yet in its pastoral following *Roe*, the bishops' Administrative Committee decided there was no right to privacy, after all, so women could not follow their consciences if abortion resulted. "The Court held that the right of privacy encompasses a woman's decision to terminate a pregnancy, although the right of privacy is not an absolute right, and is not explicitly mentioned in the Constitution," the pastoral asserted. Before the term "pro-choice" would enter the abortion lexicon, the bishops seemed to be saying that Catholic women gained a right to choose when the federal government promoted contraception, but lost it when the federal government permitted abortion.[141]

Second, the unusual unity within Catholic ranks could not dispel the yawning divisions between Catholics and non-Catholics over the abortion issue. "The most persistent charge against Catholics in the abortion debate is that they are trying to impose their will on others," *America* admitted eight months before *Roe*. Asking "how . . . can we state our position without gratuitously—and counterproductively—offending other religionists who do not agree with us?" Shaw suggested another USCC position paper, this one on "the ecumenical aspects of the abortion controversy."[142]

Cardinals Krol, Cody, Manning, and Medeiros could have used it in March 1974 when they testified on behalf of a pro-life amendment on Capitol Hill. Jean Garton, a member of the national board of the Right to Life Committee and representative of the Lutheran Church's Missouri Synod's national board of social concern, objected not to what the cardinals said but to the scheduling of their remarks immediately preceding those of non-Catholic abortion proponents. The "entire day was arranged for and reported [by the press] as a case of four members of the Catholic hierarchy trying to impose their religious values on the American public," she lamented, "a simple matter of Catholics opposing abortion and Protestants and Jews seeing no religious grounds for rejecting abortion." The general board of the American Baptist Churches USA, meanwhile, was adopting a resolution expressing concern that the bishops' lobbying for an anti-abortion amendment threatened the seven-year ecumenical dialogue between American Baptists and Catholics. The "pro-abortion" Women's Lobby was going even further, taking the United States Catholic Conference to court to challenge its tax-exempt status because of its overtly political activities.[143]

The bishops had managed to offend non-Catholics before they had even written their own amendment. As for the cardinals' appearance before Congress, "if the purpose of the testimony—from the media point of view—was to make the point that this matter is something the Catholic Church takes seriously, the purpose was achieved," the USCC's Russell Shaw concluded. "If the purpose was to avoid linking the abortion issue with the Catholic Church, the purpose was not achieved—quite the opposite." At Shaw's urging, the bishops undertook a study to determine a way not to repeat this embarrassing episode.[144]

To heal their rift with the Baptists, the bishops sent representatives to a meeting with members of the general board, at which the Baptists disagreed with the bishops' "absolute" position on abortion but agreed with their rejection of "abortion on demand." Father McHugh responded to the Women's Lobby lawsuit by noting that of a USCC budget of $17 million, only $100,000 went to the Family Life Division and $128,000 to the Office of Government Liaison, so the push for an anti-abortion amendment was hardly the "primary purpose" of the conference. Judge Aubrey Robinson of the U.S. District Court for the District of Columbia sided with the bishops, tossing the case out of his court.[145]

But if Judge Robinson did not believe that opposition to abortion was the bishops' raison d'être, a lot of others did, furnishing a third problem uncovered by the abortion issue: the perception of Catholics as a single-issue constituency. Dennis Horan, legal counsel to the National Right to Life Committee, advised the bishops in September 1973 to reject the inclusion of euthanasia in the Hogan human life amendment because "I think we unnecessarily divide the force of the amendment by including euthanasia as one of its concepts." Though the bishops in April 1973 likened medical experimentation on aborted fetuses to the "cruel and unusual punishment" of the death penalty, which the Supreme Court had ruled unconstitutional in 1972, they still refused to condemn capital punishment itself.[146] "If we oppose abortion and fight against it out of conviction, a concern for fetal life," Sister Jo Dunne suggested in March 1973, "perhaps we can accept the same process and situation of those who refuse, out of respect, for visable [sic] life-on-earth, to support *war*—and now seek amnesty."[147] The bishops had come to oppose the Vietnam War and would come to back amnesty for draft resisters. But, to many Catholics, in the anxious aftermath of *Roe v. Wade*, abortion was all that seemed to matter.

"I think the abortion issue was handled very well in that everyone felt the opportunity was there to express views and no one seemed particularly concerned that it did not make its way into the Platform," Rita Hauser, Nixon's advisor on women's issues, reflected upon her return from the Republican convention in August 1972. "I feel keenly that nothing further should be said on this issue one way or another for the duration of the campaign." Nixon privately agreed at an October White House meeting, asserting that "abortion reform [is] not the proper ground for federal action," adding, according to his chief of staff, H. R. Haldeman, that he would "never take action as president." On this increasingly volatile issue, the president chose to and could afford to remain silent. Three months later, the Supreme Court would afford many American Catholics, for better or worse, no such luxury.[148]

The performance of American Catholics in influencing the Nixon administration's policies on Vietnam, welfare reform, and abortion was decidedly mixed. In the end, however, the bishops' belated opposition to the war and growing disaffection with welfare reform, by exacerbating conflict within the Catholic rank and file, helped steer the president toward peace in Vietnam and away from the Family Assistance Plan. And the bishops' fervent defense of the unborn, by forging a fragile consensus among the Catholic rank and file, foreshadowed a national debate so rancorous that Nixon would be the last president who could avoid it.

CHAPTER FOUR

Catholics and Gerald Ford
(1974–1977)

IT HAS BECOME PART of the American mythology that "anybody can grow up to be president." But not everybody wants to be president, even a long-term minority leader of the House of Representatives and a short-term vice president who suddenly finds himself in the White House, as Gerald Ford did in 1974. And who could blame him? The Vietnam War was ignominiously winding down, with Indochinese refugees seeking a new life. Much of the world was starving. And abortion had arrived as a contentious political issue. In less than three years, however, Ford would address all of these concerns, enlisting American Catholics to help resettle the refugees and help feed the hungry. But if the president ultimately obliged many Catholics with his policies in these areas, he nonetheless frustrated them on abortion, on which his reluctance to speak his mind on *whether* to combat it only heightened their inability to make up their minds on *how* to combat it.

War and Peace: Indochinese Refugees

The U.S. military role ended in Vietnam with the signing of the flawed Treaty of Paris in January 1973, but American involvement did not. For the next eighteen months, Republican president Richard Nixon pressed the Democratic-controlled Congress to fund America's South Vietnamese allies, who had completely taken over the fighting against the North. Congress whined and wailed, and gave Nixon half of what he wanted.[1]

Then, in August 1974 Nixon's resignation gave the Congress—and the country—most of what it wanted. Gerald Ford took the oath of office and assured Americans that one "long national nightmare," the Watergate scandal, was over.[2] But the other was not. Like Nixon, Ford tried to save South Vietnam from the North and from itself. But Congress was still largely unwilling to help, and from his uneasy exile Nixon witnessed the outcome he had long dreaded. America for the first time lost a war.

Ford played a minor role in this tragedy, so history views him more as a caretaker than a co-conspirator. But since his brief stint as commander in chief arrived as the nation's longest war was departing, he confronted the issues that his predecessors had only anticipated. One of the largest items on his agenda was the fate of the Southeast Asians entering the United States after the war. Thanks in part to the interest and involvement of American Catholics in this matter, Vietnam remained on the front burner of U.S. politics and policy during the abbreviated Ford presidency. But as with the war itself, in the interaction between the Ford administration and American Catholics over the resettlement of Southeast Asian refugees, it was not always clear who was friend and who was foe.

Refugees

The U.S. surrender in Vietnam came in March 1975, when both houses of the Democratic-controlled Congress rejected Ford's request of $300 million for South Vietnam and $222 million for Cambodia. The Cambodian war finished on April 17, and the South Vietnamese conflict concluded on April 30. While the Khmer Rouge's unelected government took control of Cambodia, and North Vietnam's unelected government grabbed South Vietnam, the United States' unelected government turned its attention to the refugees fleeing the communist tyrants who had ultimately prevailed.[3]

"Many Vietnamese 'boat people' encountered pirates and storms at sea . . . , [their] girls and women raped and tortured," recalled Kou Yang of the California State University at Fresno. "The Cambodian refugees escaped by land . . . but were killed by land mines, starvation and disease. The Hmong and Lao had to cross the Mekong River between Laos and Thailand, and many drowned."[4] "We cannot responsibly turn our backs as a nation on a situation we have helped to create," Cincinnati archbishop Joseph Bernardin, the president of the United States Catholic Conference's National Conference of Catholic Bishops, said on Good Friday 1975, as the Southeast Asian dominoes fell. Quoting Pope Paul VI, Bernardin urged Americans to "do everything we can to alleviate the tragedy of those people and to prove to them that our world is not indifferent to the cries of our brethren."[5]

The USCC's general secretary, Bishop James Rausch, sent Bernardin's message to the White House and pledged to "expand existing programs or to establish new ones which would help refugees in the light of the present emergencies." The president replied with a statement of his own, ordering American naval ships to assist in the evacuation effort. Bernardin praised Ford's message in a letter to United Nations secretary-general Kurt Waldheim, offering the assistance of "Catholic Relief Services, the Migration and Refugee Services of the USCC, and, indeed, of the entire American Catholic community."[6]

The special assistant to the president for human resources, Dr. Theodore Marrs, thanked Bishop Rausch for transmitting Bernardin's statement. In words that the bishops had grown accustomed to hearing, Marrs lauded the USCC's "spiritual support of the President, who cannot afford the luxury of simplistic or superficial solutions to the complexities of today's problems." Three days later Ford established a special interagency task force, representing the Departments of State; Treasury; Defense; Health, Education, and Welfare; Justice; Interior; Labor; Housing and Urban Development; and Transportation, as well as the Agency for International Development, Office of Management and Budget, and Central Intelligence Agency, to coordinate Southeast Asian refugee resettlement.[7]

Casting aside Marrs's condescension, the bishops offered more than prayers and platitudes. In an April 16 letter to his fellow prelates, Bernardin requested a special collection for refugee assistance, to take place in all 165 Catholic dioceses. On the same day he appointed Rev. John McCarthy, the USCC's director of Migration and Refugee Services, as the national coordinator of the bishops' Southeast Asian refugee resettlement network. On April 28 Bernardin asked the bishops to begin cataloging the available resources in their dioceses that could serve Indochinese refugees. On May 8 Bernardin launched a preemptive strike against the expected backlash toward refugee resettlement in the United States. "It is natural that we should wish to put the war behind us," the archbishop conceded. "But it is inconceivable that we should turn our backs on the suffering which continues."[8] The USCC dispatched full-time staff from its Migration and Refugee Services to military camps serving as refugee staging centers. It also conducted regional meetings in San Francisco, Orlando, Kansas City, New Orleans, Newark, and Boston to train diocesan resettlement directors and Catholic Charities officials in resettlement techniques.[9]

These efforts were not in vain. By May 8, Ford wrote to Pope Paul VI, the U.S. government had "evacuated nearly 60,000 refugees from threatened areas of Vietnam." Ford encouraged the pope to "consider issuing a general appeal calling on nations throughout the world in helping these refugees start a new life." A week later, the president finally replied to Bishop Rausch, thanking him for sending Bernardin's Good Friday message and expressing his conviction that "the vast majority of Americans share your belief that these refugees must be given an opportunity to live in freedom."[10]

But a majority of Congress did not share that belief. After the House of Representatives voted down a refugee aid package, the Senate whip, Robert Byrd, Democrat of Virginia, told Ford that "there is no political support for this in this country." But the White House would not take no for an answer. The House reversed itself, the Senate went along, and on May 24 Ford signed the Indochina Migration and Refugee Assistance Act of 1975, which earmarked $455 million for refugee resettlement. "To ignore the refugees in their hour of need," the president explained, "would be to repudiate the values" of the nation he led.[11]

Asserting that "time is of the essence," Ford had already appointed a seventeen-person Advisory Committee on Refugees, chaired by John Eisenhower and including Archbishop Bernardin among its membership. The committee promised to keep the president and the public abreast of refugee developments. At its first meeting, May 23, the committee discussed, in the words of another member, White House aide Marrs, the "distinct phases in the processing of refugees—the extraction of people from Vietnam . . . , setting up of basic processing, expediting clearances . . . , establishing Vietnamese communities into the U.S. community." Bernardin informed the committee of the diocesan collections mandated by the bishops, as well as the 158 resettlement offices opened by the United States Catholic Conference throughout the country. The archbishop pronounced himself "very optimistic" that the bishops' "rather extensive refugee program" would serve the country well.[12]

"We need to move faster," Chairman Eisenhower pleaded ten days later, lamenting the release of only four thousand refugees from increasingly crowded processing centers since the previous committee meeting. The USCC's Rev. John McCarthy, the acting chair of the Committee on Refugees and Migrants of the American Council of Voluntary Agencies, nonetheless echoed Bernardin's optimism by reminding the Eisenhower Committee's second gathering that his group had successfully resettled over two million refugees of varied nationalities since World War II.[13] A week later the USCC released a status report on the Indochinese refugee problem. Noting that "a little over five weeks ago the Catholic Church, together with other religious denominations and voluntary groups, was asked by the U.S. Government to assist with the resettlement of refugees from Vietnam and Cambodia," the report documented the addition of over 150 paid and volunteer staff to the USCC's Migration and Refugee Services.[14]

On June 18 Bernardin was among a USCC contingent at the White House that conveyed to Ford its concern over North Vietnamese seizure of a refugee camp on Phu Quoc Island off the coast of South Vietnam. Bernardin also registered that concern in a letter to UN secretary-general Kurt Waldheim. On June 23 the Eisenhower Committee issued its own refugee status report as required by the Indochina Migration and Refugee Assistance Act. It counted 131,399 Indochinese refugees under American control, with 32,321 resettling in the United States and 3,756 relocating to other countries.[15] Two weeks later the White House director of correspondence, Roland Elliot, responded for the president to the bishops' disquiet over the Phu Quoc refugees. Though the United States had no control over refugees in the newly communist South Vietnam, Elliot assured Bernardin that the Justice Department would press for their repatriation to another country, if not the United States.[16]

The country they were trying to leave was far different than it had been only months earlier. White House aide Brent Scowcroft would report to Ford of the systematic government persecution of Catholic students, churchgoers, and clergy by Vietnam's communist regime. Where religious symbols formerly had appeared, only Ho Chi Minh's picture was present. The government demanded identification from parishioners as they entered Masses and registration from priests in order to preside over them. Foreign clergy had to leave the country, while indigenous clerics had to spy on each other. Those who defied the government faced imprisonment and torture in barbed-wire "tiger cages" that were only one foot high and exposed to the elements. "The Church seems to be moving in the direction of grudgingly acquiescing to the role the Communists want it to play," Scowcroft concluded, "both because it has little other choice and because its leaders believe it must do so in order to preserve its existence."[17]

Such news disheartened Pope Paul VI, who met with President Ford at the Vatican in June 1975. "I know that you are concerned about the human problems in Indochina," the president told the pontiff. "We have made an effort to bring 125,000 refugees, of which about 100,000 are in the U.S. or Guam. We want to make certain that they become part of the U.S., and we welcome them as we assimilate them in our society with the help of the people of the U.S."[18] "It is a very great and noble undertaking on your part," the Holy Father replied. "Unfortunately because of its very greatness many do not understand it or give it the wrong interpretation. We praise the actions of your country and are willing to help."[19]

Some of those who did not understand the resettlement program were native-born Americans, many of them Catholic, who objected to the arrival of ethnic outsiders and economic competitors in their often insular communities. An April 1975 Gallup Poll found 54 percent of Americans opposed to the resettlement of South Vietnamese refugees in the United States. "The 133,000 Indochinese refugees who suddenly entered the United States in the spring of 1975 found themselves in a society which was unprepared to receive them and was suffering its worst economic recession since World War II," noted social scientist Barry Stein of Michigan State University. Stein added that the fall of the South Vietnamese government came without warning, and the flood of so many new arrivals to the United States in such a short time was without precedent. Three years later, over 60 percent of white-collar refugees remained in blue-collar occupations, and two-thirds of the refugees holding white-collar jobs were doing clerical or sales work. The Indochinese newcomers were faring much worse after three years than 1970 immigrants from other regions had done after two.[20]

In his study of Ames, an Iowa college town of forty-five thousand, anthropologist Gerald Kleis of Iowa State University found that the Vietnamese population there most often chose isolation over assimilation. "Many Catholic Vietnamese in Ames," Kleis wrote, "go directly home after Mass without interacting with Americans." Christopher Thao, the United States' first Hmong lawyer, told of a fellow countryman who hanged himself in an American jail cell after his arrest for vehicular homicide because he understood neither the language of his interrogators nor the concept of bail. "Racism is like a wall," lamented Chou Lee of heavily Catholic Eau Claire, Wisconsin, where many of his fellow Hmong people relocated from Laos after fighting the communist Pathet Lao. "Unlike the Chinese, Japanese, and other Asian immigrants in America," historian Ronald Takaki pointed out, "the Indochinese refugees cannot go home."[21]

But if the resettlement of the refugees from America's longest war only seemed to lengthen it for many Americans, others were less wary and more generous, and quite often Catholic. Stein reported that within three years of their resettlement, the Indochinese had seen their male unemployment rate drop from 32 to 4.9 percent, and the percentage of households earning less than $400 a month dropped from 52.4 to 22.4 percent. "If one compares the response of the host society toward the Vietnamese with [that toward] earlier immigrant groups," Kleis observed, "one might conclude that they favor assimilation."[22]

In 1964, there had been only 603 Vietnamese living in the United States. From 1975 to 1980, church and state resettled 388,802 refugees, more than in any other country. By 1985, there would be 643,200 Vietnamese in the United States. By 1987 Indochinese people would be the largest Asian group in the nation. In August 1976, with Congress about to give the president all of the money he requested to relocate the Southeast Asians, Jim Castelli of the National Catholic News Service called the refugee effort "the high point in cooperation between the Catholic Church and the Ford Administration."[23]

A week after Ford's loss to Jimmy Carter in the 1976 presidential election, the bishops issued the "Resolution on the Pastoral Concern of the Church for People on the Move." Asserting that "massive migration from underdeveloped countries and regions is a special phenomenon of our age," the pastoral urged a new and better definition of the category of "refugee" so as to better "provide a haven for oppressed people from any part of the world regardless of their race, religion, color, and creed." Thus did the hierarchy attempt to unite a divided immigrant Church, during the bicentennial of a divided immigrant nation.[24]

Conclusions on War and Peace

In April 1975, as Saigon fell in the desperate denouement of the Vietnam War, President Gerald Ford for one last time extolled the South Vietnamese for "fighting for their freedom." The liberal journalist Richard Reeves observed that "Ford seemed to have learned nothing from Vietnam."[25] But in the waning years of the war, as their bishops successfully cooperated with the president on refugee resettlement, many American Catholics seemed to have learned a lot, even if not everyone shared their lessons.

First, they learned to oppose Ford's repeated requests for more assistance to the faltering South Vietnamese. "President Ford now tells us that we need an additional $300 million fast, to 'help South Vietnam,'" Edward Herman wrote in *America* in February 1975. "'South Vietnam' sounds like a country of people, not a Southeast Asia mafia. . . . We are backing an unrepresentative and venal clique who survive only by our largesse and force (past and threatened) and who are actually the enemy of the South Vietnamese majority."[26]

Commonweal's editors escalated their attacks on the administration's increasingly futile aid requests. "White House couriers find congressional corridors no longer predictably hospitable to financing our war by proxy abroad, in a region of the world marginal to our national security," a *Commonweal* editorial signed by "Sisyphus" opined on the eve of the war's end in April 1975. After over fifty thousand American combat deaths and over $150 billion in war expenditures, the editorial surmised, "if Congress is to be blamed," it was not because of insufficient support for the war effort, but because it "did not call a halt to the bloody business years ago."[27]

Second, many American Catholics learned to repudiate even the cause of the war. Writing in the July 1975 *Atlantic Monthly*, the U.S. ambassador to the United Nations, Daniel Patrick Moynihan, a Catholic Democrat who had served every president from Kennedy to Ford, accepted William Pfaff's early characterization of Vietnam as "American liberalism's war." Liberal idealism got the United States in; liberal guilt got the United States out.[28]

And liberalism helped sour many American Catholics on the war's origins. Writing in the pages of *America* in February 1975, Rev. Francis Winters, the director of Georgetown University's Institute for the Study of Ethics and International Affairs, pronounced just-war theory to be "militarily obsolete." Historian Michael Warner, in his study of the first seven decades of the National Catholic Welfare Conference/United States Catholic Conference, concluded that "through the 1970s, the USCC's liberal leadership, primarily Bishop [James] Rausch and [Joseph] Bernardin with their new advisor Father [Bryan] Hehir, co-opted the radical Catholic left" when they "rejected anticommunism as a motive for American foreign policy." The hierarchy's embrace of unconditional amnesty for draft resisters reflected this stance.[29]

The bishops' march to the left on the postwar peace was as inexorable as it was remarkable. While a 1980 congressional report would criticize the U.S. government's traditional preference for refugees from communist countries over those from non-communist ones, the bishops exhibited their own double standard. The USCC's failure to condemn North Vietnam's repression in the South followed a pattern of absolving leftist dictators while criticizing rightwing despots in Latin America and Africa. When Cambodian tyrant Pol Pot's slaughter of millions of his own people would lead to another refugee exodus in 1978, the bishops' Administrative Committee issued a statement denouncing "oppressive actions by new Communist regimes in Southeast Asia" while promising "to aid the refugees of any nation, regardless of religion and political ideology." The next year, however, after Vietnam had invaded Cambodia and deposed Pol Pot, the bishops released a pastoral deploring the "starvation and desperation" of the Cambodian people without mentioning the dictator. Instead, they warned their own country not to play "politics" with human lives. When confronted with the bishops' apparent inconsistency on human rights, Father Hehir defended it, arguing that the United States had more leverage over friendly right-wing governments than unfriendly left-wing regimes.[30]

The bishops' liberalism also produced some startling instances of role reversal. Lamenting the country's post-Vietnam anti-anti-communist mood, Moynihan, the bishops' erstwhile Cold War ally, noticed in July 1975 that the "American Catholic hierarchy . . . once so militant in such matters, is silent now."[31]

Even more arresting was the familiar juxtaposition of antiwar Catholic clergy and laity against their bishops. Reverends Philip and Daniel Berrigan, Dorothy Day, Thomas Cornell, Auxiliary Bishop Thomas Gumbleton of Detroit, Auxiliary Bishop John Dougherty of Newark, and Bishop Carroll Dozier of Memphis were among ninety persons who signed a letter protesting the religious and political persecution of the people of South Vietnam by their government. Only this time, the letter went to the communist government of Vietnam, and these prominent members of the Catholic Left, much to the chagrin of some of their comrades, were attacking the United States' former enemy in Vietnam. "There were those who felt it was premature to send it,"

Gumbleton apologized to his fellow liberals. "They wanted to take a wait-and-see attitude about the North Vietnamese government and not react immediately to all the bad things we were hearing. I couldn't see the rationale behind that."[32] The letter appeared in January 1977, the twenty-ninth and final month of the Ford administration, the twenty-first month since the fall of Saigon, and the fourteenth month since the United States Catholic Conference's testimony implicitly advocating full U.S. diplomatic and economic relations with communist Vietnam. "Wait and see"—the discredited mantra of Presidents Kennedy, Johnson, Nixon, and Ford regarding U.S. policy in Vietnam—was the new slogan of Gumbleton's critics on the Catholic Left who had finally achieved an end to the war they abhorred. And it was still the motto of the American Catholic hierarchy, with which they now found themselves strangely allied.

The U.S. Catholic hierarchy, with its representation on Ford's refugee committee, played a large part in shaping the administration's policies in the war's aftermath. But even as the bishops were poignantly remembering the war's victims at home and abroad, they joined most American Catholics in effectively erasing the memory of the war itself, of why many of their compatriots had fought it, and of why they had long championed those who did.

Social Justice: World Hunger

At varied times amid changing fortunes, "American exceptionalism" has invited fervent devotion or caustic derision. Virtually no American adventure, at least since the nation attained international prominence, has gone unnoticed in the eyes of the superpatriots and superpessimists. Even on the rare occasions when both groups initially agree, they soon find reason to part company. Take, for instance, world hunger. What could be a nobler undertaking than feeding the world when the world is starving, as much of it was in August 1974?

Gerald Ford assumed the presidency at an exceptional time, after superpatriots and superpessimists alike had helped remove his predecessor from office during the Watergate scandal. While both groups were absorbing their own lessons from that debacle—the system succeeded, the system failed—they diverted some of their attention to people in parts of the world most of them had hardly noticed and barely understood. Feeding the world, therefore, had to be about something else—oil or population or even communism—something they *knew*. So they argued about how to feed the world, and how not to.

President Ford found himself in the middle of this controversy as the representative of a generous people. Americans, after all, are different. American Catholics found themselves in the middle of this controversy, too, as they lived the parable of the loaves and fishes, to which they had only listened before. Catholics, after all, are different too.

Across the deserts of Africa, on the plains of South Asia, amid the lowlands of the Far East, and in the neighborhoods of the United States, American exceptionalism and Catholic exceptionalism cooperated, conflicted, and ultimately collided. But in the end, whether America's government and America's Catholics fed the people in these far-flung and familiar places was all that really mattered.

Cooperation

For the first time in twenty years, world food production declined in 1972. Poor weather, depleted grain reserves, commodity speculation, global inflation, world energy shortages, and unusually large Soviet grain purchases contributed to the crisis. As a result, the genesis of the Ford administration occurred in a world growing more hungry every day. By September 1974, between one-quarter and one-third of the people of Africa and the Far East were substantially undernourished, and almost five hundred million people around the world were malnourished.[33]

To help address this dire situation, Secretary of State Henry Kissinger had pledged to the United Nations in April 1974 that the United States would increase food aid to the developing world and take the lead in organizing a World Food Conference. Yet such gestures contravened the Ford administration's commitment to fiscal discipline in an economy gone bad.[34] So in September 1974 budget director Roy Ash presented the new president with three funding options for the FY 1975 Food for Peace program: $1.28 billion (recommended by the State Department, National Security Council, and Agency for International Development to meet the food emergency); $742 million (favored by the Office of Management and Budget, Council of International Economic Policy, Council of Economic Advisors, and Department of Agriculture to recognize the budget shortfall); and $978 million (suggested by the Treasury Department to try to do both). Given the Hobson's choice between spending too much and feeding too few, Ash warned Ford that no matter which option the president selected, he should do so quietly.[35]

In a speech before the United Nations on September 18, Ford sided with Treasury in splitting the difference between fiscal conservatism and food security. While calling upon all countries to raise their food production, establish reasonable prices, forswear national advantage, and trade fairly, the American president vowed that his country "will not only maintain the amount it spends for food shipments to nations in need, but it will increase the amount this year." And he did so quietly by omitting a dollar figure, later estimated at

$1.1 billion, too high for the administration's budget hawks and too low for its foreign aid advocates. "The U.S. cannot and should not feed the world," AID's Bob Stillman conceded to the budget balancers. But Ford's adoption of the middle figure nonetheless "bothers my moral senses."[36]

He was not alone. At the United States Catholic Conference's administrative board meeting in September, the nation's bishops proclaimed the moral imperative of "sharing our scarcity." Noting that the 6 percent of the world's population in the United States was consuming 40 percent of the world's food, the bishops asserted, "While the relationship of food and population growth is recognized as a problem, the pattern of resource consumption in wealthy or developed nations is regarded as an equally important part of the problem." To overcome poor nations' inability to pay the market price for food, the bishops proposed the sharing of a world food reserve.[37]

A couple of weeks later, 170 American Catholics, most of them nuns, descended on the nation's capital to lament, among other concerns, that "world grain reserves" were at their "lowest in thirty years" and to urge their government to ameliorate the shortage. "The ministry of justice has moved steadily from the periphery of the Church's life to the heart of her life," Rev. Bryan Hehir, the director of the USCC's Peace and Justice Division, addressed the group, aptly named Network, and so did Bobbie Kilberg of the Ford administration and several members of Congress from both parties. Writing in *Christian Century*, one of the participants, Sister Carol Coston, explained that the Washington seminar went beyond Hehir's call for a "ministry of justice" to a bipartisan campaign for "effective legislative action."[38]

New York's Terence Cardinal Cooke carried a similar message to the White House a week later when he reported on his recent trip to drought-stricken Senegal and Mauritania, where the USCC's Catholic Relief Services had combined with the Agency for International Development to furnish 40 percent of the world's attempt at preventing the starvation of twenty million people. The president promised the cardinal that his administration would increase U.S. funding and personnel to combat the drought, and the cardinal in turn pledged to back the president.[39]

Ford would not stop there. The World Food Conference envisioned by Kissinger convened in early November in Rome, and the U.S. delegation advocated more efficient food production and distribution systems in the developing countries and more assistance from the developed nations, including the creation of the kind of international grain reserve espoused by the bishops. Rev. James Rausch, the USCC general secretary, welcomed these recommendations in a November letter to the president. "The problem of conscience posed for us as a nation by the food crisis is clear and compelling," Rausch wrote.

"We cannot afford this burden spiritually, psychologically, or politically in our country today."[40]

"Since I became president the U.S. has expanded its food programs," Ford told Pope Paul VI in Rome in June. "As stated by Dr. Kissinger last week, the U.S. is an active participant in the World Food Council, so that countries can enhance their food growing capabilities." The Ford administration has "an excellent formula," the Holy Father replied, "and it points to a new world based on cooperation."[41]

Conflict

But as the bishops were cooperating with the president, they were planting the seeds for conflict. First, they expressed dismay at the paltry sums that Ford was allocating for the crisis. In his letter, Rausch urged a sizable increase in the administration's FY 1976 Food for Peace budget.[42]

Second, they went beyond soliciting aid by advocating income redistribution. In their November pastoral, "Statement on the World Food Crisis," authored by Cooke and Chicago's John Cardinal Cody among others, they espoused not only immediate assistance, but long-term planning, and not just the promotion of "economic growth" championed by conservatives like Ford, but the reduction of the "gap between the wealthy and the poor" pressed by their fellow liberals. They exhorted the American Catholic faithful to participate in a program of information, education, pastoral activities, and legislative action to increase food aid, remove trade barriers, overcome economic inequities, and "modify the operation of the free market system, especially the impact of the large corporation when it stands in the way of justice."[43]

Third, the bishops viewed the food crisis as primarily humanitarian and not geopolitical. In their November pastoral, they admonished the Ford administration to "resist efforts to use food as a political and strategic weapon." *America* applauded the pastoral for its recognition that the food crisis was less a threat to U.S. national security than a "clear-cut challenge to common human values."[44]

Fourth and most significant, the bishops helped bring the food crisis home. The Ford administration's "international position" toward the crisis "cannot be evaluated," they claimed at their November meeting, "apart from a changed domestic picture." If pleas for more robust national budgets, indictments of international inequality, and appeals to human values seemed safely familiar to American Catholics raised to give to the missions, clean their plates, and pray for world peace, this localization of the crisis's victims and villains did not. "Stories of the elderly eating dog food, of children no longer able to buy school lunches, and of a rash of petty thievery in supermarkets by people who have never stolen anything," Father Hehir reported in November to the bishops and in December to the Ad Hoc Senate Committee on the World Food Conference, "show the human face of the domestic food problem." Among Hehir's remedies were a more equitable tax system, more food stamps, more school lunches, and an accounting by the "five companies [that] control ninety percent of the world's grain reserves"—none of them especially appealing to a Republican during a recession.[45]

Collision

Not this Republican, anyway. Honoring a tradition that reverted to the Eisenhower administration and seeking to undo the damage done by agriculture secretary Earl Butz's tasteless joke at the World Food Conference about Pope Paul VI's opposition to birth control, Ford helped inaugurate the congressional session by attending the Red Mass in Washington in January 1975. "We in this country, blessed with the world's most fertile open plains, are the world's largest producers of food," the president heard Bishop Rausch preach in his homily that day. "This brings with it an awesome responsibility, one we dare not fail to meet by whatever means are available to us." But those means apparently did not include a meeting on the food crisis between the bishops and the president, as Rausch's December letter to the White House had requested.[46]

At least not yet. Although Congress had authorized the shipment of 4.5 million metric tons of U.S. food to respond to the emergency in the summer of 1974, only about one-third had traveled by March 1975. Despite the repudiation by the assistant secretary of state for economic and business affairs, Thomas Enders, of any distinction between "humanitarian" and "political" assistance, the administration had sought special shipments to war-torn South Vietnam and Cambodia, where American allies were hanging on for dear life. "If the bishops are going to focus on food aid," White House chief of staff Robert Hartman advised Ford, "the President should have something *positive* to tell them."[47]

So after appropriating a record $1.6 billion for the FY 1975 Food for Peace program and receiving a letter from the newly elected United States Catholic Conference president, Archbishop Joseph Bernardin of Cincinnati, reiterating the bishops' desire for a meeting, the chief executive finally sat down with a thirty-member delegation from the USCC in June. President Ford, Attorney General Edward Levi, Secretary of State Caspar Weinberger, and Deputy Secretary of State Robert Ingersoll cited the administration's food expenditures as well as its commitment to "import incentives . . . , technical aid . . . , and [lower] barriers to trade in agricultural products." Bernardin applauded these "recent developments" as helping to ease the crisis. But he urged even more food aid, more technical assistance, and the creation of an international food reserve. The archbishop told the president that "the American people, when given the facts, are prepared to support a generous food policy," even from a Republican, even during a recession.⁴⁸

Though the bishops had secured what United Press International dubbed "an unusual if not unprecedented" meeting with the president, in which he solicited their views on Indochinese refugees and abortion as well as the food crisis, they had not heard all the answers they were seeking. While Bernardin praised the "cordial and positive" tone of the meeting, the bishops left the White House feeling as unfulfilled as when they arrived.⁴⁹ So they and other American Catholics resumed their protest of the Ford food budgets. "While the United States provides a large portion of the food needs of the world," Father Hehir told the bishops at their September administrative board meeting, "it is still a smaller percentage than what the country had given some years ago." He prodded the bishops to back congressional measures designed to increase the American contribution.⁵⁰

Others again tried to nationalize the international food problem. In April the USCC's Department of Social Development and World Peace urged Congress to prevent the parsimonious president from enacting reductions in federal food stamps and school lunches. The department's Msgr. Francis Lally wrote to Ford in September urging him to sign the National School Lunch and Child Nutrition Amendments of 1975 in order "to maintain adequate nutrition programs for children in the United States." When Ford vetoed the legislation, citing budget constraints, the National Conference of Catholic Charities' executive director, Lawrence Corcoran, decried the president's "manifest insensitivity to the impact of the inflation-recession on poor people—in this case, people who are having to bear the brunt of trying to correct problems in our economic system."⁵¹

Then the bishops went further. In a November 1975 pastoral, "The Economy: Human Dimensions," the prelates delved below the statistics to examine the lives of ordinary Americans. "Our concern . . . is not with technical fiscal matters or the vindication of particular economic theories," they explained, as if speaking to the president, "but rather the moral aspects of economic policies and the impact of these politics on people." Lest they incur more ridicule from the hardheaded "experts" in Washington, however, they enlisted a few of their own, attaching remarks by economists Paul Samuelson, Helen Ginsberg, Robert Eisner, Dan Larkins, Lester Thurow, and Leon Keyserling to their statement. The bishops also included their own statistics—"almost forty percent of minority teenagers, twenty percent of all teenagers, 14.2 percent of all minority persons, and over eleven percent of all blue-collar workers" were out of work.⁵²

Arguing that "the right to have a share of earthly goods sufficient for oneself and one's family belongs to everyone," they espoused a more equitable tax system, a more just distribution of income, and a full-employment economy. "Fundamentally," the pastoral concluded, "our nation must provide jobs for those who can and should work, and a decent income for those who cannot." In a letter to Ford, General Secretary Rausch enclosed the bishops' message, while encouraging him to sign the Public Works Employment Act of 1975, which would provide federal grants for local public works jobs, assistance to maintain local government services, and extension of the Jobs Opportunities Training and Placement programs. "We share your concern over budget deficits and inflation," Rausch spoke for the bishops. "Yet we believe this legislation is a proper and appropriate expenditure of federal funds to get people back to work."[53]

But Ford, again invoking budget deficits and inflation, affixed one of his sixty-six vetoes to the legislation, and the bishops criticized him for it. The president did not directly respond to the bishops, however. "I do not think the reply to this should come from an economist," White House aide Dr. Theodore Marrs had advised. So Ford passed Rausch's letter on to Roland Elliot, the director of the Office of White House Correspondence, who sent the bishop a copy of the veto message, with the administration's backhanded acknowledgment of the human dimensions of the economy.[54]

Ford's veto followed his annual report to Congress on the Food for Peace program, in which he noted the "substantial" U.S. donation to drought-stricken Africa as serving the "humanitarian" as well as the "foreign policy" objectives of his government. He could have added, as Emma Rothschild did in the January 1976 *Foreign Affairs*, that the United States had become the "only genuine global exporter" of food, transporting it to 130 countries on all continents.[55] Yet the administration had fallen short of the ambitious goals of the 1974 UN World Food Conference, which had, in Rothschild's recollection, "called for international cooperation in holding reserves, in providing food as aid, and in promoting agricultural development in order to reduce the dependence of poor countries on the world food trade." Although the United States more than doubled its food aid to the poorest countries in 1975, the richer developing countries were receiving a greater share of U.S. farm exports, while only 15 percent went to the thirty poorest nations. This imbalance fostered resentment by the have-nots toward the haves, with the Arab oil embargo that stoked the 1973–1974 recession an extreme example of such backlash. America's ally the shah of Iran pointedly observed that before Middle East oil prices went up, U.S. food prices did.[56]

Along with the U.S. Catholic bishops' unread pastorals and unanswered letters, Rothschild added her voice to the growing chorus imploring the president not to employ food as a weapon. Rothschild accused the administration of postponing food aid to famine-stricken Bangladesh because it had sent jute to communist Cuba. Barbara Huddleston of the International Food Institute, who was critical of Rothschild elsewhere, concurred that "beginning in 1972, the desire to keep U.S. grain reserves low and maximize exports has also dovetailed with diplomatic objectives in the Soviet Union, Eastern Europe, and the Middle East."[57]

Not only was the administration deaf to such criticism, Rothschild wrote, but a published analysis by the Central Intelligence Agency warned that "massive migration [from a destitute country] backed by force" would become a "very live issue," and an unnamed Treasury official spoke of the "power" of letting "millions of children starve on television."[58] A decade before the birth of the Cable News Network and two decades before the ill-fated American humanitarian intervention in Somalia, members of the Ford administration were prescient in their fears if not their policies. Starvation, it seemed, could be a weapon too.

The country needed a "national food policy," Youngstown bishop James Malone of the USCC's Executive Committee told the Temporary Committee on Resolutions for the 1976 Republican National Convention in August, one that promotes the "protection of a dispersed pattern of ownership of land and resources coupled with land use planning; agricultural policies and programs to promote full production and an adequate return for farmers; and domestic food programs to meet the needs of hungry and malnourished people in the United States." Malone also pressed for a centralization of federal nutrition and health assistance programs as well as a reform of the welfare system.[59]

A month later Bernardin and several other bishops again discussed the food issue with Ford at the White House. Internationally, the archbishop again pleaded with the president to build and share food reserves with other nations. Domestically, he again advocated for more federal dollars for the poor. This time, Bernardin did receive a follow-up letter from Ford, but the president defended his food programs against the hierarchy's onslaught.[60]

The presidential election results in November 1976 rendered this defense virtually meaningless. Ford lost to Jimmy Carter, the former Georgia Democratic governor and current peanut farmer, who pledged more food aid, more attention to the world's maldistribution of income, less preoccupation with geopolitics in foreign policy, and less neglect of the hungry here at home. Though food aid was hardly a defining issue in a campaign dominated by the economy, energy, and détente, it was an important component of Carter's signature devotion to human rights, which seemed to leave lots of room for food aid but little for food as a weapon. At least for now.[61]

Conclusions on Social Justice

World hunger seemed an unlikely source of political discord. Yet many American Catholics parted with the Ford administration over the intent and extent of U.S. food programs. In so doing, they split not only with the president, but with other Catholics. Though they paid a considerable political price, they ultimately brought the president to their side.

The food controversy continued the hierarchy's liberal lurch, which had rattled Richard Nixon on welfare reform. The September 1975 statement that Archbishop Bernardin presented to Ford at the White House called for the maintenance and strengthening of the domestic food stamp program as well as the development of international food reserves. The adoption of this liberal document came only after conservative dissent, however. Bishop Thomas Donnellan of Atlanta spoke for those wary of government programs when he sought some recognition in the message of the "failures of the food stamp program." But the liberal bishops had the votes, agreeing with their associate secretary for domestic social development, Francis Butler, that "while abuses and problems existed in it, evidence did not support [such a] sweeping indictment of the food stamp program." While the final version's call for "effective reforms" was a nod to Donnellan, its overall verdict that the food stamp program was "an effective instrument of assistance to the poor and needy" rendered such lip service all but empty.[62]

The hierarchy's liberalism was in step with many of the Church faithful, who had accorded a majority of their votes to liberal Democrat Hubert Humphrey in 1968 and to Republican Richard Nixon in 1972 only after he had spent four years expanding Johnson's Great Society. So when Ford followed his March 1975 exhortation to his Domestic Council that its first priority be to "tighten up on the Food Stamp Program" with the next year's proposed cuts, the National Conference of Catholic Charities and the National Catholic Conference for Interracial Justice joined the United States Catholic Conference's attack on the president's budget.[63]

The food issue at times nonetheless pitted Catholic against Catholic. "Liberals will tend to vote for measures to ease hunger and prevent starvation, but most of them will allow abortion to continue," Howard Fetterhoff of the Pennsylvania Catholic Conference observed in his April 1976 analysis of Catholic views toward "pro-life" issues. "Conservatives, on the other hand, will vote to prevent abortion but will be less inclined to share American resources to prevent starvation abroad and poverty at home." Fetterhoff concluded that liberal Catholic resentment of the bishops' preoccupation with abortion "can be silenced only if the Church makes an equally strenuous effort to bring about American public policy which will combat starvation more effectively in developing nations."[64]

The bishops attempted to downplay the divisions within the Church, which they had fomented over the food issue. In their February 1976 presidential campaign document, "Political Responsibilities: Reflections on an Election Year," the bishops identified an "important link between faith and politics," yet disavowed "the formation of a religious voting bloc." Similarly, at the Forty-First International Eucharistic Congress, August 1–8, 1976, in Philadelphia, where the theme was "The Eucharist and the Hungers of the Human Family," the organizers tried to appeal to both factions by broadly defining hunger as "emotional, spiritual, and social" as well as "material." Ford skipped the congress's left-leaning world hunger symposium and instead addressed the group before the closing liturgy.[65]

Despite these liabilities, however, the Catholic campaign against world hunger was largely effective. First, the Church helped assure that federal spending to fight world hunger abroad would rise dramatically during Ford's tenure. At his March 1975 speech at the University of Notre Dame, the fiscally prudent Ford cited his authorization of food spending "even higher than the highest option recommended to me at the [World Food] Conference." He called the Notre Dame president, Rev. Theodore Hesburgh, "a factor in my own decision" to raise the ante on food expenditures. Hesburgh in turn praised Ford, in the words of the National Catholic News Service's Jim Castelli, "for responding to Church and other humanitarian groups and raising the amount of American food aid . . . at the height of world famine."[66]

In his September 1976 letter to Archbishop Bernardin, the president promised that his budget would provide for "six million of the ten million ton annual target" established for all countries at the World Food Conference. "Through our PL 480 [Food for Peace] program," Ford added, "we are able to use the enormous productivity of the American farmer to meet human needs with grain which the poorer nations could not otherwise afford to import." During the Ford presidency, foreign food and nutrition appropriations grew from $284 million in FY 1975 to $505 million in FY 1977.[67]

Second, Catholics also helped to elicit recognition from a fervently capitalist president of structural defects in the international economic system. At the World Food Conference in 1974, the American delegation promised more aid despite higher food prices and lower crop yields at home. In his Notre Dame address in 1975, Ford called U.S. food aid a "moral commitment." In his letter to Bernardin in 1976, Ford reassured the bishops that his policies were targeting hunger's causes as well as its symptoms. He reiterated his support for an international food reserve "to provide against the human and economic disaster which could result from a global shortfall in grain reduction"—a bulwark against the ominous uncertainties of the free market.[68]

Third, Catholics also helped ensure that food be less of a weapon in developed countries' arsenals and more of a lifeline to developing nations' people. The requirement that at least 75 percent of American food aid go to countries with a per capita gross national product of $300 or less, which Congress imposed upon the president in 1975, allowed such assistance to feed the recipients before it served the donors. By the 1976 presidential campaign, the administration had adopted this position as its own. "It is my understanding," White House aide Rob Quartel wrote in August, "that the current Administration position is that the use of food and aid as a foreign policy lever is not very effective."[69]

Finally, the Church helped move the nexus of the food emergency from obscure foreign outposts to familiar American cities and towns. Even as President Ford was distributing Whip Inflation Now buttons and vetoing one appropriations bill after another, federal domestic spending on food stamps was increasing from $4.3 billion in FY 1975 to $5.3 billion in FY 1976, and on school lunches from $1.7 billion in FY 1975 to $1.9 billion in FY 1976. Ford's 1976 attempt to lop unworthy recipients off the food stamp rolls ran afoul of the courts in July.[70] The prelates' prominent and persistent pleading thus helped the country now to hear about "hunger in America" from the same administration voices that had been uttering "never in America" only a short time before. At Notre Dame in 1975, Ford spoke of "concerns about hunger among our own people."[71]

Thanks in large measure to the cooperation, conflict, and collision between the president and Catholics, world hunger diminished to a point where some experts confessed that the crisis had been overblown, and most voters concluded that it had blown over. At the very least, the Church had succeeded in its determined mission to put a human face on a problem that had moved from across the world to down the street.[72]

The ultimate defeat for the president was not what the bishops had necessarily intended. Despite his ardent courtship of the hierarchy as well as his humble persona, private religion, and stances in favor of non-public school aid and against abortion, which endeared him to the rank and file, Ford would lose the Catholic and the overall American vote in 1976. In an election less about food than about Ford, Catholics turned out to be not that exceptional after all.[73]

Life and Death: Abortion

When asked about his role as the nation's first vice president, John Adams was uncharacteristically succinct. "I am nothing," he whispered. "But I may be everything."[74] Just as John Adams became the first elected vice president to rise to the presidency, so Gerald Ford was the first unelected understudy to earn the promotion. But Adams rode the coattails of a popular chief executive to victory in 1796, while Ford would carry the baggage of a disgraced one to defeat in 1976.

In some ways abortion had little to do with Ford's loss. After all, there was not much the president could do to influence the abortion debate. The courts had legalized it, so the courts would have to outlaw it. Ford, it seemed, could do nothing. In other ways, however, abortion had a lot to do with Ford's defeat, and the presidency that preceded it. After all, there was much the president could do to influence the abortion debate. He could mount the bully pulpit of his office, go to court, or press for a constitutional amendment to overturn *Roe v. Wade*. Ford, it seemed, could do everything.

Like Adams, Ford did nothing before he did everything. But by the time he approached the official Catholic posture on abortion, Ford's inaction had cost him time, goodwill, and political capital. In many ways, most American Catholics preferred Ford's stand on abortion, and Ford himself, to the position and personality of his opponent in 1976. They just didn't vote for him.[75]

Nothing

The new administration's first pronouncement on abortion did not come from the president but from his press secretary. "As announced by Jerry ter Horst," White House aide Ken Cole reminded Ford in September 1974, "your position seems to be that one, you favor an amendment that would let each state enact its own laws on the subject; and two, that personally, you and Mrs. Ford believe in abortions for limited situations such as rape or illness." Even First Lady Betty Ford addressed the subject before her husband did, expressing her support for *Roe v. Wade* as a godsend to American women.[76]

President Ford fittingly announced his arrival to the abortion controversy by vetoing legislation. On October 1, 1974, Ford returned to Congress an appropriations bill for the Department of Health, Education, and Welfare that prohibited Medicaid funding of abortions for welfare mothers. Although he "agree[d] with the restrictions on the use of federal funds for abortion," the president explained that he rejected the bill out of "compassion for the taxpayers." Later the same month, the Senate opened confirmation hearings on Ford's vice presidential nominee, Republican Nelson Rockefeller, the former governor of New York, whose defense of abortion rights provoked the futile opposition of the nation's Catholic bishops.[77]

With the president on the sidelines, abortion partisans had their way. On October 21, 1974, the U.S. Supreme Court refused to hear an appeal by a Minnesota hospital of a circuit court decision mandating that public hospitals provide abortion services. Four days later the Department of Health, Education, and Welfare submitted to the *Federal Register* a proposed policy for the "protection of human subjects," which defined the viability of a "fetus" as beginning after birth. Msgr. James McHugh, the director of the United States Catholic Conference's Family Life Division, protested that the HEW proposal "completely ignores the right to life of the fetus, and the societal efforts to legally protect that right."[78]

At their meeting in November the U.S. Catholic bishops listened as their general counsel, Eugene Krasicky, presented a "Legal Memorandum on Abortion," which called for a "simple," "precise," yet "broad" and "juridical" constitutional amendment to repeal *Roe v. Wade*. In the void of leadership yet to be filled at the White House, however, John Cardinal Krol of Philadelphia cautioned that the bishops could only expect "a gradual movement" toward achieving that goal.[79]

In December Ford signed PL 94-161, a foreign aid bill, which required that two-thirds of the funds earmarked for population and health programs finance family planning. The year ended with the Senate Judiciary Subcommittee on Constitutional Rights having failed to act on a number of proposals to restrict or outlaw abortion, and the comparable House panel refusing even to hold hearings on such measures.[80]

Not quite Thomas Jefferson's vaunted "wall of separation," only the altar rail divided the Catholic and American hierarchies as the new year commenced. At the traditional Red Mass ushering in a new session of Congress, President Ford listened as the homilist, the United States Catholic Conference's general secretary, Bishop James Rausch, called the right to life "our most fundamental and inalienable prerogative." Rausch would deny, however, that this thinly veiled allusion to abortion was directed at the president, calling news reports to that effect "false and misleading" while insisting that his "statements were not written or delivered for the benefit of President Ford." That's a good thing, because Rausch's remarks appeared to have little impact on the president.[81]

The invisible president and the invigorated bishops finally met at the White House in June. The five USCC representatives—Cooke, Rausch, Bernardin,

Archbishop Thomas Donnellan of Atlanta, and Bishop James Malone of Youngstown—implored Ford to, in Bernardin's words, "use the moral force of his office in support of a constitutional amendment to reverse the U.S. Supreme Court's decision." They also urged "that federal administrative policy and practice fully respect the right of Congress and the states to legislate on the matter of abortion, and that federal agencies not seek to impose permissive abortion policies." They singled out the pre-*Roe* Nixon administration edict that military hospitals should abide by state laws on abortion.[82]

The president told the bishops what they wanted to hear. "While in Congress I did favor a constitutional amendment that would allow each State to make its own laws concerning abortion," said Ford. As for the Nixon directive, Ford told the prelates that he "knew of no plan for a change" and that he "thought the present policy was a good one."[83] Then the president went back into hiding. Following the meeting, seven members of Congress appealed to the administration for a change in the military hospital policy. Ford aide Philip Buchen observed that since "it appears that the Defense Department is not contemplating a change in policy, I vigorously object to any attempt to raise this problem to the Presidential level." Ford aide James Connor concurred, noting that because Buchen "has lead [*sic*] on this one," there was no need to involve the president.[84]

"The Catholic bishops would quite justifiably feel they had been misled if, a few days after their conference [with Ford], when none of us had any idea that a policy change was planned," the secretary of Health, Education, and Welfare, Caspar Weinberger, warned about the Nixon edict, "a proposed change is publicly discussed by 'Pentagon spokesmen.'" So they privately discussed it. A review of the policy ordered by Buchen resulted in the Defense Department's assistant general counsel for manpower, health, and public affairs, Jerome Nelson, recommending that the administration reverse the policy. Nelson argued, however, that since a commander in chief had initiated the policy, another commander in chief should undo it. He thus drafted a statement, similar in format to Nixon's 1971 message, for Ford to deliver.[85]

The Nelson recommendation blindsided the president. Having read Weinberger's warning, Ford conceded that there was "some merit to Cap's comment on credibility" and wondered, "Why did DOD do it with no forewarning?" But he didn't stop it. In September the assistant secretary of defense for health and environment, James Cowan, publicly announced the termination of the Nixon policy on abortion in military hospitals. Rather than conform to state laws rendered unconstitutional by *Roe v. Wade*, these facilities would now permit virtually unfettered abortions through the first six months of pregnancy.[86] To the consternation of the Pentagon, the commander in chief said nothing.

But as the HEW secretary had predicted, the bishops said a lot. "In my pastoral role as Military Vicar [of the armed forces] I am continually edified by the efforts of military families to build stable and committed marital relationships," Cardinal Cooke responded. "Permissive abortion will make their efforts more difficult and threaten their commitment to human life, marital fidelity, and sexual responsibility."[87]

In October the Department of Health, Education, and Welfare announced that it would permit federal medical facilities to ignore state laws that were more restrictive than *Roe v. Wade*, and would leave the decision to fund abortions for welfare mothers to the states. "Although Congress had forbidden the use of federal funds where abortion is considered a method of birth control," Msgr. McHugh reacted, "HEW is reportedly ready to override congressional intent and reimburse the state up to ninety percent, which is the family planning formula." McHugh called the new policy "part of a calculated effort to institutionalize abortion on request in the United States."[88]

An effort that showed no signs of abating. Buchen warned Ford in November against rescinding the new policy on abortions in military hospitals. "Such a change," Buchen wrote, "would be legally unsupportable." In December the Senate unanimously confirmed Ford's choice to fill the vacancy on the Supreme Court created by the death of Justice William Douglas. Chicago judge John Paul Stevens, one of three candidates recommended to the president by Attorney General Edward Levi, would prove a reliable vote for abortion. Presidential aide James Cannon then prepared a set of questions and answers about the president's elusive position on abortion. To the question "Is the President pro or anti-abortion?," Buchen's answer was "both," saying that Ford supported *Roe* and a constitutional amendment to repeal *Roe* at the same time.[89]

The president would mention neither. "You have not made any public statements on abortion in public since becoming President," aides Cannon and Buchen reminded the chief executive in January 1976. As the third anniversary of *Roe v. Wade* approached, Nellie Gray of the anti-abortion March for Life Committee requested a meeting with Ford. Two weeks later, Gray, Randy Engle of the United States Coalition for Life, and Rev. Harold Brown of the Christian Action Council discussed their opposition to abortion at the White House. "Even though the government could not prohibit abortion," Gray contended, "it was not necessary to encourage and to fund abortions." Seven members of the administration attended the meeting. The president was not one of them.[90]

"I'm sure I'm not telling you anything you do not know," the USCC's director of public affairs, Russell Shaw, wrote to Msgr. McHugh and legislative liaison James Robinson at the end of January, but "abortion has already become a significant issue in 1976 politics." So the president, running for election, would finally have to address it.[91]

Or not. In what the *New York Times*'s James Naughton called a "carefully prepared statement" of what Ford termed a "moderate position," the president sought to have it both ways on abortion. In a February interview with CBS television's Walter Cronkite, Ford promised to "of course, uphold the law as interpreted by the Court," while asserting that the Court "went too far." He opposed a constitutional amendment to repeal *Roe* but supported one to return decisions about abortion to the states. Ford thus appeared to commit himself to do more of the same on abortion—nothing. The president "is not urging anything," White House press secretary Ron Nessen translated the interview, because "he has no role in the process."[92]

"Driving home last night I heard a radio report (CBS) which said Mr. Ford had stated his support for a constitutional amendment on abortion," the USCC's Russell Shaw privately recounted. "When I got up this morning, I heard a radio report (ABC) which said the President had stated that he did not support a constitutional amendment." Shaw concluded that Ford and Nessen "are trying to please anti-abortion people by saying that he is generally opposed to abortion, while simultaneously pleasing pro-abortion people by saying he doesn't plan to do anything about it." Ford's remarks were therefore "highly unacceptable" to the USCC. "Frankly, I consider his handling of the matter," Shaw minced no words, "to be both stupid and pusillanimous."[93]

The public USCC reaction was hardly more generous. Though "it would be unfair . . . to be any more critical of Mr. Ford than of other political leaders," Archbishop Bernardin spoke for the bishops, "it is regrettable that Mr. Ford's comments seem to contradict his earlier position, expressed both before and after he became president, of support for a so-called 'states' rights' amendment permitting the states to adopt meaningful legislation to restrict or prohibit abortion."[94] But hadn't Ford endorsed such an amendment? Bernardin's statement "was issued in response to a partial transcript of the interview made public by the White House several hours before it was broadcast," Bishop Rausch explained. "The President did not, in fact, state opposition to a constitutional amendment to restore to the states the right to regulate or prohibit abortions," Rausch continued. "But neither did he support such an amendment."[95]

He didn't? The full transcript shows that when asked by Cronkite, "Doesn't the Supreme Court decision itself seem to move against any possibility that the state can take any local action?" Ford awkwardly replied, "That is correct, but if there is to be a constitutional amendment, and there are some suggestions in the Congress now that would permit each state on its own through a vote of the people or through its state legislative branch to adopt its own state regulations."[96] "If there is to be one," the president continued, "I think that's a preferable answer rather than the one that's recommended by others." Cronkite added, "But under the Supreme Court decision, that would presumably take a constitutional amendment to let the states do that." And Ford responded, "That is correct."[97]

Everything

Whatever his intent, Ford's obfuscation was sufficiently evident, and the pressure from his more conservative primary rival sufficiently intense, that his days of doing nothing to oppose abortion were over. The president now embarked on a new two-pronged political strategy: do everything he could to attack abortion, and deny that he had ever done nothing.

In March 1976 the president at last climbed the bully pulpit. When asked by a reporter what he had meant by the Supreme Court going "too far" in the *Roe* case, Ford responded that "the question of where we should go or how we should handle it is a deep moral issue." He therefore rejected "ironclad decisions by a Supreme Court or an ironclad Constitutional amendment on the other side." Instead, "when these deep moral issues are involved, . . . you shouldn't be rigid in what is sought to be done by either the courts on the one hand, or the Constitution on the other."[98]

Earlier in March the bishops had received encouragement in the unlikeliest of venues, the courts. The Supreme Court did not take up a Billings, Montana, case challenging the federal law that permitted private hospitals to refuse to perform abortions and sterilizations. The USCC's Russell Shaw prepared a statement for Bishop Rausch, which saluted the Court's decision. "The law in question is essential to the American tradition of respect for the rights of conscience and religious liberty," Shaw wrote. "The Supreme Court's refusal to hear a challenge to the law is therefore supportive of these principles."[99] Solicitor general Robert Bork said much the same thing in an amicus curiae brief in *Beal v. Doe*. Speaking for the Ford administration, Bork contended that neither Title XIX of the Social Security Act nor the Fourteenth Amendment to the Constitution required a federally funded Medicaid program to pay for abortions that were not medically indicated.[100]

Things were suddenly going so well for the bishops that they worried about pressing their luck. When Republican Jesse Helms of North Carolina announced his intention to bypass the Judiciary Committee and offer his human life amendment for a test vote on the Senate floor, USCC congressional liaison

James Robinson feared the move would backfire on the pro-life forces. "A Senate vote at this time will lose by a substantial margin, far short of the two-thirds vote needed," Robinson prophesied.[101]

Robinson was right. In April Helms introduced his amendment, and after five hours of debate, his colleagues voted 47–40 to table it. But Msgr. James McHugh, chairman of the USCC's Committee for Population and Pro-life Activities, called the votes for the amendment "encouraging" because they fell only twenty-seven short of the two-thirds necessary to send it to the states. Robinson now estimated that a states' rights amendment would do even better, but still fail by ten to fifteen votes.[102]

In contrast to Robinson's gloomy prognostications, the frequent discussion of abortion in the early presidential primaries had produced, in the words of Harrisburg bishop Joseph Daley at the USCC's May meeting, "signs of hope" for the anti-abortion interests. New York's Terence Cardinal Cooke read in the election returns "a growing consensus among Americans against abortion on demand," and he voiced optimism that one of the forty-seven constitutional amendments under consideration by the Congress would soon succeed.[103]

President Ford was hearing much the same thing. In June Republican pollsters Graham Lee and Thomas Melady sent special assistant to the president Myron Kuropas their study showing that although abortion had limited appeal as an issue for most Americans, it had a special resonance for Catholics. "Though as a group Catholics are not that much more opposed to abortion than the nation as a whole," the authors argued, "those Catholics who do oppose abortion do so strongly enough that a candidate's position on this issue will be enough to determine their vote." Since Ford's primary challenger Ronald Reagan, whom most Catholic Republicans preferred, had "flip-flopped" from signing California's liberal abortion law to backing a human life amendment, and Ford's prospective general election rival, Jimmy Carter, opposed any anti-abortion amendment at all, both were "vulnerable on this issue among Catholic voters." Ford, heretofore "unable to exploit this potentially very valuable advantage," could do so, Lee and Melady concluded, by arguing that the states' rights approach he had endorsed was not substantively different from the human life amendment he had repudiated.[104] A July survey by Ford aide Henry Cashen reinforced this statement. "Even a modestly anti-abortion position could win millions of [Catholic] votes," Cashen argued.[105]

The counsel to Ford from Lee, Melady, and Cashen seemed to be: if you stick to your guns by advocating a states' rights anti-abortion amendment and by courting Catholics, you have little to fear from Republicans and much to gain from Democrats. So Ford took the advice.

In July, speaking at the Eucharistic Congress in Philadelphia, Ford brought the assembled Catholics to their feet when he deplored the "increased irreverence for life" and extolled the "supreme value of every person to whom life has been given by God." Lest there be any doubt that the president was referring to abortion, an "unidentified White House staffer" assured the *Washington Post* that he was.[106] Conservative Catholic columnist John Lofton couldn't believe his ears. Was this the same Ford, Lofton asked, who stood silently in the first year and a half of his presidency as his administration decided to fund Medicaid abortions and international family planning?[107]

But others had shorter memories. Brooklyn bishop Francis Mugavero described the response to Ford's Philadelphia speech as "quite positive," while Bishop Bernard Law of Springfield–Cape Girardeau, Missouri, called the address "a rather strong affirmation of life." A reporter wondered whether Ford's powerful remarks were the reason he left the First Lady at home.[108]

In August the six members of the USCC Executive Committee met with the Democratic challenger, Jimmy Carter, who held firm to his position of personal disapproval of abortion but resistance to a constitutional amendment to regulate it. After the meeting, Bernardin lamented that he and his colleagues "continued to be disappointed with the Governor's posistion."[109] As Ford awaited his turn with the bishops, he denied that his embrace of a states' rights amendment was incompatible with his party's endorsement of a human life amendment. "My position is that of the Republican platform," said the president, "and I will stick with it."[110]

When the USCC Executive Committee met with Ford in September, Archbishop Joseph Bernardin asked the president to clarify his position on a constitutional amendment. Ford repeated his insistence that a states' rights approach was consistent with the Republican platform. Bernardin then solicited Ford's stance on federal funding of abortion. Ford assured the archbishop that not only did he personally oppose such funding, but he had authorized a study within his administration to determine whether and how he could legally stop it. Bernardin emerged from the meeting "encouraged" by Ford's support for a constitutional amendment, but disappointed that the president had not opted for a "better approach" than the states' rights language so as to "give the maximum protection possible to the unborn."[111]

The study that Ford ordered would show that in 1975 alone the Department of Health, Education, and Welfare had financed between 250,000 and 300,000 abortions at a cost of $45–$55 million, while the Department of Defense had provided for 6,849 abortions at its own facilities and 1,087 at other locations, at a cost of $9 million. But in a letter to Bernardin following their meeting, Ford politely forsook the archbishop's "better approach" and clung to the states' rights method he had first promoted as a congressman from Grand Rapids.[112]

Although he could not completely escape his past, Ford had done so much to repudiate it that he raised inordinate expectations. In September 1976, he again vetoed an appropriations bill, this one for the Departments of Labor and HEW, despite its prohibition on federal funding of abortion. But this time, he endured criticism not only from those who backed the ban, but from those who wondered why the president had not lobbied for it. "The White House responsibility is to take a position in an area like this, I believe, as to how the laws are administered," the president protested, "not necessarily to get involved in every particular amendment that is in the process of being considered by Congress."[113]

The next day the Democratic-controlled Congress overrode Ford's veto, and the amendment proposed by Catholic Republican representative Henry Hyde of Illinois began its three-decade run. "I accept the Hyde Amendment. I think it was good, and I said so in the veto message," Ford reminded the pro-life forces, "and we will carry it out, and we are at the present time." But crusaders don't "carry things out"—bureaucrats do, and Ford's words appeared off-key and anticlimactic.[114]

It is ironic that this greatest victory of the Ford era for the pro-life movement, including many American Catholics, occurred despite the anti-abortion president, not because of him. Yet the greatest irony occurred six weeks later when Ford, the candidate forced to explain why he was wooing Catholics, lost to Carter, the candidate forced to explain why he wasn't. In a campaign gone wrong, members of the Ford administration had been right to instruct the president that the Catholic vote was important and that abortion was important to the Catholic vote. It just took their prize pupil too long to learn.

Conclusions on Life and Death

If Gerald Ford was silent on the subject of abortion for two-thirds of his presidency, American Catholics were not. Theirs was a cacophony of voices, however, which made it harder, not easier, for the president to speak. Divisions over the kind of constitutional amendment to pursue, the extent to which the bishops were acting as a political interest group, the degree to which the bishops appeared partisan, and the breadth of Catholic opposition to abortion conspired to postpone Ford's day of reckoning on abortion. In the end, Catholics were no better at playing politics than Ford was.

The first major rift that undermined the Catholic offensive against abortion concerned the type of constitutional amendment to champion. At the bishops' November 1974 meeting, the United States Catholic Conference's general counsel, Eugene Krasicky, offered four guiding principles in the formulation of an amendment:

1) It should be a simple, clear, and concise statement of the purpose which it is designed to achieve;
2) It should be broad enough to afford protection against private as well as governmental action;
3) It should contain language empowering Congress and the states to adopt legislation carrying out the purposes of the amendment, and
4) It should not be a restatement of a theological position, but rather a juridical proposition structured to achieve the purpose for which the amendment is designed.[115]

Robert Lynch, the president of the USCC's National Committee for a Human Life Amendment, proposed five options toward meeting these goals:

1) An amendment to proscribe abortion at all times. Such a possibility is remote, and no draft presently exists.
2) An amendment to proscribe abortion except when necessary to save the life of the mother. This does not have much support at the present time.
3) An amendment to guarantee protection "from the moment of implantation." No draft presently exists.
4) An amendment guaranteeing the states the right to regulate such matters. This draft exists, is popular with the senators, and has a good chance of passing the Senate.
5) To do nothing.[116]

By January 1975 the USCC's Committee on Law and Public Policy, headed by attorneys Edward Hanify and William Ball, had concluded that a states' rights amendment was, in Archbishop Joseph Bernardin's words, "the only approach with any political viability," so Bernardin asked the USCC's general secretary, Rev. James Rausch, to "begin to prepare our people for this political eventuality."[117]

Yet when such an amendment actually came up for a vote, the bishops overlooked Krasicky's fourth principle—that they argue juridically, not theologically—and sowed more complexity than clarity. In September the bishops informed the Senate Judiciary Committee's Subcommittee on Constitutional Amendments that they backed a human life amendment affirming a right to life and legal protection from conception onward, but were not opposed to the human life/states' rights combination sponsored by North Dakota Democrat Quentin Burdick. According to Honolulu bishop John Sweeney, however, Hawaii Republican Hiram Fong had promised the National Committee for a Human Life Amendment that he would "vote out a human life amendment so that the matter could be discussed by the entire Senate." Though he supported other, less restrictive amendments, Fong opposed the Burdick hybrid because he believed the bishops were against it. When Fong's nay helped sink the Burdick Amendment by a 4–4 tie vote, the USCC's Terence Cardinal Cooke wrote to the subcommittee chair, Birch Bayh of Indiana, denouncing his panel's failure to consider any of the other six anti-abortion proposals before it.[118]

Msgr. James McHugh tried to resolve this confusion in October when his Committee for Population and Pro-Life Activities met with Catholic Democratic senator Edward Kennedy of Massachusetts at the senator's Washington home. "Though the point may have remained unclear in our discussions," McHugh wrote to Kennedy following the meeting, "we realize that efforts to reverse the U.S. Supreme Court may not result in an absolute and comprehensive protection from the moment of fertilization onwards." Nevertheless, McHugh explained, "we believe that some type of constitutional protection for unborn life—albeit limited and qualified—is possible. This protection, coupled with assurance of alternatives, would do so much to reverse the present situation that allows one million abortions or more per year." At least the monsignor, unlike the bishops, appeared to realize that a states' rights amendment would not stop all abortions.[119]

Having confused Senators Fong and Kennedy, however, McHugh ultimately confused himself. A week after meeting with the Massachusetts senator, McHugh briefed his pro-life committee. "Our policy remains to push for an amendment that protects human life as much as possible," McHugh repeated his earlier statements. "However, we will also likely be faced with people in the Congress who will be more determined to pass states' rights legislation"—the kind of legislation Fong had voted against, Kennedy didn't understand, and McHugh had defended to both of them.[120]

At their November meeting the bishops attempted to help Msgr. McHugh untangle himself, only to ensnare themselves. "Bishop [Romeo] Blanchette [of Joliet, Illinois] asked whether the efforts for a constitutional amendment would extend to a compromise 'states' rights' amendment on abortion," read the minutes. "Cardinal Cooke replied that during the previous summer's regional meetings of bishops, there was a consensus of the bishops to work for an amendment that would protect all the unborn. This had been a feature of the testimony given by the Cardinals at the Senate subcommittee hearings"— which explains Cooke's all-or-nothing reaction to the Bayh subcommittee results, but not Cooke's statement after the USCC meeting to the *New York Times* that he would leave the specific wording of an amendment to Congress. The cardinal told the *Times* that the bishops writing it "would be the best way to kill an amendment because then you would be playing into the hands of those who say [abortion] is a Catholic issue." But George Dugan, who wrote the *Times* story, said that the bishops *not* specifying an amendment had killed the anti-abortion measures in the Bayh subcommittee. Thus did Dugan resurrect the ghosts of Bishop Sweeney, Senator Fong, Msgr. McHugh, and Senator Kennedy. In a classic bit of understatement, Bishop Rausch told his colleagues that on abortion, "Many of our people aren't sure what the Church's positions are."[121]

Among "our people" were the bishops themselves. Archbishop John Whealon of Hartford, Connecticut, appealed to Rome for guidance on whether a states' rights proviso would be consistent with the teachings of the magisterium on abortion. The pope's apostolic delegate to the United States, Rev. Jean Jadot, in turn wrote Bernardin, requesting his "evaluation of the proposed legislation." Bernardin replied in January 1976 that while the states' rights version was "the least desirable of the possibilities, it appears to be . . . more likely to succeed."[122]

But only if it received a hearing. The USCC legislative liaison, James Robinson, deplored the December decision by the House Judiciary Committee's Subcommittee on Civil Rights and Constitutional Rights not to let the bishops testify on an anti-abortion amendment. Robinson claimed that the USCC had "taken a restrained view of the Supreme Court decision, and . . . asked the Catholic people to use the process of representative democracy available to them." In other words, he seemed to be saying, the bishops had sought to testify in favor of an amendment that would declare abortion to be murder—except where it wasn't.[123]

If American Catholics quarreled over what kind of product they were selling, they also clashed over how to sell it. The Church's role as lobbyist furnished a second bone of contention that undercut the anti-abortion campaign. In what *Time* called a "sharp shift from uncoordinated, at times strident opposition to abortion to a more reasoned and concerted attack on it," the USCC at its November meeting issued the "Pastoral Plan for Pro-Life Activities." The plan mandated an educational campaign at the parish level and a political offensive on a national scale.[124] Noting that the pastoral plan also included a commitment to help women who had experienced abortions or problem pregnancies, *America* editorialized in December, "When the bishops announced their pastoral plan, the secular press paid no attention to the parts concerned with the care of pregnant women or with informing and educating the public.

Instead, but quite predictably, the secular media headlined the political action part of the plan."[125] "With the launch of their pastoral plan, the bishops are perceived as having 'gone political,'" the USCC's Shaw complained. "I think it's open season for Catholic-baiting," Msgr. McHugh lamented.[126]

Syndicated columnist Marianne Means estimated that in 1973, two years before the bishops inaugurated their pastoral plan, the United States Catholic Conference spent "four million dollars in anti-abortion activities for that one year." Means claimed that "never before has one religion tried so openly and emphatically to impose a view upon the political process which is opposed, according to polls, by a majority of voters and a majority of its members." "There is no basis for the four-million-dollar figure," Bishop Rausch retorted, maintaining that the bishops' National Committee for a Human Life Amendment spent about $250,000 in 1975. As for one religion dictating to others, the ecumenical American Citizens Concerned for Life rose to the bishops' defense. In a letter signed by the group's president, Marjory Mecklenburg, a Methodist; its vice president, Judith Fink, a Baptist; and Rev. Robert Holbrook, the co-ordinator of Baptists for Life, the Protestants applauded the Catholics' efforts and urged Americans "to seek solutions to these problems by becoming actively involved in citizen pro-life political action groups."[127]

American Citizens Concerned for Life was nonetheless more comfortable with the bishops' end than their means. The House Subcommittee on Civil Rights and Constitutional Rights was "moving nicely toward inclusion of testimony that abortion is not a church-state issue," Mecklenburg wrote to Bishop Rausch, "when pressure was brought to bear on [Catholic Democratic] Chairman [Peter] Rodino [of New Jersey] by the Catholic Church to include their official representatives." As a result, "a great deal of ill will was created."[128]

Despite Rausch's disclaimer that "the appearance of the four Cardinals before the Senate [in 1974] and the anticipated appearance of USCC representatives before the House Subcommittee in no way prevents others from requesting and obtaining time to testify," Mecklenburg would prove prescient. "As things now stand," the USCC's William Cox reported to Rausch three weeks before the hearings, "the Catholic bishops will be the only religious leaders testifying in favor of an amendment to the Constitution. All Protestant leaders and groups who have requested the opportunity to testify before the Subcommittee have been turned down by the Subcommittee."[129] To add insult to injury, Cox continued, "on the same day that the Bishops will be testifying, Mr. Leo Pfeffer, who will be billed as an eminent Church-State legal expert, and the Religious Coalition for Abortion Rights, which bills itself as a 'group of twenty Protestant, Jewish, and Catholic organizations,' will be testifying against an amendment." Because "the Bishops are walking into a situation which has been carefully orchestrated by the Subcommittee to embarrass the Church," Cox recommended that the USCC not testify.[130]

Bernardin and Cooke testified anyway in March 1976, but not before the USCC ignited yet another firestorm about its lobbying activities with its release of "Political Responsibility: Reflections on an Election Year," which reaffirmed the Church's claim to political legitimacy. "Never before in the two hundred years of American independence have the bishops provided such concerted, nationwide, overt political leadership," Marquette University political scientist Paul Weber wrote in *America*. "This new activism . . . raises serious questions. Stated bluntly, should the Catholic bishops . . . become so directly active politically?"[131]

Even some members of the hierarchy were uncomfortable with their colleagues' political prominence. Although the pastoral plan had passed unanimously at the bishops' November 1975 meeting, Jim Castelli noted in *America* in May 1976 that "several reliable sources indicated extreme 'discomfort' or 'uneasiness' among the bishops at the political thrust of the document." These bishops refused to make their private reservations public, Castelli explained, for fear of criticism by their fellow pro-lifers.[132] Such attacks, they worried, would provide aid and comfort to the enemy, such as the National Organization for Women, which in October asked the Internal Revenue Service to investigate whether the bishops' political activities had violated the Church's tax-exempt status. NOW board member Davlyn Jones stated that her group "didn't particularly care to have a priest dictating the law."[133]

Or a priest telling Americans how to vote. A third contentious issue among American Catholics was the appearance of partisanship cultivated by the bishops' anti-abortion campaign. In an August 1975 letter to Bishop Rausch, USCC legislative liaison James Robinson cheered the anti-abortion efforts of Minnesota congressman James Oberstar because "he represents a Democratic voice in what has been too much of a conservative Republican issue." Rausch concurred that "the media has presented the [abortion] issue as an interest of conservatives only."[134]

To correct this image, Youngstown bishop James Malone warned the hierarchy at its November meeting to exercise "caution in supporting candidates whose positions on other issues, e.g. full employment, housing, and revenue-sharing, might be unacceptable." At Malone's suggestion, the bishops inserted the word "qualified" before "candidates" in the "Pastoral Plan for Pro-Life Activities" exhortation "to work for candidates who will vote for a constitutional amendment and other pro-life issues." When the bishops released their "Political Responsibility" document in February 1976, a USCC spokesman said that it proved that "the church is interested in other issues" besides abortion.[135]

But such efforts could not dispel the notion among many Catholics that the USCC was rooting for the Republicans. Pro-life Methodist Marjory Mecklenburg accused the USCC's William Cox of pressuring her to "resign from the [Sargent] Shriver [Democratic] presidential campaign advisory committee or bring Mr. Shriver and Senator [Edward] Kennedy around to publicly backing the Human Life Amendment within a period of about two weeks, or no further cooperation with [the bishops] was possible."[136]

Even some bishops acknowledged their growing problem. Jim Castelli reported that the listing in "Political Responsibility" of seven major issues in addition to abortion was a response to the USCC's Department of Social Development and World Peace's concern over the bishops' perceived preoccupation with a "single issue," and the primary position of abortion on the alphabetically ordered list came only after the bishops rejected a proposal to substitute the words "pro-life activities" instead. At the May 1976 Executive Committee meeting, Bishop Francis Hurley of Juneau, Alaska, wished that "just as every effort was being made to avoid a sectarian level . . . so too efforts could be made to avoid a 'conservative-liberal' label."[137]

The debate continued with the bishops' input into the party platforms. When the Democrats defied the bishops on abortion, the USCC's Russell Shaw and Msgr. James McHugh argued that the USCC president, Archbishop Joseph Bernardin, should temper his public disapproval with a recognition of the historic "similarity between the priorities of the Democratic Party and Catholic social teaching."[138] Msgr. George Higgins of the Department of Social Development and World Peace wrote to Bernardin that his "statement on the Democratic platform was a mistake, not because it criticized the section on abortion, but because it said nothing about any other issue." Msgr. McHugh lamented to Bishop James Rausch the apparent leaking to the press of dissension among the bishops.[139]

"The Church does not involve itself in partisan politics," Bernardin felt obliged to announce in August. "It does not endorse or oppose particular parties or candidates." Abortion was no more a "Catholic issue," Bernardin insisted, "than our involvement in the food crisis makes that a Catholic issue." Alluding to the many pastorals issued by the bishops in recent years, Bernardin stressed that the hierarchy was "concerned about many issues."[140] Thus did the USCC president defuse the controversy over the bishops' alleged partisanship, for at least forty-eight hours. But then Bernardin lavished such praise on the Republican platform that the issue resurfaced inside and outside Catholic circles.[141]

The bishops went so far in disavowing Republican sympathies that they began to sound like Democrats. The USCC released an issue-by-issue analysis that showed that, in the words of the National Catholic News Service's Jim Castelli, "on more than a half dozen" issues other than abortion, "the Democratic platform agrees with the USCC and the Republican platform does not." After four months of zigs and zags, the bishops ultimately generated the remarkable consensus that on abortion, in Castelli's words, "There is not that much difference between Ford's and Carter's positions."[142]

If the wording of an amendment, the role of lobbying, and the perception of partisanship were not enough to divide American Catholics over abortion, the issue itself opened a final fissure. The December 1974 "Declaration on Abortion" issued by the Vatican Congregation for the Faith at the behest of Pope Paul VI proclaimed that a "Christian can never conform to a law which is in itself immoral, and such is the case of a law which would admit in principle the licitness of abortion." The statement added that a Christian may not "campaign in favor of such a law, or vote for it. Moreover, he may not collaborate in its application." Yet despite the bishops' repeated appeals for adherence, many American Catholics defied the declaration. A December 1974 poll by the National Opinion Research Center, the first of its kind since 1963, found a stunning 70 percent of American Catholics agreeing that "married women who did not want more children should be able to obtain a legal abortion."[143]

The survey unleashed an acrimonious exchange between the USCC and Rev. Andrew Greeley, the Catholic sociologist who headed the study. The USCC's associate general secretary, Rev. Thomas Kelly, charged that Greeley "appears willing to sacrifice truth to rhetoric." The USCC general counsel, Edward Hanify, sneered that the "fox is taking a poll of the chicken coop."[144] Having discredited Greeley's survey, the hierarchy undertook one of its own. The findings, released in February 1975, showed that "people expect 'guidance on moral issues' from priests even if it means that the priests will get involved in politics," and "people become more conservative as more information is given them." Msgr. McHugh interpreted the results as a clarion call for more and better education of American Catholics on abortion and other issues, especially in the parochial schools, whose products were less informed than their public school counterparts.[145] Such an education campaign could have started on Capitol Hill. Eight of fifteen Catholic senators voted in September against the Bartlett amendment prohibiting the use of public funds for abortion.[146]

If the bishops were going to educate the faithful on the evils of abortion, they first had to get them to go to church. A January 1976 American Statistical Association poll found that "a significant number of Catholics who regularly attend church disapprove of abortion under any circumstance, while the rate of disapproval among regular churchgoing Protestants is only slightly lower." However, "among those who attend church once a month or less, there is no difference between Protestants and Catholics on their attitudes toward abortion," and there "is a slight trend toward a more liberal attitude by both groups, with almost seventy-five percent of both groups approving five or six reasons for abortion by 1974."[147]

Yet if many American Catholics didn't oppose abortion because they were not attending church, some of them were not attending church because they didn't oppose abortion. The March 1976 publication of Father Greeley's complete study, in the form of a 483-page book, concluded that *Humanae Vitae*, the 1968 papal encyclical prohibiting artificial contraception and abortion, had cost the Church about one-third of its worshippers and about $1 billion in donations. Most frightening, perhaps, efforts to educate American Catholics on Church doctrine were failing abysmally, as the percentage of school-age Catholics not receiving formal religious instruction doubled from 1963 to 1976, to 43.5 percent.[148]

The USCC again responded not by acknowledging reality but by attacking Greeley. While the Catholic hierarchy was separating itself from Greeley's study, the faithful were separating themselves from the hierarchy. A March 1976 Gallup Poll found a bare majority of Catholics—54 percent of females and 51 percent of males—in favor of a constitutional amendment to outlaw abortion unless the mother's life was in danger. At the bishops' May meeting, Cardinal Cooke confessed "increasing despair about the possibility of obtaining a constitutional amendment" against abortion.[149]

When Jimmy Carter won the election in November 1976 with majority Catholic support, conservative Jesuit commentator Rev. Virgil Blum muttered that the Democratic Party could "twist a broken bone into the flesh of Catholics without a loss of votes." But before Carter could twist the bone, Gerald Ford and many American Catholics had gone a long way toward breaking it. The unforgettable Watergate scandal and the intractable economic malaise had caused many American Catholics to defect from the Republican "silent majority." And contrary to the best hopes of conservative pollsters and the worst fears of liberal pundits, abortion was not enough to bring them back.[150]

Gerald Ford's presidency was over almost before it began. But its brevity belied the enormity of the challenges that he confronted. Ford concluded the Vietnam War with compassion toward Indochinese refugees. He orchestrated an international response to the food crisis. He signed the Hyde Amendment banning federal funds for abortion, and he endorsed a constitutional amendment outlawing all abortions. On every one of these policies, American Catholics were out front, helping to take the president places where he didn't always want to go.

CHAPTER FIVE

Catholics and Jimmy Carter
(1977–1981)

AS A BORN-AGAIN BAPTIST from a region historically inhospitable to Catholics, candidate Jimmy Carter attracted many Catholic skeptics even as he collected most Catholic votes. By proposing nuclear arms control and universal health insurance and by opposing federal funding of abortion, however, President Jimmy Carter endeared himself to much of the Church power structure. But no amount of Catholic lobbying could rescue SALT II, enact health care legislation, or persuade Carter to translate personal repugnance toward abortion into political affinity for a constitutional amendment. In the end, too many American Catholics strayed from their leader in the White House and their leaders in the Church.

War and Peace: Nuclear War

In May 1977 newly elected President Carter told the graduates at the University of Notre Dame that Americans possessed an "inordinate fear of communism." Carter would receive much acclaim for this signature speech by the first president of the post-Vietnam era.[1]

Carter did more than talk. He worked assiduously to achieve a second Strategic Arms Limitation Treaty with Soviet premier Leonid Brezhnev, who had signed the first one with Richard Nixon in 1972. Before Carter could send the treaty to the Senate for ratification, however, Brezhnev had ordered the invasion of neighboring Afghanistan to prop up a friendly government. With startling suddenness, détente died, the Cold War resumed, and Carter admitted that he had been wrong about communism.

The American Catholic hierarchy was with the Southern Baptist president almost every step of the way. The bishops lauded his insistence on human rights and shared his devotion to arms control. Their preferred foreign policy was markedly similar to his: long on negotiation, short on bluster, with more conciliation than confrontation. But many of the Catholic congregants, dubi-

{169}

ous about Carter from the start, found his diplomacy naïve and his moralism grating. Theirs was the hard line of an earlier era, when Vietnam was a mission before it was a morass, and communism was godless before it was guiltless. Just as Carter underestimated the Soviets, so the bishops underappreciated their flock. But unlike Carter, the bishops would not admit their mistake.

Catholics, Carter, and SALT

Carter's focus on nuclear arms control was quite consistent with the recent teaching of the Church on nuclear war, especially Pope John XXIII's *Pacem in Terris* (1963), Pope Paul VI's *Populorum Progressio* (1967), and the International Synod of Bishops' *Justicia in Mundo* (1971). So the Catholic drumbeat for SALT II was sounding even before Carter came to Washington.[2]

Testifying before the Senate Foreign Relations Committee in January 1976, Archbishop Peter Gerety of Newark, New Jersey, quoted the Second Vatican Council's *Gaudium et Spes* ("Of Hope and Joy," 1965). This document established three principles governing the deployment of nuclear weapons:

1) Use of the weapons against cities and populated areas is prohibited in a special way because of their destructive capacity.
2) While use is prohibited, the possession of these weapons for deterrence may possibly be legitimated as the lesser of two evils.
3) Even deterrence is questionable unless it is conceived as an interim expedient accompanied by extraordinary efforts to negotiate their limitation and reduction.[3]

As soon as Carter entered the White House, the American Catholic bishops began to sing his praises. A United States Catholic Conference internal document reviewing the first six months of the new administration applauded the president's commitment to "the early resumption of SALT talks," as well as his willingness to negotiate "an exchange of limitations of cruise missiles for Soviet limitations on the Backfire bomber and their heavy ICBM's [intercontinental ballistic missiles]; and a ban on new systems such as the mobile ICBM's on both sides."[4]

In September 1977 the United States Catholic Conference president, Archbishop Joseph Bernardin of Cincinnati, and its general secretary, Bishop Thomas Kelly, received a briefing from President Carter and Vice President Walter Mondale on the administration's staunch advocacy of human rights in foreign policy. Pope Paul VI ushered in the new year with a message proclaiming "No to Violence, Yes to Peace." The USCC administrative board followed with a February 1978 pastoral, "The Gospel of Peace and the Danger of War," which declared the "primary moral imperative . . . that the arms race must be stopped and the reduction of armaments must be achieved." In April Edward

Doherty conveyed to the Senate Foreign Relations Committee Subcommittee on Arms Control, Oceans, and International Environment the bishops' dedication to the aims of the forthcoming United Nations General Assembly Special Session on Disarmament, scheduled for May 23 to June 28. Doherty praised Carter's pledge to make a "strong and positive contribution" to the gathering.⁵

Doherty cautioned, however, that the "bilateral SALT framework" was preferable to any multilateral UN effort to attain nuclear disarmament. He concluded by quoting Philadelphia archbishop John Cardinal Krol's admonition to the 1971 International Synod of Bishops that SALT needed "greater interest, encouragement, and support." Just before the United Nations special session convened, San Francisco archbishop John Quinn, the president of the USCC, urged the delegates to "demonstrate that humanity need not continue ... to tremble at the possibility of nuclear holocaust."⁶

In October 1978 Paul Warnke of the Arms Control and Disarmament Agency briefed Catholic and other religious leaders on the status of the treaty. In November Carter unveiled Americans for SALT, a high-profile lobbying effort spearheaded by the University of Notre Dame president, Rev. Theodore Hesburgh. The United States Catholic Conference was among the organizations represented on the executive committee of Americans for SALT.⁷ By the end of the year, the bishops were calling the ratification of SALT II "a principal goal for the United States." They warned Carter, however, not to "impose an increased defense budget to win support for treaty ratification." In February 1979, the USCC administrative board formally endorsed SALT II. The editors of *America* praised the bishops for joining Americans for SALT, while worrying that "the rejection of SALT II would dangerously encourage the hostility and suspicions that make disarmament so elusive."⁸

In March Warnke briefed the religious leaders again, telling them that public opinion supported SALT by 80 percent when the wording of the survey question was general, and 50 percent when it was specific. San Francisco archbishop John Quinn, Hartford archbishop John Whealon, Georgetown University president Rev. Timothy Healy, *Commonweal* editor James O'Gara, *America* editor Joseph O'Hare, and Leadership Conference of Women Religious president Sister Mary Dooley were among those at a June White House briefing on the progress of the SALT talks. Carter assured the group, "SALT II is not based on trust. The treaty will be verifiable by our own technical means of verification."⁹

Then the president left for Vienna, where he exchanged ceremonial kisses with Soviet premier Leonid Brezhnev as the two heads of state signed the second Strategic Arms Limitation Treaty at the venerable Hofburg Palace. The treaty's signatures and Carter's cheeks were barely dry when he met in July with Americans for SALT representatives from twenty-four states, including Indiana's Father Hesburgh, to discuss the battle for Senate ratification of the agreement.[10]

Philadelphia archbishop John Cardinal Krol testified on SALT II for the United States Catholic Conference before the Senate Foreign Relations Committee in September. Krol recited the three principles governing nuclear war that the Second Vatican Council had enunciated in *Gaudium et Spes*: indiscriminate attacks on civilians are always unacceptable, the arms race ultimately does not deter war, and continuation of the arms race portends "lethal ruin." He called SALT II "a limited but acceptable agreement which constrains the nuclear forces of both the U.S. and the U.S.S.R., does not jeopardize U.S. security, and can be the beginning of a continuing and necessary process for obtaining meaningful and progressive reductions." Therefore, Krol concluded, "the treaty should be ratified by the Senate." Krol reiterated these convictions in a meeting with President Carter a week later.[11]

SALT was also on the table at a White House luncheon between Carter and Archbishop Quinn later that month. Before the meeting, Carter aide Anne Wexler apprised the president of the USCC's fear, expressed by Krol, that the only way SALT could win ratification was by enticing hawkish senators with promises of more defense spending, at the expense of domestic needs.[12] The meeting of the president and the archbishop was part of White House preparations for the unprecedented visit of a pope to the American capital. Secretary of State Cyrus Vance recommended that when Carter received Pope John Paul II in October, he should note that despite the pontiff's disappointment that SALT II would not actually reduce nuclear weapons, the president welcomed the Holy Father's overall endorsement of the treaty. The Catholic national security advisor, Zbigniew Brzezinski, added that the papal visit would offer an excellent opportunity to "build on the Pope's initial support for SALT II."[13]

The president and the pope recognized this opportunity. "We must successfully conclude our arms control agreements," Carter told John Paul II, "and in this continuing effort we must find a way to end the threat of nuclear annihilation forever." The pontiff replied, "I know and appreciate this country's efforts for arms limitation, especially for nuclear weapons. With all my heart I hope there will be no relaxing of its efforts to both reduce the risk of fatal and disastrous worldwide conflagration and to secure a prudent and progressive reduction of the destructive capacity of nuclear arsenals."[14]

The American Catholic bishops seized the moment. No sooner had the pope returned home than the USCC's general secretary, Bishop Thomas Kelly, was quoting him in a letter from the bishops to every senator, urging quick approval of SALT II. Though Carter's shelving of the B-1 bomber, postponement of the neutron bomb, and futile opposition to a new nuclear aircraft carrier had already alienated congressional hardliners enough to jeopardize the treaty, Brezhnev ultimately killed it: first, by sending a Soviet brigade to Cuba in September, then by sending several to Afghanistan in December.[15]

With uncharacteristic humility, Carter admitted that he had misjudged the Soviets. "My opinion of the Russians has changed more drastically in the last week than in the two and one-half years before that," the nation's chief diplomat conceded in the final week of 1979, finally siding with Brzezinski against Vance. "On SALT, we decided to keep it on the Senate calendar, but there's no way to vote on it now," Carter wrote in his diary on January 2, 1980. "There is little doubt that we had the votes lined up in the Senate to ratify SALT II," Carter would remember, "but the Soviet invasion sent a clear indication that they were not to be trusted."[16]

Terence Cardinal Cooke stopped by the White House in January 1980. *Commonweal* urged Carter not to give up on the treaty in February, and Bishop Thomas Kelly testified in favor of SALT II before the Republican and Democratic platform committees in May and June. Carter spoke at the Catholic Charities Convention in September. In October, a month before the presidential election, Carter told the Catholic *Our Sunday Visitor* that if the country would reelect him he would "seek Senate ratification" of SALT II "as soon as that is feasible." But the country would elect the Republican former California governor, Ronald Reagan, who opposed the treaty in his campaign but would observe it while in the White House. Carter would brand SALT's failure the "most profound disappointment of my presidency."[17]

Conclusions on War and Peace

Like so many other issues, arms control divided the Catholic Church in the United States. This division helped to wound the White House campaign for the treaty even before the Soviets killed it.

First, it split the hierarchy, as SALT II incurred criticism from the more conservative bishops, such as Archbishop Philip Hannan of New Orleans. Two weeks before President Carter assured the graduating class at the nation's most famous Catholic university that they need not fear communism, Hannan warned his fellow prelates that they dare not forget it. "There is a growing tendency among a number of people, especially youth," Hannan lamented at the United States Catholic Conference's spring 1977 meeting, "to consider Marxism as a good substitute for the free enterprise system." Hannan then proposed that the bishops draft a "Pastoral Letter on Marxist Communism" to remind Catholics of the true nature of that heinous system. They would, but not until a week after Carter's electoral defeat, and in a less strident way than Hannan proposed.[18]

At the other extreme, Detroit's auxiliary bishop, Thomas Gumbleton, believed SALT II did not go far enough. Gumbleton related that when he attended a State Department briefing in October 1978 he fully expected to support the treaty. But by the end of the first morning session, he had turned against it. "I began to ponder the fact," Gumbleton recalled, "that SALT II would legitimate the destructive power of 615,000 Hiroshima bombs, the present American arsenal." At the bishops' February 1979 administrative board meeting, Bishop John O'Rourke of Peoria agreed with Gumbleton that by freezing rather than eliminating nuclear weapons, SALT II would violate the USCC's earlier repudiation of real and potential attacks on civilian populations. Archbishop Thomas Donnellan of Atlanta, Archbishop Rembert Weakland of Milwaukee, Auxiliary Bishop Austin Vaughan of New York, and Bishop Ernest Unterkoefler of Charleston therefore opposed any USCC testimony in favor of the treaty.[19]

The bishops privately addressed the increasing difficulty of reaching agreement on such troubling policy issues by trying to redefine "consensus" from a required two-thirds majority to a simple majority. But their attempt failed by a majority of one—the pope.[20] Philadelphia archbishop John Cardinal Krol publicly acknowledged the division within the hierarchy in his September 1979 testimony before the Senate Foreign Relations Committee. Though the bishops as a whole endorsed SALT II, Krol conceded, "it is not a unanimous position."[21]

Second, SALT II also exposed continued strains between Church leaders, who were moving toward the Democrats, and Church followers, who were drifting toward the Republicans. In October 1976, a month after Cincinnati archbishop Joseph Bernardin's celebrated disavowal of the hierarchy's Republican sympathies on abortion, the USCC's Rev. Bryan Hehir all but endorsed the Democratic Party platform, favorably contrasting its "more specific" proposals with the "most feeble" planks of the Republicans. A month after Carter's election, Father Hesburgh submitted a long list of his recommendations to staff the new administration, with almost all of his choices liberal, most of them Democratic, and some of them—like Secretary of State Cyrus Vance, Secretary of Health and Human Services Patricia Roberts Harris, Secretary of the Treasury Michael Blumenthal, and national security advisor Zbigniew Brzezinski—remarkably prescient. Hesburgh himself would play several roles in the Carter administration, including chair of the U.S. delegation to the United Nations Conference on Science and Technology Development, the Cambodia Crisis Committee, and the Select Commission on Immigration and Refugee

Policy, as well as co-chair of Americans for SALT and member of the President's Commission on the Holocaust.[22]

"What is the difference between God and Father Hesburgh?" was the joke circulating on campus at the time. "God is everywhere, and Father Hesburgh is everywhere but Notre Dame." That is, unless it was commencement, when the president accepted Hesburgh's invitation to speak. Carter's dovish message to the graduates in May 1977 was strikingly similar to that of the bishops, who, historian Michael Warner observed, were counseling that "in many countries it had become necessary for Catholics to collaborate with Marxists."[23]

Two months after Carter's Notre Dame address, an internal USCC memorandum called the "problems of guns and butter" the administration's "most serious disappointment." As a candidate, Carter had pledged to slash defense spending by $5–7 billion a year. Yet, much to the chagrin of most bishops, Carter's Office of Management and Budget was now projecting an increase in defense expenditures of 48 percent over two years.[24] But not to worry, the bishops would assure the president. In September 1977 the USCC's Bishop Kelly and Archbishop Bernardin visited the White House. "Toward the end of the meeting, I reminded Mr. Carter that he and I had met a year ago," Bernardin would recall. "I noted that there had been serious misperceptions of that meeting." Then the archbishop "told the president that the bishops' conference is . . . generally supportive" of Carter in areas other than "the need for a constitutional amendment to restore protection for the unborn."[25]

Many of the American Catholic faithful, however, were not as enamored of Carter and SALT as most bishops were. From the left, Joseph Fahey of Pax Christi attended the same State Department briefing that Bishop Gumbleton did and arrived at the same conclusion. Pax Christi voted in December 1978 not to endorse the treaty because it fell short of true disarmament.[26] Such dissension did not escape the notice of the bishops. "What has been the level of acceptance of our teaching, its adequacy, its influence on the consciences of ourselves and of our people?" Bishop Francis Murphy of Baltimore wondered at the USCC's November 1978 meeting. "What has been the effect of our teaching on public debate and policy formation regarding the development of armaments?"[27]

Nor did the dissension elude the Carter administration. Catholic aide Charles O'Keefe worried that the Catholics whom Carter had enlisted, such as the assistant secretary of Housing and Urban Development, Msgr. Geno Baroni, on domestic matters and Father Hesburgh on international affairs, spoke for neither the bishops nor "mainstream Catholicism."[28]

But then again, maybe they spoke for both. Former Nixon and Ford aide

Patrick Buchanan conceded that a large majority of all Americans, reaching a high of three-fourths in January 1978, were in support of SALT II. Jim Castelli would note that in every Gallup survey during the Ford and Carter administrations, Catholics were more likely than other Americans to approve of lower defense spending.[29]

Were the bishops and the ubiquitous Father Hesburgh merely reflecting American, and American Catholic, public opinion in their dovish stances? Yes and no. A White House official admitted that despite considerable support for SALT II, the administration pursued a "defensive" strategy in selling the treaty, acknowledging widespread doubts about its enforcement. Buchanan cited a February 1978 poll that showed that while 71 percent of Americans backed SALT II, 64 percent believed the Soviets would violate it. Castelli would conclude that although most American Catholics had become doves, they remained fiercely anti-communist.[30]

"Trust, yet verify." Carter's successor, Ronald Reagan, would quote an old Russian proverb to explain his arms control success in the wake of Carter's failure. To former president Jimmy Carter, abandoned by Soviet leaders and American voters, the old Russian who said it must have sounded like a Catholic.[31]

Social Justice: Health Care

Americans are impatient people. Their food must be fast, their communication must be rapid, and their gratification must be instant. Americans are good at a lot of things, but waiting is not one of them. Unless, that is, the subject is health care. Like the dog-eared magazines in the doctor's office, health care had been part of the national political debate long before Jimmy Carter assumed the presidency in January 1977. Over a generation after President Harry Truman introduced national health insurance as a political issue, Carter vowed finally to enact it. Many Americans, including many Catholics, would try to hold the chief executive to this promise.

They would be sorely disappointed. The Southern Baptist in the White House and the Catholics who helped elect him raised the issue's profile without advancing its prospects. Carter and the U.S. Catholic bishops concluded that the time had come for national health insurance. Then they decided that maybe it could wait.

Carter and Health Care

"Complex and bedeviling" is how the secretary of Health, Education, and Welfare, Joseph Califano, described national health insurance in a November 1977 memorandum to President Jimmy Carter. Califano cited five major objectives of any national health plan as viewed by the interest groups connected to the issue: improving health; protecting Americans against financial devastation from illness; making health services more accessible to all, but particularly to low-income inner-city and rural populations; making the health care delivery system more efficient (or at least less costly) and more effective; and changing the health care system's orientation from acute care to other emphases such as mental health and preventive services. For every goal, there was a potential obstacle: paying federal expenses, defining the role of private insurance companies, regulating the cost and quality of health care within the states, and devising a timetable for implementation.[32]

Of all those possible roadblocks, none would be more daunting than the federal price tag. Carter owed his election in large part to the spiraling inflation that his predecessor could not tame, so he was not about to let his administration offer a plan that stoked those inflationary embers. The president warned Califano in July 1978 that "the American people would not accept, and I will not propose, any health care plan which is inflationary."[33]

Carter had already introduced a health care plan that was not inflationary, a small-bore attempt at hospital cost control. Carter proposed a mandatory 9 percent ceiling on hospital spending increases in the first year, with lower caps in subsequent years, and a national maximum of capital expenditures by hospitals. Fierce opposition by the hospital industry and the American Medical Association led Carter to give up on the legislation in September 1977.[34]

While Carter's minor health care proposal was falling short, his major effort was taking shape. In January 1979 Califano revealed the fruits of two years of study within the administration: a national health plan that would achieve universal coverage by mandating that employers cover their employees and that the federal government cover virtually everyone else. The system would include private as well as public insurance, would establish a negotiating structure by which the federal government set payment rates, and would allow state and local governments to limit doctors' fees and hospital costs.[35]

Califano suggested that the administration publicize the tentative proposal after the State of the Union address later in the month. Then, after two to three months of consultation with legislators and interest groups, the administration should offer a comprehensive plan to be implemented in the 1983 fiscal year.[36] But domestic policy advisor Stuart Eizenstat, budget director James McIntyre, and Treasury secretary Charles Schultze successfully urged Carter to reject Califano's recommendation on financial, strategic, and political grounds. Carter would offer "Phase I," a hybrid of Medicare/Medicaid reform and catastrophic coverage, leaving a comprehensive plan for another day.[37]

In his State of the Union speech a week later, the president spoke specifically about a new hospital cost containment bill but only generally about national health insurance, promising to "submit a plan later in the year and work . . . with the Congress toward a prompt enactment of that plan." To satisfy Califano, however, Carter would present a broad outline of a comprehensive plan in a special message to Congress in June. Carter would also have to appease the Catholic Massachusetts Democrat Edward Kennedy, the loudest voice for health care in the Senate, who had presented his own comprehensive plan in October. White House aide Peter Bourne suggested a strategy of "Califano out front attacking Kennedy to keep the battle away from the president."[38]

Carter finally unveiled his plan in June 1979. The president asserted that "a fully comprehensive health plan is among the great unfinished items on our Nation's social agenda." Then he offered a plan that fell considerably short of that goal. "There are those who sincerely believe that we must insist upon a full-scale, comprehensive plan enacted all at once," Carter conceded, but added that "the idea of all or nothing has been pursued for three decades without success."[39]

And Carter had been pursuing hospital cost containment for two years without success. His latest attempt was a tepid threat to impose cost controls in 1980 only if hospitals exceeded a 9.7 percent rate of increase in 1979. The bill exempted institutions in states with successful mandatory or voluntary cost control regimes, small non-urban hospitals, hospitals less than three years old, and health maintenance organizations. Califano estimated that these exemptions would cover over half the nation's hospitals.[40]

By the time the House voted on cost containment in November, the administration bill had given way to an even feebler substitute sponsored by Missouri Democrat Richard Gephardt, which replaced mandatory caps with that time-honored monument to congressional cowardice—a presidentially appointed commission to monitor costs. Yet despite personal visits to Capitol Hill by Vice President Walter Mondale and telephone calls to wavering representatives from the president, even that measure failed on the House floor. Carter blamed the "hospital industry" for the defeat, calling it "the worst example of a powerful special interest that I have seen since I've been in office."[41]

Without hospital cost containment, Carter would not pursue Phase I. And he could not even think of seeking comprehensive coverage.

Catholics and Health Care

If the federal government was arriving late to the issue of health care, so was the American Catholic hierarchy. The bishops marked the nation's bicentennial in 1976 with an election-year call for "political responsibility" on the part of their flock. But the word "health" appeared nowhere in their three-page discussion of campaign issues, nor in the rest of the ten-page document.[42]

At their February 1977 administrative board meeting, the first since Jimmy Carter's election, Bishop Maurice Dingman of Des Moines, the chairman of the United States Catholic Conference's Committee on Health Affairs, reported "pressure ... from those in the field" for a pastoral on health care "to give a clear affirmation of the Church's role as a sponsor of health care." Dingman cited the Catholic Hospital Association, the National Conference of Diocesan Counselors of Health Affairs, and the National Association of Catholic Chaplains as the strongest advocates of such a statement. "The President is moving forward on plans for national health care," Dingman noted, "and such a pastoral would bring to the public's attention the Catholic health care program which numbers 699 hospitals and comprises about one-third of the total hospital system in the United States."[43]

Dingman's motion carried, but the bishops could not agree on what their pastoral should say. Some argued that it should focus solely on the role of Catholic hospitals, others suggested that it emphasize the importance of health care in fighting poverty, while still others urged that it address questions of medical ethics. Some wanted it to highlight national health insurance, others wanted no mention of the subject at all.[44]

While they were laboring to write their pastoral, the bishops matched President Carter's cautious campaign for national health insurance with one of their own. In October 1977 representatives of the USCC and the bishops' National Conference of Catholic Charities presented joint testimony to the Department of Health, Education, and Welfare in favor of a plan based on the assumptions that health care is a basic human right, coverage should be universal, and benefits should be comprehensive.[45]

The bishops reacted to Califano's July 1978 statement by agreeing with most of the administration's principles for a comprehensive plan but rejecting its call for "cost-sharing mechanisms such as patient deductibles that would impede access to health care." In October Msgr. Francis Lally, the secretary of the USCC's Department of Social Development and World Peace, told the Senate Subcommittee on Health that while the bishops supported the concept of comprehensive health insurance, they opposed the inclusion of contraceptive devices and abortion services in any such plan.[46] This juggling act—backing national health insurance while resisting abortion—provoked a long discussion at the USCC administrative board meeting a year later. With congressional health care plans moving from the general to the specific, the bishops clashed over the proper strategy to pursue in their quest for comprehensive coverage.

The USCC's general secretary, Bishop Thomas Kelly, presented three options for the bishops: continue to testify in favor of national health insurance and against abortion, but not take a position on any particular bill; back specific national health insurance legislation containing an abortion provision while opposing the provision; and oppose any health insurance bill that included an abortion provision.[47]

Bishop John May of Mobile argued for the first approach. Msgr. Lally, Cincinnati archbishop Joseph Bernardin, and New Orleans archbishop Philip Hannan advocated the second. Archbishop John Quinn of San Francisco, John Cardinal Krol of Philadelphia, and Bishop Norman McFarland of Reno defended the third. With the administrative board hopelessly divided, they passed the matter to their Executive Committee, which was still mulling it over a year later when Carter stood for reelection.[48]

The bishops finally finished their pastoral in 1981. "Health and Health Care" asserted that "adequate health care" was a "basic right"; any "comprehensive health system" should contain both private and public elements; public policy should include "preventive care, early intervention, and alternative delivery systems"; consumers should retain a "reasonable choice" of health care providers; "uniform standards" should govern the health care system; and a health care policy should incorporate cost control incentives. "Following on these principles," the document concluded, "we call for the development of a national health insurance program . . . that will insure a basic level of health care for all Americans." Thus did the bishops finally speak with one voice on health care, a year after the defeat of a president who largely supported their principles by a president who largely would not.[49]

Conclusions on Social Justice

Jimmy Carter waged his ideological battles with his own party on health care at the same time that the American Catholic hierarchy was often fighting its rank and file. Just as Carter and many Catholics deserved much of the credit for promoting health care reform, they also shared much of the culpability for postponing it. The president's fault in health care's failure was in deepening the rift within his party. "For Carter, as for most elected Democrats," Califano would admit, "national health insurance was more political rhetoric than potential reality, a part of the Democratic catechism more to be recited than honored."[50] Carter and his fellow Democrats, weaned on Johnsonian liberalism but reborn from the rubble of Nixon's resentment, wandered between the party's left and center, uncertain of where its real future lay. Health care perfectly embodied the Carter conundrum, with comprehensive coverage the object of the liberals and incrementalism the refuge of the centrists.

By ultimately casting his lot with his party's center on health care, Carter, in the eyes of liberals, was forsaking the people of the lower class, whom Lyndon Johnson had intended to serve and for whom Edward Kennedy purported to speak. Following a July 1978 press conference that Kennedy held "to blast us on the health care system," Carter confided in his diary that Kennedy's criticism actually helped his administration "because we've been dreading the liberal image of putting forth an expensive health care system, and Kennedy made us look responsible and conservative" in comparison. "Kennedy and [organized] labor have argued that once catastrophic coverage is passed, the demands of the middle class will be fulfilled," aides Stuart Eizenstat and Joe Onek confided to Carter in March 1979. No matter that "this argument may have had validity a decade ago. It no longer does" because "the majority of middle-class Americans now have catastrophic coverage," which is why "there is no enormous pressure for national health insurance today." To the Democratic left wing, the reality was stark: Carter was pandering to the middle class, so the poor needed a champion. Senator Kennedy would have to run for president in 1980.[51]

A similar drama was unfolding in American Catholic circles, where a more progressive power structure was losing touch with a more conservative membership. "Many people in the Catholic community, particularly ethnic Americans . . . often resent the fact that some liberal leaders have deserted them as reactionary, or prejudiced, etc.," Carter campaign aides Terry Sundy and Sister Victoria Mongiardo had warned their candidate in August 1976. "They are looking for some signs that political leaders understand their plight in an insecure economy, and their pride in their religious ethnic heritage as well." The conclusion that "urban ethnic Catholics felt that they were once again being left out of the Democratic Party" led to the belated formation of the Carter campaign's Urban Ethnic Desk in September. And it would return Msgr. Geno Baroni to the national stage.[52]

Baroni, the architect of the bishops' working-class outreach during the Nixon years, was an unofficial consultant to the Carter campaign. Though unfairly blamed for inspiring Carter's unfortunate use of the term "ethnic purity" to describe acceptable de facto residential segregation, Baroni was so successful in helping his candidate erase the doubts of urban Catholics that he became known within the campaign as "the priest who turned us around with Catholic voters." His reward was a position as Carter's assistant secretary of Housing and Urban Development. His challenge was a formidable one: to help stem white flight from the violent crime, drug trafficking, school busing, and racial diversity in the nation's cities. Thus Msgr. Baroni, one of the few Catholics around Carter, came to represent the "moderate" president.[53]

The administration's most prominent Catholic, HEW secretary Califano, would speak for the "liberal" Carter. A veteran of the Great Society, where he advised Johnson on domestic issues, Califano viewed Carter as the tribune of the underclass and argued accordingly. "Minorities have less political clout than farmers and rural Congressmen," Califano lamented, pressing for "additional health benefits to the poor."[54]

Baroni and Califano were merely reflecting the larger split among their fellow Catholics. Mary Hanna found that the closer that white Catholics lived to African-Americans, the more conservative they became on race issues. Differences between white Catholics and white northern Protestants were smallest "on the issue of minority welfare," which both groups saw as unfairly favoring the poor. Self-professed Catholic conservatives tended to be middle-aged churchgoers; Catholic liberals typically were over fifty or under thirty, and did not regularly attend church.[55] The Church hierarchy, Hanna discovered, was more liberal than the rank and file, especially those who filled the pews every Sunday. "Many 'middle Americans' feel disenfranchised, their concerns systematically shut out of the media and apparently not listened to by the government agencies," wrote James Hitchcock of the National Committee of Catholic Laymen in 1978. "Their frustration intensifies when the Church, which ought to be a voice of their discontent, seems to be merely another vehicle of expression for fashionable and elitist ideas."[56] California Republican congressman Robert Dornan was more blunt. "The majority of Catholics do not support do-good liberal positions," Dornan wrote, explaining the formation of Catholics for Christian Political Action in April 1978, "regardless of what some official Church spokespersons say."[57]

As president, Carter did much to try to overcome this divide within the American Catholic community. In 1977 he appointed a Catholic to the traditionally Protestant position of envoy to the Vatican, and he incurred the wrath of some fellow Georgia Baptists with his Catholic appointees to the Federal Communications Commission. Msgr. Baroni would trumpet the passage of the 1978 Neighborhood Self-Development and National Consumer Cooperative Bank Acts, providing grants and loans to urban ethnic organizations. *Commonweal*'s Jim Castelli remembered that over half of Irish-Americans and Italian-Americans had voted for Carter in 1976, and the Catholic Committee on Urban Ministry's Philip Murnion predicted that Carter's urban policies would influence them to do so again in 1980.[58]

If Catholic followers had some reasons to be enamored of the Carter presidency, so too did their leaders. The National Conference of Catholic Charities' executive director, Msgr. Lawrence Corcoran, said that Democrat Jimmy Carter was closer to the Church on more issues than his Republican opponent was in 1976, while Bishop Thomas Kelly would say virtually the same thing in 1980. Archbishop John Roach of Minneapolis–St. Paul gave the invocation at Carter's inauguration in January 1977. For Carter, a July 1979 meeting with religious leaders at which "Cardinal Cooke impressed me most" was the springboard for the following week's much-maligned "malaise" speech, in which the president appeared to blame Americans for the country's problems. Carter joked at the Catholic Charities convention in October 1979 that a Southern Baptist friend had noticed that he had been "spending an awful lot of time with Catholics lately," while another added, "It hasn't hurt you a bit."[59]

The health care issue had the potential to unite Catholics with their bishops as well as with their president. Mary Hanna found that three-fifths of all white Catholics believed that the government was doing too little on health care, and white Catholics were more likely than white Protestants to want the government to do more. "Given a choice," George Gallup and Jim Castelli concurred, "American Catholics would spend more for butter and less for guns."[60]

But in the end Carter could no more bring American Catholics together than he could enact health legislation. In the aftermath of Pope John Paul II's historic visit to the White House in October 1979, Carter's Irish-American aide Charles O'Keefe lamented the "unacknowledged letters to the President from the President of the National Conference of Catholic Bishops" and the "inability to discuss substantive issues and concerns with senior policy staff" at the USCC. "I don't believe we can pay so little attention to the leadership of this constituency of fifty million," said O'Keefe, "or almost one-fourth of the population."[61] Without such meaningful consultation on health care, the bishops moved further and further to the left of the administration. As early as September 1977, the USCC's Committee on Law and Public Policy argued that a bill's "explicit preservation of voluntary health care" was not necessary, but its explicit provision for the "better distribution of health care and facilities" was. As late as November 1979, Bishop May reminded the USCC administrative board to remain "adamant in their commitment to poor people" in a comprehensive health care plan.[62]

As for the other side of the Catholic divide, campaign aide Adam Walinsky had admonished Carter following the 1976 Democratic convention that underserved urban ethnic Catholics were pleading, "We need you to owe us something." Yet after serving four years in the White House, Carter's Italian-American special assistant for ethnic affairs, Stephen Aiello, regretted that "many so-called ethnics—middle-class persons . . . the majority of whom are Catholic, feel that few, if any programs developed by our party include them or address their needs." Most significantly, they still believed that they were "taxed to support these programs disproportionately."[63] Without such meaningful participation, the rank and file moved further and further to the right of the administration. In November 1980, a narrow plurality of American Catholics would cast their votes for Republican Ronald Reagan in a three-way race. The president who had sought to create Carter Catholics had instead spawned Reagan Democrats.[64]

A year before Carter's electoral defeat, the United States Catholic Conference's legislative liaison, James Robinson, had offered the president an unsolicited suggestion. If, as expected, Catholic liberal justice William Brennan retired from the Supreme Court, and if, as expected, Carter filled the vacancy with Presbyterian vice president Walter Mondale, he should make amends by appointing New York's Catholic senator, Daniel Patrick Moynihan, to the second spot on the ticket. If he became vice president, perhaps Moynihan could help bridge the yawning gaps in his party and in his church.[65]

But Brennan did not retire. Moynihan did not replace Mondale. And the national health insurance for which Carter and many Catholics had yearned remained in the waiting room.

Life and Death: Abortion

"Hopeless" is how a woman must feel when she seeks an abortion, Bishop James Rausch, representing the United States Catholic Conference, related to Georgia Democratic congressman Rev. Andrew Young, representing presidential candidate Jimmy Carter, in July 1976. "Hopeless" is also how Rausch must have felt about his fellow bishops' crusade against abortion when Young admitted that his candidate didn't know much about the issue. With the former governor "coming from a state with so few Catholics," Young said of Carter, "the need for such understanding has never held significant importance."[66]

That would begin to change the next month, when the Democratic nominee engaged the USCC's president, Archbishop Joseph Bernardin of Cincinnati, in a highly publicized conversation that exposed their rift over abortion. But below the headlines and behind the scenes, the meeting would presage four years of dialogue that, while not erasing their differences, nonetheless uncovered wide areas of agreement. For the many American Catholics opposed to abortion, most of the Carter presidency would be a time of hope, when moderation was in fashion and a middle ground seemed within reach.[67]

But the president struggled to control his party, and the bishops battled to defend the Church. By 1980, as extremists largely captured the abortion debate, there was little that Carter or the USCC could do. In many ways, the situation had become hopeless.

Despair

While he was governor of Georgia from 1971 to 1975, Jimmy Carter had penned the foreword to James Trussell and Robert Hatcher's *Women in Need* (1972), a book advocating abortion rights. He had promoted family planning services that included abortion, had backed the plaintiffs in litigation challenging the state's anti-abortion law, and had applauded the U.S. Supreme Court's legalization of abortion in *Roe v. Wade* in 1973. So there was little surprise when Carter became his party's nominee for president in 1976 that he would approve the first effectively "pro-abortion" major party platform in U.S. history.[68]

"We fully recognize the religious and ethical nature of the concerns which many Americans have on the subject of abortion," read the plank adopted by the Democrats in June 1976. "We feel, however, that it is undesirable to attempt to amend the United States Constitution to overturn the Supreme Court decision in this area." The party accepted this language over the strong objections of the nation's Catholic bishops. "Jimmy Carter and his operatives had almost complete control of the proceedings," the United States Catholic Conference's government liaison, Frank Monahan, reported from the convention in New York.[69] Archbishop Joseph Bernardin denounced the abortion plank as "irresponsible." New York's Terence Cardinal Cooke decried the implausibility of a candidate who maintains that "he's personally opposed to abortion but doesn't want to do anything about it."[70] Some Catholic critics went even further. Rev. Edward O'Donnell editorialized in the *St. Louis Review* that the abortion plank "can only offend Catholics—and who cares about them? . . . The platform makes it official. The Democrat [*sic*] Party doesn't want Catholics."[71]

The Carter campaign made matters worse. The issues coordinator, Stuart Eizenstat, asserted that Bernardin did not speak for all the bishops, that many of them were upset with him, and that some had even told him to "cool it." Chief pollster Patrick Caddell, while conceding that the abortion plank had aggravated Carter's tenuous relationship with the hierarchy, rejected the "conventional wisdom" that it had jeopardized the "Catholic vote" for his candidate. "As a Catholic," Caddell complained, "I'm offended by the idea I should be appealed to as a slogan or as a symbol of my faith. I'm an American voter first."[72] Carter denied that he had orchestrated the inclusion of the abortion language in the platform. "I did not have input personally or through my staff," the candidate insisted, "with the adoption of a particular abortion plank."[73]

The bishops responded. Archbishop Thomas Donnellan of Atlanta telephoned the campaign to deplore Eizenstat's and Caddell's "insulting" remarks. Every Catholic bishop in the country sent Carter a telegram acknowledging that Bernardin was speaking for them in his attacks on the abortion plank. And Monahan publicly released his eyewitness account of the platform committee hearings in which Carter and his lieutenants played a decisive role.[74]

While publicly refuting the bishops' version of events, the Carter campaign was privately corroborating it. Catholic campaign aides Terry Sundy and Sister Victoria Mongiardo confessed to Carter "a number of minor staff miscalculations that have contributed to a mistaken perception of a lack of concern for Catholic and/or ethnic voters and leaders." They cited "the handling of the abortion plank in the platform" and "the failure to realize that Archbishop Bernardin spoke as President of the Bishops in criticizing the abortion plank." Eizenstat followed with a public apology of sorts, maintaining that when he criticized Bernardin, he didn't realize that the archbishop was speaking for the entire USCC.[75]

Carter's August 31 meeting with Bernardin, Rausch, Cooke, John Cardinal Carberry of St. Louis, Archbishop John McGuire of New York, and Bishop James Malone of Youngstown did little to heal the rift. Though "the meeting was courteous [with] a good exchange of information," Bernardin reported, Carter would not "commit himself to supporting an amendment" to overturn *Roe v. Wade*. "We therefore continue to be disappointed with the Governor's position."[76]

Despite much hand-wringing inside and outside the Carter campaign about the Southern Baptist candidate's relations with Catholics, Carter won a majority of Catholic voters in his November election victory over Republican incumbent Gerald Ford. The role that abortion played in the election was hard to measure, though Albert Menendez tried in his 1977 book, *Religion at the Polls*. Carter's "Protestant gains . . . probably outdistanced Catholic and Jewish losses," Menendez concluded, leaving room for the reader to substitute the word "abortion" for "Protestant" and "Catholic."[77]

The news grew worse for abortion opponents after the election. In December 1976, when the Supreme Court struck down employer mandates for pregnancy benefits, the Senate rushed to pass S. 995, a bill requiring such benefits, including abortion services. In June 1977 an amendment authored by the USCC and sponsored by Missouri Catholic Democratic senator Thomas Eagleton, which would have excluded non-therapeutic abortions from the legislation, fell in a 9–4 vote in the Senate Committee on Human Resources.[78]

After the committee reported the legislation, Eagleton revived his amendment on the Senate floor, where the bill passed but the amendment failed. "I cannot stress strongly enough the consequences [that] passage of this legislation, unamended, would have for the Catholic Church," the USCC's general secretary, Bishop Thomas Kelly, argued as the measure awaited a vote in the

House of Representatives. "The Equal Employment Opportunities [sic] Commission has already stated to the Congress that H.R. 6075—the House version of S. 995—will require churches and church institutions to include abortion benefits in their medical care benefits package."[79] Despite Kelly's warning, the House Education and Labor Subcommittee on Employment Opportunities passed H.R. 6075 in February 1978 without an Eagleton-like amendment sponsored by Rhode Island Catholic Democrat Edward Beard. The full Education and Labor Committee restored the Beard amendment, 19–12, before its passage on the House floor.[80]

Though the Carter administration took no official position on the Beard amendment, the assistant director for education and women's issues, Elizabeth Abramowitz, all but dismissed it in a June letter to San Francisco archbishop John Quinn. H.R. 6075 "would not interfere with a religious institution's First Amendment rights," Abramowitz contended, "even without the amendment."[81]

The House-Senate conference report stripped the Beard amendment from the bill, replacing it with a weaker addition, sponsored by California Democratic representative Augustus Hawkins, which excluded abortion from mandatory health benefits but not from disability benefits and sick leave. After both houses of Congress passed and President Carter signed the Pregnancy Disability Benefits Act in October 1978, Bishop John May of Mobile proposed that the USCC sue to overturn the Beard-less legislation. The bishops then for the first time filed a lawsuit challenging the constitutionality of a federal statute, suing the Equal Employment Opportunity Commission and the Department of Justice on the grounds that "an element of choice must remain for an employer concerned with preserving two lives and prepared to fund an abortion only where it truly is essential to the woman's survival." A federal district judge dismissed the bishops' lawsuit in January 1980.[82]

By the end of the Carter presidency, Catholic pro-life forces had much reason to despair. About six million more abortions had occurred in the United States since Jimmy Carter took the oath of office. Not only had a constitutional amendment to undo *Roe v. Wade* not emerged from any congressional committee, but the bishops still had not agreed on what type of amendment they wanted. And despite the hierarchy's exhaustive efforts to dissuade them, a majority of American Catholics believed that abortion should continue to be legal "under certain circumstances," just as they had four years before.[83]

Hope

All was not lost, however, for the U.S. Catholic bishops and their allies. After all, when asked at a campaign rally in 1976 whether there were any circumstances under which he would support a national anti-abortion law, Carter had replied, "Yes, I suppose it is possible, though I can't think of any." The second part of his answer somehow disappeared when Iowa's *Catholic Mirror* printed the story, and he won the endorsement of pro-life Catholic priests during the Iowa caucuses. Carter attracted significant Catholic support nationwide, and he overwhelmingly defeated the lone Catholic in the race, Kennedy in-law Sargent Shriver.[84]

The Democratic platform therefore must have come as a shock to Iowa's Catholics. Though the end result opposed an anti-abortion amendment, the first draft, like 1972's final version, was silent on abortion. Only after Carter's staff was "literally mobbed by pro-abortion lobbyists," in the words of the United States Catholic Conference's Frank Monahan, did the language change. And after the revision, the candidate privately telephoned the USCC's Bishop Rausch to distance himself from the platform, winning Archbishop Bernardin's public praise for Carter's personal opposition to abortion and his contention that "it's inappropriate for the Democratic Party to seek to obstruct a change in the Constitution" that would outlaw abortion.[85]

Carter even appointed a former USCC staffer, Terry Sundy, to help lead his campaign's outreach to Catholics. Before Carter's August 1976 meeting with the bishops, Sundy encouraged the candidate to stress his resistance to the federal funding of abortion and his endorsement of active participation by religious groups in the political process. Sundy's office also helped to arrange an interview of Carter by the Italian-American magazine *I-Am*, in which the candidate reiterated that although he would not try to start an anti-abortion constitutional amendment, he wouldn't try to stop one, either.[86]

Carter's victory over Gerald Ford in November was not a complete disaster for the bishops either. "Although some have considered the outcome of the election a setback for the pro-life effort, we take a more positive approach," Cardinal Cooke told his colleagues at their meeting a week after Carter's triumph. "The Catholic presence was felt and the Democrats suffered badly from their position on abortion in the platform," a stance that their nominee had repudiated. "Although we cannot count on presidential leadership on the constitutional amendment," Cooke continued, "we should hold the President-elect to his commitments against federal funding or encouragement of permissive abortion."[87]

The bishops would hold Carter accountable, and he would largely oblige them. In May 1977 Cooke noted approvingly that "President Carter and HEW Secretary Califano have continually stated that they do not favor the use of federal funds for elective abortion through any program of National Health Insurance being proposed by the Administration." The next month, in *Beal v.*

Doe, *Maher v. Roe*, and *Poelker v. Doe*, the Supreme Court ruled on the side of the president and the bishops when it upheld Connecticut, Pennsylvania, and St. Louis, Missouri, laws prohibiting the expenditure of public funds for abortions that were not "medically necessary." Msgr. James McHugh, the executive director of the USCC's Committee for Pro-Life Activities, called the decisions "a source of encouragement to those hospitals and health care workers who have resisted becoming involved in providing abortion services against their moral and ethical convictions."[88]

The Democratic-controlled Congress followed suit in 1977 and 1978, continuing the Hyde Amendment's restrictions on Medicaid funding: paying for abortions only in the case of rape or incest, to save the life of the mother, or to protect the health of the mother in serious cases. In 1979 Congress went a step further, removing the health exception from the Hyde Amendment. The next year, under pressure from the president, it shortened the reporting period for rape from sixty days to seventy-two hours in order to prevent fraud and abuse. When asked at a February 1978 press conference whether he considered abortion to be "the taking of human life," Carter answered, "Yes, I do," while promising to tighten enforcement of the Hyde Amendment if it "is being abused by women who have not actually been raped or had a pregnancy caused by incest." The president added that Health, Education, and Welfare secretary Joseph Califano, charged with implementing the amendment, was a "devout Catholic" who shared Carter's revulsion toward abortion.[89]

To those unsettled by this mingling of church and state, Pope John Paul II's October 1979 invitation to Jimmy Carter's White House added a historic exclamation point. Pope John Paul II's "strong and repeated denunciation of permissive abortion and his passionate plea for the right to life in all stages made in the shadow of the U.S. Capitol building," *America* editorialized, "was a dramatic witness to the values American Catholics must contribute to their pluralistic society." The pope's public remonstrance provoked the president's private reflection. "I told him it was difficult for me as a politician sworn to uphold our laws," Carter wrote in his White House diary, "to live with the concept of permissive abortion." Carter would call the papal visit the "most exciting day" of his presidency.[90]

American Catholics contributed further when the Hyde Amendment came under attack in the courts. In January 1980 the United States Catholic Conference joined the Carter administration in asking the U.S. Supreme Court to reverse an Illinois district court decision that had ruled the Hyde Amendment unconstitutional.[91] The Supreme Court agreed in June in *Harris v. McRae*, narrowly upholding the Hyde Amendment. The 5–4 decision was consistent with the USCC position that "Congress has a legitimate interest in treating abortion differently from other medical procedures because it is the only procedure which involves [in the words of the Court] 'the purposeful termination of a potential life.'" And it was consistent with Carter's annual ritual of signing appropriations bills with Hyde Amendments attached, which Califano attributed to the president's "deep personal belief" in no federal funding for abortion. All this consistency overshadowed the case's grand irony: the winner was Health and Human Services (formerly HEW) secretary Patricia Roberts Harris, whose appointment to replace Califano had delighted abortion rights advocates, and the losing district court judge was John Dooling, who happened to be a Catholic.[92]

"Consistency" would also be the buzzword for Carter's reelection campaign overtures to American Catholics. In an interview with *Our Sunday Visitor*, the president asserted, "My position on abortion has been consistent throughout my public career. I am personally opposed to abortion and will do everything I can to minimize abortions in this country. I have signed legislation limiting the use of Medicaid funds for abortions."[93] Cardinal Cooke took notice, writing the president to thank him for taking so many positions on abortion that were sympathetic to those of the Church. "It is gratifying," Carter replied, "that you noted my reservations and my restatement of a consistent position regarding the serious question of abortion."[94]

Carter further endeared himself to many American Catholics by convening the White House Conference on Families, which he had promised in his first campaign. Though bickering between the Right and the Left forced the conference to relocate from Washington to regional sites in Baltimore, Minnesota, and Los Angeles, it finally convened in the summer of 1980.[95] Although the delegates did not approach a consensus on abortion, the American Catholic bishops appreciated their inclusion in the conference from start to finish, from membership on the planning committee to attendance at the proceedings. The conference dovetailed with the Church's 1980 Family Year, and the bishops issued a report on its results. "Despite disagreements at some stages in the process and at the meetings themselves," the USCC's Committee on the Conference concluded, "the top recommendations at all three meetings were in line with Catholic social teaching." Among the Catholic principles buttressed at the meetings, the committee noted, was a "respect for life."[96]

If this principle had not always been the practice in the four years of the Carter presidency, the bishops still had had much about which to be hopeful. Although Carter had kept his promise not to promote a constitutional amendment to ban abortion, he had also fulfilled his pledge not to obstruct one. With Carter on the sidelines, the USCC had adopted a four-year "master plan" to mobilize public opinion in favor of an anti-abortion addendum. Within the first year, the USCC's Committee on Pro-Life Activities had organized congressional district action committees reaching two-thirds of the members of Congress and, when combined with other right-to-life groups, touching 90 percent of congressional districts.[97]

By the bishops' count, from 1977 to 1978, support for a human life amendment on Capitol Hill increased by twenty-seven votes, and backing for a states' rights anti-abortion amendment rose by forty-three votes. In the November 1978 midterm elections, pro-life forces increased in the House by twelve votes for a human life amendment and four votes against federal abortion funding, and in the Senate by one vote for the amendment and four votes against the funding. A 1978 National Opinion Research Center poll found that although most Americans would allow abortion in cases of rape, incest, and fetal abnormality, or to save the life of the mother, most would oppose it for reasons of limiting family size, terminating an out-of-wedlock pregnancy, saving money, or providing convenience. By 1979 abortion advocates had become so defensive that they abandoned the appellation "pro-abortion" for the moniker "pro-choice."[98]

By being both "pro-choice" and "pro-life," Jimmy Carter seemed to have found a middle ground on the delicate issue of abortion. Though many American Catholics were uneasy about the first pro-choice president of the *Roe* era, they found comfort from perhaps the last pro-life Democratic president of the *Roe* era. While they had hoped to do better during his four years in the White House, they knew they could have done a lot worse.

Hysteria

Others seemed determined that the country as a whole do a lot worse. Despite the best efforts of the president and the bishops to secure a civil discourse on abortion, too many of their ostensible allies adopted a frightening rigidity, which would pollute the debate well past the Carter presidency and seemingly beyond the point of no return.

"During the recent election campaign, for the first time the abortion issue received widespread public attention and became a highly visible national issue which most political analysts have now recognized as serious and lasting," Cardinal Cooke reported to his fellow bishops in November 1976. "This is advantageous because it raises the level of public awareness regarding the 'abortion issue' and the constitutional amendment. However, it does not necessarily deepen the public understanding."[99] That was a colossal understatement. Too many of the bishops' fellow pro-lifers would poison the burgeoning public discussion of abortion. "When the United States Supreme Court legalized abortion five years ago," Lawrence Lader, the president of Abortion Rights Mobilization, complained in January 1978, "none of us who had struggled for so long about abortion rights could have predicted that this would soon polarize the nation." He cited a raid on a Norwich, Connecticut, Planned Parenthood clinic and a protest in Washington, D.C., in which the demonstrators chained themselves to the furniture in the clinic waiting room.[100]

In May 1978, a half-dozen children and adults representing Friends for Life invaded a Chicago abortion clinic, where they read a Mother's Day proclamation to a sobbing patient. In Portland, Oregon, two vanloads of parochial schoolchildren shouted "Murderers! Murderers!" at women leaving a clinic. In Anchorage, Alaska, four protesters chained themselves to a bed at a clinic. Ohio, Nebraska, and Minnesota abortion clinics went up in flames. An Arizona abortion doctor discovered gum in his office door's lock, bullet holes in his car, and poison in his dog's food.[101] Lader lamented that "the immediate losers from the rise in fanaticism are the poor" being denied access to abortion services, but "the long-term victim may be the First Amendment." *America*'s editors were more succinct. "It's hard to keep that cheery smile going," they observed, "when the other side is calling you a murderer or a Fascist."[102]

Many abortion rights proponents stopped smiling. The National Organization for Women's president, Eleanor Smeal, claiming without citation that "seventy-six percent of all Catholics support the right of women to choose a safe and legal abortion," signed a 1977 fundraising letter denouncing the "intimidation of state and national legislators" by "the Roman Catholic hierarchy and the other anti-choice forces," including "the Christian Crusade, the John Birch Society, the Ku Klux Klan, and the National States' Rights Party." Karen Mulhauser, the executive director of the National Abortion Rights Action League, made her own fundraising appeal. "With fanatical zeal and backed by hundreds of thousands of dollars," she wrote in 1977, "the so-called 'right to life' forces have made major advances in their current attack on those least able to defend themselves—the poor."[103]

The following year, Planned Parenthood Federation of America, which provided contraceptive materials and abortion services, published a booklet called "Abortion Eve." On the back cover was a familiar portrait of the Immaculate Conception of Mary, but with two glaring changes. The Virgin Mother's face was that of *Mad* magazine character Alfred E. Neuman, and the caption below the image was "What, Me Worry?"[104] When objections arose, the organization's president, Faye Wattleton, sent a letter of apology to the United States Catholic Conference president, Archbishop John Quinn of San Francisco, explaining that the publication and dissemination of the offensive material was the work of employees in Planned Parenthood's Denver and Chicago offices.

"The Board of Directors in Denver has repudiated the material; severely reprimanded the employee concerned; received an unqualified apology from the employee; and taken steps to see that such an action does not occur again," Wattleton wrote. "In Chicago . . . the staff member responsible for the material's release is no longer with the agency, but as in Denver the Directors have issued a formal repudiation of the material."[105]

Though the USCC's Russell Shaw contended that "Planned Parenthood has given different explanations of this incident at different times," USCC's general secretary, Bishop Thomas Kelly, accepted Wattleton's apology on behalf of Archbishop Quinn. The bishops "are deeply concerned about the growing incidence of anti-Catholicism in the context of the abortion controversy," Kelly wrote, but they are "pleased to learn that Planned Parenthood will work to discourage religious bias of any kind in the future."[106]

Or at least until the next presidential election. In November 1980 Wattleton sent a fundraising letter urging her members to "stand up and be counted with us to stop the zealous minority who wish to impose their dogmatic will upon us all."[107]

Conclusions on Life and Death

The leader of the country and the leaders of the Church were models of restraint as extremists threatened to wrest control of the abortion debate. They were civil in broaching and constructive in bridging their substantial differences over the issue.

The president and the bishops nevertheless were not blameless in the widening of the chasm over abortion. Carter enraged the bishops with his August 1978 appointment of Sarah Weddington, a prominent member of the National Abortion Rights Action League and plaintiff's attorney in the *Roe v. Wade* case, as his special liaison on women's issues. When Bishop Thomas Kelly wrote a letter of protest to Carter on behalf of the USCC administrative board, he received no reply from the president.[108]

White House staffer James Gammill responded instead with a form letter addressed to "Mr. Kelly," infuriating *Our Sunday Visitor* columnist Dale Francis. "I reach a circulation of more than one million with the papers that carry my syndicated column," Francis wrote to White House aide Walter Wurfel. "If I reported this story I could create outrage among many Catholics." But Francis would not report the story, and Carter would not remove Weddington.[109]

If Weddington's appointment alienated many Catholics, Carter's White House Conference on Families disillusioned others with its underrepresentation of the pro-life point of view. In July 1980, while the conference was meeting in Los Angeles, seven thousand people were gathering in Long Beach to endorse a human life amendment and a Senate investigation into the delegate selection process for the conference to which they were not invited.[110]

Carter provoked those on the other side of the divide as well. The White House rescinded its invitation to a December 1979 meeting of women's groups to National Organization for Women president Eleanor Smeal when her group's political action committee passed a resolution denouncing the administration's support for the Hyde Amendment. While Carter and Weddington presided over the meeting inside the White House, NOW picketed outside in the rain.[111]

NOW came in from the rain, however, long enough to help shape the Democratic Party platform and influence the Carter administration in June 1980. Although the organization's Judith Lonnquist introduced decidedly more pro-choice language than the party had adopted in 1976, the USCC's Frank Monahan reported, the resulting majority report retained the disclaimer that "we fully recognize the religious and ethical concerns which many Americans have on the subject of abortion." But the platform replaced 1976's relatively mild resistance to an anti-abortion constitutional amendment with unbridled opposition: "The Democratic Party supports the Supreme Court decisions on abortion rights as the law of the land and opposes any constitutional amendment to restrict or overturn those decisions." Monahan noted that "a member of the White House staff informed us that this language was worked out with the knowledge and approval of the White House staff."[112]

But Lonnquist was not finished, and the Carter administration was not done capitulating. A subcommittee presented a draft plank that said, "The Democratic Party recognizes the work of the White House Conference on Families and supports its efforts to make federal programs more sensitive to the needs of families." Lonnquist objected, contending that "the looney right-wing led by Phyllis you-know-who [Schlafly, the Catholic founder of the right-wing Eagle Forum]" had dominated the conference. She introduced a substitute plank, making no mention of the conference and expanding the definition of "family" beyond its traditional parameters. The new statement, "The Democratic Party supports efforts to make federal programs more sensitive to the needs of the family, in all its diverse forms," would become part of the platform over the protests of Catholics whom, in Monahan's words, "the Administration had begged and cajoled" to join the conference.

Gloria Steinem then proposed a section on "privacy," which contained the following language: "The Democratic Party recognizes reproductive freedom as a fundamental human right. We therefore oppose government interference in the reproductive decisions of Americans, especially those government programs or legislative restrictions that deny poor Americans their right to privacy by funding or advocating one or a limited number of reproductive choices only." Though the Carter representatives managed to squelch this rebuke to the president's support for the Hyde Amendment in the subcommittee, it gained enough votes to become a minority report, which the full subcommittee subsequently adopted as part of the platform.

As he had in 1976, Carter separated himself from his party's abortion planks. But the inability of an incumbent to rein in his convention on such a highly visible subject delivered almost as potent a message as if he had simply endorsed the platform. "Some individuals in the right-to-life movement," the National Catholic News Service noted in its interview of Carter on the eve of the 1980 election, "say you have not disassociated yourself strongly enough from the Democratic platform's call for federal funding of abortion."[113]

Just as the president was having trouble controlling his left flank, the bishops were encountering difficulty with theirs. "It would be more naïve to believe that as a result of his meeting with the [USCC] Executive Committee," liberal Bishop Rausch wrote in September 1976, "Mr. Carter will emerge having adopted our position [on abortion] lock, stock, and barrel." Two weeks later, in what American Catholic historian John Tracy Ellis called an "utterly unprecedented" action, the National Coalition of American Nuns, an organization of 1,200 sisters committed to social justice, went "lock, stock, and barrel" in the other direction, endorsing Carter for president. "Abortion," NCAN's president, Sister Dorothy Donnelly, explained, was a "red flag issue . . . which deprives people of their thinking process."[114]

If they thought more deeply, Catholic liberal journalist Colman McCarthy argued in a September 1976 column endorsing Carter, the bishops would abandon their opposition to birth control, which offered the most promising alternative to abortion. And they would recognize that a Catholic "can in perfectly good conscience oppose abortion on moral grounds and yet think a constitutional amendment on the subject a bad idea," *Commonweal* editorialized later that month, "which indeed is Mr. Carter's position." It was also the position of the Leadership Conference of Women Religious in August 1977, when it distinguished "between the ideal and the feasible," placing an antiabortion amendment in the former category.[115]

The bishops tried not to succumb to the dissension on their left. They refused to endorse Carter, with Archbishop Bernardin maintaining that they were "absolutely neutral" in the 1976 campaign, as in all campaigns. They refused to question the Church's proscription of artificial contraception, asserting at their spring meeting in 1980 that rather than undermine their arguments against abortion, the papal encyclicals *Populorum Progressio* (1967) and *Humanae Vitae* (1968) demonstrated "the coherence of Catholic teaching on social justice and the transmission of human life."[116] And they refused to give up on an anti-abortion constitutional amendment. An October 1977 meeting between the Leadership Conference of Women Religious and the United States Catholic Conference was "pleasant and cordial," Terence Cardinal Cooke reported, "but it became clear that the LCWR did not agree with the [USCC's] Pastoral Plan for Pro-Life Activities," and Cooke saw "no value in engaging in an ongoing debate with the group."[117]

By the end of the Carter era, however, the bishops had joined the president in largely caving to the critics on their left. "The bishops, widely accused of tilting toward Ford on the abortion issue in 1976, were intentionally quiet as a body this year," Jim Castelli wrote in *Commonweal* in the wake of the 1980 election. "There were no meetings with the candidates and only one token denunciation of the Democratic plank favoring legal abortion" and no celebrating of the Republican platform's support for a human life amendment.[118]

So the president and the bishops braced themselves for a backlash from their right. In 1976 televangelist Rev. Pat Robertson and a majority of his fellow evangelical Christians helped to elect one of their own as president. By 1979, however, Baptist minister Rev. Jerry Falwell and Christian educator Robert Billings had founded the Moral Majority, a political action committee of the religious Right. Due in large part to his stance on abortion and other "social issues," Jimmy Carter was not the choice of the religious Right in 1980.[119]

The bishops expressed misgivings about this mostly Protestant movement, despite its affinity with them on abortion. While conceding that "we need all the American citizen support we can get," Cardinal Cooke acknowledged to his fellow bishops in the aftermath of the November 1980 election that "the question is raised about maintaining contacts on particular issues with organizations whose full agenda does not coincide with our own." Cooke argued that while the bishops should welcome religious conservatives into the pro-life fold, they should not forsake their own participation in the "non-sectarian, bi-partisan" effort whose "primary focus" was an anti-abortion amendment.[120]

At the National Conference of Catholic Charities convention in October 1976, John Cardinal Dearden of Detroit had predicted that "one religious group cannot determine public consensus," but groups or individuals "with a religious vision" can "influence the course of society." By 1980, Dearden's prophecies had come true. The public consensus on abortion, which the religious president largely achieved and the political bishops largely accepted, had almost completely crumbled. And as the extremists on both sides poisoned the debate, the course of society would never be the same.[121]

As a self-styled moderate former governor from the New South, President Jimmy Carter pursued the elusive center in American politics. On nuclear weapons, he offered arms limitation, but not arms reduction. On health care, he proposed universal coverage, but only after cost containment. On abortion, he supported *Roe v. Wade* and the Hyde Amendment at the same time. Yet due in part to an American Catholic community divided between increasingly liberal leaders and ever more conservative followers, he shelved SALT II and health care reform. And just as he and American Catholics approached the middle on abortion, representatives from both extremes began to pull them apart.

CHAPTER SIX

Catholics and Ronald Reagan
(1981–1989)

IN SOME WAYS the American Catholic bishops never had it better than during the presidency of Ronald Reagan. After a long struggle to have their social pronouncements taken seriously by politicians, pundits, and scholars, they would produce two pastorals within three years that garnered unprecedented attention and widespread respect. After dealing with three presidents who wanted little to do with overturning *Roe v. Wade*, they welcomed a president who seemed determined to do so. But only in the arena of war and peace would the bishops register much of an impact on the Reagan administration. They, along with the pope, greatly contributed to the administration's stunning metamorphosis from developing to destroying nuclear weapons. But their statist cures for the nation's economic ills failed to win over many of the members of their church, and their campaign to amend the Constitution to outlaw abortion failed to win over the president beyond familiar words and fitful actions.

War and Peace: Nuclear War

Historians make better detectives than psychiatrists. Recording what someone did and when and where he did it has always been easier than dissecting how and why he did it. No matter how many clues a historian uncovers, trying to piece them together is often haphazard at best. Historians know that President Ronald Reagan played a role—some would say a large role—in decelerating the arms race and accelerating the fall of the Soviet Union. Yet the degree to which he intended either continues to perplex even the most astute observers. As the "evil empire" began its descent to the "ash heap of history" at the close of his presidency, Reagan was quick to say, "I told you so."[1]

But had he? Was Reagan's celebrated first-term arms build-up, followed by a "build-down" in his second term, an example of brilliant choreography or dumb luck? Would the Soviet Union have fallen regardless of who was in the White House, even an eager-to-appease dove?

Many American Catholics thought so—before, during, and after the Reagan era. Led by their bishops, these Catholics gave Reagan little credit and lots of grief. But most Catholics joined other Americans in giving him the lion's share of their votes. This Catholic majority would then greet the unprecedented and largely unforeseen denouement of the Cold War as a long-expected guest. By effectively questioning the president's conduct of the Cold War, however, the bishops and their supporters had a lot to do with its conclusion. American Catholics may have been unsure if Ronald Reagan won the Cold War. But thanks in part to their bishops' persistent, public, and productive pressure on the president, they were certain that God did.

Reagan's First Term

"War is the work of man. War is the destruction of human life, war is death," Pope John Paul II lamented in Hiroshima, Japan, in February 1981. Recalling the atomic destruction that had engulfed that city thirty-five years earlier, the pontiff declared that "humanity must make a moral about-face.... From now on, it is only through a conscious choice and through a deliberate policy that man can survive."[2]

But the administration of President Ronald Reagan seemed in no hurry to conclude the nuclear era. In May at the University of Notre Dame, the president predicted the ultimate defeat of Soviet communism.[3] Worried about the "arms build-up initiated by the Carter Administration and now enthusiastically pursued by the Reagan Administration," as well as Reagan's "cautious approach to strategic arms negotiations with the Soviet Union," reported the United States Catholic Conference's secretary of public affairs, Russell Shaw, the nation's Catholic bishops in November 1980 had appointed a special committee chaired by Archbishop Joseph Bernardin of Cincinnati to study "questions of war and peace." Writing in *America* in July 1981, the Georgetown University theologian Rev. Francis Winters encouraged his fellow Catholics to join in the bishops' effort. "If we ignore the voice of the bishops, we shall see a sign in the sky," Winters admonished. "It will be the cloud seen over Hiroshima."[4]

Reagan unveiled his first arms control initiatives in November. He called for talks on intermediate nuclear forces (INF) in Europe with the goal of their abolition, the so-called zero option. He also proposed negotiations on intercontinental nuclear weapons. Unlike SALT I and SALT II, which merely aimed to limit the construction of new weapons, these Strategic Arms Reduction Talks (START) would actually seek to reduce the two superpowers' nuclear arsenals.[5]

Reagan sent a copy of his arms control proposals to Pope John Paul II, assuring the Holy Father that "no one shares your hope for a productive outcome more than myself." The pope replied, in a letter to both Reagan and Soviet premier Leonid Brezhnev, with his hope that the INF talks commencing in Geneva would "not pass without achieving results." He also urged them to receive a delegation from the Pontifical Academy of Sciences, which would soon be issuing a report on the catastrophic consequences of nuclear war.[6]

The bishops nevertheless proceeded with their study. While granting Reagan's point that "the enormous build-up of nuclear and conventional arms pursued by the Soviet Union in recent years has done more than its share to heighten the peril of the present moment," Archbishop Bernardin defended his committee's focus on their country. "If we direct our attention particularly to the United States," Bernardin explained to his fellow bishops at their November 1981 meeting, "it is for the simple reason that we are American citizens and have a right and duty to address our government."[7] The representatives of the Pontifical Academy of Sciences, most of whom were neither American nor Catholic, presented their report to President Reagan at the White House in December. In a nuclear war, the group's spokesman, Victor Weisskopf, told the president, "the conditions of life following a nuclear attack would be so severe that the only hope for humanity is prevention of any form of nuclear war."[8]

Reagan concurred with his guests on the imperative of avoiding nuclear war. He heeded the counsel of his secretary of state, however, and added that only by correcting the strategic imbalance with the Soviet Union could his country help ensure such an outcome. He cited the book of Revelation (16:16–21), which portrays the end of the world. Then he dismissed the scientists, only fifteen minutes after they arrived and without even asking them to sit down.

Even the pope was preaching toughness toward the Soviets. John Paul II's January 1982 reply to two letters from President Reagan regarding the imposition of martial law in the Soviet satellite of Poland included an endorsement of U.S. sanctions against his native country's communist regime. "The Pope's letter," Reagan's staunchly anti-communist Catholic national security advisor, William Clark, wrote to the president, "makes it clear that," at least in Poland, "he supports our policies and shares our goals."[9]

Both sides of the argument over the arms race received a hearing at the Bernardin committee's January 1982 meeting. While conceding that the North Atlantic Treaty Organization's four-decade reliance on nuclear weapons was of "dubious morality," James Schlesinger, Gerald Ford's secretary of defense and Jimmy Carter's secretary of energy, told the bishops that these "strategies have worked well to this point." Schlesinger conveyed his unsuccessful attempt as secretary of defense to modify U.S. policy toward the Soviet Union from "mutual assured destruction," which would spare no civilians, to "city avoidance," which would have honored the Catholic just-war principle of "proportionality." The problem with adopting such a "reasonable" policy, committee staffer Rev. Bryan Hehir objected, was that it could increase, rather than decrease, the likelihood of the use of nuclear weapons.

Gerard Smith, who had helped negotiate the first Strategic Arms Limitation Treaty for Richard Nixon and had served as ambassador-at-large for nonproliferation for Jimmy Carter, followed Schlesinger's testimony with a determined defense of deterrence. Though he criticized the Reagan arms escalation as excessive, Smith urged the committee to eschew "absolute" opposition to nuclear weapons. "Bless me, Father, I have sinned," he imagined a Catholic confessing if such an approach were promoted by the bishops. "I was in a B-52 yesterday." Auxiliary Bishop Thomas Gumbleton of Detroit argued that incrementalism had brought the world to its current precarious condition. "Something has to stop us," the bishop pleaded. "We are lemmings en route to the sea." He worried that the committee's discussions were occurring within the "old framework" and were missing the "whole new attitude" that chairman Bernardin had suggested.[10]

In March Archbishop Raymond Hunthausen of Seattle condemned the U.S. Navy's decision to build a Trident nuclear submarine base in nearby Bangor, Washington. "One Trident submarine," the archbishop complained, "has the destructive equivalent of 2040 Hiroshima bombs."[11] In the same month, Bishop Francis Quinn of Sacramento urged a resumption of U.S. arms control talks with the Soviet Union, which had been stalled since the December 1979 Soviet invasion of Afghanistan, and the institution of a "multilateral freeze" by all the world's nuclear powers on the development of those weapons. Noting that "the explosive force of the stockpile of nuclear weapons our country alone has now is equivalent to 615,000 times the explosive force of the Hiroshima bomb," Quinn warned that "a nation has used atomic warheads, and there is no guarantee that some nation will not use them again."[12]

Reagan's secretary of the navy, John Lehman, denounced Hunthausen's "extremist political views" as a "deeply immoral . . . use . . . of sacred religious office." Since the United States was the primary peacemaker in the world and the staunchest defender of the "Western Judeo-Christian civilization," the Catholic secretary concluded, it was only appropriate that the Trident submarine to be based in Hunthausen's archdiocese be named "Corpus Christi."[13]

In May the Bernardin committee invited Secretary of State Alexander Haig, Secretary of Defense Caspar Weinberger, and the director of the Arms Control and Disarmament Agency, Eugene Rostow, to present their side of the nuclear story. Reminding the committee that "the United States has forsworn the use or possession of biological weapons" and "maintains a chemical warfare capacity only to the degree necessary to deter the use of chemical weapons by a potential aggressor," Haig asserted that U.S. policy was to avert, not ignite, a confrontation with the Soviet Union. Denying that the United States was seeking military supremacy over the Soviets, and claiming that deterrence had been successful, Weinberger said that "we don't believe there is a winner in a nuclear war" with the Soviets, though "they do." Allowing that nuclear proliferation was a "much greater problem" than he had anticipated when he joined the administration, Rostow contended that the nuclear option was vital as the "ultimate weapon of self-defense."[14]

"Very depressing," Bishop Gumbleton wrote in his notes on the meeting. "Unless in some miraculous way we discover a way to have no war in the world," he forecast, "these weapons will be used." Sixteen months into the Reagan administration, and five months after the Schlesinger and Smith testimony, Gumbleton was still complaining that he had heard "no *new* thinking."[15]

If nothing new was emerging from the bishops' committee, the same was not true on Capitol Hill, where 128 congressional representatives signed a resolution proposing a bilateral U.S.-U.S.S.R. "nuclear freeze." Catholic Democrat Edward Markey of Massachusetts introduced the resolution in March 1982. "Across the country," Markey observed, "religious leaders" were among those "organizing to demand a halt to the nuclear arms race." Over half of the nation's 350 Catholic bishops would soon be among those religious leaders.[16]

The administration, however, firmly rejected any hint of a nuclear freeze. Lawrence Eagleburger, Reagan's undersecretary of state for political affairs, told Archbishop Bernardin in June that "a freeze would lock in a Soviet advantage in two critical areas: land-based intercontinental ballistic missiles—the most destabilizing of the nuclear weapons—and intermediate range nuclear weapons."[17]

President Reagan and Pope John Paul II met for the first time in Rome in June 1982. Reagan called his first presidential trip to Europe a "pilgrimage for peace," with the goal of "offering new opportunities for realistic negotiations with those who may not share the values and the spirit we cherish." The pope replied that his "greatest preoccupation is for the peace of the world." He defined *peace* as "not only the absence of war" but the presence of "reciprocal trust between nations . . . manifested and proved through constructive negotiations that aim at ending the arms race." As if to emphasize that their common quest for peace was not about them, neither leader mentioned the previous year's assassination attempts that had almost cost them their lives.[18]

Four days later the Vatican's secretary of state, Agostino Casaroli, read a message from John Paul II to the United Nations' Second Special Session on Disarmament. In words that must have heartened Reagan, the pope reserved a place in the "teaching of the Catholic Church" for the "independence, freedom, and legitimate security of each and every nation." Though not an end in itself, the pontiff added that "under present conditions a discussion based on equilibrium" was a "morally acceptable" means to "progressive disarmament." Like Reagan, the pope seemed to be embracing détente and deterrence at the same time. In words that Bishop Gumbleton underlined on his copy of the speech, John Paul II quoted the warning of Pope Paul VI that "the logic underlying the request for the balance of power impels each of the adversaries to seek a certain measure of superiority, for fear of being left at a disadvantage." He judged the status quo, in which "the nations of the world are already overarmed" as "wrong," and called for a "freshness of perspective" in addressing the arms race. Like Gumbleton and Bernardin, the pope seemed to be rejecting the old ways of doing business between the Americans and the Soviets.[19]

Reagan nonetheless clung to the old ways. Speaking to the UN a week later, the American president repeated his pledge to Pope John Paul II to do "everything possible for peace and arms reduction" but warned that "such a peace would be a terrible hoax if the world were no longer blessed with freedom and human rights."[20]

The First Draft of the Peace Pastoral

If Reagan appeared to be precluding a middle ground on arms control, so too did the U.S. Catholic bishops. A few days after the president's UN address, Archbishop Bernardin released the first draft of his committee's statement on nuclear war. The document, "God's Hope in a Time of Fear," held that attacks on civilians and first strikes were never acceptable, that the threat to deploy nuclear weapons must contemplate neither attacks on civilians nor a first strike, that only limited use of nuclear weapons was justifiable, that possession of nuclear weapons was just only if the above conditions were met, and that such possession was moral only if accompanied by a serious commitment to arms reduction.[21]

The draft predictably unleashed a torrent of criticism from the administration and its allies. National security advisor William Clark complained that the document failed to credit President Reagan for his ongoing efforts toward disarmament. He maintained that the administration's "flexible response" approach, which did not rule out a first strike, had "kept the peace in Europe for over thirty years."[22] Archbishop Philip Hannan of New Orleans found his colleagues' document rife with contradictions, on the one hand seeming to rule out a first strike but on the other narrowly ruling it in. He found it imbalanced, blaming the United States but not the Soviet Union. He found it hasty, a rush to judgment in the midst of arms reduction talks. Rather than listen to his fellow bishops, Hannan urged Catholics to heed their pope, whose speech at the UN was "much more realistic, magisterial, better written, and much shorter."[23]

The administration clearly had work to do in making its case to the public. The Departments of State and Defense as well as the Arms Control and Disarmament Agency mounted a media blitz and outreach aimed at "religious, ethnic, veterans, women, and other interest groups." Clark observed that the special advisor to the president and to the secretary of state for arms control matters, Edward Rowny, would be "particularly suited for events in Wisconsin, where he is certain to have rapport with Roman Catholic and Polish segments" in influencing the state's September vote on a nuclear freeze.[24]

The president himself launched the offensive. In a major arms control address to the Knights of Columbus in Hartford, Connecticut, in August, Reagan implored the conservative Catholic organization to reject the nuclear freeze. In a meeting with Vatican secretary of state Casaroli on the day of the speech, Reagan reiterated his commitment to arms reduction and his resistance to a freeze, which would merely reward Soviet misbehavior.[25]

Two weeks after Bernardin became the archbishop of Chicago, Secretary of Defense Caspar Weinberger joined the administration campaign with his response to the pastoral letter's first draft. Quoting John Paul II's UN address, the secretary argued for the administration's "morally acceptable" deterrent over the Bernardin committee's "marginally justifiable" version, which he considered a "dangerous departure" from tradition. In October the White House nuclear policy group, chaired by Robert MacFarlane of the National Security Council, suggested that the administration "mobilize some of our political types . . . to educate the bishops" on nuclear war.[26]

"The Reagan Administration is trying to influence the work on the bishops' pastoral letter on War and Peace," a worried "group of uptown Catholics" from Chicago wrote to their new archbishop. Bernardin assured them that "in no way has the Committee become entrapped by the Administration or any other group."[27]

The Second Draft of the Peace Pastoral

That became clear a week later, with the October 1982 release of the second draft of the pastoral, retitled "The Challenge of Peace: God's Promise and Our Response." Although it explicitly repudiated unilateral disarmament, it even more strongly than before found no moral basis for nuclear war. A limited use of nuclear weapons, which the Bernardin committee again concluded was conceivable in the abstract, would undoubtedly lead to unlimited death and destruction. Any first use of nuclear weapons was therefore morally unacceptable. The second draft also criticized the administration's support for the "missile experimental" (MX) as a policy because it could "invite attack," and denounced the administration's adherence to the doctrine of "mutual assured destruction," because it targeted civilians. And just as the Reagan administration had feared, the committee implicitly endorsed an immediate, bilateral, and verifiable freeze on "the testing, production, and deployment of new strategic systems."[28]

The new document gained the support of liberal Minneapolis–St. Paul archbishop John Roach, the president of the United States Catholic Conference, who termed any use of nuclear weapons "absolutely, unequivocally immoral." And it also enlisted the backing of conservative John Cardinal Krol of Philadelphia, a former president of the USCC, who asked, "How many times can we be killed? Why should we be spending money to make a bigger hole in the earth?"[29] Krol's endorsement came not only in the wake of the imposition of martial law by the Soviet-backed government of his ancestral Poland, but in the face of the Polish pope's more moderate approval of nuclear deterrence at the UN a year earlier. Though the second draft added the papal language on deterrence, the document framed it as "strictly conditioned," a nuanced reading not shared by Archbishop Hannan, who repeated his call to replace what the committee thought the pope said with all of what the pope actually said.[30]

The Reagan administration also read the pope's words differently from the Bernardin committee. In a press conference two days after the issuance of the second draft, Weinberger interpreted John Paul II's message as indicating that "deterrence is a moral policy." Reagan dispatched roving ambassador Vernon Walters, a Catholic, to the Vatican to encourage the pope to remind the bishops what he really meant.[31]

To nuclear freeze proponents, however, such contentions smacked of desperation, as the midterm elections brought far-reaching victories for the nuclear freeze and the Democratic Party. Freeze supporters could take credit for winning referenda in eight of nine states, while the Democrats gained twenty-five seats on Capitol Hill. Though the fear that led most voters to choose the Democrats was probably more about impending unemployment in a recession than imminent death in a nuclear war, the freeze gave many another reason to rebuke the party in power.[32]

The bishops held their own election a week later at their November meeting. Even before over three hours of discussion, 195 bishops pronounced themselves "basically in agreement" with the second draft of the pastoral, while 71 had "major reservations," and only 12 were in "basic disagreement" with it. A Gallup Poll at the end of the year found American Catholics almost evenly split over the nuclear freeze their bishops were implicitly endorsing.[33]

The Third Draft of the Peace Pastoral

To win over those Catholics whom they had not yet persuaded, the bishops returned to rewriting their document, and the Reagan administration reverted to trying to reshape it. Even though the bishops turned down requests by Secretary of State George Shultz to address their November meeting and by President Reagan to receive a delegation from the gathering, they again invited administration input into the pastoral. So Reagan assigned the State Department's Office of Political and Military Affairs to negotiate with the Bernardin committee.[34]

National security advisor William Clark again weighed in, in a letter to Archbishop Bernardin. Clark applauded the committee's inclusion of Pope John Paul II's remarks at the UN permitting deterrence and precluding unilateral disarmament. Clark praised the document's search for "alternative approaches to current nuclear arsenals and strategies." But the nuclear freeze that the committee apparently espoused would "remove incentives for achieving reductions."[35] A bipartisan cohort of two dozen Catholic congressional representatives, led by Republican Henry Hyde of Illinois, also wrote to Bernardin. They asserted that the second draft downplayed the insidiousness of the Soviet ideology, underestimated the worth of deterrence, overlooked the shift in U.S. defense strategy away from targeting Soviet cities, undersold previous and current U.S. arms control efforts, and underemphasized the values for which Americans must sometimes fight.[36]

Displeasure with the second draft spread from the American government to the European Church. The Catholic hierarchies of France and West Germany attacked the document for renouncing the North Atlantic Treaty Organization's nuclear shield, which had protected the continent for almost four decades. But the Bernardin committee held its ground.[37]

Then, the president replied to *his* critics. In his first major arms control message, Reagan lamented in November 1982 that in the previous two decades, the number of American intercontinental missiles and bombers declined while the Soviets gained nuclear superiority. He therefore pledged to pursue arms reduction, but only in tandem with a meaningful nuclear deterrent.[38] "The nuclear freeze movement is one that is rapidly growing among the American public and is of particular interest to some of our major constituent groups, e.g. Catholic," White House aide Elizabeth Dole wrote to chief of staff James Baker following the Reagan speech. "We need a central focus here at the

White House to coordinate all activities related to the freeze issue so that it can be dealt with most effectively."[39]

Meanwhile, the administration continued to focus on the bishops. When Archbishop Hannan debated Bishop Gumbleton on the pastoral in *U.S. News and World Report* in December, White House aide Sharon Fairbanks entreated the administration "to show him our support for the role he is playing . . . [and] to give him the recognition he deserves."[40]

"Do not believe them! Do not trust them!" Rev. John Kmech, a Chicago priest and former prisoner in a Siberian concentration camp, warned Reagan about the Soviets in a December 1982 letter, before apologizing for "the silly ramblings of the bishops." Reagan responded, "If only more people, and yes, if the Bishops could hear and heed the words of someone like yourself who knows firsthand the Godless tyranny of Soviet totalitarianism."[41]

Pope John Paul II continued to rise above the rift between the president and the bishops. As if to acknowledge their common goal, the pontiff's World Day of Peace address, delivered December 20, noted approvingly that "peace has become . . . a major preoccupation not only for those responsible for the destiny of nations," like the president, "but even more so for the broad sections of the population," like the bishops. Yet he also recognized their common failure. "The scandal of the arms race," the Holy Father proclaimed, "only underlines the urgency for world society to equip itself with effective means of negotiations."[42]

Secretary of Defense Weinberger met with Washington, D.C., archbishop James Hickey. Weinberger reiterated his concerns about the Bernardin committee's renunciation of first use and discouragement of deterrence. Hickey, though not a member of the committee, nonetheless defended his fellow bishops for raising the "moral" issue of nuclear weapons. The meeting concluded, however, on a rare point of agreement—John Paul II's renunciation of war only two days earlier.[43]

Then the committee began to backpedal. On the day after the Reagan administration extended diplomatic recognition to the Vatican in Washington, Bernardin; the USCC's president, Archbishop John Roach of Minneapolis–St. Paul; and its general secretary, Msgr. Daniel Hoye, were meeting with European bishops and the papal secretary of state, Agostino Casaroli, in the Vatican. While Bernardin and Roach conceded that a "no first use" policy would require a change in NATO strategy, and that inclusion of the pope's statement on deterrence in the pastoral was "absolutely necessary," the American bishops said they would ultimately write their own document regardless of the European prelates' views.[44]

That was before Bernardin met the pope. In a meeting that included Casaroli; the prefect of the Congregation of Church Doctrine, Joseph Cardinal Ratzinger; and Pope John Paul II during the week following Bernardin's installation as cardinal, the pope sounded a lot like Ronald Reagan. "Nations have not only the right but the obligation to defend themselves," the pope told Bernardin. He acknowledged the need for "both superpowers to work on disarmament," but "the approach must be bilateral [and] mutually verifiable." Since "the Soviets do not subscribe to the same moral principles" as the American bishops, the Bernardin committee "may have some impact" on their own country "but not necessarily on the Soviet Union." To avoid further juxtaposition of one against the other by critics of the Bernardin committee, the pope recommended that the pastoral separate the doctrinal from the empirical. While "the Holy Father did not ask that the thrust of the Pastoral be changed," Bernardin concluded, he did request that "we keep in mind the points he had made."[45]

The next day, the new cardinal promised Ratzinger and Casaroli that his committee would try to portray the Reagan administration's policies accurately in the next version of the letter. "But I explained that we could not approve of every dimension of their strategy," Bernardin observed. "I could not envision the Government's being totally pleased with our document no matter how the final nuancing turns out."[46]

Nor would the pope be entirely pleased. In a front-page story in the February 11 *National Catholic Reporter*, Patricia Scharber Lefevere reported that in his meeting with the European and American bishops, Casaroli had given the "green light" to the Americans "to go beyond papal statements when making their national declarations on war and peace." It was one thing for the bishops to confront their president. It was quite another for the bishops to defy their pope. So the USCC scrambled to correct the record. The general secretary, Msgr. Daniel Hoye, without naming Lefevere or the *National Catholic Reporter*, blasted "inaccurate reports" of the meeting that he had attended.[47]

Cardinal Bernardin followed with a statement to Jerry Filteau of the National Catholic News Service, which attempted to correct "the impression given in some press accounts" of a meeting at which he also was present. "It is only natural that [papal] teaching must be applied to the concrete situations as they exist in various parts of the world," said Bernardin. In making such applications, "there is room for flexibility," Bernardin explained. "However, when practical, contingent judgments are made, it is important that they be clearly labeled as such. Moreover, every effort must be made to see that the Church's basic moral teaching is applied logically and correctly."[48]

Asked why an archbishop had felt compelled to comment publicly on a news report, the USCC's public affairs secretary, Russell Shaw, responded, "When a story like this puts inflammatory observations in the mouth of the Cardinal Secretary of State, it is the obligation of this Conference to point out that these things were not said by Casaroli." Undaunted by the attacks by Hoye, Bernardin, and Shaw on his newspaper's credibility, *National Catholic Reporter* publisher Jason Petosa stood by the story.[49]

Cardinal Casaroli did not. "When dealing with moral questions which are still being discussed among theologians can, and up to what point, the Bishops' teaching take an (authoritative) position?" the cardinal asked, according to the official transcript of the meeting, recorded by Rev. Ian Scholte, the secretary of the Pontifical Commission on Justice and Peace, and sent to all the American bishops. "Here is the question of magisterial responsibility—and the faculty—of individual Bishops and of Episcopal conferences (where there easily can be majorities and minorities also on points of doctrine) or at least in the application of principles accepted by all to concrete cases or situations."[50]

Though something less than the "green light" to encourage dissent within the Church that Lefevere had identified, Casaroli's words did appear to allow more "wiggle room" for the bishops than Hoye, Bernardin, and Shaw were willing to acknowledge. So the *National Catholic Reporter* story actually did the bishops a favor, offering them a pretext for publicly allying themselves with a pope who had privately separated himself from their pastoral.

And the pontiff would continue to separate himself. A confidential memorandum from Pio Laghi, the pope's apostolic delegate to the United States, speaking for Cardinal Ratzinger and other "highly placed authorities of the Holy See," urged the Bernardin committee to distinguish between mandatory Church teaching and the bishops' non-binding "opinions," to avoid the implication that pacifism is such a teaching.[51]

As the bishops struggled to keep their differences with the pope private, their dispute with the president was becoming even more public. In March, Reagan unveiled his Strategic Defense Initiative, a laser-based missile defense system that would take at least a decade to build and perhaps a trillion dollars to fund. Cardinal Bernardin joined the critics of the "Star Wars" program, pronouncing himself "very skeptical" of SDI's "consequences on the arms race."[52]

But the third draft of the pastoral, released in April 1983, was decidedly more friendly to the Reagan administration. As the European bishops and the pope had urged, the Bernardin committee issued a document that was clearer in its distinction between the teachings of the Church and the opinions of the bishops. As the White House had urged, the committee condemned Soviet repression and accepted the administration's disavowal of civilian targeting. The committee's most conservative member, Scranton bishop John O'Connor, had threatened to resign if his colleagues did not adopt these changes.[53]

Whereas the second draft had prodded the administration "to halt the testing, production, and deployment of new strategic systems," widely interpreted as endorsing a nuclear freeze, the third draft called upon the administration "to curb the testing, production, and deployment of new nuclear systems," widely interpreted as rejecting a nuclear freeze. While the third draft reiterated the second's opposition to nuclear first use as "an unjustifiable moral risk," it was now willing to postpone the dismantling of the first-use strategy until NATO could devise a viable alternative.[54] The Reagan administration was therefore decidedly more friendly to the third draft. Though "we do not share all the bishops' specific judgments," national security advisor Clark praised the new version as "an important and responsible contribution to discussion of the issue."[55]

The committee's fellow bishops, however, believed it had failed to find the proper balance. Over the objections of the White House, the bishops restored the word "halt" to the document's call for "immediate, bilateral agreements to halt the testing, production, and deployment of new nuclear weapons systems," and did not pretend that this was not a call for a nuclear freeze. They unequivocally rejected the first use of nuclear weapons. They regarded "any attack on Soviet cities" that transcended "legitimate defense" as "morally unjustifiable." They accepted deterrence only if it was not part of a nuclear war fighting strategy, did not advance nuclear superiority, and served as a negotiating tool to attain disarmament.[56]

There were 239 bishops who voted in favor of the revised third draft. Only eight voted against. The United States Catholic Conference requires two-thirds approval for its pastorals, but its "unwritten law of consensus," according to religion writer Peter Steinfels, "demands at least eighty percent." The final draft of "The Challenge of Peace" had received 96 percent approval. "Not even the letter's most ardent supporters," Steinfels marveled, "had expected that."[57]

The day after the bishops' vote, a nuclear freeze resolution sponsored by Wisconsin's Clement Zablocki passed the House of Representatives 278–179, with 82 of his 86 fellow Catholic Democrats and 15 of 38 Catholic Republicans voting in favor. There were reports of Catholics in the military and the defense industry having second thoughts about their professions. A poll by Americans United for Separation of Church and State showed 78 percent of American Catholics (compared to 82 percent of Jews and 57 percent of Protestants) in support of a nuclear freeze such as the one advocated by the bishops.[58]

Not all Catholics celebrated the hierarchy's achievement, however. Archbishop Hannan not only voted against the final draft but claimed that by considering over five hundred amendments in under two days, his fellow prelates had "railroaded this through," and he vowed to "appeal to Rome." After all, that had seemed to work the last time.[59]

Terence Cardinal Cooke of New York rushed to assure Catholics serving in the military and defense establishment that they could keep their jobs. The pastoral "does not advocate unilateral disarmament and it does not condemn deterrence or retaliatory action against unjust aggressors—although these are strictly conditioned," Cooke loosely interpreted the pastoral in a letter to military chaplains. Besides, the cardinal added, the document was not promulgating Church doctrine, but was offering "purely human judgments, which are not binding."[60]

The Reagan administration found the bishops' judgments sorely lacking. A Catholic admiral, James Watkins of the Joint Chiefs of Staff, called the pastoral an "outrage" that "mentioned nothing about the Soviets, as if somehow we had developed these weapons for our own amusement." Robert Reilly, Reagan's liaison to the Catholic community, reminded his fellow Catholics that the document was a collection of "prudential moral judgments," which were "certainly not based on infallible teaching." Reilly was "doing the White House proud," the conservative Catholic weekly the *Wanderer* cheered, by pointing out that the Reagan foreign policy was in "the mainstream of Judeo-Christian values."[61]

In January 1984 the pope wrote to President Reagan to urge him to continue his arms control efforts. Reagan assured the Holy Father that he remained "fully dedicated to the pursuit of negotiated arms control agreements," but he would not undermine "the structure of collective security that has preserved our peace and freedom for almost thirty-five years." When the two leaders met in Fairbanks, Alaska, in May, Reagan recommitted himself to "a constructive, substantive dialogue with the Soviets, especially on arms control."[62]

Reagan considered his decision to deploy Pershing II missiles, which could reach the Soviet Union within twelve minutes of their launch from Western Europe, as a means toward that end. The bishops disagreed. At the White House in April, Cardinals Bernardin and Krol, Bishops Thomas Kelly of Louisville and James Malone of Youngstown, joined O'Connor (now archbishop of New York) in asking the president to reconsider. In their testimony before the House Foreign Relations Committee in June, Bernardin and O'Connor criticized this deployment as a needless escalation of the arms race.[63]

The president obtained a victory and the bishops suffered a defeat in October when the Senate rejected the nuclear freeze. By the end of his first term in the White House, Ronald Reagan had achieved no meaningful arms control with the Soviet Union.[64]

Reagan's Second Term

But he did achieve reelection. The country's rebounding economy and rejuvenated international standing earned Reagan electoral majorities among Catholics and everywhere except Minnesota, the home state of his Democratic rival Walter Mondale, and the District of Columbia, the seat of the government that he alternately defended and derided.

Washington also housed the headquarters of the United States Catholic Conference, just a few blocks from Capitol Hill, where the bishops renewed their campaign against the administration's defense build-up. In March 1985 the USCC's president, Bishop James Malone of Youngstown, sent a letter to every member of Congress and released statements by Bernardin and O'Connor, urging a "no" vote on the funding for the MX, a more mobile and more lethal alternative to the Minuteman III missile and the centerpiece of the administration's defense modernization. The MX would cost inordinate amounts of money and increase the likelihood of an American first strike, points that Malone and O'Connor would repeat to Reagan at the White House in April.[65]

"Catholic Bishops Urge Lawmakers to Bar MX Funds" was the headline that caught William F. Buckley's eye as Congress deliberated. "Catholic Lawmakers Urge Bishops to Mind Their Own Business" was the headline he would have preferred. "Bishop Malone could be as smart as Einstein," Buckley wrote, "from which nothing whatever would follow about the intelligence of his views on the MX missile."[66] Congress found the bishops and the president equally intelligent in their assessments of the MX. The legislators voted to fund fifty of the hundred MX missiles requested by the administration.[67]

Lest his lobbying for the MX appear to compromise his commitment to arms control, Reagan sent three letters to Pope John Paul II in April attesting to his devotion to the cause. The pope responded, national security advisor Robert MacFarlane relayed to Reagan, "that he has prayed for you and implored divine guidance as you conduct the great responsibilities you bear for your country and peace in the world."[68]

Bishop Malone was also writing to the president and, for a change, agreeing with him. In June Malone thanked Reagan for the administration's adherence to the unratified SALT II treaty. Three months later Ed Rowny, the Catholic special advisor to the president and to the secretary of state for arms control matters, suggested that the president discuss such issues with John O'Connor (now a cardinal) and Bernard Cardinal Law of Boston.[69] Such meetings were not unusual. In the four years since his first election triumph, the U.S. president had met several times with his country's Catholic bishops and twice with the pope. But he had never met with any Soviet heads of state who, Reagan complained, "keep dying on me." That would finally change in November 1985 in Geneva, where Reagan sat down with the new Soviet leader, Mikhail Gorbachev.[70]

The bishops wished them well. "Men and women of good will throughout the world share the hope that President Reagan's meeting with First Secretary Gorbachev will contribute to improved relations between the United States and the Soviet Union and will begin a process of reducing military weapons and forces," Bishop Malone spoke for the USCC on the eve of the summit.[71]

It would. The two leaders agreed in principle that they would cut their nuclear arsenals in half, though they could not yet agree on how. They also concurred that, as Reagan liked to say, "a nuclear war cannot be won, and must never be fought."[72] But just when nuclear deterrence finally appeared to be paying diplomatic dividends, the bishops considered withdrawing their meager investment. At their November 1985 meeting, they voted to review their threadbare allegiance to deterrence in "The Challenge of Peace."[73]

Reagan and Gorbachev met again in Reykjavik, Iceland, in October 1986. Best known for Reagan's stunning proposal to eliminate all nuclear weapons, the summit ended in a stalemate when Gorbachev refused Reagan's offer of a mutual 50 percent reduction of strategic weapons over five years and elimination of intermediate nuclear forces in Europe because Reagan would not confine his Strategic Defense Initiative to the laboratory. A former Bernardin committee staffer, Edward Doherty, lamented that as the seventh year of the Reagan presidency dawned, "no progress" in arms control had occurred, and "arms control experts in Washington did not seem hopeful" of any breakthrough.[74]

That did not stop the president and the bishops from trying. In April 1987 Reagan sent Secretary of State George Shultz to Moscow to restart negotiations on intermediate nuclear forces. In June at the Vatican and in September in Miami, Reagan and Pope John Paul II discussed the progress of the INF and START negotiations. In August the bishops sent a representative to the UN Conference on Disarmament and Development and unsuccessfully pressed Shultz to do likewise. In October the bishops sent a letter to a House-Senate conference committee supporting provisions in the FY 1988 defense authorization bill limiting nuclear testing and observing the Anti-Ballistic Missile (ABM) and SALT II Treaties if the Soviets would. In November Bernardin, now chairing the bishops' deterrence committee, reported that since the completion of "The Challenge of Peace," the arms race had escalated, arms control progress had been largely symbolic, the Strategic Defense Initiative had gained traction, and defense expenditures had preempted vital social spending.[75]

But Bernardin had spoken too soon. The breakthrough in arms control finally occurred in Washington, D.C., in December 1987, when Reagan and Gorbachev signed the Intermediate Nuclear Forces Treaty, which mandated the first actual reduction of nuclear weapons, the elimination of an entire class of weapons, and the first agreement on verification. Gorbachev, invigorated by the historic accord and intoxicated by the hero's welcome he received on the streets of Washington, told Reagan, "I will never think of your country the way I did before."[76]

But the American Catholic bishops would. At their April 1988 meeting Cardinal Bernardin delivered the report of his Ad Hoc Committee on the Moral Evaluation of Deterrence. In the report, the committee clung to "strictly conditioned deterrence," with little enthusiasm for the recently ratified INF Treaty and even less for SDI. Quoting Pope John Paul II's January 1988 address to the Vatican diplomatic corps, the committee described the Reagan-Gorbachev treaty, which "involves only a very limited portion of the respective arsenals," as "more a point of departure than an end in itself." Though they shared SDI's goal of transcending deterrence and accepted the need for research and development of its potential, they opposed its deployment outside the parameters of the ABM Treaty as militarily, economically, and morally dubious.[77]

If Bernardin's newest panel was unwilling to embrace "Star Wars," Bishop Gumbleton, a member of both Bernardin committees, was now unwilling to condone "strictly conditioned" deterrence. His dissent became part of the report approved by his fellow prelates. So the bishops exited the Reagan era the same way they had entered: largely opposed to the administration's arms control policies.[78]

Conclusions on War and Peace

"Where's the rest of me?" actor Ronald Reagan asked in the movie *Kings Row* in 1942. This query would become the title of his autobiography, and the subject of considerable debate among historians since his time in the White House.[79] Because his detractors and admirers alike have tended to see only a one-dimensional president—an unrepentant hawk who fell into arms control or a wily genius who planned it all along—they have left history to finish the portrait of his presidency.

The role of the American Catholic bishops, and Catholics in general, in the transformation of Ronald Reagan and the disintegration of the Soviet Union is also not entirely clear. By adroitly negotiating with the administration and through the media, the bishops ensured not only that the president would hear them, but that he could not afford not to. In "The Challenge of Peace," the bishops targeted two audiences, the "civil community" and "the Catholic faithful." Advocates and adversaries alike quietly concluded that they were reaching both.⁸⁰ There nevertheless were limits to the pastoral's resonance. "A crucial deficiency lay in the bishops' failure—or more correctly *refusal*—to establish some mechanism to monitor progress in arms reduction, a basic condition for the bishops' conditional acceptance of nuclear deterrence," the new Pax Christi director, Gordon Zahn, wrote in *Commonweal* in March 1985. "Now, nearly two years later, it is obvious that the conditions have been ignored, and the pastoral had little impact on this nation's nuclear policies or the steadily escalating arms race." *U.S. Catholic*'s "R. E. B." regretted in August 1986 that "if the bishops' courageous voicing is being discussed today, it is being discussed only sporadically and quietly. And there is no real evidence that the statement has had any effect on American governmental policy."⁸¹

In many ways the president and the bishops appeared to confirm these gloomy judgments. "Actually, the letter is 45,000 words long, and all of the attention seemed to be on that one word, the change from 'curb' to 'halt,'" Reagan said in reaction to the pastoral in May 1983. "The basic emphasis of the letter aimed at the same thing we're aiming at—world peace." When asked by a reporter whether the pastoral wasn't exerting an "influence on the debate" over nuclear war, Reagan answered, "Well, is it really? Is there anyone that really favors using these weapons?" Citing "our own proposals in START and INF," the president maintained that the bishops were "not saying anything we don't say."⁸²

Nor were they apparently affecting what his administration might do. Three weeks after the issuance of "The Challenge of Peace," the Joint Chiefs of Staff testified on Capitol Hill that the administration was considering adopting a "launch-on-warning" strategy, which would enhance the kind of nuclear first strike capacity that the administration had been downplaying and the bishops were repudiating.⁸³

But not repudiating strongly enough, by their own calculations. The hierarchy "was bound to fail to move this Administration into serious arms control after having assured that the core of its strategic doctrine—namely nuclear deterrence—is morally acceptable," Bernardin staffer Edward Doherty complained in December 1986. "This result was compounded in the course of the subsequent three years by the absence on the part of the bishops' conference of any vigorous policy advocacy of its own recommendations, such as on a comprehensive test ban treaty."⁸⁴ Bernardin's Ad Hoc Committee on the Moral Evaluation of Deterrence admitted as much in its 1988 report. The "conditional acceptance" of deterrence, which the bishops reiterated five years after "The Challenge of Peace," the deterrence committee asserted, was "not an endorsement of a status quo that we find inadequate and dangerous."⁸⁵

If the bishops had seemingly not influenced the Reagan administration, had they at least persuaded their flock? Here too, to a large degree, they seemed to come up short. "The bishops do not appear to be worried about the letter being rejected by their people," Rev. Thomas Reese wrote in *America* in May 1983. "Most felt that the majority of Catholics would be with them on this issue, and in any case they had an obligation to teach, even if they were not listened to."[86] "Do you feel optimistic about people studying the letter out in the dioceses and in the parishes?" the editors of *U.S. Catholic* asked Rev. Bryan Hehir of the Bernardin committee staff. "I'm optimistic," he replied, "but that's not a guarantee of anything. I try to keep my expectations modest."[87] Which is a good thing, because two years after the nuclear freeze won at the polls, so did Ronald Reagan, with majority Catholic support, over Walter Mondale, who had heaped praise upon the pastoral. And as the Cold War began to wane four years later, most of the credit was going to Reagan, the president whom the bishops had challenged; John Paul II, the pope who had challenged the bishops; and Mikhail Gorbachev, the leader of a country where bishops dared not challenge anyone.

The U.S. Catholic bishops deserved better. Most of the evidence, after all, showed that the nuclear pastoral had a substantial and lasting impact. George Kennan, the repentant architect of containment, hailed the pastoral as "the most profound and searching inquiry [into nuclear ethics] yet conducted by any responsible collective body." The liberal Rev. Andrew Greeley gushed that the letter "appears to be the most successful intervention to change attitudes ever measured by social science."[88]

Catholic conservative George Weigel of the World without War Council of Greater Seattle chided those who "minimize the possible impact [good or ill] of the Church's engagement with war and peace issues." A former Henry Kissinger advisor, Helmut Sonnenfelt, lamented that what the bishops said "may indeed affect the public policies of the U.S. and its allies."[89]

While time would narrow the sweep of such early judgments, it nonetheless would vindicate their spirit. "A forthright condemnation of nuclear weapons . . . is not going to end the arms race, it will not lead to unilateral reductions in strategic arms by the United States, it will not alter the cast of American war planning, and it will not lessen the danger of nuclear war," Thomas Powers wrote of the unfinished pastoral in *Commonweal* in November 1982. But it "will encourage the peace movement, will push this administration and succeeding administrations to negotiate seriously, will force a crisis of conscience in many Catholics in the military or in defense industries, and will precipitate an unpleasant—perhaps an ugly—confrontation between Church and State."[90]

Powers was remarkably prescient on every count—except for the ugly confrontation between church and state, which never came. And the influence of the church was perhaps the most lasting legacy of "The Challenge of Peace." It was "startling to switch on a late-night TV show and find a bunch of bishops holding forth about the morality of U.S. nuclear arms strategy," Catholic conservative Norman Miller confessed in the *Wall Street Journal* in December 1982. "It's pretty heady stuff to pick up *Time* magazine and find Archbishop Joseph Bernardin on the cover." Miller, who rejected the pastoral's prescriptions, nonetheless rejoiced, "Thank God . . . it's not another cover story about the church and birth control, or about all the priests who have quit."[91]

Thank God, indeed. Bernardin received three standing ovations when he presented "The Challenge of Peace" to his fellow bishops in November 1983. He probably deserved a fourth—from the country, for showing the best face of a church that could wrestle with a complicated issue and take on a popular president in a reasonable, deliberate, and inclusive way. In the pastoral the bishops had promised "to help Catholics form their consciences and to contribute to the public policy debate about the morality of war." They delivered on both promises.[92]

And they did so even in ways they did not intend. The bishops' deliberations provoked Admiral James Watkins of the Joint Chiefs of Staff to step back from his initial dismissal of the pastoral long enough to search his own soul on the question of nuclear deterrence. His dialogue with fellow Catholics at the Naval War College helped lead to his advocacy of using "our applied technological genius to achieve our deterrent instead of sticking with an offensive land-based rocket exchange which they [the Soviets] will win every time." The result of Watkins's introspection was his support for the Strategic Defense Initiative, which would fascinate President Reagan and frighten the bishops.[93]

But if Watkins had made a decision that alienated the bishops of his church, he reached a conclusion that vindicated them. "The American people thought Mutually Assured Destruction morally distasteful," Watkins would recall. "It was a political loser." In painstakingly, powerfully, and publicly arriving at that judgment before the president did, the American Catholic hierarchy surely was not.[94]

Social Justice: The Economy

Perhaps no other quality endeared Ronald Reagan more to the American people than his optimism. His frequent and fervent allusions to the basic goodness of the United States provided a welcome tonic to a populace weary of the malaise of the Jimmy Carter years. In an age of televangelism Reagan, a nominally Protestant son of a lapsed Catholic father, was the perfect preacher, extolling the virtues of a work ethic sullied by too much welfare and a profit motive savaged by too much socialism. From his bully pulpit, the high priest of Reaganomics espoused self-reliance and free markets. The American people had replaced a born-again Baptist with a born-again supply-sider.

To his detractors, however, the Reagan religion was dangerously deceptive, promoting wealth more than work and entrepreneurship at the expense of equality. These critics focused on those to whom the gospel of Reaganomics did not speak. While Reagan argued that the "war on poverty" had failed, his opponents contended that it had never really begun. Among those adversaries were some American Catholics, who confronted Reagan with a potent brew of Catholic social teaching. The best way to fight the Reagan religion, they concluded, was with more religion.

In mounting this challenge, these Catholics, led by their bishops and their pope, were not only taking on a popular president, but, in largely casting their lot with a manufacturing-based, trade unionist economy, they in some ways were turning back time. Almost two decades late, the American Catholic hierarchy was acknowledging the urban ethnic working class that had filled its churches. But by the Reagan era, the overlooked Americans had become less urban, less ethnic, less working class, and even less Catholic, so the bishops and the pope turned to the voiceless poor, for whom Reagan's uplifting rhetoric left little room and for whom Reagan's penurious policies portended limited returns.

But the reach of the Catholic leaders' critique of Reaganomics exceeded their grasp of the changes in their church membership. Most of their congregants now preferred the president's economic prescriptions to those of the bishops and the pope. By empathizing with society's least valued and most vulnerable, the hearts of the Catholic hierarchy had found the right place. By defying a conventional wisdom that elevated society's most ambitious and least troubled, the minds of the Catholic hierarchy had picked the wrong time.

Reaganomics

In February 1981 the new president proposed a three-year, 30 percent across-the-board income tax cut, and a budget with $49 billion less in social spending. Reagan predicted that these actions would "stimulate growth, productivity, and employment at the same time that we move toward the elimination of inflation."[95]

Not everyone shared the president's rosy outlook. In January 1981 the United States Catholic Conference's president, Archbishop John Roach of Minneapolis–St. Paul, had asked the liberal Milwaukee archbishop, Rembert

Weakland, to chair the Ad Hoc Committee on Christianity and Capitalism, which Weakland had proposed at the November 1980 USCC general meeting. Born to a welfare widow, Weakland was now a Benedictine monk sworn to poverty. In the same month, the USCC's general secretary, Bishop Thomas Kelly, sent a letter to all members of Congress urging them to vote against the expected Reagan budget. "Our concern in this regard," Kelly wrote, "stems from our belief in the sanctity and dignity of all human beings, and from our special commitment to the poor."[96]

Kelly did not speak for the entire conference, however. Bishop Joseph McNicholas of Springfield, Illinois, while protesting that he "did not wish to give the Administration a blank check on cutting social programs," nevertheless worried that such early criticism of the president risked "the relationship of the Conference with the new Administration," which "won a landslide victory in November from an electorate that believed that the economy should be brought under control."[97]

When the USCC's director of domestic social development, Ronald Krietemeyer, sent the bishops a memorandum evaluating Reagan's economic proposals, Kelly said the memo had met Reagan in the middle, between the "old left" and the "new right." McNicholas praised Krietemeyer's analysis, warning that "while continuing to express [our] concern for the poor," the bishops "should be wary of being used by groups that are opposing the budget cuts."[98]

In August 1981 Congress passed Reagan's Economic Recovery Tax Act, mandating the largest tax reduction in U.S. history. Not only did this measure cut income taxes by 25 percent in all brackets, but it reduced the highest tax rate from 70 to 50 percent and dropped the lowest rate from 14 to 11 percent. Reagan also signed the Budget Reconciliation Act, establishing an FY 1982 budget that was $30 billion leaner than the one the Carter administration had projected.[99]

More than offset by massive increases in the Carter defense budget, which they also opposed, the Reagan social spending reductions alarmed the bishops. Unlike the administration, Archbishop Roach told his fellow prelates at their November meeting, the poor had to choose "not between guns and butter, but between bread and rent." The bishops then heard a report from the Independent Sector, an organization of voluntary agencies including the USCC, which assessed the potential impact of the Reagan budget on nonprofit groups. By 1984, the study forecast, if federal budget decreases reached $100 billion, nonprofits would be without $27.3 billion of their normal expenditures.[100]

So Roach dispatched USCC representatives to lobby Congress on behalf of the poor. In December Archbishop Edmund Szoka of Detroit told the House Ways and Means Committee that the Reagan reductions had produced "at least a one hundred percent increase in requests for modest assistance" to Catholic social service agencies in his diocese. In February 1982 Auxiliary Bishop Joseph Sullivan of Brooklyn argued before a task force of the House Committee on the Budget that "particularly in the case of food stamps, Aid to Families with Dependent Children, and Medicaid," the Reagan cuts "constitute a denial of the most basic human needs for thousands of Americans." Sullivan cited the example of a woman in Minneapolis–St. Paul who left some blankets in her unlocked car overnight. She awoke to find six adults sleeping in the vehicle, huddled together to ward off the winter.[101]

Reaganomics was not only offensive to the American Catholic hierarchy, but it risked alienating the rank and file, many of whom had voted for Reagan in 1980. The elimination of the Housing and Urban Development Department's Office of Neighborhoods and Voluntary Associations and the folding of the Ethnic Heritage Studies Act into a block grant, when added to the paucity of ethnic Americans appointed to key posts in the administration, jeopardized the support of the "Reagan Democrats" whom the president had cultivated. "In the Reagan White House," Dr. John Kromkowski, the president of the National Center for Urban Affairs, lamented in March 1981, "the concerns of neighborhoods and ethnics no longer warrant special assistants to the president," as they did in the previous two administrations.[102]

In July the president met with a group of twenty-five prominent Italian-Americans. Reagan sought to, in White House aide Elizabeth Dole's words, "solicit comments on how the Administration and the Italian-American community can work together achieving the goals of the economic recovery program."[103]

But Dole believed the administration could do a lot more. In a lengthy memo written on the eve of the November 1982 midterm elections, she urged the pursuit of an "ethnic/Catholic strategy" in order to "hold and hopefully expand the base of support Ronald Reagan received from this constituency, thus forming a base for a governing coalition now and an electoral coalition in 1984." Over "our first twenty-two months in office," Dole observed, "ethnics have not been accorded the level of recognition given Hispanics and blacks." Dole recommended "frequent visits" by the president and his surrogates "to the old industrial cities of the Northeast both large and small" and the monitoring of "unemployment very closely in these blue-collar cities." She suggested that the administration send emissaries to "groups like the Knights of Columbus, the Catholic Daughters of the Americas, the National Catholic Education Association, [and] the Chief Administrators of Catholic Education." These organizations, she maintained, were "neutral and objective." The American Catholic hierarchy was not. But even though the bishops were "extremely liberal" and "essentially opposed to our policies," Dole nonetheless considered administration contacts with the hierarchy to be beneficial window dressing. "A series of meetings with key Administration leaders and selected members of the Catholic hierarchy on issues of mutual concern," Dole contended, could "enlist support or at least minimize their opposition." At the very least, such a dialogue would project "an image of caring about Catholic views." The "substance of the consultation," she concluded, was less important than "the fact that the consultation was made at all."[104]

In response, Reagan invited Archbishop Roach to a White House meeting later that same month. "Many great questions of public policy face the country today," read the invitation drafted for the president by John Mackey, special counsel to the Ad Hoc Committee in Defense of Life. "And you have my best wishes in bringing the insights of the Christian tradition to bear on them." What he really meant, Mackey seemed to be saying in his jottings in the margins of the letter, is that he agreed with Elizabeth Dole. "Most of the time clerics [are] given [the] back of [the] hand," he wrote, "which they often welcome, as it frees them to be irresponsible." So why not surprise the bishops, Mackey intimated, by offering them the president's outstretched hand instead?[105]

If American Catholics appreciated all this attention, they had a strange way of showing it. First, in November 1982 the Catholic faithful returned in droves to the Democrats, especially in the heavily ethnic and economically battered cities of the Northeast and Midwest, as the party out of power gained twenty-six House seats. Then, with the midterm election a memory, the hierarchy resumed its assault on the administration. At their November meeting, the bishops' Domestic Office reported that Reagan's FY 1983 budget called for "large cuts in Food Stamps, Aid to Dependent Children, Medicaid, and Medicare." It warned that "coming on top of last year's cuts, these new budget reductions will have a severe impact on the poor."[106]

The bishops did not stop there. Archbishop Mark Hurley of Santa Rosa, California, introduced a resolution from the USCC Department of Social Development and World Peace deploring the "economic crisis" facing the country. Fearful that adoption of such a statement would cause the hierarchy to be "identified with one political party" (not the one in the White House), Bishop Leo Maher of San Diego urged Hurley to withdraw the resolution. The bishops then tabled the statement implicitly attacking the Reagan economic policies to resume discussion of their statement implicitly attacking the Reagan defense policies.[107]

Then they got back to Reaganomics. In March 1983 Archbishop Weakland announced that his Christianity and Capitalism Committee, originally named in response to the bishops' 1980 pastoral "Christianity and Communism," had a new title. The appellation Ad Hoc Committee on Catholic Social Teaching and the American Economy, Weakland explained, "much more accurately defines the scope and content" of the group's upcoming pastoral (and more directly targeted the Reagan administration) than its former name.[108]

In an August speech to over a hundred religious leaders, Reagan confronted his critics by noting that governments can only do so much to combat poverty. The president recalled that the Good Samaritan had not gone "running into town to look for a case worker to tell him that there was a fellow out there that needed help." Instead, Reagan said approvingly, "he took it upon himself."[109]

Some Catholics saw things differently. In a Labor Day address in San Francisco, the USCC's Msgr. George Higgins ridiculed Reagan's Good Samaritan reference as a case of "sentimental Biblical fundamentalism." Higgins countered that the president was "whistling in the dark if he thinks that the churches and other voluntary agencies, in a period of very high unemployment, can make up for his own massive budget cuts in the field of social welfare."

While the bishops prepared to meet the nation's economic Armageddon, the White House prepared to meet the bishops. In the wake of the administration's belated response to the unfolding of Bernardin's peace pastoral, a White House official cautioned in August that the administration "better be out front" on the drafting of Weakland's economic message. A September consultation between White House aide Linas Kojelis and Donald Shea, the Republican National Committee's Catholic liaison, evinced the consensus that, in Kojelis's words, "while relations with Catholic lay organizations are in fairly good shape, the White House should work to improve relations with the Catholic hierarchy, especially the bishops and the U.S. Catholic Conference." The administration could begin by inviting the archbishop of largely German-American Milwaukee to the October state dinner for Karl Carstens, the president of West Germany.[110]

White House aide Faith Whittlesey relayed Kojelis's suggestion alongside one of her own, that the president meet with some of the bishops when they arrived in Washington for their November meeting. Though Reagan had met with individual prelates, Whittlesey noted, "an invitation such as this to a reception by the President to all the bishops has not been given by this Administration before and is overdue."[111]

Anticipating the Economic Pastoral

The Reagan administration's overtures to the bishops had minimal effect. The bishops declined the invitation to the White House. Archbishop Weakland declined his dinner invitation, then announced that his committee had completed the first draft of its economic pastoral.[112]

Though Weakland promised to withhold its release until after the November 1984 presidential election to avoid the appearance of partisanship, there was little doubt about what it was going to say. "Based on the issues it will address [and] the experts who have been chosen to write position papers," *Business Week* surmised in December 1983, "the final document could sound a lot like the 1984 Democratic Presidential platform." The article cited the role of University of Notre Dame economist Charles Wilber, an advocate of government economic planning, as the committee's primary consultant, as well as the ideological predilections of five-sixths of the committee. "If you want a token conservative," Atlanta archbishop Thomas Donnellan revealed, "I'm it."[113]

"Do you have any suggestions for putting enterprise's best foot forward with these well-intentioned men?" the U.S. Chamber of Commerce's Catholic vice president, Thomas Donohue, queried the assistant to the president for Cabinet affairs, Craig Fuller, upon news of the first draft's completion. Perhaps the administration could bypass the bishops entirely and speak directly to their congregants. "The Democratic Party . . . lost its traditional hold on Catholics, as they became more affluent and moved to the suburbs," the *Business Week* article noted, citing a Harris Poll that showed that a year after the Republicans' 1982 electoral disaster, 40 percent of the nation's Catholics were Democrats and 25 percent Republicans, while in 1977, 50 percent had been Democrats and only 15 percent Republicans. "The 'shepherds,'" White House counselor Edwin Meese noticed in January 1984, "don't always reflect the views of their 'flocks.'"[114]

Nor did non-Catholics always reflect the views of Catholics. For the first time in 117 years, and with bipartisan support, Reagan restored full diplomatic relations with the Vatican in January 1984, nominating Catholic oil equipment manager and land developer William Wilson to be his ambassador there. Though the United States became the 107th nation to recognize the Vatican, Reagan's decision unleashed a storm of criticism from the National Council of Churches, the National Association of Evangelicals, and the American Jewish Congress as an infringement on the First Amendment's proscription of the "establishment" of an official religion.[115]

Any hope that the recognition of the Vatican would improve the administration's relations with the Catholic bishops soon evaporated. When asked on CBS's *Face the Nation* whether Reagan's decision would affect how Catholics voted in the upcoming election, the USCC president, Bishop James Malone of Youngstown, answered, "Probably not. It seems to me that the Catholic opinion will vary widely." Malone even raised the possibility of "a new wave of anti-Catholic bigotry" arising from the move. Rev. Joseph O'Hare, the editor of *America*, supported the change but wondered whether "upgrad[ing] the presence of the Vatican could conceivably inhibit the further development of the national identity of the U.S. bishops."[116]

There seemed little danger of that. Following Reagan's January 1984 State of the Union address, in which he proposed to further reduce the federal budget by $100 billion over five years, Brooklyn auxiliary bishop Joseph Sullivan, the USCC's liaison to the National Conference of Catholic Charities, joined that organization in labeling the president's latest economic proposals as "totally unacceptable."[117]

The Weakland committee continued to hold hearings around the country while holding its fire until after the election. As others waited, a group of Catholic conservatives acted. The Lay Commission on Catholic Social Teaching and the U.S. Economy formed in May under the aegis of the American Catholic Committee. Chaired by former Treasury secretary William Simon, the group included former secretary of state Alexander Haig, former secretary of the interior Walter Hickel, industrialist Peter Grace, theologian Michael Novak, and Clare Boothe Luce of Reagan's Foreign Intelligence Advisory Board. Their mission was to draft a conservative alternative to the bishops' expected liberal manifesto.[118]

Though he had testified three times before Weakland's committee, Novak lamented that no one seemed to be listening. "Even if you thought of us as lost sheep," Novak said of his fellow Catholic conservatives, "we are still part of the flock."[119] Archbishop Weakland needed no such reminder. He not only pronounced himself "delighted" with the formation of the Simon commission, but he met with its members in July. "Their letter will be taken for what it is, an honest attempt on the part of a few committed Catholics to reflect on the economy in hopes that their reflection will influence the subsequent discussion," Weakland magnanimously recounted after the meeting.[120]

Two months later came the news that the National Council of Churches and the National Association of Evangelicals, comprising most of the country's Protestants, had filed suit to block Reagan's recognition of the Vatican out of fear that the Catholic Church would unduly influence the U.S. government. Two Catholic groups, the National Association of Laity and the National Coalition of American Nuns, joined the suit out of fear that the U.S. government would unduly influence the Catholic Church.[121] It was peculiar litigation, because at least when it came to Reaganomics, the Vatican had been noticeably silent, neither influencing nor being influenced by the administration. That is, until Pope John Paul II traveled to Canada in September.

In Edmonton, Alberta, the pontiff decried the "imperialistic monopoly of economic and political supremacy" of the world's North over the South. In Flatrock, Newfoundland, he proclaimed that "no social assistance can fully compensate" for the "affront to the dignity of the individual" that systematic unemployment begets. The pope's remedies for these ills appeared to endorse the Canadian bishops' 1983 pastoral, "Ethical Reflections on the Cultural Crisis," which was so far to the left that the quite liberal prime minister, Pierre Trudeau, called the prelates "bad economists."[122]

Weakland provided Pope John Paul II with a private oral reading of the first draft before he presented it to his fellow American bishops. Relating the pastoral to the pope's remarks in Canada, the Vatican's ambassador to the United States, Pio Cardinal Laghi, maintained that inveighing against injustice "is among the paramount tasks of the Church in our times."[123]

But that task would have to await Reagan's landslide reelection, a forty-nine-state romp that spared only Minnesota and the District of Columbia. The country's recovering economy and rebuilding defenses meant that it was "morning in America," in the words of Reagan's highly effective television ads. So any hint of darkness after the dawn would seem a frontal assault on the national psyche.

Addressing the Economic Pastoral

Yet it would arrive anyway. The triumph of Reaganomics over the misery index and at the polls threatened to render the bishops' words irrelevant and even irreverent. But somehow the media, left and right, had not lost their appetite for the Weakland committee's recipe. Nor had the Simon commission, which preempted the release of the bishops' pastoral with its own statement, which called poverty "a personal and community problem, . . . not primarily a problem of the state."[124]

The bishops' first draft appeared a week later, on the eve of their general meeting. It promoted three "priority principles which should shape our economic policies and institutions both domestically and internationally." The first was that "the fulfillment of the basic needs of the poor is of the highest priority." The second was that "increased participation for the marginalized takes priority over the preservation of privileged concentrations of wealth, power, and income." The third was that "meeting human needs and increasing participation should be priority targets in the investment of wealth, talent, and human energy." The letter said that "current levels of unemployment are morally unjustified," and "the fact that more than fifteen percent [of] our nation's population lives below the official poverty level is a social and moral scandal." While disavowing a "statist approach to economic activity," the document nonetheless advocated a "major new policy commitment to achieve full employment," defined as between 3 and 4 percent unemployment.[125]

The reactions to the pastoral were as predictable as the document itself.

Catholic liberals loved it, but Catholic conservatives did not. The March 1985 *Religion and Society Report* divided the non-Catholic responses into favorable (e.g., *New York Times*, American Federation of Labor–Congress of Industrial Organizations, Protestant ethicist John Bennett), unfavorable (e.g., *Human Events*, the *New Republic*'s Charles Krauthammer), "not radical enough" (*Nation*), and just plain nasty (the *American Spectator*'s Tom Bethell's investigative report uncovering a $2,500 dinner bill for thirty bishops attending the meeting that ratified the first draft).[126]

There would be no review from the White House, at least not yet. Whether scarred by the bruising battle over the previous year's peace pastoral or intoxicated by his gargantuan election victory, the president would say only that he "welcomes" the bishops' letter but would not be commenting on its contents. "I don't think it would serve the purpose of dialogue within the Church or between the Administration and the Church," White House press secretary Larry Speakes asserted, for Reagan to go further.[127] The administration's public professions of neutrality were only slightly less disingenuous than Reagan's earlier assertions of basic agreement with the bishops' 1983 peace pastoral. At the same time the bishops were meeting in Washington, the assistant to the president for public liaison, Faith Whittlesey, was arranging for the Simon commission to visit the White House, and the administration was preparing a new round of budget cuts in programs for the poor.[128]

President Reagan would spend much of the summer selling his tax reform package, which would lower the individual tax ceiling from 50 to 28 percent, while taxing 85 percent of all taxpayers at a 15 percent floor. "We certainly enjoyed hearing first hand your position on the proposed tax bill," William Van Tassell of the Knights of Columbus wrote to Reagan after their White House meeting in August. "You have our continued support."[129]

Archbishop Weakland extended no such greeting. Instead, he announced in September the release of the second draft of the economic pastoral. Weakland, who received the committee chairmanship largely because of his ability to listen, showed that indeed he had. The new version was about one-fourth shorter and considerably less specific, with nods to the middle class and the private sector, a call for implementation, and a link to the peace pastoral. Yet the "core message of the document," as Weakland put it, remained the same. The committee retained the language of the "preferential option for the poor" and reiterated that "government has a positive and necessary role to play in the search for economic justice."[130]

Once again, the administration's response was privately to seethe but publicly to soothe. Behind closed doors, White House communications director Patrick Buchanan, a Catholic, called the second draft "an improvement but still altogether unsatisfactory from our viewpoint." Buchanan added, however, that "the strong counsel I am getting from Catholic allies of the president—with which I agree—is that we officially take no stand whatsoever." The pugnacious Buchanan, fresh off an extended stint as a vociferous pundit on CNN's *Crossfire*, uncharacteristically prescribed silence. "Do not engage them—which is what they want. Let the Catholic community debate it—and say, that when completed, we, of course, will take a look at it."[131]

The Catholic community *would* debate it, with liberals again lining up in favor and conservatives still opposed. And once again the pope injected himself into the debate, meeting with the United States Catholic Conference's Msgr. Daniel Hoye, Msgr. Francis Murphy, Archbishop John May, and Bishop James Malone in January 1986 in Rome. "He said that he believed it was a very important document," Hoye recorded, while the pope added that "the Church exists between both major systems, Marxism and capitalism." The Holy Father said that both doctrines were "materialistic, and the Church doesn't identify with either." As he had on the peace pastoral, the pontiff recommended that the bishops confer with their counterparts in other countries, only this time not those protected by Western Europe's nuclear shield but those practicing Latin America's "liberation theology." John Paul II concluded the meeting by saying that his "major preoccupation" was "the gap that existed between those who were too rich and those who were too poor." He noted that "how to bridge the gap . . . is the question that confronts mankind." And he professed to look to the U.S. bishops "for inspiration on how to address this issue."[132]

In June Archbishop Weakland unveiled the final version of "Economic Justice for All: Catholic Social Teaching and the U.S. Economy." The pastoral invoked the scriptures, Pope Leo XIII's encyclical *Rerum Novarum* (1893), and the Second Vatican Council's *Pastoral Constitution on the Church in the Modern World* (1965) in claiming society's responsibility to its least fortunate. Contending that unemployment and poverty had risen over the previous two decades, the document espoused an increase in government job training and job creation programs, a national minimum welfare payment, expansion of welfare to cover two-parent as well as single-parent households, and deep cuts in the military budget to help finance these reforms.[133]

In November the Simon commission released its final report, "Liberty and Justice for All." In contrast to the bishops' claims, "over thirty million jobs have been created in the United States in the last fifteen years," the report stated, "more than ten million in the last four years alone." Rather than nationalize welfare, as the bishops proposed, the commission argued that "a demand for benefits without a correlative acceptance of social duties, permissive sexual standards, pregnancies apart from marriage, separation and divorce" would only worsen an already desperate situation. Instead of simply citing the 14 percent of Americans who were poor, the bishops should have accounted for "the non-cash benefits given to the poor in 1985, benefits scarcely in existence in 1965."[134]

A week later, with the Simon commission's critique fresh in their minds, the bishops discussed, debated, and amended the final draft of their pastoral. Then they voted, 225–9, to accept it. The meeting concluded with a thunderous standing ovation for Archbishop Weakland, shattering the calm of the late afternoon.[135]

While the monk was causing a ruckus, the politician was keeping quiet. Almost six years after the Weakland committee had begun its work, President Ronald Reagan still had nothing to say about the finished product. In August 1986, he warned a group of Catholics, "You can be certain you'll be accused of mixing religion and politics." The president wasn't talking to the bishops, however, and he wasn't discussing the economic pastoral. He was on the phone with the Knights of Columbus convention in Chicago. And he was talking about abortion.[136]

Conclusions on Social Justice

From the beginning of its deliberations, the Weakland committee had struggled to affect national policy by seeking the proper balance between the ecclesiastical and the political. Issuing "Economic Justice for All" with only two years left of the Reagan administration, it aggressively pursued both these tracks, only to fall short on both.

To implement the pastoral ecclesiastically, the bishops chose a familiar tactic: create a committee. Even before the Weakland committee had finished its task, the United States Catholic Conference's president, Bishop James Malone, had appointed Bishop Anthony Pilla of Cleveland to chair a panel that would devise a follow-up plan. The Pilla committee arrived at five principles to guide the bishops' subsequent efforts: "1) make a substantive commitment, 2) integrate, don't isolate, 3) teach the moral principles, 4) institutionalize the debate, and 5) the Church itself must be an agent of reform."[137]

Within a year, the bishops were well on their way to attaining these objectives. Their "substantive commitment" was $525,000 to fund a national Office of Implementation. Attempts to "integrate, not isolate" the Church membership included the distribution of 76,000 complete texts of the pastoral; 47,000 *Origins* texts of the letter; 935,000 "Catholic Update" summaries; 86,992 summaries by Rev. James Hug; and almost 5,000 Spanish texts. Ways to "teach the moral principles" were videocassettes, plays, and liturgies in English, Spanish, Dutch, and German. Efforts to "institutionalize the debate" featured lectures, discussions, courses, conferences, and workshops on Catholic campuses. Only the last goal—"the Church itself must be an agent of reform"—seemed to be making little progress. According to a *National Catholic Reporter* poll at the end of 1987, 71 percent of adult Catholics surveyed not only hadn't read the economic pastoral, they hadn't even heard of it.[138]

One can largely attribute this startling statistic to the fact that truckloads of microphones, cameras, and reporters had stopped showing up at bishops' meetings once the peace pastoral was complete. But perhaps a bigger reason was that, as Bruce Douglass and William Gould posited at the time of the first draft's release, "the majority of Americans" were not sympathetic to "the particular line the letter takes." For the bishops, the relationship between modern economic life and the Christian faith was "problematical." But for the average American, it was "perfectly natural."[139]

If the bishops' ecclesiastical track was only partially successful, their political approach was even less so. Not that they didn't have an argument. There were still too many unemployed and underemployed Americans, especially in the nation's decaying urban core. Joseph Hogan observed that although unemployment dropped to 5 percent in Reagan's final year in office, most new jobs were in the low-paying, low-producing export service sector.[140]

The bishops also had an audience: the Democratic majorities in the House of Representatives for all eight years of the Reagan administration and in the Senate for the last two. So when Archbishop Weakland told the congressional Joint Economic Committee in December 1986 that the bishops decried "the ridiculing or downgrading of government," he was preaching to a largely liberal choir. A January 1987 letter from the National Conference of Catholic Charities' executive director, Rev. Thomas Harvey, and the Catholic Health Association's president, Jack Curley, to the House and Senate Budget Committees, House Energy and Commerce Committees, and Senate Finance Committee helped to sink Reagan's plan to cap Medicaid funding. That same month, Rev. Bryan Hehir testified for the USCC before the Senate Banking, Housing, and Urban Affairs Committee that the "1000 percent increase in homelessness since 1979" was due largely to Reagan housing cuts. Congress would soon pass an anti-homelessness bill co-sponsored by Catholic Democratic senator Daniel Patrick Moynihan of New York. By March 1987, the bishops had accepted six invitations to testify on Capitol Hill about their economic pastoral.[141]

But among their fellow American Catholics, the bishops' argument attracted a limited audience. Because even before the 1980s, while Lyndon Johnson and Richard Nixon were tending to the poor, many American Catholics were striking it rich. As they abandoned their urban neighborhoods and ethnic identities, they also relinquished much of the communitarian ethos with which their immigrant ancestors had arrived. Many had become culturally if not religiously Protestant, individualized rather than hyphenated Americans. They were not indifferent to the plight of the poor, but they were skeptical of the wisdom of the government. By the time conservatives entered the American mainstream, Catholics were there to hold the door.[142] They did not completely shed their pasts. Many remained Democrats. Most remained Catholics. But in this new era, which Richard Nixon had recognized and upon which Ronald Reagan would capitalize, some of them were fiscally conservative and voted Republican.

While the Weakland committee's theological exhortation to lift the lowly had the reassuring ring of a Sunday morning homily, its political plea to fund the government had the stale odor of a big city machine. The bishops' peace pastoral had been ahead of the curve; their economic pastoral was behind the times.

Life and Death: Abortion

In 1979, weary of liberal excess, voters gazed westward, longing for a conservative savior to restore traditional values and fiscal sanity to the nation's capital. So Canadians replaced the left-wing government of Pierre Trudeau with the right-wing promise of Joe Clark. For all of nine months, Clark said all the right things, but he said them poorly. He suffered, his opponents and even some of his supporters smirked, from "amsirahc"—"charisma" spelled backward. Liberal excess, it seemed, was not so bad after all. Canada's electorate then restored Trudeau to Ottawa. The man had style.

South of the border, Jimmy Carter had turned out to be the liberals' Joe Clark. And Ronald Reagan would be the conservatives' Pierre Trudeau. Deemed out of the mainstream in his two previous runs for the White House, in 1968 and 1976, Reagan moderated none of his previous positions in his third presidential campaign. Like Clark, he persisted in trumpeting traditional values and pleading for fiscal sanity. But unlike Clark, the former Hollywood actor had style.

Many American Catholics were therefore willing to absolve Governor Reagan for signing a liberal abortion bill in California in 1967 and for proclaiming October 24, 1974, to be World Population Day to "reflect on the necessity of population stabilization to the welfare of the peoples of the world." And, unlike many of their bishops, who labored tirelessly to spur him to action, they would be willing to forgive President Reagan for eight years of failing to effect any modifications of *Roe v. Wade*. For even as his belated half-measures alienated the hierarchy, his eloquent testimonials to the sanctity of human life appeased much of the rank and file. The man had style.[143]

Style

Ronald Reagan had barely settled into the White House when the abortion issue resurfaced. Only two days after the new president's inaugural address, in which he didn't mention the subject, sixty-five thousand backers of a constitutional amendment to ban abortion descended on Washington, D.C., to commemorate the eighth anniversary of the Supreme Court decision to which they so strenuously objected.[144]

President Reagan appeared reluctant to lead this offensive. When asked at a March press conference about a constitutional amendment to overturn *Roe v. Wade*, Reagan answered that "there really isn't any need for an amendment, because once you have determined this, the Constitution already protects human life." The president's response sounded like an endorsement of anti-abortion legislation, except that members of the administration couldn't verify what Reagan had meant. Illinois congressman Henry Hyde said, "I honestly don't know" whether the president had just endorsed his anti-abortion bill. But then Hyde wasn't sure if he endorsed his own bill, explaining that "the amendment is still our ultimate goal."[145]

The U.S. Catholic bishops wished Hyde hadn't proposed his legislation at all. Since this approach would undoubtedly invite a legal challenge and distract attention from the larger objective, which even Hyde professed, the bishops announced in March that only an amendment could offer the requisite "constitutional basis for the legal protection of the unborn."[146] But Congressman Hyde disagreed. "Many Catholics here in the Congress, including myself, as elsewhere in America, are both angry and discouraged by your very public opposition to the Human Life Bill," Hyde wrote to the United States Catholic Conference's general counsel, Wilfred Caron, in June.[147]

While Hyde and the hierarchy were divided over his proposal, they were united in their disapproval of President Reagan. When White House counselor Edwin Meese signaled in May that the administration would support a Department of Health and Human Services appropriations bill minus Hyde's annual addendum prohibiting the federal funding of abortion, White House aides Gary Bauer and Morton Blackwell warned of a pro-life backlash. The backlash arrived when North Carolina Republican senator Jesse Helms led a successful roll call vote restoring the Hyde Amendment to the HHS appropriations and, in White House aide William Gribbin's words, "embarrassing the Administration." Only an agreement by Oregon Republican senator Mark

Hatfield, Helms, and Meese to attach the Hyde Amendment in the conference committee saved the anti-abortion language, and spared the president from further antipathy from his erstwhile allies.[148]

Despite a lack of support from the bishops and the president, the Hyde human life bill (now co-sponsored by Senator Helms) passed the Senate Judiciary Committee's Separation of Powers Subcommittee in July by a party line 3–2 vote. The subcommittee chair, Helms's fellow North Carolina Republican John East, cast the deciding vote in the subcommittee, but he would block consideration of the measure in the full committee to stave off virtually certain defeat.[149]

The administration continued to antagonize its ostensible comrades in the pro-life campaign. When Reagan nominated Sandra Day O'Connor to be the first woman on the Supreme Court, he received plaudits from many precincts. The pro-life community was not one of them. "I have anger, resentment, and frustration pent up in me at this moment," Marie Craven, the Catholic former chair of Illinois Citizens Concerned for Life, wrote to the president in July 1981.[150] Reagan replied to Craven in August, assuring her that O'Connor's vote as a senator in the Arizona legislature against an amendment preventing the state's university hospitals from performing abortions was one of procedure rather than policy. Attributing Craven's misperceptions to the "talk about my appointment . . . by one person in Arizona [who] . . . has something of a record of being vindictive," Reagan added that "Mrs. O'Connor has assured me of her personal abhorrence for abortion."[151] Craven remained unpersuaded. "His blanket statement astonishes me," she lamented upon receiving the Reagan reply. "He's trying to blame the whole thing on one person."[152]

Catholic conservative columnist Patrick Buchanan explained that "the whole thing" involved more than the single O'Connor vote defended by the president. He cited Senator O'Connor's vote to "remove all legal sanctions against abortions performed by licensed physicians"; her co-sponsorship of the Family Planning Act, which made available "all medically acceptable family planning methods and information," including "surgical procedures," to anyone regardless of age; and her vote against a human life amendment. Buchanan identified Reagan's "vindictive" accuser as Carolyn Gerster, an Arizona physician to whom candidate Reagan had personally pledged his fealty to the pro-life cause.[153]

Dr. Gerster, now the vice president in charge of internal affairs for the National Right to Life Committee, wrote her own letter to the president. Gerster explained that "my criticism deals with Justice O'Connor's 1970–1974 voting record on abortion-related issues." And while she questioned Justice O'Connor's commitment to the pro-life movement, Gerster remained convinced of President Reagan's devotion, expressed to her "in January in Rye, New York, and in June in Los Angeles." As for Reagan's response to Craven, Gerster asserted, "I do not believe that you wrote the letter."[154]

As the president continued to tread the scalding waters of the abortion controversy, Utah Republican senator Orrin Hatch tried to lower the temperature. Hatch proposed a constitutional amendment that would state that "there shall be no right of abortion guaranteed by the Constitution," that Congress and the states had a "concurrent power to restrict or prohibit abortions," and that "any law of a state more restrictive with respect to the permissibility of abortions shall not be superseded by any law of Congress."[155] The bishops officially welcomed the Hatch amendment as a way to bridge the divide within the pro-life movement between the advocates of anti-abortion legislation and the proponents of a human life amendment. Archbishop John Roach of Minneapolis–St. Paul told the Senate Judiciary Committee's Subcommittee on the Constitution in November that the Hatch amendment offered an "achievable solution" with promising prospects for passage on Capitol Hill.[156]

The Reagan administration thought otherwise. Assistant attorney general Robert McConnell wrote to the subcommittee chair, Republican senator Strom Thurmond of South Carolina, that the Hatch amendment was "overly broad," written in such a way as to invite national proscription of birth control and national usurpation of state homicide laws.[157]

Few bishops took issue with the hierarchy's official position. At their November 1981 meeting, the bishops took a vote on the Hatch amendment. It passed with only five dissenters. *America*'s editors saluted the bishops' pragmatism in endorsing the states' rights strategy.[158] There was greater dissent among the rank and file. From the right, University of Notre Dame law professor Charles Rice lamented that the bishops' embrace of the Hatch amendment ran counter to their professed devotion to the personhood of the unborn. From the left, Mary Meehan, who had left the Church but not the pro-life movement, observed that the Hatch amendment had won few converts among pro-choice Catholics. Pointing out that Eleanor Smeal, the president of the National Organization for Women, and Robin Chandler Duke, the president of the National Abortion Rights Action League, were baptized Catholics, she posited that it would be a lot easier to reverse *Roe v. Wade* if there were not so many Catholic liberals in favor of it.[159] Non-Catholic pro-lifers differed over the Hatch amendment as well. Everybody who was pro-life, it seemed, had weighed in on the Hatch amendment.[160]

Everybody, that is, except the president. "I have read the many reports of division in the right-to-life movement," Reagan told about twenty pro-life leaders at the White House on the ninth anniversary of *Roe v. Wade* in January

1982. "I do not intend to take sides in the current controversy over which alternative the right-to-life community should embrace." Instead, Reagan admonished those assembled that their movement "needed to get its act together."[161]

So did the administration. Reminding Reagan that he had supported a human life amendment during the 1980 campaign, White House aide Morton Blackwell called assistant attorney general Robert McConnell's argument against the Hatch amendment a "parade of horribles." Blackwell concluded that "there is no shortage of pro-life attorneys and legal scholars except, it seems, at Justice."[162] Such bickering over the ideological purity of the Hatch amendment was beside the point, because it wasn't going to pass anyway. That was the judgment of Hatch's own legislative assistant, Stephen Markman, whose memo foretelling the doom of his boss's proviso somehow found its way into the media. Markman suggested that pro-life senators could harmlessly vote for a measure in their chamber because it had no chance of passage in the other.[163]

It would not take long to test Markman's cynical hypothesis. In March 1982 the Senate Judiciary Committee reported the Hatch amendment, 20–7, on a nearly party line vote. Catholic Democrats Joseph Biden of Delaware and Dennis DeConcini of Arizona sided with most of the committee's Republicans in backing the measure, while Catholic Republican Charles Mac Mathias of Maryland and non-Catholic Republican Arlen Specter of Pennsylvania joined the Democratic minority. The panel's passing of the Hatch proposal marked the furthest an anti-abortion constitutional amendment had advanced in the post-*Roe* era.[164]

With the outlook for congressional action against abortion looking bleak, White House aide Gary Bauer drafted a letter for Reagan to send to pro-life advocates on and off Capitol Hill in an effort to jump-start the legislative process. Bauer's draft called abortion "a great moral evil and assault on the sacredness of life." Yet the letter perpetuated the administration's ambivalence on the proper legislative tactic to eliminate the evil, simply expressing the wish that the divisions over the Helms-Hyde and Hatch proposals "be resolved in favor of the common goal." And by the time Reagan sent the letter in April, White House aide Kenneth Duberstein had adjusted Bauer's deadline for Congress to consider such legislation from "without delay" to simply "in the near future."[165]

But at least Reagan had said *something*. "Mr. Reagan's initiative has helped focus the already strong desire for pro-life action in this session of Congress," Rev. Edward Bryce, the director of the bishops' Office for Pro-Life Activities, reacted to the president's missive, choosing to ignore Reagan's evasion on the proper means to attack abortion, and to disbelieve the conventional wisdom that any anti-abortion measure was sure to fail.[166]

Perhaps Reagan should have sent the letter to members of his own administration. Dr. James Wyngaarden, the newly appointed director of the National Institutes of Health, unleashed a fury of criticism from pro-life groups when he said that abortion was properly the decision of a woman, not the Congress. "I am still convinced that President Reagan is strongly pro-life," Paul Brown, the director of the Life Amendment political action committee, reacted to Wyngaarden's remarks. "I am equally convinced that some of his advisors are not."[167]

Reagan aide Gary Bauer recommended that while the administration was waiting for the outcome in the Congress, it should shift its attention to the courts, where it could file an amicus brief in *Akron v. Akron Center for Reproductive Health*, a case testing a 1978 anti-abortion ordinance in Ohio. The Akron law mandated that a doctor must warn a patient that her abortion could "result in severe emotional disturbances" and inform her that "the unborn child is a human life from the moment of conception."[168]

As the White House attempted to heal the rift among anti-abortion groups, some Catholics threatened to reopen it. "We're against any bill or amendment about it, and consider it a matter of conscientious moral choice for women to make," Sister Donna Quinn, the president of the National Coalition of American Nuns, explained her organization's opposition to the Helms-Hyde or Hatch legislation. She worried that the hierarchy's embrace of anti-abortion legislation was "another putdown of women." The bishops felt *they* were being put down. Father Bryce, speaking for their pro-life office, attacked the nuns as "misguided," calling their resistance to pro-life measures "certainly no comfort to the unborn child."[169]

While Catholics quarreled, Reagan finally showed some fight of his own. In August he told the Knights of Columbus convention in Hartford that he was "urging the Senate" to give anti-abortion proposals "the speedy consideration they deserve." For the first time, Reagan sent letters and made phone calls to wavering senators, encouraging a "yes" vote on the Helms human life bill while refusing to disavow the Hatch states' rights amendment.[170]

The Senate considered the Helms proposal in September, this time attached to school prayer as an amendment to an amendment on a debt ceiling bill. Then, for the third time, the Senate voted not to vote on it. The senators also did not vote on the Hatch amendment because its sponsor withdrew it. Senator Hatch said that he preferred to wait for a less chaotic time than the end of the congressional session.[171]

Not all the news was bad for the pro-life cause, however. For the first time, the USCC's Legal Department reported, "President Reagan had stepped up his lobbying effort on behalf of the Helms measure in the days just before" the fateful vote. The USCC's Ad Hoc Committee on the Defense of Life praised Reagan's "all-out" support for the bill. Abortion opponents hadn't won anything, but at least their most prominent supporter had gone down fighting.[172]

Or had he? When the dust had settled on the legislative setbacks, some Catholics appeared to be having second thoughts about their standard-bearer in the White House. While "the Hatch Amendment has yet to receive an unfavorable vote at any level of Congress," Richard Doerflinger, the legislative assistant for the bishops' Committee on Pro-Life Activities, reflected, "Senators unsympathetic to the pro-life cause, as well as the President of the United States, were all too willing to seize on pro-life disunity as an excuse for inaction."[173] White House aide William Gribbin returned Doerflinger's fire. "The USCC people can't be trusted, cannot be worked with, cannot be placated," Gribbin wrote to Morton Blackwell. "And if the Administration or—Heaven forbid—any of our own people outside the Administration fall in, next year, with the USCC's 1983 version of the Hatch Amendment, we can expect gratitude from them similar to this piece of slander."[174]

If Reagan had not acted early and often enough to satisfy his pro-life critics, at least now he was listening to them. "The President must be very careful not to appear as if he is using disunity in the movement as an excuse for inaction," White House aides Michael Uhlmann and William Barr implored in eerily familiar language. They suggested that to head off further criticism of the chief executive, the administration should "encourage small-scale initiatives that will likely garner majority support, such as federal fund cut-offs and fetal experimentation bans." Then, "after getting a victory or two under our belt," the White House could mount "a more direct attack on abortion," and this time help to choose "the time, place, and most promising vehicle" for legislative success.[175]

Reagan took this advice, commemorating the tenth anniversary of *Roe v. Wade* in January 1983 by telling a group of pro-life leaders to start small—renewing the Hyde Amendment's prohibition on federal funding of abortion while fighting fetal experimentation, infanticide, and sex-selection abortions—before dreaming big: outlawing all abortions. And for his part, the president promised not to wait until the eleventh hour to join the antiabortion struggle, offering instead to "plan all our pro-life battles in the Congress long enough in advance for us in the Administration to do a better job working the Hill."[176]

Reagan stepped up his assault on abortion with an article (later a book chapter) for *Human Life Review*, in which he again endorsed both the Helms-Hyde and Hatch efforts, but this time pledged his "full support." He concluded by likening abortion to slavery. Just as the nation could not survive "half-slave and half-free," Reagan posited, it could not continue bitterly divided over the rights of the unborn.[177] White House aide Michael Uhlmann urged Reagan to publish his article before the Catholic bishops released the final draft of their pastoral letter on nuclear war, to "frame the pro-life issue in our terms rather than the political opposition's." But the bishops beat the president to the punch. At the insistence of their president, Archbishop Roach, and the drafting committee's most conservative member, Archbishop John O'Connor of New York, the bishops revised the war and peace pastoral to include anti-abortion language. Then they published their final draft in April, a month before Reagan's article appeared.[178]

Following its approval of Reagan's nomination of Catholic Margaret Heckler to be his second secretary of the Health and Human Services Department, the Senate's attention returned to the Hatch amendment, now reduced to ten words—that a "right to an abortion is not secured by this Constitution." The proposal moved from the Judiciary Committee to the Senate floor after a special motion sponsored by Catholic Democrat Joseph Biden of Delaware, a supporter turned opponent of the amendment, which allowed the measure to escape the committee despite a tie vote. "In the ten years since the Supreme Court decision legalizing abortion, it has been claimed that the abortion issue was settled as a matter of law and public policy," the USCC's general secretary, Msgr. Daniel Hoye, praised the committee's decision. "With the United States Senate now preparing to debate a constitutional amendment on abortion for the first time, that claim is patently false."[179]

At least for a few weeks. At the end of June, the Senate voted 50–49 not to ratify the Hatch amendment, not only falling eighteen votes short of the two-thirds necessary to send the amendment to the states but failing to muster even a simple majority.[180]

The third year of the Reagan administration ended with both positive and negative developments for the pro-life forces on Capitol Hill. Shortly after Reagan and the USCC's president, Bishop James Malone of Youngstown, discussed abortion at the White House, both houses of Congress passed the Hyde Amendment's prohibition of federal funding of abortion for another year. Meanwhile, the Equal Rights Amendment finally died six decades after its birth when the bishops, otherwise neutral on the proposal's merits, joined the National Right to Life Committee in backing an anti-abortion rider whose failure spawned enough pro-life defectors to sink the ERA.[181]

But the Senate rejected a clumsy attempt by Iowa Republican Roger Jepsen to attach a human life amendment similar to the Helms-Hyde version to a bill dealing with the U.S. Civil Rights Commission. "It appears this Congress is unlikely to pass any general prohibition of abortion," an administration memo gloomily concluded as Reagan addressed pro-life leaders for the fourth time in his presidency in January 1984, on the eleventh anniversary of *Roe v. Wade*.[182]

Stymied at home, the Reagan administration moved its crusade against abortion overseas. Over the objections of the Agency for International Development, Reagan broadened the 1974 congressional ban on U.S. abortion funding abroad to withhold family planning monies from any countries or organizations that financed abortions, even without American dollars.[183]

When the Catholic former New York senator and current president of Radio Free Europe/Radio Liberty, James Buckley, introduced the administration's new policy at the World Population Conference in Mexico City in August, only Costa Rica, Chile, and the Vatican expressed support. "The evidence is clear that in many developing countries," World Bank president A. W. Clausen objected to Buckley's announcement, "development will be postponed indefinitely unless slower population growth can be achieved soon." But Buckley's brother William, the publisher of *National Review*, retorted that "subsidizing compulsory sterilizations and abortions in other Third World countries will not add a single ounce of rice or bread to the tables of the hungry either abroad or at home."[184]

Just when it looked as if substance had finally supplanted style as the watchword of the Reagan administration's abortion posture, critics and choir alike proceeded to dispel such notions. The hostile *New Republic*, carping that the population policy shift "had less to do with the Mexico City conference than with the Dallas convention" of Republicans who had just renominated Reagan, pointed out that "abortion money" accounted for "less than one percent of the budget of the International Planned Parenthood Federation," one of the leading targets of the administration's wrath. In his speech in Mexico City, James Buckley said that even without the abortion-related funds, the U.S. government would be increasing its budget to reach "forty-four percent of the total population assistance provided by the developed nations."[185]

Despite his heightened religiosity toward the pro-life cause, Reagan remained agnostic on the messy details of how to remake history. A week before the November election, he ducked a question from the National Catholic News Service as to which anti-abortion constitutional amendment he really preferred.[186]

Even Reagan's landslide reelection victory over the pro-choice Democratic ticket of former vice president Walter Mondale and Catholic representative Geraldine Ferraro of New York, in which he captured forty-nine states and 61 percent of the Catholic vote, would not embolden the president to walk a few blocks to address the seventy thousand marchers protesting the twelfth anniversary of *Roe v. Wade* in January 1985. For the fifth year in a row, Reagan spoke to the protesters by phone, improbably telling them that "the momentum is with us," even if the Congress, the courts, and most of the public were not. When Nellie Gray, the Catholic president of March for Life, proclaimed with equal imprecision at the perennial White House meeting with pro-life leaders that the "pro-life movement is united now" behind the "Paramount Human Life Amendment with no compromises," the president responded, "Good for you, and I support you." Then the meeting adjourned for another year, and the president went to work on other things.[187]

If the president was delusional, at least he was not lonely. In July the United States Catholic Conference joined the administration in filing amicus briefs in support of Pennsylvania and Illinois "informed consent" abortion laws. The bishops also backed Reagan's new population policy, which passed Congress in the summer of 1985.[188]

The bishops and the president also had to ward off attacks from their ostensible allies. *All News*, the self-described "official weekly of the pro-life movement," criticized the bishops' amicus brief for avoiding mention of the part of the Illinois statute that required doctors to inform patients that some birth control drugs and devices promoted abortion. The New Orleans archbishop, Philip Hannan, took his colleagues to task for implicitly upholding abortion by explicitly defending informed consent.[189]

When New York Republican representative Jack Kemp attached an amendment to the Title X family planning services appropriations bill that would have outlawed the use of such funds for abortion counseling or referrals, it lost to a counterproposal by Illinois's anti-abortion Catholic Democrat Richard Durbin to preserve the status quo. Durbin was not the only abortion opponent in the way of the Kemp amendment: Reagan's Office of Management and Budget had expressed its preference for a "clean bill" without the anti-abortion language.[190]

After pro-life Catholic Republicans Christopher Smith of New Jersey and Robert Dornan of California successfully amended the House appropriations bill for the District of Columbia to exclude abortion funding in that city, which at the time had three abortions for every two births, Helms fought the good fight in the Senate—and lost. When the conference committee prohibited D.C. from receiving federal payments for abortion but permitted local abortion financing, March for Life president Nellie Gray urged Reagan to veto the legislation. But Reagan signed it.[191]

"I am sick at heart with only pretty words about the humanity of preborn children," Gray wrote to Reagan. But pro-life House Republicans Kemp, Smith, Hyde, and Vin Weber of Minnesota and pro-life Republican senator Gordon Humphrey of New Hampshire had not heard enough. On the thirteenth anniversary of *Roe v. Wade* on January 22, 1986, they wrote to the president recommending a nationally televised address on abortion. Instead of the president speaking on television, however, he spoke at a meeting of pro-life leaders at the White House.[192]

In a letter, Teresa Ashcraft implored Reagan to move beyond "the talk, the smile, and the wave of the hand to pro-lifers each January 22," and to "take pro-life action off the back burner where it has been the last six years." Words like "the time to act is now . . . to seek to overturn *Roe v. Wade* in the courts or in the legislature as soon as possible" were what Ashcraft would have liked to hear from the president. Instead, they came in April from Virgil Dechant, the leader of the Knights of Columbus.[193]

Reagan got around to answering Ashcraft's letter in July. He acknowledged that "these years have gone by and we haven't been able to get the necessary legislation to change the Constitution, which is the only way to reverse the Court opinion"—a sentiment that not only recounted the defeat of the Hatch states' rights amendment, but that appeared to preclude Reagan's support for the Helms-Hyde human life bill. He nonetheless promised to "keep trying" and to continue to "wave to the pro-lifers because their effort to mobilize public opinion is most important to the cause." It would not be surprising if Ashcraft suggested that maybe mobilizing public opinion was what a *president* was supposed to do.[194]

In the absence of legislative progress, the pro-life movement focused on two "immediate priorities," which the special assistant to the president for public liaison, Carl Anderson, identified as Reagan's appointment of pro-life federal judges, such as Catholic Antonin Scalia, appointed to the Supreme Court to replace retiring pro-choice justice Lewis Powell in 1986, and the retention of the Republican majority in the Senate to confirm them, to help undo decisions like the Supreme Court's June 1986 rejection of Pennsylvania's "informed consent" law. As for anti-abortion legislation, Anderson shared the pessimism of Gray, Ashcraft, and the *National Catholic Register*. He forecast "no Senate floor action in 1986." Anderson also shared the prescription of his pro-life compatriots, that Reagan seize the initiative on the abortion issue. Anderson proposed that the president devise a bill of his own.[195]

Reagan would continue to resist proposing his own bill, however, preferring simply to give more speeches on the subject. In August he encouraged the Knights of Columbus not to give up flying the pro-life banner. "You can be certain you'll be accused of mixing religion and politics," the first draft of Reagan's remarks noted. "I receive the same criticism myself for supporting a pro-life amendment to the Constitution." But his pro-life critics pointed out that the Hatch amendment backed by the president was more supportive of states' rights than the right to life. So the final draft of the speech said, "I receive the same criticism for supporting pro-life legislation." But as his pro-life critics also pointed out, Reagan had never come out in favor of the Helms-Hyde human life bill, so he hadn't really supported pro-life legislation either.[196]

The seventh year of the Reagan presidency began in the usual way, with March for Life president Nellie Gray inviting Reagan to speak at the group's rally on the fourteenth anniversary of *Roe v. Wade*, Reagan speaking only at a distance before summoning Gray and other pro-life leaders to the White House, and Gray exhorting Reagan to do more than just talk. "Mr. President, it is a puzzlement and great disappointment that actions of your Executive Branch," Gray scolded, "do not follow your good words."[197]

Action against abortion seemed even more elusive as the new year commenced. Reagan's third secretary of Health and Human Services, the former Indiana Republican governor Dr. Otis Bowen, overrode the decision of his deputy assistant secretary, Joan Gaspar, to withhold federal subsidies to Planned Parenthood. The anti-abortion American Life League counted only thirty-five members of the newly Democratic Senate as dependably pro-life, far short of the fifty needed to pass a human life bill and the sixty-seven necessary to send a constitutional amendment to the states. Worst of all, "abortion fatigue" seemed to have set in on all sides of the debate. Rev. James Burtchaell, a pro-life theologian at the University of Notre Dame, sighed in January 1987 that "even Catholics don't like to bring the subject up."[198]

Substance

The cumulative disappointment of the first six years of the Reagan administration for the pro-life forces meant that when the president at last began to deliver on the promises of his 1980 campaign, they didn't seem to believe him. In February 1987 Reagan finally took Carl Anderson's advice and proposed his own anti-abortion bill, calling for a permanent ban on the federal funding of abortion, which would replace the annual renewals of the Hyde Amendment, and a prohibition on domestic nongovernmental organizations receiving federal family planning money, which would revive the Kemp amendment's revision of Title X. In a rare moment of agreement, Catholic Douglas Johnson of National Right to Life and non-Catholic Eve Paul of Planned Parenthood viewed the proposal as an empty political gesture doomed to fail. "Most pro-life groups appreciate this effort by the administration, but understand that the legislation does not stand a good chance of passage," White House aide Alfred Kingon conceded. "They are understandably dismayed."[199]

Pro-life Republican legislators Smith, Dornan, Kemp, Hyde, and Weber vouched for Reagan's sincerity in advancing his proposal, but questioned the dedication of his lieutenants to the anti-abortion cause. As if to prove them wrong, HHS secretary Bowen reversed his earlier decision and suspended federal aid to Planned Parenthood, a response not only to his fellow Republicans' plea, but to the twenty thousand letters and twenty-seven thousand telephone calls his office had received from pro-life advocates incensed at his initial directive.[200]

And the president decided to lead. Reagan's pro-life legislation, nicknamed the "Superbill," gathered 115 co-sponsors in the House of Representatives and reclaimed the allegiance of much of the pro-life movement. "The President's Pro-Life Bill is an historic event," Angela Grimm of the anti-abortion newsletter the *Light* applauded. "It represents the first time a president has promised such a measure, and perhaps the first measure with real strategic impact for the pro-life movement." The administration rewarded such confidence with a vow to mount a "big push for passage" of the Superbill.[201] Not all pro-life advocates were on board, however. The Catholic conservative law professor Charles Rice of Notre Dame considered the Superbill a halfway measure. Rice spoke forcefully against the bill, while the U.S. Catholic bishops spoke not at all. *Lifeletter* wondered, "How [to] explain the almost total lack of 'official' Roman Catholic support for [the] Superbill?"[202]

While the bishops dithered, the president dared. Not only was he initiating legislation, but he was proposing a new paradigm for the abortion debate. To break the impasse in Congress and in the country, Catholic White House aide Dinesh D'Souza pressed Reagan to treat abortion more like smoking, something that was legal yet, as most smokers and nonsmokers agreed, in need of regulation. "Within a framework of legal abortion, the government can take a number of steps to discourage women from having abortions," D'Souza suggested. Among these steps were moves to defund abortion, such as ordering Surgeon General C. Everett Koop to draft new regulations to exclude the use of federal family planning funds for abortion counseling and referral, which Reagan did in July. Reagan did not just announce what the Associated Press called "the first substantive change" on abortion that "the administration has proposed on its own." He did so at a meeting of pro-life leaders at the White House, in what aide Carl Anderson admitted was "the first major Presidential address on the pro-life issue" in the seven years of the Reagan era.[203]

"The gift of life, God's special gift, is no less beautiful when it is accompanied by illness or weakness, hunger or poverty, mental or physical hardships, loneliness or old age," Reagan eloquently quoted the late Terence Cardinal Cooke of New York, the long-time chairman of the USCC's Committee for Pro-Life Activities. "It is in and through the weakest of human vessels that the

Lord continues to reveal the power of His love." Though he was "used to a little skepticism," Reagan compared the legislative prospects for the Superbill to those for his 1986 tax reform, which had gone from unlikely to "inevitable."[204]

Reagan's newfound ardor reawakened the Catholic bishops. The USCC Ad Hoc Committee in Defense of Life cheered that the Superbill "has what no other previous anti-abortion legislation has had: President Reagan's clear support and authorship." The support of the American Life League president, Judie Brown, was more temperate. "I wish President Reagan had done this six years ago," she conceded. "But it's better late than never."[205]

The White House agreed with Brown on both counts. First, the Reagan initiative was indeed late. The White House communications director, Tom Griscom, had hesitated before adding the policy changes to the Superbill in Reagan's speech because he wondered why, if these revisions were so simple, they had waited over six years to receive a hearing. Citing the Iran-Contra scandal and the contentious battle over pro-life judge Robert Bork's nomination to the Supreme Court (which would force Reagan to nominate Catholic Anthony Kennedy instead), an anonymous "senior Reagan adviser" told *U.S. News and World Report*'s Michael Kramer that it was "ridiculous to move on this issue at this time."[206] Second, the Superbill was nonetheless welcome. "I don't think the Presidency comes to a stop in the last eighteen months," an unnamed "senior Administration official" told the *New York Times*'s Steven Roberts. "There are still things we want to accomplish and this is one of them," Kramer's source concurred.[207]

If the president heard the clock ticking on his tenure in office, so too did the pope on his September 1987 visit to the United States. Appearing with Vice President George Bush at the Detroit airport on the last stop of his nine-city tour, John Paul II said that the "ultimate test of America's greatness is the way you treat every human being, especially the weakest and most defenseless ones, those as yet unborn."[208]

At their September Administrative Committee meeting the U.S. Catholic bishops saluted the pope's words and the president's actions. The USCC Committee on Pro-Life Activities urged Reagan to "convince members of Congress" that the "significant reforms" that he had proposed were "both reasonable and necessary."[209]

While the bishops lobbied, the president led. He accepted Nellie Gray's suggestion by proclaiming January 17, 1988, to be National Sanctity of Life Day. "I have asked the legislative branch to declare the 'humanity of the unborn child' and the compelling interest of the several states to protect the life of each person before birth," Reagan reminded the public of his Superbill, now languishing on Capitol Hill. But "this duty to declare on so fundamental a matter falls to the Executive as well." Or so, the president might have added, he had been told.[210]

Rather than be told yet again, Reagan marked the fifteenth anniversary of *Roe v. Wade* on January 22 by meeting not with the leaders of the annual March for Life but with the rank-and-file marchers, the volunteers on the "front lines" of the abortion wars in places like crisis pregnancy centers and maternity homes. "You rarely speak about pro-life policy without referring to the importance of compassionate alternatives to abortion," White House aide Rebecca Range had sold the idea to the president. For one final time on the anniversary of *Roe*, Reagan promoted the actions he had taken to undo the Supreme Court's damage: the constitutional amendment that went nowhere, the Superbill that was going nowhere, and now a federal task force on model state approaches to adoption that, beyond the power of suggestion, had nowhere to go. "I will make a concerted effort this year to remove barriers to adoption," Reagan pledged, incorporating another of Dinesh D'Souza's recommendations, "so that women experiencing a crisis pregnancy will have more alternatives to abortion."[211]

"Let us unite as a nation and protect the unborn," Reagan exhorted in his final State of the Union address a few days later. Then he further divided the nation by issuing his long-awaited Title X revisions, which not only prevented the funding of groups that performed abortions but prohibited personnel at federally funded family planning clinics from even mentioning abortion, even if pregnancy would endanger a woman's life. Such a "gag rule" was "unethical, bad medicine, and inhumane," according to Dr. John Graham of the American College of Obstetricians and Gynecologists. The American Civil Liberties Union promised to challenge the edict in court.[212]

The president, the bishops, and the rest of the pro-life movement were not strong enough to help pass "Super Hyde," and Congress opted not only to restore the traditional one-year Hyde Amendment but to add exceptions for rape and incest.[213] A Reagan veto threat helped to remove the exceptions, and the new Hyde Amendment that Congress passed in September 1988 was essentially the same one it had been passing since 1976. Two weeks later, following two House-Senate conference committees, another Reagan veto threat, and pressure by the Democratic leadership to enact all thirteen bills on its agenda before the end of the session, the FY 1989 District of Columbia spending measure passed both houses with a Hyde-type amendment attached. Unlike in previous years, however, the addendum prohibited, as pro-lifers had long urged but Reagan had resisted, "local" as well as federal funding of abortion in the nation's capital. Reagan signed the bill on October 1, 1988.[214]

Two days later, the city-operated District of Columbia General Hospital, where 577 abortions had occurred the previous year, announced that neither Medicaid nor the hospital could pay for abortions anymore. Rebuffed by Congress and the president, city officials contemplated taking their pro-choice case to the federal courts. But Reagan had appointed nearly half of all federal judges in the previous eight years, including three pro-life Supreme Court justices, two of them Catholic. So winning in court would not be easy either.[215]

Conclusions on Life and Death

Scholars of all ideological stripes concur that the Ronald Reagan era was transformative in shifting the international diplomatic debate from how to win the Cold War to how to end it, and in altering the domestic political conversation from how to grow the federal government to how to gut it. On abortion, however, Reagan wrought no such transformation. In the absence of presidential leadership for most of Reagan's two terms, the pope and the bishops could not propel enough American Catholics to propel enough other Americans to shift the political winds on abortion.

Preoccupied for much of the era with foreign policy and the economy, Reagan was in large part unwilling to lead. When asked at the end of his presidency whether he would endeavor to achieve as an ex-president what he couldn't attain as a president in the struggle against abortion, Reagan challenged the premise of the question. He cited the renewal of the Hyde Amendment, the introduction of the Mexico City policy, and the unprecedented proposal of pro-life legislation.[216]

After the Catholic League for Religious and Civil Rights encouraged the president to respond to what the sociologist Rev. Andrew Greeley called the "acceptable bigotry" of anti-Catholicism, White House aide Michael Uhlmann suggested a presidential address on the subject of religious prejudice—a speech Reagan never delivered. Reagan's outreach to Catholics at the end of his presidency, when he met with the pro-life Knights of Columbus, Catholic Daughters of the Americas, and Catholic Golden Age, looked very much the way it did at the beginning, when he met with the leaders of the January 22, 1981, March for Life. Although his percentage of the Catholic vote rose by fourteen points from 1980 to 1984, the Great Communicator changed few Catholic minds on abortion. "It was not my role to lead the spiritual revival," Reagan admitted at the conclusion of his eight years in the White House, "but to encourage the spiritual people of this land to follow the spiritual guidance of their clergy."[217]

Undercut by Reagan's disinterest in abortion, the bishops were in large part unable to lead. The bishops' own great communicator, Joseph Cardinal Bernardin of Chicago, made a noble attempt to reach out to the Catholic liberals whom Reagan largely dismissed. In December 1983 at Fordham University, Bernardin formally connected the twin causes with which he was most identified—the peril of nuclear war, which alarmed the Catholic Left, and the scourge of abortion, which unsettled the Catholic Right. Citing John Courtney Murray and Popes Paul VI and John Paul II, Bernardin announced that his fellow bishops' condemnations of both of these evils were "specific applications" of a "consistent ethic of life." Bernardin spent much of the next year expanding upon this theme to include aversion to euthanasia, capital punishment, and poverty. His speaking tour concluded at the University of Notre Dame, where he appeared alongside the more conservative Archbishop John O'Connor of New York to dramatize the hierarchy's emerging consensus toward what Bernardin termed the "seamless garment" of life.[218]

If Bernardin's Fordham address was the speech Reagan never gave, it was because the president couldn't give it. In a memo to the Republican National Committee's Catholic chair, Frank Fahrenkopf, the committee's religious liaison, Father Donald Shea, called Bernardin's words "of great importance," and noted that it was "not by chance" that the cardinal who had authored the bishops' anti-nuclear pastoral would now be leading its anti-abortion committee. This was not a welcome development in the Reagan White House. Bernardin's nuclear war–abortion hybrid was a clever way to "redefine pro-life to include disarmament," an anonymous internal White House memo reacted to the cardinal, "thereby making Teddy [Kennedy] as 'pro-life' as Jesse Helms, and stopping the drift of Catholic voters toward conservative candidates."[219] Such alarmism notwithstanding, Bernardin's message was not transformative either, as Catholic conservatives helped the still hawkish Reagan win forty-nine states a year later. And few Catholic liberals started calling themselves "pro-life."

Least of all Teddy Kennedy. Speaking at Moral Majority co-founder Jerry Falwell's Liberty Baptist College two months before the Bernardin speech, Senator Kennedy challenged the bishops of his church. "I am an American and a Catholic; I love my country and I treasure my faith," Kennedy said. "But I do not assume that my concept of patriotism or policy is invariably correct—or that my convictions about religion should command any greater respect than any other faith in this pluralistic society."[220] Nine months after the Bernardin speech, Kennedy tailored his remarks to address the cardinal's "seamless garment" analogy. But the anti-nuclear senator had not become anti-abortion. Issues like nuclear arms, he asserted in a speech in New York City in September 1984, "are inherently public in nature" and properly subject to public judgment. "Personal choices like abortion should be questions for public debate," Kennedy added, "but in the end the answers cannot be matters for public decision."[221]

Mario Cuomo explained why. Following a summer of verbal sparring with Archbishop O'Connor, the pro-choice Catholic New York governor spoke a week after Kennedy in a speech before the Theology Department at the University of Notre Dame. Cuomo's eight thousand words distinguished between private morality and public consensus, between believing for oneself and legislating for others. "Yes, we create our public morality through consensus, and in this country that consensus reflects to some extent [the] religious values of a great majority of Americans," Cuomo allowed. "But no, all religiously based values don't have an *a priori* place in our public morality." So Cuomo's personal abhorrence toward abortion should not override society's public tolerance for it.[222]

Rep. Henry Hyde followed Cuomo to Notre Dame, where he told the law school that the governor's assertion that American religion had always been "intensely private ... between the individual and God" would have shocked John Winthrop, Jonathan Edwards, and John Courtney Murray (not to mention all those members of Congress who voted for the Hyde Amendment). Yet the appearance of the pro-life congressman so soon after the pro-choice governor had left town made it hard for the Church hierarchy to deny a diversity of views on abortion when the nation's most prominent Catholic university seemed to be celebrating it.[223] "I called for a dialogue," Bernardin mused to his fellow bishops. "We are getting it!"[224]

But the dialogue that Bernardin ignited had a minimal short-term impact on his church. Three years after Bernardin's Fordham lecture, a majority of New York Catholics helped to return Mario Cuomo to the governor's mansion. Four years after the "seamless garment" speech, as Pope John Paul II arrived in the United States in 1987, the *New York Times* and CBS took a poll to determine how closely American Catholics were listening to the Church hierarchy. Only 21 percent of American Catholics "believed that abortion should be as widely available under law as it is today," and 61 percent thought abortion was "murder." Yet 48 percent would permit abortion "to save the mother or in cases of rape or incest"—exceptions not accommodated by Church doctrine. Eighty-five percent agreed that "a woman who has an abortion can still be a good Catholic," a definition decidedly at odds with that of the hierarchy.[225]

A study by the pro-choice Guttmacher Institute found that Catholic women not only were as likely to have abortions as the rest of the American population, but more likely than Protestant and Jewish women. "There is some fuzziness, some confusion, about what the Church really teaches," the United

States Catholic Conference's president, Archbishop John May of Miami, said as he sought to explain the yawning gap between prelate and parishioner on abortion and other issues, "and some fuzziness as to what Catholics really believe."[226]

If Reagan largely wouldn't lead and the bishops largely couldn't lead, then disillusioned and divided American Catholics were hardly in a position to bring other Americans into the pro-life fold. The Reagan era finished with *U.S. News and World Report* proclaiming the perpetually polarized abortion controversy to be "America's Civil War," as the country weathered twenty-eight abortions for every thousand women ages fifteen to forty-four, a higher rate than in any Western nation.[227] On January 22, 1988, the fifteenth anniversary of the verdict that he authored, Supreme Court justice Harry Blackmun predicted that *Roe v. Wade* would soon "go down the drain." But despite the efforts of Ronald Reagan and Joseph Bernardin to eradicate the evil of abortion, Justice Blackmun would get it wrong again.[228]

When Ronald Reagan departed from the White House in January 1989, much had changed in the realms of war and peace and of social justice from when he entered eight years earlier. Largely because of the efforts of the pope and the American Catholic bishops, the nuclear arms race between the United States and the Soviet Union was easing. And largely in spite of the efforts of the pope and the bishops, the U.S. economy was booming. On the life-and-death matter of abortion, however, despite the efforts of the pope and the bishops, little had changed. The president who had seized so many opportunities to defuse the Cold War and to defeat the recession had squandered too many opportunities to combat abortion.

CHAPTER SEVEN

Catholics and George H. W. Bush
(1989–1993)

IN DEMEANOR AS WELL AS IDEOLOGY, Republican George Herbert Walker Bush was the epitome of moderation. In the Persian Gulf War, he would order United Nations troops to stop short of Baghdad. In the urban crisis, he would propose less than a Marshall Plan for cities. On abortion, he would never offer a proposal to repeal *Roe v. Wade*. If his moderation often exasperated liberals in the other party and conservatives in his own, however, it often endeared him to American Catholics, whose bishops were moving to the middle as well.

Though wary of his war in the Gulf, dissatisfied with his aid to the cities, and disappointed with his reluctance on abortion, the prelates nonetheless found Bush far more receptive to their ideas than his predecessor had been. With his devotion to just-war theory, compassion for the urban underclass, and commitment to the unborn, Bush gained the support of the Catholic hierarchy before he lost the loyalty of the rank and file.

War and Peace: The Persian Gulf

Perhaps no other American president was so equipped to lead the nation's armed forces. World War II pilot, Central Intelligence Agency director, United Nations ambassador, China representative, congressman, and vice president—George H. W. Bush had accumulated a foreign policy resume that any presidential candidate would envy.

The U.S. Catholic bishops possessed no such credentials. Yet by the time of the Bush presidency, the bishops had become familiar players in the debate over American foreign policy. They had supported the Vietnam War before they opposed it, pressed for arms control when Ronald Reagan postponed it, and foresaw the end of the Cold War before Reagan helped prepare for it. So when Reagan's highly capable successor dispatched U.S. troops to fight the hot war that the East-West struggle had never permitted, the bishops along with other American Catholics helped to supply the rationale.

While the war with Iraq would transform President Bush's image from the embodiment of vacillation to the enshrinement of decisiveness, it would propel the bishops in the opposite direction, from clarity against nuclear war to ambiguity toward the non-nuclear war in the Persian Gulf. Their discomfort with Bush's means of resolving the crisis in Kuwait, however, could not obscure their contribution to his ends. And for a fleeting moment in history, as the United States recovered its global stature and American Catholics reinforced their moral relevance, both seemed better for it.

Before the War

With Palestinians talking to Israelis, and the U.S.S.R.'s neighbors speaking of Soviet domination in the past tense, history appeared to be on holiday as the Bush administration got under way in January 1989. But not everyone would observe the truce. Humiliated by an eight-year war with Iran that had cost his country hundreds of thousands of lives and left it $80 billion in debt, Saddam Hussein was badly in need of a victory. Accusing neighboring Kuwait of stealing Iraqi oil, refusing to write off Iraqi war debts, and exceeding its oil production quota, the Iraqi dictator dispatched his tanks against the tiny kingdom along the Persian Gulf on August 2, 1990.[1]

With one-quarter of the world's oil supply under Iraqi control and the 15 percent of American oil imports that came from Saudi Arabia in imminent danger, President Bush now recognized after the fact what he had overlooked before it: the United States had to act so that this invasion "will not stand." Following sixty-two calls to foreign heads of state in the first month of the crisis, Bush issued an executive order, endorsed by both houses of Congress, imposing a total U.S. embargo on Iraq. Then he assembled a multinational coalition of troops in Saudi Arabia to fend off a possible Iraqi attack. In October both houses of Congress overwhelmingly approved of Bush's troop deployment. By November there were over 230,000 American forces in the Persian Gulf region.[2]

Though the Democratic Congress had given the Republican president all he had asked for in the Gulf crisis, some members of the opposition worried that they had given him too much. Catholic New York senator Daniel Patrick Moynihan feared that the Senate vote "would turn into a Tonkin Gulf resolution for the 1990s," dooming the country to the type of open-ended involvement that had failed in Vietnam. Catholic Massachusetts senator Edward Kennedy echoed Moynihan's Vietnam comparison, while Catholic Maine senator George Mitchell, the majority leader, warned Bush, "If there is to be a war in the Persian Gulf or anywhere else, it requires a formal act of Congress to commit to it."[3]

These legislators were not the only members of the Church wary of the administration's next move in the Gulf. Denver archbishop Francis Stafford wrote to the president in September, calling the UN sanctions "an appropriate response to the crisis," but warning that "military actions which flow from a policy of maintaining a standard of living" for North Americans and Europeans would be "extremely difficult to defend." In October the Maryknoll sisters sent a letter to Bush and UN secretary-general Javier Pérez de Cuéllar to "strongly protest even the consideration of military action" in the Gulf. Pax Christi issued a similar statement.[4]

America editorialized in November that such militarization would contravene all the tenets of just-war theory. "Given the destructiveness of modern weapons," the editors maintained, "a war of 'retribution'" would not furnish a "just cause." Since the international coalition constructed by the administration would likely "dissipate" if a U.S. attack occurred, no "competent authority" would be waging war. Since such a conflict would be more about oil than "rights" and "values," it would not meet the criterion of "comparative justice." The administration's dismissal of negotiations with Iraq undermined the "right intention" necessary to fight a war. A rush to abandon sanctions would violate the prerequisite that war be a "last resort." The "volatility of the region" argued against the "probability of success" needed to prosecute a war. As for the final criterion of "proportionality," the editors quoted from the bishops' pastoral "The Challenge of Peace": "For today it becomes increasingly difficult to make a decision to use any kind of armed force, however limited initially in intention and in the destructive power of the weapons deployed, without facing at least the possibility of escalation to broader or even total war and to the use of weapons of horrendous destructive potential."[5] Joseph Cardinal Bernardin had written those words in 1983, when the threat of nuclear war between the United States and the Soviet Union loomed. Seven years, one Intermediate Nuclear Forces Treaty, and several rounds of Strategic Arms Reduction Talks later, such a threat, by Cardinal Bernardin's own admission, had diminished considerably. So what did the bishops say now?

Well, they said pretty much the same thing as before. The Persian Gulf crisis topped the bishops' agenda at the November 1990 United States Catholic Conference meeting in Washington. By a vote of 249–14 they endorsed a letter sent by Los Angeles archbishop Roger Mahony, chairman of their International Policy Committee, to Secretary of State James Baker, which warned that war in the Gulf would endanger the just-war principles. New York's John Cardinal O'Connor criticized the administration for spending so much money to send American troops to Saudi Arabia and so little to address the worsening economy at home. Michael Kenny of Juneau, Alaska, urged his fellow bishops to be more specific in their admonition of a potential war. "It seems to me that we don't hesitate to tell people what to do in regard to abortion or in regard to use of a condom," Kenny noted. "Are we willing to be so clear in reference to weapons of incalculable destruction?"[6]

The answer this time was no. Following a spirited debate, the bishops voted to follow Mahony's letter to the secretary of state with one from their president, Archbishop Daniel Pilarczyk of Cincinnati, to the nation's chief executive. Mahony's letter received thirty-five minutes of airtime on public television, including reactions from Ronald Reagan's Catholic secretary of state, Alexander Haig; Reagan's secretary of the navy, James Webb; and Wisconsin Democratic congressman Les Aspin, chair of the House Armed Services Committee. Pilarczyk viewed the letter as emblematic of the "Church at its finest," asserting a "leadership role" in "provoking serious discussion as it relates to one of the burning issues of our time." Just in case Baker had not shared Mahony's letter with his boss, Pilarczyk's missive to Bush reiterated the just-war conditions while adding that "moving beyond the deployment of military forces in an effort to deter Iraqi aggression to the undertaking of offensive military action could well violate these criteria." While saying that such a war *could* be unjust, however, the letter did not fulfill Bishop Kenny's wish by stating that it *would* be unjust. And the decision to keep the bishops' deliberations secret was a nod toward Boston's Bernard Cardinal Law, the prelate closest to Bush. "That vote deprived the whole Church and the world," Bishop William McManus of Fort Wayne–South Bend regretted, "of their reasonable right to know" how the bishops reached their "moral conclusions."[7]

The National Council of Churches, whose thirty-two denominations represented about forty-two million Protestants, reached its own moral conclusions at a conference in Portland, Oregon, a few days later. Attacking the Bush administration for "reckless rhetoric" and "imprudent behavior" while condemning the "illogical logic of militarism and war," the council unanimously advocated the immediate withdrawal of most U.S. troops from the Gulf region, leaving a much smaller force under UN command. Fifteen Catholic bishops, including Seattle archbishop Raymond Hunthausen and Detroit auxiliary bishop Thomas Gumbleton, as well as Benedictine sister Joan Chitteser, Adrian Dominican sister Nadine Foley, Jesuit priest Richard McSorley, and Catholic feminist theologian Monika Hellwig, signed the NCC resolution.[8]

The pope endorsed neither the USCC nor the NCC position. Before meeting a second time with Soviet premier Mikhail Gorbachev in Rome, John Paul II ended his Sunday Mass with an impassioned plea for peace in Kuwait. Urging "an end to the suffering of those who have been stricken by the crisis and by the measures that have followed it," the pope wished that "humanity will not know the horrors of a new conflict."⁹

As 1990 drew to a close, so too did Saddam Hussein's window for avoiding such a conflict. "As I write this letter at year's end there is still some hope that Iraq's dictator will pull out of Kuwait," President Bush wrote to his children following a family New Year's Eve celebration at Camp David. "I have the peace of mind that comes from knowing that we have tried hard for peace." Nonetheless, Bush continued, "principle must be adhered to—Saddam cannot profit in any way from his aggression. So, dear kids, better batten down the hatches."¹⁰ Then the president appealed to Congress. On January 12, 1991, following debates that included forty-five references to Neville Chamberlain, forty-six to Winston Churchill, 198 to Adolf Hitler, and 413 to Vietnam, the Senate and House voted to authorize the use of force against Iraq.¹¹

"War seems imminent," the USCC's president, Archbishop Daniel Pilarczyk, acknowledged as Iraq's January 15 deadline for leaving Kuwait arrived. Speaking for the bishops, Pilarczyk posited that "offensive force would likely violate the principles of last resort and proportionality" integral to a "just war." In a letter to Bush and Saddam Hussein on the same day, Pope John Paul II warned, "We cannot pretend that the use of arms, and especially of today's highly sophisticated weaponry, would not give rise, in addition to suffering and destruction, to new and perhaps worse injustices."¹²

"I am grateful that you have invoked your moral authority to appeal once more to President Saddam Hussein to choose peace over war," Bush responded to the pope. "I pray that he will heed the call."¹³

During the War

He would not. On January 17, 1991, in the early morning skies over Baghdad, American pilots unleashed Stealth bombers to initiate the war that the pope had feared and the president had dreaded. The president went on national television to tell the American people why. "This military action, taken in accord with United Nations resolutions and with the consent of the United States Congress, follows months of constant and virtually endless diplomatic activity on the part of the United Nations, the United States and many, many other countries," Bush recalled. "Now, the twenty-eight countries with forces in the Gulf area have exhausted all reasonable efforts to reach a peaceful solution." The UN therefore had "no choice but to drive Saddam from Kuwait by force," a mission in which "we will not fail."¹⁴

Protestant evangelists Rev. Pat Robertson, the host of television's *700 Club*, and Rev. Billy Graham, who spent the first night of the war at the White House, rallied to Bush's defense, as did the Protestant *Christian Century*'s James Johnson. Many Catholics joined the chorus of support for the war, including Cardinals Bernard Law of Boston and James Hickey of Washington, D.C., and the director of the Ethics and Public Policy Center, George Weigel. Rev. Joseph Ryan, the archbishop for the armed forces, quoted the pope in arguing that military resistance to aggression was just. The pontiff whom Ryan chose to cite was not John Paul II, however, but Pius XII, in his 1948 Christmas address.[15] Philip Caputo, the renowned Catholic veteran and critic of the Vietnam War, also weighed in on the side of the administration. "Saddam Hussein's conduct . . . has shown why the war was necessary and just," Caputo wrote. "He has allowed his legions to pillage Kuwait with a barbarism worthy of Tamerlane."[16]

Other Catholics took a different view. Rev. Bryan Hehir, who had helped Archbishop Bernardin draft "The Challenge of Peace," contended that the Persian Gulf conflict failed to meet the just-war theory's criterion of "last resort." Los Angeles archbishop Roger Mahony lamented that Bush's decision showed that "nations are more effective in preparing and waging war than in building and achieving peace." The fifteen Catholic bishops who had joined the NCC in November in opposition to the approach of war joined the NCC again in February in opposition to the advent of war. *America* cited the U.S. Catholic hierarchy's misgivings in November about the prospect of war as it voiced its dissent in February to the reality of war. Catholic historian David O'Brien of Holy Cross College concurred, asserting that "sanctions, diplomacy, political maneuvers, an enhanced blockade [and] cautious military pressure under U.N., not U.S. command" could have averted war. The pacifists of Pax Christi condemned not just the war, but the American appetite for oil that helped to launch it.[17]

If President Bush had not heeded these religious critics of his wartime leadership, at least he had heard them. "The war in the Gulf is not a Christian war, a Jewish war, or a Muslim war," the president told the National Religious Broadcasters convention ten days after the fighting began, "it is a just war." The theologian in chief then invoked several criteria for a "just war": the "just cause" of Iraq's expulsion from Kuwait, the "legitimate authority" of twelve United Nations Security Council resolutions and twenty-eight nations from six continents, and the "last resort" after two hundred meetings, ten diplomatic missions, ten appearances before Congress, and 103,000 miles traveled in 166 days of diplomacy by members of his administration.[18]

Whichever posture American Catholics assumed in relation to Operation Desert Storm, they could take comfort in the knowledge that their church had largely defined the terms of the debate. "There rarely has been such a sustained and in many respects impressive grappling with the moral criteria and political logic of the just war tradition," observed George Weigel, who considered the war to be just. "Never has a president inclined his head so often to the moralists" with "all the talk about a just war," noted *Commonweal* managing editor Daniel Jordan, who considered the war to be unjust. "It seems to have been the American bishops," Georgetown University theologian Rev. Francis Winters concluded, "who set the tone of the public discussion of the war in their own traditional just-war terms."[19]

Whether just or not, the war was a rapid and resounding success. Everybody loves a winner, sometimes even those who didn't want to play. The Los Angeles archbishop, Roger Mahony, reversed his resistance to the war in time to pen an article in the *Los Angeles Times* commending the United Nations for acting "in concert to condemn the Iraqi aggression and to repel it." San Francisco's archbishop, John Quinn, lamented that modern weaponry was making "just war" less and less likely, but stopped short of labeling this war unjust. Chicago's Joseph Cardinal Bernardin announced that although he still opposed the war, he now concluded that it was just.[20]

"We are not ready with George Bush to declare this a just war," *Commonweal* editorialized. "But neither do we see evidence that it is manifestly unjust." Speaker of the House Thomas Foley of Washington and Senate majority leader George Mitchell of Maine, Catholic Democrats who had voted against the authorization of force, now sponsored resolutions lauding the president's handling of the war, which passed almost unanimously in the House and unanimously in the Senate. The USCC's Father Bryan Hehir admitted his change of heart, conceding that "on January 17, if asked, I would have maintained that force should not be used" against Iraq. On February 22, however, he concluded that because it met the tests of discrimination between military and civilian casualties and proportionality to Iraq's provocation, the war was now "just but unwise." But Archbishop Pilarczyk would not own up to his revisionism, which now sugarcoated his prewar doubts as "let's not rush into this" and camouflaged his wartime reservations as "let's be sure we wage war justly."[21]

The people in the pews underwent similar transformations. When her parish discussed the war on February 3, *Commonweal* editor Margaret O'Brien Steinfels related, a self-described "habitual anti-war person" rose to speak in favor of fighting Iraq. Less than a decade earlier, over two-thirds of American Catholics had embraced the nuclear freeze proposed by their bishops. During the war in the Gulf, however, almost half endorsed the potential use of tactical nuclear weapons against Iraq.[22]

After the War

"Kuwait is liberated. Iraq's army is defeated. Our military objectives are met," said President Bush as he announced the cessation of hostilities on February 27. "Aggression is defeated," Bush told a joint session of Congress on March 6. "The war is over."[23]

But the theological debate over the war's worthiness was not. "We deeply regret that the intense diplomacy of the past few weeks did not lead to a rapid Iraqi withdrawal from Kuwait," Archbishop Roach, chairman of the bishops' International Policy Committee, lamented two days before the ceasefire. "We know that shaping a lasting peace may be far more difficult than waging a war." Archbishop Mahony, who would become a cardinal in June, complained that "the environmental and ecological damage created through the Persian Gulf conflict opens a new and deadly chapter in warmaking."[24]

In March Pope John Paul II convened Church leaders in those countries directly involved in the war—seven Middle Eastern patriarchs and eight heads of bishops' conferences—for a Vatican summit. "That which we must call a war," the pontiff addressed the participants, "has had and will continue to have repercussions on all the region and its surrounding areas." It was the fifty-sixth statement by the pope on the Persian Gulf crisis since Iraq had invaded Kuwait seven months earlier.[25]

The communiqué that resulted from the conference echoed Pope Paul VI's plea for "never again war" and Pope John Paul II's allusion to the Persian Gulf War as a sign of the "decline of humanity." The attendees concluded that recognition of the "unity, independence, and sovereignty of Lebanon," the "inalienable right of the Palestinians to a country," and the right of "the Israeli people to be able to live within more secure boundaries and in harmony with their neighbors" was indispensable to lasting peace in the Middle East. Archbishop Pilarczyk, representing the United States Catholic Conference in Rome, pledged the assistance of his country's Catholics in working toward this goal. While the U.S. hierarchy never "as a body expressed a definitive and common position about whether the war was morally justified," Pilarczyk recalled, "our conference was united in expressing concern about the moral questions relating to the war and the pursuit of peace."[26]

If the American bishops continued to mince their words in the war's aftermath, the pope's message remained loud and clear. In contrast to the light that Christ's resurrection shone on the world, the Holy Father intoned on Easter Sunday a month after the war's end, the violence in the Persian Gulf had needlessly brought "darkness" to all those affected.[27]

And the pope's gloom stood in stark contrast to the president's giddiness, as Bush basked in the afterglow of an adventure approved by nine of every ten Americans, many of them Catholic. "The relationship between the Catholic Church and Islam clearly takes precedence for the Vatican over the relationship between the Catholic Church and Judaism," Italian columnist Furio Colombo attempted to explain this dichotomy. "And even over the one between the Catholic Church and the Western World."[28]

As with the hierarchy, there remained a divergence of opinion on the war among the Catholic faithful. *America*'s editors, *Commonweal*'s Abigail McCarthy, Georgetown's Rev. Francis Winters, the Center on Conscience and War's Gordon Zahn, and the Conference of Major Superiors of Men's Justice and Peace Committee aligned themselves with the pope. When Bush answered the USCC's September 1992 questionnaire by defending the Persian Gulf War as "just," his Justice Department approved the president's language as "important to some Catholics." The war's opponents and proponents alike could agree with Winters that the conflict had been "a fair test of just-war theory," and with President Bush that the road to peace in the Middle East "does not end with the liberation of Kuwait."[29]

Conclusions on War and Peace

The first Bush presidency would end quickly. Bush's stratospheric popularity would fall almost as rapidly as it had risen. Raising taxes, struggling with a recession, and appearing not to care about either would doom the foreign policy wizard to one term. Bush would depart the world scene shortly after Mikhail Gorbachev's Soviet Union, and long before Saddam Hussein's Iraq. Before Bush left the White House, however, American Catholics, with or without the president, had taught the nation a number of important historical lessons.

First, the U.S. Catholic bishops reached an accommodation with the president on foreign policy. In March 1983, following George Bush's harsh criticism of the bishops' tacit support for the Marxist government of Nicaragua, Archbishop John Roach complained to the vice president that the Reagan administration "feels the Church is out of its league . . . on disarmament." Roach told Bush that none of the bishops "thinks the Administration is immoral," but some "think you are wrong." Yet only eight and a half years later, following a war fought largely on their terms, the bishops received a seat at the peace table. In October 1991, Archbishop Pilarczyk wrote Bush to commend him on his elimination of tactical nuclear arms, removal of tactical nuclear weapons from American ships, termination of the alert status for nuclear bombers and some nuclear missiles, and openness to negotiating the extermination of land-based multiple-warhead missiles. "In our 1983 pastoral on nuclear arms and in our 1988 report on nuclear deterrence," Pilarczyk reminded the president, "we urged such 'independent initiatives' to reduce nuclear arsenals and to bring greater stability and safety to the world."[30]

Pilarczyk also praised Bush's persistence in seeking peace between Palestinians and Israelis, opposition to the United Nations General Assembly vote to brand Zionism as a form of racism, and denunciation of Israeli settlements in the occupied territories. The archbishop cited the bishops' 1989 and 1991 statements on the Middle East, which endorsed the "land for peace" formula of UN Resolutions 242 and 338, and Pope John Paul II's conviction that both Israelis and Palestinians have "a fundamental right to have their own homeland in which they live in freedom, dignity, and security, in harmony with their neighbors."[31] "It's good to know we have the backing of so many of our nation's Catholic leaders for our initiatives to reduce the number and alter the deployment of America's nuclear weapons," Bush replied to Pilarczyk. "I also appreciate your strong support for our efforts to advance the peace process in the Middle East."[32]

Boston's Bernard Cardinal Law had dispatched a communication of his own to the White House, wiring his support for the president's "international leadership." The cardinal then sent so many similar messages to the president that Bush's Office of Public Liaison wondered if the White House had to answer them all.[33]

In May 1992 Bush met with Cardinal O'Connor, recently returned from Lebanon. The cardinal briefed the president on his consultations not only with Lebanese in the Middle East, but with Lebanese-Americans in New York.[34]

A second lesson was that if the president and the bishops now seemed to be singing from the same hymnal, the Vatican remained on a different page. Archbishop Donato Squicciarini, the papal delegate to the International Atomic Energy Agency, condemned "the disastrous consequences which even a limited war can have in our times [as] clearly demonstrated in the Persian Gulf War," while lamenting that international efforts toward nuclear nonproliferation relied too heavily on the "good faith" of national governments. The Vatican, meanwhile, relied heavily on Italian taxpayers. "You don't measure faith with taxes," Italian bishop Altilio Nicora admitted after nonetheless acknowledging that his country's taxpayers were choosing to fund the Church instead of their own government. The bishops' leading fundraiser, Pierluigi Bongiovanni, considered the Italians' largesse an endorsement of the pope's opposition to the war.[35]

A third lesson was that, in contrast to the White House and in concert with the Vatican, American Catholics not only had started the debate over whether the Persian Gulf War was just, but they seemed in no hurry to finish it. Nearly three years after implying that UN sanctions against Iraq were a more humane realty developers, hospitals turned over to community boards, publications disappear—even some colleges." As white ethnics deserted the cities, they left behind a church not only less wealthy, but less white—and less Catholic. In 1989 over one-fifth of American Catholics belonged to minority groups—16 percent Hispanic, 3 percent African-American, and 3 percent Asian. The percentage of non-Catholics attending Catholic schools grew from 2.7 percent in 1969 to 11.2 percent in 1989. "So what if we only had eight baptisms here last year," commented a parishioner at the once-thriving Polish-American Transfiguration Church in Detroit. "Does the Cardinal expect eighty-year-old women to have babies?"[48]

Belatedly acknowledging this changed environment, the Catholic hierarchy struggled to catch up. The U.S. bishops adopted a pastoral plan for Hispanic ministry in 1987. In November 1988 Pope John Paul II celebrated Mass in Rome with African-American auxiliary bishop Joseph Francis of Newark, New Jersey. The following February the Holy Father condemned racism as sinful, singling out the American Catholic Church for its historical complicity in slavery and segregation. In June the U.S. Catholic bishops joined hands and sang along with Sister Thea Bowman of Canton, Mississippi, following her impassioned address on the problems facing her fellow African-American Catholics. All of these measures helped to double the number of black Catholics between 1985 and 1989.[49]

Yet these efforts were too little, too late for some prominent African-Americans. "It seems odd that the Church's 1100 black parishes are headed by 1040 white priests and only sixty black priests," the Harvard theologian Preston Williams wrote in March 1990. Rev. Philip Murnion, the director of the National Pastoral Life Center, observed in December 1990 that "the current inner city populations are either largely non-Catholic black or Oriental people or Hispanic Catholics . . . who lack priests of their own nationality and other supports for seeing the parish as 'their own.'" The next year Rev. James Lyke, the apostolic administrator for the Archdiocese of Atlanta, lamented that there was still no "major study of African-American Catholics."[50] Rev. George Stallings, the black pastor of a black parish in the predominantly black city of Washington, D.C., went a step further. "The reality is that a split exists in the American Church just as it exists in American society," Father Stallings asserted, "and its cause is racism." So he left the American Catholic Church in July 1989 and formed his own Imani Temple. The interdenominational National Black Clergy Caucus endorsed Stallings's action while calling for an African-American rite within the Catholic Church.[51]

The Church that Stallings abandoned heeded his message. At their November 1989 meeting the bishops vowed to increase the number of African-

alternative to war, the bishops suggested that the sanctions may have been virtually as destructive as the war that followed. Having applied the just-war theory to the war, the bishops at their November 1993 meeting applied the just-war theory to the sanctions. Like war, they argued, sanctions should be a measured last resort.[36]

By that time, of course, George Bush was no longer president. Arkansas Democratic governor Bill Clinton had triumphed in a three-way race with Bush and Texas billionaire Ross Perot that dwelled little on foreign policy in a post–Gulf War, post–Cold War environment. As the country climbed out of its economic doldrums, Americans forsook the war hero they "wouldn't have to train" for the draft resister they didn't want to.

American Catholics helped to teach this fourth and final lesson: the limits of foreign policy as a political issue. "I know the economy is an important matter," Thomas Melady, Bush's ambassador to the Vatican, wrote to the administration in January 1992. "But other issues are also important" to his fellow Catholics. Not important enough, however, as Catholics gave 47 percent of their votes to Clinton and only 35 percent to Bush in the November election. The Persian Gulf War, which had once put the unbending president and the uncertain bishops together on center stage, was now but a sideshow. The "just war" had become just a war.[37]

Social Justice: The Urban Crisis

George Bush's triumph in the Persian Gulf would quickly become as much political curse as geopolitical blessing. He would have to explain to the pundits and the voters why his center-right ideology did not reflect a dismissal of all things domestic. Bush, however, the butt of late-night comics and the bane of latent grammarians, was not very good at explaining. So in April and May 1992, Bush would stammer while Los Angeles burned.

Many Catholics who had applauded Bush's certitude in international affairs now derided his equivocation toward the urban crisis in their country and in their church. As the streets of South Central simmered, it no longer seemed to matter that Bush had spoken early, often, and even eloquently of the nation's urban ills, nor that his words and actions had largely dovetailed with those of the Catholics he so earnestly courted. So as the cities continued to wither, the Bush presidency died.

The Country's Urban Crisis

By the time Vice President Bush ran for president in 1988, the poverty rate in the nation's central cities was 18 percent, five points above the national average.

The federal government was spending over $10 billion to help the homeless, over $10 billion for Supplemental Security Income (a guaranteed payment for the elderly, blind, and disabled), and over $9 billion for Aid to Families with Dependent Children.[38]

Candidate Bush wanted to spend more—and less. During the campaign he pronounced himself "haunted" by the "violence and horror" of the inner cities, and pledged more Head Start and Medicaid funding for the poor. His acceptance speech at the Republican National Convention in New Orleans called for a "kinder and gentler nation." But he told his fellow Republicans that the nation's cities were decaying because, not in spite of, Democratic social programs, which had discouraged personal responsibility and stifled individual initiative. So in his best Clint Eastwood impression, the Republican nominee memorably mouthed to the camera, "Read my lips—no new taxes."[39] But within two years Bush would violate his pledge on taxes, and within four years he would fulfill his pledge on the urban crisis.

A routine traffic stop resulting in the videotaped pummeling of a young African-American man, Rodney King, by four white police officers preceded the acquittal in April 1992 of all the cops of all the charges. In response to the verdict, a riot in the impoverished South Central neighborhoods, not unlike the one that had devastated nearby Watts three decades earlier, killed 52, injured 2,500, destroyed almost $500 million worth of property, and focused the nation's attention on the inner cities it had tried to forget. On the first day of the riots, with "smoke still coming out of the buildings," the commander in chief dispatched 3,000 National Guardsmen, 3,000 infantry soldiers, 1,500 marines, and 1,000 federal law enforcement officials to the city.[40] "Now let's talk about the beating of Rodney King," the president addressed the nation on May 1 after meeting with civil rights leaders. Pronouncing himself "stunned" at the verdict, Bush ordered the Justice Department "to move into high gear on its own independent, criminal investigation of the case." But Bush's sympathy for King did not extend to the rioters. "What we saw last night and the night before is not about civil rights. . . . It's not a message of protest," Bush maintained. "It's the brutality of a mob, pure and simple."[41]

"We will do everything we can," Bush told reporters after a Cabinet meeting on the riots three days later, "to help get to the core of the problem." Echoing statements from earlier in his presidency, Bush related that the "dissolution and decline of the American family" was the "number one concern" of mayors throughout the country. Yet when pressed to name his solutions to address the root causes of the disturbances, Bush could say only that "we think homeownership is a very good concept."[42] And when Bush continued to blame Great Society programs for the country's urban maladies, a reporter wondered which policies the president had in mind. "There is no point trying to go into your question answering the specifics, trying to assign blame," the president posited, so he didn't try.[43]

Bush finally appeared in Los Angeles five days after the riots. Upon his return to Washington, Bush introduced his urban aid package.[44] "Did it take the riots to do all this for you?" a reporter quizzed the president. "No, because some of these things have been proposed before," Bush accurately recalled. Yet unlike before, "we're going to fight for them to get passed."[45]

Bush's fight culminated with his signature on a billion-dollar emergency aid bill for Los Angeles and Chicago (ravaged by April floods) and a billion-dollar package combining his Weed and Seed anti-drug initiative, a summer youth jobs program, and that old Great Society standby, Head Start. But in an election year with a congressional majority from the other party, he received little credit. Liberals from the Democratic side of the aisle lamented that the president was spending too little; conservatives from his own party grumbled that he was spending too much. Vice President Dan Quayle would recall that in an administration of mixed messages, Bush's response to the riots—castigating somebody else's government spending while promoting his own—was only the most recent. And the president's attention span, like the public's, could be fleeting. After returning home from Los Angeles, Bush passed up an opportunity to visit the inner cities of Cleveland and Philadelphia.[46]

Yet the riots had done what Bush had been unable to do: galvanize the nation's concentration on its neglected urban populations. One could forgive the president for saying "I told you so," if only he could find the words.

The Church's Urban Crisis

At the dawn of the Bush presidency, the sun appeared to be setting on urban American Catholic Church. From 1978 to 1988, the Archdiocese of cago closed twenty-five schools. In October 1988 the Archdiocese of D announced that it was closing forty-three churches. In 1976 there ha almost two hundred thousand Catholic households in Detroit. By 1 were fewer than fifty thousand. The Archdiocese of New York ann December 1990 that its subsidies to parochial schools would decli quarter. In 1920 there had been one priest for every 806 Catholic l the United States. In 1989 there was one for every 912. "I don't thi find a single historical parallel to this," the eminent historian M Ellis of Catholic University said as he surveyed the damage to

"In a generation's time," wrote former *Commonweal* man Deedy in November 1989, "we have seen thousands of closed . . . , convents converted to other purposes, semina

American priests and to incorporate African-American culture into the liturgy. In 1990 the black monastic historian Rev. Cyprian Davis published *The History of Black Catholics* (of which Father Lyke apparently was unaware). By 1992 there were offices dealing with black Catholic concerns in over half the nation's dioceses, and the National Black Congress voted to study the establishment of an African-American rite within the Catholic liturgy. The Church's urban crisis had not abated, but it was finally receiving much-needed attention.[52]

The Common Crisis

When church and state finally appeared at the scene of the urban crisis, they arrived together. Newark archbishop Theodore McCarrick urged the 1988 presidential candidates to be "faithful to the Constitution" in their treatment of the poor. The group Catholics for Bush insisted that their candidate "believes, as did the framers of the Constitution, that the God-given rights of the family come before those of government." Ronald Reagan's Catholic ambassador to Burundi and Uganda, Thomas Melady, implored Bush and his opponent, Massachusetts Democratic governor Michael Dukakis, to remember those "communities, especially those long dependent on welfare," who "are not benefitting from the American dream." Bush told the U.S. Catholic bishops that he favored "reducing dependency on the federal government." The bishops backed "federal action to provide significant new resources and creative partnerships to effectively combat hunger, homelessness, and poverty in the United States." Bush agreed that "we must be sure that the safety net for Americans in need has no holes in it."[53]

Bush won election with the support of a plurality of American Catholics, and he was determined not to govern without them. "There are increasing pressures in and out of government to sweep religion from the public scene all together [sic]," the newly elected United States Catholic Conference general secretary, Rev. Robert Lynch, wrote to Bush's incoming chief of staff, John Sununu, a Catholic, in December 1988. "I know that President-elect Bush does not share that view of America nor do the Catholic bishops of the United States."[54]

Father Lynch had a point. Bush appointed a record number of Catholics (five) to his Cabinet. A group of Catholics within the administration began meeting on the first Friday of every month. Within a month of his inauguration, Bush had met with the five active U.S. cardinals: Boston's Bernard Law, Chicago's Joseph Bernardin, Detroit's Edmund Szoka, New York's John O'Connor, and Washington, D.C.'s James Hickey. "We have more contact and involvement with the cardinals now than they did with the previous administration," Bush's special assistant and informal Catholic liaison, Douglas Wead, would boast. "That might not have been possible before," when the bishops lunged to the left while the Reagan administration steered to the right.[55] "To reinforce the President's strong ties with the American Catholic Church," as Wead put it, Bush met in March with prominent lay Catholic supporters, including *National Review* founder William F. Buckley, Knights of Columbus vice president Carl Anderson, and Bradley Foundation chair Dr. Michael Joyce. "We are in a desperate struggle for the souls of a new generation in the battle with drugs," the president told his guests.[56]

In April 1989 the bishops wrote to Bush urging his support for child care legislation that combined the administration's tax credits and inclusion of religious providers with the Democratic Senate's vouchers. A meeting of Catholic child care providers with representatives from the administration and the Senate failed to produce consensus or congressional action. "The Bush people came in and said that a tax credit would help you—it's wonderful, and the providers said, 'Well it wouldn't help many of our poor families,'" said John Carr of the USCC, who attended the meeting. "Then the Democrats came in and said, 'We have this proposal . . . but your church-state stuff would cut us out.'"[57]

In August Vice President Quayle praised the Knights of Columbus at their Baltimore convention for their adherence to "family life," "loyalty," "public service," and "volunteerism at its best." Quayle noted that "government at all levels" was trying to "cope with . . . the breakdown in family life, in delinquency, in welfare dependency, and homelessness, in abandonment of the elderly and abuse of our children."[58]

In September, at the invitation of Cardinal Law, Bush attended the Red Mass for Catholic lawyers in Boston. "We must devote special attention to the problems of those on the margins," Bush told the attorneys, "those lacking adequate food or shelter, those addicted or mentally ill, those whose neighborhoods have been decimated by crime." In December Bush spoke at a fundraiser for Catholic University in Washington, where he likened the Church's commitment to "service to others" to his own "thousand points of light."[59]

By the end of 1989 Bush had met with Catholic educators and had received an invitation to visit a Catholic school. Cardinals Law and O'Connor had spent the night at the White House. "The president never talked about, publicized, or let anyone know about his relationship with Cardinal Law through the political campaign," Wead recalled, adding that their friendship "would have been a very interesting story—the Cardinal of Boston [and Bush], with [Massachusetts Democratic governor Michael] Dukakis running [against Bush]." As for the president's other overnight guest, the administration was "not afraid to call Cardinal O'Connor if we have a troubling political question."[60] "This has been a Catholic year at the White House," Wead, a Presbyterian, marveled in December. Bush, whose maternal ancestors were Catholic, "has been more sensitive and more accessible to the needs of the Catholic Church than any president I know of in American history."[61]

If the volume of the president's interaction with the Catholic community would decline in the following three years, the value would not. The administration and the Church continued their remarkably congruent course. In January 1990 the board of directors of Catholic Golden Age conveyed to President Bush its endorsement of Clarence Thomas for a seat on the U.S. Court of Appeals. In words that would later prove vital, the group's president, Joseph Leary, wrote, "Please count on us for further support."[62]

In March, amid a controversy over the public funding of Robert Mapplethorpe's allegedly anti-Catholic art, Wead recommended that the administration place restrictions on the National Endowment for the Humanities. At Seton Hall University, a Catholic institution in South Orange, New Jersey, which Bush's Catholic ambassador to the Vatican, Thomas Melady, would call "sympathetic to President Bush and his programs," Quayle defended the justness of the UN embargo against Iraq in November 1990. In January 1991 HUD secretary Kemp addressed the urban crisis in a speech to the USCC's Department of Social Development and World Peace.[63]

Pope John Paul II sounded a lot like President Bush in his May 1991 encyclical, *Centesimus Annus* ("The Hundredth Year"), in which he reiterated the Church's embrace of both organized labor and private property, which Pope Leo XIII had enunciated in *Rerum Novarum* ("Of New Things") a century before. Like the leader of the capitalist world, the pope espoused a kinder, gentler market economy, regulated by "a strong juridical framework which places it at the service of human freedom in its totality and which sees it as a particular aspect of that freedom, the core of which is ethical and religious."[64] Like the fervently anti-communist president, the fervently anti-communist pope clothed his defense of the Right in the lexicon of the Left. The conservative editor of *First Things*, Rev. Richard Neuhaus, viewed the document as a repudiation of the U.S. bishops' 1986 pastoral, "Economic Justice for All." But the liberal author of that pastoral, Archbishop Rembert Weakland of Milwaukee, read the pope's words as his own.[65]

More than rhetoric linked Rome and Washington. The U.S. ambassador to the Vatican, Thomas Melady, wrote to President Bush in July after attending the installation of two new American cardinals. Melady's conversation with members of the American hierarchy in town for the ceremony had persuaded the ambassador that "your Administration is receiving very high grades from them," notably on Bush's "commitment to family and community values." At

Melady's suggestion, Bush met in September in Philadelphia with the newly installed cardinal, Anthony Bevilacqua, and his predecessor, John Cardinal Krol, both "great supporters" of the administration, according to the ambassador. In the same month, Bush met with American Catholic seminarians and with the pope in Rome.[66]

The next month *Commonweal* criticized Bush's nomination of African-American Clarence Thomas to the Supreme Court as "clever and cynical," then cleverly and cynically supported the choice because "succeeding nominees were unlikely to be an improvement." *America* opposed the nomination, but reprinted a speech by the Catholic comedian Steve Allen to a group of Jesuits in Milwaukee that likened Thomas's self-described "high-tech lynching" by Senate liberals during his confirmation hearings to the racist reception the judge had received as a young Catholic seminarian.[67]

In November 1991 Bush discussed the safety net for the elderly with liberal and conservative representatives of the Catholic Golden Age, Catholic Daughters of the Americas, Catholic Charities, Knights of Columbus, National Council of Catholic Women, Catholic Health Association, National Catholic Education Association, and United States Catholic Conference. Later in the month, when Bush changed his mind and signed the Civil Rights Act of 1991, he found himself on the same side as Catholic liberals like Massachusetts Democratic senator Edward Kennedy, David Carlin of *Commonweal*, and the editors of *America*, and on the opposite side from Catholic conservatives like William F. Buckley and William McGurn, who had backed his veto of a similar bill the year before.[68]

In their November pastoral, "Putting Children and Families First," the U.S. Catholic bishops found themselves on both sides. Government can "support . . . families as they cope with the moral, social, and economic stresses of caring for children," the bishops nodded to the liberals. But "no government can love a child, and no policy can substitute for a father's care," the bishops bowed to the conservatives.[69]

Pope John Paul II had tackled the same subject in much the same way in *Centesimus Annus*. "It is the task of the state to provide for the defense and preservation of common good," said the Holy Father, but the "first and fundamental structure . . . is the family." Bush lavished praise on the pope's message at the commencement ceremonies at the University of Notre Dame in May 1992. "I was impressed to learn that more than two-thirds of Notre Dame's students participate in community service," the president remarked to the graduates of the nation's most famous Catholic university. In a senior class of about fifteen hundred, that added up to roughly a "thousand points of light."[70]

As the head of state was speaking in South Bend, Indiana, the head of the Church was cleaning up in South Central Los Angeles. Like President Bush, Los Angeles's Roger Cardinal Mahony on April 30 had condemned the riots but confirmed their roots. "Unprovoked physical attacks by individuals on others, the brazen looting of stores by bands of youth, adults, and even children . . . , the senseless torching of buildings block after block," the cardinal reiterated to his archdiocese on May 3, were unjustified reactions to the "perceived lack of justice in the Rodney King verdict." Yet the violence exposed the "potent and lethal realities" of "racial discrimination," "systemic injustice," "substandard housing," "substandard education," and "unemployment."[71] And, like the president, the cardinal advocated spending money to resurrect the city. On April 29 Mahony authorized Catholic Charities of Los Angeles, the St. Vincent de Paul Society, and his own Cardinal McIntyre Fund (named after his predecessor) to devote $1 million to disaster relief and recovery. Mahony also pledged to cooperate with Los Angeles mayor Tom Bradley's Rebuild L.A. and Hope in Youth reconstruction endeavors. But also like Bush, Mahony acknowledged the limits of the public sector's ability to respond, as "excessive regulations" and "bureaucratic delays" could undermine the relief efforts. So the cardinal appealed to a higher power, through a "special novena" in the city's Catholic parishes from May 29 to June 6, "asking the Holy Spirit to heal riot-torn Los Angeles."[72]

To Vice President Quayle, who spoke in San Francisco two days after Bush's Notre Dame address, the South Central riots were symptomatic of the "poverty of values" that was spawning single-parent households throughout the country. The media's preoccupation with the messenger, the oft-caricatured intellectual lightweight who couldn't spell "potato," obscured the message of Quayle's attack on the CBS comedy *Murphy Brown* for glamorizing single motherhood as a "lifestyle choice." Though his headline-grabbing popular culture reference was new, the born-again Presbyterian vice president who sent his children to Catholic schools was not saying anything that he, the president, the pope, and the bishops hadn't said before. Quayle was simply putting a white, middle-class face on what Lyndon Johnson's Catholic assistant secretary of labor, Daniel Patrick Moynihan, had identified as a black, lower-class problem a generation earlier.[73]

Some Catholic liberals had dismissed Moynihan as a racist; others now derided Quayle as a rube. But many Catholics made the connection between burning cities and broken homes. In 1970 fewer than 11 percent of children in the United States were born out of wedlock. By 1986 over 23 percent of births occurred outside of marriage. Among blacks, the percentage almost doubled, to 61.2. Among whites, it tripled, to 15.7. Since 1987 a majority of recipients of Aid to Families with Dependent Children had become eligible through out-of-wedlock births, prompting Bush's insistence on the inclusion of family planning in his administration's anti-poverty initiatives in 1990. "Basically, Catholics are Democrats" with trust in governments, Bush aides Leigh Ann Metzger, Jane Leonard, and Kathy Rust learned while preparing their candidate for his 1992 reelection campaign. "But they have moved to the Republican camp because of the traditional values platform" and its faith in families. To the "thirty percent of the President's constituency" who were Catholic, messages like Quayle's affirmed that the administration shared their values.[74]

Bush's ambassador to the Vatican, Thomas Melady, offered a similar campaign analysis. "While understanding and compassionate about human weakness," as liberals viewed themselves, Melady wrote in September 1992, white ethnic Catholics "overwhelmingly supported traditional values on what is right and wrong," as conservatives saw themselves.[75]

So American Catholics and the American president continued to split the difference between dependence on governments and devotion to families. In their 1992 campaign questionnaire, the bishops asked the presidential candidates, "Do you support a national policy which would provide decent jobs for those who can work and adequate assistance for those who cannot . . . including increased resources for job creation and job training for the unemployed?" Bush's response promoted more government spending for his Job Training 2000 initiative, and less government spending—"without the creation of an intrusive government-dominated national policy"—at the same time. The president might as well have said that he was "putting families first," as the bishops had a year earlier.[76]

Not all American Catholics, however, believed that the Bush administration spoke for them. Before he could claim his party's nomination for a second term, Bush had to fend off a challenge from his right by Patrick Buchanan, the former White House aide who had honed Richard Nixon's strategy and Ronald Reagan's message. True to his ethnic roots, Buchanan sought to return his party and his country to a simpler time before big government raised too many taxes and big business removed too many tariffs. Though he never won a primary, Buchanan succeeded in landing a prime-time speaking role at the Republican convention in Houston in August. The media outcry that greeted Buchanan's verbal assault on gay rights and illegal immigration virtually overshadowed Bush's acceptance speech and post-convention public opinion "bounce." Though Buchanan would reconcile with Bush, some of his supporters would not, and the wounded incumbent limped all the way to defeat in November.[77]

Conclusions on Social Justice

The cooperation between the Republican president and Catholic leaders in addressing the urban crisis marked a notable departure from the confrontation over the economy that had estranged the nation's bishops from the president, and from their own rank and file, during the previous administration. George H. W. Bush's liberal willingness to tax and spend more than Ronald Reagan, while expanding upon his predecessor's conservative attachment to the traditional family, facilitated this fulfilling, if flawed, partnership. Yet as another Republican president who largely welcomed additional changes among American Catholic congregants, he ultimately could not overcome the continuity that would return many Catholics to their Democratic roots, and return George Bush to private life.

Many Americans were redefining what it meant to be a Catholic. The number of Catholics in the United States had doubled from 26 million in 1948 to 53.5 million in 1988. No longer members of an overwhelmingly European-American church, American Catholics now included substantial numbers of persons of color. From 1978 to 1988, the country's Latino population grew five times faster than the rest of Americans. Compared to most of their fellow citizens, Hispanic-Americans were disproportionately Catholic, and disproportionately poor.[78]

As these newest Americans flocked to the cities, their older, whiter brethren headed for the suburbs. In the process, many of the latter shed their religious identities. "The postwar suburbanization of America has been doubly destructive of the patriotic sense of Catholic uniqueness," the theologian Rev. Joseph McShane of LeMoyne College lamented in April 1989. "It has lured Catholics out of the cities and away from their institutionalized empires, frustrating bishops and pastors who have attempted to duplicate the network that made urban Catholicism a way of life and a world apart." The theologian Rev. Avery Dulles of Fordham University noted in January 1990 that "middle-age adults constitute the last generation of Catholics raised with a strong sense of Catholic identity." An April 1990 poll of its readers by *U.S. Catholic* discovered 57 percent unwilling to involve themselves more in their parishes. Two centuries after John Carroll became the nation's first Catholic bishop, fellow Jesuits Rev. Joseph Fitzpatrick and Rev. John Coleman worried that the middle-class values embraced by most American Catholics were more American than Catholic.[79]

Some Catholics also left their devotion to Catholic social teaching behind. According to a 1986 Lilly Foundation study, only 39 percent of Catholic adults believed that "the Catholic bishops should take public stands on some political issues such as the arms race or the American economic system." Liberal auxiliary bishop Robert Donnelly of Toledo estimated that "less than one percent of the people in the Church" typically read the bishops' pastoral letters. The conservative editor Rev. Richard Neuhaus of *First Things* noted that not all Catholics shared the hierarchy's susceptibility to "the lie that politics is the 'real world.'" Rev. Thomas Reese, whose 1992 book, *A Flock of Shepherds*, examined the role of the United States Catholic Conference, concluded that "both on the left and on the right, we have an anti-clericalism. The one thing that the two groups agree on is that the bishops do not know what they are doing."[80] But the bishops *were* aware of the diminished level of commitment of many parishioners. "I would agree that often we are not in the same ballpark as our people," Cardinal Bernardin conceded in October 1992.[81]

Some Catholics left the Democratic Party behind as well. "Delivering the poor in the aftershocks of the Reagan-Bushquake will demand the full power of the two thousand years of experience in the works of mercy," the Catholic novelist Susan Cahill wrote, assessing the damage in November 1989. The Catholic march to the right, the Notre Dame theologian Rev. Richard McBrien contended in August 1992, was allowing Catholic conservatives to reposition the center so that liberals were about to, in the words of *Commonweal*'s editor, Margaret O'Brien Steinfels, "fall off the map."[82] To these members of the Catholic Left, there was no end in sight to the conservative avalanche inside and outside the Church. Just as Ronald Reagan's judicial appointments would long outlive his presidency, Philip Berryman wrote in May 1989, so Pope John Paul II's choices for the episcopate "may outlive him by half a generation or more."[83]

If American Catholics had become less religious, less activist, and less Democratic, they had not entirely relinquished their past. Writing in *America* in November 1992, Dennis Castillo concluded that when one measured the percentages of priests and nuns versus the percentages of Catholics in the population, it was clear that the decline in numbers of priests and nuns had begun not during Vatican II, but during World War II. "The immigrants' interest group–style persists," Catholic historian David O'Brien of Holy Cross College contended, "in the assertion of single-issue absolutes and in persistent efforts to mobilize poor and working-class people around bread-and-butter economic objectives." Writing in November 1989, almost a year into the Bush presidency and almost three years before the Rodney King verdict, O'Brien appreciated the "once common blend of internal conservatism and external championing of labor and minority interests" that was "reappearing in places like Los Angeles."[84] The Church was still second only to the federal government in dispensing social services in the United States. A 1993 Gallup Poll found 83 percent of Catholics satisfied with the Church's "social services provided to the poor and needy" in their communities.[85]

Not only was Catholic social teaching alive and well, but political involvement was still winning converts in the Catholic community. The Church's leaders "not only have a right to speak to political and social issues," Rev. William Barry, the rector of the Jesuit community at Boston College, wrote in August 1989, "but *must* do so." While most Catholic adults disapproved of their bishops' political activism in the 1986 Lilly survey, most Catholic college students approved. Three-quarters of the readers of *U.S. Catholic* agreed in 1990 that "in the next ten to fifteen years I'd like to hear more from the American bishops on social issues." The bishops were willing to oblige. "It is very difficult to say, 'Well, we are not going to take any interest in that,'" Cardinal Bernardin protested in October 1992. "There is a great deal of pressure on the Conference to make its thoughts known on virtually every conceivable topic."[86]

And rather than knowing less than the government about pressing political issues, the bishops sometimes knew more. When the bishops' representatives met with Housing and Urban Development secretary Jack Kemp to discuss the urban crisis, the USCC's John Carr remembered in October 1992, "we had our regular committee, but we brought in six or eight people from around the country who we heard were doing the best housing stuff." Not only were the bishops not out of their league, some had become experts. "We were doing it before it was trendy," Carr explained of the USCC's concern for the inner city. "Very few people know as much about homelessness as we do."[87]

As for the Republican Party's foothold among American Catholics, it was hardly firm. Just when the hierarchy was belatedly turning right to meet the Church and the country halfway, the Church and the country began turning left. In the Congress that had greeted the new, more moderate Republican president in January 1989, not only were most of the 538 members Democrats, but so were most of the 138 Catholics. As for the bishops, like the pope who was appointing them, they could still be as Democratic as they were Republican. "Many political observers cannot understand how the bishops can be conservative on one issue," Father Reese wrote in *A Flock of Shepherds*, "and liberal on another." When asked in 1992 to identify the ideological inclinations of the United States Catholic Conference, Carr shrugged, "We're very unpredictable."[88]

Although the bishops and much of their flock resembled the administration in their philosophical gymnastics, they often considered the president not liberal enough in his spending priorities before and after the Los Angeles riots. "There is some truth" to the "conservative complaint," the liberal Father Reese admitted in 1992, that the bishops "focus on the federal government as the solution to all social and economic problems." Archbishop Pilarczyk's September 1992 letter urging Bush's support of family leave legislation went unanswered, and the president remained opposed. And despite the inroads that Ronald Reagan had made within the Church, George Bush barely won the Catholic vote over his Democratic opponent in 1988 before losing it in 1992.[89]

As they veered between change and continuity, Right and Left, American Catholics approached the urban crisis with essentially the same mixture of dismay, dollars, and disappointment as the Bush administration did. "You make policy at home, quietly," the liberal Archbishop Weakland described the more centrist role of the bishops' conference in October 1992. "You try to move things there, not in Washington." George Bush could not have said it better.[90]

But Bush at times was too quiet, and he struggled to convey empathy for the plight of the urban poor, which his words and actions, alongside those of the Church, so evocatively if unevenly exhibited. With the country mired in a recession, the patrician stiffening of his upper lip would be no match for Arkansas governor Bill Clinton's populist biting of his lower lip in the 1992 presidential campaign, and many Catholics returned to the Democratic fold. The president who had won election by asking the American people to read his lips lost reelection by asking them to read his mind.

Life and Death: Abortion

By the time George Bush entered the White House, it had been almost a generation since the right to an abortion had become the law of the land. But it had been less than a decade since Bush had initially advocated its repeal. When he ran for president for the first time in 1980, Bush had supported *Roe v. Wade*. When Ronald Reagan chose his chief primary rival to be his running mate, he asked Bush to reverse his position on abortion. So Bush did.[91]

Bush's "deathbed conversion" on abortion gave him a new political life, but, like his ideological meandering on the urban crisis, it made him suspect in the eyes of many conservative Republicans. In this instance, however, he should not have been. Perhaps to overcompensate for his youthful indiscretion, George Bush became the most anti-abortion president yet in U.S. history. He thus aligned himself, as he had on the Persian Gulf War and the urban crisis, with many American Catholics. Because of his, and their, past experiences, they nonetheless approached him warily. After all, the last two pro-life Republican presidents, Gerald Ford and Ronald Reagan, had largely let them down—Ford by talking too little about abortion and Reagan by talking too much.

George Bush would not let them down. The president not known for his talking didn't really have a choice. Several court cases and countless pieces of legislation would force him to act. But preoccupied by the deteriorating economy, too many pro-life Catholics would let George Bush down. First he lost their attention. Then he lost their votes.

Before Webster

If he had any question whether abortion would be a major preoccupation of his presidency, George Bush didn't need to wait long to find out. On January 5, 1989, two weeks before Bush's inauguration, Boston's Bernard Cardinal Law wrote to his friend requesting his presence at the annual March for Life in the nation's capital on Monday, January 23, the new president's first workday. At the very least, Law implored, could Bush follow the example of his predecessor, who telephoned the marchers and met with their leaders at the White House? Since Bush had been vice president for eight years while Ronald Reagan did this, Law concluded that "in all likelihood" some acknowledgment of the march was "already figured in your schedule for that weekend."92

Yes, it was. "I think the Supreme Court's decision in *Roe v. Wade* was wrong and should be overturned," Bush told the marchers via one-way telephone in the early hours of his presidency. "I think America needs a human life amendment." Bush would not meet with the leaders of the March for Life, however; he dispatched Vice President Dan Quayle instead. But on the same day that Bush was telling the pro-life protesters that he supported a constitutional amendment to outlaw abortion, Bush's Catholic chief of staff, John Sununu, who attended the meeting of the protest's leaders with Quayle, was telling them that he didn't.93

"Are you going to have any White House initiatives [on abortion]," a reporter asked the president four days later, "or are you going to wait for the Supreme Court?" Bush replied, "I think probably [I'll wait], but I have been pledged, you know, to an amendment. But I'd like to see the Supreme Court decision as soon as possible"—so he wouldn't have to fulfill his pledge.94 Instead, the Bush administration would be arguing in the Supreme Court case of *Webster v. Reproductive Health Services*, in which lower federal courts had struck down a Missouri law declaring that life begins at conception, prohibiting abortions at public hospitals except when a mother's life was in danger, and preventing the use of public funds for abortion counseling. True to the president's word, the Bush administration sought not only to uphold the Missouri law, but to upend *Roe v. Wade* entirely.95

The administration had a lot of company. The United States Catholic Conference filed an amicus brief in the *Webster* case that urged *Roe*'s repeal. The brief argued that the Supreme Court should abide by its promise in *Roe*'s companion case, *Doe v. Bolton*, to "readjust its view and emphasis in light of the advanced knowledge and techniques of the day." The USCC cited such post-*Doe* developments as a sixfold rise in abortions, increasingly frequent maternal deaths due to abortions, a sharp reduction in the number of adoptions of out-of-wedlock children, and the extreme psychological effects of abortion on women who had them.[96] The Catholic fraternal organization the Knights of Columbus filed its own amicus brief, seeking *Roe v. Wade*'s removal on Fourteenth Amendment grounds. The "only reasonable reading of the word 'person' is that it includes an unborn child," the Knights wrote. "[The] expansive design for the amendment, combined with the predominant anti-abortion sentiment and legislation of the time in which it was proposed and ratified, inexorably lead to the inclusion of the unborn as 'persons' under the Fourteenth Amendment."[97]

Bush's decision to deploy the Justice Department on the front lines of the battle to overturn *Roe v. Wade* stirred a small revolt. Over two hundred career attorneys in the department sent a petition to Attorney General Richard Thornburgh asserting that "every woman has the right to make her own decision about whether or not to continue her pregnancy, in accordance with the guidelines set forth in *Roe v. Wade*." The petition had little effect, except to irritate the president. "One of the things that complicates the whole concept is the propensity of career people to try to shape policy in a way that is unacceptable to the President," Bush complained to Sununu. "I ran opposed to abortion. My opponent ran in favor."[98]

The bishops' brief also flew in the face of legal advice. The USCC counsel Mark Chopko had told the bishops that the best they could hope for in the *Webster* decision was that *Roe* would be "trimmed back," but it would not be reversed. The brief also defied the finding by President Reagan's pro-life surgeon general, C. Everett Koop, released in March 1989, that "the available scientific evidence about the psychological sequelae of abortion cannot support either the pre-conceived beliefs of those pro-life [emphasizing the negative physical effects of abortion] or those pro-choice [downplaying them]." And the attempts by the administration, the bishops, and the Knights of Columbus to overthrow *Roe v. Wade* contravened public opinion, since 53 percent of Americans in a March 1989 *Boston Globe* poll were in favor of the right to abortion in cases of "rape, incest, potential or definite genetic deformity," and to protect the health or save the life of the mother.[99]

Bush nonetheless told a group of key lay Catholic supporters at the end of March that he saw "a very good chance that *Roe v. Wade* may be overturned [in] these next few months." At least one of the attendees, *National Review* editor William F. Buckley, agreed with the president. Sounding like Bush, Buckley reminded his readers, "Just six months ago, a pro-choice candidate and a pro-life candidate were running for president. The latter is in the White House. The former was sent back to Boston."[100]

Webster

As the highly anticipated *Webster* case unfolded at the end of April 1989, U.S. solicitor general Charles Fried, siding with the defendant, Missouri attorney general William Webster, urged the Supreme Court to repeal *Roe v. Wade*. "We are not asking the Court to unravel the fabric of unenumerated and privacy rights that the Court has woven," Fried spoke for the Bush administration. "Rather, we are asking the Court to pull this one thread." Frank Susman, representing the plaintiff, Reproductive Health Services, urged the Court to leave *Roe v. Wade* alone. "I think the Solicitor General's submission is somewhat disingenuous when he suggests to this Court that he does not seek to unravel the whole cloth of constitutional rights, but merely to pull a thread," Susman countered. "It has always been my personal experience that when I pull a thread, my sleeve falls off."[101]

When Susman reminded the Court that the *Brown v. Board of Education* decision had rejected the argument that fundamental rights be decided by state legislatures, Justice Antonin Scalia, a Catholic Reagan appointee, questioned the analogy to abortion. "What conclusion does that lead you to?" Scalia asked Susman. "That, therefore, there must be a fundamental right on the part of the woman to destroy this thing that we don't know what it is, or, rather, that whether there is or isn't is a matter that you vote upon?"[102] Then, taking Scalia's lead, the Court voted to overturn *Roe v. Wade*—before it didn't. Justice Sandra O'Connor, Ronald Reagan's first appointee to the Court, changed her mind and wrote her own opinion in which she sided with Webster against Reproductive Health Services but avoided *Roe v. Wade* completely. "When the constitutional invalidity of a State's abortion statute actually turns on the constitutionality of *Roe v. Wade*," O'Connor wrote, "there will be time enough to reexamine *Roe*."[103]

No longer having the votes to rescind *Roe v. Wade*, Chief Justice William Rehnquist narrowed his opinion, signed by Justices Byron White and Anthony Kennedy, another Catholic Reagan appointee, to side with Missouri without addressing *Roe*. "Nothing in the Constitution," Rehnquist wrote, "requires states to remain in the business of performing abortions." Yet apparently nothing in the Constitution could stop them either.[104]

The Court unanimously upheld Missouri's ban on the public funding of abortion, ruled 5–4 in favor of the state's prohibition on public hospitals performing abortions, and decided 5–4 to accept the state's reduction of *Roe*'s viability threshold from twenty-four to twenty weeks of pregnancy. Of the nine justices, three of them Catholic, only Scalia argued to overturn *Roe v. Wade*.[105]

The Bush administration and the American Catholic hierarchy nevertheless hailed the verdict. "We welcome the decision. By upholding the Missouri statute, the Court appears to have begun to restore to the people the ability to protect the unborn," the White House announced, while adding, "we continue to believe that *Roe v. Wade* was incorrectly decided and should be reversed." To the USCC's Office of General Counsel, "the decision clearly marks a turning point in abortion jurisprudence."[106] Much of the pro-life community was ecstatic. "The abortion question that so many thought settled in 1973 is now again before the American people," Burke Balch, the state legislative coordinator of the National Right to Life Committee, rejoiced. *Webster* had achieved, the Fordham University sociologist James Kelly cheered, what "no student of the pro-life movement predicted."[107]

But not all pro-life Catholics shared in the euphoria. Helen Alvare, the USCC's director of pro-life planning and information, said that she was "appalled that the Supreme Court had explicitly reaffirmed its 1973 abortion decision and failed to give even minimal consideration to the lives of unborn children." The editors of *Commonweal* worried that by not uprooting *Roe v. Wade*, the Court had left intact "an abortion ethic so deeply rooted in our culture that overturning or narrowing *Roe* may have minimal effect on the number of abortions."[108]

And not all Catholics were part of the pro-life movement. Frances Kissling, the president of Catholics for a Free Choice, lamented that *Webster* "has made it abundantly clear that a fundamental right—the right to obtain an abortion without government intrusion—no longer exists in this country." Self-described Catholic feminist Mary Segers, an associate professor of political science at Rutgers University, protested, "I do not think Catholics should be pleased with a judicial ruling" that, by outlawing abortions in public hospitals, "so victimizes the young and the poor."[109] Fifty percent of Catholics told Gallup's pollsters that they disapproved of the *Webster* decision, while 42 percent approved. But this disapproval should not be seen as disappointment that the decision did not go further: 55 percent opposed overturning *Roe v. Wade*, while only 38 percent were in favor.[110]

After Webster

Rather than demoralize the pro-choice movement, the *Webster* decision appeared to energize it. A 1989 *Time*/CNN poll found 34 percent of women supporting abortion on demand before *Webster*, and 43 percent in favor after the ruling. To pro-life scholar James Kelly, "things have changed," in that "now pro-life activists bear the burden of proof."¹¹¹

The bishops welcomed the burden. "We didn't want pro-life citizens thinking that the Court decision had done the whole job," Camden, New Jersey, bishop James McHugh, a member of the USCC's Committee for Pro-Life Activities, explained in August. The committee issued a statement advocating alternatives to abortion, government programs for prenatal and maternal care, parental leave, child care, job assistance, adoption services, and aid to the disadvantaged. In so doing, the bishops sought to dispel the charge by pro-choice forces that pro-life Catholics cared "only for life before birth."¹¹²

The president resisted the burden. Following Bush's White House meeting with Boston's Bernard Cardinal Law in August, a reporter wondered whether the president was feeling "pressure from groups like the Catholic Church to do something [to] enforce your position on pro-life." Bush denied any pressure, and did nothing to shore up his pro-life credentials.¹¹³

Indeed, much of the pressure on the president was coming from the opposite direction. On Capitol Hill, pro-choice Democrats were enjoying what *Congressional Quarterly* called "their strongest legislative showing in a decade." The Senate narrowly passed an amendment to a foreign operations funding measure sponsored by Catholic Democratic senator Barbara Mikulski of Maryland that restored U.S. population assistance to organizations engaged in promoting abortion or sterilization. Douglas Johnson, the Catholic legislative director of the National Right to Life Committee, urged Bush "not to gut a major pro-life victory of the Reagan years."¹¹⁴ California Democratic senator Barbara Boxer modified the Hyde anti-abortion amendment to appropriations for the Departments of Labor, Health and Human Services, and Education to allow for exceptions in the case of rape and incest. James Cardinal Hickey of Washington, D.C., urged the president not to revoke "the present policy which prohibits the use of government funds for abortion."¹¹⁵

The House Appropriations Committee approved the first allocation for the District of Columbia without a ban on abortion funding. Johnson expressed confidence that the president would veto the bill, ridiculing the prediction of Dwight Cropp of the D.C. Office of Intergovernmental Operations that "I don't think we need to worry about our bill being vetoed." When the House Appropriations Committee then approved a second D.C. appropriations bill, which outlawed the federal but not local funding of abortion, Johnson again urged the president to veto the bill.¹¹⁶

Bush vetoed all four bills, and Congress overcame none of the vetoes. "If I have to err," the president wrote to Senate majority leader Robert Byrd of West Virginia in October 1989, "I prefer to err on the side of human life." Thus did the president stem the tide of pro-choice sentiment in the Congress and the country, and reassure the pro-life community that he was in their camp.[117]

Some Catholics were showing too much passion for the pro-life cause. In October Randall Terry, the head of Operation Rescue, went to prison for preventing access to an Atlanta abortion clinic.[118] Other Catholics, however, were preaching moderation.

At the November 1989 United States Catholic Conference meeting in Baltimore, the bishops adopted a resolution in which they expressed themselves "encouraged" by the "reason to hope" offered by the *Webster* decision yet discouraged that it did not overturn *Roe v. Wade*. They addressed their liberal critics by endorsing "support to pregnant women for prenatal care and extended support for low-income women and their children." They confronted their feminist opponents by recognizing "the anguish of women who face issues that we never will." They acknowledged the momentum of the pro-choice coalition, which had "formed new political parties and . . . intensified efforts to defeat politicians who do not support permissive abortion." And, in a statement added to the resolution, they admonished that public advocacy of a woman's "choice" was not an acceptable position for Catholic politicians privately opposed to abortion.[119]

Yet they stopped short of identifying sanctions for these pro-choice Catholic officeholders. "You can't jump from that text to the statement that now you can't vote for any pro-choice candidates," New York's John Cardinal O'Connor, the newly appointed chairman of the USCC's Committee for Pro-Life Activities, explained.[120]

While the bishops were exhibiting their leadership in the battle against abortion, their ally in the White House was abdicating his. On the same day that the bishops issued their resolution calling abortion "the fundamental human rights issue for all men and women of goodwill," a reporter asked the president whether his priorities were the same. No, Bush responded, implying that politics, not principle, was the primary determinant of his policies. "I don't believe that most voters are single-issue voters," said the president, sounding as if he had defected to the pro-choice camp. "I can tell you that that issue [abortion] ranks about ninth to fourteenth if you talk to a pollster like [the White House's] Bob Teeter." Rather than defend his pro-life colors, Bush virtually apologized for them. He reminded the press that he had been "out front for family planning for a long time and as a member of Congress way back there"—way back when Bush was pro-choice.[121]

New Jersey's pro-choice Catholic governor, Thomas Kean, seemed to be reading the same polls as the president. "When you try to make an issue of religion or conscience as a matter of public policy, you run into trouble," Kean contended at the Republican Governors Conference a week later, urging his party to avoid talking about abortion. Bush largely obliged, even before sympathetic audiences. Having said nothing about abortion before the Catholic Lawyers Guild (and Cardinal Law) in Boston in September, he devoted only two general sentences to it at a Catholic University dinner (attended by Cardinal Hickey) in Washington in December.[122]

But the president *was* listening. "Let me assure you that this president stands with you on this issue of life," Bush telephoned to the participants in the January 22, 1990, March for Life. And unlike the year before, Bush did not delegate the task of meeting with the leaders of the march. The day after the protest, Bush told his fellow pro-lifers that he stood with them in opposition to Massachusetts Catholic Democratic senator Edward Kennedy's proposed revision of the Title X family planning bill to permit abortion counseling and referrals.[123]

Abortion was also on the agenda when Bush met with a group of Catholic bishops on March 22, and with members of the Catholic Golden Age and Catholic Daughters of the Americas eight days later. "We firmly support your stand on right to life," Joseph Leary, the president of Catholic Golden Age, wrote to the president, thanking him for the meeting.[124]

The same month the House Foreign Affairs Committee voted to nullify two Reagan-era pro-life measures—the "Mexico City policy," which prohibited federal population assistance funds from going to the performing of, promoting of, or lobbying for abortion, and the Kemp-Kasten Amendment to foreign aid appropriations, which denied federal population funds to any organization that abetted coercive abortion or sterilization. "We need help from the White House" in defeating these efforts, the National Right to Life Committee's Johnson wrote to Chief of Staff John Sununu in April. The pro-life forces received help in the form of White House pressure on Congress, and the Title X, Mexico City, and Kemp-Kasten anti-abortion policies would survive the congressional session without the need for Bush's veto.[125]

Another Bush administration wish came true in New York City in March 1990. A federal district court dismissed a lawsuit by Planned Parenthood against the Mexico City policy.[126]

While the Bush administration was executing its legislative strategy, the U.S. Catholic bishops were honing theirs. In a major address at Georgetown University in March, Joseph Cardinal Bernardin outlined the bishops' legislative aims. Like the administration, they hoped to enact a constitutional amendment to protect the unborn, and they intended to seek limits on abortion until such an amendment became politically possible. Though the *Webster* decision had advanced the latter goal, Bernardin observed, there remained "much work to be done in terms of public opinion" to achieve the former. Bernardin nonetheless urged Catholics not to give up the fight against abortion, citing polls that showed most Americans in favor of informed consent, parental notification, testing for fetal viability, and bans on the federal funding of abortion.[127]

To help shape public opinion, the bishops decided that they needed better marketing of their message. So the Knights of Columbus provided the bishops with $1 million a year for three to five years toward the hiring of the Hill and Knowlton public relations firm and the Wirthlin polling group. Cardinal O'Connor dismissed as a "myth" the perception that Catholics "have this huge educational network, and all of our pulpits are at the service of the pro-life movement." He said that at Sunday Mass "maybe once, maybe twice a year there would be a formal homily on abortion—of varying lengths, and of varying quality."[128]

If the bishops' influence over national abortion policy was a "myth," it was one they themselves had effectively cultivated ever since *Roe v. Wade*. And it was one in which their adversaries and at least some of their allies fervently believed. Though *Commonweal*'s John Garvey and *America*'s editors rushed to the bishops' defense, the Hill and Knowlton vice chair, Frank Manckiewicz, a former Democratic Party operative, called the decision "a bigger public relations disaster for us than the church because we know better." There were 136 Hill and Knowlton employees who signed a petition protesting the firm's contract with the Church. Others offered to provide pro bono advertising services to abortion rights groups.[129]

The furor over the bishops' public relations offensive reignited the controversy over the American Catholic hierarchy's political role. Pro-choice organizations accused the bishops of violating the First Amendment's separation of church and state. They had made the same argument in 1980, when Abortion Rights Mobilization filed suit against the United States Catholic Conference, accusing the bishops of violating the restriction on political campaign activity in section 501 of the Internal Revenue Code. Yet the bishops continued their public relations campaign. And in April 1990 the Supreme Court dismissed the lawsuit.[130]

But the criticism of the bishops' public relations effort would not go away. "If some of the hostility, bitterness, and anger can be directed at me to leave you free to do the work of God," Cardinal O'Connor alluded to the controversy at a pro-life rally in Washington in April, "then thanks be to God." President Bush was also free to do the work of God from a comfortable distance, addressing the rally by telephone.[131] The cardinal, meanwhile, kept right on throwing punches. O'Connor said in June that Catholic public officials who "are perceived not only as treating Church teaching on abortion with contempt, but helping to multiply abortions by advocating legislation supporting abortion or by making public funds available for abortion" could be subject to excommunication. In less than a year O'Connor had gone from disavowing any penalty for pro-choice Catholic politicians to suggesting the ultimate sanction. "It is upsetting," said New York Democratic governor Mario Cuomo. New York Democratic congressman Charles Rangel found O'Connor's words "mean-spirited." New York Democratic congressman José Serrano said he was "saddened." All three were the kind of pro-choice Catholic politicians O'Connor had in mind.[132]

Yet none of them would face excommunication. "I have no intention of excommunicating anybody," O'Connor reconsidered three days later, explaining that by raising the specter of excommunication, he had actually been discouraging it. Rather than say that bishops *should* consider such a draconian step, the cardinal clarified, he said that they *may* consider it.[133] Once Cardinal O'Connor had persuaded himself of what he had said, he tried to convince the members of his archdiocese. Seventy percent of New York Catholics disapproved of the excommunication of pro-choice politicians by the Church, and even 62 percent of those who had a favorable opinion of Cardinal O'Connor disapproved of what he said.[134]

"Confusion and anger" had resulted from the cardinal's mixed messages, Brooklyn auxiliary bishop Joseph Sullivan complained. "It's got to be solved by the bishops talking to the bishops." Milwaukee archbishop Rembert Weakland talked to O'Connor, maintaining that moral beliefs cannot become legal precepts until there is a "consensus of the population." Weakland argued that politicians grappling with the abortion issue should receive "as much latitude as reason permits." Weakland's moderation would cost him an honorary degree from the University of Fribourg in Switzerland, which the Vatican withheld because of the "confusion" sowed by Weakland's remarks.[135]

All this confusion threatened to obscure two more legal victories for the bishops and the Bush administration. In June, after the state of Illinois settled the *Turnock v. Ragsdale* case out of court, the Supreme Court announced its decisions in the *Akron v. Akron Center for Reproductive Health* and *Hodgson v. Minnesota* parental notification abortion cases. As it had in the *Webster* ruling, the Court upheld the states' abortion restrictions without overturning *Roe v. Wade*, a fact that Justice Scalia ruefully observed in his concurring and dissenting opinions in *Hodgson*. For the bishops, who filed amicus briefs in both cases; the administration, which filed an amicus brief in *Hodgson*; and their pro-choice adversaries, these decisions nonetheless constituted significant legal strides toward repealing *Roe*.[136]

Meanwhile, much of the public remained confused. According to a 1990 survey by the Wirthlin Group, the polling organization hired by the bishops, 47 percent of American voters believed there were fewer than five hundred thousand abortions per year in the United States. Their guess was low by one million. The respondents estimated that 46 percent of abortions occurred to save a mother's life or following rape or incest. Their guess was high by over 45 percent. And although they overwhelmingly backed such restrictions on abortion as parental notification and informed consent, almost half of American Catholics called themselves "pro-choice." The bishops therefore approved a television commercial produced by Hill and Knowlton to advertise the public's estrangement from reality—and to justify their contract with Hill and Knowlton. When the ad noted the actual frequency of abortions in the country, it showed the Statue of Liberty shedding a tear.[137] "We try to link the value of life with the value of freedom," a USCC spokesperson, Helen Alvare, explained the commercial. "Some women's groups and abortion rights advocates have been able to tie the notion of women's freedom closely with abortion, as if abortion were a ticket to freedom," Alvare continued. It was no coincidence that the spokesperson was a woman.[138]

While the bishops' female appointee was making waves, President Bush was pondering whether to make his own splash. The pro-choice Catholic Supreme Court justice William Brennan was to retire at the end of the Court's 1989–1990 term, and Bush was looking for a replacement. One of the two finalists in the administration's search was Judge Edith Jones of the U.S. Court of Appeals for the Fifth Circuit, who had no record on abortion but was so dependably conservative that her nickname was "Scalia in a Skirt."[139] But Bush would not choose her. Instead he selected the other finalist, Judge David Souter of the U.S. Court of Appeals for the First Circuit, who had no judicial record on abortion and little record on anything else. But he was the favorite of Bush's pro-life Catholic chief of staff, John Sununu, who, like Souter, was a native of New Hampshire. So despite Souter's even stronger ties to New Hampshire's pro-choice Republican senator, Warren Rudman, Sununu persuaded Bush that Souter would be a vote against *Roe v. Wade*. Eager to avoid a protracted confirmation process, Bush appointed the little-known Souter as a "safer" choice than Jones.[140]

It was perhaps fitting that Souter won a seat on the Supreme Court in part because he had done nothing on abortion in 1990. In the same year, Bush didn't veto a bill, allow his Justice Department to argue a case, or give a speech. Yet he won in Congress, he won in court, and he won by not opening his mouth.

The year 1991 ushered in the old with the new. Just as he had in the first two years of his presidency, George Bush telephoned the participants of the March for Life on January 22. "I am encouraged by the progress which has taken place. Attempts by Congress to expand . . . federal funding for abortions have been defeated, and the Supreme Court has taken welcome steps toward reversing its *Roe v. Wade* decision," the president told the marchers. "Despite these successes, much needs to be done."[141] And just as in the first year of his presidency, Bush did not meet at the White House with the leadership of the protest. Instead, in the first week of the Persian Gulf War, the commander in chief delegated that responsibility to Sununu.[142]

The Supreme Court remained an ally of the president. In May, in *Rust v. Sullivan*, the Court upheld Title X's exclusion of the federal funding of abortion. The decision was a triumph not only for the Bush administration, but for the United States Catholic Conference, which had filed an amicus brief in favor of the restriction.[143]

Capitol Hill also looked eerily familiar. The November 1990 midterm elections had brought a few more abortion proponents to Congress, so there would be more pro-choice bills for the president to oppose. In June, while Pope John Paul II was berating the Polish legislature for failing to pass an anti-abortion bill, Bush sent a letter to the U.S. legislature threatening to veto any pro-abortion bills. Included among those measures was an effort to amend Title X in a way that, in the words of White House aide Brian Waidmann, "weakens the family planning regulations recently upheld by the Supreme Court." And included among the Bush aides attending a July White House meeting to plot legislative strategy on the Title X bill was the Catholic deputy solicitor general John Roberts, who would head the high court a little over two decades later.[144]

The June 1991 resignation of Lyndon Johnson's pro-choice appointee Justice Thurgood Marshall offered the opening for Bush to replace him with Catholic Clarence Thomas. Thomas's explosive Senate confirmation hearings in October became mostly about his former employee Anita Hill, who accused him of sexual harassment, but they did not entirely neglect abortion. The Catholic Democratic senator George Mitchell of Maine, that body's majority leader, managed to interrupt the soap opera for his own pro-choice commercial. And "the most intense opposition" to Thomas, *Commonweal*'s David Carlin reported, "came from the pro-choice lobby."[145]

Thomas's narrow confirmation capped off another successful year for the pro-life Bush administration. Not only would Thomas eventually prove a pro-life counterweight to Souter, but Bush repeatedly stymied the increasingly pro-choice Congress. Five times Congress added pro-choice provisions to legislation. But two vetoes of the District of Columbia and the Labor/HHS/Education appropriations bills as well as three veto threats—against a reauthorization of the National Institutes of Health that eliminated a ban on experimentation using fetal tissue, and foreign aid appropriations bills that would have provided abortion-related financing of the United Nations Population Fund—forestalled any new abortion legislation in 1991.[146]

It had also been a good year for pro-life Catholics. Not only was the Bush administration firmly on their side, but more Americans seemed to be as well. A 1991 Gallup Poll commissioned by Americans United for Life, the leading anti-abortion legal organization, found that most Americans opposed most abortions. Sixty-nine percent favored parental notification and viability testing, while 86 percent backed informed consent. And among non-Catholics, the favorability rating of the Catholic Church was ten points higher than the rating of the National Abortion Rights Action League.[147]

But not all the news was good for pro-life Catholics. In the same AUL poll, Planned Parenthood's favorability was ten points higher than that of the Catholic Church. And most alarmingly, another Gallup Poll at the end of 1991 showed only 27 percent of Catholics in favor, and 68 percent opposed, to the overturning of *Roe v. Wade*. So the firm on Madison Avenue and the salesman on Pennsylvania Avenue in whom the U.S. Catholic hierarchy had invested so much still had work to do.[148]

The Supreme Court would make sure of that. The Bush administration and the USCC filed amicus briefs on the side of the defendant, Pennsylvania governor Robert Casey, in *Planned Parenthood v. Casey*, a challenge to the parental notification, spousal notification, informed consent, twenty-four-hour waiting period, and filing of reports by abortion providers required by state law. In addition to offering another opportunity for the president and the bishops to seek *Roe*'s repeal, the case would showcase an endangered species—a Catholic Democratic officeholder opposed to abortion. Since the Democrats were the party of "choice," they would deny Casey a speaking slot at their convention in New York the following summer.[149]

The president denied himself a speaking role on abortion. In March he told the National Association of Evangelicals that if Congress passed the Freedom of Choice Act, codifying *Roe v. Wade*, "it will not become law as long as I am president of the United States of America." But when he delivered the commencement address at the University of Notre Dame in May, he said nothing about abortion. And as Bush looked on, the nation's foremost Catholic university awarded its highest honor, the Laetare Medal, to New York's pro-choice Catholic Democratic senator, Daniel Patrick Moynihan. The next month, when the bishops held their annual spring meeting at Notre Dame, Cardinal O'Connor and several other prelates stayed home to protest the university's decision.[150]

If Notre Dame was deciding against the bishops, the Supreme Court was not. In June the Court upheld Pennsylvania's Abortion Control Act of 1992 (except for the spousal permission requirement). "I am pleased with the Supreme Court's decision upholding most of Pennsylvania's reasonable restrictions on abortion," was the White House reaction to the ruling, this time (unlike after the *Webster* decision) invoking first-person singular. *America*'s editors had written before the verdict that a favorable decision would be "the sort of legislative compromise the nation needs."[151] As with *Webster*, however, it was a partial victory. By a 5–4 margin, the Court again refused to overturn *Roe v. Wade*. Bush appointee Clarence Thomas joined fellow Catholic Antonin Scalia in the minority. But Bush appointee David Souter and Catholic Reagan appointee Anthony Kennedy were in the majority. *Commonweal*'s editors condemned the Court for "going out of its way to endorse *Roe*'s agnosticism about fetal life."[152]

But partial victories are still victories, and *Casey*, like *Webster*, mobilized the pro-choice majority on Capitol Hill, eager to undo the decisions. By August, when he addressed the Knights of Columbus convention in New York City, Bush had nixed three more abortion-related bills. "Seven times I have ignored the polls and acted on what I believe is fundamental principle," the president reviewed his record for the Knights, "and vetoed . . . abortion legislation."[153] Bush soon added three more vetoes—rejecting the abortion components of a Title X family planning bill and a D.C. appropriations measure in September, and spurning provisions for abortion in overseas military hospitals in the Military Health Care Initiatives Act in October. Of the forty-four vetoes of his presidency, almost a quarter were in opposition to abortion.[154]

But the president had not "ignored the polls." He couldn't if he wanted to—there were so many of them. And in an election year, he certainly didn't want to—especially when they vindicated his actions. The most prevalent argument against Bush's vetoes was that they unfairly penalized poor (and, often, minority) women who could not afford abortion services without government assistance. Yet a 1992 poll by the bishops' Wirthlin Group showed that although most Americans earning over $60,000 per year supported the public funding of abortion, most Americans earning under $15,000 a year opposed it.[155]

Undermined by a primary challenge by pro-life protectionist Patrick Buchanan and unnerved by a general election fight from pro-choice budget hawk Ross Perot, Bush ran a lackluster reelection campaign that started late and never really caught up. A *USA Today* poll placed abortion tenth on a list of issues most important to voters in the 1992 election—about where Bush had put it three years earlier.[156]

The bishops' campaign had been nearly as futile. A 1991 Gallup Poll found that only 43 percent of Catholics were aware of groups like Birthright, Alternatives to Abortion, and Catholic Charities, which offered free medical counseling and pre- and postnatal services for women contemplating abortion. A 1992 study by sociologists James Davis Hunter of the University of Virginia and Carl Bowman of Bridgewater College concluded that "outside of the rank-and-file of the anti-abortion movement, the average American . . . tends to view the anti-abortion movement in the same negative way as the pro-choice coalitions do." Or, as Cunningham put it, "People who believe abortion to be wrong resent those who remind them of it."[157]

George Bush would not be reminding them of it after November. But then, he hadn't offered too many reminders during the previous four years either. The bishops' campaign continued, however, after the president's ended. Two weeks after Bush's defeat by a plurality of American Catholics, the Church issued a new catechism, which listed abortion as a modern sin.[158]

There were a lot of sinners. A 1992 survey by the University of Chicago sociologist Rev. Andrew Greeley found that by 1988 one in four American women born between 1958 and 1965 had had an abortion, while 17 percent of Catholic women in this cohort had undergone the procedure. Though Greeley found this difference "statistically significant," he admitted that "Catholic conservatives" would find the rates for Catholic women disgracefully high.[159]

Conclusions on Life and Death

The years since *Roe v. Wade* have offered few unalloyed victories for either side of the abortion standoff. On balance, the Bush era produced significant, if incomplete, progress for the pro-life cause.

It would nevertheless be easy to characterize the George Bush presidency as one of retreat for pro-life Catholics. First, not only did the Supreme Court in *Webster, Rust, Akron, Hodgson,* and *Casey* refuse to reverse *Roe v. Wade,* but the Court in some ways actually strengthened it. In their joint opinion in the *Casey* case, Justices Sandra Day O'Connor, Anthony Kennedy, and David Souter referred to the "life of the fetus," "prenatal life," the "life of the unborn," and the "developing child." They even admitted that "some of us [as] individuals find abortion offensive to our most basic principles of morality." Yet they reached the conclusion that the "life" and "child" to which they repeatedly alluded was not a "person" under the Constitution. These three justices, one of them Catholic and all of them appointed by pro-life Republicans, were not just upholding *Roe v. Wade.* They were leaving little hope that what Harvard professor Mary Ann Glendon dubbed "the most permissive abortion laws in the industrial West" would disappear anytime soon.[160]

A second step back for pro-life Catholics was the growing realization that the reversal of *Roe* was likely not going to happen outside of court. "I support a constitutional amendment that would reverse the Supreme Court's decision in *Roe v. Wade*," President Bush wrote in his first year of office. "I also support a human life amendment." Bush repeated these positions in his last year in office. In between he worked for neither. Thus did Bush perpetuate his party's recent tradition of proposing constitutional amendments—to reinstate school prayer, to balance the budget, to prohibit burning the flag—with little if any hope of passage. *America*'s editors were more candid than the president. "We have never favored a constitutional amendment to prohibit abortion," they explained in February 1990, "not just because we think it unattainable, but because we think it futile, given the lack of consensus in the nation about the morality of abortion."[161] The U.S. Catholic bishops also backed a constitutional amendment to ban abortion, but they weren't working for it either. In the face of majorities in the nation and in the Church in favor of *Roe v. Wade*, they were largely settling instead for the piecemeal restrictions imposed by the executive, legislative, and judicial branches.

Of course, if they had been working for an amendment, they would not have been lobbying for the same approach as the president. This constituted a third step back for pro-life Catholics—in some ways the president wasn't really one of them. Bush's amendments excepted the victims of rape and incest and allowed exceptions to spare the life of the mother, while the official Catholic position never permitted abortion. Bush backed artificial contraception; the bishops opposed it. Bush's "moderate" stance on abortion, Donald Burrill contended in *Christian Century* in April 1990, was "wholly incompatible with the pro-life principle."[162]

A fourth setback for pro-life Catholics during the Bush era was the often vicious polarization of the abortion debate reignited by the *Webster* decision. "It's War!" screamed the scarlet letters of *Ms.* magazine's August 1989 cover. "The New Civil War," ABC News dubbed the conflict in a November 1990 documentary. "I have been disappointed in the public dialogue since *Webster*," Cardinal Bernardin wrote in March 1990, "because so much attention has been focused on protest and power, and so little on what is at stake substantively in our society."[163]

Catholicism itself became a convenient target for some in the abortion debate. In January 1991 Episcopal bishop John Spong of Newark urged women to leave the "insulting, retrograde" Catholic Church "for the sake of their humanity." The city's Catholic archbishop, Theodore McCarrick, lamented that "Catholic bashing" was "alive and well in New Jersey." In August 1991 Virginia governor Douglas Wilder, an African-American, a Democrat, and a Protestant, criticized President Bush's selection of Judge Clarence Thomas, an African-American, a Republican, and a Catholic, for the Supreme Court. "The question is," said the governor, resuscitating an accusation last leveled at presidential candidate John Kennedy by the Ku Klux Klan in 1960, "how much allegiance is there to the Pope?"[164] Bishop Spong unleashed another assault on Catholics in April 1992, calling the Church "prejudiced, hypocritical, and repressive," while encouraging an end to Episcopalian-Catholic dialogue. Archbishop McCarrick defended Catholics again, writing to Bishop Spong, "I truly regret that you have decided to move in the direction of such personal attacks on the Catholic Church by making a parody of our teaching and a caricature of our theology."[165]

The media furor over Cardinal O'Connor's excommunication threat evinced the perils associated with a fifth step back for pro-life Catholics: the return of the abortion issue to the states. "It was easy to have successes in state legislatures and even in Congress," said Auxiliary Bishop Edward O'Donnell of St. Louis, a member of the USCC's Committee for Pro-Life Activities, while the courts stood in the way of pro-life legislation. Now that the courts were cooperating with the pro-life forces, O'Donnell posited after *Webster*, the stakes at the state and federal legislative levels would be higher, and pro-life statutes would be more difficult to attain. Because of *Webster*, *Commonweal*'s David Carlin wrote, when Americans vote "for their fifty governors and 7461 state legislators, they will be forced to take into consideration the position candidates hold on the abortion/choice question." As a result, "small-scale warfare is about to be replaced by total war."[166] "While the Supreme Court teases the nation with a patchwork process allowing some restrictions and turning down others," *Commonweal* editorialized, "the acrimonious scramble for influence in the fifty state houses and state legislatures for pro-life and pro-choice forces will be poisonous to our whole political system." Or, as the New York Assembly speaker, Mel Miller, put it, "It's terrible to have this issue back again."[167]

This decentralization of the abortion controversy shifted the issue's nexus from Washington, where the Republican administration, the Democratic Congress, and the United States Catholic Conference sought a national consensus, to the states, where individual politicians and prelates spoke only for themselves and received more attention than they deserved. "One Catholic bishop, not noted for his sagacity, trumpeted that several Catholics holding public positions on his turf whose views on abortion did not coincide with his would henceforth be anathema," R.E. B. wrote in *U.S. Catholic* in October 1990, "unless, presumably, they did penance by walking the length of his cathedral on their knees." The fact that "approximately 400 other Catholic bishops did not act in so high-handed a manner" mattered less now that there were fifty abortion battlegrounds instead of one.[168]

For each of these backward steps, however, there was a more significant forward thrust for pro-life Catholics in the Bush era. First, although *Roe v. Wade* remained substantially intact, the collective impact of *Webster*, *Rust*, *Akron*, *Hodgson*, and *Casey* showed that it was not impregnable. And the pro-life forces not only had public opinion on their side on parental notification, informed consent, and a waiting period, but they increasingly had science on their side in their quest to upend *Roe* altogether. "The growing medical interest in fetal research and the widespread use of the sonogram allowing a woman to see her fetus *in utero*," Daniel Callahan noted in November 1990, "have brought the fetus more squarely into the public eye."[169]

Second, President Bush's lack of proselytizing on abortion could not overshadow his considerable achievements in preserving the status quo. Not only did all of his abortion vetoes stick, but his veto threats and statements comprised components of the speech he never gave. "The President's 1989 veto message could hardly have been more explicit," the National Right to Life Committee's Douglas Johnson lauded Bush's rejection of foreign aid appropriations permitting abortion funding. "The President's June 26, 1990, letter promising to veto any foreign aid bill that weakened the Mexico City or Kemp-Kasten anti-coercion law," an administration memo concluded, "played a key role in framing that issue and in the eventual defeat of the pro-abortion amendments in Congress."[170]

Third, Bush's differences with pro-life Catholics over abortion for rape and incest victims and on family planning were less significant than they appeared. After all, there were very few instances of rape or incest victims having abortions. A 1992 Planned Parenthood study discovered that 76 percent of women who had had abortions were "concerned about how having a baby could change [their] life," 68 percent said they could not afford a baby, 51 percent wanted "to avoid single parenthood" or were having "problems with a relationship," and 7 percent had a "health problem." Only 1 percent cited rape or incest as the reason for their abortions.[171]

Rape and incest victims having abortions were not only unusual, but legislating an exception for them was unrealistic. Bush's pro-choice aide Bobbie Kilberg successfully urged the president to veto the FY 1990 Labor/HHS/Education appropriations bill despite its apparent alignment with Bush's position—no federal funding of abortion except in cases of rape or incest. "A rape and incest exception to the prohibition against federal funding of abortions would be impossible to police," Kilberg wrote in October 1989. "It would either weigh down the courts with thousands of disputed claims, or amount to an 'open door' presenting no real restrictions to anyone determined to get a Medicaid-paid abortion." An anti-abortion constitutional amendment with the same exceptions, as advocated by Bush, would presumably possess the same risks.[172]

Bush's division with the bishops over family planning actually worked to the benefit of both by shining some political daylight between church and state. "The pro-abortion lobby, and the press, are already beginning to beat the drums that the President is 'against family planning,'" the National Right to Life Committee's Johnson and Darla St. Martin warned Chief of Staff Sununu in February 1990. "I understand your position on abortion and you clearly cannot change that," David Packard wrote to Bush in June 1992. "You can, however, come out with a strong position on population control." Bush replied to Packard from Air Force One that "what I will do as a result of your letter is get out a strong statement of support for international family planning." The statement followed, with Bush trumpeting his Agency for International Development's record spending on population control and calling for a "blue ribbon Commission on Population and the Future."[173]

While separating the president from the bishops, his family planning stance also united them. It constituted Bush's version of Cardinal Bernardin's "consistent ethic of life," by which the president and the bishops disarmed those critics who charged that they cared less about the born than the unborn. To the bishops, "abortion is of overriding concern," Cardinal O'Connor explained in November 1989, "because it negates two of our most fundamental moral imperatives: respect for innocent life, and preferred concern for the weak and defenseless." Those imperatives underscored the bishops' advocacy of public assistance for adoption, child care, and parental leave, as well as their opposition to capital punishment.[174]

A fourth step forward for pro-life Catholics in the Bush era was the realization by many non-Catholics and Catholics alike that polarization is ultimately self-defeating. A pluralistic society has "to learn to live uncomfortably with this issue," *Life*'s Roger Rosenblatt, a non-Catholic, wrote of abortion in November 1990. "Let's not toss the charge of anti-Catholicism about too casually, thereby adding Catholics to the list of those who refuse to debate, who prefer to silence their critics by charging them with some psychological infirmity or moral depravity," *Commonweal*'s David Carlin, a Catholic, appealed in June 1991. After all, *Webster* was a victory not just for Catholics, but for Agudath Israel, the National Organization of Episcopalians for Life, Presbyterians Pro-life, American Baptists' Friends for Life, Moravians for Life, United Church of Christ's Friends for Life, the Task Force of United Methodists on Abortion and Sexuality, and the Christian Action Council. All of these religious groups had signed amicus briefs in favor of Missouri in the *Webster* case, and none of them was complaining about religious prejudice. A May 1990 Gallup Poll found that neither age, gender, race, political party, nor religion was an accurate predictor of one's views on abortion.[175]

A fifth and final forward movement for pro-life Catholics was the momentum generated by *Webster* in state legislatures throughout the country. Two days after the decision, Louisiana overwhelmingly passed a resolution to enforce its abortion restrictions. In Michigan and Wisconsin, the legislatures prepared to consider parental notification bills. In Illinois, the House overrode a veto by the pro-choice Republican governor, James Thompson, of a bill banning research using aborted fetuses. The transfer of the abortion issue to the states was not just fomenting friction; for the right-to-life community, it was producing progress.[176]

As for the uncontrollable utterances of errant bishops, they were the exception rather than the rule. "Bishops in Wisconsin, Montana, and Ohio have issued effective statements on abortion," *Commonweal* editorialized, "some of them published in response to statements by local politicians, without applying ecclesiastical penalties or even hinting that they would." Not only did no American Catholic politician face excommunication, but there was only one such case in all of the Western nations. And the Vatican still had no policy on the matter.[177]

During the Bush presidency, the debate shifted from whether legalized abortion to whither legalized abortion. But this move from moral absolutism to moral relativism was not entirely negative for pro-life Catholics. The reawakening of the pro-choice campaign between the judicial bookends of *Webster* and *Casey* meant that its foot soldiers, many of them Catholic, were alarmed. And they had good reason to be. *Webster* signaled that there were now more than two sides to the abortion question, and for pro-choice activists, most of them were bad. "By 1992, as the [pro-life] Republican platform abundantly showed," Walter Burnham wrote, "abortion had become a prime, talismanic issue."[178] Thanks largely to a president whose career had put him on almost every side, a pro-life movement some had given up for dead was still breathing. And many Catholics had helped George Bush keep it very much alive.

In the eyes of many American Catholics, there was much that President George Bush could have done differently. He could have waited longer before forsaking economic sanctions for war against Iraq. He could have acted sooner to arrest the decline of America's cities. And he could have spoken more forcefully and more frequently in defense of the unborn. But while they quarreled with his methods, they nevertheless shared his aims. And before he dispatched international forces to Kuwait, sent federal dollars to Los Angeles, and promoted pro-life policies in all three branches of the national government, he invited Catholic input and incorporated Catholic ideas. Bush was not a Catholic president, but in many ways he was a president for Catholics.

CHAPTER EIGHT

Catholics and Bill Clinton
(1993–2001)

A PLURALITY OF AMERICAN CATHOLIC VOTERS returned to the Democratic Party in 1992 after choosing Republicans in the three previous presidential elections. In many ways they received little in return for their votes for Bill Clinton. He started two wars about which they were unsure, failed to enact health care reform about which they were hopeful, and promoted abortion to such an extent that they were appalled. But thanks largely to the leadership of their church, they would have a powerful voice on all of these issues. Then, when peace interrupted war and prosperity arrived without health care reform, they swallowed their reservations on abortion and voted for him all over again.

War and Peace: Bosnia and Kosovo

The "American Century," as Americans like to call it, began and ended on the Balkan Peninsula. Within a hundred years, "Balkanize" would debut as a verb and depart as a virtue. But war remained a vice. To Democratic presidents Woodrow Wilson and Bill Clinton it was an evil to be averted. "He kept us out of war" was the pacifist slogan that helped to reelect Wilson in 1916. "It's the economy, stupid" was the parochial sentiment that helped to elect Clinton in 1992.

Neither president could achieve peace through diplomacy, however, so they resorted to war. Wilson's war would enable Yugoslavia. Clinton's wars would disable it. Wilson's war introduced air power as a supplement to ground forces. Clinton's wars introduced air power as a substitute for ground forces. Yet the wars that both commanders in chief fought, and the peace that they forged, were the residue of their liberal internationalist designs—measured, multilateral, and moralistic.

Unlike the First World War, which Congress declared, and the Treaty of Versailles, which Wilson himself negotiated, the wars in Bosnia and Kosovo, and the peace that followed them, garnered little attention and demanded

{293}

minimal sacrifice from the American people. And the pronouncements of the American Catholic hierarchy about the latter conflicts were often as confusing as they had been clear about the former. World War I had made the world "safe for democracy." The Bosnian and Kosovo wars would make the former Yugoslavia safe for demography. If liberal internationalists had relinquished all perspective in the excesses of the twentieth century's first U.S. war, they regained it within the limits of the last. By reluctantly endorsing Clinton's carefully circumscribed U.S. military role on the Balkan Peninsula, Catholic leaders and most of their followers indicated that they still wanted their country to save the world—just not all of it, and not all at once.

Bosnia

Shortly after an assassin's bullet deprived Austria-Hungary of its next ruler, the bloodiest war yet ravaged the globe in the summer of 1914. After four years and sixteen million dead, there was a new map of the world and a reluctant empire in charge of it. Among the new nations that emerged from the ruins of a century of imperialism was Yugoslavia, a makeshift monument to Slavic self-determination.

With the death of communist dictator Marshal Josip Broz Tito in 1980, however, this anxious amalgam of six republics, five nations, four languages, three religions, and two alphabets lost the solid sum of its brittle parts. When Slovenia and Macedonia sought to secede a decade later, Yugoslavia's Serb strongman, Slobodan Milošević, begrudgingly let them go. But when Croatia and Bosnia tried, a triangular civil war erupted in 1992 between the mostly Eastern Orthodox Serbs, the mostly Catholic Croats, and the mostly Muslim Bosnians. The results, according to the U.S. Department of State, were rape, torture, and death camps perpetrated by the Serbs, which approached the actions of the Nazis in World War II.[1]

After the United Nations Security Council passed Resolution 770, encouraging all nations to take "all measures necessary" to extend humanitarian aid to the war's victims, both houses of Congress passed their own resolutions in August 1992 supporting the UN action. But with the arrival in Washington the next year of a new president inexperienced in the ways of the world, America again became a reluctant empire.[2]

In the absence of executive initiative, the legislative branch took the lead on U.S. policy toward Yugoslavia's civil war in 1993. Congress approved nonbinding resolutions urging President Bill Clinton to disregard the arms embargo imposed by the United Nations on all parties to the conflict, because it was inadvertently favoring the heavily armed Bosnian Serbs. Clinton agreed that the embargo should end, and he announced his support for air strikes against

Bosnian Serb targets, but only if the UN voted to take these measures. Fearing that a lifting of the embargo and the introduction of air strikes would endanger its peacekeepers on the ground in Bosnia-Herzegovina, the UN refused.[3]

The leaders of the Catholic Church appeared to side with both Congress and Clinton. As Milošević escalated his genocidal campaign against Croats and Bosnian Muslims, Pope John Paul II prodded the "international community" to "show more clearly its political will not to accept . . . the aberration of 'ethnic cleansing.'" When "populations are succumbing to the attacks of an unjust aggressor," the pontiff told the Vatican diplomatic corps in January 1993, "states no longer have a right to indifference." He called for "all forms of action aimed at disarming the aggressor."[4] In February a national Catholic organization, the Leadership Conference of Women Religious, urged the United Nations to condemn the mass rape in Bosnia and implored the United States to send humanitarian aid to the victims. In March Archbishop John Quinn addressed Slovenian and Croat parishes in his San Francisco archdiocese, pleading for the safeguarding of human rights and the commitment to self-determination in the former Yugoslavia. The same month the administrative board of the United States Catholic Conference, while maintaining that "there is no real military solution in the former Yugoslavia," nonetheless advocated U.S. military deployment to protect safe areas, refugees, and humanitarian aid shipments, as well as to enforce economic sanctions and a "no-fly" zone.[5]

Archbishop John Roach of Minneapolis–St. Paul, chairman of the bishops' International Justice and Peace Committee, reiterated the administrative board's position in a letter to Secretary of State Warren Christopher two months later. "Given the atrocities committed on all sides in this war, the lack of accountability of many of the militias fighting in Bosnia, and the likelihood that the war would escalate and widen," the archbishop nonetheless questioned whether President Clinton's proposal to arm the Bosnians and bomb the Serbs would fulfill the Church's just-war criteria.[6] When some press reports described Roach's letter as a call for U.S. military intervention in Bosnia, the archbishop hurried to issue a clarification. Repeating his distinction between limited defensive actions and broader offensive tactics, Roach insisted that his letter "rejects the arguments that the United States has no role or responsibility in stopping the slaughter in Bosnia," but it also "rejects the premise that there is a true military solution to the crisis."[7]

Ten years after his pastoral "The Challenge of Peace" had challenged Ronald Reagan to do more to halt the nuclear arms race with the Soviet Union, Joseph Cardinal Bernardin of Chicago called in May for "effective steps . . . to protect the innocent and to stop the horror of the ethnic cleansing" in Bosnia.

Fifteen years into his papacy, at a meeting with the president in Denver in August, John Paul II challenged Bill Clinton to "do more" to halt the massacre in the Balkans.[8] But "doing more" did not mean doing wrong, the American bishops reminded the nation at their November meeting in Washington. In their pastoral "The Harvest of Justice Is Sown in Peace," they revisited the Church's just-war tradition, which "aims at clarifying when force may be used, limiting the resort to force, and restraining the damage done by military forces during war." But while reiterating the basic tenets of a just war—"just cause, comparative justice, legitimate authority, right intention, probability of success, proportionality, last resort, and noncombatant immunity"—they did not address whether and how U.S. military intervention in Bosnia could meet these criteria.[9]

Neither did the pope. In January 1994 in Rome, the Holy Father presided over a two-day meeting on the Balkan crucible. He called for "humanitarian intervention" but stopped short of advocating military action. His Pontifical Council of Justice and Peace issued a ten-point statement urging the international community to "do everything possible not to let the problem of minorities be solved by expulsion, transfer, and, still less, extermination of peoples," without saying what "everything" would entail.[10] "The seemingly intractable nature of this conflict is not an excuse for indifference or inaction," Bishop Daniel Reilly of Worcester, chairman of the USCC's Committee on International Policy, agreed with the Vatican. But he suggested no particular action.[11]

Though Americans saw no national interest in Bosnia and divided over a moral obligation to intervene, Clinton obtained approval from NATO to bomb selected Serb targets in Sarajevo. But before NATO pilots could drop the bombs, Serb forces evacuated the Bosnian capital, taking most of their heavy artillery with them. "NATO is trying in its imperfect way to respond," Newark archbishop Theodore McCarrick approved, after returning from the war-torn Bosnian diocese of Banja Luka, whose Catholic population had shrunk by two-thirds in three years. While he embraced the threat of air strikes, McCarrick opposed lifting the embargo, calling instead for tighter sanctions to cripple the Serbs. "When the history of this terrible conflict is written," McCarrick lamented about the administration's foot dragging, "the United States will not come off well."[12]

The United States did not come off well in an ABC documentary hosted by Peter Jennings in March 1994. Titled *While America Watched: The Bosnian Tragedy*, the program implicated the Bush and Clinton administrations in the deaths of two hundred thousand Bosnian civilians in three years at the hands of Croats and Serbs. "This could all have been stopped before that," Archbishop Vinko Puljic of Sarajevo asserted in an interview with *America*, "when the Yugoslav army made its move against Slovenian independence." The archbishop maintained that "if the world had reacted seriously then," it would not have so much blood on its hands now.[13]

At the same time that the Croatian National Union of the United States and Canada was criticizing Clinton's "lack of leadership" in "the tragic war of aggression being waged by the Bosnian Serbs," Archbishop Puljic was admitting that some of the culprits in the conflict were Catholic. "There were crimes committed by Croats against Muslims," the archbishop recounted, "and by Muslims against Croats." He therefore welcomed the Clinton administration's successful brokering of a federation between Croats and Muslims, and between this federation and the republic of Croatia.[14] "The threat of intervention by Croatian troops has ended," Clinton's United Nations representative, Madeleine Albright, agreed with Archbishop Puljic in April. She also conceded, however, that "the road ahead remains steep."[15]

The road was indeed steep in Bosnia, where the Serbs followed their exit of Sarajevo with a violation of the UN no-fly zone, leading to the downing of Serb planes by U.S. pilots in NATO's first combat operation in its forty-five-year history. And the road was steep on Capitol Hill, where this aerial success failed to secure support for Clinton's new strategy from lawmakers still wedded to an elimination of the arms embargo. "The president . . . will have to clearly explain to the American people the stake the United States and the international community has in Bosnia," the Republican Senate majority leader, Robert Dole, urged, and a lifting of the embargo would buttress such an explanation.[16]

Among those calling for a unilateral repeal of the embargo was New York's Catholic Democratic senator Daniel Patrick Moynihan, who infuriated Clinton not just with the content but with the moment of his criticism. "That's just a freebie for him," Clinton privately fumed, outraged that Moynihan had chosen to voice his popular position so soon after NATO air strikes had spectacularly driven Serb troops from the Muslim stronghold of Goražde, where the Serbs had killed seven hundred and wounded two thousand more.[17]

In June 1994, by a vote of 244–178, the House of Representatives amended the FY 1995 defense authorization bill with language compelling Clinton to lift the embargo. As the House was expressing disapproval in Washington, the president was seeking approval in Rome. Bosnia was among the subjects that Clinton discussed with Pope John Paul II at the Vatican in June, picking up the conversation where it had left off during their telephone call the previous month.[18]

A year later, after the unlikely rescue of Captain Scott O'Grady, the first American shot down in sixty-nine thousand UN-NATO sorties over Bosnia,

Clinton accorded the young pilot a hero's welcome at the White House. Alone with O'Grady in the Oval Office, Clinton asked him for advice about Bosnia. Whatever you do, the airman counseled, don't send ground troops into the forbidding highlands of the region.[19] O'Grady, a devout Catholic, believed that the Virgin Mary had saved him from capture by the enemy. But he couldn't save Clinton's faltering Bosnia policy. "Not even a fortnight of pumped-up celebration after the nearly miraculous rescue of Air Force Captain Scott O'Grady," Daniel Wackerman wrote in *America*, "can clear from our minds those images now two years old, of emaciated bodies peering through the barbed wire of Serb war camps."[20]

In August 1995, two and a half years into his presidency, Bill Clinton finally arrived at a coherent strategy on Bosnia. After yet another Serb massacre killed thirty-seven civilians in Sarajevo, Clinton issued the bombing order he had hoped he would never have to give. The NATO airmen would join Croatian infantry in a major escalation of the war. And just in case, NATO massed tens of thousands of ground forces in southeastern Europe.[21]

Just as the president was finally getting specific, so too were the bishops. In their September 1995 document, "Proclaiming the Gospel of Life: Protecting the Least among Us and Pursuing the Common Good," the bishops echoed Archbishop Roach's letter two years earlier in asserting that "the international community has a right and duty to intervene" in Bosnia and in espousing a "limited use of force to protect vulnerable civilian populations, to enable relief supplies to get through, and to implement a peace settlement." Yet this time they went further, adding that "U.N. peacekeeping and humanitarian protection should be strengthened so that it can more effectively prevent 'ethnic cleansing' and meet its commitment to humanitarian protection." Although they did not rule in NATO air strikes to help attain these goals, this time they did not rule them out.[22]

Clinton and John Paul II would again cross paths, on their way to commemorate the fiftieth anniversary of the United Nations, the beacon of multilateralism, which the pope had relentlessly invoked and the president had restlessly ignored during the Bosnian air campaign. When the president greeted the pope in Newark in October, they again discussed Bosnia, as they had in Denver and Rome. But this time, as Clinton eloquently put it, "horror was giving way to hope."[23]

And war was giving way to peace. The day after Clinton's meeting with Pope John Paul II, a cease-fire started in Bosnia. Upon his return to Rome, the pope convoked the bishops of Bosnia-Herzegovina, Croatia, Macedonia, Slovenia, and Yugoslavia to help reconcile the warring factions within their countries and, in the words of the meeting's official communiqué, "to hasten the advent of lasting peace."²⁴

At the beginning of November the assistant secretary of state, Richard Holbrooke, assembled the leaders of Bosnia, Croatia, and Yugoslavia in Dayton, Ohio. For the next three weeks Holbrooke would broker peace negotiations with Alija Izetbegović, Franjo Tuđman, and Slobodan Milošević. By the end of the month the principals in Dayton had come to an agreement. The ceasefire would remain, UN-NATO peacekeepers would arrive, and Bosnia would be 51 percent Muslim and Croat, 49 percent Serb. When Clinton announced the Dayton Accords to the nation on November 27, he recalled Pope John Paul II's plea at their Newark meeting that the twentieth century not end the way it began, with a war in Sarajevo.²⁵

"With John Paul II, we welcome the Peace Agreement, which offers a long-awaited hope for a permanent peace," the bishops wrote in reaction to the unusually upbeat news about Bosnia. "These goals cannot be achieved without strong support from the United States." John Hart, the Clinton administration's liaison to the Catholic community, welcomed the bishops' statement, which he considered their "most supportive to date on the President's position in Bosnia." The administration arranged a meeting with several bishops and sent a summary of the Dayton Accords to all of the American cardinals, the heads of major Catholic humanitarian organizations, the chairmen of relevant USCC committees, and the bishops in "high priority" states. Then the commander in chief advocated a U.S. contribution to the international peacekeeping force, which, Clinton promised, would be home within a year, just in time for the presidential election. And the bishops successfully lobbied Congress to deploy the peacekeepers.²⁶

The peacekeepers would not come home, but it didn't seem to matter. The peace agreement held, and although Clinton's rival in the 1996 campaign would be Senator Dole, Bosnia would not be an issue. The questionnaire that the bishops sent to the candidates in September contained no questions about the recently completed war.²⁷

In 1997 Pope John Paul II journeyed to Sarajevo. Local police removed two dozen freshly planted mines from the route of the Holy Father's motorcade. Shadowed by Bosnian soldiers on rooftops and NATO pilots in helicopters, the frail yet gallant pilgrim traveled down the street known as Snipers Alley, in a city known for war. The pope preached forgiveness to the leaders of Bosnia's fledgling government, a combustible collection of Serbs, Croats, and Muslims who had hardly finished putting away their guns. Amid the rubble of what was barely Bosnia were more than 1,100 mosques and more than 600 Catholic churches. "The war is over, we believe," said Dusko Ladan, an electrical engineer who had left his home at one o'clock in the morning to make the four-hour trek to see the pope. "The reality is that we must be ready for peace or war. That is the destiny of this region."[28]

Kosovo

Within two short years, war was again Yugoslavia's destiny. In 1990 Yugoslav president Slobodan Milošević had revoked the autonomy of Kosovo, the country's southernmost province with a population about 90 percent Albanian Muslim and only 8 percent Serb. Two years later, U.S. president George H. W. Bush admonished Milošević about repression of the Kosovar majority, a warning to be repeated several times by Bush's successor, Bill Clinton. Milošević disregarded these warnings, and Serbs continually violated the human rights of Kosovar Albanians.[29]

As in Bosnia, the nature and scale of the violence in Kosovo demanded American and Catholic attention. In March 1998, in the village of Donji Prekaz, Serb secret police slaughtered fifty-eight members of the family of local Kosovo Liberation Army leader Adem Jashari, including eighteen women and ten children. "This crisis is not an internal affair," Clinton's Catholic secretary of state, Madeleine Albright, now admitted. "It is long past time," the bishops of her church concurred, "for the Yugoslav government to end its repression in Kosovo and take concrete step[s] to recognize [the] basic rights of the Albanian community there." The author of this statement by the American bishops, Newark archbishop Theodore McCarrick, returned from Kosovo in August with a call for a cease-fire, the restoration of Kosovar autonomy within Yugoslavia, and protection of the rights of Kosovo's majority and minorities.[30]

Stung by criticism in a book by his chief Bosnian negotiator, Richard Holbrooke, that he had moved too slowly to stanch the bleeding there, President Clinton quickly attempted to find a diplomatic solution to the second Balkan crisis of his presidency. He wouldn't succeed. In January 1999 Serbs killed forty-five Albanian civilians in the village of Račak. "Last week's massacre of more than forty civilians," Archbishop McCarrick wrote after the carnage, "is simply the most egregious example of grave and ongoing human rights violations committed against civilians."[31]

In February 1999 there was yet another set of negotiations with the Serbs, begun under NATO auspices in Rambouillet, France. "The Holy See deeply appreciates the commitment on the part of the international community, particularly of European countries, shown in these days at Rambouillet," the Vatican saluted the talks, "to help all walk the path of sincere dialogue."[32] But when the talks resulted in a request for an autonomous Kosovo to be policed by almost thirty thousand NATO troops, the Serbs balked. So, as he had in Bosnia, Clinton selected a military option to resolve the crisis. "Let's do it," the commander in chief ordered, and NATO warplanes opened a barrage on the Yugoslav capital. "The inexorable press to begin bombing in Yugoslavia," *Commonweal* editorialized, "had an air of fateful necessity." But the director of the Vatican Press Office, Joaquin Navarro-Walls, quoted Pope Pius XII, "Nothing is lost with peace. All can be lost with war."[33]

Within less than a month, NATO jets flew 1,700 sorties. Every hour, a thousand refugees fled Kosovo to neighboring Bulgaria, Albania, Macedonia, and Greece, as Catholic relief agencies struggled to keep up. "How can we speak of peace when people are forced to flee, when they are hunted down and their homes are burned to the ground," Pope John Paul II scolded the combatants for shattering the hope of the Easter season, "when the heavens are rent to the din of war, when the whistle of shells is heard around people's homes, and the ravaging fire of bombs consumes towns and villages?"[34]

The pope appealed for an end to the NATO air strikes and the construction of a "humanitarian corridor" to shield the refugees from the bombs. He instructed the Vatican secretary of state, Angelo Soldano, to convene a special meeting of the ambassadors of the sixteen NATO and UN Security Council countries to expedite the end to hostilities, the delivery of humanitarian assistance, and the start of a UN-sponsored peace process. Soldano's assistant, Archbishop Jean-Louis Tauran, delivered a personal appeal from the pope to Milošević to stop the fighting.[35] Many Catholics shared the Holy Father's revulsion toward the Serb aggressors and compassion toward the Kosovar refugees. The USCC's president, Bishop Joseph Fiorenza of Galveston-Houston, deplored the "unjustifiable and intolerable aggression and ethnic cleansing against Kosovar civilians."[36] The bishops' Catholic Relief Services called for "protecting civilian populations" and spent $600,000 to assist the refugees. "The Church is doing very much," Archbishop Paul Cordes, the head of Cor Unum, the Vatican's humanitarian organization, observed, singling out Caritas, the international Catholic aid agency. "They are doing a lot," he reiterated, but due to the enormity of the tragedy, "it is still too little."[37]

The NATO air offensive evoked no such consensus. The bombing campaign raised "difficult moral and policy questions on which persons of goodwill may disagree," *Commonweal* conceded in April,[38] and there was much disagreement—even though the human cost for Americans was so low. There had been no American casualties in Bosnia, and only two, from a helicopter crash during a training exercise, in Kosovo. "If one can say of any war that it is ethical," the former Czech president and disaffected Catholic Václav Havel marveled at NATO's scrupulous aerial surgery, "it is this . . . war."[39]

"The NATO air strikes challenge Catholics to dust off the just war theory and consider if this war fits the criteria for legitimate humanitarian intervention," *America*'s editor, Rev. Thomas Reese, observed in April. To Rev. Bryan Hehir, the Serbs' premeditated, systematic ethnic cleansing furnished a "just cause," the multilateralism of NATO's response ensured a "legitimate authority," the precision of the air power facilitated "discrimination" and the probability of "success," and the failure of diplomacy made the war a "last resort." Reese determined that the war in Kosovo met the requirements of a "just cause" ("the prevention of ethnic cleansing and genocide by Serbian military and security forces"), "legitimate authority" (the newly enlarged NATO alliance), and a "last resort" (Milošević had "thumbed his nose at all diplomatic efforts to find a solution"). Though the "probability of success" and "proportionality" of the conflict, Reese admitted, were "less clear," these uncertainties argued for, not against, intervention—a longer, more robust one, involving ground troops.[40]

But some Catholics opposed the war. The Yale political scientist Bruce Russett found himself on the opposite side of his fellow "Challenge of Peace" consultant Father Hehir. Russett argued that the NATO bombing undermined the "just cause" criterion by accelerating Milošević's "ethnic cleansing'"; in circumventing the UN, NATO was not acting as a "legitimate authority"; and the fear of American casualties jeopardized the war's "discrimination, proportionality and probability of success." After "months of botched preparations and the hubris of coercive diplomacy," Russett concluded, the war was not a "last resort."[41]

But it was a war fought at a safe distance from its victims. The fireworks launched from fifteen thousand feet raised new questions about the morality of warfare. "That the military was saved from casualties at the price of greater casualties and suffering on the part of civilians is a scandal," Rev. Drew Christiansen protested in *America*. "Who are these soldiers," Father John Kavanaugh quoted the allusion by France's commander in Bosnia to NATO's pinball pilots, "who are ready to kill and not ready to die?"[42]

To these critiques from the Left one could add some consternation from Catholics on the Right. "The sorry lesson awaiting the West," a former Reagan special assistant, Robert Reilly, wrote, "is that Greater Albanian nationalism is not morally superior to Serbian nationalism." Pope John Paul II "saw from the beginning that American bombs could do nothing," Tom Hoopes, the executive editor of the conservative *National Catholic Register*, asserted, "but unwittingly aid the violent at the expense of the just."[43]

While these Catholics debated how and whether to make war, the Church's hierarchy was striving to make peace. Pope John Paul II ushered in April by meeting with the UN high commissioner for refugees, Sadako Ogata, about the plight of the Kosovar Albanians. He finished the month by writing to UN secretary-general Kofi Annan to wish him well in his peace mission to Belgrade. In between, Archbishop Jean-Louis Tauran, the Vatican secretary for relations with states, put forward an outline for peace in Kosovo. In separate letters to Presidents Milošević and Clinton, the eight American cardinals quoted the pope, "There is always time for peace. It is never too late to negotiate."[44]

When not bombing Serbs, NATO was also talking peace. President Clinton spent the first week in May in Europe, first at NATO headquarters in Brussels, then at the Group of Eight summit in Bonn. At the latter conference, all eight countries—the United States, Canada, France, Germany, Italy, Great Britain, Japan, and most significantly, Serb supporter Russia—agreed to a Kosovo peace plan that would stop the fighting, disarm the fighters, return the refugees, grant autonomy to Kosovo, and invite peacekeepers under UN, not NATO, command.[45] "We welcome the news of the proposed framework for negotiations on Kosovo reached by the United States, the other G-7 nations and Russia," the USCC's president, Bishop Joseph Fiorenza of Galveston-Houston, said in reaction to the news from Europe. "We urge the Yugoslav authorities to halt immediately their campaign of ethnic cleansing and to seize the opportunity represented by this diplomatic initiative."[46]

"How is it, at the end of this century and in the middle of the conflict in Kosovo, when it seems as though evil never retreats," a Catholic priest asked Holocaust survivor and Nobel Prize–winning author Elie Wiesel at his White House lecture in early June, "[that] you tell us there is a future that can be positive?" Wiesel replied with a question of his own, "What choice do we have?"[47] And NATO replied with more bombs. Finally, after seventy-eight days and tens of thousands of deaths, the allies again, just as in Bosnia, bombed Milošević to the peace table. The Serb dictator unhappily accepted the G-8 peace plan on June 10. "We welcome the end of the Kosovo conflict," Bishop Fiorenza spoke for the American Catholic hierarchy.[48]

"I'm scared of going back in," Sanha Rusiti, an ethnic Albanian, confessed from a refugee camp in Macedonia, "even if NATO forces escort me by the hand." Seven thousand Americans would be among those peacekeeping forces, adding to the six thousand still in Bosnia. In what was becoming the motto of America's global police, a U.S. Army official announced, "We're here for the long haul."[49]

Conclusions on War and Peace

No president wishes for war. But when he did finally and forcefully intervene in Bosnia and Kosovo, as Michael O'Hanlon observed, Bill Clinton helped to secure triumphs of American might and right. The Clinton administration heard the din of war on the Balkan Peninsula, according to former Notre Dame president Rev. Theodore Hesburgh, who visited refugee camps in Kosovo with a UN delegation in 1999, and "quieted it down." For the president and the many Catholics who successfully pressed him for U.S. military involvement, the noble end justified the messy means.[50]

But for liberal internationalists, the means must justify the end. And neither the president who twice chose war, nor the pope and bishops who advised him to do so, spoke persuasively or acted decisively. Clinton was remarkably reticent about explaining his actions in Bosnia and Kosovo. Like the president, the American Catholic episcopate often addressed these conflicts in excruciatingly inchoate ways. During the Bosnian war, Archbishop Roach's letter to Secretary Christopher, which seemed to promote U.S. military intervention, and his clarification of that letter, which seemed to preclude U.S. military intervention, provoked an undiplomatic exchange in the *National Catholic Reporter* between Catholic pacifist Colman McCarthy and the United States Catholic Conference's Gerard Powers. During the Kosovo war, Philadelphia's Anthony Cardinal Bevilacqua contended that NATO bombs were "not an acceptable solution," but then signed a letter to President Clinton, along with the seven other American cardinals, accepting the necessity for such ordnance after the Serbs scuttled the Rambouillet agreement.[51]

The bishops at once acknowledged that it "might be unwise to commit U.S. forces to combat," Michael Warner wrote of their pronouncements on Bosnia, while hinting that "the Bosnia conflict had met the just-war criteria for the use of force." The inverse was true of the prelates' March 24, March 31, and May 7, 1999, statements about Kosovo, which Bishop Fiorenza summarized as support for the "principle of humanitarian intervention" but concern that NATO's "strategic bombing risked violating relevant norms of discrimination, proportionality, and likelihood of success." The bishops' "fine line between pacifism and the strictest possible application of just-war criteria," Warner concluded, "has sometimes blurred toward meaninglessness."[52]

Even the Church hierarchy in the war zone appeared unable to make up their minds. In March 1995 Sarajevo's Vinko Cardinal Puljic admonished that the introduction of more weapons would only cause "more destruction to complete cataclysm in Bosnia-Herzegovina." Yet in December 1994 Puljic had joined his fellow cardinal, Franjo Kuharić of Zagreb, Croatia, in lamenting that "everything reaching the people about negotiations by the great powers and international institutions bewilders them even further and drives them to despair." Thus did the Balkan prelates pillory both war and peace.[53]

The pope's abhorrence toward war at times seemed to mute his repugnance toward the evils that sometimes justify it. The official Vatican newspaper *L'Osservatore Romano* in July 1995 defended "humanitarian intervention" in Bosnia, only to backpedal that "war will never be a true solution." Clinton's Catholic ambassador to the Vatican, Raymond Flynn, called the Holy See "officially pacifist on moral grounds," while admitting that Pope John Paul II had followed his taut embrace of the Bosnian government's military action against the Bosnian Serbs as a "just, defensive war" with slippery statements "implying" a "reluctant endorsement" of "appropriate forceful means" by the "international community."[54]

Indicting Muslims and Croats as well as Serbs, Francesco Monterisi, the papal nuncio in Bosnia, claimed in February 1994 that the "aggressor" whom John Paul II sought to "disarm" was plural. "Can we remain neutral in the face of systematic violations of the most elementary human rights?" the Vatican secretary of state, Angelo Soldano, asked ten months later, decrying a European continent "paralyzed" by inaction. Then he answered his own question affirmatively, quoting Pope Paul VI's dictum "war, never again," offering a recipe for more inaction. Between "declaring 'the aggressor must be disarmed' in Bosnia and that 'war will never be the appropriate way to solve problems'" in Kosovo, Peter Steinfels wrote, "John Paul II swings between just-war teaching and something approaching pacifism." To political scientist Robert Shellady, "The Vatican's critique of U.S. policy has not been that influential. Given the Vatican's rhetoric, it is unclear if any situation will ever meet the Vatican's criteria of permissive war."[55]

Approvingly quoting the USCC's Rev. Bryan Hehir, Clinton's Catholic secretary of state, Madeleine Albright, would regret that neither she nor the president really listened to the churches on Kosovo. When Slobodan Milošević announced a unilateral cease-fire in Kosovo in April 1999, the pope welcomed it but the president rebuffed it. Msgr. Mato Zovkić, the vicar general of the Catholic Archdiocese of Sarajevo, would recall that Holbrooke never comprehended the potent "force of ethnicity" in the region.[56]

Despite their lack of clarity and consistency, however, there was substantial evidence that the leaders of the Catholic Church played a significant role in the formulation of U.S. policy toward Bosnia and Kosovo. And in some ways their imprecision was not only understandable but essential in conveying the complexity of both the Balkan drama and the Church's role in it. "Our ethical tradition is neither simple nor easy to apply," Archbishop Roach spoke for his fellow prelates. "We address these issues as citizens," Cardinal McCarrick added, "not political leaders or foreign policy experts."[57]

Yet, as their anti–nuclear war pastoral "The Challenge of Peace" had demonstrated a decade earlier, their words could be authoritative and effective.

"Religious leaders have a responsibility," Cleveland archbishop Anthony Pilla convincingly argued, "to continue to lift up the human and moral consequences of this conflict" in the former Yugoslavia.[58]

So they did—with significant results. The American Catholic bishops' repeated reminders of the moral ramifications of U.S. policy in the Balkans helped to prompt Holbrooke to include human rights expert John Shattuck in the Dayton peace talks. When Lisa Misol and Eric Schwartz briefed national security advisor Samuel Berger for his August 1997 meeting with Archbishop McCarrick, they described the archbishop as "a leader in mobilizing support for Bosnia policy (including our intervention)." At the meeting, when an aide mentioned that McCarrick had been to the Balkans in the 1990s almost as often as Holbrooke, Berger replied, "And with greater effect." Clinton would acknowledge this influence by awarding McCarrick the Eleanor Roosevelt Award for Human Rights and the Presidential Medal of Freedom.[59]

Pope John Paul II's even-handed assessments of the Balkan crises—pleading for an end to both Serb genocide and NATO bombardment—similarly appeared reasonable and statesmanlike, rising above the political fray. Biographer Carl Bernstein lauded the pope's "innovative concept of international law known as 'humanitarian interference,'" a necessarily nebulous doctrine for wars that defied easy solutions. Passing such judgments on martial matters, Archbishop Tauran credibly claimed, was always a "delicate" yet morally irresistible rhetorical dance for the Holy Father.[60]

It was also a largely successful one. Pope John Paul II discussed Bosnia with Clinton at their unprecedented three meetings in three years, and the president cited the pope in his Bosnian victory speech. In ambassador Flynn's recollection, the pope's October 1995 meeting with the bishops of the former Yugoslavia "complemented" the Dayton negotiations. "The influence of John Paul II is extraordinary; the president understands it," Flynn asserted, even if "there are people in Congress and people in the Administration who don't."[61]

The bishops and the pope reinforced what Bill Clinton already knew, that the black-and-white world of the Cold War had faded to shades of gray. In an increasingly isolationist nation, Bishop Daniel Reilly observed in the middle of the 1990s, "there is no single international issue . . . that has Americans up in arms on one side against fellow Americans on the other." While two-thirds of Americans had favored the entrance of U.S. ground troops into Bosnia in October 1995, less than a third would tolerate as few as twenty-five American combat deaths. Clinton knew, his communications director, George Stephanopolous, would write of Bosnia, "that any casualties would cost him his presidency."[62]

The leaders of the country and the Church faced an arduous task in rallying the American people behind the wars in Bosnia and Kosovo. And, however tortured in their arguments and tentative in their actions, they ultimately won at home and abroad, just as they had almost a century before.

Social Justice: Health Care

In his 1991 Senate campaign in Pennsylvania, Catholic Democrat Harris Wofford advocated the enactment of national health insurance. "If criminals have a right to a lawyer," the former U.S. assistant attorney general for civil rights insisted, "working Americans should have the right to a doctor." Despite the logical fallacies of Wofford's syllogism—while governments indict, they do not infect—Wofford, and national health insurance, were political winners.[63]

In his 1992 presidential campaign, Democrat Bill Clinton noted that he, too, considered the lack of health insurance for nearly a quarter of the American population to be a crime. Upon his election, Clinton would follow a long line of his predecessors—most recently, Jimmy Carter—in attempting to deploy the federal government to cover the uninsured. Like Carter, Clinton would enlist widespread Catholic support for his program. Like Carter, he would encounter not only staunch opposition from Republicans, but divisions among Democrats and Catholics over the cost and character of health care reform. And like Carter, Clinton would fail to attain the primary objective on his domestic agenda. But the tale of Clinton's health care plan was not merely a reprise of the Carter saga. In many ways the Clinton effort attracted more public scrutiny, was more politically shrewd, and was more marketable than the Carter proposal. The Clinton plan nevertheless died amid accusations of excessive privacy in its formulation, in the face of charges of political naïveté in its composition, and as the victim of a superior rival sales job in its presentation.[64]

The defeat of Clinton's health care reform was a setback for many American Catholics, whose leadership initially lined up strongly behind the administration. But it was also a victory for many of these same Catholics, when the Clinton plan became one they could no longer fully support.

The Task Force

Before he took the oath of office, President-elect Bill Clinton received a memorandum from his transition team warning that a difficult road lay ahead for his bid for universal health insurance because of its enormous expense in a time of massive budget deficits and because of the inevitable resistance by powerful interest groups. "If we don't get this done this year," First Lady Hillary Clinton repeated the transition team's warning, "we are three years away from the benefits, so we've got to get it done right away, or we're going to be beaten in 1996."⁶⁵

"Right away" began five days after the inauguration, when Mrs. Clinton's husband made history by appointing her to lead a task force to devise his administration's health care package. Ira Magaziner, a fellow Rhodes Scholar who had met Bill Clinton at Oxford before becoming a high-powered business consultant, would co-chair the panel. In the liberal Democratic tradition of the New Deal, the task force quickly sprouted twenty-eight committees with five hundred experts. And in the mold of Franklin Roosevelt, Bill Clinton gave the task force a hundred days to prepare its program.⁶⁶

To help offset the expected opposition to its proposal, the task force moved rapidly to attract interest groups favorable to its cause, including Catholic ones. In February 1993 Mike Lux of Hillary Clinton's staff suggested that the United States Catholic Conference would want to testify before the task force. A month later the wife of the Catholic Democratic Speaker of the House, Thomas Foley of Washington, provided Mrs. Clinton with a description of interest groups identified with health care. Among those listed was the Catholic Health Association, which, Heather Strachan Foley explained, "represents all the Catholic hospitals in the country."⁶⁷

It was not long before the USCC and the CHA professed their allegiance to the goals of the task force. The administration's talking points for the new president's first meeting with the USCC's president, Archbishop William Keeler of Baltimore, in March 1993 noted that Clinton had often quoted the bishops' pastoral "Putting Children and Families First," and the bishops had long championed universal health care. Keeler's statement following the meeting acknowledged the bishops' "common ground" with the president on health care. Auxiliary Bishop John Ricard of Baltimore, chairman of the USCC's Domestic Policy Committee, wrote to Mrs. Clinton in April, voicing "our strong support for comprehensive reform of the nation's health care system." Citing the bishops' 1981 pastoral, "Health and Health Care," Ricard asserted their long-standing endorsement of "universal access to comprehensive quality care subject to cost containment and controls, characterized by equitable financing and genuine respect for human life and dignity."⁶⁸

Rev. Fred Kammer, the president of the bishops' Catholic Charities U.S.A. and a friend of the president since their teen years, wrote to Hillary Clinton the same month, noting that Catholic Charities had advocated "national health care reform for more than twenty-five years." Revs. Ricard and Kammer joined Sister Jane Brady, Sister Bernice Coreil, Jack Bresch of the CHA; James Cardinal Hickey of Washington, D.C.; and John Carr of the USCC in conveying their positions to Mrs. Clinton and Health and Human Services secretary Donna Shalala in a late April meeting at the White House.[69]

In May the CHA released a report, "Controlling Expenditures under National Healthcare Reform: An Assessment of Options." The paper resurrected the CHA's 1992 proposal for a universal "integrated delivery network" from which consumers would choose their health care providers. "Unlike rate-setting," the paper argued, "a more promising approach is managed competition, based on capitated payments (i.e., annual per person) to the networks."[70]

If the Catholic leadership was open to one politically risky strategy being considered by the task force, however, it was not amenable to all. At their White House meeting at the end of April, the Catholic representatives told the First Lady that the inclusion of abortion services in the administration's health care bill would be an unforgivable moral and political error. Since 10 percent of the nation's hospitals and 15 percent of the nation's hospital beds were under Catholic Health Association auspices, such a provision would antagonize a potentially critical component of the coalition needed to pass the Clinton proposal.[71] But as Catholic leaders were warning against the inclusion of abortion in the Clinton plan, the administration was moving in the opposite direction. In May the White House created an interdepartmental working group on "abortion and choice." Representatives of the USCC, CHA, and Catholic Charities responded to this ominous development with a closed-door conference a few days later. "The hush-hush meeting in Chicago signals that a long-time nightmare of the bishops and their Washington staff is well on its way to being a reality," *Our Sunday Visitor* reported, "a comprehensive healthcare proposal that has a chance for passage which includes abortion."[72]

The Clinton administration's strategy was to accentuate the existing consensus it shared with the Catholic interests and to overlook the potential conflict. When asked at the end of May whether abortion would be permissible under his health care proposal, President Clinton first cited the Hyde Amendment's prohibition on the federal funding of abortion, then noted that "most private health insurance plans permit some broader coverage for abortion." But despite his campaign promise to include abortion, he claimed that the task force had not yet decided whether to do so.[73] Hillary Clinton spoke via satellite in June to the CHA's membership assembly gathered in New Orleans. "Your proposal is right in line with what we're thinking," she noted, citing the CHA's commitments to managed competition, universal access, cost control, and inclusion of religious hospitals. Recalling her father's stay at the Catholic St. Vincent's Infirmary in Little Rock, the First Lady maintained that "the opportunities for not-for-profit, tax-exempt hospitals and their affiliated organizations should only increase in the years to come." Recognizing that "you're on the front lines," Mrs. Clinton told the assembly that "we do not have to accept the status quo."⁷⁴

When the CHA left New Orleans, the American Catholic bishops arrived. Their message was the same. "Health care in the United States serves too few and costs too much" was the opening sentence of the resolution "A Framework for Comprehensive Health Care Reform," which they adopted at their June meeting. They advocated universal access, cost containment, and inclusion of religious providers in any reform. But they warned that "it would be a moral tragedy, a serious policy misjudgment, and a political mistake to burden health care reform with abortion coverage that most Americans oppose and the federal government has not funded for the last seventeen years."⁷⁵ The bishops had a point. According to a 1993 CBS/*New York Times* poll, almost three-quarters of Americans, including most Catholics, believed that abortion funding had no place in a health care bill. And the Hyde Amendment, named for Catholic Republican representative Henry Hyde of Illinois, had prevented the federal financing of abortion for almost two decades.⁷⁶

By September, as President Clinton put the finishing touches on his health care bill, he had taken time out to sign a revision of the Hyde Amendment to exempt victims of rape and incest from the law's proscription of federal abortion aid. He extended such assistance to federal employees and, in an MTV interview, promised to do so in his health care legislation.⁷⁷

The Life of the Plan

The proceedings of the Clinton-Magaziner task force spilled past the hundred-day deadline, beyond the spring and into the summer. Finally, on the second day of autumn, President Clinton unveiled his health reform package before both houses of Congress and a prime-time national television audience. The plan provided universal coverage, an employer mandate of up to 80 percent of benefits, state health care alliances to regulate the competition among insurers and providers, a National Health Board to establish standards and review benefits, and a ceiling on annual price increases of health insurance premiums. There was no mention of abortion.⁷⁸

Among those watching the Clinton speech was the Catholic Health Association president, Jack Curley. He was in the East Room of the White House, and he joined the president and First Lady at a private reception after the address. "We look forward to continued involvement with the Administration," Curley assured them. "It's Here!" the CHA's newsletter, *Catholic Health World*, marked the long-awaited arrival of the Clinton plan with a banner headline and glowing reviews. And Curley was still there, at the White House, as the administration kicked off its campaign to pass the bill. Curley sat directly behind the president and the First Lady at a "presidential pep rally" the day after the Clinton speech. Sister Maryanna Coyle, the CHA's board chair, who also attended the event, said that she "felt in the midst of history. It was important for the CHA to be present. We've had a very significant influence on the debate that is unfolding, and it's obvious that we will continue to have one."[79]

Curley and Sister Coyle would make sure of that. In a letter to President Clinton after the pep rally, they cited the similarities between the 1992 CHA health care proposal and the 1993 Clinton plan. Noting that the CHA had been "waiting for this day since 1986 when we called for universal coverage in a redesigned health care system," they "promised to do everything in their power to make health care reform a reality."[80] The Curley-Coyle letter was not entirely supportive, however. The CHA leaders found the administration's cost estimates "unrealistically rapid and uneven." They questioned the administration's "top-down" approach to budgeting, preferring the CHA's "top-down, bottom-up" method. As in the president's speech, however, there was no mention of abortion.[81]

"It really makes me feel good," Dr. Ronald Blankenbaker related after a White House meeting with the Clintons; Vice President Al Gore and his wife, Tipper; and Ira Magaziner, to note so many similarities between the Clinton plan and the 1992 CHA proposal the doctor had helped to write. When Mrs. Clinton testified before House and Senate subcommittees on the administration's Health Security Act, she too acknowledged the CHA's handiwork. "Two years before my husband was even elected president," she responded to a question from Catholic Democratic senator Barbara Mikulski of Maryland, the CHA "came up with a plan in which they talked about having networks of health care providers competing for business that would be provided to people in their communities, and individuals would be making those kinds of choices." Hillary Clinton assured Catholic Democratic representative Barbara Kennelly of Connecticut that the administration bill would incorporate a "conscience clause for Catholic health plans, as discussed in our conservations with the CHA."[82]

When asked on television if abortion services would be part of the Clinton plan, however, the First Lady answered affirmatively, noting that they would be "widely available." This comment led Indiana Republican congressman Dan Coats to propose an amendment removing abortion from the legislation.[83] And it led the CHA to break its recent silence on the issue. "Human dignity requires that all persons be guaranteed a right to a uniform, comprehensive package of health care services," Sister Maryanna Coyle applauded the Clinton plan before the Senate Committee on Labor and Human Resources, chaired by Catholic Democratic senator Edward Kennedy of Massachusetts, in October. But for the first time since the president's speech, she spoke against the inclusion of abortion and in favor of the incorporation of a conscience clause in the legislation.[84]

Abortion was on the minds of other Catholics as well. Bishop Ricard called the Clinton plan a "major step forward . . . in its strong commitment to universal access." But it was a "tragic step backward in its inclusion of abortion coverage as an integral part of national health care reform." The National Right to Life Committee, which counted many Catholic members among its three thousand local chapters, expressed its concern that abortion would be among the "family planning and pregnancy related services" provided by the Clinton proposal.[85]

The Clinton administration didn't appear to be concerned. "There seems to be a consensus both among White House staff and external allies that there are five major issue areas that will dominate the legislation and public debate over this plan," Mike Lux wrote to Magaziner and Mrs. Clinton at the end of September. He named the "employer mandate, global budget/cost controls, overall financing, size and structure of health alliances, and 'new' benefits: prescription drugs, long-term care, mental health." Abortion did not make the list.[86]

A week later Lux was even more dismissive of abortion opponents. Under the heading "Groups Most Enthusiastic," defined as "close allies, ninety percent or more with us" on the health care bill, Lux included the CHA. The CHA was such a stalwart, Lux decided, that it ranked above the National Abortion and Reproductive Rights Action League, which he considered "mostly sympathetic, but still arm's length because of one issue or another, or because their internal decision-making process isn't finalized yet."[87]

Just before Thanksgiving, the administration completed its draft of the Health Security Act and sent it to Capitol Hill. Three committees in the House began deliberating on the bill, while two Senate committees clashed over who had jurisdiction over the measure.[88] "A winning coalition is essentially in place," Lux assured the president in the middle of December. Lux worried, however, that much of the public remained uneducated about the plan, that advertising by the opposition was expensive and effective, and that some of the administration's advocates were "nit-picking over the ten percent they didn't get."[89]

Such as abortion. Though President and Mrs. Clinton assiduously avoided the subject, Health and Human Services secretary Donna Shalala had suggested in April that abortion services would be a piece of the Clinton health care reform. Then the United States Catholic Conference's Bishop Ricard testified before the Senate Committee on Labor and Human Resources in February 1994. Citing "six hundred hospitals, three hundred long-term facilities, and hundreds of clinics and other health ministries," Ricard asserted that "no community has more at stake or more to contribute to this debate than the Catholic community." While expressing the bishops' support for the principles of universal coverage and cost containment embodied in the Clinton legislation, Ricard nonetheless stopped short of an endorsement. Noting the CBS/*New York Times* poll results and recent congressional votes against the federal funding of abortion, Ricard warned that "however long it may take to eliminate the violence of legalized abortion from our society, pro-life citizens should not be forced to pay for this destruction, and abortion on demand should not be made an integral part of health care. The sooner this burden is lifted, the better the cause of reform." And if the administration persisted in fighting to keep abortion in the legislation, the bishops would escalate their offensive to keep it out. "We have a constituency," the bishop warned. "Because of our size, presence, and principles, we can make a significant impact on the health care reform debate."[90]

In March the Clintons and the Gores invited two hundred hospital administrators, doctors, nurses, social workers, and pharmacists to an "Event with Front-Line Providers" on the South Lawn of the White House. Introducing the president was Sister Bernice Coreil, the chair of the CHA's Leadership Task Force on National Health Policy Reform. In her introduction, Sister Coreil maintained that "there is no excuse, moral or otherwise, for making millions of working families wait for coverage while attempts are made to lower costs to those who are lucky enough to have coverage now." Turning to the president, she added, "You know this, Mr. President, and the American people know it. Some of the critics of your reform proposal do not." But Sister Coreil had her own critics. "I write to present my serious concern about the presentation made by Sister Bernice Coreil to President Clinton," Bishop Edward Hughes of Metuchen, New Jersey, wrote to CHA president Jack Curley in March. "While it is perfectly appropriate and in accord with the approach of the bishops for Sister to emphasize that the health care reform plan should include universal coverage," Hughes protested, "it is highly offensive to praise President Clinton when that program includes abortion coverage."[91]

Optimism nonetheless infused the CHA's annual assembly in June, when South Dakota Catholic Democratic senator Tom Daschle and the deputy director of the Office of Management and Budget, Alice Rivlin, joined Republican senator John Danforth of Missouri in addressing the gathering. Despite the hardening of party lines, Danforth concurred with the Democratic speakers that health care reform was likely to pass in 1994. If it did, Rivlin observed, it would be in no small measure due to the "centuries' old Catholic tradition," which has been "brought to bear on the national health care debate."[92]

The Death of the Plan

But the survival of the Clinton health care reform was in grave doubt. The Health Insurance Association of America had run so many hostile television commercials since the Clinton speech that the fictional couple "Harry and Louise" depicted in the ads had become almost as familiar as the Clintons. Newer versions of the Clinton proposal circulated through Congress, toppling some or all of the pillars of universal coverage, employer mandates, cost controls, managed competition, and premium caps that had once so rigidly anchored the Clinton plan. By the summer of 1994, Democratic congressional leaders told the president that, with too little consensus on Capitol Hill and an off-year election approaching, health care reform was dead.[93]

The Clintons chose not to believe them. In August the president and First Lady met at the White House with representatives of the CHA. Hillary Clinton praised the organization's latest study—which showed that incremental, as opposed to universal, health care coverage would shift and raise health care costs—as "the best thing that has happened on health care in the last two months."[94] That wasn't saying much. Following their August meeting, CHA president Jack Curley wrote to Clinton urging him not to give up on health care. But Congress would adjourn for the election season without a health care bill. Health and Human Services secretary Donna Shalala took issue with the Clintons and the CHA. Finally saying publicly what she had long thought privately, the secretary lamented that her boss's health care reform had called for too much government, too soon.[95]

Following the November 1994 congressional elections, which transferred control of Capitol Hill to the Republican Party for the first time in four decades, the chastened Democratic president had no choice but to give up on the course charted by the CHA and settle for the piecemeal approach advocated by Shalala. In 1996 Clinton signed the Health Insurance Portability and Accountability Act, co-sponsored by Edward Kennedy and Kansas Republican senator Nancy Kassebaum, which mandated that people be able to keep their health insurance when they change their jobs. In 1997 Clinton enacted the State Children's Health Insurance Program, co-sponsored by Kennedy and Utah Republican senator Orrin Hatch, which extended federal health insurance through the states to low-income children. By that time Clinton had easily won reelection over former Kansas Republican senator Robert Dole, whose incremental health care proposal Clinton had once derided. But now it was Bill Clinton who was thinking small—and winning big.[96]

Conclusions on Social Justice

While Ira Magaziner, Hillary Clinton, and President Clinton were the major influences on the life of the administration's health care plan, Catholics were in many ways a major influence on *them*. Catholics helped to devise the Clinton plan, but they also helped to defeat it.

The Catholic imprint on the conception of the Clinton proposal was evident from the outset of the administration. In February 1993 White House press secretary Dee Dee Myers reminded reporters that the new president was "Jesuit-educated," with "a lot of close relationships with Catholics and Catholic priests" who "share many goals, including social and economic justice." At a roundtable with the Catholic press two and a half years later, Clinton shared his long-held belief that the Church "over the life of this country, has probably done more to help the poor than any other institution in America." The First Lady, Magaziner, and the president met frequently with leaders of the Catholic Health Association, and borrowed heavily from the CHA's 1992 health care proposal.[97]

Along with the CHA and Catholic Charities, the American bishops were quite active in pressing for some form of the Clinton plan. Anthropologist Michael Angrosino of the University of South Florida, a member of the health care task force for the St. Petersburg Diocese, lauded the bishops for linking the issue of national health insurance to Catholic social teaching. Conceding that most of the Catholic hierarchy's documents gather dust on the shelves of dioceses throughout the country, Angrosino recalled that the St. Petersburg task force distributed and discussed the 1993 health care pastoral at numerous forums while the Clinton plan made its way through Washington. "Even the task force's conservatives came to recognize that seemingly radical initiatives were, in fact, reflections of long-standing values," Angrosino remembered, in contrast to the Clinton bill's uphill climb on Capitol Hill.[98]

The Catholic health care campaign also appeared on television, as Jesuit Productions of St. Louis created a national program, *Body and Soul*, narrated by Catholic actor Martin Sheen, which advocated national health insurance. And it showed up in many other places. "The grassroots advocacy was unprecedented—millions of postcards, countless letters, homilies and bulletin inserts, hundreds of columns and ads, and an impressive number of face-to-face and telephone visits with legislators," Bishop Ricard would recollect of the United States Catholic Conference's extensive lobbying efforts in and out of the nation's capital.[99] And those efforts paid off. A 1994 survey of its readers by

U.S. Catholic revealed that an overwhelming 85 percent believed that health care was a "basic human right," 67 percent favored "mandatory universal care," 59 percent were willing to pay more taxes for universal health insurance, and a plurality of 35 percent accorded the largest role in regulating health care to the federal government, versus only 14 percent who would leave it to "market forces."[100]

Like the Clinton administration, the Catholic lobbyists to a large degree were unwilling to compromise their devotion to the principles of health care reform. "Our message of no to abortion mandates and yes to universal coverage clearly reflected our teaching," said Bishop Ricard. "We didn't choose between priorities," the bishop would remember, and in the end "the Catholic community did a better job on health care reform than the Congress."[101] Perhaps that is why Sister Coreil did not allude to abortion when she introduced President Clinton. To ensure the political viability of health care reform and the financial security of Catholic health institutions, Angrosino argued, "the position taken by the CHA and the bishops through 1994 was that reform should be pursued even though there might continue to be debate over the status of abortion as health care." While the CHA and the bishops demanded a "conscience clause" in the Clinton plan, which the administration and most members of Congress were willing to accept, they merely requested the exclusion of abortion services from the legislation, a concession that the Church was, in Angrosino's view, "probably not in a political position to win."[102]

Just as Catholics abetted the rise of Clinton's health care reform, however, so they greased its fall. While Bishop Ricard stressed the advocacy of universal coverage as a non-negotiable demand throughout the Clinton bill's legislative odyssey, he would nonetheless admit, "I seemed to spend most of my time making the case in the media and on Capitol Hill against abortion mandates."[103] "Opponents of abortion will oppose any inclusion in the benefit package, and there is relatively little compromise that could reduce their opposition," Linda Bergthold of the Clinton-Magaziner task force accurately predicted in March 1993. "Therefore it seems foolish to disguise or finesse the issue in any way." Fellow task force member Robert Valdez countered at the time that "explicitly identifying abortion" would have "the potential to derail the entire health care reform initiative by opponents of abortion." Bergthold and Valdez nevertheless agreed that Clinton should keep his campaign promise to include abortion in the package in order to avoid antagonizing his pro-choice allies.[104]

President Clinton himself admitted on ABC television the day after his September 1993 speech that the retention of abortion in the bill would be a "political minefield." So when not lavishing praise on the CHA's commitment to universal coverage in her remarks at its June 1994 assembly, OMB deputy director Alice Rivlin was acknowledging the "strong differences" that separated the Clinton administration and the CHA over the inclusion of abortion in health care legislation.[105]

On the morning of July 13, 1994, every member of Congress received a letter from Cardinal Mahony, Archbishop Keeler, and Bishop Ricard of the USCC explaining that universal coverage and abortion exclusion were the bishops' "two essential priorities" in any health care legislation. They attached to the letter the results of a USCC survey administered by Tarrance and Company, which found that while 70 percent of Americans supported universal coverage, 65 percent opposed "taxpayer-subsidized abortion coverage," 58 percent rejected "mandating family abortion coverage," and 49 percent objected to "mandatory insurance coverage for abortion." And most significantly, in response to Angrosino's claim that the Catholic hierarchy's resistance to abortion services was politically unwise, the survey argued the opposite. Sixty percent of the supporters of universal health coverage, the poll discovered, would switch to the opposition if taxpayer-subsidized abortion remained part of health care reform.[106] So by the evening of July 13, 1994, seventy House Democrats announced that they would not vote for any health care bill that included abortion. "Most of the proposals before Congress now include a requirement that Americans be offered a standard package of benefits including 'pregnancy-related services,' a phrase taken to include abortion," the *New York Times*'s Gustav Niebuhr reported in August. "But this provision is certain to provoke bitter debate if and when the House and Senate begin serious efforts to pass legislation."[107]

It already had. But the bitter debate between the Catholic Health Association and Bishop Hughes over Sister Coreil's introduction of President Clinton had lasted only until CHA president Jack Curley had time to defuse it, with an anti-abortion proclamation every bit as fierce as that of the prelate who confronted his organization. And the CHA was still sending this message to the Clintons, as Angrosino acknowledged, at their White House meeting in August 1994. "On the issue of abortion and pregnancy-related services, CHA has communicated strong opposition to the Administration," the White House talking points for the meeting noted. "Because of the abortion issue, we have respected their concern that we *not* state that they have endorsed the Health Security Act."[108]

And contrary to Angrosino's contention, the CHA and the bishops were *not* willing to settle for a conscience clause in the Clinton legislation. In her testimony before the Senate Labor and Human Resources Committee in October 1993 the CHA's Sister Maryanna Coyle asserted that her organization "firmly supports" the addition of a conscience clause while adding that the

CHA "strongly opposes" the inclusion of abortion services. "Strong conscience clauses are necessary to deal with a variety of medical/moral issues, but are not sufficient to protect Catholic and other providers who find abortion morally objectionable," Cardinal Bernardin explained the bishops' position in May 1994. "The only remedy is not to link needed reform to abortion mandates." Above the words "conscience clause" on the minutes of Ira Magaziner's May 1994 White House health care briefing, a staffer scribbled, "doesn't fix the abortion problem."[109]

And the longer abortion remained in the Clinton legislation, the more Catholics threatened to undo the progress toward health care reform. Fifty-nine percent of Americans, and 57 percent of Catholics, told Gallup's pollsters in July 1994 that they opposed the inclusion of abortion in any health care plan. In their "Ethical and Religious Directives for Catholic Health Care Services," issued in November 1994, the bishops reiterated that at Catholic health facilities, "abortion is never permitted."[110]

The Clinton health care proposal would never become law. In its failure, however, it had almost as great an impact on the president and American Catholics as if it had succeeded. The defeat of Clinton's health care reform helped lead to the defeat of Clinton's party in the November 1994 congressional elections. Armed with a ten-point "Contract with America," the Republicans conquered Capitol Hill for the first time in four decades, leaving Clinton feeling suddenly alone and even irrelevant in the White House. So he turned to a trusted old friend, Dick Morris, the political guru who had helped to resurrect Governor Clinton's career in Arkansas a decade earlier. Morris, better known for advising Republicans, helped to steer Clinton to the right—but not as far as the House.

A 1996 poll by the Pew Research Center for the People and the Press revealed that more white Catholics were Democratic or independent than Republican, but more were moderate or conservative than liberal. In a reversal of the findings from a generation earlier, 50 percent said their churches should "express views on social and political matters," and 49 percent said they should not. Yet only 28 percent believed it was "sometimes right for clergy to discuss political candidates or issues from the pulpit," while 70 percent believed that it was never right.[111]

And, in a pattern presaged by the moderate Bush administration, the times demanded political pirouettes from the president and the bishops alike. Speaking at Notre Dame in September 1992, candidate Clinton saluted the liberal tenets of Catholic social teaching and "Economic Justice for All," the conservative Catholic respect for tradition, and the arguments that they spawned. "How I love those arguments," said the would-be president. When Clinton was asked by the Catholic News Service in 1992 and again at a 1994 meeting with religious leaders, including a representative from the Catholic conservative magazine *Crisis*, what he had learned from the sisters in grade school in Arkansas and the Jesuits at Georgetown University, he again offered something for both the Left and the Right. The nuns had taught him "the social mission of the Church." The priests had taught him "intellectual rigor."[112]

In 1996, when the USCC's president, Bishop Anthony Pilla of Cleveland, explained the political responsibility of the bishops, he too deftly navigated the political spectrum. "The Conference's public policy agenda is sometimes in agreement with both parties," the bishop asserted, "and at times with neither." The hierarchy's celebrated consensus seeker, Chicago's Joseph Cardinal Bernardin, then embarked on a "common ground" expedition to explore the inner reaches of the Catholic center. "While others have pulled people apart," Clinton said while awarding him the Presidential Medal of Freedom in 1996, "Cardinal Bernardin has sought common ground." There was so much agreement at the bishops' November 1997 meeting in Washington that they went home a day early.[113]

For Bill Clinton and many American Catholics, the defeat of health care reform portended a political crisis of identity. With the renewal of the nation's prosperity and the president's popularity, however, this ideological ambiguity didn't seem to matter.

Life and Death: Abortion

Following the nation's most pro-life administration, President Bill Clinton and many of his pro-choice cohorts believed that the federal government's 1973 protection for abortion was under siege. He therefore vowed to keep abortion "safe, legal, and rare."[114]

With the approval of much of the public and the ability to appoint federal judges all the way to the Supreme Court, however, Clinton helped the abortion rights movement not only survive, but in many ways thrive, during his two terms in office. Bill Clinton did not just meet the most dire expectations of pro-life Catholics—he exceeded them. Abortion remained safe and legal, but hardly rare.

The Democratic Congress

Even before the polls closed on Election Day in November 1992, pro-life Catholics had suffered a major setback. The District of Columbia Court of Appeals had overturned the outgoing George H. W. Bush administration's ban on abortion counseling at family planning clinics receiving federal funds.[115]

It took only two days for the Vatican newspaper *L'Osservatore Romano* to deliver its analysis of the election. Bush had shown "political wisdom" in "fundamental aspects of domestic and international life," including most prominently "the defense of life." It warned Clinton, "In the difficult years to come, do not ever let freedom be deformed into devastating models of behavior elevated to norms of life, nor into license to strike the weakest, from yet unborn infants to the elderly on the margins of society."[116]

Not all of the air had escaped the pro-life balloon, however. Wanda Frantz, the president of the National Right to Life Committee, which counted many Catholics among its members, pledged an all-out battle to prevent the proposed Freedom of Choice Act, a long-standing legislative effort to codify *Roe v. Wade*, from becoming law. She rallied her followers with the reminder that Bill Clinton would be the "first pro-abortion president."[117]

In the eyes of abortion opponents, Clinton would earn that moniker all in one day. In a series of executive orders issued on January 22, 1993, only two days after his inauguration, Clinton reversed the Reagan-Bush policies prohibiting abortion counseling and referrals at federally funded family planning clinics, barring privately paid abortions at overseas military facilities, preventing the federal financing of research using tissue from aborted fetuses, and outlawing American aid to international planning organizations that promoted abortion (the so-called Mexico City policy). Clinton also instructed the Food and Drug Administration to investigate and possibly to rescind the ban on the abortion pill RU-486.[118]

The reaction of pro-life Catholics to the new president's directives was swift and sure. Archbishop Joseph Dimino of the Archdiocese for Military Services wrote to Clinton to object to his authorization of abortions at military hospitals. Gail Quinn, the executive director of the United States Catholic Conference's Secretariat for Pro-Life Activities, wrote to members of Congress protesting the introduction of a bill to implement Clinton's decision to fund research on aborted fetuses.[119] *L'Osservatore Romano* denounced Clinton for leading his country down "the pathway of death and violence against innocent human beings." Roger Cardinal Mahony of Los Angeles recalled that "during the campaign President Clinton vowed to reduce abortions in our country." The cardinal asserted, however, that "you cannot reduce abortions by promoting abortion as just another method of birth control, . . . by fueling a market for tiny unborn bodies of unborn children, [and] by exporting abortion to the poor in the Third World." Mahony found the president's actions especially offensive because they occurred on the twentieth anniversary of *Roe v. Wade*, and just a few blocks away from the annual March for Life.[120]

Before the month had ended, the Supreme Court had ruled that federal judges could not preclude protesters from attempting to block access to abortion clinics. But the Court did not sanction murder. In March Michael Frederick Griffin, a member of the anti-abortion group Rescue America, fired three shots into the back of Dr. David Gunn as he arrived at a women's health services clinic in Pensacola, Florida. Though Dr. Gunn's picture and identifying information had circulated at an Operation Rescue rally, Randall Terry, the Catholic leader of the radical anti-abortion organization, disassociated his group from the homicide.[121] The killing of Dr. Gunn was only the latest in a series of violent incidents prompted by pro-life demonstrations at medical facilities throughout the country. These confrontations, which included two more shootings, gathered momentum for passage of the proposed Freedom of Access to Clinic Entrances Act, which would make it a federal crime to use or threaten force to intimidate employees or patients at clinics offering reproductive health care services.[122]

The pro-choice forces were just getting started. Shortly after an abortion clinic in Montana suspiciously caught fire, President Clinton announced that he wanted to put the Hyde Amendment to the torch. The sixteen-year-old rider had banned the federal funding of most abortions. Previously supported by the last pro-choice Democrat in the White House, Jimmy Carter, the ban remained extremely popular, with over two-thirds of Americans behind it.[123] So when it came to a vote in the House of Representatives, many Democrats defied their president and sided with Republicans in continuing the Hyde Amendment by a 255–178 vote. The president backed down. Clinton's short-lived decision to buck public opinion was rare, even if, contrary to his campaign rhetoric, abortion was not.[124]

As other abortion legislation was making its way through Congress, Pope John Paul II was making his way toward the United States. Two weeks after reaffirming the Church's unyielding stand against artificial contraception, the pontiff visited Denver in August for the World Youth Day celebration. In his fifth trip to the United States and fifth meeting with an American head of state, the Holy Father placed himself squarely in opposition to the new president's abortion policies. "The inalienable dignity of every human being and the rights which flow from that dignity—including the right to life and the defense of life—are at the heart of the Church's message and action in the world," the stern pope lectured the stunned president on the tarmac at Denver's Stapleton International Airport, as he departed from his prepared text.[125]

The pope was not the only one who surprised Clinton. Fred Barnes of the *New Republic* reported that the president had not anticipated the strength of the pro-life forces. Perhaps, Barnes speculated, that was because only two of Clinton's top aides—Catholics Raymond Flynn, the ambassador to the Vatican, and Paul Begala, an unofficial political advisor—opposed abortion. The political scientist James Guth would observe that Catholics failed to receive appointments in the administration proportionate to their population within the Democratic Party. It would take almost two years for Clinton to begin the kind of formal Catholic outreach his predecessor had launched from the outset.[126]

And some members of the administration approached the furthest boundary of the other side. In August the Justice Department arranged meetings with representatives from both abortion camps. It solicited the American Catholic bishops to suggest participants from the pro-life community so that Reta Lewis of the White House Office of Political Affairs could compile a list of, in her words, "anti-choice groups." The office's senior liaison, Bob Hessey, politely asked the bishops to "confine their recommendations to those groups who do not engage in violent activity."[127]

Meanwhile, Clinton was surprising no one. "When I took office I absolved the gag rule [on abortion counseling]. I absolved the ban on fetal tissue research," Clinton boasted at a town meeting in Sacramento in October. He also noted his appointment of Justice Ruth Bader Ginsburg, "who believes in the constitutional right to choose," to a seat on the Supreme Court. Clinton called his pro-choice record "clear and unblemished."[128] By the end of the year Clinton added another pro-choice trophy when he signed a modified version of the Hyde Amendment, attached to the FY 1994 Departments of Labor and Health and Human Services appropriations, which contained new exceptions for rape and incest (in addition to safeguards for the life of the mother). When objections to the Freedom of Choice Act's proscriptions on parental consent and a twenty-four-hour waiting period forestalled a floor vote in Congress, however, Clinton decided it wasn't worth a fight.[129]

He was too busy fighting Catholics, and the president even seemed to be picking some of these fights. At Clinton's invitation, the Nobel Prize–winning humanitarian Mother Teresa traveled from the impoverished slums of Calcutta to the privileged corridors of Washington to speak at the annual National Prayer Breakfast in February 1994. "Every abortion," she told the guests "is the denial of receiving Jesus." For that heartfelt sentiment, the saintly wisp of a woman received a standing ovation from most of those in the room—but not from President and Mrs. Clinton or Vice President and Mrs. Gore. When the applause subsided, Mother Teresa resumed her remarks. She added that "any country that accepts abortion is not teaching its people to love one another but to use violence to get what they want." President Clinton apologized to Mother Teresa after her speech, not for his support of abortion, but for the Clintons so conspicuously refusing to applaud her words. Mother Teresa magnanimously forgave them, and the First Lady in turn would help raise awareness and funds for the Mother Teresa Home for Infant Children, which would open a year later in Washington as a halfway house for mothers waiting to give up their babies for adoption.[130]

The Cairo Conference

To pro-life Catholics, Clinton was making abortion more common not only in the nation, but in the world. "Abortion, which destroys existing human life, is a heinous evil, and it is never an acceptable method of family planning," Pope John Paul II declared in March 1994, "as was recognized by consensus at the Mexico City United Nations International Conference on Population." The pope was not only explicitly rejecting the pro-choice draft document of the UN International Conference on Population and Development to be held in Cairo in September, but he was implicitly reproaching the Clinton administration's reversal of U.S. adherence to the Mexico City policy.[131]

The pope's criticism of the administration hit closer to home in April, when he penned a letter to the American president and all other heads of state. The Cairo document's "numerous proposals for general international recognition of a completely unrestricted right to abortion," the pope protested, "goes well beyond what is already unfortunately permitted by the legislation of certain nations."[132] Such as the United States, where President Clinton took a call from Pope John Paul II two weeks later. The April dialogue was the result of feverish damage control by the U.S. ambassador to the Vatican, Raymond Flynn, who had shuttled between Rome and Washington at the behest of the pope. "The principal topic of conversation" on the telephone, Vatican spokesman Joaquin Navarro-Walls related, "was the position of the Catholic Church on moral problems raised by the preparatory meeting" for the population conference. The cardinal denied, however, that the tone of the discussion was confrontational.[133]

In a May letter, the United States Catholic Conference president, Archbishop William Keeler of Baltimore, joined the six active American cardinals in urging Clinton to withdraw his support of the draft, "which continues to advocate abortion as a way of controlling population growth and promiscuity." As for the document's claim that more contraception would lead to less abortion, *America*'s editors asked, "Can anyone honestly point to the United States and say, that in a land where contraceptives are so available, abortion has been reduced?"[134]

Bill Clinton would have, but he was preoccupied with the pope. At their second meeting in Rome in June, a week after Clinton signed the Freedom of Access to Clinic Entrances Act, the pope conveyed to the president the "grave ethical problems," in the words of Vatican spokesman Joaquin Cardinal Navarro-Walls, regarding the "defense and promotion of life and promotion of the family in particular" posed by the accessibility of abortion. Speaking to a group of American seminarians after the meeting with the pope, Clinton claimed to share the Holy Father's opposition to abortion as a form of birth control while adding that his primary concern was "the tens of millions of abortions that are occurring in unsafe ways that are putting women at risk."[135] Clinton asserted that he and the pontiff had made "great progress" at their meeting, but there was scant evidence of that. Ambassador Flynn wrote to Clinton complaining that the president had ignored the pope's (and Flynn's) special pleading on the Cairo draft, and accusing some members of his administration of having an "ugly, anti-Catholic bias."[136]

A plea by John Cardinal O'Connor of New York that the Cairo conference not countenance "abortion on demand" attracted the signatures of 114 of the world's 139 cardinals. The American Catholic bishops, meeting in San Diego in June, unanimously adopted a resolution that described the prelates as "outraged that our government is leading the effort to foster global acceptance of abortion."[137] President Clinton and Vice President Gore attempted to allay the Catholic hysteria. "Abortion should not be encouraged as a method of family planning," Clinton replied to Rev. Hickey and the cardinals at the end of June. "The United States has not sought, does not seek, and will not seek to establish any international right to an abortion," Gore insisted two weeks before departing for Cairo to head the American delegation.[138]

The Catholic hierarchy remained unpersuaded. "The draft document, which has the United States administration as its principal sponsor," Cardinal Navarro-Walls retorted, "contradicts in reality Mr. Gore's statement." In an "Open Letter to Pope John Paul II" published in the *New York Times* on the eve of the conference with over 3,500 signatures, however, the American organization Catholics Speak Out assailed the Church's resistance to contraception.[139]

When the long-awaited conference finally convened in Cairo in September, the Vatican decided that it could wait a little longer. After Gore opened the meeting by repeating his disclaimer, the Holy See, backed by several small nations, sponsored a move to return the draft document's abortion language to committee.[140] Then, on the fifth day of the nine-day gathering, the majority maneuvered, and the Vatican caved. The delegates reversed the order of two sentences so that the disputed paragraph now began with "In no case should abortion be promoted as a method of family planning." Following immediately was "All governments and relevant intergovernmental and nongovernmental organizations are urged to strengthen the commitment to women's health to deal with the health impact of unsafe abortion as a major public health concern, and to reduce the recourse to abortion through expanded, improved family planning services." Rather than "prolong the discussion," Cardinal Navarro-Walls explained, the Vatican called off its filibuster. The undersecretary of state for global affairs, Timothy Wirth, applauded the Holy See's "benign" gesture, adding that while "they don't agree with everything in there, neither do we."[141]

"We didn't start this fight, they did," Msgr. Peter Elliott, an Australian member of the Vatican delegation, defended the Holy See's performance in Cairo. "They" were the pro-choice feminists who constituted a portion of the American contingent, led by former New York Democratic congresswoman Bella Abzug, she of the floppy hats and fiery harangues. "Many intemperate comments were made by nongovernmental officials in the U.S. delegation," ambassador Flynn said, deploring the American women's spiteful swipes at the Church's all-male gerontocracy.[142] The fight ended when, unlike at previous UN population conferences in 1968 and 1984, the Vatican signed the document, choosing only to express reservations about the report's references to "sexual and reproductive health." But the quarrel would leave scars. The meeting adjourned with the Non-Governmental Organization Forum circulating a petition calling for the removal of the Vatican's permanent observer status.[143]

"Partial-Birth" Abortion

Following the historic 1994 midterm elections, the predominantly pro-life Republican Party now controlled Congress for the first time in forty years. So Clinton's top domestic priority shifted from health care reform to welfare reform, and his rhetoric tilted toward the center. When asked in February 1995 whether his welfare reform proposal, by shedding unwed mothers from the public dole, would invite more abortions, Clinton answered negatively. "The abortion rate has been going down in America," said the president, even though it wasn't. It had held steady at about 1.5 million per year since *Roe v. Wade*.[144]

Having spent two years ensuring that abortion remain legal, the president set about trying to convince the country that it was becoming rare. And he was even willing to credit the pro-life movement as one of the reasons. The bishops weren't buying the president's contrived consanguinity, however. In the statement "Faithful for Life: A Moral Reflection," which they adopted at their June 1995 meeting, they decried the "abortion mentality" that celebrated "unlimited personal choice" as "the prerequisite for every satisfying human experience, even within the family."[145] The pope also wasn't buying it. In October, in his second visit to the United States during the Clinton presidency and the first since issuing the encyclical *Evangelium Vitae* ("Gospel of Life"),

Pope John Paul II again publicly and privately berated the president for his complicity in the crime of abortion. "No American politician," the veteran journalist Charles Morris said in wonder at the pope's adulatory reception, "could have pulled it off." So in Newark as he had in Denver, the president exercised his right to remain silent.[146]

And in the end Clinton wasn't buying it, either. "Since abortion is under attack in Congress," MTV's Tabitha Soren asked the president in August 1995, "do you think that you should be doing more to support the pro-choice movement?" Clinton replied, "I'm doing everything I can," adding, "I don't know what else I could do."[147]

Having battled to keep abortion legal and to prove that it was becoming rare, the president also fought to make it safe. "The abortion is performed by partially delivering the baby (leaving the head in the birth canal) and then puncturing the base of the skull with scissors in order to insert a catheter," Mark Stricherz would describe a ghastly late-term abortion procedure. "The baby's brain is then sucked out, causing the skull to collapse, killing the child." Pro-life advocates called this process "partial-birth" abortion. Pro-choice partisans preferred not to talk about it at all. But as a bill to ban this operation wended through Congress in 1996, Clinton had no choice.[148] He carved a position that condoned the practice while appearing to condemn it. In a letter to Congress in February 1996, he stipulated that he could sign a ban if it contained an exception protecting the health of the mother.[149]

Such an exception, the American Catholic bishops responded in a full-page ad in the *Washington Post* in March, "can be defined as just about anything." They noted that women sought abortions, even in the late term, for reasons as varied as preventing the birth of a Down syndrome child, "interfering with career goals," or not being able to "fit into a prom dress." Cardinals Joseph Bernardin of Chicago, James Hickey of Washington, and Bernard Law of Boston then conducted a vigil outside the White House urging a "partial-birth" abortion ban. After both houses of Congress passed a ban without a health exception in April, Bernardin and Hickey wrote to Clinton urging him to sign it.[150]

"This is a difficult and disturbing issue, one which I have studied and prayed about for many months," Clinton replied to the cardinals on April 10. "I am against late-term abortions and have long opposed them. As governor of Arkansas, I signed into law a bill that barred third-trimester abortions, with an appropriate exception for life and health, and I would sign one now."[151] Then the president vetoed the ban. Surrounded by five women who had experienced the procedure formally known as "intact dilation and evacuation" (IDE), Clinton told the country, as he had told the cardinals, that he could not enact a law that jeopardized the health of women such as those appearing with him.[152]

"Shortly after your inauguration, you sent me a letter in which you stated that you do not support abortion in the third trimester after viability had occurred," Philadelphia's Anthony Cardinal Bevilacqua reminded Clinton. "Today you had an opportunity to act on that conviction and protect the lives of children, and you did not!" Cardinals Law and Hickey took the extraordinary step of urging Catholics to vote against Bill Clinton in November.[153]

"Cardinal letters AGAIN," White House aide Kyle Baker wrote as the United States Catholic Conference president, Bishop Anthony Pilla of Cleveland, joined the eight active American cardinals in writing to Clinton to convey their "deepest sorrow and dismay" at the president's decision. "At the veto ceremony, you told the American people that you 'had no choice but to veto the bill,'" the prelates recalled. Citing a 1996 poll showing 78 percent of American female voters in favor of a ban, they added that these women "have made their choice." The National Council of Catholic Women and the Vatican endorsed the USCC letter, and the U.S. bishops prepared a national postcard campaign in their churches to encourage a congressional veto override.[154]

"The procedure is grossly misrepresented by the press, our elected officials and the ... Catholic bishops," Mary Dorothy Line, a self-described pro-life Catholic who had appeared with Clinton, wrote of her "partial-birth" abortion in a letter to *Commonweal*'s editors in June. "No scissors were used and no one sucked out our baby's brain. I was under general anesthesia during all parts of the procedure." Then, as the president had stated, Mrs. Line explained that "not only was our son dying, but the complications of the pregnancy put my health in danger. With no hope for our baby, my doctor recommended an IDE as the best procedure to protect my health." *Commonweal*'s editors, while sympathizing with Mrs. Line, "as who could not," considered the production in which Mrs. Line had starred disconcerting and even dishonest. "Congressional hearings on the partial-birth abortion ban indicate that the majority of such procedures are elective, and not representative of the situations described by Mrs. Line."[155]

Even some abortion rights supporters would admit that. A month before the administration undertook an "open dialogue" with the bishops on abortion, the executive board of the College of Obstetricians and Gynecologists concluded in January 1997 that there were "no circumstances under which this [IDE] procedure would be the only option to save the life of the mother or preserve the health of the mother."[156] "I lied through my teeth," Ron Fitzsimmons, the executive director of the National Coalition of Abortion Providers confessed in February, recanting his claim on ABC television a year and a half earlier that cases of "partial-birth" abortion were highly unusual, with only about 450 such procedures occurring each year. The number, he now conceded, could be as great as ten times that many.¹⁵⁷ The *Bergen Record* reported that in one New Jersey facility alone, doctors "performed three thousand abortions a year on fetuses between twenty and twenty-four weeks," of which at least half were "partial-birth" procedures. The *Washington Post* cited a doctor "who had performed hundreds of these [IDE] abortions" yet admitted that "eighty percent of his patients had no medical reason for abortion."¹⁵⁸

"The public has learned that partial-birth abortions are performed not a few hundred times a year but hundreds of times each year," Bishop Pilla and the cardinals wrote to Clinton in March. "The public has also learned that the vast majority of these procedures are performed on the healthy babies of healthy women." They therefore urged Clinton to "explain that you were misled, as were most Americans."¹⁵⁹ John Hart, the White House director of Catholic outreach, privately conceded that the prelates now had "momentum on their side." So domestic policy advisor Elena Kagan devised talking points to stem the deluge of unwelcome evidence. "The president has never claimed that partial-birth abortions are used only, or even primarily, to prevent death or serious harm," Kagan wrote. "The president has recognized that some doctors may use the procedure for elective reasons and has called for an end to this procedure."¹⁶⁰

Then Clinton tossed aside the talking points. "The facts are just as we all said they are," the president insisted at a March 1997 press conference. While there may be as many as "five thousand" IDE abortions per year, he argued, only "maybe ten percent or so are like those five women I had in the White House," whose "babies they were carrying could be dead." Those "few thousand people a year, they don't have much [*sic*] votes or influence," Clinton reflected, "but they're the people I'm concerned about."¹⁶¹ Clinton's advisors were concerned about the president. "We probably should let him know that the number of women whose health is potentially at risk here is very small—not the few hundred he said at the press conference—and that principles more than lives are at stake," domestic policy advisor Bruce Reed suggested to Kagan after Clinton's misstatements. "That won't make him feel better."¹⁶²

But it might prevent more embarrassing press conferences. So Kagan, along with her Domestic Policy Council colleagues John Hilley and Tracey Thornton, set the president straight. "You have asked whether the so-called partial-birth procedure is ever necessary to save the life of a woman or avert serious harm to her health," they wrote to Clinton. "Perhaps the most reliable opinion," they propounded, was that of the College of Obstetricians and Gynecologists. So the answer was "no" on both counts. Now that the House had overwhelmingly passed a ban, the three advisors recommended that Clinton answer "yes" to a proposed amendment to the Senate "partial-birth" abortion bill sponsored by the pro-choice Catholic Democratic minority leader, Tom Daschle of South Dakota. The addendum would simply outlaw all third-trimester abortions, with a narrower health exception than the one Clinton had previously favored. The president heeded the counsel. At the top of the memo, he scribbled, "Any possibility we can get any Catholics to support the Daschle bill?"[163]

Not any pro-life Catholics. "It is extremely doubtful that the Daschle proposal would have any impact on the thousands of partial-birth procedures performed each year," Bernard Cardinal Law, chairman of the bishops' Committee for Pro-Life Activities, wrote to all the members of the Senate in May, "both because most are performed in the fifth and six months of pregnancy, after viability, and because any 'health' exception will be subject to [the] broad interpretation of federal courts and the subjective judgment of abortion practitioners."[164]

Thanks in part to the bishops' lobbying, the Daschle amendment failed, 64–36. An amendment similar to Daschle's, sponsored by California Democrat Dianne Feinstein, fell 72–28. Then the "partial-birth" abortion ban, sponsored by Catholic Republican Rick Santorum of Pennsylvania, passed 64–36, three short of the two-thirds majority that would be needed to override a second Clinton veto. Daschle, chafing under pressure from his bishop, Rev. Robert Carlson of Sioux Falls, reversed himself and voted for the Santorum bill.[165] Then, "for exactly the same reasons I returned an identical version of this bill," Clinton vetoed a ban on "partial-birth" abortion in October 1997. Despite an unprecedented press conference by the bishops, and a prayer service by the American cardinals on the steps of the Capitol, Congress again upheld the veto, with ten pro-choice Catholic senators, nine of them Democrats, siding with the president.[166]

Thus did the politician addicted to polls and the president committed to consensus again defy both. "Recent polling we have conducted for the Center on Reproductive Law and Policy shows clearly that playing defense . . . in the partial birth abortion debate is a dangerous proposition," White House advisor Rahm Emanuel confided in July 1998, "because it gives the other side too much freedom to define their position as mainstream and the President's as 'radical.'"[167] But the Republican Congress kept the Democratic president on the defensive. In October 1998 he vetoed the Foreign Affairs and Restructuring Act, which linked the payment of U.S. dues to the United Nations to a restoration of the Mexico City policy.[168]

In January 1999 Pope John Paul II spoke in St. Louis, origin of the famed *Dred Scott* case, which would reach the U.S. Supreme Court. The pope's analogy of abortion to slavery, while hardly novel, undoubtedly hit close to home for the president, who was an eleven-year-old boy in Hot Springs, Arkansas, when federal troops desegregated Little Rock's Central High School. But in his remarks Clinton praised the pope and the Church while steering clear of slavery and abortion.[169]

In June 2000, with Clinton's second appointee, Justice Stephen Breyer, writing for the majority, the Supreme Court by 5–4 struck down Nebraska's ban on "partial-birth" abortion. Breyer said that under the Supreme Court's 1992 *Casey* decision, the Nebraska statute was unconstitutional because it placed an "undue burden" on a woman seeking an abortion. In the case, *Stenberg v. Carhart*, the Court mandated an exemption to protect the health of the mother in any similar future legislation. In a fitting climax to the turbulent eight years of the Clinton era, pro-choice activist Janet Benshoof greeted the verdict with "champagne and shivers"—euphoria at the outcome but unease with the margin.[170]

There were only shivers, however, among most Americans and most Catholics, including the bishops who had filed a friend-of-the-court brief on the side of Nebraska. Twenty-seven years after *Roe v. Wade*, the Supreme Court was still no friend of theirs.[171]

Conclusions on Life and Death

Pro-life Catholics, spearheaded by their pope and their bishops, tried desperately to change Bill Clinton's mind on abortion. But when the president known for political expediency demonstrated ideological consistency, pro-life Catholics were on the losing side for most of the Clinton era.

Clinton's resolute representation of the pro-choice position challenged many American Catholics in a way no president had. Yet there was some evidence that Catholics were up to the task. Their bishops mounted a passionate defense of the rights of the unborn. Their pope lent his considerable charisma and commitment to the pro-life cause in his unprecedented three meetings with an American president. The impact of these efforts percolated from the pulpits to the pews. A CBS/*New York Times* poll released on the twenty-fifth anniversary of *Roe v. Wade* showed that almost 80 percent of Americans backed parental consent (supported by Clinton) and waiting periods for abortion (opposed by Clinton), while only 32 percent supported "generally available legal abortion" (as did Clinton), with women no more likely to approve abortion than men.[172]

A 2000 study by Annette Tomal, an economics professor from Wheaton College in Illinois, discerned that the more religious a girl was, the more likely she was to tell her parents she was pregnant and to forgo an abortion. A 2000 University of Michigan survey as well as a 2001 article by Paul Perl of the Center for Applied Research and James McClintock of the University of Notre Dame discovered that, although their effect was limited, the bishops in the previous decade had nudged more Catholics, regardless of gender or ideology, toward the "consistent ethic of life" against abortion and capital punishment (both supported by Clinton).[173]

And even with a pro-choice president throughout the Clinton era, pro-life Catholics registered some notable political successes. Millions of postcards from the bishops through their parishes to Capitol Hill helped to derail the Freedom of Choice Act. Clinton's reluctant signing of the 1996 Defense Authorization Act as well as the passage, before Clinton's vetoes, of the two "partial-birth" abortion bans in 1996 and 1997 were additional omens that the right-to-life movement had not run its course. Helen Alvare, the director of planning and information for the United States Catholic Conference's Secretariat for Pro-Life Activities, acknowledged three "firsts" in the debate over "partial-birth" abortion: the American Medical Association opposed an abortion method, an abortion advocate confessed a lie, and the media reported his confession.[174] The "power of the pro-life right and the Catholic leadership," Dorothy McBride Stetson, the director of the pro-choice Abortion Issue Network, would grudgingly acknowledge, led "even long-standing abortion-rights allies to waver and vote for the ban." According to *Crisis* magazine's Catholic Voter Project, 55 percent of Catholics believed that abortion was always immoral, while 26 percent thought that it was usually immoral. And from 1996 to 1999, whether in spite of, or because of, the pro-choice president, the abortion rate declined for the first time since *Roe v. Wade*, from 1.5 million to 1.3 million per year. "In the nineties abortions are going down, attitudes are changing dramatically," Michael Taylor, the executive director of the USCC's National Committee for a Human Life Amendment, would recall, "and even pro-choice people are saying abortion is wrong."[175]

Bill Clinton was one of them. "Everyone knows life begins biologically at conception," he would write in his memoir.[176]

Despite these optimistic indicators, however, there were more clues that the Clinton era was a time of retrenchment for pro-life Catholics. Clinton's first term featured executive orders undoing the pro-life edicts of the Reagan-Bush years, two pro-choice appointees to the Supreme Court, the clamorous Cairo conference, and the veto of the first "partial-birth" abortion bill. Clinton's reward for thrusting these daggers into the hearts of the right-to-life community was to win reelection easily, with the votes of a majority of Catholics, over a pro-life opponent whom New York's John Cardinal O'Connor had all but endorsed, in what Bishop James McHugh of Camden, New Jersey, called a "failure" of the USCC's pro-life campaign. American Catholics, the administration's

Office of Catholic Outreach had accurately predicted in May 1996, were not single-issue voters, and "while the issue of abortion is paramount, the Church is concerned with a broad array of issues" supported by the president.[177]

In the middle of Clinton's second term, after his second veto of a "partial-birth" abortion ban, the president celebrated a quarter-century of *Roe v. Wade* by hailing its "positive impact." Thanks to the Supreme Court, Clinton cheered, "safe, legal abortion has all but eliminated the dangerous, clandestine conditions that claimed too many women's lives when the procedure was illegal." The U.S. Catholic bishops commemorated *Roe v. Wade*'s silver anniversary through a radically different lens: "more than thirty-five million children have been killed, and reasons used to justify abortions are now extended to include infanticide."[178]

The pro-choice Catholic columnist Mary McGrory of the *Washington Post*, who opposed "partial-birth" abortion, opined that Congress's failure to override Clinton's veto showed that "clerical clout" was "a thing of the past." The U.S. ambassador to the Vatican, Raymond Flynn, who had judged Pope John Paul II to be a consequential player in the Balkan crises, nevertheless concluded that "the Vatican has less influence in Western countries," most of which "have legalized abortion." Health and Human Services secretary Donna Shalala would remember that the Catholic "influence on abortion policy" during the Clinton administration "was minimal."[179]

While more Catholics were heeding the political counsel of their hierarchy, many Americans, inside and outside of the Clinton administration, were not. "The Pope's still pretty cool for a Polish guy," Clinton aide Gordon Bendick quipped in January 1997. "Except for his stands on abortion, women in the priesthood, celibacy, and a bunch of other stuff, I think he's nearly infallible!" Nearly half the respondents in the 1998 CBS/*New York Times* poll described abortion opponents as "extremists," while far more found abortion proponents "reasonable."[180] Pro-life Catholics' deteriorating image may have had to do with their increasing association in the public mind with the religious Right. The formation of the Catholic Alliance within the largely Protestant evangelical Christian Coalition intensified this impression, causing consternation at the bishops' November 1995 meeting. Noting that the Catholic Alliance shared the USCC's view on abortion, Cardinal Law cited the distance between the two groups on other issues, such as health care. "To our knowledge, the Catholic Alliance leadership has never asked nor received from any bishop permission to use the word 'Catholic,'" Law wrote in February 1996. "Therefore, the group has no official recognition as a Catholic organization."[181]

In his mastery of the pro-choice message, Bill Clinton in some ways affected pro-life Catholics even more than they influenced him. While he did not alter their principles, he inadvertently helped to adjust their presentation. Clinton's inclusive imagery and feminist fealty offered potent weapons with which to restock the pro-life arsenal. And reeling from false charges of sexual abuse aimed at the beatific Cardinal Bernardin, a renewed effort to ordain women, and a discomforting liaison with Islamic radicals against the Cairo draft document, the Church was ripe for rearmament.[182]

So, like President Clinton, the Catholic hierarchy went out of its way to curry favor with the no-longer weaker sex. "I say this without in any way wishing to reduce the importance of securing justice and equity for women," Pope John Paul II assured Nafis Sadik of the United Nations before launching his tirade against the Cairo population proposal in March 1994.[183] The fourth chapter of the pope's March 1995 encyclical, *Evangelium Vitae*, called for a "new feminism," which would usher in a "new culture" centered on a respect for life. In August the pope renounced all forms of discrimination against women, inside and outside the Church. The next month a synod of the world's bishops in Rome began to implement the papal mandate, promising a greater role for nuns in the governance of the Church.[184]

The pope wasn't finished. On the recommendation of Clinton's ambassador to the Vatican, Raymond Flynn, Pope John Paul II appointed the Harvard law professor Mary Ann Glendon to represent him at the UN's Fourth World Conference on Women in September 1995 in Beijing, where Hillary Clinton would speak for the administration.[185] There would be much "common ground" between Glendon and Clinton in Beijing. In their speeches on the same day, both women skewered the host country's policies of coercive abortion, sterilization, and female infanticide.[186]

Following their addresses, Professor Glendon and Mrs. Clinton met for twenty minutes, again stressing their areas of agreement. The next day, the Catholic U.S. ambassador to the UN, Madeleine Albright, told the assembly, "We believe, with John Paul II, in the equality of spouses with respect to family rights." Following her remarks, Albright told the Catholic News Service in Beijing that the relationship between the administration and the Vatican was "excellent," with "many, many subjects on which we agree in terms of social and economic issues." Flynn concurred, noting that Glendon was the first American to head a Vatican delegation, and one-third of the Church's representatives to the conference were from the United States.[187]

The American bishops followed the pope's lead in reaching out to women. "No woman in need with a child, born or unborn, whether she is Catholic or not, should feel herself without help," the prelates pleaded in "Faithful for Life," their June 1995 message. "We pledge the hearts and heads of the Church to help mothers and fathers in need to find pregnancy counseling, pre- and postnatal care, housing and material support, and adoption services." At the Catholic Press Association convention in May 1996, Helen Alvare, the spokesperson for the bishops' Secretariat for Pro-Life Activities, suggested that "Christianity could be the source of a new feminism" to displace the discredited "old feminism" of pro-choice partisans. At their November 1997 meeting, the bishops saluted "the work of more than three thousand pregnancy centers, as well as those hospitals, agencies, and medical centers in radical solidarity with women in need of counseling, pre- and postnatal care, housing, material support, and adoption services."[188] Like the president, the leaders of the Catholic Church recognized the political imperative of securing their base. The 1993 Gallup Poll had concluded that American Catholic women were more religious than their male counterparts.[189]

In a scene captured in an iconic photograph, seventeen-year-old Bill Clinton had shaken hands with President John Kennedy at the White House as part of a tour by the American Legion's Boys Nation group in July 1963. The first Catholic president and the first president to graduate from a Catholic university would have much in common—roguish charm, easy eloquence, pliable liberalism, and an aversion to the Sixth Commandment. But much would change between the thirty-fifth and forty-second chief executives. Perhaps most dramatically, the political nuisance of birth control would yield to the political albatross of abortion.

A lightening of the legal and emotional burden of abortion demanded the agility of an attorney and the empathy of a caregiver. Bill Clinton, the master politician of his age, steadfastly summoned a formidable combination of both. And for pro-life Catholics, who tried but ultimately failed to beat him at his own game, faith and perseverance proved no match for either.

The word "lobbying" too often conjures up twisted arms and greased palms. So the Catholic hierarchy would shrink from the term. Whatever one called it, the pope and the bishops, on behalf of most American Catholics, succeeded in pressing Bill Clinton to intervene in the wars in the Balkans and to propose, then withdraw, a plan to enact universal health insurance. But they failed to dislodge him from his intractable defense of abortion. And in the process, the chief lobbyist in the White House in some ways had a greater impact on them than they had on him.

CHAPTER NINE

Catholics and George W. Bush
(2001–2004)

IN THE WAKE OF THE NATION's closest presidential election, George Walker Bush promised to unite a bitterly divided country. And within nine months of taking office, he would: by sending U.S. troops into Afghanistan to hunt the Al Qaeda militants who had dared to attack the United States. But by the time he ran for reelection, the nation had again splintered, this time over the ill-fated U.S. occupation of Iraq. In between, Bush took significant strides to advance his faith-based initiative and to restrict abortion, only to fall short of his ultimate objectives in the Congress and the courts. Throughout his first term Bush listened so closely to Catholic leaders, and wooed so many Catholic voters, that some were calling him more "Catholic" than the Catholic opponent he would defeat in 2004. But by changing course earlier in Iraq and pressing harder for faith-based legislation and against abortion, he could have won over even more Catholic hearts and collected even more Catholic votes.

War and Peace: Iraq

"What if?" is the question that historians hate to ask but that leaders have to ask. For U.S. presidents from Harry S. Truman to George H. W. Bush, that query occupied the center of their anti-Soviet foreign policies. They expended countless hours, dollars, and lives preparing for the attack on American soil that never came.

A decade after the end of the Cold War, however, the hypothetical became real. On the morning of September 11, 2001, nineteen Al Qaeda terrorists killed almost three thousand people in their suicidal aerial destruction of part of the Pentagon and all of New York's World Trade Center, as well as the crash of a hijacked plane in Pennsylvania. The first incursion across the borders of the United States since the Japanese assault on Pearl Harbor sixty years earlier introduced Americans to an even more perilous world than the one from which their Cold War commanders in chief had successfully defended them.

It now fell upon George W. Bush, the former Texas governor with the threadbare Electoral College majority, to rally the nation behind its newest war, which offered no compass and portended no conclusion. Backed by a compliant Congress and an aroused public, Bush dispatched U.S. troops to fight Al Qaeda and its Taliban enablers in Afghanistan. Then, the real became hypothetical. Just in case another anti-American Muslim was hatching his own 9/11, the president announced in March 2003 that the United States would also be sending combat forces to Saddam Hussein's Iraq. Once again, Congress complied and most Americans approved.

Unlike when he went to war in Afghanistan, Bush defied the pope and the U.S. bishops by invading Iraq. Most Americans voted to prolong the Iraq war by reelecting the president, as did most American Catholics. But if the hierarchy did not speak for most of the Church or the country, they nonetheless contributed to American wartime diplomacy by raising their own age-old questions for a troubling new era.

Prelude to Iraq

On the first anniversary of the September 11 attacks, President George W. Bush addressed the nation on television. "We will not allow any terrorist or tyrant to threaten civilization with weapons of mass destruction," said the president, without naming Saddam Hussein or Iraq. The next day he addressed the United Nations, urging action to disarm Iraq. On September 20 Bush announced his National Security Strategy, which argued that, in an era of chemical, biological, and nuclear weapons, and with the omnipresent threat of these weapons falling into the hands of rogue nations or terrorist networks, the United States must prepare for war even when a threat is not imminent. On September 26 Bush asked Secretary of Defense Donald Rumsfeld, according to the secretary's notes, to "develop a plan to invade Iraq." In November the Bush administration successfully pressed the UN Security Council to adopt a unanimous resolution calling upon Iraq to disarm or face "serious consequences."[1]

Many Catholics were wary of a second war. In a September 2002 letter to President Bush, which he hand-delivered to national security advisor Condoleezza Rice, Bishop Wilton Gregory of Belleville, Illinois, the president of the United States Conference of Catholic Bishops (formerly the United States Catholic Conference), asserted that without "clear and adequate evidence of Iraqi involvement in the attacks of September 11 or an imminent attack of a grave nature," an assault on Iraq "would not meet the strict conditions of Catholic teaching for overriding the strong presumption against the use of military force." Gregory defined such conditions as "just cause, right authority, probability of success, proportionality, and noncombat immunity." Pope

John Paul II wrote to Bush in October, pleading for more time for diplomatic efforts, economic sanctions, and weapons inspections to postpone war.[2]

The bishops took up Gregory's letter at their November 2002 meeting in Washington. "We are on the brink of war," Bishop Walter Sullivan of Richmond, Virginia, stated, "and I think we have to be very clear that we are all against the [potential] war in Iraq." But "all of us" were not against a war. Recalling his own experience ministering to victims at liberated Nazi concentration camps in World War II, New Orleans archbishop Philip Hannan allowed that he would approve of a war to topple a "despotic power" like Saddam Hussein.[3]

The bishops stopped short of an absolutist pronouncement. Citing the Catholic Catechism number 2039's definition of a "just cause" as one in which "the damage initiated by the aggressor on the nation [is] lasting, grave, and certain," the bishops questioned the existence of such a premise for commencing hostilities. They called upon the "legitimate authority" of Congress and the UN Security Council to debate such a move, worried that "unpredictable consequences" could undermine the "probability of success," and advocated adherence to the "norms of conduct governing the war," particularly as they related to civilian casualties. But because they could "not predict what will happen in the coming weeks," they reached "no definitive conclusions."[4]

In a January 2003 address to the Vatican diplomatic corps, John Paul II twice referred to Iraq, exhorting the world to say "no to war." The American bishops quoted the pope's words in a February statement issued by Bishop Gregory: "With the Holy See and many religious leaders throughout the world, we believe that resort to war would not meet the strict conditions in Catholic teaching for the use of military force." The bishops fortified their previous reluctance, only to hedge their bets once again. "If the decision to use force is taken," the prelates advised, "the moral and legal constraints on the conduct of war must be observed."[5]

The bishops weren't the only Catholics quoting the pope. When "you examine carefully what the Pope said," Bush's ambassador to the Vatican, James Nicholson, noted after attending the pontiff's March speech to the Sant'Egidio movement, "he said that war is not inevitable—and we agree." Nicholson invited the Catholic conservative theologian Michael Novak to address a symposium on Iraq in Vatican City. "Under the original Catholic doctrine of *justum bellum* [just war], a limited and carefully conducted war to bring about a change of regime in Iraq," Novak contended, "is, as a last resort, morally obligatory."[6]

"You're never going to hear the Holy Father say, 'Go to war,'" Rev. Edward Hathaway, the pastor of St. John's Catholic Church in McLean, Virginia, told a group of parishioners gathered in March to discuss the potential confrontation with Iraq. The son of a navy pilot and brother of two graduates of the Air Force Academy, Father Hathaway suggested that they view the impending conflict not as a preemptive strike but, as Novak argued, the long-delayed conclusion of the Persian Gulf War. "I expect the Holy Father to pray for peace," one congregant noted approvingly, "and the U.S. Marines to bring it about."[7]

The Holy Father was not just praying. He welcomed British prime minister Tony Blair, Spanish prime minister José María Aznar, UN secretary-general Kofi Annan, Iran Parliament leader Seyed Mohammad Reza Khatami, and Iraq deputy prime minister Tariq Aziz to the Vatican in February to try to stave off war. He sent diplomats to the United Nations, Baghdad, and Washington. Italian archbishop Celestino Migliore, the Holy See's nuncio to the UN, told that body in February that while the "disarmament of arsenals of mass destruction" was a worthy end, a "resort to force" would not be a defensible means. French cardinal Roger Etchegarry, a former president of the Pontifical Council for Justice and Peace, emerged from his February meeting with Saddam Hussein convinced that the Iraqi dictator was anxious to avoid war. Italian cardinal Pio Laghi, a former Vatican ambassador to the United States and a friend of Bush's father, headed to Washington.[8]

Before Bush met with Cardinal Laghi, he requested a meeting between national security advisor Condoleezza Rice and representatives of the American Catholic hierarchy. Cardinals Theodore McCarrick of Washington, Anthony Bevilacqua of Philadelphia, Edward Egan of New York, and William Keeler of Baltimore answered the call. "Dr. Rice received us very graciously and went over the concerns of the Administration," McCarrick recounted of the gathering. Venturing further than the hierarchy had ever gone before, the cardinals told her that the American Catholic bishops now opposed a "pre-emptive strike against Iraq."[9]

For all the speeches, statements, and letters, no representative of the Catholic power structure had personally told the president what he had only heard and read. So Cardinal Laghi's visit assumed a special niche in the Catholic campaign to dissuade the Methodist commander in chief from attacking the Muslim nation. "I told the president that today, on Ash Wednesday, Catholics around the world are following the Pope's request to fast and pray for peace," Laghi summarized the March meeting. "The Holy See maintains that there are still peaceful avenues within the context of the vast patrimony of international law and institutions which exist for that purpose." From the Vatican point of view, Laghi elaborated, "a decision regarding the use of military force can only be taken within the framework of the United Nations."[10]

The president shared the pope's faith in God. "I am working hard to keep the peace and avoid a war," Bush had written to his twin daughters, Barbara and Jenna, away at Yale and the University of Texas, as 2003 dawned. "I pray that the man in Iraq will disarm in a peaceful way."[11] But the president did not share the pope's faith in the United Nations. When inspector Hans Blix informed the UN that Saddam Hussein was defying Resolution 1441 by submitting a false declaration of his weapons systems, Bush dispatched Secretary of State Colin Powell to New York to plead for a new Security Council resolution—this time, to authorize the use of force. But this time, the votes were not there. On March 17, 2003, the United States withdrew the resolution.[12]

Iraq

"The United Nations Security Council has not lived up to its responsibility, so we will rise to ours," President Bush addressed the nation that evening. "Saddam Hussein and his sons must leave Iraq within forty-eight hours. Their refusal to do so will result in military conflict, commenced at a time of our choosing."[13]

The Vatican issued a terse one-sentence rejoinder the day after Bush's speech: "Whoever decides that all the peaceful means made available under international law are exhausted assumes a grave responsibility before God, his conscience, and history." Almost half of the nation's practicing Catholics, according to a *Crisis* magazine poll, disapproved of U.S. entry into the war. But for the pope, the bishops, and those Catholics who continued to counsel patience, the president had an answer. "It had been more than a decade since the Gulf War resolutions had demanded that Saddam disarm, over four years since he had kicked out the weapons inspectors, six months since Resolution 1441 had given Saddam his 'final opportunity,' and three months to fully disclose his WMD [weapons of mass destruction]," Bush would recall. "Diplomacy did not feel rushed. It felt like it was taking forever."[14]

So would the war. Within a month the uneven thirty-three-nation "coalition of the willing" that Bush had cobbled together without the United Nations had secured Baghdad, the prize that the first President Bush had forsaken a dozen years before. In May in San Diego, arrayed in a flight suit aboard the USS *Abraham Lincoln* with a Mission Accomplished banner prominently displayed behind him, the second President Bush declared the end of combat operations in Iraq, and the beginning of the postwar occupation.[15] Bush not only saluted the outcome of Operation Iraqi Freedom, but the path that the coalition forces had followed to achieve it. Two decades after the American Catholic bishops had suggested that modern warfare was inherently immoral, Bush implied that it was actually less immoral than its more primitive predecessors. "No device of man can remove tragedy from war," said the commander in chief, "yet it is a great moral advance when the guilty have more to fear from war than the innocent."[16]

The Vatican remained dubious. "There were not sufficient reasons for moving against Iraq because the country did not constitute a true threat for the United States and its allies," the Vatican-approved Jesuit periodical *La Civiltà Cattolica* insisted later the same month. "I wish for everyone the peace that only God, through Jesus Christ, can give—the peace that is the work of justice, truth, love, and solidarity, the peace from which people can benefit when they follow the law of God, the peace that makes them feel like brothers," John Paul II said to thousands of Spaniards in Madrid. "He did not mention Iraq," the *New York Times*'s Frank Bruni reported, "nor did he have to."[17] Michael Griffin, a Holy Cross seminarian at the University of Notre Dame, could not help but notice the contrast between the triumphant president and the troubled pope. "President Bush claims a victory for preventive force," Griffin wrote in *America* in June. "The Pope laments a defeat for lasting peace."[18]

As the occupation under the direction of Catholic convert Paul Bremer quickly turned bloody, the pope appeared a prophet while the president played the fool. Rev. Timothy Hogan, a Catholic chaplain in Iraq, was working overtime counseling U.S. marines who were not only "witnessing the shock of dead bodies on the side of the road" but viewing "children and adults begging for food." Despite Bush's disclaimer, Jack Miles, a Catholic member of the Pacific Council on International Policy, worried that "Gulf War II will cost twice as many Iraqi lives as Gulf War I did." Estimating "Gulf War I casualties at the lower-end consensus figure of 30,000 (12,500 military plus 17,500 civilian)," Miles calculated in *Commonweal* in July, "it would then seem conservative to estimate that sixty thousand Iraqis may die as a result of the current conflict." Miles claimed that the only thing worse than the abundance of civilian casualties in Iraq was the Bush administration's apparent disinclination to report them.[19]

The administration was also not reporting evidence of Iraqi weapons of mass destruction, because there wasn't any. The absence of WMDs, "Rob 1" editorialized in the *National Catholic Register* in June and Professor Gregory Foster of the National Defense University observed in *Commonweal* in August, rekindled the debate over the justness of the Iraq war. At the outset of the war, "Rob 1" reflected, "most Catholics were willing to give the president the benefit of the doubt in the hope that the administration had access to intelligence that it was unable to share." But without WMDs, "the case for urgency . . . is going to be undercut," and "just-war principles *demand* that urgency." Without the WMDs, Foster wondered, was the cause just, the resort to war final, the intention right, the authority legitimate, and the conflict proportionate and

{340} CHAPTER NINE

discriminating with a high probability of success? In other words, were *any* of the just-war criteria being met, Foster inquired, in the Bush administration's preemptive war against a largely disarmed Iraq?[20]

If weapons of mass destruction were proving elusive, Saddam Hussein was not. The Iraqi dictator's December 2003 capture by the U.S. Delta Team helped to pry the war's proponents from the defensive in the debate over Iraq. "We savor the all-too-rare spectacle of a brute brought low," William F. Buckley rhapsodized, "and brought to justice."[21] "Saddam had three weapons with him, including a pistol that the men presented to me in a glass box," Bush would reflect on the visit of the Iraqi leader's captors to the White House a few months later. "I told them I would display the gift in the private study off the Oval Office and one day in my Presidential Library," Bush remembered. "The pistol always reminded me that a brutal dictator, responsible for so much death and suffering, had surrendered to our troops while cowering in a hole."[22]

The Vatican would not be requesting one of the other weapons. "I felt pity to see this man destroyed," Renato Cardinal Martino said in Rome in reaction to the capture of Saddam Hussein. "Seeing him like this, a man in his tragedy, despite all the heavy blame he bears, I had a sense of compassion for him."[23] If the Catholic hierarchy was less enthused about the apprehension of Saddam Hussein than was the U.S. government, it nevertheless shared President Bush's aversion to withdrawing from Iraq. "The Vatican clearly said 'no' to the war," a Church official explained. "But at a certain point you have to manage the situation that has been created in the way that does the least damage. If the military pulls out of Iraq now, the country will fall into chaos."[24]

So Cardinal Martino, a former papal envoy to the United Nations who had opposed the United States' "unilateral" action in Iraq, now hoped that Saddam Hussein's capture would prove a "watershed" in the worsening war. In January 2004, when Vice President Dick Cheney and the ambassador to the Vatican, James Nicholson, met in Rome with the Vatican secretary of state, Angelo Cardinal Soldano, a vocal critic of the invasion, they addressed the Israeli-Palestinian conflict instead. When Cheney met with Pope John Paul II, the pope didn't mention Iraq either, beyond an oblique allusion to "international cooperation and solidarity in the service of peace." The vice president presented the pope with a gift far different from the one that the president would receive from the Delta Team—a crystal dove of peace.[25]

"Based on an assessment of the data we collected over the past ten years, it would have been difficult for analysts to come to any different conclusions than the ones reached in October of 2002," George Tenet, the Catholic director of the Central Intelligence Agency, addressed the missing WMDs in a February 2004 speech at Georgetown University. "However, in our business, that is not good enough." To the war's growing covey of critics, however, the administration's damage control was not good enough either.[26]

American Catholics had been hearing a lot more from their president than from their prelates about the war's first year. The latter were too busy defending or defrocking priests in their dioceses, inside or outside of court, amid the charges of sexual abuse that had rocked the Church since 2002. So as American bishops initiated their cycle of fifth-year consultations in Rome, they heard Vatican officials plead with them to change the subject. In a March 30, 2004, meeting with Archbishop Giovanni Lajolo, the Vatican's foreign affairs specialist, bishops from Florida, Georgia, and North Carolina discussed terrorism and the preventive, "unilateral" war the United States was fighting in Iraq.[27]

A different kind of abuse—the appalling treatment of Iraqi prisoners by U.S. soldiers at the Abu Ghraib facility—offered the bishops an opening to reenter the public discourse on the war. Internet images of beatings, prisoners on dog leashes, and sexual humiliation shocked the world. "The abuse and torture of Iraqi prisoners," Bishop John Ricard of Pensacola-Tallahassee, Florida, the chairman of the International Policy Committee of the United States Conference of Catholic Bishops, reacted in May, "have brought shame upon the nation."[28] Bush offered a public apology. Secretary of Defense Donald Rumsfeld offered his resignation (which Bush twice refused). A U.S. government investigation would exonerate all except the soldiers on the scene. But the horrific memories of Abu Ghraib stained the nation's conscience.

Abu Ghraib was "a heavier blow to the United States than September 11," the Vatican foreign minister, Archbishop Giovanni Lajolo, contended, because "the blow was not inflicted by terrorists but by the Americans themselves." He urged the UN to help conclude a war that never should have started. It never would have, the archbishop added wistfully, if only the president had listened to the pope.[29] The president finally *would* listen to the pope, on his visit to Rome in June. John Paul II reminded Bush of the "unequivocal position of the Holy See" against the war, while entreating him to enlist "the international community and the United Nations" in hastening the end of hostilities in Iraq. In an apparent reference to Abu Ghraib, the pope lamented the "other deplorable events [that] have come to light which have troubled the civic and religious conscience of all and made more difficult a serene and resolute commitment to shared human values." Bush presented John Paul II with the Presidential Medal of Freedom, which cited the pope's successful effort to help curtail the Cold War but made no mention of his unsuccessful effort to help forestall the Iraq war.[30]

While Bush was uncharacteristically avoiding the subject of Iraq, the United States Conference of Catholic Bishops was uncharacteristically addressing it.

Speaking for the bishops two weeks after Bush's meeting with the Holy Father, the USCCB's president, Bishop Wilton Gregory, reminded the president of "the grave moral concerns previously expressed by our episcopal conference about the military intervention in Iraq and the unpredictable and uncontrollable negative consequences of an invasion and occupation."[31]

Dissatisfaction with President Bush's conduct of the Iraq war penetrated every corner of American Catholic society. "The war in Iraq was a mistake and unnecessary," Deacon Mike Solomon, a Catholic pilgrimage operator and fundraiser from Florida, told the *National Catholic Register* in July. "We were lied to about weapons of mass destruction in Iraq," Tracy Hutchinson, a Catholic hospice worker in Massachusetts, agreed, "and now innocent women and children are being killed every day." Writing in *Commonweal* in July under the pseudonym "Mary Jony," the Catholic mother of a twenty-one-year-old Army Ranger in Iraq lamented that her "moral universe has been conscripted, held hostage." She harbored "one final illusion—that of keeping my son alive."[32]

American Catholics, from right to left, top to bottom, had become disillusioned with a war many of them had once embraced. A June 2004 survey by the Washington, D.C., polling firm Belden, Russonello, and Stewart found the war to be the top election-year issue for American Catholics, with only 54 percent of them still confident in Bush's ability to resolve it and 46 percent having lost confidence. Almost two-thirds of American Catholics in a September Pew Research Center poll cited Iraq as a "very important" issue in the upcoming presidential election, compared to less than half who named abortion. The sociologist Rev. Andrew Greeley reported that Catholics were more likely to oppose the war than were Protestants. And Protestants weren't exactly applauding the president: a July ABC News/*Washington Post* survey found only 44 percent of all Americans in support of the war.[33]

By this time, the Democrats were running a candidate against Bush, and he was a Catholic. A Vietnam veteran who had voted to authorize the war only to wish he hadn't, Massachusetts Democratic senator John Kerry promised a phased withdrawal of U.S. troops from Iraq. And if Kerry couldn't persuade Americans, perhaps other Catholics could. In Rome in November the Pontifical Council for Justice and Peace released a revised *Compendium of the Social Doctrine of the Church*. When a nation is under attack, the new version held, it may resort to "the force of arms" to defend itself. But "engaging in a preventive war without clear proof that an attack is imminent cannot fail to raise serious moral and juridical questions."[34]

"I believe that if a secret ballot were to be held in the Vatican, Kerry would beat Bush, 60–40," the *National Catholic Reporter*'s Vatican commentator John Allen wrote on the eve of the American election, claiming that Iraq even trumped abortion in Rome. But the pope didn't have a vote. Millions of American Catholics cast theirs for Bush, more than voted for one of their own. Most of those voting to reelect the president agreed with the Vatican that the war was more important than abortion. They just didn't agree why. A Georgetown University study found that most Catholic voters opted for Bush because of his firm stance against terrorism.[35]

Conclusions on War and Peace

The ineffectiveness of the pope, the bishops, and many American Catholics in swaying the Bush administration on the war in Iraq as they had influenced the Nixon administration on the war in Vietnam stemmed from several factors. Despite several similarities—the murky strategy, the cultural arrogance, the moral superiority, and the obstacles posed by guerrilla warfare in the field and declining public support at home—Iraq was not Vietnam, and antiwar Catholics could not repeat their success. Their efforts nonetheless were not completely in vain.

The first reason Iraq was not Vietnam is that during the Iraq war, there were no draft cards to burn, no reasons to flee to Canada, and no major mobilization of young people against the war—because there was no draft. A majority of Americans surveyed by Gallup in October 2003 said that the war had not affected them personally. "The whole burden [of the war in Iraq] is being borne by a small cadre of Americans—the soldiers, their families and reservists," Thomas Friedman of the *New York Times* wrote in February 2004, "and the rest of us are just sailing along, as if it had nothing to do with us."[36] So if the faces of the Catholic Left in the Vietnam era were the Berrigan brothers destroying draft records, the face of the Catholic Left in the Iraq era was Cindy Sheehan mourning her son's death on the battlefield. Cindy Sheehan repudiated the war; Casey Sheehan had reenlisted for it.[37]

Second, not only did the all-volunteer military mark an important shift from Vietnam, but public attitudes toward the members of that force dramatically changed as well. Reviled by war opponents as a "baby killer," the U.S. soldier returned home from Vietnam as an outcast in his own land. Revered by war opponents and proponents alike as a "wounded warrior," the U.S. soldier returned home from Iraq as *Time*'s Person of the Year. There were some, like Catholic conscientious objector Stephen Frank of the Marine Corps, who opposed the war. But he had little company. "No one knows about co's in my generation," Frank observed, noting that in the days of Vietnam conscription there were two hundred thousand, but during the all-volunteer Persian Gulf War there were only about a hundred. "Thank you for these men," military chaplain Lt. Col. Tommy Preston prayed on behalf of much of the country as he sent off members of the Fourth Infantry to Iraq in December 2004, "who care about your Word more than for their own lives."[38]

So if it was hard for Vietnam-era protesters to separate the soldiers compelled to fight the war from the politicians who sent them there, so it was difficult for Iraq-era protesters to separate the soldiers choosing to fight the war from the politicians who sent them there. Only this time, the connection worked to the advantage of the government. With an all-volunteer force, it was difficult for other Americans to tell the soldiers it was time to come home, when not only did the soldiers want to stay and fight, but they knew that none of those other Americans would be taking their place. Much to the chagrin of Art Laffin of the pacifist Dorothy Day Catholic Worker movement in Washington, the bishops acceded to Catholic soldiers engaging in an unjust war. "Everyone tells you that you did what you had to do," Sergeant Brendan O'Byrne muttered before redeploying to Afghanistan. "And I just hate that, because I didn't have to do any of it."[39]

Third, unlike in Vietnam, there emerged an uneasy agreement among many antiwar as well as pro-war Catholics that the coalition troops should stay in Iraq to finish the job—and there was even remarkable congruence on what that job was. Pope John Paul II "never took sides or condemned military actions as immoral" once the war was under way, Bush's Catholic ambassador to the Vatican, James Nicholson, maintained. Before he failed to persuade President Bush to avoid war with Iraq, papal envoy Pio Cardinal Laghi noted that the pope and the president shared a devotion to "democracy"—which could not come to Saddam Hussein's Iraq without war. After he met with President Bush as the war that he had denounced entered its second year, Pope John Paul II saluted "the recent appointment of a head of state in Iraq and the formation of an interim Iraqi government," then assisted the United States with Iraq's humanitarian relief and reconstruction—developments that would not have happened without war. In their statement during the war's second year, the U.S. Catholic bishops, who had opposed the conflict from the outset, nevertheless maintained that "the United States now has responsibility for sustained, long-term efforts to help the Iraqi people build a stable, pluralistic, democratic, and prosperous Iraq"—efforts that would not have existed without war. "I do see the benefit in ending a cruel dictatorship, and preventing the mass murder that had been present, but that did not seem at the time to be the reason that we went in," Cardinal McCarrick equivocated in the war's second year. Thus the war "may or may not have been just for the good of the people over there."[40]

The antiwar Catholic presidential candidate seemed to want to have it both ways as well, voting for Iraq war appropriations in 2004 before voting against them. In his opportunistic ambiguity on Iraq, Senator Kerry barely resembled his former self, the forthright Lieutenant Kerry, movingly urging the Senate Foreign Relations Committee on behalf of Vietnam Veterans against the War in 1971 not to permit any more young Americans to "die for a mistake."[41]

If Kerry was too indecisive on the war, Bush was too decisive, furnishing a fourth reason for the president's inattention to the Catholic chorus against the war. While Kerry couldn't make up his mind, Bush had his mind made up. "For months I had solicited advice, listened to a variety of opinions, and considered the counterarguments," Bush would claim of the build-up to the Iraq invasion. But others would spin a different tale. In Robert Woodward's view, Bush had decided to invade Iraq by early January 2003. "Look, we're going to have to do this, I'm afraid," Bush had told Rumsfeld. "I didn't see how we're going to get him [Saddam Hussein] to a position where he will do something in a manner that's consistent with the U.N. requirements, and we've got to make an assumption that we're not." George Tenet would remember that Bush opted for war in Iraq before December 2002. Bush "had probably made up his own mind about the war sometime early in 2002," James Pfiffner also concluded, "but other members of his Administration became aware of his decision at different times over the next year."[42]

The president's obduracy seemed consistent with his dualistic worldview, a Calvinist conviction that alarmed many Catholics. On his unsuccessful peace mission to Washington, Cardinal Laghi detected "something Calvinistic" about the U.S. president's resolve to intervene in Iraq. "We have a concept of sin and evil, too," a Vatican official intimated, "but we also believe in grace and redemption."[43] Perhaps that is why, when the pope, the bishops, and their representatives pressed Bush to call off his war, Bush and members of his administration were so utterly unresponsive. "In hours together on the road I often tried to raise theological issues and questions about justification for war, etc.," Bush advisor Douglas Wead would recall of the 2000 campaign. "Although he professed faith, he had absolutely no interest whatsoever in God or theology except as a political discussion."[44]

The Vatican secretary of state, Angelo Cardinal Soldano, described Bush's discussion of Iraq in their June 2004 meeting in Rome as "generic." After the president's meeting that same day with the pope, Bush said nothing about Iraq. After the vice president's earlier meeting with the pope, Cheney had said nothing at all. When asked about the pope's arguments, national security advisor Condoleezza Rice, a Presbyterian minister's daughter and former University of Notre Dame graduate student, said she didn't understand them. "I didn't see how it could be immoral to prevent the deaths of tens of thousands, maybe hundreds of thousands, maybe millions of people," she explained, "against a brutal regime that has already been responsible for the deaths of 100,000 people."⁴⁵

Of course, it didn't help the antiwar Catholics' case that their pope was ailing and their bishops were reeling—a fifth cause of Catholic weakness. "The Holy Father's energy had given way to frailty," Bush would recall in his memoir of his first encounter with Pope John Paul II, three years before they discussed Iraq at the Vatican in a meeting that the memoir wouldn't record. Crippled by Parkinson's disease, the octogenarian pontiff had long since entered what the *New York Times*'s Alessandra Stanley termed "the twilight of his papacy." Unable to walk without assistance and barely able to talk, the once loquacious pilgrim seldom left Rome. Forty percent of American Catholics in a May 2002 Gallup Poll believed that the pope should resign because of his poor health. "I think the people around him should tell him he must stop," Metropolitan Simeon, the head of the Orthodox Church in Central and Western Europe, commented after meeting with Pope John Paul II in May 2002. "He is suffering like Christ."⁴⁶

The U.S. Catholic bishops were suffering, too, upon a cross largely of their own making. The sexual abuse scandal, which erupted in Bernard Cardinal Law's Archdiocese of Boston in January 2002 and continued for much of the year with almost daily accounts of abusive priests there and elsewhere, shamed the bishops into silence and shredded their credibility on Iraq and other issues. "American churchgoers, while supportive of their parish priests, have vented their fury at the Church's hierarchy," the *New York Times*'s Laurie Goodstein wrote in April 2002, "withholding donations to bishops' fundraising campaigns, picketing churches and news conferences, and calling for the resignation of Cardinal Law of Boston." A CBS News poll discovered that a majority of American Catholics were critical of the Church's national leaders.⁴⁷

Ultimately, *when* the pope and the bishops spoke was more important than *whether* they spoke, adding a sixth and final explanation for the feebleness of the Catholic antiwar lobby. The Bush administration was not always listening to American Catholics, but American Catholics were often listening to the Bush administration. Like the twin towers of the World Trade Center, the two pillars of George W. Bush's post-9/11 foreign policy—Afghanistan and Iraq—remained inseparable in the minds of many. Despite any firm connection between September 11 and Saddam Hussein, the administration made no significant attempt to correct the American public's conflation of the two and instead, at least to its critics, eagerly exploited this misconception. Though Al Qaeda had infiltrated Iraq, and suicide bombings there fit the textbook definition of "terrorism," the war's critics deplored this linkage between the "good" war on terror and the "bad" war in Iraq.⁴⁸

Yet, like Bush, they kept tethering the two. The papal envoy Cardinal Laghi failed to persuade the president to forestall war in March 2003, but Bush induced Laghi to denounce terrorism. When not separating himself from Bush on Iraq in his remarks after their June 2004 meeting, Pope John Paul II was allying himself with Bush on terrorism, describing it as "a source of constant concern." When not distancing themselves from Bush on Iraq in their June 2004 statement, the U.S. Catholic bishops were expressing sympathy for Bush's resistance to "terrorists who want to make Iraq a battleground for a clash of civilizations between Islam and the West." In trying to compensate for the war they opposed by citing the war they supported, these antiwar Catholics seemed not all that different from the pro-war president.[49]

In April 2005, Pope John Paul II died. George W. Bush became the first U.S. president to attend a pope's funeral, joined by former presidents George H. W. Bush and Bill Clinton. "As we knelt at the communion rail to pray over his body," George W. Bush would recall, his wife, Laura, whispered to him, "Now is the time to pray for miracles."[50] The miracles would appear a couple of years later. For his critics the miracle was that Bush finally changed his mind about Iraq—not about whether to keep fighting, but how. He authorized more troops, something Lyndon Johnson and Richard Nixon had resisted in Vietnam and Donald Rumsfeld (before his firing at the end of 2006) had talked him out of in Iraq. For his supporters the miracle was that Bush's "surge" actually succeeded, snatching apparent victory from the jaws of all-but-certain defeat.

It is doubtful that the Catholics who had criticized Bush had much to do with his change of mind on Iraq. The deteriorating situation on the ground there and the dismal prospects for Republicans in the 2006 midterm elections, which would cost them control of Congress, were far more influential. And it is certain that antiwar Catholics had nothing to do with his decision to escalate the war, beyond helping to convince him that his present course was disastrous.[51]

But Catholics, both those who supported and those who opposed Bush's wars and elections, did in the end have some impact on this president. In the age of Al Qaeda, they helped to teach the president the lessons of Aquinas. "President Bush made clear that he sought to abide by the precepts of a just war," ambassador Nicholson would recall. Both the pope and President Bush believed that war should be the last resort. Both recognized that decisions of war and peace must be made by legitimate civil authorities. Where they differed, however, was over "whether all diplomatic means to achieve Iraqi disarmament had been exhausted before resorting to military action."[52]

The campaign of the Church hierarchy to dissuade the president from going to war in Iraq was not a total failure. With their just-war theology and faith-based reasoning, the pope and his fellow Catholics reminded George W. Bush that "what if?" is only the second question a commander in chief must ask before sending Americans to die. The first, which Bush struggled to answer in two wars with too many rationales, is "what for?"

Social Justice: The Faith-Based Initiative

According to Article VI, clause 3, of the U.S. Constitution, there is no religious test to hold office in the federal government. But at least when it comes to the presidency, there might as well be. Americans do not elect atheists. Belief in a higher power has become an unofficial qualification for the nation's highest office. So presidential candidates routinely visit churches, cite scripture, and invoke God's name.

If the American electorate demands religion of its presidents, it is nonetheless wary of religiosity in its presidents. Presidents who do not wear their religion lightly risk alienating a large segment of the public whose faith does not move them to pray or lead them to church. Americans want their leaders to practice, but they do not want them to preach. To many Americans, therefore, when George W. Bush entered the White House in January 2001, he was skating on thin ice. During his barely successful run for the presidency, Bush had maintained that God called him to serve, had named his campaign biography after the Methodist hymn "A Charge to Keep," and had spoken often of the "compassion" by which "churches and synagogues and mosques and cathedrals . . . warm the cold of life."[53]

Candidate Bush's "God talk" became the foundation for his proposal to enlarge the "charitable choice" provisions of Bill Clinton's 1996 welfare reform law to ensure a greater federal role for faith-based entities in rescuing the downtrodden. Catholic organizations were among those that stood to benefit from such an expansion.

Although most Catholics would support Bush's faith-based initiative, some feared that presidential piety would engender political excess, fiscal irresponsibility, and constitutional overreach. As a result, the Catholic reaction to Bush's effort would be at times incoherent and underwhelming. In the end, however, Bush impressively answered Catholics' request to serve the disadvantaged, even when some of them stopped asking.

The Proposal

Bush's faith-based initiative had its roots in *The Tragedy of American Compassion* (1992), a book by the evangelical Christian professor Marvin Olasky of the University of Texas, in which he attacked government responses to poverty while extolling churches' anti-poverty efforts. In 1996 the Republican-controlled House of Representatives and Senate amended the welfare reform bill (which Democratic president Bill Clinton would reluctantly sign during his reelection campaign) to include a "charitable choice" provision. The amendment permitted the federal funding of social services administered by religious groups and hiring by these groups on the basis of religion, while preventing these groups from using federal monies to advance a religious agenda or hiring on the basis of race, color, sex, national origin, visual impairment, disability, or age. "Charitable choice" would expand to three other social service programs, and Clinton appointed a Catholic priest to coordinate "community and interfaith" partnerships at the Department of Housing and Urban Development. But the Clinton administration otherwise largely neglected it. Governor George W. Bush's Texas was one of only a few states to implement "charitable choice."[54]

In a November 1998 article in the conservative Catholic magazine *Crisis*, pollster Steven Wagner wrote that churchgoing Catholics had grown weary of the Church's quest for "economic justice" and instead were seeking "social renewal." As Governor Bush pondered a run for the White House, his pollster Karl Rove seized upon the article as inviting Republican outreach to these disaffected Catholics, a potential equivalent to the "soccer mom" swing voters who chose Clinton in 1996.[55]

Four months later, in a meeting in Austin, Governor Bush asked his guests for "one big new idea on compassion." Bush then sat in stunned silence as University of Pennsylvania political scientist John DiIulio, a Catholic and a Democrat, informed him of the over two million children of prisoners in need of adult mentors. "In almost every subsequent communication I had with Bush before he became president," DiIulio would recall, "we discussed mentoring for the children of prisoners."[56]

The Bush campaign received more ideas from more Catholics. Bush met with a group of Catholic leaders in September 1999. Writer Michael Novak, *First Things* editor Rev. Richard Neuhaus, and *Crisis* editor Deal Hudson advised the candidate throughout the campaign, infusing Bush's speeches with such Catholic notions as "solidarity," "subsidiarity," and the "common good."[57] DiIulio, who, one observer said, "talked like a longshoreman, reasoned like Einstein, and cared like Mother Teresa," counseled the campaigns of both Bush and his Democratic rival, Vice President Al Gore. Both candidates would advocate spending increases and tax credits to encourage more services by, and larger contributions to, faith-based organizations.[58]

In November 2000 the Democrat won more Catholic votes and more votes overall, only to lose the election in Florida, where Bush's Catholic brother was the governor. So DiIulio stopped advising Gore and kept advising Bush.[59] "Together we will address some of society's deepest problems one person at a time, by encouraging and empowering the good hearts and good works of the American people," Bush promised in his first speech as president-elect in December 2000. "This is the essence of compassionate conservatism."[60]

Only a week later in Austin Bush convened about thirty clergy from various denominations. "You can see that there was a real interest here," said Rev. Robert Sirico, the Catholic leader of the Acton Institute for the Study of Religion and Liberty in Grand Rapids, who attended the meeting. "This is a man who has had a religious experience, who understands the influence of religion in a very dramatic way." Bishop Joseph Fiorenza of Houston and Galveston came away from the meeting convinced that Bush "really wants to bridge the gap that exists among the different groups in this country." The bishop added that Bush "was looking for some ideas which he could put in his inaugural address that could make the country realize he is sincere about bringing the country together."[61]

Bush expressed those ideas in his inaugural address in January 2001. "In the quiet of American conscience, we know that deep, persistent poverty is unworthy of our nation's promise," said the new president. "Church and charity, synagogue and mosque lend our communities their humanity, and they will have an honored place" in the fight against poverty. The "compassion" portion of Bush's speech was its longest.[62] The next day Bush became the first president to accept an invitation to the residence of an American cardinal. "These are men of great faith, huge compassion for the poor and the oppressed," Bush described the Washington, D.C., cardinal-designate, Rev. Theodore McCarrick, who extended the invitation, as well as his predecessor, James Cardinal Hickey; the papal nuncio, Archbishop Gabriel Montalvo; and Bishop William Lori of Bridgeport, Connecticut, who accepted it. The dinner helped lead to McCarrick's endorsement of Bush's faith-based initiative, as long as it did not become "an excuse for the government to abandon its own responsibilities to the poor."[63]

The president did not see that happening. The federal government "will never be replaced by charities and community groups," Bush assured a gathering of Catholics, Protestants, Jews, Muslims, and nonbelievers at the White House on January 29. Yet "when we see social needs in America," his administration would "look first to faith-based programs and community groups, which have proven their power to save and change lives." To fulfill that objective, the president signed two executive orders creating a White House Office of Faith-Based and Community Initiatives and instituting branches in the

Departments of Housing and Urban Development, Labor, and Education to implement the office's programs. Bush appointed DiIulio to head the new office for six months until, as he requested, he would return to academia.[64]

"On your faith-based initiative," a reporter queried Bush after his announcement, "could you address the concern that some people have that this is an erosion of [the separation of] church and state, and that this will somehow be an office of evangelicals in the White House?" Bush answered the first part of the question. "I am convinced that our plan is constitutional," he explained, because "we will not fund a church or a synagogue or a mosque or any religion but instead will be funding programs that affect people in a positive way."[65] Had the president chosen to answer the second part of the reporter's question—the part about evangelicals dominating the faith-based initiative—he might have simply pointed to the Catholic who would head the office or the thirty other Catholics with whom he was to discuss the subject the next day. "The president and his advisors know very well that for their faith-based program to work it must establish a full partnership with existing Catholic social service providers," explained Deal Hudson, who helped arrange the meeting. Another attendee, Archbishop Charles Chaput of Denver, praised Bush for having the "courage to raise these issues in a new and helpful way." He urged his fellow Catholics to "give the president's creative programs a hearing and hope for their success."[66]

"We listened to him and he listened to us," said Rev. Edward Egan, the cardinal-designate of New York. "The meeting was a dialogue, a conversation." Archbishop John Favarola of Miami said that Bush had reassured him that the faith-based initiative would augment rather than supplant the government's role. But Rev. Val Peter of Girls and Boys Town lamented that the president had not assuaged his concerns about the quality of the faith-based programs.[67] Father Peter need not worry, the president told the leaders of Catholic Charities in a White House meeting the following day. "During my travels around the country, I have been most impressed not only by the quality of leadership of the men and women who make up the Catholic hierarchy," said Bush, "but also the unwavering commitment to the poor and to the disadvantaged and to those who are unable to defend themselves."[68]

The hierarchy returned the compliment. "The men who wrote the United States Constitution never intended to erect a huge and impregnable wall of separation between church and state," Philadelphia's Anthony Cardinal Bevilacqua wrote in support of the administration's "expanded partnerships" between religion and government. "The United States Catholic Conference acknowledges President Bush's priority on overcoming poverty as he begins to lead our nation," Roger Cardinal Mahony of Los Angeles, the chairman of the bishops' Domestic Policy Committee, added. Mahony looked forward to "a fuller dialogue on the specifics of the initiative."[69]

The dialogue had already begun. On February 27, addressing a joint session of Congress on the goals of his administration, Bush promoted his plan to allow non-itemizing taxpayers to deduct their charitable contributions, a reform of the tax code that he claimed would encourage as much as $14 billion in new philanthropy. He also committed $700 million over ten years to a federal Compassion Capital Fund, which would fund existing faith-based efforts against illiteracy, teen pregnancy, and drug addiction, and would implement DiIulio's proposal of adult mentors for the children of prisoners. Bush promised that his "mission" would be a "focused and narrow" one.[70]

The Campaign

The Bush faith-based initiative was off to a running start in the American Catholic community. "Churches do a great deal of good for considerably less resource investment than we pay via other institutional means," DiIulio contended, and many of his fellow Catholics agreed. "Faith-based institutions not only work better than their secular counterparts," said William Donohue, head of the Catholic League for Religious and Civil Rights, "they do so at a fraction of the cost." Eighty-one percent of Catholics polled by the Pew Research Center in March 2001 "favored allowing faith-based groups to apply for government funding."[71]

Those who had studied existing faith-based programs, however, could find no reason for such enthusiasm. If DiIulio was part preacher, he was all professor, and one of the conditions of his accepting the position in the Bush administration was that no legislation precede an unprecedented review of federal funding of religious groups.[72]

DiIulio would get his review, but not before the introduction of faith-based legislation. Rather than wait and devise a bill of its own, the administration allowed Republican J. C. Watts of Oklahoma and Democrat Tony Hall of Ohio, along with forty-four co-sponsors, to offer H.R. 7, the Community Solutions Act of 2001. The bill, which originated in the House Joint Committee on Taxation in March, included tax deductions for charitable donations by non-itemizing taxpayers and "individual development accounts" for low-income earners, which allocated up to $500 a year for "higher education, first-time home buying, business capitalization, roll-overs, or death benefit pay-outs." But there was no mention of Bush's Compassion Capital Fund, or the money to finance it.[73]

"The Catholic Church is fortunate to have such strong, capable, decent leadership," the president said as he welcomed about sixty bishops to the White

House in March, hailing the Church's "universal care for the weak and suffering." Then, in what had become a political rite of passage for U.S. presidents or presidential candidates, Bush spoke at the University of Notre Dame in May. After the obligatory quip about the former university president Rev. Theodore Hesburgh's record haul of honorary degrees, Bush added federal programs promoting homeownership and providing drug treatment to his faith-based proposal. Like his father a decade earlier, he criticized the unfulfilled promise of Lyndon Johnson's War on Poverty. But he moved beyond the private voluntarism of his father's "thousand points of light" to the public policy of his own "armies of compassion." The first President George Bush had assailed the War on Poverty because it had not been effective. The second President George Bush was attacking it because it had not been inclusive. "The War on Poverty turned too many citizens into bystanders," he lamented, "convinced that compassion had become the work of government alone." Noting that public money already helped to fund faith-based groups like Catholic Charities, Bush wondered of his opponents, "Do the critics really want to cut them off?"[74]

The bishops didn't. Decrying the "polarized ideological" opposition to the faith-based initiative by liberals wary of religion overtaking government and conservatives fearful of government overtaking religion, Los Angeles's Roger Cardinal Mahony spoke for his fellow prelates in a June endorsement of H.R. 7. Two weeks later the president thanked the bishops for their support of the House bill in a speech that also acknowledged the backing of the Church of God in Christ, the Prison Fellowship, Alianza Ministerial Evangelical Nacional, Latino ministries, and the Salvation Army.[75]

Two days after Bush said that there was "no more important initiative" than his faith-based proposal, the bill passed the House in July, 233–198, along a near party line vote. The president praised the House action, prodding the Senate to "act quickly to unleash this enormous force for good." The bishops also approved, entreating the Senate to "look beyond partisan politics in its work on companion legislation."[76]

In August came the release of the report DiIulio had demanded. Titled *Unlevel Playing Field*, it confirmed what DiIulio and Bush had been saying all along—that the government had underfunded religious organizations that offered social services. The report also revealed that the government had undercounted them, with members of the administration unsure of which groups were or were not faith-based. With the review completed, DiIulio could do as he promised, albeit two months late—resign and return to campus.[77]

As it did to just about everything else, the September 11 terrorist attacks on the United States diverted attention from the faith-based initiative, as Bush spoke and acted less often on his "compassion" agenda. The attention returned in February 2002 with Bush's appointment of DiIulio's replacement, a Catholic Democratic attorney named James Towey. DiIulio's compassion had linked him to Mother Teresa, while Towey's caseload had connected him to Mother Teresa, as her legal counsel for twelve years. Bush would muse that in the litigious climate of the day, "even Mother Teresa needs a lawyer."[78]

The new year also brought a new bill, S. 192, the Charity, Aid, Recovery, and Empowerment Act (CARE), introduced by Bush, Jewish Democratic senator Joe Lieberman of Connecticut, and Catholic Republican senator Rick Santorum of Pennsylvania at a White House meeting in February. CARE included a "large charitable deduction for non-itemizers, new provisions to encourage contributions from individual retirement accounts, a large increase in social service block grants, expanded individual development accounts, compassion capital funds, and a few narrowly tailored 'religious freedom' provisions."[79]

In March the Department of Housing and Urban Development, acting on the recommendations of the *Unlevel Playing Field* report, facilitated the provision of faith-based social services for the residents of public housing. In April the Department of Labor expanded job training and counseling programs to include religious groups. In May Americans for Community and Faith-Centered Enterprise, a conservative group headed by Catholic philanthropist Michael Joyce, organized a CARE Advocacy Day on which about six hundred activists descended on the nation's capital to lobby senators to pass the faith-based bill. In June Catholic Democratic senator John Kerry of Massachusetts, despite his misgivings about the non-itemizer deduction, endorsed the whole bill. Yet despite all of this activity, CARE died before the completion of the 2002 congressional session.[80]

The Alternative

But the faith-based initiative was still alive. "As Catholics, we must come together with a common conviction that we can no longer tolerate the moral scandal of poverty in our land," the bishops declared in their November 2002 pastoral, "A Place at the Table: A Catholic Recommitment to Overcome Poverty and to Respect the Dignity of All God's Children." They added, "In the United States the growing attention to faith-based and other community institutions is overdue recognition of the work of Catholic schools, Catholic health care institutions, Catholic Charities, the Catholic Campaign for Human Development, and other groups."[81]

And if Congress was not going to provide that recognition, the president would do it himself. In December 2002, with Anthony Cardinal Bevilacqua among those in attendance at the White House Conference on Faith-Based and Community Initiatives in Philadelphia, Bush issued an executive order prohibiting discrimination against religious organizations in the distribution of federal funds for social services, establishing offices for faith-based initiatives in the Department of Agriculture and the Agency for International Development, and including church groups as recipients of disaster relief.[82]

At over a dozen conferences attended by more than twenty thousand religious and community leaders, members of his administration instructed social service organizations in the art of receiving. At the White House Conference on Faith-Based and Community Initiatives in Washington in June 2004, the president did the teaching himself. He assured an audience that included Archbishop Harry Flynn of Minneapolis, Bishop Donald Wuerl of Pittsburgh, and Mark Franken, the executive director of the United States Conference of Catholic Bishops' Migration and Refugee Services, that "there's a lot more money available."[83]

And there was. At the Knights of Columbus convention in Dallas in August, Bush announced federal grants of $45.5 million to religious and community organizations to provide adult mentors to children of prisoners; $43 million to help fund soup kitchens, homeless shelters, drug treatment centers, and job training programs; and $100 million to states and Indian tribes for drug treatment vouchers. "Jeb knows, as I do, that your works of mercy are making our society more compassionate, changing the lives of millions of citizens," the president told the gathering, invoking the name of his brother, the Florida governor, who was not only a Catholic but a third degree knight. The audience, which included New York's Edward Cardinal Egan and Washington, D.C.'s Theodore Cardinal McCarrick, responded with several standing ovations.[84]

Senator Kerry did not have any dollars to dispense, but he was not above pandering to his fellow Catholics. In the October 8 presidential candidates' debate in St. Louis, Kerry described himself as a "Catholic" whose "faith affects everything I do," particularly "[my] fight against poverty." The Massachusetts senator was not only a Catholic, but he had been an altar boy, a credential Bush's brother, an adult convert, couldn't claim. And just in case any Catholics had missed the reference, Kerry repeated it in the next debate.[85]

In a speech in Fort Lauderdale less than two weeks before the election, Kerry finally spoke as a Catholic first, a candidate second. He invoked Catholic social teaching in explaining how his commitments to "solidarity" and the "common good" had "sustained me in the best and worst of times," and "which I will carry with me every day as president." Perhaps he had to. A poll showed that a majority of Catholics didn't even know that Kerry was one of them.[86]

While the Catholic presidential candidate was suddenly flaunting his religion to attract voters, his Methodist rival was suddenly downplaying his to avoid scaring them away. In the first two weeks of his tenure Bush had mentioned God over twenty times. In the last two weeks before the election he mentioned God hardly at all. "He's commander-in-chief, not chaplain-in-chief," Towey told the convention of the Religious Newswriters Association in Washington. "I haven't seen him lost in prayer or levitating."[87]

In the end, both candidates' religiosity and support for a faith-based initiative largely neutralized those factors in the November election. While most churchgoers selected Bush and most nonbelievers sided with Kerry, their votes had a lot more to do with Iraq, terrorism, and the economy. On these issues, most Americans, and most Catholics, opted to stay the course.[88] So the incumbent who had worn religion on his sleeve until election eve defeated the challenger who had kept religion up his sleeve until election eve. "I was always wary of people who used faith as a political weapon," Bush would write in his memoir, prolonging the October charade. Then he quoted the Bible.[89]

Conclusions on Social Justice

The historical jury on the faith-based initiative—and the Catholic role in it—is still out. But the early indicators were mostly positive. The inability of the Bush administration to pass the program through Congress, however, produced much soul-searching, considerable hand-wringing, and a lot of scapegoating. To the Catholic conservative Joseph Bottum of *First Things*, Bush's faith-based initiative "collapsed into a clown show of political missteps, fumbled chances, and administrative infighting."[90]

Some blamed the president. In a December 2002 interview with *Esquire* reporter Ron Suskind, DiIulio criticized Karl Rove and Bush's political team for rushing to endorse H.R. 7 without adequate planning or funding. In his 2006 book David Kuo, Towey's deputy director, charged that Bush had put his mouth where his money wasn't. In his memoir Bush would claim that his faith-based initiative had expended $20 billion in eight years, a number that Kuo would surely challenge.[91]

One could also blame Catholics. Though they strongly backed the initiative, the bishops and other Catholics at times acted as if their hearts were not in the fight. Part of the reason was the political discomfort of backing a Republican president who, when he wasn't singing the praises of faith-based social services, was attacking the alleged waste in non-faith-based social services. And Bush's attempt to blur the distinction between the two so as to inflate the tallies of his faith-based spending (as he did in a May 2001 speech to the leaders of Hispanic faith-based organizations) did not please many in the

Catholic community. The October 2001 Senate testimony by Catholic Charities coupled a firm endorsement of the faith-based initiative with an equally pointed disclaimer that it had other priorities, such as universal health insurance and a repeal of tax cuts for the wealthy, both of which Bush opposed. While the United States Conference of Catholic Bishops "has been a strong and consistent supporter of the president's community and faith-based initiative," the USCCB's president, Bishop Wilton Gregory of Illinois, wrote to the members of the Senate in March 2003, it "must be accompanied by a commitment to adequate funding of these programs." A majority of Hispanic Catholics and "committed" non-Hispanic Catholics in a 2004 Pew survey believed that "the government should help the needy, even if it means more debt."[92]

Another piece of the explanation for Catholic culpability in the demise of Bush's faith-based legislation was that maybe Catholics just didn't need it. There was a "sense that we're already doing this," said Timothy Goeglein, Bush's deputy director of the White House Office of Public Liaison, recalling the attitudes of some Catholic organizations toward the administration's project. In 1999, two-thirds of Catholic Charities' $2.3 billion budget came from government. So opening the federal coffers to competitors might have meant less, not more, cash for Catholic Charities. No wonder Catholic Charities took no position on H.R. 7 two years later. "The focus of this debate should be on the needs on the poor," Towey said, welcoming this competition. But Catholic Charities did not.[93]

Yet another possible reason for the less-than-robust endorsement of the faith-based initiative by Catholic groups was that some of them weren't that Catholic anyway. In 1996, Catholic Charities received 64 percent of its funding from federal, state, and local governments, and only 5 percent from the Catholic Church. A 2003 study by the psychologist Charles Degeneffe of California State University discovered that local chapters of Catholic Charities varied greatly in the extent to which they followed Church teachings on such matters as abortion and contraception.[94] That is, if such teachings still existed. In their 2004 research Daniel Rigney, Jerome Matz, and Armando Abney found "little empirical support for the existence of a distinctive Catholic ethic of sharing as reflected in self-reported volunteer behavior." No wonder that only a third of American Catholics in that presidential election year said that they even occasionally cast faith-based votes.[95]

If Catholics did not seem to be learning, perhaps it was because their teachers were not teaching. The sexual abuse scandal that exploded in 2002 severely undercut the hierarchy's influence inside and outside the Church. Weekly church attendance declined from 52 percent of Catholics in 2000 to 35 percent in 2003, and donations from Catholics to the Church fell by half from 2002 to 2004. Seventy percent of Catholics in June 2004 said that the views of their bishops were not important factors to consider when they voted.[96]

So rather than the bishops commenting on the president, the president found himself commenting on the bishops. "I'm confident the church will clean up its business and do the right thing," Bush asserted in March 2002, before offering no opinion on whether his friend Bernard Cardinal Law of Boston should resign. Law *would* resign in December.[97]

He was not the only one. In 1986 Archbishop Rembert Weakland of Milwaukee had established himself as the hierarchy's leading advocate for the poor as the principal author of "Economic Justice for All," the bishops' stinging rebuke to Reaganomics. Yet in July 2002, when President Bush came to Milwaukee to promote his faith-based outreach to the poor, Weakland was nowhere to be found. Already under suspicion for a lax response to the predator priests of his archdiocese, Weakland had resigned in disgrace two months earlier, when an extortion scheme by a man who accused the archbishop of sexual assault become public.[98]

Yet despite this unfortunate alignment of forces inside the Bush administration, on the Right and the Left, and within the Catholic Church, it is nonetheless plausible to portray the faith-based initiative as a success for President Bush and for American Catholics. However one splits the difference between Bush's exuberance and Kuo's exasperation, between disciple DiIulio's inspiration and dissident DiIulio's indignation, billions of dollars flowed from the president's executive orders and the office he created.

And if the Catholic hands receiving much of that money bore the calluses of doubt and division, they had nonetheless endured and even grown stronger in the face of adversity. In 1997, only five years before the scandal broke, Catholics ages twenty to thirty-nine considered "the sacraments" and "devotion to Mary" two of the three "most essential" elements of their faith. The third was "special attention to helping the poor." A majority of Catholic voters in 2000 wanted the new president to "spend more on hunger." A 2001 poll by the bishops' Catholic Campaign for Human Development discovered that half the general public was more committed to helping the poor after September 11 than before. In the same year, a Public Agenda poll found that almost half the general public understood the fundamental beliefs of Catholicism, almost double their knowledge of any other religion.[99]

Even after the scandal, American Catholics displayed uncommon resilience. In their November 2002 pastoral the bishops reminded American Catholics that the Church was "the largest nongovernmental provider of education, health care and human services in our nation." Their increasingly poor and Latino congregations needed no such reminder. In 2004, two years after the scandal broke, two-thirds of the readers of *U.S. Catholic* were still donating to the bishops' annual appeal.[100]

Despite the scandal, conservative Brian Simboli wrote in the *American Spectator* in June 2003, there was still an identifiable "Catholic vision," composed of "interlocking societies, organizations, and communities that mediate between the twin dangers of monolithic statism and the atomizing individualism of capitalism gone awry." The bishops, liberal and conservative alike, agreed. "Our own public struggles, shortcomings, and inconsistencies," Los Angeles's Roger Cardinal Mahony spoke for his fellow prelates in October 2003, "do not negate a centuries-old tradition." The bishops invoked that tradition in their pre-election-year document "Faithful Citizenship" in 2003.[101] This tradition had not just been a major influence on Bush's 2000 campaign, but it remained a key ingredient of his presidency. William McGurn, a Catholic Bush speechwriter, would quip that the president had more Catholics writing his speeches than were in "any Notre Dame starting line-up in the past half-century." Bush's Republican fealty to "federalism," *U.S. Catholic* senior editor Kevin Clarke would note at the end of his first term, "makes a good fit with Catholic social teaching's concept of subsidiarity, essentially the notion that justice and communities are best served when the appropriate level of government authority is displayed to most effectively deal with a social problem." DiIulio was more succinct. He simply said that Bush "intuitively got" Catholic social teaching.[102]

Although he could have spent more time, money, and political capital on his faith-based effort, with greater opportunities to serve the needy and to assist those Catholics who ministered to them, Bush achieved gains not so easily measured. "We're trying to change the culture of Washington to welcome people of faith in helping meet social objectives," he told the White House Conference on Faith-Based and Community Initiatives in Los Angeles in March 2004. In many ways he was already effecting such a metamorphosis. Professor Robert Tuttle of the George Washington University School of Law judged the Bush initiative "a success that doesn't really have a parallel in contemporary administrative law, where you have a complete change in culture."[103]

At the beginning of the Bush administration 40 percent of Americans believed that churches better fed the homeless, while only 28 percent thought that governments were more effective. By the end of Bush's second term, 52 percent would say "churches," and only 21 percent would say "governments." Thus did Bush redefine Christian conservatism, the Heritage Foundation's Joseph LoConte applauded in *First Things* in May 2002, from a "politics of protest" to a "fuller portrait of the faithful." As a result, "religious charities are regularly invited to congressional hearings, get frequent presidential visits, enjoy lots of favorable media, and are the hottest topic at conferences on religion in America."[104]

Bush's culture change overcame sectarian barriers and traversed party lines. "Bush was able to cut a path between conservatives in his own party who oppose activist government, and liberal Democrats, whose defense of existing programs ironically painted them as conservatives," the political scientists John Wells of Carson Newman College and David Cohen of the University of Akron would decide. "The CARE Act isn't a Republican or Democratic plan," Bush quoted the Catholic Democratic Senate majority leader, Tom Daschle of South Dakota, in his speech at Holy Redeemer Institutional Church of Christ in Milwaukee in July 2002. "It's a bipartisan proposal that strikes the right balance between harnessing the forces of faith in our public life without infringing on the First Amendment." CARE would not pass the Senate, but Bush's and Daschle's sentiments would ultimately carry the day.[105]

The evidence was overwhelming. The Bush administration, according to a study by the Nelson Rockefeller Institute of Government's Roundtable on Religion and Social Welfare Policy, had rewritten sixteen federal rules to "provide government services on a 'level playing field' with secular groups and without diminishing their religious character, [and] training and assistance [was] provided to more than 100,000 religious and secular grassroots organizations through regional conferences around the country." By 2008, thirty-three states and dozens of local governments had established faith-based programs. Bush's successor, liberal Democrat Barack Obama, would not only retain the federal Office of Faith-Based and Community Initiatives but would expand it. By 2009, large majorities from both parties, and more Democrats than Republicans, would support a federal faith-based initiative.[106]

When asked about his legacy almost four years into his presidency, three years after 9/11 and over a year into the Iraq war, Bush mentioned only one issue. "I believe that government ought to welcome faith-based programs that work," said the president, "and give them access to federal monies." Though the success of their missions and their accessibility to federal funds were hardly universal, faith-based organizations did become an important part of the Bush legacy. In his resignation letter two and a half years into the Bush presidency and two and a half years before his radical reassessment, David Kuo lauded the president's "unwavering support for this initiative." Six years after his resignation, DiIulio conceded that "faith-based is in the public vernacular. Some good things have happened. Certainly some very good things have happened at the state and local level."[107]

Although Bush and members of his administration did not secure faith-based legislation and made many mistakes along the way, the president's religious and rhetorical commitment to the issue enlisted many Catholic allies, helped him spend a few more Catholic dollars, and may have earned him a few more Catholic votes. Lay and clerical Catholic representatives, Bush's public liaison Timothy Goeglein would remember, were "extremely involved" in the Bush endeavor from inception through implementation, in a fitting climax to over four decades of growing Catholic participation in the political process.[108] While his critics were defending a wall, George W. Bush was building a bridge.

Life and Death: Abortion

At forty years of age, suffering through one more hangover and fearing for his marriage, George W. Bush swore off alcohol and accepted Jesus Christ as his personal savior. Yet he shunned the characterization "born again" and remained a Methodist. He resisted the urge to evangelize, and when he became president, he seldom even went to church.[109] Though his speeches were rife with theological references and his worldview seemed as much Old Testament as New World Order (a term used by the first President Bush), Bush's social conservatism fell short of fanaticism and rarely evinced passion. On abortion, he said all the right things and took several meaningful steps to promote what he called a "culture of life." But he not only was unable to reverse *Roe v. Wade*. He appeared unwilling to try.[110] As a result, President Bush forfeited a lot of goodwill in the American Catholic community. Though most Catholics supported him throughout his first term, and helped elect him to a second, they resigned themselves to Bush more than they rallied behind him.

The forty-third president, so inwardly religious and outwardly self-righteous, came up short on the highest moral priority for the Catholic leadership and many of its followers. In a presidency that aspired to big things, abortion had seldom seemed so small.

An Old Beginning

With the return of a pro-life Republican president after eight years of a pro-choice Democrat, the incoming administration spent its early days trying to restore what the outgoing administration had removed. Only two days after his inauguration, George W. Bush followed the precedent established by Ronald Reagan by addressing the annual March for Life on the anniversary of *Roe v. Wade*. Like Reagan and the first President Bush, however, he chose to do so from a politically secure distance. "We share a great goal," said a statement issued by the White House to the protesters, "to work toward a day when every child is welcomed in life and protected in law."¹¹¹

Bush followed this statement five days later with his first executive order, reinstating Reagan's Mexico City policy, which Bill Clinton had rescinded eight years before. As a result no U.S. funds could finance abortions abroad. In April the Department of Health and Human Services limited the use of the abortion pill RU-486 to "extreme circumstances," and added that state requirements such as a twenty-four-hour waiting period, parental notification, and counseling should apply to RU-486. The administration also closed Clinton's White House Office for Women's Initiatives and Outreach, which it considered a refuge for pro-choice activists.¹¹²

The president and the Catholic hierarchy shared the stage that same month at the unveiling of the Pope John Paul II Cultural Center in Washington. "In the culture of life we must make room for the stranger. We must comfort the sick. We must care for the aged. We must welcome the immigrant. We must teach our children to be gentle with one another," Bush addressed an audience that included the seven American cardinals. "We must defend in love the innocent child waiting to be born."¹¹³ In his remarks Adam Cardinal Maida of Detroit explained why Pope John Paul II had wanted the center to be in Washington rather than in Warsaw or Krakow in his home country of Poland. "He sees Washington, D.C.," the cardinal noted, "as the crossroads of the world."¹¹⁴

In July Bush bestowed the Congressional Gold Medal on the late John Cardinal O'Connor of New York. Bush called the cardinal "the gallant defender of children and their vulnerability, innocence, and right to be born."¹¹⁵

A New Turn

The "right to be born" was very much on the president's mind as his administration grappled with the contentious concern about the federal funding of embryonic stem cell research, which Bush had opposed during the campaign but which advocates viewed as a potential avenue toward a cure for such fatal diseases as Alzheimer's and Parkinson's. Vice President Dick Cheney and Chief of Staff Andrew Card were among those inside the administration lobbying for such funding. Nancy Reagan, who lost her husband, the former pro-life Republican president, to Alzheimer's, was among its most vocal proponents outside the White House.¹¹⁶

And Pope John Paul II, battling Parkinson's, was among its most vocal opponents. The Holy Father met with President Bush for the first time in August at Castel Gandolfo, the pope's summer residence southwest of Rome. The pontiff told the president that "proposals for the creation for research purposes of human embryos destined to destruction in the process" demonstrated a "tragic coarsening of conscience." Lest anyone misinterpret the pope's words as permitting research on existing stem cell lines formed from previously destroyed embryos, the Vatican issued, and the American bishops released, a clarification later in the day.[117]

John Paul II wasn't making Bush's impending decision any easier. "Mr. President, was it a surprise for you to hear today from the Holy Father on his declaration on manipulations of embryos?" a reporter asked Bush after the meeting. The president maintained that it was not, explaining that "I hear that message from his cardinals and bishops . . . throughout our country. One of the things about the Catholic Church that I admire [is that] it's a church that stands on consistent and solid principle." "Frankly I do not care what the political polls say," Bush had said earlier, referring to the choice he was about to make. "I do care about the opinions of people, particularly someone as profound as the Holy Father."[118]

The president's much-anticipated decision in late August, however, was no closer to the pope than to the polls. "As I thought about this issue I kept referring to the fundamental questions," said Bush. "First, are these frozen embryos human life and therefore something precious to be protected? And second, if they're going to be destroyed anyway, shouldn't they be used for a greater good, for research that has the potential to save and improve other lives?" Heeding the counsel of his Catholic secretary of Health and Human Services, Tommy Thompson, Bush answered both questions affirmatively, prohibiting federal funding of research on new stem cell lines while allowing federal dollars to continue research on the over sixty existing stem cell lines already created from aborted fetuses. Thus did the president's executive order offend not only Pope John Paul II, but the majority of Americans, including most white Catholics, who did not favor the federal funding of any stem cell research.[119]

Bush's "trade-off" between permitting the bankrolling of old stem cell lines while preventing the subsidizing of new lines was "morally unacceptable" to Bishop Joseph Fiorenza of Galveston-Houston, the president of the bishops' conference. "The existing stem cell lines to be used for federally financed research have themselves come from deliberately destroyed embryos," William Cardinal Keeler of Baltimore, chairman of the United States Conference of Catholic Bishops' Committee for Pro-Life Activities, protested, "and the researchers who destroyed them will profit from the new federal policy." Cardinals Edward Egan of New York, Anthony Bevilacqua of Philadelphia, and Bernard Law of Boston, as well as Donald Shea of the National Right to Life Committee, Rev. Michael Place of the Catholic Hospital Association, and Carl Anderson of the Knights of Columbus added their voices to the chorus of Catholic criticism of the Bush directive. Msgr. John Stynkowski, the executive director of the bishops' Secretariat for Doctrine and Pastoral Practices, pointedly reminded the president of the pope's largely futile plea at Castel Gandolfo.[120]

In January 2002 Bush telephoned the protesters at the March for Life. "My Administration opposes partial-birth abortion and public funding for abortions," said the president, adding that it supported "teen abstinence and crisis pregnancy programs" as well as "adoption and parental notification laws." Speaking from a manufacturing plant in West Virginia, Bush promised to sign a cloning ban that had overwhelmingly passed the House and was certain to pass the Senate. He made no mention of stem cell research.[121]

The Church Becomes Distracted

While the president was compromising on matters of life and death, the U.S. Catholic bishops were compromising their own moral standing. The American Church's sexual abuse scandal, which originated in Boston in January 2002 and would implicate over eleven thousand priests in 95 percent of the country's dioceses, raised the hierarchy's profile in uncomfortable ways. In April Pope John Paul II summoned the American bishops to Rome for an extraordinary meeting to address the crisis.[122]

When the bishops returned home, their anti-abortion activities largely occurred out of the public eye. They quietly sent a letter to the Department of Health and Human Services supporting its new rule including unborn children in the benefits of the Clinton-era State Children's Health Insurance Program, which had expanded health insurance for low-income children under nineteen years old. For the first time, a federal policy defined life as beginning at conception. The National Right to Life Committee and the Catholic Health Association added their endorsements of the change. When pro-choice groups objected to the new policy, HHS secretary Thompson insisted that it had nothing to do with abortion.[123]

With the bishops nursing their self-inflicted wounds, some American Catholics looked to the pope to fill the leadership void in the pro-life struggle. Yet John Paul II appeared neither willing nor able. He met with Bush again in Rome at the end of May, but this time there was no public counsel for the pope to offer and the president to reject. In July the pontiff traveled to North America—but not to the United States.[124] In August in his native Poland, the pope lamented that "frequently man . . . claims for himself the Creator's right to interfere in the mystery of human life." When some members of the audience exhorted the pope to "stay with us" and not return to the Vatican, the Holy Father joked that "they're trying to get me to abandon Rome."[125]

Many American Catholics had already abandoned Rome. According to a 2002 CBS News/*New York Times* poll, one-third of American Catholics would outlaw all abortions, 40 percent would accept some limits on abortion, and one-quarter would support the "general availability" of abortion.[126]

Slowly Moving Forward

In August 2002 in Pittsburgh, after it passed by voice vote in the House of Representatives and unanimous consent in the Senate, Bush signed the Born-Alive Infants Protection Act. The legislation, co-sponsored by Catholic Republican senator Rick Santorum of Pennsylvania and Catholic representative Steve Chabot of Ohio and backed through letters to Congress by the bishops, provided legal safeguards for infants born alive following the failure of induced abortion. So on January 22, 2003, when he telephoned the March for Life from St. Louis, Bush could cite one more piece of evidence that "we're making progress" in fulfilling a "commitment to building a culture of life in America." He also added the prevention of "the destruction of embryos from stem cell research" to the litany of his administration's strides against abortion. Bush didn't mention the part of his controversial executive order with which the marchers disagreed. And on the thirtieth anniversary of *Roe v. Wade*, the pro-life president made no mention of *Roe v. Wade*.[127]

And why should he? A November 2002 survey by the Catholic conservative periodical *Crisis* unearthed only 36 percent of "inactive" Catholics and 55 percent of "active" Catholics in favor of "enacting legal restrictions on abortion in order to reduce the number of abortions being performed." A Gallup Poll marking *Roe*'s three decades found that 53 percent of Americans considered the decision legalizing abortion a "good thing" for the country. Almost halfway through Bush's first term, only 30 percent thought it was a "bad thing."[128]

Overwhelming numbers of Americans, however, believed that "partial-birth" abortion was a bad thing. A late October 2003 Gallup/*USA Today* poll showed that 77 percent of Americans ages eighteen to twenty-nine and 68 percent of those ages thirty and older wanted a ban on the late-term procedure formally known as "intact dilation and evacuation." After such a prohibition easily passed both houses of Congress, Bush signed it in November 2003. "The best case against partial-birth abortion is a simple description of what happens," the president explained as Edward Cardinal Egan of New York looked on. "It involves the partial delivery of a live boy or girl, and a sudden, violent end of that life."[129]

Denver archbishop Charles Caput, the chairman of the United States Conference of Catholic Bishops' Committee for Pro-Life Activities, which had testified in favor of such a ban in 1996 and had sent letters to Congress in 2003 urging its passage, conveyed the "deep gratitude" of the bishops to the president "for signing into law a ban on one of the most inhumane procedures ever inflicted on a human child." The Knights of Columbus's Carl Anderson applauded "President Bush and Congress for enacting a Partial Birth Abortion Ban" and rewarding "the firm and unwavering resolve" of the "American people" to enact it. But an amendment to the legislation sponsored by Iowa Catholic Democrat Tom Harkin, which endorsed *Roe v. Wade*, passed the Republican-controlled Senate, 52–46. "We won't stand by silently," Kim Gandy, the Catholic president of the pro-choice National Organization for Women, said in reaction to the votes, "as this Administration attempts to erode our rights."[130]

The bishops were not standing by either. Though large numbers of American Catholics had long defied the Church's proscription of artificial contraception, the bishops' Committee for Pro-Life Activities launched a new attempt to epoxy contraception to abortion at their November meeting in Washington.[131] Also discussed at the meeting was the "Doctrinal Note on Some Questions regarding the Participation of Catholics in Political Life," which the Vatican's Congregation of the Doctrine of the Faith, headed by Joseph Cardinal Ratzinger of Germany, had issued the previous year. The note said that Catholic legislators had a "grave and clear obligation to oppose any law that attacks human life. For them as any Catholic, it is impossible to promote such laws or vote for them." So the bishops appointed a task force, to be chaired by Washington's Theodore Cardinal McCarrick, to determine their proper response to those Catholics who violated this instruction.[132]

Two months later the March for Life was in Washington, and the president was not. For the third consecutive year Bush addressed the marchers by telephone, this time adding the Partial-Birth Abortion Ban Act of 2003 to the list of his administration's efforts to protect the unborn. For the fourth consecutive year, Bush did not allude to overturning *Roe v. Wade*, the cause about which the marchers cared most.[133]

The Church Becomes a Distraction

If the president was reluctant to press the fight against *Roe v. Wade*, some bishops were not. Just before his installation as the archbishop of St. Louis, Bishop Raymond Burke gave the pro-choice Catholic lawmakers of his Wisconsin diocese a going-away gift they had not requested. "Catholic legislators who are members of the faithful of the Diocese of La Crosse and who continue to support procured abortion or euthanasia may not present themselves to receive

Holy Communion," the bishop announced in January 2004, not waiting for the McCarrick task force's report. Among the targets of Burke's canonical notification was veteran Democratic congressman David Obey.[134]

Boston archbishop Sean O'Malley, who had replaced the beleaguered Bernard Cardinal Law, saw the Burke edict as an opportunity for dialogue. He agreed with Burke that pro-choice Catholic politicians should not be receiving communion, but he was not going to try to prevent them. "A priest or a Eucharistic minister is not a police officer," O'Malley spokesman Rev. Christopher Coyne countered. "The proper place for a conversation is not in a communion line, but before or after."[135]

Perhaps the most famous communicant in O'Malley's archdiocese was Senator John Kerry, now the frontrunner for the Democratic presidential nomination, who had received the sacrament at O'Malley's installation the previous July. Kerry was so proud of his pro-choice credentials that he inflated them, erroneously claiming that his first speech as a senator was in defense of a woman's right to an abortion.[136]

In February 2004 Bush heartened the pro-life community when his commissioner of the Food and Drug Administration, Dr. Mark McClellan, refused to make "Plan B," the "morning-after" pill that prevents pregnancy after sexual intercourse, available without a prescription. In March, after the conservative *Crisis* editor and Bush advisor Deal Hudson objected to Ono Ekeh's position as the founder and moderator of the Catholics for Kerry email discussion list, Ekeh, the pro-choice program coordinator for the USCCB's Secretariat for African-American Catholics, lost his job. Kerry took time off from his presidential campaign to cast a rare vote on the Senate floor, against a bill that would make harming a fetus a separate offense during the commission of a crime. The measure nonetheless easily passed the Senate, as it had the House. "We applaud the Senate for voting for justice for women and their children," said Cathy Cleaver Rose, the director of planning and information for the bishops' Secretariat for Pro-Life Activities, which had sent letters to both houses of Congress urging passage. "No woman should ever be told she lost nothing when she loses her child to a brutal attacker."[137]

When Bush signed the Unborn Victims of Violence Act in April, for the first time federal law recognized what statutes in thirty-four states had already acknowledged—that a fetus is a "person," and when a fetus dies during a crime, the perpetrator has committed a homicide. If the pregnant woman also dies, the perpetrator has committed a double homicide.[138]

Three months after Bush had been a no-show at the March for Life, Kerry was a featured speaker at the NARAL Pro-Choice America March for Women's Lives in Washington. As Kerry resumed his campaign, the McCarrick task force continued its deliberations. In April a task force member, Bishop John Ricard of Pensacola-Tallahassee, was part of a delegation of prelates from Florida, Georgia, North Carolina, and South Carolina that visited the Vatican in April. "They are basically struggling with this, as we are," said Ricard of the process that had begun in Rome two years earlier.[139]

The U.S. bishops would have to struggle some more. "The norm of the Church is clear," Francis Cardinal Arinze of Nigeria, the prefect of the Congregation for Divine Worship and the Discipline of the Sacraments, proclaimed at a news conference in Rome three weeks after the bishops departed. Since pro-choice Catholic politicians were "not fit" to partake in communion, the bishops should not allow them to do so. "If they should not receive," said Cardinal Arinze, "they should not be given." Bishops Fabian Bruskewitz of Lincoln, Nebraska, and Joseph Galante of Camden, New Jersey, reacted to the cardinal's statement with approval, announcing that they would be denying communion to pro-choice Catholic politicians in their dioceses. Bishop Wilton Gregory of Belleville, Illinois, the president of the United States Conference of Catholic Bishops, reacted to the cardinal's statement with equivocation. "Each diocesan bishop has the right and duty to address such issues of serious pastoral concern as he judges best in his local church," the bishop waffled, "in accord with pastoral and canonical norms." Senator Kerry reacted to the cardinal's statement with defiance. "We are going to have a change of leadership in this country," said the senator, while accepting the first-ever presidential endorsement of the Planned Parenthood Action Fund, "to protect the right of choice."[140]

Cardinals McCarrick and Roger Mahony of Los Angeles responded to Cardinal Arinze with sympathy—for Kerry. McCarrick said that after speaking to the cardinal in Rome, he interpreted Arinze's remarks as suggesting that Kerry should voluntarily forgo communion. "Your goal is to bring them to the faith," McCarrick spokesperson Susan Gibbs observed after the cardinal's meeting with the senator in May, adding that McCarrick had no plans to deny communion to any pro-choice Catholic legislators. "I do not favor a confrontation at the altar rail," Cardinal Mahony agreed after his meeting with Kerry, "with the sacred body of the Lord Jesus in my hand." Francis Cardinal George of Chicago quipped, "I've been asked that question so often lately that I have considered a policy of denying communion to reporters."[141]

All the attention being paid to Kerry and other pro-choice Catholic office-holders had obscured the other potential offenders: the Catholics who voted for them. Colorado seemed a good place to revive this half of the communion equation. After all, that state was the home of Denver archbishop Charles

Caput, a Potawatomi whose name means "the wind that rustles the trees." As chairman of the bishops' Committee for Pro-Life Activities, he had written that "real Catholics" should determine whether candidates' positions on abortion were consistent with Church teaching, then "vote accordingly." It was also the home of Rev. Bill Carmody, a Catholic priest who had led the state's House of Representatives in prayer, imploring the members of the chamber to be "the antithesis of John Kerry" by "letting faith influence and guide every vote they take."[142] And Colorado was the home of Bishop Michael Sheridan of Colorado Springs, who announced in May that he would deny communion to any pro-choice Catholic in his diocese, whether or not they held public office. "I'm not making a political statement," said Bishop Sheridan. "I'm making a statement about Church teaching."[143]

Some Catholics thought that the bishop was doing both. In June forty-eight Catholic Democratic congressional representatives, led by minority leader Nancy Pelosi of California, wrote to Cardinal McCarrick requesting a meeting. "Allowing a bishop to take actions that lead to involvement in partisan politics," the mostly pro-choice legislators wrote, "would be detrimental to the Church." The Catholic liberal sociologist Rev. Andrew Greeley concurred. By concentrating so much on Kerry's abortion record, Father Greeley lamented, Bishop Sheridan and others "appear to be doing the Republican National Committee's work for it."[144]

Hoping to defuse the controversy, the bishops traveled to their June meeting in, of all places, Colorado. There the bishops debated the interim report of the McCarrick task force, titled "Catholics in Political Life." The report stated, "Our task force does not advocate the denial of communion for Catholic politicians or Catholic voters." But the task force also did not rule it out. "Every bishop has the right and duty to address these realities in his own diocese," the statement hedged. When the closed-door discussion was over, the bishops took a vote on the interim communiqué. There were 183 ayes, with only 6 nays. McCarrick's final report, to be issued after the November 2004 elections, would simply pass the interim findings on to the bishops' Doctrine Committee for more study. The support in Denver for denying communion to pro-choice politicians and voters turned out to be a mile high and an inch deep.[145]

And baffling all around. In July the Italian magazine *L'Espresso* published online the six-point memorandum that Joseph Cardinal Ratzinger, the prefect of the Vatican's Congregation for the Doctrine of Faith, had sent to Cardinal McCarrick to inform his task force of the pope's position on the communion question. Ratzinger's memo said that "a Catholic would be guilty of formal cooperation in evil, and so unworthy to present himself for Holy Communion, if he were to deliberately vote for a candidate precisely because of the candidate's permissive stand on abortion and/or euthanasia." It added, however, that "when a Catholic does not share a candidate's stand in favor of abortion and/or euthanasia, but votes for that candidate for other reasons, it is considered remote material cooperation, which can be permitted in the presence of proportionate reasons." The cardinal seemed to be saying that it was impermissible for a pro-choice Catholic to vote for a pro-choice candidate, but permissible for a pro-life Catholic to vote for a pro-choice candidate. No wonder the bishops were confused.[146]

Amid all the confusion, one thing seemed clear. The biggest winner in Denver wasn't even there. Not only did the Catholic bishops vote indecisively to welcome John Kerry to the altar rail, but three-quarters of the Catholics in a June *Time* poll voted decisively to do so. Perhaps most encouraging for Kerry was that, despite all the publicity surrounding the communion conundrum, still only a third of Americans knew that he was a Catholic.[147]

If John Kerry gained the most from the Denver meeting, George W. Bush may have gained the least. At Bush's request, the president had met with Pope John Paul II in Rome a week before the bishops' meeting. Bush applauded the pope's defense of "the unique dignity of every life," and the pope praised Bush's "promotion of moral values in American society, particularly with regard to respect for life." After his conversation with the pope, Bush talked with the Vatican secretary of state, Angelo Cardinal Soldano. "Not all the American bishops are with me," the president told the cardinal, imploring the Vatican to press the prelates to speak more forcefully and more frequently on "life" issues.[148]

A week later, even fewer of the American bishops were with Bush. The interim report of the McCarrick committee not only failed to censure Bush's November opponent, but it released a lot of air from the media balloon, which had directly damaged Kerry and indirectly benefited Bush. The longer the public focused on Kerry's battle with the bishops, the less it noticed Bush's negligible progress toward outlawing abortion. So Bush political advisor Karl Rove's frequent meetings with Deal Hudson and other Catholic conservatives had aimed to keep the dispute alive.[149] And the Democrats tried to kill it. Though the party adopted a pro-choice platform, as it had since 1976, it did so with little fanfare. Eager to put the communion furor behind them and to unite the party for the fall campaign, neither Kerry nor his running mate, the pro-choice North Carolina senator John Edwards, mentioned abortion in their acceptance speeches.[150]

President Bush didn't mention abortion either—at least not directly. Before attending his own party's convention, Bush stopped in Dallas for the conference of the Knights of Columbus. Bush's recollection of his most recent "awesome" meeting with Pope John Paul II, in which the Holy Father challenged "our nation and the entire world to embrace the culture of life," was the president's only allusion to abortion in his speech to the conservative Catholic fraternal organization, which did not invite Kerry. In his acceptance speech at the Republican National Convention in New York the next month, Bush devoted only one line to the subject. "Because a caring society will value its weakest members," said the president, "we must make a place for the unborn child."[151]

With the two major party presidential candidates trying to bury the abortion issue, it remained for the bishops to try to resurrect it. In August Bishop David Ricken of Cheyenne, Wyoming, issued "A Letter to Catholic Politicians and Public Officials on the Subject of Abortion and the Law." Writing "as a friend to those brave Catholic men and women in public life, in the legislature, and in public service," Ricken reflected more on law and science than on religion. Citing everyone from the late seventeenth-century English jurist Sir William Blackstone to the early twentieth-century U.S. justice Oliver Wendell Holmes, Ricken argued that the view of abortion as "a violent assault on human life" was "imbedded in the very fabric of civilized peoples, and can be held by civilized peoples apart from its religious context."[152]

The pro-choice rejoinder to Bishop Ricken arrived swiftly, delivered by another Catholic Democrat named Casey. Richard Casey, a blind federal judge for the Southern District of New York, was a graduate of Holy Cross College and Georgetown University Law School and had received the Blessed Hyacinth Cormier O.P. Medal from Pope John Paul II in Rome for his "outstanding leadership in the promotion of Gospel Values in the field of justice and ethics." At the end of August 2004, Judge Casey, who had granted a restraining order against the Partial-Birth Abortion Ban Act of 2003 the day after Bush signed it, rendered his judgment on the constitutionality of the measure. He agreed with Bishop Ricken that abortion—in this case "partial-birth" abortion—was "gruesome, brutal, barbaric, and uncivilized." But he disagreed that the Supreme Court had wrongly decided *Roe v. Wade* or *Stenberg v. Carhart*, the 2000 decision that repudiated Nebraska's partial-birth ban. "While medical science and ideology are no more happy companions than *Roe* and its progeny have shown law and ideology to be," wrote Casey, as if referring to Bishop Ricken's letter, "*Stenberg* remains the law of the land." And since the federal law, like the Nebraska statute, provided no exception to safeguard the health of the mother, it too was unconstitutional.[153]

Most Americans, and for the first time since 1924 an even greater percentage of Catholics, chose Bush in November. But they voted largely on the basis of other issues besides abortion. On this at least the president and the Catholic liberals who rejected him agreed: *Roe v. Wade* wasn't going away anytime soon. And although Bush's second term finally allowed him to make two appointments to the Supreme Court—pro-life Catholics John Roberts and Samuel Alito—it ended with *Roe* firmly intact. Even a Court with its first Catholic majority could not erase three decades of history. Catholics helped to reelect a pro-life president, but they couldn't reverse pro-choice precedent.[154]

The election of 2004 had been bittersweet for pro-life Catholics. George W. Bush went back to the White House. But John Kerry went back to communion.

Conclusions on Life and Death

It is easy to make the case that President George W. Bush's first term was a time of progress for most Catholics on the life-and-death matter of abortion. Yet it is easier to argue that Bush could have done more.

Pro-life Catholics could indeed point to several successes in the Bush administration. The restoration of the Mexico City policy, the restrictions on the use of the abortion pill RU-486, the broadened prohibition of federal funding of abortion (upheld by the U.S. Court of Appeals for the Federal Circuit in 2004), the Born-Alive Infants Protection Act, and the Partial-Birth Abortion Ban Act (upheld by the Supreme Court in 2007) significantly diluted the federal commitment to legal abortion. Bush also sided with pro-life Catholics in appointing pro-life judges and supporting informed consent state abortion laws, such as the Indiana statute upheld by the federal Seventh Circuit Court in 2002 with a concurring opinion that cited the amicus brief of the United States Catholic Conference. Pro-life Catholics could also allude to Bush's rhetorical role in promoting the "culture of life" of which he spoke so eloquently and often.[155]

There were plenty of data to buttress these claims of Bush's leadership on the pro-life issue. An April 2004 Zogby survey found that 50 percent of Americans believed that abortion should either never be legal or legal only when the mother's life was in danger or in cases of rape or incest; 63 percent opposed embryonic stem cell research. A May 2004 poll by Quinnipiac University discovered that two-thirds of Catholic voters opposed abortion in most or all cases. In the 2004 election, according to an Edison/Mitovsky exit poll, "moral values" topped the list of Americans' reasons for voting, with Bush garnering eight of ten of these "values voters" and three of four abortion opponents. From 2000 to 2008, the national abortion rate would drop by 8 percent.[156]

If the American people were moving in the Catholic Church's direction on the abortion issue, however, it was not nearly as evident that George W. Bush was leading them there. From his debut on the presidential campaign trail in 2000 through his encore performance four years later, Bush in many ways was more prevaricator than prophet in the crusade against abortion. Scott

McClellan, Bush's campaign press secretary who would follow him to Washington, would remember Texas governor Bush's stance as a "middle ground" that sought "practical ways to reduce the number of abortions," such as parental notification and adoption. "On abortion . . . he embraced the conservative Christian position, saying he was against it except for special circumstances, and he was in favor of a constitutional amendment banning abortions," David Kuo, Bush's deputy director of the Office of Faith-Based and Community Initiatives, would recall of presidential candidate Bush's views in 2000. "Yet he quickly followed that statement by saying that Americans wouldn't go for it, and it was pointless to talk about it."[157]

Bush's stem cell research speech similarly was as political as it was principled. Where Karl Rove saw moral conviction at the base of Bush's decision, others saw Karl Rove. Bush had "not only protected but actually expanded his image as a moderate," Bush speechwriter David Frum would recall. "It was a masterstroke."[158]

So was the Democrats' nomination of Kerry—for the Republicans. Bush's opponent was so extreme that the incumbent never really had to defend his record to pro-life Catholics in the 2004 campaign. The "perfect storm" of a pro-choice Catholic candidate and a pro-life Catholic hierarchy was too enticing for the media, Catholic and non-Catholic alike, to overlook. So with every joust against Kerry by Catholic bishops came the corresponding attacks on Catholic bishops by the Kerry camp—their obsession with a single issue, their insensitivity to women, their telling Catholics how to vote, their acting in a partisan manner. Less than two weeks before the election, Kerry gave a speech establishing his Catholic credentials. "I know there are some bishops who have suggested that as a public official I must cast votes or take public positions—on issues like a woman's right to choose and stem cell research—that carry out the tenets of the Catholic Church," Kerry said in Fort Lauderdale, Florida. "I love my church; I respect the bishops; but I respectfully disagree." It sounded as if Kerry were running against the bishops, not the president.[159]

"Some Catholic archbishops are telling their Church members that it would be a sin to vote for a candidate like you because you support a woman's right to choose abortion and unlimited stem cell research," CBS's Bob Schieffer asked Kerry in the third presidential debate in October 2004. "What is your reaction to that?" Kerry struggled to answer. Bush didn't have to.[160]

Kerry not only had to answer to his church, but he had to answer to the American people, with whom he disagreed on so many aspects of the abortion question. According to the National Right to Life Committee, as of July 2004 Senator Kerry had voted seventy-nine times in favor of abortion, including six times in favor of "partial-birth" abortion. "My opponent has voted against sen-sible bipartisan measures like parental notification laws," Bush noted in a radio address in October 2004. In the third presidential debate the same month, Bush attacked Kerry's support for "partial-birth abortion" as "out of the mainstream."[161]

Bush was firmly within the mainstream where, in many ways, he had become much too comfortable. And while the president wasn't willing to do more to stop abortions, the bishops weren't able. The 2002 sexual abuse revelations and the 2004 communion contretemps delivered a public relations battering from which the Catholic hierarchy would not fully recover. The similarly timid president and the badly tattered bishops thus largely failed to push the needle of public opinion, inside and outside of the Church, on the abortion issue. "Sir, in your last campaign, you said that the American public was not ready for a complete ban on abortion," a reporter reminded Bush in October 2003. "Do you believe that the climate has changed since the last campaign, and all abortions should be banned?" "No," Bush replied, almost three years into his presidency. "I don't think the culture has changed to the extent that the American people or the Congress would totally ban abortions."[162]

Thus did the president who so mightily moved the American people (if not the Congress) on his faith-based initiative tacitly admit that he was not similarly transforming the dialogue on abortion. "I know you will redouble your efforts to change hearts and minds," Bush told the January 2004 March for Life. But he did not redouble his.[163] As a result, in 2004, 55 percent of Americans said abortion should be "legal in some circumstances," 24 percent said it should be "legal under any circumstances," and 19 percent said it should be "illegal in all circumstances." Gallup reported that these numbers not only had remained constant since 1996, but they were consistent with the survey's findings from the mid-1970s through the 1980s. As for those "values voters" of November, a *Los Angeles Times* survey concluded that their percentage in 2004, after one term of the pro-life George W. Bush, was the same as in 1996, after one term of the pro-choice Bill Clinton.[164]

Kerry's line of attack on Bush in their third presidential debate in October 2004 therefore targeted not the president's passion against abortion but his indifference toward it. "I will not allow somebody to come in and change *Roe v. Wade*," said Kerry. "The president has never said whether or not he would do that."[165]

When the bishops sent Kerry and Bush their quadrennial election-year questionnaire on abortion and some forty other issues, neither candidate returned it. Perhaps it was because for the first time, the bishops demanded one-word answers—"support" or "oppose."[166] Thus did the "Catholic" president resemble the Puritans of his ancestral seventeenth-century New England who, afraid of losing followers, eliminated the requirement of a conversion experience for church membership, settling instead on baptism as a means of joining their congregation. Their compact with God thus became a "half-way covenant," which compromised their beliefs but helped sustain their existence.[167]

George W. Bush likewise met pro-life Catholics halfway. His presidency was better than the one that preceded it and preferable to the one promised by his pro-choice Catholic opponent. But it was not what it could have been. Despite the presence of a Republican Congress for over half of his first term, he never proposed a human life amendment to the Constitution, never pressed for legislation that would severely limit abortions, and never extended himself on the abortion issue in a way that would jeopardize his reelection. Bush sincerely wanted to save the unborn. But like the Puritans, first he wanted to save himself.

On election night in November 2004, with U.S. troops still in Iraq, faith-based legislation a forlorn hope, and *Roe v. Wade* still the law of the land, George W. Bush and the Catholic majority who voted for him had little to celebrate. In choosing the incumbent over his Catholic challenger, however, these Catholics improbably voted for change. Thanks in part to the efforts of Catholic leaders, by the end of his second term Bush changed his strategy in Iraq, changed the culture on faith-based government programs, and changed the composition of the federal courts. While these were no small accomplishments, they still left many Catholics wishing for more.

Conclusion

MOST OF THE ONE IN FOUR American Catholics who regularly attend Sunday Mass listen intently to the priest's homily, which draws a lesson from that day's gospel reading. The preacher intends that his parable follow the parishioners out of church and accompany them during the week ahead, at least until the next Sunday, when the process begins anew.[1] While many of the people in the pews endeavor in good faith to heed their pastor's insights, others leave his scriptural wisdom at the church door. They find it too abstruse, too utopian, or too remote from their everyday lives. They have bills to pay, mouths to feed, and deadlines to meet. Their hour of scriptural diversion is over, and it is time to reconnect with the rugged reality with which God has saddled them.

So it was with the relationship between American Catholics and the power structure of the Church from 1960 to 2004. In the years between electing and rejecting one of their own as the leader of their government, American Catholics alternately followed and forsook the dictates of the leaders of their church. On elements of war and peace, social justice, and life and death, American Catholics evinced the political prowess befitting one-quarter of the country's population. But they also displayed a diversity of opinion reflecting their dissonance along lines of race, class, gender, and political affiliation. While their numbers always demanded the attention of U.S. presidents, their differences often lightened their imprint on U.S. presidencies. Yet because of those numbers and despite those differences, American Catholics exhibited a substantial impact on a secular government in a Protestant culture.

In the realm of war and peace, American Catholics and their presidents would no doubt concur that from 1960 to 2004 there was too much of the former and too little of the latter. Whether confronting communism, genocide, or terrorism, every president of the age exerted the awesome authority of commander in chief. And hovering balefully over the entire epoch was the specter of a nuclear apocalypse, at risk of being ignited by the superpowers' escalation of the arms race or the terrorists' infiltration of the arms trade.

For a peace-loving Catholic Church, which sanctions war only when it is just, this era created abundant angst. As early as 1965, Pope Paul VI was renouncing war, and as early as 1968 the U.S. Catholic bishops were raising questions about the Vietnam conflict. Yet Presidents Johnson, Nixon, and Ford extended the strife in Southeast Asia for seven more years. Twice within a dozen years U.S. presidents named Bush fought wars against Iraq that, Pope John Paul II and the American bishops implied in 1991 and amplified in 2003, were unjust. In the Balkans from 1993 to 1995 and again from 1998 to 1999, President Clinton acted less swiftly and less decisively to arrest the humanitarian horror than the Catholic hierarchy often appeared to be demanding.

Pope John XXIII's efforts to stave off nuclear war over Cuba did not preclude Kennedy and Khrushchev from taking the world to the brink in 1962. The bishops' campaigns for SALT II and a virtual nuclear freeze could not deter Carter from withholding the treaty when Brezhnev chose to invade Afghanistan in 1979, nor could they deter Reagan from intensifying the arms race when Soviet leader Yuri Andropov chose to build in kind in 1983. "I don't think you can claim that specific recommendations that the bishops made have been followed in any way," the United States Catholic Conference's Rev. Bryan Hehir admitted four years after "The Challenge of Peace." In the early years of Reagan's presidency, Notre Dame's Rev. Theodore Hesburgh would remember, the president remained committed to mutual assured destruction.[2]

American Catholics nonetheless achieved measurable success in helping to move American presidents and the American people in their direction on matters of war and peace. The United States waded into Vietnam largely because of Catholics: the communist oppression of the Church there galvanized Senator John Kennedy's interest in the region, which would result in thousands of American military advisors and millions of American dollars going to Southeast Asia at President John Kennedy's request. And the United States wobbled out of Vietnam largely because of Catholics: the Catholic Left helped to push the bishops to break with Nixon over the war in 1971, and the bishops helped to press Ford to address the refugee crisis in which Catholic Charities played a leading role in 1975.

In the Persian Gulf, the pope and the bishops ultimately may have lost the argument, but to a large degree they had started it. The first President Bush had to explain why his war against Saddam Hussein was just. The second President Bush had to admit that the primary cause of his war with Saddam Hussein was not.

On the Balkan Peninsula, Clinton may have been painfully slow to react, but when he did, he responded successfully. Like the pope and the bishops, President Clinton argued that a war must be just not only in its origin but in its execution. So while the periods he waited to intervene in Bosnia and Kosovo were agonizingly long, the wars he waged were mercifully short, saving the lives of Slavs without sacrificing the lives of Americans. If Catholics, especially in Croatia, in some ways stoked the fire in the Balkans, Catholics, especially in the United States, in some ways helped to put it out.

And though the nuclear nightmare never escaped the realm of the possible, it never entered the realm of the probable. After Khrushchev warily waved off his nuclear missiles from Cuba, Kennedy proudly waved his copy of Pope John XXIII's *Pacem in Terris*. Though the U.S. Senate never ratified his treaty, Carter and his successors observed its terms, which the bishops, Father Hesburgh, and other Catholic members of Americans for SALT II had fervidly championed. Though Reagan and the Catholic leadership commenced his presidency far apart over nuclear arms escalation, they finished it close together on nuclear arms reduction. "There is a widespread impression that the bishops' letter pushed the Administration in that direction"—away from mutual assured destruction—Father Hehir said of the link between "The Challenge of Peace" and the Strategic Defense Initiative, the key bargaining chip in the Reagan administration's arms talks with the Soviets. "Did we shape the dialogue?" Hehir would ask. "I think that we did."[3] Father Hesburgh, who helped to organize a 1982 Vatican meeting of scientists committed to abolishing nuclear weapons, would recall that although Reagan started slowly in the pursuit of arms reduction, "he wound up on the right side." Thanks in part to American Catholics, "Reagan and Gorbachev saved the world."[4]

In the area of social justice, American Catholics similarly struggled at times to direct the decisions of American presidents. The Church leadership withstood the same resistance to civil rights, first from the state laws of the South, then from the city neighborhoods of the North, that the presidents did. The American bishops could not prod Presidents Kennedy and Johnson on civil rights, however, until they first persuaded their congregants and themselves of the moral urgency of the cause.

The civil rights backlash felt by the Catholic prelates and the Democratic presidents presaged a repudiation of their increasingly statist conception of social justice. "Traditionalist Catholics, of whom there were more then than now," Nixon, Ford, and Reagan aide Patrick Buchanan would remember, launched this rightward ricochet. As a result, the first President Bush's special assistant Douglas Wead would recall, Catholics became "two-party voters," liberated from the conventions of the New Deal coalition and open to the highest political bidder. The rise of Catholic Republicans, from "old movement" conservatives like William F. Buckley and Phyllis Schlafly to "new movement" conservatives like William Bennett, Ann Coulter, and "practically the whole line-up of the Fox News Channel," according to Wead, helped to elect most of the American heads of state from 1968 to 2004.[5]

In this more conservative environment, the bishops' liberal case against Nixon's welfare reform and the domestic budgets of Ford, Reagan, Bush, and Bush, as well as their progressive embrace of Carter's and Clinton's health care reforms, often fell on deaf ears in the nation's churches and the nation's capital. "The Counsil [sic] of Bishops . . . favored the Democrat[ic] Party," Wead would reminisce, so "I organized a concerted effort to reach out to the American Cardinals and ignore the Counsil [sic]." The Republican National Committee's chairman of Catholic outreach, Deal Hudson, would agree that "there was an amazing alienation that took place as the Catholic Conference turned hard left," so, according to the *New Yorker*'s Peter Boyer, Catholic conservatives like Hudson's Catholic Working Group largely replaced the United States Conference of Catholic Bishops as "the conduit between the Church and the government" in the George W. Bush White House. The USCCB's gravest weakness, Rev. John Coleman of Loyola Marymount University concluded, was its "relative failure to engage grassroots support for its position." Whether liberal or conservative, pollster John Zogby determined in 2004, Catholics were "Americans first."[6]

But the Church hierarchy's efforts were not in vain. Kennedy unveiled, and Johnson enacted, the most far-reaching civil rights legislation in the country's history. Nixon's welfare reform perished in Congress, and Ford's food expenditures and Reagan's social spending grew. The willingness of Bush the father to spend public money to address the urban crisis paved the way for Bush the son to spend public money on his faith-based programs. Clinton learned from Carter's mistakes and more aggressively pursued universal health insurance, then learned from his own and enacted piecemeal health reforms.

Though they sometimes seemed out of touch with their flock, the Church's shepherds rarely strayed from their course. Their constant invocation of the social justice tenets of their faith assured an audience, if not an allegiance, in the Oval Office. Where Deal Hudson perceived the bishops making a permanent left turn engineered by progressives like Rev. Bryan Hehir, Father Hehir would view the prelates as pushing forward, toward the middle, in the best tradition of Catholic social teaching. The USCCB's greatest strength, according to Father Coleman, was its "moral authority." So although they visited valleys as well as peaks, they ultimately gained much along the way. The twenty-first century would usher in the nation's most "Catholic" president, followed by its most liberal, and most Catholics would help to reelect the former and elect the latter.[7]

On matters of life and death, American Catholics made their greatest contribution. Once again, however, much of their effort seemed an exercise in futility. All the presidents from 1960 to 2004, like the overwhelming majority of American Catholics, opposed the Church's dogma on birth control. So it disappeared as a political issue in the United States after 1973, and only occasionally reappeared in bishops' meetings or in papal pronouncements.

Abortion performed no such vanishing act. Both of the Democratic presidents since *Roe v. Wade* defended the decision; none of the five Republicans tried to overturn it. Neither the Democratic nor Republican chief executives translated the Church's "consistent ethic of life" against abortion and capital punishment into public policy. According to the American Life League, almost half of the 144 Catholics in Congress in 2004 were "vocal abortion supporters." And despite the very persistent and very public pleading of popes and bishops, polls continued to show most American Catholics sympathetic to capital punishment as well as to abortion. Among American Catholics, "there does not appear to be a constituency," the University of Nevada–Las Vegas political scientist Ted Jelen concluded from his polling in 2004, "for what Cardinal Joseph Bernardin has termed a 'consistent ethic of life.'" On questions of life and death, Zogby concluded in 2004, American Catholics "have more in common with American Protestants than they have in common with Catholics in other nations."[8]

Even the incremental inroads that the Catholic hierarchy helped to forge against *Roe* were often tentative and temporary, easily undone by liberal judges or Democratic presidents. "[The Church] could do more, a lot more, to educate lay Catholics," Richard Doerflinger, the associate director of the USCCB's Secretariat for Pro-Life Activities, conceded in 2004. When asked why Catholics did not hold greater sway over U.S. presidents, Father Hesburgh replied that there were not enough Catholics with a direct line to the White House. What the Church needed, he seemed to be saying, was a few more Father Hesburghs.[9] To Mary Segers, the costs of the Church's crusade against abortion outweighed its benefits. Its disassociation from modern feminism, implicit association with the violence against abortion clinics, inability to appreciate the complex demands of public service, failure to distinguish between law and morality, and elevation of abortion above all other concerns did more harm than good.[10]

Yet beneath the soil of the Catholic leaders' gravest disappointment lay the seeds of their fondest hope. Though Republican judicial appointees often proved even less reliable for pro-life Catholics than the chief executives who selected them, the Supreme Court remained only one vote away from reversing *Roe*. While most Americans backed the ruling, many Catholics did not. Most Americans, most Catholics, and most of the Supreme Court opposed abortion on demand and "partial-birth" abortion, while endorsing such encroachments on "the right to choose" as parental consent and waiting periods. And if Presidents Nixon, Ford, Reagan, Bush, and Bush had not been as determined in their defense of the unborn as many American Catholics had hoped, Presidents Carter and Clinton were not as ferocious in their protection of abortion rights as many American Catholics had feared. Carter did not only say he was personally opposed to abortion, but this belief led him to reject federal financing. Clinton may have been the most pro-choice president in U.S. history, but he spent much of his presidency on the defensive.

"The fight against abortion," Margaret Ross Sammon would surmise, "clearly illustrates the hierarchy's ability to organize, raise money, lobby members of Congress, and address individual Catholics at the parish level." Michele Dillon would add that by invoking the U.S. Constitution and the Declaration of Independence, the bishops' arguments were as American as they were Catholic. Michael Taylor, the executive director of the USCCB's National Committee for a Human Life Amendment during the Clinton and both Bush presidencies, claimed that the bishops' biggest accomplishment on abortion was in "keeping the issue alive. In 1973 the [Supreme] Court said this is the law of the land. Go home. [But] it didn't happen."[11]

Popes, bishops, and priests, as they have repeatedly reminded Americans, do not engage in partisan politics and do not make public policy. All they can really do to influence both is to talk—and then talk some more. But a pope's encyclical, a bishop's pastoral, and a priest's homily are not merely words. They can be, if the authors are effective and the audience is engaged, a powerful call to action. So despite the festering factionalism within their church, a majority of American Catholics in a 2004 poll by the Center for Applied Research in the Apostolate pronounced themselves "satisfied" with the performance of their clerical superiors. And an even greater percentage, almost three-fourths, of non-Catholics perceived the Catholic faithful as marching in lockstep with the hierarchy.[12]

From 1960 to 2004, American Catholics did not always win the debates surrounding the policies of their presidents. But whether espousing the just-war doctrine, Catholic social teaching, or the consistent ethic of life, American Catholics often certified that those debates ensued. Catholics put thoughts into the minds of the American people and words into the mouths of American presidents. Though at times crippled by dissent and crushed by scandal, the Church somehow remained resourceful and resilient. The U.S. presidents at times disregarded and defied it. But they dared not ignore it. "There is no 'Catholic vote,'" the Catholic liberal columnist E. J. Dionne wrote in June 2000, yet, as the "ultimate swing vote, it matters."[13]

Catholics, for so long on the periphery of American society and politics, have secured their place on the inside of American history. And though it has not been everything they imagined, the view is still much better from there.

NOTES

ABBREVIATIONS

AAB	Archives of the Archdiocese of Boston
AANO	Archives of the Archdiocese of New Orleans
ACA	Archdiocese of Chicago Archives
ALAAC	Archdiocese of Los Angeles Archival Center
AMA	Archdiocese of Milwaukee Archives
CUA	Catholic University Archives, Washington, D.C.
FOIA	Freedom of Information Act
GBPL	George Bush Presidential Library, College Station, Tex.
GRFPL	Gerald R. Ford Presidential Library, Ann Arbor, Mich.
JCPL	Jimmy Carter Presidential Library, Atlanta, Ga.
JFKPL	John F. Kennedy Presidential Library, Boston, Mass.
LBJPL	Lyndon B. Johnson Presidential Library, Austin, Tex.
MUA	Marquette University Archives, Milwaukee, Wis.
NA	National Archives, College Park, Md.
RRPL	Ronald Reagan Presidential Library, Simi Valley, Calif.
UMA	University of Minnesota Archives, Minneapolis
UNDA	University of Notre Dame Archives, Notre Dame, Ind.
USCCBA	United States Conference of Catholic Bishops Archives, Washington, D.C.
WHORM	White House Office of Records Management
WJCPL	William J. Clinton Presidential Library, Little Rock, Ark.

INTRODUCTION

1. Jay Dolan, *The American Catholic Experience* (Notre Dame, Ind.: University of Notre Dame Press, 1992), 20–22.

2. Ibid., 16.

3. Jay Dolan, *In Search of an American Catholicism* (New York: Oxford University Press, 2002), 14, 15, 29.

4. Dolan, *The American Catholic Experience*, 127, 134.

5. Lawrence J. McAndrews, *The Era of Education: The Presidents and the Schools, 1965–2001* (Urbana: University of Illinois Press, 2006), 4.

6. Dolan, *The American Catholic Experience*, 143.

7. William Prendergast, *The Catholic Voter in American Politics* (Washington, D.C.: Georgetown University Press, 1999), 138; Dolan, *The American Catholic Experience*, 357.

8. Lawrence J. McAndrews, *Broken Ground: John F. Kennedy and the Politics of Education* (New York: Garland, 1991), 24–25.

9. Ibid.

10. Michael Warner, *Changing Witness: Catholic Bishops and Public Policy, 1917–1994* (Grand Rapids, Mich.: Eerdmans, 1995), 2; "A Short History of the USCCB," *Fifth Column*, 29 March 2011, http://skellmeyer.blogspot.com/2011/03/short-history-of-usccb.html, 1.

11. Timothy Byrnes, "The Politics of the American Catholic Hierarchy," *Political Science Quarterly* 108 (Fall 1993): 498; Mark Stricherz, "Inside the Bishops' Conference, Part I: Why the American Bishops Lack Accountability," *Crisis*, 1 October 2003, http://crisismagazine.com/october2003, 1, 3.

12. Mark Evans, "Moral Theory and the Idea of Just War," in *Just War Theory*, ed. Mark Evans (New York: Palgrave Macmillan, 2005), 2–3.

13. Ibid.

14. Lawrence Cunningham, *The Catholic Heritage* (New York: Crossroad, 1983), 79.

15. George Weigel, "War, Peace, and the Christian Conscience," in *Just War and the Gulf War*, ed. George Weigel and James Turner Johnson (Lanham, Md.: Ethics and Public Policy Center, 1991), 63.

16. United States Catholic Bishops, "A Pastoral Message: Living with Faith and Hope after September 11," USCCB, 14 November 2001, http://www.usccb.org/sdwp/sept11.shtml, 4; Neta Crawford, "The Justice of Pre-emptive and Preventive War Doctrines," in Evans, 45–46.

17. D. Paul Sullins, "Introduction," in *Catholic Social Thought*, ed. D. Paul Sullins and Anthony J. Blasi (Lanham, Md.: Rowman and Littlefield, 2009), 15–17.

18. Dolan, *The American Catholic Experience*, 334, 344.

19. Qtd. in Thomas Storck, "Catholic Social Teaching: St. Pius X through Pius XI," *Distributist Review*, 30 August 2010, http://distributistreview.com/mag/2010/08, 6; "Teacher Yes, Mother No," *Time*, 29 September 1961, http://www.time.com/time/magazine/article/0,9171,895721,00html, 1.

20. Dolan, *In Search of an American Catholicism*, 201.

21. Karen O'Connor, *No Neutral Ground?* (Boulder, Colo.: Westview, 1996), 20; John McGreevy, "Catholics in America: Antipathy and Assimilation," in *American Catholics, American Culture*, ed. Margaret O'Brien Steinfels (Lanham, Md.: Rowman and Littlefield, 2004), 15–16; "Birth Control," *America*, 24 October 1964, 477; Donald Critchlow, *Intended Consequences: Birth Control, Abortion, and the Federal Government in Modern America* (New York: Oxford University Press, 1999), 116–117.

22. Critchlow, 138.

23. George Weigel, *The Courage to Be Catholic* (New York: Basic, 2002), 68, 106; O'Connor, 60; Margaret Ross Sammon, "The Politics of the U.S. Catholic Bishops," in *Catholics and Politics*, ed. Kristin Heyer, Mark Rozell, and Michael Genovese (Washington, D.C.: Georgetown University Press, 2008), 16–17; E. Christian Brugger, *Capital Punishment and Roman Catholic Moral Traditions* (Notre Dame, Ind.: University of Notre Dame, 2003), 136–137.

24. James Hennesey, *American Catholics* (New York: Oxford University Press, 1981); Charles Morris, *American Catholic* (New York: Times Books, 1997); Mark Massa, *Catholics and American Culture* (New York: Crossroad, 1999); John McGreevy, *Catholicism and American Freedom* (New York: Norton, 2003); Patrick Carey, *Catholics in America* (Westport, Conn.: Praeger, 2004); James Fisher, *Communion of Immigrants* (New York: Oxford University Press, 2008).

25. Mary Hanna, *Catholics and American Politics* (Cambridge, Mass.: Harvard University Press, 1979); George Gallup and Jim Castelli, *The American Catholic People* (Garden City, N.Y.: Doubleday, 1987); Prendergast; Steinfels, *American Catholics, American Culture*; Heyer et al., *Catholics and Politics*; Deal Hudson, *Onward, Christian Soldiers* (New York: Simon and Schuster, 2008); Timothy Byrnes, *Catholic Bishops in American Politics* (Princeton, N.J.: Princeton University Press,1991); Thomas Reese, *A Flock of Shepherds* (Kansas City, Mo.: Sheed and Ward, 1992); Michael Warner, *Changing Witness* (Grand Rapids, Mich.: Eerdmans, 1995); Hugh Heclo and Wilfred McClay, eds., *Religion Returns to the Public Square* (Baltimore, Md.: Johns Hopkins University Press, 2003).

26. Weigel and Johnson, eds.; John McGreevy, *Parish Boundaries: The Catholic Encounter with Race in the Twentieth Century Urban North* (Chicago: University of Chicago Press, 1996); Critchlow; Leslie Tentler, *Catholics and Contraception* (Ithaca, N.Y.: Cornell University Press, 2004); David Settje, *Faith and War* (New York: New York University Press, 2011); Lawrence J. McAndrews, *Broken Ground: John F. Kennedy and the Politics of Education* (New York: Garland, 1991); and McAndrews, *The Era of Education*; Thomas Carty, "White House Outreach to Catholics," in Heyer et al., 175–198.

27. John Kenneth White and William D'Antonio, "Catholics and the Politics of Change: The Presidential Campaign of Two JFK's," in *Religion and the Bush Presidency*, ed. Mark Rozell and Gleaves Whitney (New York: Palgrave Macmillan, 2007), 58.

CHAPTER ONE. Catholics and John Kennedy

1. John F. Kennedy, "Inaugural Address," 20 January 1961, *Public Papers of the Presidents of the United States: John F. Kennedy, 1961* (Washington, D.C.: U.S. Government Printing Office, 1962), 1.

2. John F. Kennedy, "Commencement Address at American University in Washington," 10 June 1963, *Public Papers of the Presidents of the United States: John F. Kennedy, January 1–November 22, 1963* (Washington, D.C.: U.S. Government Printing Office, 1964), 462.

3. "On Fighting Communism," *America*, 22 April 1961, 170–171; George Dunne and C. J. McNaspy, "How We Look to Others," *America*, 13 May 1961, 274; Arnaldo Cortesi, "Pope's Easter Message Voices 'Anxiety' over Communist Acts," *New York Times*, 3 April 1961, L25.

4. Richard Reeves, *President Kennedy* (New York: Simon and Schuster, 1993), 177; Richard Cardinal Cushing, "Sermon in Honor of the Centenary of the 101st Regiment, Cathedral of Holy Cross," 18 June 1961, box 33, folder: Centenary of 101st Regiment, Cathedral of Holy Cross, Richard Cardinal Cushing Papers, AAB, 4.

5. "Pope's Encyclical Urges Rich Nations to Aid Poor; Deplores Fear in the World," *New York Times*, 15 July 1961, L1, 8.

6. Kathleen Teltsch, "U.S. and Soviets Endorse Ideals of Disarmament," *New York Times*, 21 September 1961, L1; "Kennedy Favors Shelters for All," *New York Times*, 7 October 1961, L1; Arnaldo Cortesi, "World Threats Deplored by Pope," *New York Times*, 5 November 1961, L1; Arnaldo Cortesi, "Pope Urges Peace in Christmas Talk," *New York Times*, 22 December 1961, L12.

7. "Twenty-Five Thousand Worshippers Attend Red Mass," *New York Times*, 2 October 1961, 6, 7; "Text of Catholic Bishops' Statement Issued at Close of Annual Meeting," *New York Times*, 19 November 1961, 6, 82; "Memorandum on Briefing Organized by Conference Group of U.S. National Organizations on the United Nations," 15 November 1961, General Administration Series, subser. 1.1: Alphabetical Subject Files, box 52, folder: International Affairs: United Nations, 1961, National Catholic Welfare Conference Papers, CUA, 2.

8. Theodore Sorensen, "The Kennedy Record in Foreign Affairs," 29 December 1961, White House Staff Files: Lee C. White File, Legislation File, box 10, John F. Kennedy Presidential Papers, JFKPL, 3; "The Necessity of Peace," *Commonweal*, 12 January 1962, 399.

9. Memorandum from McGeorge Bundy to Ralph Dungan, 3 April 1962, White House Staff Files: Ralph Dungan, box 1, folder: State Department, JFKPL; E. W. Kenwothy, "Kennedy Pledges Speed in Applying Any Arms Accord," *New York Times*, 14 March 1962, L1; Reeves, *President Kennedy*, 514.

10. Letter from Richard Cardinal Cushing to Mother Paula, 11 January 1963, box 14, folder: January–June 1963, AAB, 1; "Clearing the Record," *Tidings*, 4 March 1962, in General Administration Series, subser. 1.1: Alphabetical Subject Files, box 33, folder: Information, Media-Publications, January–June 1962, Subject: "Communism: A Threat to Freedom" by John F. Cronin, S.S., CUA; letter from Rev. Albert Bauman to Richard Cardinal Cushing, 19 December 1961, box 10, folder: Correspondence, AAB, 1; letter from Catherine Schaefer to Msgr. Paul Tanner, 9 April 1962, General Administration Series, subser. 3.6: Alphabetical Subject Files, box 174, folder: CAIP, Rita Schaefer Correspondence, 1946–1969, CUA, 1–3.

11. Memorandum from Elizabeth Zepf, 13 April 1962, General Administration Series, subser. 1.1: Alphabetical Subject Files, box 52, folder: International Affairs: United Nations, January–June 1962, CUA, 1; letter from Msgr. Paul Tanner to Most Rev. Egidio Vagnozzi, 22 May 1962, General Administration Series, subser. 1.1: Alphabetical Subject Files, box 52, folder: International Affairs: United Nations, January–June 1962, CUA.

12. Letter from William O'Brien to Eileen Egan, 11 June 1962, and letter from Eileen Egan to William O'Brien, 14 May 1962, General Administration Series, subser. 1.1: Alphabetical Subject Files, box 52, folder: International Affairs: United Nations, January–June 1962, CUA. For explanation of CAIP, see John Leo, "On the Peace Circuit," *Commonweal*, 25 October 1963, 123.

13. Letter from Msgr. Francis Lally to Richard Cardinal Cushing, 25 May 1962, box 12, folder: Correspondence, May 1962, AAB, 1; letter from Richard Cardinal Cushing to Concepcion Nodarse, 19 July 1962, box 13, folder: Correspondence, July 17–20, 1962, AAB.

14. Norman Cousins, "The Improbable Triumvirate," *Saturday Review*, 30 October 1971, 25.

15. Ibid.

16. Arnaldo Cortesi, "Pope Bids Rulers Save the Peace," *New York Times*, 26 October 1962, L1; "Catholics Pray for World Peace on Plea of U.S. Bishops in Rome," *New York Times*, 29 October 1962, L43.

17. "Pope Makes Plea for Peace as Fourth Year in Vatican Ends," *New York Times*,

29 October 1962, L17; Herbert Parmet, *JFK: The Presidency of John F. Kennedy* (New York: Penguin, 1984), 310.

18. Cousins, 26.
19. Parmet, *JFK*, 315; Reeves, *President Kennedy*, 439.
20. Cousins, 30.
21. Ibid., 30, 32.
22. Ibid., 27.
23. Parmet, *JFK*, 311; "The Choice," *Commonweal*, 19 April 1963, 85; Arnaldo Cortesi, "Pope John Urges a World Nation to Guard Peace," *New York Times*, 11 April 1963, L1.
24. "Peace Encyclical Wins Red Cheers," *New York Times*, 13 April 1963, L3; "Cardinal Koenig on Papal Mission to Better Ties with Reds," *New York Times*, 4 May 1963, L2; "TASS Hails Pope John; Cites Fruitful Activity," *New York Times*, 4 June 1963, L21.
25. "U.S. Praises Encyclical," *New York Times*, 13 April 1963, L3; John F. Kennedy, "Address at the Boston College Centennial Ceremonies," 20 April 1963, *Public Papers, 1963*, 336.
26. Victor Ferkiss, "*Pacem in Terris*: An Opening to the Left?," *Catholic World*, November 1963, 108; William Purdy, "The New Vatican Approach to Communism," *Catholic World*, July 1963, 201; "*Pacem in Terris*," *Commonweal*, 26 April 1963, 123; memorandum from Ed Bayley to Ralph Dugan, 11 February 1963, Ralph Dungan Special Assistant Files, box 11, folder: Miscellaneous, 1962–1963, JFKPL.
27. Letter from John Kennedy to Pope John XXIII, 4 May 1963, and letter from Norman Cousins to Ralph Dungan, 25 April 1963, Ralph Dungan Special Assistant Files, box 7, folder: Correspondence, May 1963, JFKPL; Tom Wicker, "Kennedy to Visit Pope Late in June," *New York Times*, 18 May 1963, L1.
28. M. S. Handler, "Washington Mourns Loss of Great Force of Peace," *New York Times*, 4 June 1963, L1; "TASS Hails Pope John," *New York Times*, 4 June 1963, L21.
29. Kennedy, "Commencement Address at American University in Washington," *Public Papers, 1963*, 461, 464.
30. Letter from Catherine Schaefer to Msgr. George Higgins, 26 June 1963, General Administration Series, subser. 1.1: Alphabetical Subject Files, box 52, folder: International Affairs—United Nations, 1963, CUA, 1–2.
31. Arnaldo Cortesi, "President and Pope Confer for Forty Minutes," *New York Times*, 3 July 1963, L1.
32. John F. Kennedy, "Radio and Television Address to the American People on the Nuclear Test Ban Threat," 26 July 1963, *Public Papers, 1963*, 602.
33. "A Sermon at the First Anniversary Memorial Mass for the Late President John F. Kennedy," 22 November 1964, box 35, folder: First Anniversary Memorial Mass for the Late President John. F. Kennedy, Cathedral of the Holy Cross, AAB, 2.
34. Interview of Rev. Theodore Hesburgh by author, 17 August 2011; Albert Menendez, *John F. Kennedy: Catholic and Humanist* (Buffalo: Prometheus, 1978), 77; Lawrence Fuchs, *John F. Kennedy and American Catholicism* (New York: Meredith, 1967), 207; Menendez, *John F. Kennedy*, 62; "POAU: No Sectarian Bias in Appointments of President Kennedy," 23 May 1962, White House Central Files, Subject File: Religious Matters, box 885, folder: RM 5/16/62–1/25/63, JFKPL; Eugene Armao, "Geno-Slander Used: Winchell Attacks Italian Leadership," *Il Populo Italiano*, n.d., White House Cen-

tral Files, Subject File: Religious Matters, box 888, folder: 361 FG 295 4-16-61, JFKPL; letter from Edward Swanstrom to Richard Cardinal Cushing, 23 August 1962, box 13, folder: Correspondence, August 21–25, 1962, AAB, 2.

35. "Church and President," *America*, 13 January 1962, 461–462; letter from Robert Kennedy to Sister Mary Rita, 8 February 1962, White House Central Files, Subject File: Religious Matters, box 886, folder RM 3-1, 1962, JFKPL.

36. Letter from Norman Cousins to Ralph Dungan, 28 January 1963; telegram from Norman Cousins to Ralph Dungan, 16 January 1963; and memorandum from Ralph Dungan to President John F. Kennedy, 19 January 1963, Ralph Dungan Special Assistant Files, box 11, folder: Catholic Church—General, JFKPL; Norman Cousins, *The Improbable Triumvirate* (New York: Norton, 1972), 111.

37. Memorandum from Msgr. Paul Tanner, 28 February 1961, General Administration Files, Alphabetical Subject File, box 10, folder: Church—Church and State: Federal Aid to Education, 1961, January–February, CUA, 8; Lawrence J. McAndrews, *Broken Ground: John F. Kennedy and the Politics of Education* (New York: Garland, 1991), 72–81.

38. Memorandum from Ralph Dungan to President John Kennedy, 22 June 1963, and memorandum for President Lyndon B. Johnson, July 1964, Ralph Dungan Special Assistant Files, box 11, folder: Catholic Church—General, JFKPL.

39. Letter from Msgr. Paul Tanner to James Cardinal McIntyre, 23 March 1962, General Administration subser. 1.1, Alphabetical Subject File, box 33, folder: Information Media: Publications January–June 1962, CUA; "Minutes of the Meeting of the Administrative Board of the National Catholic Welfare Conference," 23 April 1963, General Administration Series, subser. 1.1, Alphabetical Subject File, box 25, folder, NCWC Administrative Board, 1963, CUA, 1068; "Communism and the Pope," *Commonweal*, 24 May 1963, 235–236.

40. Letter from Msgr. George Higgins to Catherine Schaefer, 27 June 1963, General Administration Series, subser. 3.6, Alphabetical Subject File, box 174, folder: CAIP, Rita Schaefer Correspondence, 1946–1969, CUA, 1; "Agenda for Special Meeting of Administrative Board, Chicago," 6 August 1963, subser. 1.1; General Administration Files, Alphabetical Subject File, box 25, folder: NCWC Administrative Board, 1963, CUA.

41. Reeves, *President Kennedy*, 537; interview of James Wine by John Stewart, 26 January 1967, Oral History Collection, JFKPL, 54–55.

42. Fuchs, 207; interview of Brooks Hays by Warren Cinkins, May–June 1964, Oral History Collection, JFKPL, 35; letter from Ralph Dungan to William O'Brien, 9 January 1962, box 10, folder: Correspondence, AAB.

43. Memorandum from Brooks Hays to President John Kennedy, 7 March 1962, Ralph Dungan Special Assistant Files, box 5, folder: Correspondence, 3/62 [2 of 2], JFKPL.

44. "Sermon by Richard Cardinal Cushing at the First Anniversary Memorial Mass for the Late President John F. Kennedy," 1; Menendez, *John F. Kennedy*, 61.

45. James Hennesey, *American Catholics* (New York: Oxford University Press, 1981), 305; "Rough Draft of Section B of Memorandum to Ecumenical Council from National Catholic Council for Interracial Justice," n.d., ser. 28, box 1, folder: NCCIJ, American Bishops, Memo to, 1963, National Catholic Conference for Interracial Justice Papers, MUA, 1.

46. United States Catholic Bishops, "Discrimination and the Christian Conscience," 1958, in National Catholic Conference for Interracial Justice, 1956–, ser. 20, box 2, folder: Bishops, 1960–1963, MUA, 1–5; letter from Rev. John LaFarge to "Your Excellency," n.d., ser. 20, box 2, folder: Bishops, 1960–1963, MUA.

47. "Interracial Frontier," *America*, 11 February 1961, 621–622.

48. "Pastoral Letter for First Sunday of Lent," attached to letter from Rev. Paul Hallinan to Msgr. Paul Tanner, 13 February 1961, General Administration Series, subser. 1.1, box 89, folder: Social Action, Race Relations 1960–62, CUA.

49. James Graham Cook, *The Segregationists* (New York: Appleton-Century-Crofts, 1962), 229; Committee to Study Catholic Schools in the Archdiocese of New Orleans, "Statistical Summary of Questionnaire on Desegregation," 13 June 1955, Desegregation File, box 2, folder: Desegregation Institute (1955–1967), AANO.

50. Letter from Mathew Ahmann to Rev. Patrick O'Boyle, 27 April 1961, ser. 20, box 2, folder: Bishops, 1960–1963, MUA; interview with Bishop Joseph Vath and Monsignor Charles Plausche, by Charles Nolan, 30 August 1980, Desegregation File, no box, no folder, AANO, 7.

51. Anthony Lewis, "Kennedy Speaks for Integration and Vows Action," *New York Times*, 8 February 1961, A1.

52. "Appeal for Civil Rights," *America*, 23 October 1961, 114; memorandum from Frederick Dutton to the President, 30 November 1961, White House Central Files, Subject File—Human Rights, box 358, folder: HU 1/20/61–5/10/61, JFKPL.

53. "Appeal for Civil Rights," 114; interview of Rev. Theodore Hesburgh by author, 17 August 2011.

54. Letter from President John Kennedy to Mathew Ahmann, 25 August 1961, White House Central Files, Subject File—Religious Matters, box 886, folder: RM 3-1 Catholic 1961, JFKPL; letter from Lee White to Mathew Ahmann, 16 December 1961, ser. 20, box 31, folder: U.S. Government, 1960–1965, MUA; Mark Stern, *Calculating Visions: Kennedy, Johnson, and Civil Rights* (New Brunswick, N.J.: Rutgers University Press, 1992), 52.

55. Memorandum from Rev. John Cronin to Msgr. Paul Tanner, 8 January 1962, and Reply from Tanner to Cronin, 9 January 1962, General Administration Series, subser. 1.1, box 88, folder: Social Action, Labor Relations, 1961–1963, CUA; "Formal Announcement by Archbishop Rummel that all Schools at all Grade Levels Would be Open to all Catholic Children, Regardless of Race," 27 March 1962, Desegregation File, box 2, folder: Catholic School Integration—Department of Health, Education, and Welfare (1954–1972), AANO; Philip Grant, "Archbishop Joseph Rummel and the 1962 Desegregation Crisis," *Records of the American Catholic Historical Society* 91 (March–December 1980): 63.

56. Letter from John Siegenthaler to Henry Cabirac, 3 November 1961, ser. 20, box 31, folder: U.S. Government, 1960–1965, MUA; letter from Henry Cabirac to Burke Marshall, 4 April 1962, ser. 20, box 31, folder: U.S. Government, 1960–1965, MUA; letter from Henry Cabirac to Burke Marshall, 29 August 1962, ser. 20, box 31, folder: U.S. Government, 1960–1965, MUA.

57. Letter from Mathew Ahmann to Burke Marshall, 24 April 1962, and Reply from Marshall to Ahmann, n.d., ser. 20, box 31, folder: U.S. Government, 1960–1965, MUA.

58. Letter from Henry Cabirac to Burke Marshall, 3 October 1962, ser. 20, box 31, folder: U.S. Government, 1960–1965, MUA.

59. "Civil Rights Achievements since January 1961," White House Central Files, Subject File—box 888, folder: RSI Administration Accomplishments 1/20/61–7/6/61, JFKPL, 1; letter from John McDermott to Ralph Dungan, 6 June 1962, White House Central Files, Subject File—Religious Matters, box 885, folder: RM 1/26/63, JFKPL.

60. "Negro Bishops," *America*, 29 June 1963, 897; memorandum from John McDermott to Members of the Steering Committee, 30 January 1963, ser. 7, box 2, folder: NCRR Executive Committee, MUA; John Cronin, "Religion and Race," *Extension*, February 1963, 1, attached to memorandum from Cronin to Msgr. Paul Tanner, 6 February 1963, General Administration Series, subser. 1.1, box 89, folder: Social Action—Race Relations, 1963 January–July, CUA; "An Appeal to the Conscience of the American People," General Administration Series, subser. 1.1, box 85, folder: Social Action—Civil Rights, 1963, CUA; Mathew Ahmann, "Report to Leaders of National Conference on Religion and Race," 6 October 1963, ser. 7, box 2, folder: NCRR Reports, MUA, 1.

61. Cronin, "Religion and Race," 1; John Kennedy, "Special Message to the Congress on Civil Rights," 28 February 1963, *Public Papers of the Presidents of the United States: John Kennedy, January 1–November 22, 1963* (Washington, D.C.: U.S. Government Printing Office, 1964), 222.

62. Theodore Sorensen, *Kennedy* (New York: Harper and Row, 1965), 494.

63. McAndrews, *Broken Ground*, 136; Stern, 79; Arthur Schlesinger, *A Thousand Days: John F. Kennedy in the White House* (Boston: Houghton Mifflin, 1965), 966.

64. "Concession to Common Sense," *America*, 13 April 1963, 482; National Catholic Conference for Interracial Justice, "Commitment," May 1963, General Administration Series, subser. 1.1, box 89, folder: Social Action—Race Relations, 1963 January–July, CUA, 2.

65. "National Conference on Religion and Race Newsletter," 23 August 1963, ser. 7, box 2, folder: Conferences, Workshops, Institutes (NCRR), Newsletters, March 1963–February 1964, MUA, 6; "Memorandum from the Steering Committee of the St. Louis Ministers and Laymen's Association for Equal Opportunity to the Executive Committee of the St. Louis Conference on Religion and Race," 10 May 1963, 1–3, attached to memorandum from Rev. Arthur Walmsley to Members of Steering and Follow-up Committees, 28 May 1963, ser. 7, box 2, folder: NCRR Clergy and Contacts, MUA.

66. "The Religion and Race Conference," *St. Louis Review*, 20 May 1963, 14, attached to memorandum from Walmsley to Steering and Follow-up Committees.

67. "Armistice, Not Peace," *America*, 25 May 1963, 738.

68. "How Much Liberty?" *Commonweal*, 21 June 1963, 340; Stern, 93.

69. John Kennedy, "Radio and Television Report to the American People on Civil Rights," 11 June 1963, *Public Papers, 1963*, 470, 469; Stern, 91.

70. Memorandum from Ralph Dungan to the President, 14 June 1963, Ralph Dungan Special Assistant Files, box 8, folder: Correspondence, June 1963, JFKPL, 1–2.

71. Telegram from Msgr. Paul Tanner to Bishops, 12 June 1963, General Administration Series, subser. 1.1, box 85, folder: Social Action—Civil Rights, 1963, CUA; "Church Leaders Stand Up to Be Counted," *America*, 29 June 1963, 897.

72. Letter from Rev. John Cronin to Ralph Dungan, 19 June 1963, General Ad-

ministration Series, subser. 1.1, box 85, folder: Social Action—Civil Rights, 1963, CUA; letter from Lee White to Mathew Ahmann, 11 July 1963, White House Central Files, Subject File, Religious Matters, box 886, folder: RM Religious Matters, JFKPL; letter from Irwin Miller to President John Kennedy, 23 July 1963, White House Staff Files: Ralph Dungan, box 1, folder: Civil Rights, JFKPL; letter from President John Kennedy to Rev. Irwin Miller, n.d., White House Staff Files: Ralph Dungan, box 1, folder: Civil Rights, JFKPL.

73. McAndrews, *Broken Ground*, 138; telegram from President John Kennedy to Msgr. Francis Hurley, 15 June 1963, General Administration Series, subser. 1.1, box 85, folder: Civil Rights, 1963, CUA.

74. "Memorandum of Meeting in the Office of Ralph Dungan, the White House, Washington," 20 June 1963, ser. 7, box 2, NCRR Executive Committee, MUA, 1–4.

75. "Request for Testimony on Civil Rights Legislation," 19 June 1963, General Administration Series, subser. 1.1, box 85, folder: Social Action—Civil Rights, 1963, CUA, 2.

76. "Immediate Action by NCCW Re Civil Rights Program," 15 July 1963, General Administration Series, subser. 1.1, box 89, folder: Social Action—Race Relations, 1963 January–July, CUA, 1–2; "Meeting of Leadership Conference on Civil Rights, Mitts Building, Washington, D.C.," 17 July 1963, General Administration Series, subser. 1.1, box 89, folder: Social Action—Race Relations, 1963; "Testimony on Civil Rights Legislation Presented to Committee on Judiciary, House of Representatives, by National Catholic Welfare Conference, Synagogue Council of America, and National Council of Churches of Christ," 24 July 1963, General Administration Series, subser. 1.1, box 85, folder: Social Action—Civil Rights, 1963, CUA, 1–10.

77. Letter from Henry Cabirac to Galen Weaver, 18 July 1963, ser. 7, box 2, folder: Conferences, Workshops, Institutes (NCRR)—Weaver (1963–64), MUA; interview of Vath and Plausche, 7.

78. Letter from Rev. Patrick O'Boyle to "Your Excellency," 18 July 1963, General Administration Series, subser. 1.1, box 89, folder: Social Action—Race Relations 1963 January–July, CUA; United States Catholic Bishops, "On Racial Harmony," 25 August 1963, General Administration Series, subser. 1.1, box 89, folder: Social Action—Race Relations, August 1963—, CUA, 1–2; letter from Rev. Patrick O'Boyle to "His Excellency," 9 August 1963, General Administration Series, subser. 1.1, box 89, folder: Social Action—Race Relations, August 1963—, CUA, 1.

79. "NCRR Newsletter," 23 August 1963, 5–6; John Kennedy,"The President's News Conference of July 17, 1963," *Public Papers, 1963*, 572.

80. "NCRR Newsletter," 23 August 1963, 10; "March on Washington," *America*, 10 August 1963, 131.

81. Sorensen, 504; "Text of Speech Originally Planned to be Delivered at Lincoln Memorial," 23 August 1963, General Administration Series, subser. 1.1, box 85, folder: Social Action—Civil Rights, 1963, CUA, 4; letter from Rev. Patrick O'Boyle to Msgr. Paul Tanner 4 September 1963, General Administration Series, subser. 1.1, box 85, folder: Social Action—Civil Rights, 1963, CUA, 1.

82. Reeves, *President Kennedy*, 583–584; Taylor Branch, *Parting the Waters* (New York: Simon and Schuster, 1988), 874–879; O'Boyle to Tanner, 4 September 1963, 1.

83. Reeves, *President Kennedy*, 583–584.

84. Ibid., 585; Taylor Branch, *Pillar of Fire: America in the King Years* (New York: Simon and Schuster, 1998), 138; "National Conference on Religion and Race Newsletter," November–December 1963, ser. 7, box 2, folder: NCRR Newsletters, MUA, 4, 2–3.

85. "NCRR Newsletter," November–December 1963, 3; "National Conference on Religion and Race Newsletter," November 19, 1963, ser. 7, box 2, folder: NCRR Newsletters, MUA, 1; "Text of Appeal for Unity by U.S. Catholic Bishops," *Washington Post*, 17 November 1963, D31; George Dugan, "Catholics Uphold Biracial Couples," *New York Times*, 18 November 1963, L47.

86. "NCRR Newsletter," November–December 1963, 13; "Rough Draft of Section B," n.d., 4.

87. David Southern, *John LaFarge and the Limits of Catholic Interracialism* (Baton Rouge: Louisiana State University Press, 1996), 348; "Rough Draft of Section B," n.d., 6, 3.

88. Memorandum from Rev. John Wagner to Msgr. Paul Tanner, 27 September 1963, General Administration Series, subser. 1.1, box 85, folder: Social Action—Civil Rights, 1963, CUA, 1–2.

89. John Donovan, *Crusader in the Cold War* (New York: Peter Lang, 2005), 149.

90. Schlesinger, 74.

91. James Giglio, *The Presidency of John F. Kennedy* (Lawrence: University of Kansas Press, 1991), 195.

92. Jay Dolan, *The American Catholic Experience* (Notre Dame, Ind.: University of Notre Dame Press, 1992), 424; "Ouster of Racists in South Forecast," *New York Times*, 27 August 1961, L4; Milton Bracker, "U.S. Bishops at Rome Ask Clear Equality Stand," *New York Times*, 25 October 1963, L1, 15; Cronin, "Religion and Race," 1; "Commitment," May 1963, 18.

93. Branch, *Pillar of Fire*, 22; Peter Finney, "Laypersons Launched 1961 Desegregation Drive," *New Orleans Clarion Herald*, 18 January 2001, n.p., Desegregation File, box 1, folder: Desegregation—Archbishop Rummel, AANO.

94. Mathew Ahmann, "Report to Leaders of National Conference on Religion and Race," 6 October 1963, ser. 7, box 2, folder: Conferences, Workshops, Institutes, (NCRR) Reports, 1963, MUA, 3; James Findlay, "Religion and Politics in the Sixties: The Churches and the Civil Rights Act of 1964," *Journal of American History* 77 (June 1990): 71.

95. "Rough Draft of Section B," n.d., 2.

96. Reeves, *President Kennedy*, 429.

97. NCRR Newsletter, 19 November 1963, 1–2.

98. Giglio, 202; John McGreevy, *Parish Boundaries: The Catholic Encounter with Race in the Twentieth-Century Urban North* (Chicago: University of Chicago Press, 1996), 151; letter from Rev. Robert Tracy to Members of the Clergy, Diocese of Baton Rouge, 30 March 1962, Desegregation File, box 1, folder: Desegregation—Archbishop Rummel, AANO; NCRR Newsletter, 19 November 1963, 1–2.

99. Reeves, *President Kennedy*, 277; memorandum from Harris Wofford to the President, 29 May 1961, Personal Papers of Ralph Dungan, box 2, folder: Special Assistant Files—Correspondence, JFKPL.

100. McGreevy, *Parish Boundaries*, 136–149; Niebuhr qtd. in John McGreevy, *Catholicism and American Freedom* (New York: Norton, 2003), 211.

101. "Memorandum for all Department and Agency Heads," n.d., White House Staff Files, Lee C. White File, Civil Rights, box 19, folder: Civil Rights, General, 6/18/62–11/16/63, JFKPL; letter from Rev. John Cronin to Henry Cabirac, 5 June 1963, ser. 34, box 18, folder: USCC Social Action Department, Msgr. Higgins and Fr. Cronin, 1962–1968, MUA, 1; "Status of National Conference on Religion and Race," June 1962, General Administration Series, subser. 1.1, box 89, folder: Social Action—Race Relations, 1960–1962, CUA; Rev. John Cronin, "Report to Archbishop Cousins on Steering Committee Meeting, National Conference on Religion and Race," 17 April 1963, General Administration Series, subser. 1.1, box 89, folder: Social Action and Race Relations, 1963, CUA.

102. Giglio, 202; John Kennedy, "The President's News Conference of September 12, 1963," *Public Papers, 1963*, 677; "Discrimination and the Christian Conscience," 1.

103. Giglio, 202; "The President's News Conference of September 12, 1963," 677; letter from Msgr. Paul Tanner to Mathew Ahmann, 11 December 1961, General Administration Series, subser. 1.1, folder: NCWC Administrative Board, 1961, CUA; letter from Alba Zizzamia to Grace Teti, General Administration Series, subser. 3.6, box 174, folder: CAIP Correspondence, 2, 1950–1967, CUA.

104. "Rough Draft of Section B," n.d.; "Waking Up to Race," *Time*, 4 October 1963, 80; "That Awful Fatalism," *Time*, 25 January 1963, 66; John LaFarge, Letter to the Editor, *Time*, 15 February 1963, 14; letters from Mathew Ahmann and Joseph Neusse to the *Washington Post*, 18 November 1963, General Administration Series, subser. 1.1, box 89, folder: Social Action—Race Relations, 1963, September–December, CUA; Southern, 364.

105. Giglio, 173.

106. Memorandum from Rev. John Cronin to Msgr. Paul Tanner, 30 October 1963, General Administration Series, subser. 1.1, box 85, folder: Social Action—Civil Rights, CUA.

107. Thomas Reeves, *A Question of Character* (New York: Free Press, 1991), 336–337; "NCRR Newsletter," 23 August 1963, 6; "Report to NCRR," 6 October 1963, 2; "Waking Up to Race," 79.

108. Kennedy supported the Court's decision in *Abingdon Township School District v. Schempp*, but of 950 pieces of correspondence received by the White House after the decision, only thirteen agreed with Kennedy, in memorandum from William J. Hopkins to Ralph Dungan, 9 July 1963, White House Central Files, Subject File—Religious Matters, box 886, folder RM2/ED 9/1/62, JFKPL; "Memorandum of Meeting in the Office of Ralph Dungan, the White House, Washington," 20 June 1963.

109. Letter from Frank Hall to Msgr. Paul Tanner, 22 August 1961, General Administration Series, subser. 1.1, box 89, folder: Social Action—Race Relations, 1960–62, CUA, 2; letter from Rev. John Cronin to Henry Cabirac, 5 June 1963, ser. 34, box 17, folder: USCC Social Action Department, Msgr. Higgins and Fr. Cronin, 1962–1968, MUA, 1.

110. Memorandum from Msgr. Francis Hurley to Msgr. Paul Tanner, 12 July 1963, General Administration Series, subser. 1.1, box 89, folder: Social Action and Race Relations, 1963 January–July, CUA, 2; memorandum from Msgr. Francis Hurley to Ms. Peggy Roach, 22 July 1963, General Administration Series, subser. 1.1, box 85, folder: Social Action—Civil Rights, 1963, CUA; memorandum from Msgr. Francis Hurley to

Msgr. Paul Tanner, 21 September 1963, General Administration Series, subser. 1.1, box 85, folder: Social Action—Civil Rights, CUA.

111. James Hilty, *Robert Kennedy: Brother Protector* (Philadelphia, Pa.: Temple University Press, 1997), 168; "Radio and Television Report to the American People on Civil Rights," 11 June 1963, 469.

112. "News and Comment," *Science*, 20 December 1963, 1554; "Statement on Population Issued by the Bishops of the United States 1959," General Administration Series, subser. 1.1, box 93, folder: U.S. Government, Birth Control, 1966, CUA, 2.

113. "News and Comment," 1554.

114. Theodore Sorensen, *Kennedy* (New York: Harper and Row, 1965), 364.

115. David Broder, "Fertility Study Points Up Delicate Policy Question," *Washington Star*, 25 April 1962, A13; John F. Kennedy, "The President's News Conference of July 19, 1961," *Public Papers, 1961*, 518.

116. Broder, A13.

117. Ibid.

118. "Memorandum of Conversation," 3 January 1962, White House Staff Files: Ralph Dungan, box 2, folder: Population Control, JFKPL, 2.

119. "News and Comment," *Science*, 14 December 1962, 1249; "News and Comment," *Science*, 21 June 1963, 1291.

120. John F. Kennedy, "The President's News Conference of April 24, 1963," *Public Papers, 1963*, 344; George Barrett, "Catholics and Birth Control: A Bold Re-Examination," *Reader's Digest*, November 1963, 81; "News and Comment," *Science*, 20 December 1963, 1554.

121. "Pope Pius XII on Population," 20 January 1958, General Administration Series, subser. 1.1, box 86, folder: Family Life Bureau, 1959, Subject—Population and Future U.S. Policy, CUA.

122. Letter from Catherine Schaefer to Rev. James Griffiths, 18 January 1961, General Administration Series, subser. 1.1, box 86, folder: Social Action: Family Life Bureau—Birth Control 1961–62, CUA; memorandum from Harmon Burns to Msgr. Paul Tanner, 29 September 1961, General Administration Series, subser. 1.1, box 86, folder: Social Action: Family Life Bureau—Birth Control, 1961–1962, CUA.

123. Memorandum from Rev. James Vizzard to Msgr. Paul Tanner, 6 November 1961, General Administration Series, subser. 1.1, box 86, folder: Social Action: Family Life Bureau, 1961–62, CUA.

124. Memorandum from Msgr. Francis Hurley to Msgr. Paul Tanner, 7 December 1962, General Administration Series, subser. 1.1, box 86, folder: Social Action: Family Life Bureau—Birth Control, 1963, CUA.

125. Letter from Catherine Schaefer to the President, 31 July 1962, General Administration Series, subser. 1.1, box 86, folder: Social Action: Family Life Bureau—Birth Control, 1961–1962, CUA, 1–2.

126. Memorandum from Harmon Burns to Msgr. Francis Hurley, 21 November 1962, General Administration Series, subser. 1.1, box 86, folder: Social Action: Family Life Bureau—Birth Control, 1961–1962, CUA; memorandum from Msgr. Francis Hurley to Msgr. Paul Tanner, 14 December 1962, General Administration Series, subser. 1.1, box 86, folder: Social Action: Family Life Bureau—Birth Control, 1961–1962, CUA; "Statement by Richard N. Gardner, Deputy Assistant Secretary of State for Interna-

tional Organization Affairs, in Committee II, on Population Growth and Economic Development," 10 December 1962, General Administration Series, subser. 1.1, box 52, folder: International Affairs: UN, 1962, July–December, CUA, 5.

127. "Birth Control and the Catholic," *Time*, 5 September 1961, 75; "The Population Bomb," *America*, 27 May 1961, 364; "President Approves Population Studies," *Christian Century*, 8 May 1963, 605.

128. "The Population Bomb," 365; "Birth Control and the Catholic," 70; "Family Planning," *Commonweal*, 20 October 1961, 85.

129. "News and Comment," *Science*, 30 November 1962, 960–961; "Accenting the Positive," *America*, 23 March 1963, 389; letter from Alan Guttmacher to President John Kennedy, 23 April 1963, White House Central Files, Subject File—Religious Matters, box 19, folder: RM 2/21/63—, JFKPL; "Birth Control: How Much Federal Help?," *U.S. News and World Report*, 29 April 1963, 11; "News and Comment," *Science*, 20 December 1963, 1555.

130. Schaefer to Griffiths; "Minutes of the Meeting on International Affairs," 19 July 1961, General Administration Series, subser. 1.1, box 36, folder: International Affairs—General, CUA, 1.

131. Memorandum from Catherine Schaefer, 20 October 1961, General Administration Series, subser. 1.1, box 173, folder: Memorandums: FY 1961–1962, CUA; memorandum from Rev. James Vizzard to Msgr. Paul Tanner, 9 November 1961, General Administration Series, subser. 1.1, box 86, folder: Social Action: Family Life Bureau—Birth Control, 1961–62, CUA.

132. "Memo for Clergymen," *America*, 17 February 1962, 638; letter from Msgr. Francis Hurley to Father Knott, 7 December 1962, General Administration Series, subser. 1.1, box 86, folder: Social Action: Family Life Bureau—Birth Control, 1963, CUA; Hurley to Tanner, 14 December 1962.

133. "Memorandum for Briefing for Non-Governmental Organizations at the U.S. Mission to the U.N., February 13, 1963, with Leighton Van Nort of the Bureau of International Affairs, Department of State," 20 February 1963, General Administration Series, subser. 1.1, box 52, folder: International Affairs—United Nations, 1963, CUA, 1.

134. "The President's News Conference of April 24, 1963," 344; "Notes and Comment," *Science*, 30 November 1962, 961–962; "Birth Control and Policy," *America*, 11 May 1963, 662; "Notes and Comment," *Science*, 20 December 1963, 1554; letter from Thomas Benham to Msgr. Francis Hurley, 27 December 1963, General Administration Series, subser. 1.1, box 86, folder: Social Action: Family Life Bureau—Birth Control, 1963, CUA.

135. McAndrews, *Broken Ground*, 70–71; memorandum from Ralph Dungan to the Files, 16 April 1962, Ralph Dungan Special Assistant Files, box 5, folder: Correspondence, 4/62 [2 of 3], JFKPL; memorandum from Donald Wilson to Ralph Dungan, 6 July 1962, Ralph Dungan Special Assistant Files, box 6, folder: Correspondence, 7/62 [1 of 2], JFKPL; "News and Comment," *Science*, 30 October 1962, 961; "News and Comment," *Science*, 21 June 1963, 1291.

136. Eve Edstrom, "Population Parley Asks Birth Curbs," *Washington Post*, 18 November 1963, A1; "Regulating Reproduction," *Washington Post*, 20 November 1963, A22.

137. Letter from Rev. Theodore McCarrick to Msgr. Paul Tanner, 20 November

1963, General Administration Series, subser. 1.1, box 86, folder: Social Action: Family Life Bureau—Birth Control, 1963, CUA; letter from Rev. Theodore McCarrick to Rev. John McGuire, 18 November 1963, General Administration Series, subser. 1.1, box 86, folder: Social Action: Family Life Bureau—Birth Control, 1963, CUA.

138. "News and Comment," *Science*, 20 December 1963, 1554–1555.

139. Letter from Msgr. Paul Tanner to Msgr. Francis Hurley, 18 October 1963, General Administration Series, subser. 1.1, box 86, folder: Social Action: Family Life Bureau—Birth Control, January–June 1964, CUA; McAndrews, *Broken Ground*, 173.

140. Fuchs, 167; interview of Kitty and John Kenneth Galbraith by Vicki Daitch, 10 September 2002, Oral History Collection, JFKPL, 43.

141. Interview of Richard Cardinal Cushing by Sen. Edward Kennedy, n.d., Oral History Collection, JFKPL, 5.

142. Letter from Msgr. Francis Hurley to Thomas Benham, 30 November 1963, General Administration Series, subser. 1.1, box 86, folder: Social Action: Family Life Bureau—Birth Control, 1963, CUA.

CHAPTER TWO. Catholics and Lyndon Johnson

1. Paul Conkin, *Big Daddy from the Pedernales: Lyndon Johnson* (Boston: Twayne, 1986), 195–196.

2. Bruce Schulman, *Lyndon B. Johnson and American Liberalism* (Boston: Bedford, 1995), 135; Robert Dallek, *Flawed Giant: Lyndon Johnson and His Times* (New York: Oxford University Press, 1998), 247–248.

3. Robert Doty, "Pontiff Appeals for Peace Effort," *New York Times*, 12 February 1965, L1; "Peace in Vietnam Is Sought by Pope," *New York Times*, 21 February 1965, L24.

4. Memorandum from Bill Moyers to "Mr. President," 16 April 1965, White House Central Files, Name File—N, box 24, LBJPL.

5. Memorandum from Jack Valenti to President Lyndon Johnson, 26 February 1965, White House Central Files, Subject File—Religious Matters, box 6, LBJPL, 1–2; Jack Languuth, "Saigon Catholics Fearful of Buddhist Army Purge," *New York Times*, 13 April 1965, L1,4.

6. "Text of Encyclical by Pope Paul Deploring Armed Conflicts," *New York Times*, 1 May 1965, L9; Jack Languuth, "Saigon Catholics Contend Regime Is Easy on Reds," *New York Times*, 10 May 1965, L1; Jack Languuth, "Saigon Generals Striving to Form a Stable Regime," *New York Times*, 12 June 1965, L1.

7. Robert Doty, "Papal Encyclical a Plea for Peace," *New York Times*, 1 May 1965, L9; "Memorandum for the President: Talking Points for the Pope," n.d., Appointment File (Diary Back-up), box 23, LBJPL, 1.

8. "Excerpts from Papal Address," *New York Times*, 4 October 1965, L2; Tom Wicker, "Two Leaders Meet: Paul and President Confer Forty-Six Minutes on World Issues," *New York Times*, 4 October 1965, L2.

9. E. W. Kenworthy, "Mansfield Report Seen as Urging U.S. to Get Peace Pact Quickly," *New York Times*, 9 January 1966, L1.

10. Transcript, Bill Moyers Press Conference, 4 October 1964, Appointment File (Diary Back-up), box 23, LBJPL, 7; Robert Doty, "Pope's Christmas Plea: 'Sincere Ne-

gotiation,'" *New York Times*, 24 December 1965, L1; Robert Doty, "Pope Sends Pleas: Pontiff Exhorts Hanoi, Saigon, Washington to Pursue Peace," *New York Times*, L1; Jack Raymond, "U.S. is Pessimistic as War Is Resumed," *New York Times*, 26 December 1965, L1.

11. "Pope Regrets His Peace Bids' Failure," *New York Times*, 25 June 1966, L5; letter from President Lyndon Johnson to Senator Mike Mansfield, 22 June 1966, White House Central Files, Name File, box 72, LBJPL, 2–3.

12. Letter from Martin Riley to President Lyndon Johnson, 1 July 1966, White House Central Files, Name File, box 141, LBJPL.

13. "Text of Pope's Encyclical on Peace," *New York Times*, 20 September 1966, L18; memorandum from Tom Johnson to President Lyndon Johnson, 3 October 1966, White House Central Files, Subject File—Peace, box 1, LBJPL; "Report to the Bishops," USCC Office for United Nations Affairs, September 1966, General Administration Series, subser. 3.3, box 165, folder: Report to Bishops, USCC Papers, CUA, 1.

14. "Papal Peace Vow Sent to Vietnam," *New York Times*, 1 October 1966, L4; Robert Doty, "150,000 Join Pope in Plea for Peace by Negotiations," *New York Times*, 5 October 1966, L1,4; Robert Doty, "Pope Paul Urges Truce Extension, Then Peace Talks," *New York Times*, 9 December 1966, L1, 17; "Rusk Pessimistic on Lengthy Truce," *New York Times*, 9 December 1966, L17.

15. "Pope to Receive Soviet President," *New York Times*, 4 January 1967, L6; Robert Doty, "Podgorny Meets Pope at Vatican," *New York Times*, L1, 16; "The Pope's Message," *New York Times*, 9 February 1967, L2; "Meeting of the Pope and the President," 13 December 1967, Special Files—Meeting Notes File, box 2, LBJPL, 4–5; "The President's Reply," *New York Times*, 9 February 1967, L2; "Ho Chi Minh Reply to Pope," *New York Times*, 14 February 1967, L8; "Saigon Catholics Stage a Protest," *New York Times*, 25 February 1967, L3.

16. "Thant Hails Pope on Peace Efforts," *New York Times*, 27 April 1967, L9; "Text of Sermon by Pope Paul and Shrine of Fatima," *New York Times*, 14 May 1967, L47; "Pope Melancholy on Peace Outlook," *New York Times*, 17 August 1967, L15.

17. "Meeting of the Pope and the President," 4–14.

18. Bernard Weinraub, "Bishops of South Vietnam, Asking Peace, Score Thieu," *New York Times*, L3.

19. "Meeting of the Pope and the President," 2; Schulman, 148.

20. "Poetic Justice in Vietnam?" *America*, 20 June 1964, 837; "Memorandum," National Catholic Welfare Conference Office for United Nations Affairs, 20 July 1964, General Administration Series, subser. 3.5, box 173, CUA, 1; "Protest in Saigon," *America*, 27 June 1964, 862.

21. "Vatican Appeals for Saigon Calm," *New York Times*, 30 August 1964, L3.

22. Msgr. George Higgins, "National Policy and the Clergy," CAIP News, May 1965, General Administration Series, subser. 3.6, box 174, folder: CAIP News, 1964–65, CUA, 6–7; letter from Rev. Robert Lucey to Jack Valenti, 10 May 1965, White House Central Files, Subject File—Religious Matters, box 6, LBJPL, 1; Charles O'Donnell, "Statement on the War in Vietnam by the CAIP World Order Committee," 17 July 1965, General Administration Series, subser. 3.6, box 174, folder: CAIP News, 1964–65, CUA, 6–7.

23. Arthur Goldberg, "Efforts for Peace," 4 December 1965, in *Social Digest*, July–

August 1966, General Administration Series, subser. 3.6, box 174, folder: CAIP Annual Convention, 1965, CUA, 219, 217–218.

24. Douglas Robinson, "Catholics Picket Spellman Office," *New York Times*, 5 December 1965, L1, 10; "Spellman Arrives for Five Day Visit with Vietnam G.I.'s," *New York Times*, 24 December 1965, L6.

25. "The Bishops and Vietnam," *Commonweal*, 15 April 1966, 93; John Cogley, "'Never Again War,'" *New York Times*, 5 October 1966, L4.

26. "Peace and Patriotism," *America*, 16 July 1966, 50; "Peace and Vietnam," National Council of Catholic Bishops, USCC, 18 November 1966, in *Quest for Justice: A Compendium of Statements of the United States Bishops on the Political and Social Order 1966–1980*, ed. J. Brian Benestad and Francis Butler (Washington, D.C.: United States Catholic Conference, 1981), 53.

27. "Statement on Peace," 18 November 1966, General Administration Series, subser. 1.1, box 70, folder: NCWC Bishops General Meeting Minutes, 1963–66, CUA, 192; "Open Letter to American Catholic Bishops," n.d., General Administration Series, subser. 1.1, box 7, folder: Administration—Letters to Bishops, April–December 1966, CUA, 2; "Text of Pope's Encyclical on Peace," 18; "Spellman's View Decried in Rome," *New York Times*, 28 December 1966, L3; John Cogley, "The Spellman Dispute," *New York Times*, 29 December 1966, L3; "Spellman's View on War Called Outrageous by Episcopal Bishop," *New York Times*, 4 February 1967, L3; John Sheerin, "Who Speaks for the Church on Vietnam?," *Catholic World*, November 1966, 72.

28. "Catholics Seek a Review on War," *New York Times*, 19 March 1967, L3; Daniel Callahan, "America's Catholic Bishops," *Atlantic Monthly*, April 1967, 69.

29. "In Recent Peace Plea Bishop Asks Withdrawal from Vietnam," CAIP News, October 1967, General Administration Series, subser. 3.6, box 174, folder: CAIP News, 1966–67, CUA, 7–8; "Bishops Endorsing Negotiation Now," CAIP News, October 1967, General Administration Series, subser. 3.6, box 174, folder: CAIP News, 1966–67, CUA, 6–7; William O'Brien, "Statement on Bombing Population Centers in North Vietnam," CAIP News, October 1967, General Administration Series, subser. 3.6, box 174, folder: CAIP News, 1966–67, CUA, 5.

30. "On Peace," NCCB, USCC, 16 November 1967, in Benestad and Butler, 56–57; "Resolution on Peace," NCCB, USCC, Fourth General Meeting, 23–24 April 1968, USCC Papers, USCCBA, 64–65; "Up Bishops' Sleeves," *Newsweek*, 24 April 1967, 88.

31. "White House Rebuttal to Vietnam Critics," *Catholic World*, October 1966, 53.

32. Memorandum from Joseph Califano to President Lyndon Johnson, 18 September 1967, White House Central Files, Subject File—Religious Matters, box 6, LBJPL; Lyndon Johnson, "Statement by the President," 2 December 1967, White House Central Files, Subject File—Religious Matters, box 6, LBJPL; memorandum from Marvin Watson, 28 March 1968, White House Central Files, Subject File—Religious Matters, box 6, LBJPL.

33. James O'Gara, "Banning the Bomb," *Commonweal*, 23 July 1965, 522.

34. Charles Meconis, *With Clumsy Grace: The American Catholic Left, 1961–1975* (New York: Seabury, 1979), 9; "Men of Peace," *Commonweal*, 19 March 1965, 779; Anthony Bouscaren, "The Catholic Peaceniks," *National Review*, 8 March 1966, 202.

35. Meconis, 13; Bouscaren, 202; John Sheerin, "The Morality of the Vietnam War," *Catholic World*, March 1966, 330.

36. Melvin Small, *Antiwarriors: The Vietnam War and the Battle for America's Hearts and Minds* (Wilmington, Del.: Scholarly Resources, 2002), 51; Charles Palms, "Peace and the Catholic Conscience," *Catholic World*, June 1966, 145–146; "Getting Out," *Commonweal*, 23 December 1966, 335.

37. Emanuel Perlmulter, "Twelve Clerics Criticize Johnson on Hanoi Bombing," *New York Times*, 27 December 1966, L6; "Arkansas Priest Leads Fight on War," *New York Times*, 26 February 1967, L9.

38. "Says Vietnam War Defends Christian Values," CAIP News, January 1966, General Administration Series, subser. 3.6, box 174, folder: CAIP News, 1966–67, CUA, 11; Bouscaren, 202.

39. Andrew Greeley, "Peaceniks Have a Lot to Learn," CAIP News, June 1965, General Administration Series, subser. 3.6, box 174, folder: CAIP News, 1964–65, CUA, 7–8.

40. Robert McNamara et al., *Argument without End* (Washington, D.C.: Public Affairs, 2000); "President Lyndon Johnson Explains Why Americans Fight in Vietnam, 1965," in *Major Problems in American Foreign Relations*, ed. Dennis Merrill and Thomas Paterson (Lexington, Mass.: Heath, 1978), 2:450.

41. James O'Gara, "Catholics and Peace," *Commonweal*, 11 November 1966, 158; "Campus Poll Shows Catholics Back War, Decry Draft Lottery," *New York Times*, 20 November 1966, 16; Jeffrey Jones, "The Protestant and Catholic Vote," http://www.gallup.com/poll/11911/Protestant-Catholic-Vote,aspx?.

42. "At a General Audience," CAIP News, October 1966, General Administration Series, subser. 3.6, box 174, folder: CAIP News, 1966–67, CUA, 6.

43. "Our War in Vietnam," *Commonweal*, 6 August 1965, 547; James Hennesey, *American Catholics* (New York: Oxford University Press, 1981), 319; Jay Dolan, *The American Catholic Experience* (Notre Dame, Ind.: University of Notre Dame Press, 1992), 451.

44. "The Churches: What Should We Say?" *Newsweek*, 10 July 1967, 82; Dolan, *The American Catholic Experience*, 426; "Human Life in Our Day: Chapter II, 'The Family of Nations,'" NCCB, 15 November 1968, in Benestad and Butler, 60, 65; John Donovan, *Crusader in the Cold War* (New York: Peter Lang, 2005), 187.

45. "Human Life in Our Day," 59, 67–68.

46. John Sheerin, "The Bishops and the Vietnam War," *Catholic World*, January 1967, 197.

47. "Our War in Vietnam," *Commonweal*, 5 August 1965, 548; James Fraser, *Between Church and State* (New York: St. Martin's, 1999), 155; Small, *Antiwarriors*, 6–7; Hennesey, 320; Dolan, *The American Catholic Experience*, 426; Meconis, ix; M. S. Handler, "Clergymen Clash on Role in Major National Issues," *New York Times*, 1 March 1965, L78; "The Churches: What Should We Say?" 81–82.

48. "The Churches: What Should We Say?" 82; James Shannon, "Catholic Bishops and Vietnam," *Commonweal*, 17 March 1967, 671; "The Bishops Taken to Task," *America*, 11 March 1967, 337.

49. John Corry, "The Catholic Student Protest: Priest Calls Support of Liberal Clergy 'Argument within the Family,'" *New York Times*, 26 December 1965, L55.

50. Lyndon Johnson, "Remarks at the University of Michigan," 22 May 1964, *Public Papers of the Presidents of the United States: Lyndon B. Johnson, 1963–1964*, vol. 1:

November 22, 1963–June 30, 1964 (Washington, D.C.: U.S. Government Printing Office, 1965), 706.

51. Schulman, 111.

52. Lyndon Johnson, "Address before a Joint Session of the Congress," 27 November 1963, *Public Papers, 1963–1964*, 1:9.

53. Letter from Isacc Franck to Galen Weaver, 6 December 1963, subser. 1.1, box 89, folder: Social Action—Race Relations, 1963, September–December, CUA; Gene Currivan, "Prelate Appeals for Racial Justice," *New York Times*, 14 February 1964, L33; John Cronin, "Religion and Race," *America*, 28–30 June 1964, 472.

54. Jeff Shesol, *Mutual Contempt: Lyndon Johnson, Robert Kennedy, and the Feud That Defined a Decade* (New York: Norton, 1997), 162; Ben Franklin, "Interfaith Rally in Capital Backs Civil Rights Bill," *New York Times*, 29 April 1964, L1; E. W. Kenworthy, "The Coming Filibuster," *New York Times*, 23 February 1964, E, 10.

55. Letter from James Cardinal McIntyre to Archbishop Patrick O'Boyle, 26 March 1964; letter from Archbishop Albert Meyer to O'Boyle, 29 February 1964; and letter from O'Boyle to "Your Excellency," 26 February 1964, General Administration Series, subser. 1.1, box 89, folder: Social Action—Race Relations, 1964–1966, CUA.

56. John McGreevy, *Parish Boundaries: The Catholic Encounter with Race in the Twentieth-Century Urban North* (Chicago: University of Chicago Press, 1996), 151; letter from Rev. John Cronin to Bishop William Cousins, 20 March 1964, General Administration Series, subser. 1.1, box 85, folder: Social Action—Civil Rights, 1964, CUA, 2; James Findlay, "Religion and Politics in the Sixties: The Churches and the Civil Rights Act of 1964," *Journal of American History* 77 (June 1990): 80; McGreevy, *Parish Boundaries*, 151.

57. Findlay, 80; letter from Mathew Ahmann to Burke Marshall, 1 May 1964, ser. 20, box 31, folder: U.S. Government—Department of Justice, National Catholic Conference for Interracial Justice Papers, MUA.

58. *Congressional Record*, Senate, 29 April 1964, 9251, 9243–9244.

59. Memorandum from Ralph Dungan to Bill Moyers, 24 April 1964, White House Central Files, Subject File—Religious Matters, folder: RM 11/23/63–9/23/66, LBJPL; "Statement of Archbishop Patrick O'Boyle to President Johnson," 29 April 1964, box 85, folder: Social Action—Civil Rights, 1964; Statement by Rev. John Cronin, 10 April 1964, General Administration Series, subser. 1.1, box 89, folder: Social Action—Race Relations, 1964–66, CUA, 1.

60. Lyndon B. Johnson, *The Vantage Point: Perspectives of the Presidency* (New York: Holt, Rinehart, and Winston, 1971), 160; "Civil Rights," *Congress and the Nation*, vol. 1: *1945–1964* (Washington, D.C.: Congressional Quarterly, 1965), 1636–1637; "Two Faiths Set Up Panels on Rights," 20 June 1964, *New York Times*, L16.

61. Donovan, 152.

62. Johnson, *Vantage Point*, 159; Donovan, 152.

63. Jones; letter from Burke Marshall to Mathew Ahmann, 6 January 1965, box 20, ser. 31, folder: U.S. Government—Department of Justice, MUA.

64. Taylor Branch, *Pillar of Fire: America in the King Years* (New York: Simon and Schuster, 1998), 519.

65. Morris MacGregor, *Steadfast in the Faith: The Life of Patrick Cardinal O'Boyle* (Washington, D.C.: Catholic University Press, 2006), 321.

66. MacGregor, 324.

67. John McGreevy, "Racial Justice and the People of God," *Religion and American Culture* (Summer 1994): 221.

68. David Lawrence,"Ignorance of the Law, Constitution," *Washington Evening Star*, 15 March 1965, A11; letter from Msgr. George Higgins to David Lawrence, 17 March 1965, General Administration Series, subser. 1.1, box 85, folder: Social Action—Civil Rights, 1965–66, CUA, 1–2.

69. Lyndon Johnson, "The President's News Conference of March 13, 1965," *Public Papers of the Presidents of the United States: Lyndon B. Johnson, 1965*, vol. 1: *January 1–May 31, 1965* (Washington, D.C.: U.S. Government Printing Office, 1966), 277; Msgr. George Higgins, "The Yardstick," National Catholic News Service, 22 March 1965, 2, attached to Higgins to Lawrence, 17 March 1965.

70. Lyndon Johnson, "Special Message to the Congress on the Right to Vote," 15 March 1965, *Public Papers, 1965*, 1:283; Schulman, 110; Donovan, 153; Dallek, 218–219.

71. MacGregor, 323.

72. Rev. John Cronin, "Testimony on Voting Rights Legislation Presented to Committee on Judiciary, House of Representatives, by Commission on Religion and Race, National Council of Churches in the United States of America; Social Action Department, National Catholic Welfare Conference; Social Action Commission, Synagogue Council of America," 25 March 1965, General Administration Series, subser. 1.1, box 85, folder: Social Action—Civil Rights, 1965–66, CUA; Donovan, 154.

73. Michael Stone, "Project Equality Today," *Christian Century*, 21 January 1970, 79.

74. John Cronin, "Report on Interreligious Clearing House Meeting, New York, July 13–14, 1965," General Administration Series, subser. 1.1, box 89, folder: Social Action—Race Relations, 1964–66, CUA.

75. "Civil Rights," *Congress and the Nation*, vol. 2: *1965–1968* (Washington, D.C.: Congressional Quarterly, 1969), 361; Rev. John Cronin, "Defeat of Dirksen Amendment Seen as Important," *Catholic Messenger*, 12 August 1965, 3, ser. 34, box 17, folder: USCC Social Action Department, Msgr. Higgins and Fr. Cronin, 1962–

76. Donovan, 156.

77. McGreevy,"Racial Justice and the People of God," 233–234; Cronin, "Report on Interreligious Clearing House Meeting."

78. MacGregor, 325; "Housing Racial Bias Is Scored by Prelate as an 'Immoral' Act," *New York Times*, 23 May 1966, L18; "Testimony of Representatives of the National Council of Churches, National Catholic Welfare Conference, and Synagogue Council of America, before Subcommittee No. 5, House Judiciary Committee, in Support of H.R. 14765, the Proposed Civil Rights Act of 1966," 18 May 1966, General Administration Series, subser. 1.1, box 88, folder: Social Action—Housing 1956–66, CUA, 3–4.

79. Roy Reed, "Meredith Is Shot in Back on Walk into Mississippi," *New York Times*, 7 June 1966, L1, 29; letters from James McGuire to John Doar, 5 July 1966, and Doar to McGuire, 12 July 1966, ser. 20, box 31, folder: U.S. Government—Justice Department, MUA.

80. McGreevy, "Racial Justice and the People of God," 234.

81. Shesol, 347; Johnson, *Vantage Point*, 176; "On Race Relations and Poverty, Pastoral Statement of the National Conference of Catholic Bishops," 18 November

1966, General Administration Series, subser. 1.1, box 65, folder: NCWC Administrative Statements 1965–66, CUA, 1–2; "Minutes, Annual Meeting, National Conference of Catholic Bishops, 11/14–18/66," General Administration Series, subser. 1.1, box 70, folder: NCWC Bishops' General Meeting Minutes, 1962–66, CUA, 180; letter from Robert Weaver to Rev. John Dearden, 23 December 1966, General Administration Series, subser. 1.1, box 69, folder: NCWC Annual Reports—Correspondence, 1966, CUA.

82. MacGregor, 325; McGreevy, "Racial Justice and the People of God," 240–241.

83. "Testimony of Representatives of the National Council of Churches, United States Catholic Conference, and Synagogue Council of America before the Subcommittee on Housing and Urban Affairs of the Senate Committee on Banking and Commerce in Support of S. 1538," 23 August 1967, ser. 28, box 1, folder: Federal Fair Housing Act, 1968, MUA, 6; MacGregor, 330, 326–327.

84. "Civil Rights," *Congress and the Nation*, 2:381, 383; memorandum from Arnold Aronson to Participating Organizations, 18 April 1968, 1–6, and letter from Peggy Roach to Rev. Kevin Kelly, 3 April 1968, ser. 28, box 1, folder: Federal Fair Housing Act, 1968, MUA.

85. "A Law to Assure Fair Housing and to Protect Rights against Interference (A Brief History of H.R. 2516)," attached to Aronson to Participating Organizations, 2; The "Mrs. Murphy" clause in the 1968 law reduced the maximum exemption from five to four rental units; see *Congress and the Nation*, 2:383.

86. "Statement on the National Race Crisis, 1968," in Minutes of the Administrative Board, National Conference of Catholic Bishops Fourth General Meeting, 4/23–24, 1968, CUA, 15–18.

87. Memorandum from Joseph Califano to the President, 10 April 1968, White House Central Files, Confidential File, box 56 [1 of 2], folder: HU2 Equality of Races [1967–] [5 of 5], LBJPL.

88. MacGregor, 331.

89. Letter from Rev. Philip Hannan to Mother A. Richard, 6 May 1968, Desegregation File, folder: Catholic School Integration: Department of Health, Education, and Welfare (1954–1972), AANO.

90. McGreevy, *Parish Boundaries*, 213–214.

91. Letter from Mathew Ahmann to Floyd Agostinelli, 21 February 1964, ser. 28, box 1, folder: Legislative Issues, Miscellaneous, 1964–68, MUA; David Southern, *John LaFarge and the Limits of Catholic Interracialism* (Baton Rouge: Louisiana State University Press, 1996), 348.

92. Letter from John Kenna to John Sisson, 5 November 1964, ser. 34, box 17, folder: USCC Social Development Department Division of Family Life, McHugh, Fr. James, 1964–66, 71, MUA; memorandums from Rev. John Cronin to Msgr. Francis Hurley, 13 November 1964, and Hurley to Cronin, 18 November 1964, General Administration Series, subser. 1.1, box 89, folder: Social Action—Race Relations, 1964–66, CUA; "Selma, Civil Rights, and the Church Militant," *Newsweek*, 29 March 1965, 76.

93. David Garrow, *The FBI and Martin Luther King Jr.* (New York: Penguin, 1988); memorandum from Rev. John Cronin to Msgr. Paul Tanner, 1 March 1965, General Administration Series, subser. 1.1, box 89, folder: Social Action—Race Relations, 1964–1966, CUA.

94. "Alabama Bishop Attacks Marches by Priests, Nuns," *New York Herald Tribune*,

19 March 1965, attached to letters from Msgr. Francis Hurley to Rev. Egidio Vagnozzi, 28 July 1965, and Vagnozzi to Hurley, 29 July 1965, General Administration Series, subser. 1.1, box 85, folder: Social Action—Civil Rights, 1965–66, CUA.

95. "Beyond Civil Rights," *America*, 19 June 1965, 875; letter from Msgr. Paul Tanner to Rev. Patrick O'Boyle, 26 August 1965, General Administration Series, subser. 1.1, box 89, folder: Social Action—Race Relations, 1964–1966, CUA.

96. Letter from Rev. William Cort to "Dear Member," 10 September 1966, and "The Georgetown Meeting," *Ave Maria*, n.d., n.p., in ser. 34, box 17, folder: USCC National Catholic Social Action Conference, 1963–69, MUA; Daniel Callahan, "America's Catholic Bishops," *Atlantic Monthly*, April 1967, 66, 69; "How Catholics View Their Church," *Newsweek*, 20 March 1967, 69–70.

97. Callahan, 66; "The Catholic Vote," *America*, 12 December 1964, 766.

98. Conkin, 219.

99. Pope Paul VI, *Constitution on the Church in the Modern World (Gaudium et Spes)*, 7 December 1965, http://www.vatican.va/archive/hist_councils/ii_vatican_council /documents.

100. "Population: New U.S. Interest in Offering Assistance Reveals Lag in Underdeveloped Nations," *Science*, 6 March 1964, 1016; "Welfare Birth Control," *America*, 1 February 1964, 157.

101. "Birth Control," *America*, 24 October 1964, 477; memorandum from Msgr. Francis Hurley to Msgr. Paul Tanner, 19 August 1965, General Administration Series, subser. 1.1, box 86, folder: Social Action—Family Life Bureau, Birth Control, CUA, 1.

102. "AID Told to Cooperate on Latin Birth Control," *Washington Post*, 25 April 1964, A9; "Now It's Official: U.S. Backs Birth Control Aid," *U.S. News and World Report*, 22 March 1965, 65; *Griswold v. Connecticut*, 381 U.S. 419 (1965); "Birth Control Laws," *America*, 7 November 1964, 544–545.

103. "Birth Control," *America*, 24 October 1964, 477; letter from Rev. Egidio Vagnozzi to Msgr. Paul Tanner, 12 March 1964, General Administration Series, subser. 1.1, box 86, folder: Social Action—Family Life Bureau, Birth Control, 1964 January–June, CUA.

104. Letter from Msgr. Paul Tanner to Rev. Egidio Vagnozzi, 18 March 1964, General Administration Series, subser. 1.1, box 86, folder: Social Action—Family Life Bureau, Birth Control, 1964 January–June, CUA; memorandum from Harmon Burns to William Consedine, 8 May 1964, General Administration Series, subser. 1.1, box 86, folder: Social Action—Family Life Bureau, Birth Control, 1964 January–June, CUA; Catherine Schaefer, "Summary of Trends and Activities in the Field of Reproduction," 30 May 1964, General Administration Series, subser. 1.1, box 52, folder: International Affairs—UN, 1964–65, CUA.

105. "Fifth Question," attached to letter from Rev. Patrick O'Boyle to Egidio Vagnozzi, 13 May 1964, General Administration Series, subser. 1.1, box 86, folder: Social Action—Family Life Bureau, Birth Control, 1964 January–June, CUA, 1–3.

106. Memorandum from Msgr. Francis Hurley to Rev. Patrick O'Boyle, 14 August 1965, General Administration Series, subser. 1.1, box 86, folder: Social Action—Family Life, Birth Control, August 1965, CUA; "Say a Little, Do a Lot," *Time*, 29 January 1965, 55.

107. "Promoting Birth Control," *America*, 20 February 1965, 238; "Public Birth

Control," *America*, 17 April 1965, 513; letter from Catherine Schaefer to World Union of Catholic Women's Organizations, 23 April 1965, General Administration Series, subser. 3.4, box 170, folder: Population: Memo 1, 1947–1965, CUA, 2.

108. "Special Conditions Applicable to the Use of OEO Grant Funds for Family Planning Programs," 12 March 1965, Sargent Shriver Personal Papers, box 63, folder: Birth Control Issue, JFKPL, 1–3.

109. Letter from Richard Cardinal Cushing to Sargent Shriver, 8 April 1965, Sargent Shriver Personal Papers, box 63, folder: Birth Control Issue, JFKPL.

110. "Stand on Johnson's Population Statement Priest's, Not Church's, Journals Claim," Religious News Service, 21 January 1965, General Administration Series, subser. 1.1, box 86, folder: Social Action—Family Life Bureau, Birth Control, 1964–1965, CUA; memorandum from Msgr. Francis Hurley to Rev. John Cronin, 15 February 1965, General Administration Series, subser. 1.1, box 95, folder: U.S. Government—Poverty, Family Planning and Public Policy Draft Statements, 1965, CUA; letter from Msgr. Paul Tanner to Msgr. Frank Rodimer, 10 March 1965, General Administration Series, subser. 1.1, box 86, folder: Social Action—Family Life, Birth Control, January–July 1965, CUA, 2; letter from Msgr. Paul Tanner to Rev. Egidio Vagnozzi, 3 August 1965, General Administration Series, subser. 1.1, box 86, folder: Social Action—Family Life, Birth Control, August 1965, CUA.

111. Memorandum from Msgr. Francis Hurley to Msgr. Paul Tanner, 19 August 1965, General Administration Series, subser. 1.1, box 86, folder: Social Action—Family Life, Birth Control, August 1965, CUA, 3.

112. Lyndon Johnson, "Address in San Francisco at the Twentieth Anniversary Commemorative Session of the United Nations," 25 June 1965, *Public Papers of the Presidents of the United States: Lyndon Johnson, 1965*, vol. 2: *June 1–December 31, 1965* (Washington, D.C.: U.S. Government Printing Office, 1966), 705; letter from Msgr. Francis Hurley to Bill Moyers, 16 July 1965, White House Central Files—Name File, box 24, folder: National Catholic, U–Z, LBJPL; "Health, Education, and Welfare," *Congress and the Nation*, 2:684.

113. Memorandums from Msgr. Francis Hurley to Msgr. Paul Tanner, 13 August 1965, 1–2, 13 August 1965, 2, and 23 August 1965, General Administration Series, subser. 1.1, box 86, folder: Social Action—Family Life, Birth Control, August 1965, CUA.

114. Memorandum from Harmon Burns to William Consedine, 11 August 1965, General Administration Series, subser. 1.1, box 86, folder: Social Action—Family Life, Birth Control, August 1965, CUA; "The Silence Is Broken," *America*, 11 September 1965, 256; Jean White, "Two Catholic Views Heard on Birth Control Bill," *Washington Post*, 25 August 1965, A1, 9; Michael Schiltz, "Did the Archbishop Mean to Commit Us?" *New City*, 15 September 1965, 3; "Testimony of William Ball," 24 August 1965, General Administration Series, subser. 1.1, box 93, folder: U.S. Government—Birth Control, CUA, 9.

115. Pope Paul VI, "Speech to the United Nations Organization," 4 October 1965, http://www.vatican.va/holy-father/paul-vi/speeches/1965/index.htm; memorandum from Donald Baker to Joseph Kershaw, Sargent Shriver, and Bernard Boutin, 19 October 1965, Sargent Shriver Personal Papers, OEO Correspondence, box 40, folder: Staff—Poverty Memos, 1965, JFKPL, 1–2.

116. "Birth Control Notes," 3 November 1965, General Administration Series, subser. 1.1, box 93, folder: U.S. Government—Birth Control, 1965, 1–11.

117. "NCWC Policy on Birth Control," 8 November 1965, General Administration Series, subser. 1.1, box 93, folder: U.S. Government—Birth Control, 1965, CUA, 1–11; memorandum from Msgr. Paul Tanner to Rev. James McNulty, 14 March 1966, General Administration Series, subser. 1.1, box 93, folder: U.S. Government—Birth Control, 1966 March, CUA.

118. "Health, Education, and Welfare," *Congress and the Nation*, 2:684; "Coming: More Federal Help on Birth Control," *U.S. News and World Report*, 15 November 1965, 11.

119. Memorandum from William Consedine to the Files, 15 December 1965, General Administration Series, subser. 1.1, box 93, folder: U.S. Government—Birth Control, 1965, CUA, 1–3.

120. Rowland Evans and Robert Novak, "Birth De-Control," *Washington Post*, 10 December 1965, A29.

121. Memorandum from Sargent Shriver to Bernard Boutin, Donald Baker, and Herbert Kramer, 13 December 1965, Sargent Shriver Personal Papers, OEO Correspondence, box 40, folder: Staff—Poverty Memos, 1965, JFKPL, 1–4.

122. Memorandum from Msgr. Francis Hurley to Msgr. Paul Tanner, 24 January 1966, General Administration Series, subser. 1.1, box 93, folder: U.S. Government—Birth Control, January 1966, CUA, 1.

123. "Health, Education, and Welfare," *Congress and the Nation*, 2:684; John Richmond, "Birth Control Showdown Near," *St. Louis Review*, 11 March 1966, n.p., General Administration Series, subser. 1.1, box 93, folder: U.S. Government—Birth Control 1966, March, CUA; Wilbur Cohen, "Freedom to Choose," 5 May 1966, General Administration Series, subser. 1.1, box 93, folder: U.S. Government—Birth Control, 1966, May, CUA; "Birth Control in High Gear," *America*, 25 June 1966, 869; Statement by Sargent Shriver, 3 July 1966, General Administration Series, subser. 1.1, box 93, folder: U.S. Government—Birth Control, 1966, July, CUA.

124. "Minutes of the Meeting of the Administrative Board," April 1966, National Catholic Welfare Conference Papers, UNDA, 8–10.

125. *Congressional Record*, 31 March 1966, H6980; "NCWC Official Scores OEO on Birth Control," *Jefferson City Catholic Missourian*, n.p., 10 July 1966, General Administration Series, subser. 1.1, box 86, folder: Social Action—Family Life Bureau, Birth Control, 1966, CUA; memorandum from Harmon Burns to William Consedine, 4 April 1966, General Administration Series, subser. 1.1, box 93, folder: U.S. Government—Birth Control 1966, April, CUA.

126. Memorandum from Rev. James McHugh to Rev. Paul Tanner, 26 September 1966, General Administration Series, subser. 1.1, box 93, folder: U.S. Government—Birth Control, 1966, August–September, CUA, 1; letter from Rev. Paul Tanner to Harley Staggers, 11 October 1966, General Administration Series, subser. 1.1, box 86, folder: Social Action—Family Life Bureau, Birth Control, 1966, CUA, 1–3; memorandum from Wilbur Cohen to Douglass Cater, 7 November 1966, White House Central Files, Subject File—Religious Matters, LBJPL.

127. NCCB, "On the Government and Birth Control," 14 November 1966, General

Administration Series, subser. 1.1, box 86, folder: Social Action—Family Life Bureau, Birth Control, 1966, CUA.

128. George Dugan, "Catholic Bishops Say U.S. Coerces Poor over Births," *New York Times*, 15 November 1966, L1, 24; memorandum from Douglass Cater to Lyndon Johnson, 29 November 1966, White House Central Files, Name File, box 24, folder: National Catholic U–Z, LBJPL; Joseph Califano, *The Triumph and Tragedy of Lyndon Johnson* (New York: Simon and Schuster, 1991), 157.

129. Califano, *Triumph and Tragedy of Lyndon Johnson*, 158; letter from Msgr. Francis Hurley to Rev. Patrick O'Boyle, 10 September 1965, General Administration Series, subser. 1.1, box 86, folder: Social Action—Family Life, Birth Control, 1965, CUA.

130. Dallek, 521; Califano, *Triumph and Tragedy of Lyndon Johnson*, 157–158.

131. Cater to Johnson, 29 November 1966; memorandum from Joseph Califano to Lyndon Johnson, 15 November 1966, White House Central Files, Name File, box 24, folder: National Catholic, U–Z, LBJPL.

132. Califano, *Triumph and Tragedy of Lyndon Johnson*, 157; "The Bishops Meet," *Commonweal*, 2 December 1966, 245–246; Cater to Johnson, 29 November 1966.

133. John Leo, "News and Views," *Commonweal*, 2 December 1966, 244; McCarthy qtd. in John Leo, "News and Views," *Commonweal*, 6 January 1967, 358.

134. "Minutes, National Conference of Catholic Bishops, Forty-Eighth Annual Meeting," 14–18 November 1966, CUA, 2–3.

135. "Background Information," 27; memorandum from Donald Baker to Sargent Shriver, 15 November 1966, General Administration Series, subser. 1.1, box 93, folder: U.S. Government—Birth Control 1966 October–December, CUA, 2–5.

136. "About-Face on Birth Control," *Time*, 9 December 1996, 30; memorandum from Msgr. Francis Hurley to Rev. Paul Tanner, 18 January 1967, box 140, folder: U.S. Government—Birth Control, 1967–70, USCCBA.

137. "Health, Education, and Welfare," *Congress and the Nation*, 2:747, 703; Johnson, *Vantage Point*, 348; Lady Bird Johnson, *A White House Diary* (New York: Holt, Rinehart, and Winston, 1970), 569.

138. Lyndon Johnson, "Annual Message to the Congress on the State of the Union," 17 January 1968, *Public Papers of the Presidents of the United States: Lyndon B. Johnson, 1968*, vol. 1: *January 1–June 30, 1968* (Washington, D.C.: U.S. Government Printing Office, 1969), 27; Lyndon Johnson, "Annual Budget Message to the Congress, Fiscal Year 1969," 29 January 1968, *Public Papers, 1968*, 1:89, 104; Johnson, *Vantage Point*, 340; memorandum from Msgr. Francis Hurley to Rev. Joseph Bernardin, 3 September 1968, box 140, folder: U.S. Government—Birth Control, 1967–70, USCCBA, 2.

139. Pope Paul VI, *Humanae Vitae*, 25 July 1968, http://www.vatican.va/holy_father/paul_vi/encyclicals/documents/hf_p-vi_enc_25071968_humanae-vitae_en.html.

140. Leslie Tentler, *Catholics and Contraception* (Ithaca, N.Y.: Cornell University Press, 2004), 270; United States Catholic Bishops, "Human Life in Our Day," November 1968, box 34, folder: *Humanae Vitae*, John Cardinal Dearden Papers, UNDA, 18–19.

141. Hurley to Bernardin, 2; Johnson, *Vantage Point*, 340.

142. Johnson, *Vantage Point*, 339–340; Califano, *Triumph and Tragedy of Lyndon Johnson*, 157; "Poverty Office in Peril," *Chicago Sun-Times*, n.p., box 140, folder: U.S. Government—Poverty, 1967 January–June, USCCBA; interview of Sargent Shriver by Michael Gillette, 23 August 1980, Oral History Collection, JFKPL, 2:55.

143. Memorandum from Msgr. Francis Hurley to Msgr. Paul Tanner, 1 October 1965, General Administration Series, subser. 1.1, box 86, folder: Social Action—Family Life Bureau, Birth Control, 1965, CUA, 2; "Minutes of November Meeting," attached to letter from Rev. Paul Tanner to Rev. James McHugh, 14 March 1966, General Administration Series, subser. 1.1, box 86, folder: Social Action—Family Life Bureau, Birth Control, 1966, CUA.

144. "Birth Control Programs and the Anti-Poverty Legislation: The Chronology of Events," 18 April 1966, General Administration Series, subser. 1.1, box 93, folder: U.S. Government—Birth Control, 1966, April, CUA, 11.

145. "News and Views," *Commonweal*, 28 April 1967, 162.

146. Letter from Rev. Egidio Vagnozzi to Rev. John Dearden, 12 April 1967, box 140, folder: U.S. Government—Birth Control, 1967–70, USCCBA, 1–2.

147. Memorandum from Father Neill to William Consedine, 25 August 1967, box 140, folder: U.S. Government—Birth Control, 1967–70, USCCBA.

148. Interview of Shriver by Gillette, 1:1–4.

149. Memorandum from Msgr. Francis Hurley to Rev. Frederick Hochwalt and William Consedine, 20 February 1964, General Administration Series, subser. 1.1, box 95, folder: U.S. Government—Poverty, 1964 January–May, CUA, 2.

150. Memorandum from Harmon Burns to William Consedine, 28 July 1964, General Administration Series, subser. 1.1, box 86, folder: Social Action—Birth Control, 1964 July–December, CUA, 1; "United Nations Population Commission," 23 March–5 April 1965, General Administration Series, subser. 3.3, box 165, folder: Population, 1961–1965, CUA, 9–10; letter from Donald Barrett to Catherine Schaefer, 7 May 1965, General Administration Series, subser. 3.1, box 162, folder: B: Correspondence, 1959–1969, CUA.

151. Leo Pfeffer, "Letter to the Editor," *New York Times*, 18 June 1965, L34; letter from Hyman Bookbinder to Editor of the *New York Times*, 26 June 1965, n.p., General Administration Series, subser. 1.1, box 95, folder: U.S. Government—Poverty, Interreligious Committee, January–December 1965, CUA.

152. "Birth Control," n.d., Sargent Shriver Personal Papers, box 63, folder: Birth Control Issue, JFKPL, 6, 8, 9.

153. Memorandum from Msgr. Francis Hurley to Msgr. Paul Tanner, 13 August 1965, General Administration Series, subser. 1.1, box 86, folder: Social Action—Family Life Bureau, Birth Control, August 1965, CUA, 2; letter from Msgr. Francis Hurley to Rev. Paul Tanner, 17 November 1965, General Administration Series, subser. 1.1, box 86, folder: Social Action—Family Life Bureau, Birth Control, 1965, CUA, 1; John Gardner, "Memorandum to Heads of Operating Agencies," 24 January 1966, General Administration Series, subser. 1.1, box 86, folder: Social Action—Family Life Bureau, Birth Control, 1966, CUA, 1.

154. Shriver to Boutin, Baker, and Kramer, 13 December 1965, 4.

155. Sargent Shriver, "The Moral Basis for the War on Poverty," *Christian Century*, 14 December 1966, 1533.

156. Andrew Greeley, "U.S. Catholicism: Growth or Decline?" *America*, 24 December 1964, 482–483; *The Gallup Poll: Public Opinion, 1935–1971*, vol. 2: *1959–1971*, ed. George Gallup (New York: Random House, 1972), 1937.

157. Louis Harris, "How Catholics Feel about Church Ban," *Chicago Daily News*,

10 February, n.p., General Administration Series, subser. 1.1, box 86, folder: Family Life Bureau, Birth Control, 1964 January–June, CUA.

158. "Two Meetings: Will They Meet?" *America*, 11 May 1968, 630.

CHAPTER THREE. Catholics and Richard Nixon

1. Melvin Small, *The Presidency of Richard Nixon* (Lawrence: University of Kansas Press, 1999), 66.

2. Ibid.; William Pfaff, "This Way Out," *Commonweal*, 14 February 1969, 611.

3. "Ultimatum," *Commonweal*, 7 March 1969; 696; William Pfaff, "After Vietnam, What?" *Commonweal*, 21 March 1969, 7; Richard Nixon, "Remarks at a Meeting with Pope Paul VI," 2 March 1969, *Public Papers of the Presidents of the United States: Richard Nixon, 1969* (Washington, D.C.: U.S. Government Printing Office, 1970), 173; Robert Doty, "Pope Emphasizes Message of Joy in Easter Speech," *New York Times*, 7 April 1969, L1, 8.

4. Memorandum from Patrick Buchanan to the President, 11 April 1969, President's Office Files, President's Handwriting, box 7, folder: President's Handwriting, April 1969, Richard M. Nixon Presidential Papers, NA.

5. "And Now, Two Peace Plans," *Commonweal*, 10 May 1969, 307; John Sheerin, "A Cease-Fire Now in Vietnam," *Catholic World*, November 1969, 51; "The Anachronistic War," *Commonweal*, 19 September 1969, 555.

6. "Shaking the Dust," *Commonweal*, 3 October 1969, 3; Michael Novak, "Vietnam's Tomorrow," *Commonweal*, 10 October 1969, 45.

7. Mary McGrory, "More of the Same in Store," *America*, 1 November 1969, 376; *The Gallup Poll: Public Opinion, 1935–1971*, vol. 2: *1959–1971*, ed. George Gallup (New York: Random House, 1972), 2217; Small, *Presidency of Richard Nixon*, 74; George Dugan, "Religious Leaders Endorse Vietnam Moratorium," *New York Times*, 11 October 1969, L25; "This Way Out," *Commonweal*, 7 November 1969, 171.

8. "An Appeal to the Silent Majority," *America*, 11 November 1969, 452; Robert Doty, "Pontiff Applauds Nixon on Vietnam," *New York Times*, 18 November 1969, C11; memorandum from Alexander Butterfield to Peter Flanigan, Bradford Keogh, and Charles Colson, 18 November 1969, White House Special Files, Staff Member and Office Files: Charles Colson, box 46, folder: Catholic War Veterans, NA.

9. Mary McGrory, "What Did It All Mean?" *America*, 29 November 1969, 518; "Remobilizing for Peace," *Commonweal*, 27 February 1970, 571.

10. "Remobilizing for Peace," 571–572.

11. Memorandum from the American Consul General, Munich, to the Department of State, 7 July 1970, White House Special Files, Staff Member and Office Files: Charles Colson, box 52, folder: Consultation on Christian Concern for Peace, NA; Kathleen Teltsch, "Catholic Leaders Back U.S. China Policy," *New York Times*, 10 May 1970, L28.

12. Letter from William O'Brien to Catholic Association for International Peace Members, 7 May 1969, General Administration Series, subser. 3.6, box 174, folder: CAIP Correspondence, 1950–1967, USCC Papers, CUA, 2; "And Now, Two Peace Plans," 308.

13. James Fleck, "What to Do about Joe Mulligan?" *America*, 20 September 1969, 184; "Priest Presses Suit to Back War Dissent," *New York Times*, 30 June 1969, L11;

"Eight Admit Vandalizing Offices of Two Draft Boards Here; Three Priests in Group," *New York Times*, 22 August 1969, 10.

14. "The Anachronistic War," 555; "The Course We're On," *Commonweal*, 10 October 1969, 35.

15. Dugan, "Religious Leaders Endorse," 25; Michael O'Brien, *Hesburgh* (Washington, D.C.: Catholic University of America Press, 1998), 114; "The Moratorium, the War, and the Empire," *Ramparts*, December 1969, 6.

16. John Sheerin, "A Cease-Fire Now in Vietnam," *Catholic World*, November 1969, 50–51; John Fenton, "Mass Politics: A Priestly Hat Is Thrown in the Ring," *New York Times*, 23 February 1970, L18; Richard Robbins, "The Night the Peace Bus Left New Harley," *Catholic World*, February 1970, 260.

17. NCCB, "Prisoners of War," 14 November 1969, in *Quest for Justice*, ed. J. Brian Benestad and Francis J. Butler (Washington, D.C.: United States Catholic Conference, 1981), 69; Albin Krebs, "Cardinal's First Two Years: Renewal Amid Problems," *New York Times*, 6 April 1970, L41.

18. Herbert Parmet, *Richard M. Nixon: An Enigma* (New York: Pearson Longman, 2008), 128.

19. Memorandum from Charles Colson to H. R. Haldeman, 1 May 1970, White House Special Files, Staff Member and Office Files: Charles Colson, box 46, folder: Catholic War Veterans, NA, 2.

20. "The Indo-China War," attached to letter from Leno Delmolino to George Bell, 19 May 1970, White House Special Files, Staff Member and Office Files: Charles Colson, box 46, folder: Catholic War Veterans, NA.

21. Andrew Greeley, "Turning Off 'the People,'" *New Republic*, 27 June 1970, 14–16.

22. George Dugan, "Catholic Superiors Take Activist Role," *New York Times*, 27 June 1970, L16; "Where to Find the Leaders?" *Newsweek*, 4 October 1971, 82; "USCC International Affairs Committee on the War," 11 May 1970, box 15, folder: Newsletters, 1967–1973, John Cardinal Dearden Papers, UNDA; "Bishop Chastises Jesuit Candidate," *New York Times*, 23 August 1970, L56.

23. Paul Hoffman, "Papal Letter Sets as Goal a New Democratic Society," *New York Times*, 12 May 1971, L1, 10; Minutes, NCCB, September 1971, box 3, folder: NCCB Administrative Board, John Cardinal Dearden Papers, UNDA, 13.

24. Robert Hoyt, "Baffled Bishops," *Harper's*, October 1971, 77, 80.

25. Letter from Rosemary Cass, Irene Dalgiewicz, Eileen Egan, Rev. Edward Rooney, and Miriam Rooney, to Rev. Joseph Bernardin, 19 November 1971, General Administration Series, subser. 3.1, box 159, folder: Bernardin, Joseph, General Secretary USCC Correspondence, 1968–72, CUA, 2; "Annual Report, Division for United Nations Affairs," 1971, box 162, folder: Division for UN Affairs, Annual Report, 1971, CUA, 1.

26. Memorandum from Henry Kissinger and Peter Flanigan to the President, 19 January 1972, White House Central Files, Subject Files—Religious Matters, box 18, folder: RM 3-1, Catholic 1/1/71–12/72, NA, 1; telephone conversation between Rev. Terence Cooke and Richard Nixon, 20 January 1972, telephone conversation 652-13, NA.

27. Small, *Presidency of Richard Nixon*, 79; O'Brien, *Hesburgh*, 121–22.

28. "Cease-Fire," *Commonweal*, 25 September 1970, 475; "USCC International Affairs Committee on the War," 3–4.

29. Homer Bigart, "Prison Denies Berrigan Is Mistreated," *New York Times*, 30 July 1970, L70; "Fugitive Priest Seized by FBI," 12 August 1970, L1, 12; "Father Berrigan Begins Three-Year Sentence for Destroying Draft Records," *New York Times*, 13 August 1970, 11.

30. Robert McFadden, "Army Officer Wins Objector Discharge Basing Case Solely on Roman Catholic Tenets," *New York Times*, 30 August 1970, L35; memorandum from William Consedine to Rev. Joseph Bernardin, 13 November 1970, General Administration Series, subser. 3.6, box 159, folder: Bernardin, Joseph, General Secretary USCC Correspondence 1968–1972, CUA, 2; memorandum from Msgr. Marvin Bordelon to Rev. Joseph Bernardin, 12 February 1971, General Administration Series, subser. 3.6, box 159, folder: Bernardin, General Secretary USCC Correspondence, CUA, 1–3.

31. Richard Nixon, "Remarks following Meeting with Pope Paul VI in the Vatican," 28 September 1970, *Public Papers of the Presidents of the United States: Richard Nixon, 1970* (Washington, D.C.: U.S. Government Printing Office, 1971), 779.

32. Memorandum from Robert Odle to Charles Colson, 11 March 1971, White House Central Files, Subject File—Religious Matters, box 18, folder: RM 3-1 Catholic 1/1/71–12/72, NA.

33. Peter Steinfels, "Why I Went to Jail," *Commonweal*, 23 April 1971, 158; John Kerry, "Where Are the Leaders of Our Country?" *Commonweal*, 8 May 1971, 17.

34. "Another Plea for Peace... and a Resolution," *America*, 8 May 1971, 474; George Gallup, ed., *The Gallup Poll: Public Opinion, 1935–1971*, vol. 2: *1935–1971* (New York: Random House), 2291; Ralph Blumenthal, "Chaplains' Role Questioned Because They Support War," *New York Times*, 22 June 1971, L37, 70; "Cornell vs. Wichita," 9 July 1971, 346.

35. NCCB, "Resolution on Southeast Asia," in Benestad and Butler, 78; Paul Hoffman, "Appeal by Pope Calls for Peace Based on Justice, Not Power," *New York Times*, 17 December 1971, L2; memorandum from Peter Flanigan for the President's File, 3 January 1972, White House Staff Member and Office Files, Subject Files 1969–1974, box 10, folder: Presidential Meetings, Agenda and Briefs/Memos to File (April 1971–July 1974), NA.

36. Edward Fiske, "Religious Assembly Terms Vietnam Policy Immoral," *New York Times*, 17 January 1972, L35.

37. Memorandum from Brig. Gen. Alexander Haig and Peter Flanigan for the President's File, 20 January 1972, White House Staff Member and Office Files, Subject Files 1969–1974, box 10, folder: Presidential Meetings, Agenda and Briefs/Memos to File (April 1971–July 1974), NA.

38. Small, *Presidency of Richard Nixon*, 90; Eleanor Blau, "Priests' Convention Backs Harrisburg Seven; Denies Membership to Married Clergy," *New York Times*, 17 March 1972, L20.

39. H. R. Haldeman Notes, 20 April 1972, White House Special Files, Staff Member and Office Files, box 45, folder: H. R. Haldeman Notes, April–June 1972 (April 1–May 15, 1972), part I, NA; memorandum from Charles Colson to the President, 15 May 1972, White House Special Files, Staff Member and Office Files, Charles W. Colson, box 46, folder: Catholic Vote, NA, 2.

40. Emanuel Perlmutter,"Seven Nuns Arrested in Antiwar Protest inside St. Pat-

rick's," *New York Times*, 1 May 1972, L1, 14; George Dugan, "Cardinal Cooke Calls for a 'Speedy End' to the War in Southeast Asia," *New York Times*, 1 May 1972, L12.

41. George Dugan, "Berrigan Walks Out of Peace Mass at St. Patrick's," *New York Times*, 5 June 1972, L36.

42. Paul Hoffman, "Pope Paul Pleads for End to War," *New York Times*, 10 July 1972, L5.

43. "Ad Hoc Committee for a Resolution of the War in Southeast Asia," NCCB, Eleventh General Meeting, 15–19 November 1971, USCCBA, 62–63.

44. Peter Steinfels, "Calley and the Public Conscience," *Commonweal*, 16 April 1971, 128; Michael Novak, "The Battle Hymn of Lieutenant Calley . . . and the Republic," *Commonweal*, 30 April 1971, 183.

45. "The Church in South Vietnam," attached to letter from David O'Brien and Joanne O'Brien to "Dear Friend," 23 December 1971, box 3, folder: The Church in Vietnam 2, Thomas Gumbleton Papers, UNDA, 3; Richard Griffin, "Our Catholic 'Enemies,'" *Commonweal*, 6 August 1971, 403–404; Harry Bury, "The Catholics of South Vietnam Have a Message," *Lamp*, June 1972, 11.

46. Charles Meconis, *With Clumsy Grace: The American Catholic Left, 1961–1975* (New York: Seabury, 1979), 170, 142.

47. Buchanan to the President, 11 April 1969; Haig and Flanigan for the President's File, 20 January 1972, 1; "The Real America," *Commonweal*, 26 May 1972, 275; Colson to the President, 15 May 1972, 1.

48. "Resolution on Southeast Asia," 77–78; Russell Shaw, "Correspondence," *Commonweal*, 4 February 1972, 429.

49. "Scores Fourteen Bishops for Vietnam Withdrawal Statement," n.d., box 41, folder: Vietnam, "On the Morality of War," Thomas Gumbleton Papers, UNDA; Thomas Gumbleton, "On the Morality of War," *New York Times*, 2 July 1971, L33.

50. "World Justice," NCCB, Tenth General Meeting, 27–29 April 1971, USCCBA, 37; "Ad Hoc Committee for a Resolution of the War in Southeast Asia," 61.

51. "Ad Hoc Committee for a Resolution of the War in Southeast Asia," 61, 63.

52. Ibid., 64.

53. Eleanor Blau, "U.S. Catholic Bishops Call for an End to the Indochina War," *New York Times*, 20 November 1971, 1, 13.

54. Kathleen Tesch, "Catholic Leaders Back U.S. China Policy," *New York Times*, 10 May 1970, 28; Paul Hoffman, "Pope Cautions Asia on Militant Atheism," *New York Times*, 29 November 1970, L1, 14.

55. Colson to the President, 15 May 1972, 3; Telephone Conversation between Rev. John Krol and Richard Nixon, 6 June 1972, telephone conversation 25-9, NA.

56. David Settje, *Faith and War* (New York: New York University Press, 2011), 14–15, 118–119.

57. Mary Hanna, *Catholics and American Politics* (Cambridge, Mass.: Harvard University Press, 1979), 217; Meconis, 143–144.

58. "Nixon: Verbal Fence-Mending," *National Review*, 26 April 1972, 442; Jay Dolan, *The American Catholic Experience* (Notre Dame, Ind.: University of Notre Dame Press, 1992), 437, 433.

59. "Pope Emphasizes Peace Efforts in Vietnam and the Middle East," *New York*

Times, 23 June 1971, L10; "Ad Hoc Committee for a Resolution of the War in Southeast Asia," 61.

60. Memorandum from Roy Morey to Kenneth Cole and Edwin Harper, 10 December 1971; "Ad Hoc Committee for a Resolution of the War in Southeast Asia," 63–64.

61. Alexander Sigur, "Detroit's Cardinal Dearden: A Cautious Progressive," *Christian Century*, 26 May 1971, 671–672; "Where to Find the Leaders?" *Newsweek*, 4 November 1971, 83.

62. Jeffrey Jones, "The Protestant and Catholic Vote," June 2004, http://www.gallup.com/poll/1911/Protestant-Catholic-Vote-aspx?.

63. Robert Mason, *Richard Nixon and the Quest for a New Majority* (Chapel Hill: University of North Carolina Press, 2004), 117.

64. Daniel Patrick Moynihan, "Income by Right—I," *New Yorker*, 13 January 1973, 50.

65. Mason, 154.

66. Moynihan, 52; Joan Hoff, *Nixon Reconsidered* (New York: Basic, 1994), 122–123.

67. Moynihan, 52.

68. George Dugan, "Catholics Scored on Social Issues," *New York Times*, 26 March 1969, L28; "Social Action Department," Minutes of the United States Catholic Conference Sixth General Meeting, 15–19 April 1969, USCCBA, 6.

69. "Social Action Department," 7.

70. Hoff, 128, 124.

71. Richard Nixon, "Address to the Nation on Domestic Programs," 8 August 1969, *Public Papers, 1969*, 639, 641.

72. Parmet, *Richard M. Nixon*, 188; "Statement of Rev. James J. McHugh, Director of the Family Life Division of the United States Catholic Conference, Commenting on the Message of President Nixon on Welfare Reform," 8 August 1969, box 140, folder: USCC-U.S. Government, Family Planning, USCCBA, 1; "Welfare, Manpower Training, Revenue Sharing," *America*, 30 August 1969, 112.

73. Hoff, 135; memorandum from Msgr. Aloysius Welsh to Rev. Joseph Bernardin, Msgr. Francis Hurley, Msgr. George Higgins, John Cosgrove, and Rev. James McHugh, November 1969, box 140, folder: USCC-U.S. Government, Poverty, 1967, July–December, USCCBA.

74. "Testimony of John E. Cosgrove, Director, Department of Social Development, United States Catholic Conference," 12 November 1969, box 140, folder: USCC-U.S. Government, Poverty, 1967, July–December, USCCBA, 2, 3, 4, 13, 17, 19, 20.

75. Minutes, Administrative Board Meeting, USCC, February 1970, box 25, folder: USCC Administrative Board Minutes, February 1970, NCCB, John Cardinal Dearden Papers, UNDA, 13; memorandum from Thomas Cosgrove through Carol Khosrovi to Donald Webster, 20 February 1970, White House Special Files, Staff Member and Office Files, Charles W. Colson, box 63, folder: Family Assistance Plan, NA, 1–2.

76. "Family Assistance—1970 Action," *Congress and the Nation*, vol. 3: *1969–1972* (Washington, D.C.: Congressional Quarterly, 1973), 624; Rev. James McHugh, "Special Memorandum on Family Assistance Plan," 10 March 1970, White House Special Files, Staff Member and Office Files, Charles W. Colson, box 63, folder: Family Assistance Plan, NA, 1–5.

77. Memorandum from Daniel Patrick Moynihan to Donald Webster, 13 March 1970, White House Special Files, Staff Member and Office Files, Charles W. Colson, box 63, folder: Family Assistance Plan, NA; memorandum from Dwight Chapin to Rose Mary Woods and Connie Stuart, 22 March 1970, White House Central Files, Subject File—Religious Matters, box 18, folder: RM 3-1 Catholic [69/70], NA; "Heads of Three Major Religious Organizations Urge Congress to Pass Welfare Reform Bill," *New York Times*, 6 April 1970, L21.

78. "Family Assistance—1970 Action," 624; "United States Catholic Conference Resolution, Welfare Reform Legislation, 1970," box 16, folder: Reports, 1970, John Cardinal Dearden Papers, UNDA, n.p.; "The Family Assistance Program," Minutes of the United States Catholic Conference Eighth General Meeting, 21–23 April 1970, USCCBA, 12; memorandum from Rev. Joseph Bernardin to All Catholic Dioceses, Religious Orders, Institutions, and Organizations, May 1970, box 140, folder: USCC-U.S. Government, Poverty, 1970–72, USCCBA, 1–3.

79. Daniel Patrick Moynihan, "A Moment Touched with Glory," 22 April 1970, attached to letter from Moynihan to Rev. Joseph Bernardin, 22 April 1970, box 140, folder: USCC-U.S. Government, Poverty, 1970–72, USCCBA, 12.

80. Memorandum from Charles Colson to the President, 17 August 1970, President's Office Files, box 1, folder: President's Handwriting, August 1970–October 1970, 2.

81. "Family Assistance—1971 Action," *Congress and the Nation*, 3:626; "Broad Coalition Lobbies for FAP," ibid., 625.

82. "Family Assistance—1971 Action," 626.

83. Memorandum from James Robinson to Rev. Joseph Bernardin, 2 April 1971, box 140, folder: USCC-U.S. Government, Family Planning, 1971, USCCBA, 1–3.

84. Memorandum from James Robinson to Rev. Joseph Bernardin, 6 April 1971, box 140, folder: USCC-U.S. Government, Family Planning, 1971, USCCBA.

85. Memorandum from John Cosgrove to Rev. Joseph Bernardin, 5 April 1971, box 140, folder: USCC-U.S. Government, Family Planning, 1971, USCCBA, 2–3.

86. "Family Assistance—1971 Action," 626.

87. "Big Package of Welfare Reform," *America*, 29 May 1971, 557; Robert Kennedy, "Explained: One Nay Vote," *America*, 26 June 1971, 656; "Minutes of the Eleventh General Meeting," 15–19 November 1971, box 18, folder: NCCB General Meeting Agenda Report Documentation, November 1971, UNDA, 103–104.

88. "Punishing the Poor," *Commonweal*, 24 September 1971, 471.

89. "Conference Official Asks Improvements in Family Assistance Proposals," USCC News, 1 February 1972, box 140, folder: USCC-U.S. Government, Family Planning, 1971, USCCBA, 1–2.

90. "Family Assistance—1972 Action," *Congress and the Nation*, 626–627.

91. Hoff, 132–133; USCC, Department of Social Development and World Peace, "Welfare Reform in the 1970s," 25 February 1977, in Benestad and Butler, 270–279.

92. Richard Nixon, "Address to the Nation on the War in Vietnam," 3 November 1969, *Public Papers, 1969*, 909; Gene Halus, "Monsignor Geno Baroni and the Politics of Ethnicity, 1960–1984," *U.S. Catholic Historian* 25 (Fall 2007): 148–149; Linda Major, "Ford Grant Awarded Msgr. Baroni for Urban Ethnic Work," National Catholic News Service, 12 January 1971, box 38, folder: Statement Phasing Out Task Force, 25 November 1970, Monsignor Geno Baroni Papers, UNDA, 12.

93. "Reports from Regional Discussion Groups," Minutes of the Seventh General Meeting, USCC, 36, 38, 39, 41, 42, 43, 45.

94. Ibid., 50; "Report of the Ad Hoc Committee on the Proposal for a Central Office for Black Catholics," Minutes of the Seventh General Meeting, USCC, 11.

95. Memorandum from John Brown to Harry Dent, 19 December 1969, White House Central Files, Subject File—Religious Matters, box 18, folder: RM 3-1 Catholic [69/70], NA.

96. Ibid.

97. Memorandum from Jerome Rosow to the Secretary, 16 April 1970, attached to memorandum from Colson to the President, 17 August 1970, 6, 8; 15.

98. "Workshop on Urban Ethnic Community Development," 15–19 June 1970, box 38, folder: Urban Ethnic Community Workshop, Msgr. Geno Baroni Papers, UNDA, 3.

99. Ibid., 3; letter from Msgr. Geno Baroni to the President, 29 June 1970, White House Central Files, Subject File—Religious Matters, box 18, folder: RM 3-1 Catholic [69/70], NA, 2.

100. Memorandum from Peter Flanigan to Hugh Sloan, 15 July 1970, White House Central Files, Subject File—Religious Matters, box 18, folder: RM 3-1 Catholic [69/70], NA; Colson to the President, 17 August 1970, 2.

101. Msgr. George Higgins and Msgr. Geno Baroni, "1970 Labor Day Statement," attached to letter from Baroni to Mr. Harris, 29 July 1970, ser. 20, box 31, folder: USCC Task Force on Urban Problems, MUA, 1–2.

102. Memorandum from Charles Colson to H. R. Haldeman, 13 November 1970, White House Special Files, Staff Member and Office Files—Charles W. Colson, box 46, folder: Catholic Vote, NA, 1–2.

103. Memorandum from H. R. Haldeman to Robert Finch, 27 November 1970, White House Special Files, Staff Member and Office Files—Charles W. Colson, box 46, folder: Catholic Vote, NA; memorandum from Roy Morey to Kenneth Cole and Edwin Harper, 16 September 1971, White House Special Files, Staff Member and Office Files—Charles W. Colson, box 46, folder: Catholic Vote, NA, 5.

104. Memorandum from Patrick Buchanan to John Ehrlichman, H. R. Haldeman, and Charles Colson, 23 September 1971, White House Special Files, Staff Member and Office Files—Charles W. Colson, box 46, folder: Catholic Vote, NA, 4–5.

105. Buchanan to Ehrlichman, Haldeman and Colson, 23 September 1971, 4, 15; memorandum from Patrick Buchanan to Charles Colson, 20 September 1971, White House Special Files, Staff Member and Office Files—Charles W. Colson, box 46, folder: Catholic Vote, NA, 1.

106. Letter from Thomas Melady to Patrick Buchanan, 27 September 1971, attached to memorandum from Buchanan to John Ehrlichman, H. R. Haldeman, and Charles Colson, 29 September 1971, box 46, folder: Catholic Vote, NA, 1–2.

107. Letter from Arthur Finkelstein to Robert Marik, 16 December 1971, attached to memorandum from Roy Morey to John Ehrlichman, 24 September 1971, White House Central Files, Subject File—Religious Matters, box 18, folder: RM 3-1 Catholic 1/1/71–12/72, NA.

108. Mason, 59.

109. William Safire, *Before the Fall* (Garden City, N.Y.: Doubleday, 1975), 557.

110. Memorandum from Msgr. Geno Baroni to Rev. Joseph Bernardin and Rev.

James Rausch, 7 November 1970, box 38, folder: Statement Phasing Out Task Force, November 25, 1970, Msgr. Geno Baroni Papers, UNDA, 1–2; "Statement of Most Rev. Joseph L. Bernardin, General Secretary, United States Catholic Conference," 25 November 1970, box 38, folder: Statement Phasing Out Task Force, November 25, 1970, Msgr. Geno Baroni Papers, UNDA.

111. Linda Major, "Ford Grant Awarded Msgr. Baroni for Urban Ethnic Work," National Catholic News Service, 12 January 1971, box 38, folder: Statement Phasing Out Task Force, November 25, 1970, Msgr. Geno Baroni Papers, UNDA, 14.

112. Robinson to Bernardin, 2 April 1971, 3; "Report of Division of Urban Affairs," Minutes of the Thirteenth General Meeting, NCCB, 11–13 November 1972, box 18, folder: NCCB General Meeting Agenda Report Documentation, November 1972, John Cardinal Dearden Papers, UNDA, 57.

113. Memorandum from Charles Colson to Dwight Chapin, 12 February 1971, and memorandum from William Galvin to H. R. Haldeman, 17 February 1971, White House Special Files, Staff Member and Office Files—Charles W. Colson, box 91, folder: Knights of Columbus [1971], NA; Richard Nixon, "Remarks to the Eighty-Seventh Annual International Meeting of the Knights of Columbus in New York City," 17 August 1971, *Public Papers of the Presidents of the United States: Richard Nixon, 1971* (Washington, D.C.: U.S. Government Printing Office, 1972), 893–898; memorandum from Peter Flanigan to the President, 21 January 1972, White House Staff Files, Staff Member and Office Files—Peter Flanigan, box 10, folder: Presidential Meetings, Agendas and Briefs/Memos to File [April 1971–July 1974], NA; Richard Nixon, "Remarks at the Annual Convention of the National Catholic Educational Association in Philadelphia, Pennsylvania," 6 April 1972, *Public Papers of the Presidents of the United States: Richard Nixon, 1972* (Washington, D.C.: U.S. Government Printing Office, 1973), 517–523; interview of Rev. Theodore Hesburgh by author, 17 August 2011.

114. Halus, 146; Patrick Buchanan, *Right from the Beginning* (Boston: Little, Brown, 1988), 21.

115. "Where to Find the Leaders?" 82. Nixon obtained the minimum income and subsidies to the states which he had sought in FAP, without the political costs which FAP would have incurred, when Congress passed the Supplemental Security Income program for the elderly, blind, and disabled in October 1972; see Hoff, 134; and Parmet, *Richard M. Nixon*, 189.

116. Hoff, 109–110; Safire, 557–558.

117. Warren Weaver, "High Court Rules Abortion Legal in the First Three Months," *New York Times*, 23 January 1973, L1.

118. Memorandum from Robert Beusse to Rev. James Rausch, 23 January 1973, box 65, folder: NCCB Ad Hoc Committee, Pro-Life Activities, 1973, January–February, USCCBA.

119. "Statements by Two Cardinals," *New York Times*, 23 January 1973, L20; "Family Life Leader Says Court Ruling Will 'Energize' Pro-Life Movement," *National Catholic News*, 23 January 1973, 1–2.

120. Memorandum from Russell Shaw to Rev. James Rausch, 25 January 1973, box 62, folder: NCCB Ad Hoc Committee, Pro-Life Activities, 1973, January–February, USCCBA, 1–7.

121. Memorandum from John Cosgrove through Msgr. Harold Murray to Rev.

James Rausch, 2 February 1973, box 62, folder: NCCB Ad Hoc Committee, Pro-Life Activities, 1973, January–February, USCCBA, 1–4; memorandum from Rev. James McHugh to Rev. John Cody, 12 February 1973, box 62, folder: NCCB Ad Hoc Committee, Pro-Life Activities, 1973, January–February, USCCBA, 1–2.

122. NCCB, "Pastoral Message of the Administrative Committee," 13 February 1973, in Benestad and Butler, 155–156; "Catholics Warned to Avoid Abortion," *New York Times*, 15 February 1973, 20.

123. Hanna, 183; Herbert Denton, "Hogan's Assault on Abortion Finds Congress on Obstacles," *Washington Post*, 15 May 1973, C1, 3; memorandum from Father Sheehan to Father Monticello, 4 April 1973, box 62, folder: NCCB Ad Hoc Committee, Pro-Life Activities, 1973 April–June, USCCBA; "Constitutional Amendments—Abortion," attached to letter from William Ball to Charles Tobin, box 38, folder: USCC Church—Church and State, Law and Public Policy, 1973, April–June, USCCBA, 1–2.

124. "Text of Statement by John Cardinal Krol in the Name of the Executive Committee of the United States Catholic Conference," 11 April 1973, box 62, folder: NCCB Ad Hoc Committee, Pro-Life Activities, 1973 April–June, USCCBA; "Cardinal Krol, Bishops Denounce Experts on Aborted Babies; Cardinal Urges Prompt End to Abuse," *National Catholic News*, 11 April 1973, 2; "Statement by Dr. Robert Berliner, Deputy Director for Science, National Institutes of Health," 17 April 1973, box 38, folder: USCC Church—Church and State, Law and Public Policy, 1973 April–June, USCCBA, 1.

125. "Bishops' Administrative Committee Gives Backing to Human Life Amendment," *National Catholic News*, 20 June 1973, box 62, folder: NCCB Ad Hoc Committee, Pro-Life Activities, 1973 April–June, USCCBA, 1–2; "Report of the Ad Hoc Committee on Pro-Life Activities to the NCCB Administrative Committee Meeting," 5 July 1973, box 62, folder: NCCB Ad Hoc Committee, Pro-Life Activities, 1973 July–August, USCCBA, 1–4.

126. Letter from William Ball to "Your Eminences and Your Excellencies," 20 June 1973, box 62, folder: NCCB Ad Hoc Committee, Pro-Life Activities, 1973 April–June, USCCBA, 8.

127. "Constitutional Amendment on Abortion," attached to memorandum from Rev. James McHugh to Family Life Directors, Respect Life Coordinators, and State Catholic Conference Coordinators, 12 July 1973, box 62, folder: NCCB Ad Hoc Committee, Pro-Life Activities, 1973 July–August, USCCBA, 4; "Confidential Minutes of the Executive Session of the General Meeting," 15 November 1973, box 16, folder: NCCB General Meeting Minutes, 1973, John Cardinal Dearden Papers, UNDA, 6–7.

128. Letter from William Ball to Dennis Horan, 19 February 1974, box 38, folder: Church—Church and State, Law and Public Policy, 1974 January–June, USCCBA, 1–4.

129. "Four American Cardinals Testify on Behalf of Pro-Life Amendment," *National Catholic News*, 5 March 1974, 3, 5.

130. Memorandum from Rev. James Rausch to File, 4 July 1974, box 38, folder: Church—Church and State, Law and Public Policy, 1974 October, USCCBA, 1–2.

131. Safire, 558; Richard Nixon, "The President's News Conference of January 31, 1973," *Public Papers of the Presidents of the United States: Richard Nixon, 1973* (Washington, D.C.: U.S. Government Printing Office, 1975), 53–63; letter from Rev. James Rausch to Rev. Justin Driscoll, 3 July 1973, box 62, folder: NCCB Ad Hoc Committee, Pro-Life Activities, 1973 April–June, USCCBA, 1–2; letter from Rev. John Cody to "Your

Excellency," 6 August 1973, box 62, folder: NCCB Ad Hoc Committee, Pro-Life Activities, 1973 July–August, USCCBA, 2.

132. Memorandum from David Parker to James Cavanaugh and Geoffrey Shephard, 21 February 1974, White House Central Files, Subject File—Religious Matters, box 18, folder: RM 3 Catholic 1/1/73–[6/74], NA.

133. Leslie Tentler, *Catholics and Contraception* (Ithaca, N.Y.: Cornell University Press, 2004), 266; memorandum from Rev. James McHugh to Rev. Joseph Bernardin, 10 September 1970, box 140, folder: USCC-U.S. Government, Poverty, Family Planning (Birth Control), USCCBA, 9.

134. "Catholic Forum Assails Abortion," *New York Times*, 21 June 1971, L15; "Letdown in Washington," *Commonweal*, 8 December 1972, 220; memorandum from Rev. James Rausch to File, 5 July 1974, box 38, folder: Church—Church and State, Law and Public Policy, 1974 October, USCCBA, 2.

135. Edward Fiske, "Catholic Bishops Resist Changes in Church," *New York Times*, 30 April 1971, L36; Edward Fiske, "Report Finds Most Priests Oppose Paul's 1967 [*sic*] Birth Edict," *New York Times*, 8 August 1971, L52; Rev. John Dearden, "Address of the Conference President," Minutes, NCCB, 15–19 November 1971, USCCBA, 93; memorandum from Russell Shaw to Jack O'Neill, 21 February 1973, box 62, folder: NCCB Ad Hoc Committee, Pro-Life Activities, 1973 January–February, USCCBA, 2; Robert Drinan, "The Abortion Decision," *Commonweal*, 16 February 1973, 440.

136. *The Gallup Poll: Public Opinion, 1972–1977*, vol. 1: *1972–1975*, ed. George Gallup (Wilmington, Del.: Scholarly Resources, 1978), 247–249; memorandum from Sr. Jo Dunne to Jack O'Neill, 8 March 1973, box 62, folder: NCCB Ad Hoc Committee, Pro-Life Activities, 1973 March, USCCBA, 2.

137. Letter from Edward Hanify to Rev. Joseph Bernardin, 26 May 1972, box 62, folder: NCCB Ad Hoc Committee, Pro-Life Activities, USCCBA, 2.

138. Paul Weber, "Perverse Observations on Abortion," *Catholic World*, November 1970, 77; Dunne to O'Neill, 8 March 1973, 1–2.

139. Mary Daly, "Abortion and Sexual Caste," *Commonweal*, 4 February 1972, 418; memorandum from Russell Shaw to Rev. James Rausch, 25 January 1973, box 62, folder: NCCB Ad Hoc Committee, Pro-Life Activities, 1973 January–February, USCCBA, 3.

140. Norman Miller, "Opposition to Birth Control Law Wanes," *Wall Street Journal*, 14 August 1970, 8; memorandum from Russell Shaw to Robert Beusse and Father Sullivan, 22 February 1973, box 62, folder: NCCB Ad Hoc Committee, Pro-Life Committee, 1973 January–February, USCCBA, 2.

141. "Testimony of Msgr. James McHugh before the Special Committee on Human Resources on the Joint Resolution Declaring a Policy of Population Stablization," 3 November 1971, box 140, folder: USCC-U.S. Government, Poverty, Family Planning, 1971, USCCBA, 3; "Pastoral Message of the Administrative Committee," 13 February 1973, 154.

142. "Abortion, Coercion, and Anti-Catholicism," *America*, 13 May 1972, 502.

143. "Pro-Life Leaders Says Senate Committee Set Up Catholic v. Protestant Scenario," *Religious News Service*, 14 March 1974, 1; "A Report to the General Board Concerning Implementation of its Communication of Concern regarding Current Efforts of the National Conference of Catholic Bishops to Seek a Constitutional Amendment

to Guarantee the Right to Life of the Pre-Born Child," box 62, folder: NCCB Ad Hoc Committee, Pro-Life Activities, 1974 January–June, USCCBA, 1; "Catholic Conference Is Sued as Lobbyist," *New York Times*, 21 May 1974, 33.

144. "Confidential Minutes of the Meeting of the Committee on Law and Public Policy, USCC," 21–22 March 1974, box 38, folder: Church—Church and State, Law and Public Policy, 1974 January–June, USCCBA, 2; memorandum from Russell Shaw to Rev. James Rausch et al., 29 March 1974, box 62, folder: NCCB Ad Hoc Committee, Pro-Life Activities, 1974 January–June, USCCBA.

145. "A Report to the General Board" and memorandum from John Hotchkin to Rev. James Rausch, 7 June 1974, box 62, folder: NCCB, Ad Hoc Committee, Pro-Life Committee, 1974 January–June, USCCBA, 3; "Court Rejects Suit Asserting Catholics Lobby on Abortion," *New York Times*, 25 May 1974, L14.

146. Memorandum from Dennis J. Horan to Law and Public Policy Committee, 5 September 1973, box 38, folder: Church—Church and State, Law and Public Policy, 1973 July–December, USCCBA, 3. Though the National Catholic Conference for Interracial Justice and the National Coalition of American Nuns filed amicus briefs, and the United States Catholic Conference's Department of Social Development prepared a seven-page statement, against the death penalty in *Furman v. Georgia*, the bishops would not take an official stand until November 1974. See James McGivern, *The Death Penalty: A Historical and Theological Survey* (New York: Paulist Press, 1997), 339–345.

147. Dunne to O'Neill, 8 March 1973, 2.

148. Memorandum from Rita Hauser to John Ehrlichman, 28 August 1972, White House Special Files, Staff Member and Office Files, Charles W. Colson, box 28, folder: Abortion, NA; H. R. Haldeman Notes, 15 October 1972, White House Special Files, Staff Member and Office Files, box 42, folder: Haldeman Notes, October–December 1972 [10/11–19/1972], part I, NA.

CHAPTER FOUR. Catholics and Gerald Ford

1. American troops withdrew, but none of the other provisions occurred. See Joseph Conlin, *The American Past* (Orlando, Fla.: Harcourt, 2001), 974.

2. Gerald Ford, "Remarks on Taking Oath of Office," 9 August 1974, *Public Papers of the Presidents of the United States: Gerald Ford, 1974*, vol. 2: *August 9–December 31, 1974* (Washington, D.C.: U.S. Government Printing Office, 1975), 2.

3. "Indochina Act," *Congress and the Nation*, vol. 4: *1973–1976* (Washington, D.C.: Congressional Quarterly, 1977), 896.

4. Kou Yang, *From Indochina to Fresno: A Brief Look at the Plight of the Indochinese* (Fresno: California State University, Southeast Asian Student Services, 1990), xxii.

5. "Catholic Bishops' President Calls for Speedy Humanitarian Aid to Vietnam," National Catholic News Service, 27 March 1975, 1, 3.

6. Letter from Rev. James Rausch to Gerald Ford, 2 April 1975, Theodore Marrs Files, box 50, folder: National Conference of Catholic Bishops (2), GRFPL; Gerald Ford, "Statement Announcing Humanitarian Assistance for Refugees in the Republic of Vietnam," 29 March 1975, *Public Papers of the Presidents of the United States: Gerald Ford, 1975*, vol. 1: *January 1–July 17, 1975* (Washington, D.C.: U.S. Government Printing Office, 1976), 406; letter from Rev. Joseph Bernardin to Kurt Waldheim, 4 Febru-

ary 1975, Theodore Marrs Files, box 64, folder: 6/18/75, National Conference of Catholic Bishops (2), GRFPL.

7. Letter from Theodore Marrs to Rev. James Rausch, 15 April 1975, Theodore Marrs Files, box 50, folder: National Conference of Catholic Bishops (2), GRFPL; "Fact Sheet: Status Report—Refugees from Indochina," 23 June 1975, Theodore Marrs Files, box 11, folder: President's Advisory Committee: Meeting, 6/23/75, GRFPL, 1.

8. "Southeast Asian Refugee Resettlement: U.S. Catholic Involvement," n.d., Theodore Marrs Files, box 64, folder: National Conference of Catholic Bishops (2),GRFPL, 1.

9. Ibid., 1–2.

10. Letter from Gerald Ford to Pope Paul VI, 8 May 1975, White House Central Files, Presidential Name File, box 2531, folder: Pope Paul VI, GRFPL; letter from Gerald Ford to Rev. James Rausch, 16 May 1975, White House Central Files, Presidential Name File, box 2603, folder: Rausch, James S., GRFPL.

11. Gerald Ford, *A Time to Heal* (New York: Harper and Row), 257; "Refugee Act," *Congress and the Nation*, 4:898.

12. Linda Charlton, "Refugees Panel, after Vague Start, Seeking to Speed Resettlement," *New York Times*, 19 June 1975, L18; "President's Advisory Committee on Refugees, Minutes of Meeting #1," 23 May 1975, Theodore Marrs Files, box 11, folder: Indochina Refugees—President's Advisory Committee—General (2), GRFPL, 1–2, 4.

13. "President's Advisory Committee on Refugees, Minutes of Meeting #2," 3 June 1975, Theodore Marrs Files, box 11, folder: Indochina Refugees—President's Advisory Committee: Meeting, 6/3/75, GRFPL, 2–3.

14. USCC, "The Southeast Asian Refugee Program: A Status Report," 10 June 1975, Theodore Marrs Files, box 11, folder: Indochina Refugees—President's Advisory Committee: Meeting, 6/23/75, GRFPL, 1.

15. Letter from Roland Elliot to Rev. Joseph Bernardin, 7 July 1975, White House Central Files, Name File, box 3243, folder: U.S. Catholic Conference, GRFPL, 1–2; "Fact Sheet," 1.

16. Elliot to Bernardin, 7 July 1975.

17. Memorandum from Brent Scowcroft to Gerald Ford, 9 March 1976, National Security Advisor Presidential Country Files for East Asia and the Pacific, box 20, folder: Vietnam (29), GRFPL, 1–2.

18. "Draft Memorandum of Conversation—Meeting of President Ford with Pope Paul VI, Vatican City," 3 June 1975, National Security Advisor Memoranda of Conversations Files, box 12, folder: June 3, 1976—Ford, Kissinger, Pope Paul VI, Archbishop Casaroli, GRFPL, 8.

19. Ibid., 8.

20. *The Gallup Poll: Public Opinion, 1972–1977*, vol. 1: *1972–1975*, ed. George Gallup (Wilmington, Del.: Scholarly Resources, 1976), 457; Barry Stein, "Occupational Adjustment of Refugees: The Vietnamese Refugees in the United States," n.d., ser. 8, box 8, folder: Stein, Barry, "Occupational Adjustment of Refugees: The Vietnamese Refugees in the U.S.," Refugee Studies Center, UMA, 10, 13.

21. Gerald Kleis, "Assimilation vs. Accommodation: The Alternative Strategies of Vietnamese Refugee Adaptation," n.d., ser. 8, box 8, folder: Kleis, Gerald, "Assimilation vs. Accommodation: The Alternative Strategies of Vietnamese Refugee Adaptation," UMA, 14; Christopher Thao, "Torn between Cultures: Southeast Asian Immi-

grants in Minnesota," *Bench and Bar of Minnesota*, October 1987, 24; Ronald Takaki, *Strangers from a Distant Shore: A History of Asian Americans* (New York: Penguin, 1989), 463, 471.

22. Stein, 13; Kleis, 18.

23. Takaki, 448; Astri Suhrke, "Indochinese Refugees: The Impact on First Asylum Countries and Implications for American Policy: A Study Prepared for the Use of the Joint Economic Committee, Congress of the United States, 25 November 1980," in ser. 8, box 8, folder: "Congress: Indochinese Refugees," UMA, 28; Takaki, 454; Sue Bell and Michael Whitefield, "Southeast Asians in the United States: Anthropologists and the Refugee Situation of the Past Decade," *Practicing Anthropology* 9 (April 1987): n.p., in ser. 3, box 1, folder: Old U.S. Statistics, UMA; "Foreign Aid Appropriations, Fiscal 1974–77," *Congress and the Nation*, vol. 4: *1973–1976* (Washington, D.C.: Congressional Quarterly, 1977), 868; Jim Castelli, "Catholics and Ford: Cordial Relations, Mixed Reviews," National Catholic News Service, 26 August 1976, n.p., box 63, folder: NCCB Ad Hoc Committee, Pro-Life Activities, 1976, July–September, USCCBA.

24. NCCB, "Resolution on the Pastoral Concern of the Church for People on the Move," in Minutes of the National Conference of Catholic Bishops Eighteenth General Meeting, 8–11 November 1976, USCCBA, 17, 19–20.

25. Richard Reeves, *A Ford, Not a Lincoln* (New York: Harper, Brace, Jovanovich, 1975), 189.

26. Edward Herman, "On Helping South Vietnam," *America*, 14 February 1975, 392.

27. Sisyphus, "Now Comes the Winter of . . . ," *Commonweal*, 11 April 1975, 37.

28. Daniel Patrick Moynihan, "How Much Does Freedom Matter?" *Atlantic Monthly*, July 1975, 22.

29. Francis Winters, "Morality in the War Room," *America*, 15 February 1975, 106; Michael Warner, *Changing Witness: Catholic Bishops and Public Policy* (Grand Rapids, Mich.: William Eerdmans, 1995), 120–121.

30. Suhrke, 30; NCCB Administrative Committee, "Statement on Small-Boat Refugees in Southeast Asia," 16 February 1978, in *Quest for Justice*, ed. J. Brian Benestad and Francis J. Butler (Washington, D.C.: United States Catholic Conference, 1981), 139, 141; Warner, 120.

31. Moynihan, "How Much Does Freedom Matter?" 24.

32. "Bishop Gumbleton Joins Protest of Vietnam Policy," *Michigan Catholic*, 14 January 1977, in box 41, folder: Vietnam—Letter to the Vietnamese Government, 1973–1977, Bishop Thomas Gumbleton Papers, UNDA, Notre Dame, Ind., 3.

33. "Assessment of the World Food Situation, Present and Future," 5 September 1974, Council of Economic Advisors Records, Paul McAvoy Files, box 108, folder: Food Deputies Groups (2), GRFPL, 1–3.

34. Memorandum from Roy Ash to the President, 16 September 1974, Council of Economic Advisors Records, Alan Greenspan Files, box 45, folder: Food (2),GRFPL, 3.

35. Ibid., 3, 5.

36. Gerald Ford, "Address to the Twenty-Ninth Session of the General Assembly of the United Nations," 18 September 1974, *Public Papers, 1974*, 159–160; memorandum from Bob Stillman to Ed Schuh, 24 September 1974, Council of Economic Advisors Records (Stillman), box 173, folder: Stillman, Subject—Food Aid, GRFPL, 2.

37. USCC Administrative Board, "Proposed Agenda and Supporting Documents," September 1974, box 24, folder: "Proposed Agenda and Supporting Documents," John Cardinal Dearden Papers, UNDA, 13–14.

38. Carol Coston, "Network's Third Legislative Seminar: Social Justice and Politics?" *Christian Century*, 16 October 1974, 971–972.

39. "Meeting with His Eminence Cardinal Terence J. Cooke, Archdiocese of New York," 23 October 1974, National Security Advisor Presidential Name File, box 1, folder: Cooke, Cardinal Terence J., GRFPL, 2–3.

40. "World Food Conference Meets at Rome," *Department of State Bulletin*, 16 December 1974, 821–837; letter from Rev. James Rausch to the President, 13 November 1974, Theodore Marrs Files, box 50, folder: NCCB (2), GRFPL.

41. "Draft Memorandum of Conversation/Meeting of President Ford with Pope Paul VI, Vatican City," 3 June 1975, National Security Advisor Memorandum of Conversations Files, box 12, folder: June 3, 1976—Ford, Kissinger, Pope Paul VI, Archbishop Casaroli, GRFPL, 7–8.

42. Rausch to the President, 13 November 1974.

43. NCCB, "Statement on the World Food Crisis: A Pastoral Plan of Action," 21 November 1974, in Benestad and Butler, 102–103.

44. Ibid., 103; "U.S. Bishops and Human Rights," *America*, 7 December 1974, 359.

45. NCCB, "Minutes of the Fifteenth General Meeting," November 1974, box 22, folder: General Meeting Minutes 1974, John Cardinal Dearden Papers, UNDA, 6–13; Bryan Hehir, "Statement of the United States Catholic Conference on the Global Food Crisis, Ad Hoc Senate Committee Report on Rome—The Challenge of Food and Population, U.S. Senate," 18 December 1974, Theodore Marrs Files, box 64, folder: 6/18/75, Meeting—National Conference of Catholic Bishops—United States Catholic Conference—#2, GRFPL, 1–10.

46. At the World Food Conference in Rome in November, Secretary Butz said of Pope Paul VI's opposition to artificial contraception, while feigning an Italian accent, "He no playa the game, he no maka the rules." See also letter from Max Friedersdorf to Rep. Dominick Daniels, 6 December 1974, White House Central Files, Subject File—Religious Matters, box 2, folder: RM 3–1, Catholics, 8/9/74–6/30/75, GRFPL, 1; Jim Castelli, "Meeting between President, Bishops Unresolved," National Catholic News Service, 25 March 1975, 1–2; letter from Rev. James Rausch to the President, 9 December 1974, Theodore Marrs Files, box 50, folder: National Conference of Catholic Bishops (2), GRFPL, 1–2.

47. "The Politics of Food," *Time*, 17 March 1975, 6; "Department Discusses Food Aid and World's Security," *Department of State Bulletin*, 17 March 1975, 356–357; handwritten notes by Robert Hartman on memorandum from Warren Rustand to Hartman et al., 18 February 1975, William Baroody Files, box 16, folder: Wed. Meetings—6/18/75: USCC, GRFPL.

48. Castelli,"Meeting," 5; "Meeting with the United States Catholic Conference and the National Conference of Catholic Bishops," 18 June 1975, Theodore Marrs Files, box 64 folder: 6/18/75, Meeting—National Conference of Catholic Bishops—United States Catholic Conference—#1, GRFPL, 1, 3; "The World Food Problem and the American Public," n.d., William Baroody Files, box 16, folder: Wed. Meetings, 6/18/75: USCC, GRFPL, 1; "Bishops Meet with President Ford," *Origins*, 3 July 1975, 84.

49. "President Meeting with Bishops," United Press International, 21 June 1975, Theodore Marrs Files, box 50, folder: National Conference of Catholic Bishops (3), GRFPL.

50. USCC, "Confidential Minutes of the Administrative Board," 10–11 September 1975, folder: USCC Administrative Board Minutes 1975, John Cardinal Dearden Papers, UNDA, 16.

51. USCC, Department of Social Development and World Peace, "Statement on Feeding the Hungry: Toward a U.S. Domestic Food Policy," 16 April 1975, in Benestad and Butler, 259; "Child Nutrition/Food Policy," *Origins*, 2 October 1975, 253.

52. USCC, "The Economy: Human Dimensions," 20 November 1975, box 33, folder: AEI Meeting [American Enterprise Institute, 1975–1980], John Cardinal Dearden Papers, UNDA, 8.

53. Ibid., 6; letter from Rev. James Rausch to the President, 30 January 1976, White House Central Files, Name File, box 2603, folder: Rausch, James S., GRFPL, 1–2.

54. John Robert Greene, *The Presidency of Gerald R. Ford* (Lawrence: University of Kansas Press, 1995), 77; letter from Theodore Marrs to Bill Seidman, 6 February 1976, Theodore Marrs Files, box 50, folder: National Conference of Catholic Bishops (3), GRFPL; letter from Roland Elliot to Bishop James Rausch, 18 February 1976, White House Central File, Name File, box 2603, folder: Rausch, James S.,GRFPL.

55. "Annual Food for Peace Report Transmitted to Congress," *Department of State Bulletin*, 28 January 1976, 188; Emma Rothschild, "Food Politics," *Foreign Affairs* (January 1976): 288.

56. Rothschild, 291, 295–296, 297, 300.

57. Ibid., 296; Barbara Huddleston, "Food and Free Enterprise," Letter to the Editor, *Foreign Affairs* (February 1976): 823.

58. Rothschild, 294.

59. Rev. James Malone, "Statement of United States Catholic Conference before the Temporary Committee on Resolutions, Republican National Convention," 9 August 1976, Michael Raoul—Duval Files, box 27, folder: Republican Party Platform—Catholic Issues, GRFPL, 4.

60. "The Bishops Meet Ford," *Origins*, 23 September 1976, 216; Gerald Ford, "Letter to the Archbishop of Cincinnati following a Meeting with the Executive Committee of the National Conference of Catholic Bishops," 10 September 1976, *Public Papers of the Presidents of the United States: Gerald Ford, 1976–1977*, vol. 3: *July 10, 1976–January 20, 1977* (Washington, D.C.: U.S. Government Printing Office, 1979), 2232.

61. Clyde Farnsworth, "Carter Said to Plan a Food Reserve," *New York Times*, 19 November 1976, A17. In a ranking of "issues important to voters" from an October 1976 poll in *The Gallup Poll: Public Opinion, 1972–1977*, vol. 2: *1976–1977*, ed. George Gallup (Wilmington, Del.: Scholarly Resources, 1978), 879–881, inflation finished first, government spending was second, and unemployment and crime tied for third. Food was not on the list.

62. USCC, "Confidential Minutes of the Administrative Board," 10–11 September 1975, 16–17.

63. Jeffrey Jones, "The Protestant and Catholic Vote," http://gallup.com/poll/11911/Protestant-Catholic-Vote.aspx?; memorandum from Jerry Jones to James Connor, 4 March 1975, Philip Buchen Files, box 1, folder: Agriculture, GRFPL; Castelli, "Meet-

ing," 3–4; Kevin Phillips, *The Emerging Republican Majority* (New Rochelle, N.Y.: Arlington House, 1969), and Phillips, *Post-Conservative America* (New York: Random House, 1982).

64. Howard Fetterhoff, "The Politics of Abortion," April 1976, box 39, folder: Church—Church and State, Law and Public Policy, 1976–78, USCCBA, 10–11.

65. Letter from Rev. John Krol to the President, 2 April 1976, White House Central Files, Presidential Name File, box 1790, folder: Krol, John, GRFPL, 1; Gerald Ford, "Remarks at the Conclusion of the International Eucharistic Congress in Philadelphia, Pennsylvania," 8 August 1976, *Public Papers of the Presidents of the United States: Gerald Ford, 1976–1977*, vol. 2: *April 9–July 9, 1976* (Washington, D.C.: U.S. Government Printing Office, 1978), 2138.

66. Gerald Ford, "Address at a University of Notre Dame Convocation," 17 March 1975, *Public Papers, 1975*, 1:137; Castelli, "Catholics and Ford," 1.

67. Ford, "Letter to the Archbishop of Cincinnati," 2232; "Foreign Aid Appropriations, Fiscal 1974–77," *Congress and the Nation, 1973–1976*, 4:868.

68. Ford, "Address at a University of Notre Dame Convocation," 137; Ford, "Letter to the Archbishop of Cincinnati," 2232.

69. "Foreign Policy," *Congress and the Nation*, 4:869; memorandum from Rob Quartel to Foster Channock, 2 August 1976, President Ford Committee Campaign Records, box B10, folder: Voter Groups—Catholics, GRFPL.

70. Greene, *Gerald R. Ford*, 72; "Federal Food Programs, 1950–75," *Congress and the Nation*, 4:409; "U.S. Judge Holds Up Cut in Food Stamps," *New York Times*, 1 August 1976, L28.

71. Ford, "Address at a University of Notre Dame Convocation," 137.

72. Greene, *Gerald R. Ford*, 80–81; Boyce Rensberger, "Serious World Food Gap Is Seen over the Long Term by Experts," *New York Times*, 5 December 1976, A17.

73. Jones.

74. Lawrence McAndrews, "Nothing Yet Everything: The Vice Presidencies of George Clinton, Elbridge Gerry, and Daniel Tompkins," unpublished master's thesis, Millersville University, 1981, 1.

75. Letter from Henry Cashen to Mike Duval, 14 July 1976, White House Special Files, Michael Raoul—Duval Files, box 27, folder: Republican Party Platform—Catholic Issues, GRFPL, 2.

76. Memorandum from Ken Cole to President, 6 September 1974, Presidential Handwriting File, box 51, folder: Welfare, Abortions, GRFPL, 3.

77. "On File," *Origins*, 17 October 1974, 258; memorandum from Rev. James McHugh to Rev. John Cody and Members of the Committee on Population and Pro-Life Activities, 23 October 1974, box 63, folder: NCCB Ad Hoc Committee, Pro-Life Activities, 1974, October–December, USCCBA, 2.

78. "On File," *Origins*, 28 November 1974, 354; letter from Rev. James McHugh to Donald Chalkley, 20 November 1974, box 63, folder: NCCB Ad Hoc Committee, Pro-Life Activities, 1974, October–December, USCCBA, 2.

79. "Confidential Minutes of the Executive Session of the General Meeting," 21 November 1974, box 22, folder: NCCB General Meeting Minutes, 1974, John Cardinal Dearden Papers, UNDA, 2, 4.

80. "Foreign Policy," 869; "Health Programs," *Congress and the Nation*, 4:345.

81. "On File," *Origins*, 6 February 1975, 514; letter from Rev. James Rausch to Philip Geyelin, Editor, *Washington Post*, 28 January 1975, box 38, folder: NCCB Ad Hoc Committee, Pro-Life Activities, 1975, January–June, USCCBA.

82. "Bishops Discuss Issues with President at White House Meeting," USCC, n.d., 1, 4–5; "Catholic Bishops Hear President," *Lynchburg News*, n.d., n.p., Theodore Marrs Files, box 50, folder: National Conference of Catholic Bishops (3), GRFPL.

83. "Talking Points: Abortion," 18 June 1975, Theodore Marrs Files, box 64, folder: 6/18/75, Meeting—National Conference of Catholic Bishops—United States Catholic Conference—#1, GRFPL.

84. Memorandum from Philip Buchen to James Connor, 1 July 1975, box 19, folder: Health, Education, and Welfare (1), and memorandum from James Connor to Philip Buchen, 1 July 1975, box 37, folder: 1975 July (10), Philip Buchen Files, GRFPL.

85. Memorandum from Caspar Weinberger to the President, 24 June 1975, box 19, folder: Health, Education, and Welfare (1), and memorandum from Jerome Nelson to Martin Hoffman via Leonard Niederlehner, 4 August 1975, box 9, folder: Defense Department—Abortion Policy (2), Philip Buchen Files, GRFPL, 5.

86. Ford's handwritten notes on memorandum from James Connor to the President, 11 July 1975, Presidential Handwriting File, box 51, GRFPL; memorandum from James Connor to Philip Buchen, 15 July 1975, Philip Buchen Files, box 19, folder: Health, Education, and Welfare (1), GRFPL; memorandum from James Cowan to Assistant Secretaries of the Military Departments, 17 September 1975, box 63, folder: NCCB Ad Hoc Committee, Pro-Life Activities, 1975, July–December, USCCBA, 1–2.

87. "Statement of Terence Cardinal Cooke," 29 September 1975, NCCB Ad Hoc Committee, Pro-Life Activities, 1975, July–December, USCCBA, 1.

88. Lyle Denniston, "HEW Plans Change in Abortion Policy," *Washington Star*, 12 October 1975, A1, 14; memorandum from Rev. James McHugh to NCCB Pro-Life Committee, 14 October 1975, box 63, folder: NCCB Ad Hoc Committee, Pro-Life Activities, 1975, July–December, USCCBA, 1–2.

89. Memorandum from Philip Buchen to the President, 10 November 1975, Philip Buchen Files, box 1, folder: Abortion (1), GRFPL; Greene, *Gerald R. Ford*, 99; memorandum from James Cannon to Philip Buchen et al., 17 December 1975, and memorandum from Bobbie Kilberg to Cannon and Sara Massengale, 21 November 1975, 2, Philip Buchen Files, box 1, folder: Abortion (1), GRFPL.

90. Memorandum from James Cannon and Philip Buchen to the President, 16 January 1976; memorandum from William Nicholson to Sarah Massengale, 4 November 1975, Philip Buchen Files, box 1, folder: Abortion (1), GRFPL; memorandum from Massengale to File, 27 January 1976, Philip Buchen Files, box 1, folder: Abortion (2), GRFPL.

91. George Wilson, "Military Role on Abortion Liberalized," *Washington Post*, 27 September 1975, A3; memorandum from Russell Shaw to Rev. James McHugh and James Robinson, 30 January 1976, box 63, folder: NCCB Ad Hoc Committee, Pro-Life Activities, 1976, January, USCCBA.

92. James Naughton, "Ford Says Court Went Too Far on Abortion in '73," *New York Times*, 4 February 1976, L1, 49.

93. Memorandum from Russell Shaw to Rev. James Rausch, 4 February 1976, box 63, folder: NCCB Ad Hoc Committee, Pro-Life Activities, 1976, February, USCCBA.

94. "Catholic Leader Calls Abortion Views, Food, Others 'Confused,'" *United States Catholic Conference News*, 3 February 1976, 2–3.

95. Letter from Rev. James Rausch to "Your Excellency," 6 February 1976, box 63, box 63, folder: NCCB Ad Hoc Committee, Pro-Life Activities, 1976, February, USCCBA.

96. "Transcript of Ford Interview," *New York Times*, 4 February 1976, L53.

97. Ibid.

98. Gerald Ford, "Remarks and a Question-and-Answer Session in Buffalo Grove, Illinois," 12 March 1976, *Public Papers of the Presidents of the United States: Gerald Ford, 1976–1977*, vol. 1: *January 1–April 8, 1976* (Washington, D.C.: U.S. Government Printing Office, 1977), 672.

99. Memorandum from Russell Shaw to Rev. James Rausch, 2 March 1976, box 63, folder: NCCB Ad Hoc Committee, Pro-Life Activities, 1976, March, USCCBA, 2.

100. Memorandum from Bobbie Kilberg to James Cavanaugh, 4 September 1976, Philip Buchen Files, box 1, folder: Abortion (2), GRFPL, 2.

101. Memorandum from James Robinson to Rev. James Rausch, 8 March 1976, box 63, folder: NCCB Ad Hoc Committee, Pro-Life Activities, 1976, March, USCCBA, 1.

102. "On File," *Origins*, 13 May 1976, 742; memorandum from James Robinson to Rev. James Rausch, 30 April 1976, box 63, folder: NCCB Ad Hoc Committee, Pro-Life Activities, 1976, April–May, USCCBA, 1–2.

103. "Confidential Minutes of the Executive Session of the General Meeting, NCCB," 5 May 1976, box 22, folder: NCCB General Meeting Minutes 1976, John Cardinal Dearden Papers, UNDA, 1; "National Conference of Catholic Bishops, Seventeenth General Meeting," 4–6 May 1976, USCCBA, 32.

104. Memorandum from Graham Lee and Thomas Melady to Myron Kuropas, 25 June 1976, David Gergen Files, box 1, folder: Abortion (1), GRFPL, 1–2.

105. Memorandum from Henry Cashen to Michael Duval, 14 July 1976, Michael Raoul—Duval Files, box 27, folder: Republican Party Platform—Catholic Issues, GRFPL, 2.

106. "100,000 at World Mass as Catholic Parley Closes," *New York Times*, 9 August 1976, L1, 36; Janis Johnson, "President Hits Abortion 'Concern,'" *Washington Post*, 9 August 1976, A10.

107. John Lofton, "Catholics Cheer Ford, but Why?" *Human Events*, 21 August 1976, 26, in Wanda Phelan Files, box 16, folder: Lofton, John D., Jr., GRFPL.

108. "100,000 at World Mass," 36; Ron Nessen, "News Conference," 9 August 1976, Ronald Nessen Files, box 21, folder: August 9, 1976 (no. 555), GRFPL, 2.

109. "Report on the Meetings of the NCCB Executive Committee with the Democratic and Republican Candidates," 14 September 1976, box 63, folder: NCCB Ad Hoc Committee, Pro-Life Activities, 1976, July–September, USCCBA, 2; William Shannon, "Jimmy Carter and the Catholic Bishops," *New York Times*, 5 September 1976, E, 13.

110. Aldo Beckman, "Abortion Issue Key for Ford," *Chicago Tribune*, 10 September 1976, 1, 2.

111. "Report on the Meetings," 3–4; Harry Rosenthal, "Politics Round-up," Associated Press, 10 September 1976, n.p., box 63, folder: NCCB Ad Hoc Committee, Pro-Life Activities, 1976, July–September, USCCBA.

112. Memorandum from James Cannon to the President, 21 September 1976, Philip Buchen Files, box 1, folder: Abortion (2), GRFPL, 4–5; letter from Gerald Ford to Rev.

Joseph Bernardin, 10 September 1976, box 63, folder: NCCB Ad Hoc Committee, Pro-Life Activities, 1976, July–September, USCCBA, 2.

113. "Health Programs," *Congress and the Nation*, vol. 4: *1973–1976* (Washington, D.C.: Congressional Quarterly, 1977), 365–366.

114. Jim Castelli, "President Ford on Abortion, Butz, and Compassion," National Catholic News Service, 22 October 1976, 2.

115. "Confidential Minutes of the Executive Session of the General Meeting," 21 November 1974, box 22, folder: NCCB General Meeting Minutes, 1974, John Cardinal Dearden Papers, UNDA, 2–3.

116. Ibid., 4.

117. Memorandum from Rev. Joseph Bernardin to John Cardinal Wright, 27 December 1974, box 63, folder: NCCB Ad Hoc Committee, Pro-Life Activities, 1975, January–June, USCCBA, 1; letter from Rev. Joseph Bernardin to Rev. James Rausch, 3 January 1975, box 63, folder: NCCB Ad Hoc Committee, Pro-Life Activities, 1975, January–June, USCCBA.

118. "Human Life Amendment—Senator Bayh Explains His Opposition," *Origins*, 2 October 1975, 225, 231–232.

119. Letter from Rev. James McHugh to Sen. Edward Kennedy, 10 October 1975, box 63, folder: NCCB Ad Hoc Committee, Pro-Life Activities, 1975, July–December, USCCBA, 1.

120. Memorandum from Rev. James McHugh to NCCB Pro-Life Committee, 14 October 1975, box 63, folder: NCCB Ad Hoc Committee, Pro-Life Activities, 1975, July–December, USCCBA, 1.

121. "Confidential Minutes of the Executive Session of the General Meeting," 19 November 1975, box 22, folder: NCCB General Meeting Minutes, 1975, John Cardinal Dearden Papers, UNDA, 2; George Dugan, "Catholic Bishops Approve a Plan to Mobilize Public Support against Abortions on Request," *New York Times*, 21 November 1975, L19.

122. Letter from Rev. John Whealon to Rev. Jean Jadot, 9 December 1975, letter from Jadot to Rev. Joseph Bernardin, 11 December 1975, and letter from Bernardin to Jadot, 12 January 1976, all in box 63, folder: NCCB Ad Hoc Committee, Pro-Life Activities, 1976, January, USCCBA.

123. Memorandum from James Robinson to Rev. James Rausch, Rev. James McHugh, and William Cox, 30 December 1975, box 63, folder: NCCB Ad Hoc Committee, Pro-Life Activities, 1975, July–December, USCCBA, 1–2.

124. "Strategy on Abortion," *Time*, 1 December 1975, 59; William Willoughby, "Catholic Bishops: Abortion the Issue," n.p., 19 December 1975, 35, in box 63, folder: NCCB Ad Hoc Committee, Pro-Life Activities, 1975, June–December, USCCBA.

125. "The Bishops' Plan for Pro-Life Activities," *America*, 27 December 1975, 485.

126. Memorandum, from Russell Shaw to Rev. James McHugh and James Robinson, 30 January 1976, and memorandum from Rev. James McHugh to Rev. Terence Cooke, box 63, folder: NCCB Ad Hoc Committee, Pro-Life Activities, 1976, January–February, USCCBA.

127. Marianne Means, "The Pope and Politics," *Rochester News-American*, 10 February 1976, n.p., box 63, folder: NCCB Ad Hoc Committee, Pro-Life Activities, 1976, February, USCCBA; letter from Rev. James McHugh to John Sweeney, 23 February 1976,

and "Protestant Pro-Life Leaders Challenge Religious Coalition for Abortion Rights," 3 February 1976, 1–2, both in box 63, folder: NCCB Ad Hoc Committee, Pro-Life Activities, 1976, February, USCCBA.

128. Letter from Marjory Mecklenburg to Rev. James Rausch, 24 February 1976, box 63, folder: NCCB Ad Hoc Committee, Pro-Life Activities, 1976, February, USCCBA, 1–2.

129. Letter from Rev. James Rausch to Marjory Mecklenburg, 26 February 1976, 1, and memorandum from William Cox to Rev. James Rausch, 4 March 1976, 1–2, both in box 63, folder: NCCB Ad Hoc Committee, Pro-Life Activities, February–March, USCCBA.

130. Cox to Rausch, 4 March 1976, 2.

131. Paul Weber, "Bishops in Politics," *America*, 20 March 1976, 220.

132. Jim Castelli, "Anti-Abortion, the Bishops, and the Crusaders," *America*, 22 May 1976, 442.

133. Harry Farrell, "NOW Takes on the Church," *San Jose Mercury News*, 10 October 1976, n.p., box 63, folder: NCCB Ad Hoc Committee, Pro-Life Activities, 1976, July–December, USCCBA.

134. Memorandum from James Robinson to Rev. James Rausch, 4 August 1975, and letter from Rausch to Rev. John Wright, 7 October 1975, box 63, folder: NCCB Ad Hoc Committee, Pro-Life Activities, 1975, July–December, USCCBA.

135. "NCCB Confidential Minutes of the Executive Session of the General Meeting," 12 February 1976, 2.

136. Weber, "Bishops in Politics," 223; Fetterhoff, 5–6.

137. Castelli, "Anti-Abortion, the Bishops, and the Crusaders," 443; "National Conference of Catholic Bishops, Seventeenth General Meeting," 4–6 May 1976, 3.

138. Memorandum from Rev. James McHugh to Rev. James Rausch, 22 June 1976, box 63, folder: NCCB Ad Hoc Committee, Pro-Life Activities, 1976, June, USCCBA, 1.

139. Letter from Rev. George Higgins to Rev. Joseph Bernardin, 22 June 1976, and memorandum from Rev. James McHugh to Rev. James Rausch, 25 June 1976, box 63, folder: NCCB Ad Hoc Committee, Pro-Life Activities, 1976, June, USCCBA.

140. William Ryan, "Archbishop Bernardin on Church's Role: Not Involved in Partisan Politics," USCC News Service, 16 August 1976, 1–4.

141. Robert Wonderly, "Republican Pro-Life Plank Said 'Timely and Important,'" 18 August 1976, *United States Catholic News Service*, 1–2.

142. Jim Castelli, "The Bishops and the Party Platforms," National Catholic News Service, 24 September 1976, 1.

143. "Vatican Declaration on Abortion," *Origins*, 12 December 1974, 385; Kenneth Briggs, "Poll Finds Catholics Loyal to Parochial School Concept," *Boston Sunday Herald Advertiser*, 29 December 1974, 1, 12.

144. Letter from Rev. Thomas Kelly to Rev. Joseph Bernardin, 28 July 1975, box 63, folder: NCCB Ad Hoc Committee, Pro-Life Activities, 1976, March, USCCBA, 1; letter from Edward Hanify to Eugene Krasicky, 31 December 1974, box 39, folder: Church—Church and State, Law, and Public Policy, 1975, November–December, USCCBA.

145. Rev. James McHugh, "Recommendations to Dioceses for Implementation of DeVries Study," April 1975, box 63, folder: NCCB Ad Hoc Committee, Pro-Life Activities, 1975, January–June, USCCBA, 2–4.

146. Edward Kennedy, "Alternatives to Abortion Needed," *Hospital Progress*, September 1976, 11.

147. "Shifts in Public Opinion toward Abortion," *Intellect*, January 1976, 280.

148. Kenneth Briggs, "Papal Birth Stand to Hurt Church," *New York Times*, 24 March 1976, L1; Kenneth Woodward, "The Birth Control Factor," *Newsweek*, 5 April 1976, 57.

149. Robert Wonderly, "Archbishop Bernardin Statement on 'Declining Church' Study," *United States Catholic Conference News*, 22 March 1976, 1–2; memorandum from Rev. James McHugh to Rev. Joseph Bernardin, 14 April 1976, box 63, folder: NCCB Ad Hoc Committee, Pro-Life Activities, 1976 April–May, USCCBA, 1–2; "National Conference of Catholic Bishops, Seventeenth General Meeting," 32; *The Gallup Poll: Public Opinion, 1972–1977*, vol. 1: *1976–1977*, ed. George Gallup (Wilmington, Del.: Scholarly Resources, 1978), 671, 673.

150. "On File," *Origins*, 18 November 1976, 306.

CHAPTER FIVE. Catholics and Jimmy Carter

1. H. W. Brands, *The Devil We Knew* (New York: Oxford University Press, 1993), 142–143.

2. Peter Gerety, "U.S. Foreign Policy: A Critique from Catholic Tradition, Submitted to the Senate Foreign Relations Committee," January 1976, box 39, folder: USCC Church—Church and State, Law and Public Policy, 1976–78, USCCBA, 1.

3. Ibid., 3,5.

4. "National Security/Defense/Military Spending," 28 July 1977, box 39, folder: USCC Church—Church and State, Law and Public Policy, 1977, USCCBA, 2.

5. Letter from Rev. Thomas Kelly to Zbigniew Brzezinski, 23 September 1977, White House Central Files, Subject File—Religious Matters, box 2, folder: RM 3, 1/20/77–12/31/77, Jimmy Carter Presidential Papers, JCPL; USCC Administrative Board, "The Gospel of Peace and the Danger of War," in *Pastoral Letters of the United States Catholic Bishops*, vol. 4: *1975–1983*, ed. Hugh Nolan (Washington, D.C.: United States Catholic Conference, 1984), 1–2; "Testimony of Edward Doherty for the United States Catholic Conference before the Subcommittee on Arms Control, Oceans, and International Environment of the Senate Foreign Relations Committee, on the United Nations Special Session on Disarmament,"24 April 1978, box 45501, 02, folder: NCCB Ad Hoc Committee on War and Peace: Archbishop Bernardin, Joseph Bernardin Papers, ACA, 8.

6. Ibid., 12–13; "On File," *Origins*, 1 June 1978, 18.

7. Joseph Fahey, "SALT II," *America*, 24 February 1979, 128; "The Case for and against SALT II," *Congress and the Nation*, vol. 5: *1977–1980* (Washington, D.C.: Congressional Quarterly, 1981), 201.

8. Letter from Rev. Thomas Kelly, Rabbi Daniel Polish, and Claire Randall, 8 December 1978, White House Central Files, Subject File—Religious Matters, box RM 2, folder: RM 3, 1/1/78–9/30/78, JCPL, 2; "Confidential Minutes of the United States Catholic Conference Administrative Board," 14–15 February 1979, box 25, folder: USCC Administrative Board Minutes, 1979, John Cardinal Dearden Papers, UNDA, 31; "The Churches, Disarmament, and SALT II," *America*, 24 February 1979, 124–125.

9. "Acceptance List for Americans for SALT," 7 March 1979, Presidential Papers—Staff Offices, Ethnic Affairs, Aiello, box 20, folder: Bureau of Public Affairs, Special Briefing on SALT II, 3/79, JCPL; memorandum from Anne Wexler and Hamilton Jordan to the President, 11 June 1979, Presidential Papers—Staff Offices, Ethnic Affairs, Aiello, box 20, folder: Bureau of Public Affairs, Special Briefing on SALT II, 3/79, JCPL; "Briefing on SALT for National Leaders," 12 June 1979, Presidential Papers—Staff Offices, Ethnic Affairs, Aiello, box 20, folder: Breakfast Briefing on SALT II for Ethnics, 7/78–1/80, JCPL.

10. John Blum et al., *The National Experience* (New York: Harcourt Brace Jovanovich, 1985), 875; memorandum from Anne Wexler to the President, 19 July 1979, Presidential Papers—Staff Offices, Ethnic Affairs, Aiello, box 20, folder: Breakfast Briefing on SALT II for Ethnics, 7/78–1/80, JCPL.

11. "Testimony of Cardinal John Krol, Archbishop of Philadelphia for the United States Catholic Conference before the Senate Foreign Relations Committee on SALT II Treaty," 6 September 1979, Presidential Papers—Staff Offices, Ethnic Affairs, Aiello, box 20, folder: Pamphlets and Reports on SALT II, 7/79, JCPL, 10, 15; Michael Novak, "Arms and the Church," *Commentary* 73 (March 1982): 37.

12. Memorandum from Anne Wexler to the President, 10 September 1979, Presidential Papers—Staff Offices, Ethnic Affairs, Aiello, box 20, folder: Catholic Charities Conference, 10/79, JCPL, 2.

13. Memorandum from Cyrus Vance to the President, n.d., and from Zbigniew Brzezinski to the President, n.d., White House Central Files, Staff Office Files—Press, Jody Powell, box 69, folder: John Paul II—Visit to United States, 9/79 [CF, OA 588], JCPL.

14. "Exchange of Remarks between the President and His Holiness John Paul II, South Lawn," 6 October 1979, White House Central Files, Staff Office Files—Press, Jody Powell, box 69, folder: Pope John Paul II—Visit to U.S., 9/79, JCPL, 3, 6.

15. William Ryan, "Senate Ratification of SALT II Urged by Catholic Bishops' Aide," *United States Catholic Conference News*, 16 October 1979, 2.

16. "Carter Presidency," *Congress and the Nation*, 5:969; Brands, 160; "Interview with Jimmy Carter, President of the United States," *U.S. News and World Report*, 19 September 1980, 22; Erwin Hargrove, *Jimmy Carter as President* (Baton Rouge: Louisiana State University Press, 1988), 153–154; Jimmy Carter, *White House Diary* (New York: Farrar, Straus and Giroux, 2010), 383, 387.

17. Memorandum from "Fran" to "Les," 10 January 1980, White House Central Files, Name File, no box, folder: Cooke, Terence Cardinal, JCPL; Russell Shaw, "Catholic Conference Official Presents Platform Testimony," USCC News, 8 May 1980, 2; memorandum from Frank Monahan to Bishop Thomas Kelly, 26 June 1980, box 140, folder: USCC: U.S. Gov't: Election Issues, 1980, USCCBA, 2; "An End of SALT?" *Commonweal*, 29 February 1980, 99–100; memorandum from Stephen Aiello to Philip Wise, 21 August 1980, Presidential Papers, Staff Offices, Ethnic Affairs, Aiello, box 19, folder: Catholic Charities Convention—Rochester, N.Y., 9/80, JCPL; Jimmy Carter, *Keeping Faith* (Fayetteville: University of Arkansas Press, 1995), 271.

18. "Minutes, National Conference of Catholic Bishops, Nineteenth General Meeting," 3–5 May 1977, USCCBA, 42–43; "NCCB Pastoral Letter on Marxist Communism Background Notes," November 1980, box 21, folder: NCCB General Meeting Supplemen-

tary Documentation, November 1980, John Cardinal Dearden Papers, UNDA, 1; NCCB, "Pastoral Letter on Marxist Communism," 12 November 1980, in Nolan, 380–400.

19. Thomas Gumbleton, "Chaplains Blessing the Bombers," *Commonweal*, 2 March 1979, 1005; "Confidential Minutes," 14–15 February 1979, 27.

20. "Minutes, National Conference of Catholic Bishops, Twenty-Second General Meeting," 13–16 November 1978, USCCBA, 22.

21. "Testimony of Krol," 2.

22. Bryan Hehir, "Sermon Delivered at the Washington National Cathedral of Sts. Peter and Paul," 3 October 1976, Presidential Papers, Staff Offices—Ethnic Affairs, Aiello, box 19, folder: Catholic Articles and Clippings, 11/76–11/79, JCPL, 11–12; memorandum from Liz Stevens to John Carlin, 16 December 1976, White House Central Files, Name File, no box, folder: Hesburgh (Father), 12/16/76–5/9/79, JCPL, 1–2; Michael O'Brien, *Hesburgh: A Biography* (Washington, D.C.: Catholic University of America Press, 1998), 149–156.

23. Memorandum from Fran Voorde to the President, 8 March 1977, White House Central Files, Name File, no box, folder: Hesburgh, Theodore (Father), 12/16/76–5/9/76, JCPL; Michael Warner, *Changing Witness: Catholic Bishops and Public Policy, 1917–1994* (Grand Rapids, Mich.: Eerdmans, 1995), 118.

24. "National Security/Defense/Military Spending," 1.

25. Letter from Rev. Thomas Kelly to Zbigniew Brzezinski, 23 September 1977, White House Central Files, Subject File—Religious Matters, box 2, folder: RM 3, 1/20/77–12/31/77, Jimmy Carter Presidential Papers, JCPL.

26. Fahey, 128; Patrick Buchanan, "How to Defeat the Treaty," *Public Opinion*, November–December 1978, 45.

27. "Minutes, Twenty-Second General Meeting," 13–16 November 1978, 21.

28. Memorandum from Charles O'Keefe to Anne Wexler, 13 November 1979, Presidential Papers, Staff Offices—Ethnic Affairs, Aiello, box 20, folder: Catholic Issues 1/79–10/80, JCPL, 2.

29. Buchanan, "How to Defeat the Treaty," 41; George Gallup and Jim Castelli, *The American Catholic People* (Garden City, N.Y.: Doubleday, 1987), 80.

30. George Wilson and Michael Getler, "Arms Control: Is There Life after Suspended Animation?" *Washington Post*, 11 July 1980, A15; Buchanan, "How to Defeat the Treaty," 45; Gallup and Castelli, 77.

31. Arms Control Association, "Trust, but Don't Verify," 2004, http://www.armscontrol.org/act/200409/Focus.

32. Memorandum from Joseph Califano to the President, 3 November 1977, White House Central Files, Subject File—Health, box 1, folder: HE 7/1/77–1/20/81, JCPL, 2.

33. Memorandum from the President to the Secretary of Health, Education, and Welfare, 29 July 1978, White House Central Files, Subject File—Health, box 2, folder: HE 4/1/78–11/16/78, JCPL, 2.

34. "Hospital Cost Control," *Congress and the Nation*, 5:616.

35. Memorandum from Joseph Califano to the President, 8 January 1979, White House Central Files, Subject File—Health, box 2, folder: HE 11/17/78–3/20/79, JCPL, 1–16.

36. Ibid., 14.

37. Memorandum from Stuart Eizenstat, James McIntyre, and Charles Schultze to

the President, 17 January 1979, White House Central Files, Subject File—Health, box 2, folder: HE 11/17/78–3/20/79, JCPL, 1–8.

38. Memorandum from Stuart Eizenstat to the President, 17 January 1979, White House Central Files, Subject File—Health, box 2, folder: HE 11/17/78–3/30/79, JCPL; Jimmy Carter, "The State of the Union," 25 January 1979, *Public Papers of the Presidents of the United States: Jimmy Carter, 1979*, vol. 1: *January 1–June 22, 1979* (Washington, D.C.: U.S. Government Printing Office, 1980), 123–124, 133–134; memorandum from Stuart Eizenstat to the President, 22 February 1979, White House Central Files, Subject File—Health, box 2, folder: HE 11/17/78–3/20/79, JCPL, 1–2; memorandum from Peter Bourne to Hamilton Jordan, 28 January 1979, White House Central Files, Subject File—Health, box 1, folder: HE 7/1/77–1/20/81, JCPL.

39. Jimmy Carter, "National Health Plan," 12 June 1979, *Public Papers of the Presidents of the United States: Jimmy Carter, 1979*, vol. 2: *June 23–December 31, 1979* (Washington, D.C.: U.S. Government Printing Office, 1980), 1025.

40. "Hospital Cost Control," 630–633.

41. Ibid; Carter, *White House Diary*, 370.

42. USCC, "Political Responsibility," 12 February 1976, Pre-Presidential Papers, 1976 Presidential Campaign, Director's Office—Urban Affairs, Subject File—Abortion, box 304, folder: Bishops' Bicentennial Conference, JCPL, 1–10.

43. "Confidential Minutes of the Administrative Board," 16–17 February 1977, box 25, folder: USCC Administrative Board Minutes, John Cardinal Dearden Papers, UNDA, 24–25.

44. "Confidential Minutes of the Administrative Board, USCC," 12–14 February 1980, box 25, folder: USCC Administrative Board Minutes, 1980, John Cardinal Dearden Papers, UNDA, 9–14, 17.

45. "Agenda Report Documentation for General Meeting," USCC, 14–17 November 1977, box 18, folder: NCCB General Meeting Agenda Report Documentation, November 1977, John Cardinal Dearden Papers, UNDA, 75.

46. "Agenda Report Documentation for General Meeting," n.d., box 18, folder: NCCB General Meeting Agenda, November 1978, UNDA, 84.

47. "Confidential Minutes of the Administrative Board, USCC," 10 November 1979, box 25, folder: USCC Administrative Board Minutes, 1979, John Cardinal Dearden Papers, UNDA, 4–10.

48. Ibid.

49. NCCB, "Health and Health Care," 19 November 1981, in Nolan, 483–485.

50. Joseph Califano, *Governing America* (New York: Simon and Schuster, 1991), 92.

51. Carter, *White House Diary*, 209–210; memorandum from Stuart Eizenstat and Joe Onek to the President, 20 March 1979, White House Central Files, Subject File-Health, box 2, folder: HE 11/17/78–3/20/79, JCPL.

52. Memorandum from Terry Sundy and Victoria Mongiardo to the President, 31 August 1976, Pre-Presidential Campaign, Director's Office—Urban Affairs, Subject File: Abortion, box 304, folder: Bishops' Bicentennial Conference, JCPL, 8; memorandum from Urban Ethnic Desk to Landon Butler, 6 November 1976, White House Central Files, box 102, folder: Office of Public Liaison—Constanza, JCPL, 1, 8.

53. Lawrence O'Rourke, *Geno: The Life and Mission of Geno Baroni* (New York: Paulist Press, 1991), 123, 125, 133.

54. Califano, *Governing America*, 157.

55. Mary Hanna, *Catholics and American Politics* (Cambridge, Mass.: Harvard University Press, 1979), 103–120.

56. Ibid., 122; James Hitchcock, "On the Present Position of Catholics in America, 1978," Presidential Papers, Staff Offices, Ethnic Affairs—Aiello, box 20, folder: Catholic Positions, 1978, JCPL.

57. Letter from Robert Dornan to "Dear Friend," 12 April 1978, box 63, folder: NCCB Ad Hoc Committee, Pro-Life Activities, 1978, January–June, USCCBA, 2–3.

58. Brooks Flippen, *Jimmy Carter, the Politics of Family, and the Rise of the Religious Right* (Athens: University of Georgia Press, 2011), 109, 191; letter from Rev. Geno Baroni to "Friend," 19 January 1981, CNUEA Files, box 46, folder: HUD Neighborhood Organization Development, Geno Baroni Papers, UNDA, 2; Jim Castelli, "How Catholics Voted," *Commonweal*, 3 December 1976, 780–781; Philip Murnion, "Carter and Catholics," Presidential Papers, Staff Offices—Ethnic Affairs, Aiello, box 20, folder: Catholic Issues, 4/79–6/79, JCPL, 3.

59. "Carter Backs NCCC Program More than Ford," National Catholic News Service, 4 October 1976, 1–4; Thomas Kelly, "USCC Testimony before Platform Committee," *Origins* 19 June 1980, 67; Carter, *White House Diary*, 343–344; Jimmy Carter, "Remarks at the Annual Convention of the National Conference of Catholic Charities," 15 October 1979, *Public Papers, 1979*, 2:1925.

60. Hanna, 122; Gallup and Castelli, 76.

61. Memorandum from Charles O'Keefe to Anne Wexler, 13 November 1979, Presidential Papers, Staff Offices, Ethnic Affairs—Aiello, box 20, folder: Catholic Issues, 1/79–10/80, JCPL, 2.

62. "Proposed Actions of USCC, CHA, and NCCC in Regard to National Health Insurance," 7 September 1977, box 39, folder: USCC, Church—Church and State, Law and Public Policy, USCCBA; "Confidential Minutes," 10 November 1979, 9.

63. "Memorandum to Governor Jimmy Carter from Adam Walinsky," n.d., Morton Blackwell Papers, box 7, folder: Catholic Strategy (1 of 3), Ronald Reagan Presidential Papers, RRPL; memorandum from Stephen Aiello to the President, 10 November 1980, Presidential Papers—Staff Offices, Ethnic Affairs—Aiello, box 20, folder: Catholic Issues 1/79–1/80, JCPL, 2.

64. Jeffrey Jones, "The Protestant and Catholic Vote," http//www.gallup.com/poll/11911/Protestant-Catholic-vote.aspx.

65. Memorandum from James Robinson to Rev. Thomas Kelly, 19 November 1979, box 39, folder: USCC Church—Church and State, Law and Public Policy, 1978–79, USCCBA.

66. Memorandum from Rev. James Rausch to Files, 20 July 1976, box 17, folder: Correspondence 1973–1977, John Cardinal Dearden Papers, UNDA, 1–3.

67. William Ryan, "Bishops' Executive Committee Meets with Governor Jimmy Carter," *United States Catholic Conference News*, 1 September 1976, 2.

68. Scott Stossel, *Sarge: The Life and Times of Sargent Shriver* (Washington, D.C.: Smithsonian Books, 2004), 633.

69. Memorandums from Rev. James Rausch to Frank Monahan and Monahan to Rausch, 17 June 1976, box 63, folder: NCCB Ad Hoc Committee: Pro-Life Archives, 1976, June, USCCBA, 3, 6.

70. "The Abortion Plank," *New World*, 23 July 1976, n.p., in Pre-Presidential Papers, 1976 Presidential Campaign Director's Office—Urban Ethnic Affairs, Subject File: Abortion, box 304, folder: Abortion [3], JCPL.

71. Ibid.; O'Donnell qtd. in Haynes Johnson, "Catholics Seen as Problem for Carter," *Washington Post*, 16 July 1976, A19.

72. Press Release, Catholic League for Religious and Civil Rights, 15 July 1976, n.p., in Pre-Presidential Papers, 1976 Presidential Campaign, Director's Office—Urban Affairs, Subject File: Abortion, box 304, folder: Abortion [3], JCPL; Haynes Johnson, 19.

73. Patrick Riley, "Carter's Aides Drafted Plank," *National Catholic Register*, 1 August 1976, n.p., in Pre-Presidential Papers, 1976 Presidential Campaign, Director's Office—Urban Affairs, Subject File: Abortion, box 304, folder: Abortion [3], JCPL.

74. Memorandum from DeJonge Franklin to Landon Butler, 28 July 1976, White House Central Files, box 102, folder: White House Office of Public Liaison—Constanza, JCPL; "The Abortion Plank"; Riley, "Carter's Aides Drafted Plank."

75. Memorandum from Terry Sundy and Victoria Mongiardo to the President, 31 August 1976, and letter from Stuart Eizenstat to Patrick Riley, 22 July 1976, Pre-Presidential Campaign, Director's Office—Urban Affairs, Subject File: Abortion, box 304, folder: Bishops' Bicentennial Conference, JCPL, 8.

76. Ryan, "Bishops' Executive Committee Meets with Governor Jimmy Carter," 2.

77. Albert Menendez, *Religion at the Polls* (Philadelphia, Pa.: Westminster, 1977), 188–189.

78. Memorandum from Michael Bennett to James Robinson, 16 June 1977, and memorandum from Rev. Thomas Kelly to Most Rev. Archbishops, Bishops, State Catholic Conference Directors, 29 September 1977, box 63, folder: NCCB Ad Hoc Committee: Pro-Life Activities, 1977 July–December, USCCBA.

79. Kelly to Most Rev. Archbishops, 29 September 1977, 2.

80. Memorandum from Rev. Thomas Kelly to Most Rev. Archbishops, Bishops, State Catholic Conference Directors, Other Interested Persons, 8 February 1978, box 63, folder: NCCBB Ad Hoc Committee: Pro-Life Committee, 1978, January–June, USCCBA, 1.

81. Letter from Elizabeth Abramowitz to Rev. John Quinn, 5 June 1978, box 63, folder: NCCB Ad Hoc Committee: Pro-Life Activities, 1978, January–June, USCCBA.

82. "Law Briefs," USCC, n.d., USCCBA, 5–7; "Minutes, National Conference of Catholic Bishops, Executive Session, Twenty-Third General Meeting," 2 May 1979, USCCBA, 13–14; "Law Briefs," USCC, n.d., USCCBA, 1–2.

83. "Minutes, Twenty-Third General Meeting," 1–3 May 1979, 18; "Minutes, National Conference of Catholic Bishops Executive Session, Twenty-Fifth General Meeting," 30 April 1980, USCCBA, 6–7; "Abortion," 28 August 1980, in *Gallup Poll: Public Opinion, 1980*, ed. George Gallup (Wilmington, Del.: Scholarly Resources, 1981), 172; Lawrence Lader, "Abortion Opponents' Tactics," 11 January 1978, *New York Times*, A19.

84. Stossel, 635–636.

85. Monahan to Rausch, 17 June 1976, 3; Jim Castelli, "Archbishop Bernardin Says Carter Still 'Inconsistent' on Abortion, but Praises His Rejection of Abortion Plank," National Catholic News Service, 16 August 1976, 6–7.

86. Kenneth Briggs, "Carter Campaign, Moving to Mollify Catholics after Dispute over Democratic Party's Platform Stand," *New York Times*, 26 August 1976, A20;

Sundy and Mongiardo to the President, 8, 5; "Carter Says Claims of Catholic Prejudice against Him Are 'Grossly Exaggerated,'" *National Catholic News Service*, n.d., 1, in Pre-Presidential Papers, 1976 Presidential Campaign Director's Office—Urban Ethnic Affairs, box 304, folder: Abortion [1], JCPL.

87. "National Conference of Catholic Bishops Confidential Minutes of the Executive Session of the General Meeting," November 1976, box 22, folder: NCCB General Meeting Minutes, 1976, John Cardinal Dearden Papers, UNDA, 15.

88. "National Conference of Catholic Bishops Confidential Minutes of the Executive Session of the General Meeting," May 1977, box 22, folder: NCCB General Meeting Minutes, 1977, John Cardinal Dearden Papers, UNDA, 10; "Supreme Court on Medicaid and Abortion," *Origins*, 30 June 1977, 86.

89. "Individual Rights," *Congress and the Nation*, 5:812–813; Jimmy Carter, "Remarks and a Question-and-Answer Session at a Town Meeting," 17 February 1978, *Public Papers of the Presidents of the United States: Jimmy Carter, 1978*, vol. 1: *January 1–June 30, 1978* (Washington, D.C.: U.S. Government Printing Office, 1978), 362, 356, 363; Califano, *Governing America*, 86.

90. "The Pope and Pluralism," *America*, 20 October 1979, 205; Carter, *White House Diary*, 361; Jimmy Carter, "Remarks and a Question-and-Answer Session of a Town Meeting," 22 September 1980, *Public Papers of the Presidents of the United States: Jimmy Carter, 1980*, vol. 2: *May 24–September 26, 1980* (Washington, D.C.: U.S. Government Printing Office, 1981), 1876.

91. Russell Shaw, "Catholic Conference Asks Supreme Court to Reverse Decision on Abortion Funding," *United States Catholic Conference News*, 16 January 1980, 1, 3.

92. "National Conference of Catholic Bishops Agenda Report Documentation for General Meeting," November 1980, box 18, folder: NCCB General Meeting Agenda Report Documentation November 1980, John Cardinal Dearden Papers, UNDA, 30; "Individual Rights," 811–813; Califano, *Governing America*, 76; "Abortion and the Poor," *America*, 2 February 1980, 73.

93. Memorandum from Ray Jenkins to Stephen Aiello, 10 October 1980, Presidential Papers, Staff Offices, Ethnic Affairs—Aiello, box 20, folder: Catholic Issues, 1/79–10/80, JCPL, 3.

94. Letter from Jimmy Carter to Terence Cardinal Cooke, 4 September 1980, White House Central Files, no box, folder: Cooke, Terence Cardinal, JCPL.

95. Ellen Goodman, "A Relative Consensus," *Washington Post*, 11 June 1980, A19.

96. "National Conference of Catholic Bishops Agenda Report Documentation for General Meeting," 29 April–1 May 1980, box 18, folder: NCCB General Meeting Agenda Report Documentation April–May 1980, John Cardinal Dearden Papers, UNDA, 60; "National Conference of Catholic Bishops Agenda Report Documentation for General Meeting," 10–13 November 1980, box 18, folder: NCCB General Meeting Agenda Report Documentation November 1980, John Cardinal Dearden Papers, UNDA, 69.

97. "National Conference of Catholic Bishops Confidential Minutes of the Executive Session of the General Meeting," 3 May 1978, box 22, folder: NCCB General Meeting Minutes, 1978, John Cardinal Dearden Papers, UNDA, 8–9.

98. Ibid., 9–10; "National Conference of Catholic Bishops Confidential Minutes of the Executive Session of the General Meeting," 15 November 1978, box 22,

folder: NCCB General Meeting Minutes, 1978, John Cardinal Dearden Papers, UNDA, 3. Though Alan Olten was the first to use the term "pro-choice" in print, in a *Wall Street Journal* article, the term "pro-abortion" continued to appear in the mainstream media throughout 1979. See Olten, "Abortion," *Wall Street Journal*, 20 March 1975, 22.

99. NCCB, "Confidential Minutes of the Executive Session of the General Meeting," November 1976, 14.

100. Lader, 19.

101. "Abortion under Attack," *Newsweek*, 5 September 1978, 37.

102. Lader, 19; "Of Many Things," *America*, 3 February 1979, 17.

103. Letter from Eleanor Smeal to "Dear Friend," n.d., box 63, folder: NCCB Ad Hoc Committee: Pro-Life Activities, 1977 July–December, USCCBA, 1–2; letter from Karen Mulhauser to "Dear Friend," n.d., box 63, folder: NCCB Ad Hoc Committee: Pro-Life Activities, 1977 July–December, USCCBA, 1, 3.

104. Letter from Father Collins with Attachment, 14 May 1978, box 63, folder: NCCB Committee, Pro-Life Activities, 1978 January–June, USCCBA, 1–2.

105. Letter from Faye Wattleton to Rev. John Quinn, 5 May 1978, box 63, folder: NCCB Ad Hoc Committee, Pro-Life Activities, 1978 January–June, USCCBA, 1.

106. Memorandum from Russell Shaw, 15 May 1978, box 63, folder: NCCB Ad Hoc Committee: Pro-Life Activities, 1978 January–June, USCCBA; letter from Rev. Thomas Kelly to Faye Wattleton, 17 May 1978, box 63, folder: NCCB Ad Hoc Committee: Pro-Life Activities, 1978 January–June, USCCBA.

107. "Minutes, NCCB Executive Session, Twenty-Sixth General Meeting," 12–13 November 1980, USCCBA, 4.

108. Letter from Rev. Thomas Kelly to "Mr. President," 31 August 1978, box 63, folder: NCCB Ad Hoc Committee: Pro-Life Activities, 1978 January–June, USCCBA.

109. Letter from Dale Francis to Walter Wurfel, 14 September 1978, Presidential Papers, Staff Offices, Ethnic Affairs—Aiello, box 19, folder: Catholic, Carter and Abortion, JCPL, 1–2.

110. Sharon Johnson, "After Heated Debate, Family Parley Ends Quietly," *New York Times*, 14 July 1980, B12.

111. Leslie Bennets, "NOW Leader Barred from Carter Parley," *New York Times*, 14 December 1979, A1; B10.

112. Monahan to Kelly, 26 June 1980, 1–12. Quotations in the following paragraphs are from the same source.

113. "Interview with Jimmy Carter," 9.

114. Memorandum from Rev. James Rausch to the Files, 2 September 1976, box 63, folder: NCCB Ad Hoc Committee: Pro-Life Activities, 1976, July–September, 1; "Nuns Group Endorses Carter," National Catholic News Service, 16 September 1976, 1.

115. Colman McCarthy, "Carter, Catholics, and Abortion," *Washington Post*, 16 September 1976, A15; "Carter and the Bishops," *Commonweal*, 24 September 1976, 612; "LCWR Thinks No Effective Anti-Abortion Law Possible," *Our Sunday Visitor*, 21 August 1977, n.p., box 63, folder: NCCB Ad Hoc Committee: Pro-Life Activities, 1977 July–December, USCCBA.

116. Philip Shabecoff, "Archbishop Asserts Church Is Neutral in White House Race," *New York Times*, 17 September 1976, A16; "Minutes, USCC Twenty-Fifth General Meeting," 29 April–1 May 1980, USCCBA, 5.

117. "Confidential Minutes of the Executive Session of the General Meeting, NCCB," 17 November 1977, USCCBA, 9.

118. Jim Castelli, "The Religious Vote," *Commonweal*, 21 December 1980, 650.

119. James Reichley, *Religion in American Public Life* (Washington, D.C.: Brookings, 1985), 316, 317, 321–326.

120. "Minutes, NCCB Executive Session, Twenty-Sixth General Meeting," 12–13 November 1980, 5.

121. James Fiedler, "Public Policy Will Not Always Reflect Catholic View," National Catholic News Service, 7 October 1976, 1.

CHAPTER SIX. Catholics and Ronald Reagan

1. Elizabeth Edwards Spalding, "The Origins and Meaning of Reagan's Cold War," in *The Reagan Presidency*, ed. W. Elliot Brownlee and Hugh Davis Graham (Lawrence: University Press of Kansas, 2003), 65.

2. Henry Scott Stokes, "At Site of Blast in Hiroshima, Pope Appeals for Peace," *New York Times*, 5 February 1981, A2.

3. Paul Kengor, *God and Ronald Reagan* (New York: HarperCollins, 2006), 206.

4. "By Russell Shaw," n.d., box 45501.02, folder: NCCB Ad Hoc Committee on War and Peace—Archbishop Bernardin, Joseph Cardinal Bernardin War and Peace Papers, ACA, 1–2; Francis Winters, "The Bow or the Cloud? American Bishops Challenge the Arms Race," *America*, 25 July 1981, 30.

5. "Arms Control," *Congress and the Nation*, vol. 6: *1981–1984* (Washington, D.C.: Congressional Quarterly, 1985), 251.

6. Telegram from Ronald Reagan to Pope John Paul II, 23 November 1981, Executive Secretariat, National Security Council Collection, box 41, folder: The Vatican—Pope John Paul II, Cables (1 of 2), Ronald Reagan Presidential Papers, RRPL, 1; memorandum from James Vance to the President, 4 December 1981, Executive Secretariat, National Security Council Collection, box 41, folder: The Vatican—Pope John Paul II, Cables (2 of 2), RRPL; Kenneth Doyle, "Pope Writes to Reagan, Brezhnev Urging Nuclear Disarmament," National Catholic News Service, 30 November 1981, 19.

7. Joseph Bernardin, "NCCB Ad Hoc Committee on War and Peace Report," November 1981, box 21, folder: NCCB General Meeting November 1981, John Cardinal Dearden Papers, UNDA.

8. "Statement by Victor Weisskopf to President Ronald Reagan," 14 December 1981, no box, no folder, USCCBA, 1, 3.

9. "Pope Sends Warning of Nuclear Dangers," *Physics Today*, April 1982, 58; memorandum from William Clark to the President, 11 January 1982, Executive Secretariat, National Security Council, box 41, folder: Pope John Paul II (8107378–8200051), RRPL; Paul Kengor, *The Crusader* (New York: Regan Books, 2006), 112.

10. "Ad Hoc Committee on War and Peace, Session Four," 20 January 1982, box 41, folder: WPP Committee Minutes, Notes, Correspondence, Bishop Thomas Gumbleton Papers, UNDA, 1–2, 3, 5, 6, 10, 11, 13, 14, 18.

11. "Statement by Archbishop Raymond Hunthausen," *Origins*, 1 April 1982, 674.

12. Francis Quinn, "The Case for a Nuclear Freeze," *Origins*, 1 April 1982, 675.

13. John Lehman, "The Immorality of Nuclear Disarmament," *Origins*, 1 April 1982, 673–674.

14. Memorandum from Bryan Hehir to M. Hartley, V. Price, and M. Murphy, 19 April 1982, box 45501.02, folder: May 13th, ACA, 1; letter from Alexander Haig to Rev. Joseph Bernardin, 23 March 1982, box 45501.02, untitled folder, ACA; "Notes," 13 May 1982, box 41, folder: WPP Committee Minutes, Notes, Correspondence, May–July 1982, Bishop Thomas Gumbleton Papers, UNDA, 1–2.

15. "Notes," 13 May 1982, 1–2.

16. *Congressional Record*, 10 March 1982, H808; Marjorie Hyer, "Nuclear Weapon Use Immoral, Bishops State," *Washington Post*, 19 June 1982, A7.

17. Letter from Lawrence Eagleburger to Rev. Joseph Bernardin, 5 June 1982, box 44, folder: WPP Correspondence for U.S. Government Officials, June–December 1982, Bishop Thomas Gumbleton Papers, UNDA, 3–4.

18. "Remarks of the President and His Holiness the Pope following Their Meeting, the Papal Library, the Vatican," 7 June 1982, Executive Secretariat, National Security Council, box 41, folder: The Vatican—Pope John Paul II (820555-8204184), RRPL; Lou Cannon, "Pope Asks Reagan to Seek Peace, Aid Poor," *Washington Post*, 8 June 1982, A13.

19. "Message of His Holiness Pope John Paul II, Delivered by His Eminence Agostino Casaroli, Secretary of State, on the Occasion of the Second Special Session of the General Assembly Devoted to Disarmament," and Bishop Thomas Gumbleton's handwritten notes, box 44, folder: WPP Materials Covering Position of Vatican toward War 1982, Bishop Thomas Gumbleton Papers, UNDA, 7, 3, 4, 6.

20. Ronald Reagan, "Agenda for Peace," 17 June 1982, U.S. Department of State, Bureau of Public Affairs, box 45501.02, untitled folder, Joseph Cardinal Bernardin Papers, ACA, 3–4.

21. Hyer, A7.

22. Letter from William Clark to Clare Boothe Luce, 30 July 1982, box 45501.02, untitled folder, ACA, 2, 4.

23. Letter from Rev. Philip Hannan to Rev. Joseph Bernardin, 10 July 1982, box 45501.02, untitled folder, ACA, 1.

24. Memorandum from William Clark to James Baker, 16 August 1982, Morton Blackwell Files, box 6, folder: Nuclear Freeze (7 of 10), RRPL.

25. Ronald Reagan, "Remarks at the Meeting of the Supreme Council of the Knights of Columbus," 3 August 1982, *Public Papers of the Presidents of the United States: Ronald Reagan, 1982*, vol. 2: *July 3–December 31, 1982* (Washington, D.C.: U.S. Government Printing Office, 1983), 1012; memorandum from William Clark to the President, 3 August 1982, Peter Sommer Files, box 2, folder: Vatican 1983–1984 (6 of 10), RRPL, 1.

26. Andrew Malcolm, "New Bishop Takes Over Archdiocese of Chicago," *New York Times*, 25 August 1982, B4; letter from Caspar Weinberger to Rev. Joseph Bernardin, 13 September 1982, box 44, folder: WPP Correspondence from U.S. Government Office, June–December 1982, Bishop Thomas Gumbleton Papers, UNDA, 1, 2, 4; memorandum from William Triplett to Red Cavaney, 26 October 1982, RRPL.

27. Letter from "A Group of Uptown Catholics" to Rev. Joseph Bernardin, n.d.,

and letter from Bernardin to "Dear Friends," 20 October 1982, box 45501.01, folder: Current Matters, ACA.

28. Joseph O'Hare, "The Bishops' Pastoral on War and Peace I," *America*, 13 November 1982, 284; Joseph O'Hare, "The Bishops on War and Peace II," *America*, 20 November 1982, 305; Kenneth Woodward and Jane Whitmore, "The President vs. the Bishops," *Newsweek*, 29 November 1982, 41.

29. Jerry Filteau, "Nuclear Debate Heats Up with U.S. Bishops in the Middle," National Catholic News Service, 1 November 1982, 12, 13.

30. "Pastoral Letter: Blueprint for Unilateral Disarmament," *Human Events*, 6 November 1982, 1.

31. Filteau, "Nuclear Debate," 13; letter from Rep. Patricia Schroeder to Ronald Reagan, 19 November 1982, Peter Sommer Files, box 2, folder: Vatican 1983–84 (6 of 10), RRPL.

32. Woodward and Whitmore, 41; "Arms Control," 256; Gerhard Peters, "Seats in Congress Gained/Lost by the President's Party in Mid-Term Elections," *American Presidency Project*, http://www.presidency.ucsb.edu/data/mid-term_elections.php.

33. "Results of the Table Poll," 15 November 1982, untitled box, folder: Bishops' Response to Second Draft December 1982–February 1983, A–H, JCBWPP, ACA; James Mann and Michael Lose, "Impact of Bishops' Call for Nuclear Freeze," *U.S. News and World Report*, 16 May 1983, 33.

34. Richard Halloran, "Minuet with Catholic Bishops over Nuclear War," *New York Times*, 16 December 1982, B16.

35. Letter from William Clark to Rev. Joseph Bernardin, 16 November 1982, box 21, folder: NCCB General Meeting, November 1982, John Cardinal Dearden Papers, UNDA, 4, 2, 3, 5.

36. Letter from Rep. Henry Hyde et al. to Rev. Joseph Bernardin, box 44, folder: WPP Correspondence from U.S. Government Officials, June–December 1982, Bishop Thomas Gumbleton Papers, UNDA, 1–7.

37. Philip Hannan, "A Bishop's Response to the Bishops," *Human Events*, 4 December 1982, 5–6.

38. Ronald Reagan, "Address to the Nation on Strategic Arms Reduction and Nuclear Deterrence," 22 November 1982, *Public Papers, 1982*, 2:1506.

39. Memorandum from Elizabeth Dole to James Baker, 23 November 1982, Morton Blackwell Files, box 7, folder: Nuclear Freeze (2), RRPL.

40. Thomas Gumbleton and Philip Hannan, "Should Church Oppose Nuclear Freeze?" *U.S. News and World Report*, 20 December 1982, 47–48; memorandum from Sharon Fairbanks to Jack Burgess through Roger Porter, 20 December 1982, Morton Blackwell Files, box 7, folder: Nuclear Freeze (1), RRPL.

41. Paul Kengor and Patricia Clark Doerner, *The Judge* (San Francisco, Calif.: Ignatius, 2007), 191–192.

42. Pope John Paul II, "1982 World Day of Peace Message," *Origins Online*, 1 January 1983, http://originsplus.catholicnews.com/plweb-cgi/fastweb?state.

43. Memorandum from Rev. James Hickey to Rev. Joseph Bernardin, 22 December 1982, untitled box, folder: Bishops' Response to Second Draft, December 1982–February 1983, A–H, Joseph Cardinal Bernardin Papers, ACA, 1–2.

44. Memorandum from Tyrus Cobb and Peter Sommer to Robert MacFarlane,

17 January 1983, Peter Sommer Files, box 2, folder: Vatican 1983–84 (4 of 10), RRPL; "Bishops in Vatican for Nuclear Talks," *New York Times*, 19 January 1983, A10.

45. Memorandum from Rev. Joseph Bernardin to Rev. John Roach et al., 9 February 1983, box 43, folder: WPP Committee Correspondence Re: Informal Consultation with Vatican, January–March 1983, Bishop Thomas Gumbleton Papers, UNDA, 1–4.

46. Ibid., 1–4.

47. Jerry Filteau, "Bishops' Spokesman Raps NCR Article on War and Peace Meeting," National Catholic News Service, 15 February 1983, 1.

48. "Statement by Joseph Cardinal Bernardin to Jerry Filteau of N.C. News Re: Episcopal Conference—January 18–19, 1983, Rome," untitled box, untitled folder, Joseph Cardinal Bernardin Papers, ACA.

49. Filteau, "Bishops' Spokesman Raps NCR Article."

50. "Intervention of Agostino Cardinal Casaroli," 19 January 1983, box 43, folder: WPP Committee Correspondence Re: Informal Consultation with Vatican, January–March 1983, Bishop Thomas Gumbleton Papers, UNDA, 3–4.

51. Letter from Pio Laghi to Rev. Joseph Bernardin, 6 April 1983, untitled box, folder: Between First and Second Draft, Joseph Cardinal Bernardin Papers, ACA, 1–2.

52. "Arms Control," 253; Joseph Bernardin, "Morality and Foreign Policy," *Origins Online*, 7 March 1983.

53. Thomas Reese, "The Third Draft of the Peace Pastoral," *America*, 23 April 1983, 320; Peter Steinfels, "Pastoral Proceedings," *New Republic*, 30 March 1983, 15.

54. Jerry Filteau, "Second Draft's Critics Praise Pastoral's Third Draft," National Catholic News Service, 7 April 1983, 1.

55. Jim Lackey, "Washington Letter: U.S. Policy and the Third Draft," National Catholic News Service, 5 April 1983, 1.

56. Gerard Powers, "The U.S. Bishops and War since the Peace Pastoral," *U.S. Catholic Historian* 27 (Spring 2009): 76; Mann and Lose, 33.

57. Mann and Lose, 33; Steinfels, "Pastoral Proceedings," 16.

58. Mann and Lose, 33; James Dougherty, *The Bishops and Nuclear Weapons* (Hamden, Conn.: Archon, 1984), 200; Jim Castelli, *The Bishops and the Bomb* (Garden City, N.Y.: Doubleday, 1983), 178.

59. Mann and Lose, 33.

60. Kenneth Briggs, "Cooke Letter on Arms Offers Advice to Catholics in Service," *New York Times*, 8 June 1983, A12.

61. Lou Cannon, *President Reagan: The Role of a Lifetime* (New York: Simon and Schuster, 1991), 283; Steve Askin, "Liaison Works to Align White House, Catholics," *National Catholic Reporter*, 30 December 1983, n.p., in Morton Blackwell Files, box 7, folder: Catholic Strategy (1 of 3), RRPL; "White House Staffer Defends Just Wars," *Wanderer*, 22 December 1983, 12.

62. Telegram from Ronald Reagan to Pope John Paul II, 3 January 1984, and "Talking Points for President's Meeting with John Paul II," 2 May 1984, both in Peter Sommer Files, box 2, folder: Vatican 1983–84 (5 of 10), RRPL.

63. "Arms Control," 253; "Bishops See Reagan Rap Court Action," *Milwaukee Journal*, 19 April 1984, 1, 6; "Arms Control: Questions of Politics, Strategy, and Ethics," *Origins Online*, 9 August 1984.

64. "Arms Control," *Congress and the Nation*, 6:257.

65. "Agenda Report Documentation for General Meeting," November 1985, box 18, folder: NCCB General Meeting Report Documentation, John Cardinal Dearden Papers, UNDA, 117; "On File," *Origins Online*, 3 May 1985.

66. William F. Buckley, "Button Thy Lip, Thy Grace," *National Review*, 19 April 1985, 54.

67. "On File," *Origins Online*, 3 May 1985.

68. Memorandum from Robert MacFarlane to the President, 23 July 1985, Nelson Ledsky Files, box 3, folder: Vatican City, The Holy See 1987–88, RRPL.

69. "On File," *Origins Online*, 4 July 1985; letter from Edward Rowny to Frederick Ryan, 25 September 1985, White House Office of Records, Management Files, box 7, folder: RM 031 Catholic (340000–599999), RRPL.

70. Peter Beinart, "The Myth of the Wall's Fall," *Daily Beast*, http://www.thedailybeast.com/blogs-and-stories/2009-11-08/the-myth-of-the-walls-fall/fall.

71. "On File," *Origins Online*, 21 November 1985.

72. Jack Matlock, "Ronald Reagan and the End of the Cold War," in *Ronald Reagan and the 1980s*, ed. Cheryl Hudson and Gareth Davies (New York: Palgrave Macmillan, 2008), 67–68.

73. Edward Doherty, "The Challenge of Peace: Nuclear Deterrence Reconsidered," *America*, 20 December 1986, 386.

74. Matlock, 70; Doherty, "The Challenge of Peace," 397.

75. Matlock, 71; Ronald Reagan, "Remarks following Discussions with Pope John Paul II in Vatican City," 6 June 1987, *Public Papers of the Presidents of the United States: Ronald Reagan, 1987*, vol. 1: *January 1–July 3, 1987* (Washington, D.C.: U.S. Government Printing Office, 1989), 614; Ronald Reagan, "Remarks following Discussions with Pope John Paul II in Miami, Florida," 10 September 1987, *Public Papers of the Presidents of the United States: Ronald Reagan, 1987*, vol. 2: *July 4–December 31, 1987* (Washington, D.C.: U.S. Government Printing Office, 1989), 1018; "Agenda Report Documentation for General Meeting," 16–19 November 1987, box 19, folder: NCCB General Meeting Agenda Report Documentation, November 1987, John Cardinal Dearden Papers, UNDA, 136; Thomas Fox, "Catholics Debate Papal Nuclear Shift," *Bulletin of the Atomic Scientists*, May 1988, 31.

76. Matlock, 71–72.

77. "Report on the 'Challenge of Peace' and Policy Developments, 1983–1988," *Origins Online*, 21 July 1988, 20–28.

78. Powers, 77.

79. Ronald Reagan, *Where's the Rest of Me?* (New York: Best, 1965).

80. NCCB, "The Challenge of Peace: God's Promise and Our Response," 3 May 1983, in *Pastoral Letters of the United States Catholic Bishops*, vol. 4: *1975–1983*, ed. Hugh Nolan (Washington, D.C.: United States Catholic Conference, 1984), 497.

81. Gordon Zahn, "On Not Writing a Dead Letter," *Commonweal*, 8 March 1985, 142; R. E. B., "Stand Up for Something or You'll Fall for Anything," *U.S. Catholic*, August 1986, 2.

82. Ronald Reagan, "Interview with Allan Dale of WOAI Radio in San Antonio, Texas, on Domestic and Foreign Policy Issues," 5 May 1983, 648–649, and Ronald Reagan, "Question-and-Answer Session with Reporters on Domestic and Foreign Policy Issues," 4 May 1983, 636, in *Public Papers of the Presidents of the United States: Ronald*

Reagan, vol. 1: *January 1–July 1, 1983* (Washington, D.C.: U.S. Government Printing Office, 1984).

83. "What Do Bishops Know about Nukes?" *U.S. Catholic*, January 1984, 30.
84. Doherty, "The Challenge of Peace Reconsidered," 398.
85. "Report on the 'Challenge of Peace' and Policy Developments, 1983–1988," 1.
86. Thomas Reese, "The Bishops' Challenge of Peace," *America*, 21 May 1983, 395.
87. "What Do Bishops Know about Nukes?" 30.
88. Powers, 73.
89. George Weigel, "Testimony Submitted to the Ad Hoc Committee on War and Peace of the National Conference of Catholic Bishops," 22 March 1982, box 41, folder: WPP Committee Minutes, Notes, Correspondence, March–April 1982, Bishop Thomas Gumbleton Papers, UNDA; Daniel K. Williams, "Reagan's Religious Right," in Hudson and Davies, 144; Bruce Van Voorst, "The Churches and Nuclear Deterrence," *Foreign Affairs* (Winter–Spring 1983): 851.
90. Thomas Powers, "The Moment to Say No," *Commonweal*, 5 November 1982, 583.
91. Norman Miller, "A Catholic Looks at the Bishops' Pastoral Letter," *Wall Street Journal*, 9 December 1982, 22.
92. "The Challenge of Peace," in Nolan, 49.
93. Cannon, *President Reagan*, 283.
94. Ibid.
95. Ronald Reagan, "Message to the Congress Transmitting the Proposed Package on the Program for Economic Recovery," 18 February 1981, *Public Papers of the Presidents of the United States: Ronald Reagan, 1981* (Washington, D.C.: U.S. Government Printing Office, 1982), 123, 120, 132.
96. William Ryan, "First Draft on Catholic Teaching and Economy to be Ready in Middle of 1984," *United States Catholic Conference News*, 23 May 1983, 1–2; "The Bishops Start New Controversy," *Dun's Business Month*, March 1984, 31; Edmund Szoka, "Effects of the Reagan Budget Cuts," *Origins*, 7 January 1982, 484.
97. "Confidential Minutes of the Administrative Board, United States Catholic Conference," 24–26 March 1981, box 25, folder: USCC Administrative Board Minutes, 1981, John Cardinal Dearden Papers, UNDA, 11–12.
98. Ibid., 15.
99. James Roark et al., *The American Promise: A History of the United States* (Boston: Bedford/St. Martin's, 2002), 1118; "President, Congress, and the Budget, 1980–85," *Congress and the Nation*, 6:36.
100. John Roach, "The Need for Public Dialogue on Religion and Policies," *Origins*, 3 December 1981, 389; "Agenda Report Documentation for General Meeting," 16–19 November 1981, box 18, folder: General Meeting Agenda Report Documentation, November 1981, John Cardinal Dearden Papers, UNDA, 84.
101. Szoka, 484; Joseph Sullivan, "The Harsh Reality of the Economic System," *Origins*, 18 March 1982, 629.
102. "The Novak Report on the New Ethnicity," March 1981, box 45, folder: Correspondence, Memos—L. Manick, 1980, Monsignor Geno Baroni Papers, UNDA, 2, 4.
103. Memorandum from Elizabeth Dole to the President, 13 July 1981, Morton Blackwell Files, box 7, folder: Catholic Strategy (1 of 3), OA 12450, RRPL, 1.

104. "Memorandum from Elizabeth Dole to Edwin Meese, James Baker, and Michael Deaver, 2 November 1982, Morton Blackwell Files, box 7, folder: Catholic Strategy (1 of 3), OA 12450, RRPL; Elizabeth Dole, "General Plan of Appeal to Catholics," n.d., Morton Blackwell Files, box 7, folder: Catholic Strategy (3 of 3) OA 12450, RRPL, 1, 2, 9, 8, 9, 33, 38, 45.

105. Draft letter from Ronald Reagan to Rev. John Roach, attached to letter from John Mackey to Stephen Galesbach, 5 November 1982, Morton Blackwell Files, box 7, folder: Catholic Strategy (1 of 3), OA 12450, RRPL.

106. "House Vote: Major Midterm Setback for the Republicans," *Congressional Quarterly Almanac, 1982* (Washington, D.C.: Congressional Quarterly, 1983), 5-B; "Agenda Report Documentation for General Meeting," 15–18 November 1982, box 18, folder: NCCB General Meeting Agenda Report Documentation, November 1982, John Cardinal Dearden Papers, UNDA, 98.

107. "Minutes, United States Catholic Conference Twenty-Eighth General Meeting," 15–18 November 1982, no box, no folder, USCCBA, 33–35.

108. William Ryan, "First Draft on Catholic Teaching and Economy to Be Ready in Middle of 1984," USCC News, 23 May 1983, 2–3.

109. George Higgins, "Address Delivered at Labor Day Conference," 5 September 1983, box 212, folder: Higgins, Monsignor Geno Baroni Papers, UNDA, 8. The quotations in the next paragraph are from the same source.

110. Eugene Kennedy, "America's Activist Bishops," *New York Times Magazine*, 12 August 1984, 15; memorandum from "Linas" to "Faith," 14 September 1983, and memorandum from Faith Whittlesey to Gail Hodges, 14 September 1983, Robert Reilly Files, box 1, folder: Catholic Church—General, OA 9747, RRPL.

111. Memorandum from Faith Whittlesey to Frederick Ryan, 31 October 1983, Robert Reilly Files, box 1, folder: Catholic Church—General, OA9747, RRPL, 1–2.

112. "List of Attendees for State Dinner for Karl Carstens," 4 October 1983, Presidential Diary, Storage and Information Retrieval System, RRPL.

113. "Bishops' Take on Conservative Economics," *Business Week*, 19 December 1983, 79.

114. Letter from Thomas Donohue to Craig Fuller, 12 December 1983, WHORM File, box 6, folder: RMO 31 Catholic (125000–232368), RRPL; "Bishops' Take on Conservative Economics," 79; letter from Edwin Meese to Paul Cane, 9 January 1984, WHORM File, box 6, folder: RMO 31 Catholic (125000–232368), RRPL.

115. Kenneth Briggs, "Church Groups Denounce Reagan Move," *New York Times*, 11 January 1984, A4; Russell Chandler, "Catholic Bishops Look at Economic Capitalism," *Los Angeles Times*, 24 December 1983, 2:4.

116. "CBS's Face the Nation," White House News Summary, 16 January 1984, Faith Whittlesey Files, box 1, folder: Churches—Vatican, RRPL, B.

117. Ronald Reagan, "Address before a Joint Session of the Congress on the State of the Union," 25 January 1984, *Public Papers of the Presidents of the United States: Ronald Reagan, 1984*, vol. 1: *January 1–June 29, 1984* (Washington, D.C.: U.S. Government Printing Office, 1986), 89; "Catholic Charities Criticizes State of the Union Message," *Origins Online*, 9 February 1984.

118. Marjorie Hyer, "Group Plans to Counter Bishops' Letter," *Washington Post*, 19 May 1984, B8.

119. Letter from Michael Novak to Rev. Roger Mahony, 14 June 1984, box 8, folder: Novak, Michael, Archbishop Rembert Weakland Papers, AMA, 1, 3, 4.

120. Pat Windsor, "Writers of Lay 'Letter' Want to 'Contribute,'" *Catholic Herald*, 26 July 1984, n.p., in box 9, folder: July, August, September, October 1984, Archbishop Rembert Weakland Papers, AMA.

121. Marjorie Hyer, "Churches File Suit to Block U.S. Ties to Vatican," *Washington Post*, 22 September 1984, B6.

122. Jerry Filteau, "The Pope on Economics and the U.S. Pastoral," National Catholic News Service, 19 September 1984, 1.

123. Robert McClory," Discord Pascale," *Quill*, October 1984, 15; Barb Fraze, "Vatican Ambassador Offers Encouragement on Economic Pastoral," National Catholic News Service, 13 November 1984, 17.

124. J. Madeline Nash, John Greenwald, and James Castelli, "Am I My Brother's Keeper?" *Time*, http//www.time.com/time/magazine/article/0,9171,927000-2,00.html, 2.

125. "First Draft of Bishops' Pastoral Letter on Catholic Social Teaching and the U.S. Economy," *Origins Online*, 15 November 1984, 1–2.

126. "Catholic Bishops and American Economics," *Religion and Society Report*, March 1985, B1–8.

127. James Dickenson, "President Welcomes Draft of Bishops' Pastoral Letter," *Washington Post*, 14 November 1984, A15.

128. Memorandum from Faith Whittlesey to Frederick Ryan, 13 November 1984, Robert Reilly Files, box 1, folder: Catholic Church—General, OA 9747, RRPL, 1; David Hoffman, "Deficit Forecast Revised Upward," *Washington Post*, 14 November 1984, A1, 15.

129. "Congress Enacts Sweeping Overhaul of Tax Law," *Congressional Quarterly Almanac* (Washington, D.C.: Congressional Quarterly, 1987), 491; letter from William Van Tassell to Ronald Reagan, 5 September 1985, Mariam Bell Files, box 2, folder: Knights of Columbus (2 of 3), OA 17960, RRPL.

130. Rembert Weakland, "The Economic Pastoral: Draft Two," *America*, 21 September 1985, 129–132.

131. Memorandum from Patrick Buchanan to the Chiefs of Staff, 30 September 1985, Robert Reilly Files, box 1, folder: U.S. Catholic Conference, RRPL.

132. Memorandum from Rev. Daniel Hoye to Rev. Rembert Weakland and Rev. Bryan Hehir, 6 February 1986, box 8, folder: Miami, April 17–18, '86, Archbishop Rembert Weakland Papers, AMA, 2.

133. "Economic Justice for All," http://www.osjspm.org/economic_justice_for_all.aspx.

134. "Liberty and Justice for All: Report on the Final Draft (June 1986) of the U.S. Catholic Bishops' Pastoral Letter by the Lay Commission on Catholic Social Teaching and the U.S. Economy," 5 November 1986, box 8, folder: Committee on Laity, AMA, 16, 21.

135. "Minutes of the Thirty-Fourth General Meeting," 10–13 November 1986, box 23, folder: NCCB General Meeting Minutes, 1986, John Cardinal Dearden Papers, UNDA, 32–41.

136. Ronald Reagan, "Remarks by Telephone to the Annual Convention of the

Knights of Columbus in Chicago, Illinois," 5 August 1986, *Public Papers of the Presidents of the United States: Ronald Reagan, 1986*, vol. 2: *June 28–December 31, 1986* (Washington, D.C.: U.S. Government Printing Office, 1988), 1054.

137. Anthony Pilla, "How to Implement 'Economic Justice for All,'" *America*, 31 January 1987, 76–78.

138. Karen Sue Smith, "What's Become of the Pastoral?" *Commonweal*, 18 December 1987, 742.

139. Qtd. in Robert Bellah, "Resurrecting the Common Good," *Commonweal*, 18 December 1987, 736.

140. Joseph Hogan, "Reaganomics and Economic Policy," in *The Reagan Presidency: An Incomplete Revolution*, ed. Dilys Hill, Raymond Moore, and Phil Williams (New York: St. Martin's, 1990), 157.

141. "Statement of the Most Rev. Rembert Weakland, Archbishop of Milwaukee, Wisconsin, Hearings before the U.S. Senate Joint Economic Committee on 'The Catholic Church Speaks Out on Poverty: Ethics and Economics,'" 22 December 1986, box 9, folder: Weakland/Hollenbach, U.S. Congress, Joint Economic Committee, Archbishop Rembert Weakland Papers, AMA, 1; "On File," *Origins Online*, 26 February 1987; Bryan Hehir, "Testimony on Homelessness," *Origins Online*, 6 February 1987; "Confidential Minutes of the Administrative Board, United States Catholic Conference," 25–27 March 1987, no box, folder: USCC Administrative Board Minutes, 1987, John Cardinal Dearden Papers, UNDA, 6.

142. Peter Steinfels, "On Understanding the Reactions to the Economic Pastoral," *Origins Online*, 11 June 1987; David O'Brien, "America's Catholics: Who They Are," *Christianity Today*, November 1986, 19.

143. Daniel K. Williams, "Reagan's Religious Right," in *The Reagan Presidency*, ed. Paul Kengor and Peter Schweizer (New York: Rowman and Littlefield, 2000), 136.

144. "Abortion Prompts Emotional Lobbying," *Congressional Quarterly*, 18 February 1981, 384; William F. Buckley, "Right to Life Breakthrough," *National Review*, 20 March 1981, 313; "Pro-Life Interest Groups Try a New Tactic in Effort to Crack Down on Abortion," *Congressional Quarterly*, 28 February 1981, 383.

145. Timothy Noah, "The Right-to-Life Split," *New Republic*, 21 March 1981, 8.

146. "Confidential Minutes of the Administrative Committee, National Conference of Catholic Bishops," 24–26 March 1981, John Cardinal Dearden Papers, UNDA, 20; "On File," *Origins*, 16 April 1981, 690; "Life and the Fourteenth Amendment," *America*, 16 May 1981, 397.

147. "Disagreement over Proposed Human Life Bill," *Origins*, 2 July 1981, 100–101.

148. Memorandum from Gary Bauer to Ed Gray and Ron Frankum, 14 May 1981, and memorandum from Morton Blackwell to Elizabeth Dole, 15 May 1981, Morton Blackwell Files, box 8, folder: Pro-Life Continued #213, OA 12450, RRPL; memorandum from William Gribbin to Dennis Thomas, 12 September 1981, and memorandum from Gribbin to Thomas, n.d., Edwin Meese Files, box 16, folder: Abortion (1) OA 9447, RRPL.

149. National Right to Life Committee, "Legislative Alert," 22 March 1982, Dee Jepsen Papers, box 1, folder: Abortion (7), OA 10770, RRPL, 2–3.

150. "Text of Reagan's, Craven's Letters," *National Right to Life News*, 24 August

1981, Morton Blackwell Papers, box 7, folder: Pro-Life Continued #2 (1) OA 12450, RRPL, 10.

151. Letter from Ronald Reagan to Marie Craven, 3 August 1981, Morton Blackwell Files, box 7, folder: Pro-Life Continued #2 (1) OA 12450, RRPL.

152. Patrick Buchanan, "Reagan's Run-In with the Right-to-Lifers," *New York Daily News*, 11 August 1981, A30.

153. Ibid.

154. Letter from Carolyn Gerster to Ronald Reagan, 9 September 1981, Morton Blackwell Files, box 7, folder: Pro-Life Continued #2 (2) OA 12450, RRPL, 1.

155. "Confidential Minutes of the Administrative Committee, National Conference of Catholic Bishops," 15–17 September 1981, box 26, folder: NCCB Administrative Committee Minutes, 1981, John Cardinal Dearden Papers, UNDA, 18; *Congressional Record*, 22 September 1981, S10197.

156. "Law Briefs," USCC, October 1981, 1.

157. Letter from Robert McConnell to Strom Thurmond, n.d., Morton Blackwell Files, box 7, folder: Pro-Life Continued #2 (3) OA 12450, RRPL, 2–3.

158. "Minutes of the Twenty-Seventh General Meeting," 16–19 November 1981, box 23, folder: NCCB General Meeting Minutes, John Cardinal Dearden Papers, UNDA, 13; "The Bishops and the Abortion Amendment," *America*, 21 November 1981, 312.

159. William F. Buckley, "The Bishops and the Hatch Amendment," *National Review*, 5 February 1982, 133; John Mulloy, "The Warning of History to the American Bishops," *Wanderer*, 10 June 1982, Morton Blackwell Files, box 7, folder: Pro-Life Continued (2), OA 12450, RRPL, 1; Mary Meehan, "Catholic Liberals and Abortion," *Commonweal*, 20 November 1981, 650.

160. James Wallis, "Right-to-Life Activists Split on Federal Tactics," *Christian Century*, 23 December 1981, 1332–1333.

161. Memorandum from Gary Bauer to Martin Anderson and Edward Gray, 19 January 1982, Morton Blackwell Files, box 7, folder: Pro-Life Continued #2 (3) OA 12450, RRPL; "News from Senator Tom Eagleton," 3 October 1982, Dee Jepsen Papers, box 1, folder: Abortion (3), OA 10770, RRPL, 2.

162. Memorandum from Morton Blackwell to Elizabeth Dole, 4 February 1982, Morton Blackwell Files, box 7, folder: Pro-Life Continued #2 (3) OA 12450, RRPL, 1–2.

163. Buckley, "The Bishops and the Hatch Amendment," 133; Paul Foster, "'Smoking Gun' Memorandum Sets 'Hatch' Scenario," *Wanderer*, n.d., Morton Blackwell Files, box 7, folder: Pro-Life (4), OA 12450, RRPL, 1.

164. "Law Briefs," USCC, February 1982, 4; "On File," *Origins*, 8 April 1982, 678.

165. Bauer to Harper, 11 March and 23 March 1982; letter from Ronald Reagan, 10 March 1982, and memorandum from Kenneth Duberstein to Edwin Harper, 30 March 1982, all in Wendy Borchert Files, box 6, folder: Abortion, OA 7115, RRPL.

166. Russell Shaw, "Hatch Amendment Supporters See New Unity among Pro-Life Groups," *United States Catholic Conference News*, 30 April 1982, Morton Blackwell Files, box 7, folder: Pro-Life Continued #2 (1) OA 12450, RRPL, 1.

167. Betty Anne Williams, "Wyngaarden-Abortion," Associated Press, 13 April 1982, Morton Blackwell Files, box 7, folder: Pro-Life Continued #2 (1) OA 12450, RRPL.

168. Memorandum from Gary Bauer to Edwin Harper, 2 June 1982, Edwin Meese

Files, box 16, folder: Abortion (1) OA 9447, RRPL, 1; Stuart Taylor, "U.S. to Support States in Regulating Abortions," *New York Times*, 29 July 1982, A17.

169. "Nuns' Group Splits with Bishops in Backing Top Court on Abortion," *Chicago Tribune*, 30 May 1982, 1, 2.

170. "President Reagan's Address to the Knights of Columbus Convention," *Origins Online*, 3 August 1982; memorandum from Red Caveney to Jack Burgess et al., 8 September 1982, Dee Jepsen Files, box 1, folder: Abortion (3) OA 10770, RRPL.

171. "With Friends like These," *Commonweal*, 24 September 1982, 483.

172. "Helms Stopped by Single Vote in Senate Despite All-Out Support by President," *Lifeletter*, n.d., Morton Blackwell Files, box 7, folder: Pro-Life (1) OA 12450, RRPL; "Law Briefs," USCC, September 1982, 4.

173. Memorandum from Richard Doerflinger to Pro-Life and Respect Life Coordinators and State Catholic Conference Directors, 17 September 1982, Morton Blackwell Files, box 7, folder: Pro-Life Continued (1) OA 12450, RRPL, 2.

174. Memorandum from William Gribbin to Morton Blackwell, n.d., Morton Blackwell Files, box 8, folder: Pro-Life (1) OA 12450, RRPL.

175. Memorandum from Michael Uhlmann and William Barr to Ronald Reagan, 20 January 1983, Edwin Meese Files, box 16, folder: Abortion (1) OA 9447, RRPL.

176. Memorandum from Elizabeth Dole to Ronald Reagan, 20 January 1983, 2, and "Meeting with Pro-Life Leadership," 21 January 1983, both in Elizabeth Dole Files, box 92, folder: Pro-Life Organizations, OA 5233, RRPL.

177. Ronald Reagan, "Abortion and the Conscience of the Nation," *Human Life Review*, Spring 1983, Morton Blackwell Files, box 7, folder: Right to Life OA 12448, RRPL, 13, 16.

178. Memorandum from Michael Uhlmann to Edwin Harper, 23 March 1983, Morton Blackwell Files, box 8, folder: Pro-Life (4) OA 12450, RRPL; memorandum from Rev. John O'Connor to Rev. Joseph Bernardin, no box, no folder, Joseph Cardinal Bernardin Papers, ACA, 1–2.

179. "Law Briefs," USCC, April 1983, 6; William Ryan, "Senate Debate on Abortion Is Hailed by Bishops' Spokesman," *United States Catholic Conference News*, 14 June 1983, 1.

180. "Choice Decision," *Time*, 11 July 1983 21.

181. "Agenda Report Documentation," 58; Steve Askin, "Abortion Clause Fight Kills ERA," *National Catholic Reporter*, 25 November 1983, Dee Jepsen Files, box 1, folder: Abortion (2) OA 17770, RRPL, n.p.

182. "Law Briefs," USCC, December 1983, 7; "Meeting with National Leaders of Pro-Life Movement," 23 January 1984, Morton Blackwell Files, box 7, folder: Right to Life OA 12448, RRPL, 1.

183. "Hard-Line Stand," *Time*, 2 July 1984, 21.

184. "Population: Trading Places," *Newsweek*, 20 October 1984, 50; William F. Buckley, "Talking Sense on Population," *National Review*, 10 August 1984, 15–16.

185. "Grandstand Play," *New Republic*, 7 August 1984, 9; James Buckley, "Conference on Population Family Planning Programs," *Vital Speeches of the Day*, 8 August 1984, 677.

186. Ronald Reagan, "Response to Questions from the National Catholic News Service," 26 October 1984, WHORM Files, box 6, folder: RM 031 Catholic (340000–599999), RRPL, 1.

187. Jeffrey Jones, "The Protestant and Catholic Vote," 8 June 2004, http://gallup.poll/11911/Protestant-Catholic-vote.aspx; "On File," *Origins Online*, 31 January 1985.

188. "Law Briefs," USCC, July 1985, 1–2; "Agenda Report Documentation for General Meeting," 11–15 November 1985, box 18, folder: NCCB General Meeting Agenda Report Documentation, November 1985, John Cardinal Dearden Papers, UNDA, 87–88.

189. "USCC Sells Out Catholic Dogma in Supreme Court Amicus Brief," *All News*, 23 August 1985, Mariam Bell Files, RRPL; *Origins Online*, 5 September 1985; and "US Catholic Conference Officials Comment on Friend-of-the Court Brief in Abortion Law Case," *Origins Online*, 12 September 1985.

190. Letter from Anne Higgins to Ronald Reagan, n.d., Mariam Bell Files, box 5, folder: Abortion (Federal Finding F) OA17964, RRPL.

191. Ibid., 2; letter from Nellie Gray to Ronald Reagan, 29 November 1985, Mariam Bell Files, box, 5: Abortion—D.C. Appropriations (2), RRPL.

192. Gray to Reagan, 29 November 1985; letter from Christopher Smith et al. to Ronald Reagan, 22 January 1986, Mariam Bell Files, box 2, folder: March for Life OA 17961, RRPL, 1; J. C. Willkie, "Meeting the President: Turning Triumphs into Trouble," *National Right to Life News*, 13 February 1986, Mariam Bell Files, box 2, folder: March for Life OA 17961, RRPL, 3.

193. Letter from Teresa Ashcraft to Ronald Reagan, n.d., Marian Bell Files, box 4, folder: Abortion (4) OA 17964, RRPL; "Remarks of Virgil C. Dechant on Reception of the Lantern Award Given by the Massachusetts State Council," 1 April 1986, Mariam Bell Files, box 2, folder: Knights of Columbus (2 of 3) OA 17960, RRPL.

194. Letter from Ronald Reagan to Teresa Ashcraft, 16 July 1986, Mariam Bell Files, box 4, folder: Abortion (4) OA 17964, RRPL.

195. Memorandum from Carl Anderson to John Tuck, 20 June 1986, Mariam Bell Files, box 5, folder: Abortion (General) (1) OA 17964, RRPL, 1–2.

196. Ronald Reagan, "Presidential Remarks: Satellite Address to Knights of Columbus Convention, 5 August 1986," Mariam Bell Files, box 2, folder: Knights of Columbus (1 of 3), RRPL, 3.

197. Memorandum from Mari Maseng to James Miller, 19 March 1987, Mariam Bell Files, box 5; letter from Nellie Gray to Ronald Reagan, 12 January 1987, Mariam Bell Files, box 1, folder: Pro-Life (2) OA 17955, RRPL.

198. "HHS Seeks Ban on Abortion Funds," *Washington Times*, 12 February 1987, A3; Charlotte Law, "Whose Right to Choose?" *Insight*, 26 January 1987, Mariam Bell Files box 4, folder: Abortion (3) OA 17964, RRPL, 16.

199. Maggie Gallagher, "One Step Forward," *National Review*, 13 March 1987, 29; memorandum from Alfred Kingon to Donald Regan, 18 February 1987, Mariam Bell Files, box 6, folder: (Abortion) Title X OA 17965, RRPL, 1.

200. Letter from Christopher Smith et al., to Gary Bauer, 11 February 1987, Mariam Bell Files, box 1, folder: Pro-Life (2) OA 17955, RRPL; "HHS Seeks Ban," 3.

201. Mary Jean Moriarty, "Superbill Hits 125 Backers; White House Vows 'Big Push,'" *Lifeletter*, 11 July 1987; Angela Grimm, "The Birth of Strategy in the Pro-Life Movement," *The Light*, May 1987, Mariam Bell Files, box 1, folder: Pro-Life (2) OA 17955, RRPL, 1.

202. Grimm, 6; "Oh Yes, the Same Fundraiser," *Lifeletter*, 27 May 1987, Mariam Bell Files, box 1, folder: Pro-Life (2) OA 17955, RRPL, 3.

203. Fred Barnes, "Bringing Up Baby," *New Republic*, 24 August 1987, 10; "Reagan Could Bar Funds for Abortion Counseling," *Washington Post*, 23 July 1987 3; memorandum from Carl Anderson to Ronald Reagan, 29 July 1987, Gary Bauer Files, box 4, folder: Pro-Life OA 19224, RRPL, 1.

204. Ronald Reagan, "Remarks by the President in Briefing for Right to Life Leaders," 30 July 1987, Gary Bauer Files, box 4, folder: Pro-Life OA 19224, RRPL, 1–4.

205. Letter from the Ad Hoc Committee in Defense of Human Life to Anti-Abortion Leaders, 30 July 1987, and "President Orders De-Funding of Abortion Advocacy Groups; Strongly Condemns the 'Civil Rights Restoration Act,'" National Right-to-Life Committee Press Release, 30 July 1987, Mariam Bell Files, box 1, folder: Pro-Life (2) OA 17955, RRPL, 1; George Archibald and Amy Bayer, "Anti-Abortion War Resumed by Reagan," *Washington Times*, 31 July 1987, A12.

206. Barnes, "Bringing Up Baby," 12; Michael Kramer, "Reagan's Backdoor War on Abortion," *U.S. News and World Report*, 17 August 1987, 14.

207. Steven Roberts, "U.S. Proposes Curb on Clinics Giving Abortion Advice," *New York Times*, 31 July 1987, B8; Kramer, 14.

208. Robert Suro, "Pope Condemns Abortion in U.S. as He Ends Visit," *New York Times*, 20 September 1987, A1.

209. "Confidential Minutes of the Administrative Committee, National Conference of Catholic Bishops," 22–24 September 1987 box 26, folder: NCCB Administrative Committee Minutes, 1987, John Cardinal Dearden Papers, UNDA, 24.

210. Ronald Reagan, "National Sanctity of Life Day, 1988," 15 January 1988, Gary Bauer Files, box 2, folder: Abortion OA 19222, RRPL, 2

211. Memorandum from Rebecca Range to Ronald Reagan, 21 January 1988, 1, and "Suggested Talking Points for Meeting with Right to Life Volunteers," n.d., Gary Bauer Files, box 2, folder: Abortion OA 19222, RRPL.

212. "A 'Gag Rule' on Abortion," *Time*, 15 February 1988, 22.

213. Memorandum from Juanita Duggan to Rebecca Range, 28 July 1988, Gary Bauer Files, box 2, folder: Abortion OA 1922, RRPL.

214. "Reagan Veto Threat, House Pressure Lead Senate to Cave In on Abortion Funding Expansion," *Planned Parenthood Washington Memo*, 28 September 1988, Gary Bauer Files, box 2, folder: Abortion OA 19222, 1.

215. Ibid.; Lawrence McAndrews, *The Era of Education: The Presidents and the Schools, 1965–2001* (Urbana: University of Illinois Press, 2006), 175.

216. Interview of Ronald Reagan, n.d., n.p., Mariam Bell Files, box 11, folder: President's Accomplishments, Pro-Life, OA 19273, RRPL.

217. Bill Lynch and Liam Quinlan, "Anti-Catholicism in the U.S.A.," *Catholic League Newsletter*, n.d., and memorandum from Michael Uhlmann to William Barr, 29 June 1983, William Barr Files, box 2, folder: Catholic League, OA 9094, RRPL; Jones; memorandum from Rebecca Range to Frederick Ryan, 6 October 1988, Mariam Bell Files, box 2, folder: Knights of Columbus (2 of 3) OA 17960, RRPL; interview of Reagan.

218. Joseph Bernardin, "A Consistent Ethic of Life," 6 December 1983, WHORM Files, box 6, folder: RM 031 Catholic (265000–339999), RRPL, 8; Kenneth Briggs, "Cardinal Presses Catholics to Attack Wide Range of Social Issues," *New York Times*, 26 October 1984, A16; Joseph Berger, "2 Cardinals Join on Abortion Issue," *New York Times*, 2 October 1985, A12.

219. Memorandum from Donald Shea to Frank Fahrenkopf, 19 December 1983, WHORM Files, box 6, folder: RM 031 Catholic (265000–339999), RRPL; "The Bishops, the Bomb, and Abortion," 4 May 1983, Dee Jepsen Files, box 1, folder: Abortion (9) OA 10770, RRPL.

220. "Tolerance and Truth in America: Address of Senator Edward Kennedy at Liberty Baptist College," *Origins Online*, 19 November 1983.

221. "Address of Senator Edward Kennedy on Religion and Politics," *Origins Online*, 20 September 1984.

222. Mario Cuomo, "The Church and Politics: Address at Notre Dame University," *Origins Online*, 27 September 1984.

223. Henry Hyde, "Religious Values and Public Life: The Issue of Abortion," *Origins Online*, 11 October 1984.

224. "Confidential Minutes of the Administrative Committee, National Conference of Catholic Bishops," 20–22 March 1984, box 26, folder: NCCB Administrative Committee Minutes 1984, John Cardinal Dearden Papers, UNDA, 14.

225. Joseph Berger, "Catholics, in Poll, Admire Pope but Disagree," *New York Times*, 10 September 1987, A1, B10.

226. Memorandum from Thomas Melady to George H. W. Bush, 10 November 1986, George Bush Vice Presidential Records, Philip Brady Files, no box number, folder: Catholic Issues (3), GBPL; James Kelly, "Catholics, Abortion Rates, and the Abortion Controversy," *America*, 4 February 1989, 82; Berger, "Catholics, in Poll," 10.

227. Merril McLoughlin, "America's Civil War," *U.S. News and World Report*, 3 October 1988, 23, 25.

228. Ibid., 25.

CHAPTER SEVEN. Catholics and George H. W. Bush

1. "Special Report: Persian Gulf War," *Congress and the Nation*, vol. 8: *1989–1992* (Washington, D.C.: Congressional Quarterly, 1993), 299.

2. Michael Duffy and Dan Goodgame, *Marching in Place: The Status Quo Presidency of George Bush* (New York: Simon and Schuster, 1992), 153; "Special Report," 303–304.

3. "Special Report," 305.

4. Francis Stafford, "Letter to President Bush on the Persian Gulf Crisis," 15 November 1990, *Origins Online*, http://originsplus.catholicnews.com, 1; "Margin Notes," *Origins Online*, 15 November 1990, 3–4.

5. "To Attack or Not?" *America*, 10 November 1990, 339.

6. Peter Steinfels, "Debate on Persian Gulf Enlivens Bishops' Meeting," *New York Times*, 13 November 1990, A22.

7. Gregory Waldrup, "U.S. Bishops' Meeting," *America*, 1 December 1990, 420; Peter Steinfels, "Bishops Prefer Problems on Outside," *New York Times*, 16 November 1990, A23.

8. Ari Goldman, "Council of Churches Condemns U.S. Policy in the Gulf," *New York Times*, 16 November 1990, A13; "Margin Notes," *Origins Online*, 28 February 1991, 6.

9. Clyde Haberman, "Gorbachev Is Firm on Gulf Solution," *New York Times*, 19 November 1990, A13.

10. John Robert Greene, *The Presidency of George Bush* (Lawrence: University of Kansas Press, 2000), 129.

11. Thomas Leckey, "Teaching History at High Noon," *Commonweal*, 5 April 1991, 223; "Special Report," 310.

12. Daniel Pilarczyk, "Statement of U.S. Bishops' Conference President on the Threat of War," *Origins Online*, 24 January 1991, 1; John Paul II, "January 15 Letter of the Pope to President Bush," *Origins Online*, 24 January 1991, 1.

13. "Margin Notes," *Origins Online*, 7 February 1991, 7.

14. "Bush Announcement at Start of War," *Congress and the Nation*, 8:1202.

15. "Leaders Wrestle with Faith and War," *Christianity Today*, 11 February 1991, 50; James Johnson, "Just War Tradition and the War in the Gulf," *Christian Century*, 6–13 February 1991, 134; Francis Winters, "The 'Just War' War," *Commonweal*, 5 April 1991, 220–221; George Weigel, "A War about America," *Commonweal*, 22 February 1991, 121.

16. Philip Caputo, "War Torn," *New York Times Magazine*, 24 February 1991, 36.

17. Kenneth Woodward, "Ancient Theory and Modern War," *Newsweek*, 11 February 1991, 47; "Margin Notes," *Origins Online*, 7 February 1991, 36; "The Road Taken," *America*, 2 February 1991, 75; David O'Brien, "Daunting Questions for Both Sides," *Commonweal*, 8 February 1991, 85; George Weigel, "The Churches and the War in the Gulf," *First Things*, http://www.firstthings.com, 9.

18. George Bush, "Address to Religious Broadcasters," *Origins Online*, 7 February 1991, 1–3.

19. Weigel, "Churches and the War," 1; Daniel Jordan, "A No-Hands-Tied War," *Commonweal*, 8 March 1991, 148; Winters, "The 'Just War' War," 220.

20. "Margin Notes," *Origins Online*, 7 February 1991, 5–6; John Quinn, "Can There Be a Just War Today?" *Origins Online*, 25 April 1991, 1; Michael Warner, *Changing Witness: Catholic Bishops and Public Policy* (Grand Rapids, Mich.: Eerdmans, 1995), 154.

21. "Engulfed," *Commonweal*, 22 February 1991, 5–6; "Special Report," 312; J. Bryan Hehir, "The Moral Calculus of War," *Commonweal*, 22 February 1991, 126; Thomas Reese, *A Flock of Shepherds* (Kansas City, Mo.: Sheed and Ward, 1992), 63.

22. Margaret O'Brien Steinfels, "Heads and Hearts at Odds," *Commonweal*, 5 April 1991, 213; *The Gallup Poll: Public Opinion, 1983*, ed. George Gallup (Wilmington, Del.: Scholarly Resources, 1984), 74; *The Gallup Poll: Public Opinion, 1991*, ed. George Gallup (Wilmington, Del.: Scholarly Resources, 1991), 43.

23. "Bush Address on Cease-Fire in Gulf War," 27 February 1991, *Congress and the Nation*, 8:1203.

24. John Roach, "The Persian Gulf's Pastoral Challenges and Moral Questions," *Origins Online*, 14 March 1991, 5; "Margin Notes," *Origins Online*, 10 October 1991, 3.

25. Pope John Paul II, "Opening Address to the Vatican Summit on the Persian Gulf War," *Origins Online*, 4 March 1991, 2; Jean-Louis Tauran, "The Pope's Approach to the War," *Origins Online*, 21 March 1991, 1.

26. "Communiqué of the Vatican Summit Participants," *Origins Online*, 21 March 1991, 3; "Margin Notes," *Origins Online*, 21 March 1991, 5.

27. Clyde Haberman, "Pope Denounces the Gulf War as 'Darkness,'" *New York Times*, 1 April 1991, A6.

28. Ryan Barilleaux and Mark Rozell, *Power and Prudence: The Presidency of George H. W. Bush* (College Station: Texas A&M Press, 2004), 31; Furio Colombo, "Vaticant," *New Republic*, 6 April 1991, 14.

29. "Draft, President Bush's Response to United States Catholic Conference," 1 October 1992, FOIA Files, no. 2006-1149-1, George Bush Presidential Papers, GBPL, 31; "Questions the War Left Behind," *America*, 16 March 1991, 283; Abigail McCarthy, "The Gulf War: A Question Remains," *Commonweal*, 19 April 1991, 248–249; Gordon Zahn, "An Infamous Victory," *Commonweal*, 1 June 1991, 366–368; "Justice and Peace Committee of the Conference of Major Superiors of Men," *Origins Online*, 4 April 1991, 1–4; Francis Winters, "Freedom to Resist Coercion," *Commonweal*, 1 June 1991, 372; "Bush Speech on Victory in the Persian Gulf War," 6 March 1991, *Congress and the Nation*, 8:1204.

30. George Bush, Notes on Meeting with Archbishop John Roach, 21 March 1983, FOIA Files, no. 2006-1149-F, George Bush Vice Presidential Papers, GBPL; letter from Daniel Pilarczyk to George Bush, 4 October 1991, FOIA Files, no. 2006-1149-F, GBPL, 1–4.

31. Pilarczyk to Bush, 1–4.

32. Letter from George Bush to Rev. Daniel Pilarczyk, 3 November 1991, FOIA Files, no. 2006-1149-F, GBPL.

33. Telegram from Rev. Bernard Law to George Bush, 30 September 1991, FOIA Files, no. 2006-1149-F, GBPL; handwritten note by "Greg F." on letter from Leigh Ann Metzger to "Your Eminence," 21 October 1991, FOIA Files, no. 2006-1149-F, GBPL.

34. Memorandum from Cece Kramer and Leigh Ann Metzger to Kathy Super, 4 May 1992, FOIA Files, no. 2006-1149-F, GBPL.

35. Donato Squicciarini, "Countering Clandestine Nuclear Arms Programs," *Origins Online*, 10 October 1991, 2; Clyde Haberman, "Taxes Flow to the Church; Its Cup Runneth Over," *New York Times*, 14 June 1991, A4.

36. Peter Steinfels,"Beliefs," *New York Times*, 8 January 1994, A9.

37. Letter from Thomas Melady to Philip Brady, 9 January 1992, FOIA Files, GBPL; Jeffrey Jones, "The Protestant and Catholic Vote," 8 June 2004, http://gallup.poll/11911/Protestant-Catholic-vote,aspx.

38. "The President's National Urban Policy," 5 March 1991, FOIA Files, no. 2006-1149-F, GBPL, 1; "Text of Presidential Candidates' Responses to U.S.C.C. Questionnaire," *Origins Online*, 20 October 1988, 5; Gareth Davies, *From Opportunity to Entitlement: The Transformation and Decline of Great Society Liberalism* (Lawrence: University of Kansas Press, 1996), 290.

39. Herbert Parmet, *George Bush: The Life of a Lone Star Yankee* (New York: Scribner, 1997), 351, 348; Duffy and Goodgame, 28.

40. Greene, *George Bush*, 169; Roger Biles, *The Fate of the Cities* (Lawrence: University of Kansas Press, 2011), 306.

41. George Bush, "Address to the Nation on the Civil Disturbances in Los Angeles," 1 May 1992, *Public Papers of the Presidents of the United States: George Bush, 1992–1993*, vol. 1: *January 1–July 31, 1992* (Washington, D.C.: U.S. Government Printing Office, 1993), 685.

42. George Bush, "Exchange with Reporters prior to Meeting with Cabinet Members," 4 May 1992, *Public Papers, 1992–1993*, 1:687–688.

43. George Bush, "The President's News Conference with President Leonid Kravchuk of Ukraine," 6 May 1992, *Public Papers, 1992–1993*, 1:697–698.

44. George Bush, "Remarks to Community Leaders in Los Angeles," ibid., 1:732; George Bush, "Statement on Urban Aid Initiatives," 12 May 1992, ibid., 1:748–749.

45. Bush, "Statement on Urban Aid Initiatives," 750–751.

46. "Urban Aid," *Congress and the Nation*, 8:699; Barilleaux and Rozell, 42; "Long Range Scheduling Meeting #141," 6 May 1992, FOIA Files, no. 2006-1149-F, GBPL, 1, 4.

47. Dirk Johnson, "Catholic Schools Reach Out to Serve Poor and to Borrow," *New York Times*, 10 September 1988, A1; Isabel Wilkerson, "Detroit Catholics Vow to Fight Closings," *New York Times*, 3 October 1988, A1; Peter Steinfels, "Archdiocese Plans Big Cuts in School Aid," *New York Times*, 6 December 1990, B1; James Kelly, "Data and Mystery: A Decade of Study on Catholic Leadership," *America*, 15 November 1989, 345.

48. John Deedy, "Challenges Facing U.S. Catholics," *Commonweal*, 17 November 1989, 622; Johnson, "Catholic Schools Reach Out," 1; Wilkerson, 1.

49. Reese, *Flock of Shepherds*, 61; Anthony DePalma, "Catholic Churches Move to Embrace Blacks," *New York Times*, 24 January 1989, B6; "John Paul Issues a Plea for Minority Rights," *New York Times*, 2 January 1989, H6; "Excerpts from Vatican's Declaration on Racism," *New York Times*, 11 February 1989, 4; Peter Steinfels, "Bishops Approve Plan on Disputes," *New York Times*, 18 June 1989, A25; Drummer Ayres, "Black Priest Is Termed Threat to Catholic Unity," *New York Times*, 15 July 1989, A6.

50. Preston Williams, "A More Perfect Union: The Silence of the Church," *America*, 31 March 1990, 316; Philip Murnion, "The Future of the Church in the Inner City," *America*, 15 December 1990, 483, 485; James Lyke, "Toward a Promised Land," *America*, 13 April 1991, 347.

51. Peter Kilburn, "Black Priest Defies Church, Forming Own Congregation," *New York Times*, 3 July 1989, L8; Ronald Smothers, "Breakaway Priest Wins Few Followers," *New York Times*, 6 August 1989, A20.

52. "U.S. Catholic Bishops Convene," *Christian Century*, 22 November 1989, 1080; Raymond Studzinski, "Cyprian Davis—Monk, Historian, Teacher, Agent of Hope," *U.S. Catholic Historian* 28 (Winter 2010): 97; Peter Steinfels, "Joyful Mood at Black Catholic Meeting," *New York Times*, 14 July 1992, A20.

53. Tracy Early, "New York Prelate Gives Guidelines for Catholics and the 1988 Election," *Boston Pilot*, n.d., 4, attached to memorandum from Thomas Melady to George Bush, 6 May 1987, FOIA Files, no. 2006-1149-F, George Bush Vice Presidential Papers, GBPL; "Catholics for Bush," n.d., FOIA Files, no. 2006-1149-F, GBPL; "Text of Presidential Candidates' Responses to U.S.C.C. Questionnaire," *Origins Online*, 20 October 1988, 6–7.

54. Letter from Robert Lynch to John Sununu, 21 December 1988, FOIA Files, GBPL.

55. Joe Feuerherd, "Bush Hobnobs with Cardinals to Woo Church," *National Catholic Reporter*, n.d., n.p., FOIA Files, GBPL; memorandum from Leigh Ann Metzger, Jane Leonard, and Kathy Rust to Sherrie Rollins, 5 February 1992, FOIA Files, no. 2006-1149-F, GBPL, 2.

56. Memorandum from Douglas Wead to George Bush, and "Talking Points," 27 March 1989, White House Office of Appointments and Scheduling Files, box 3, folder: Presidential Daily Diary—Backup, GBPL, 1–2.

57. Kenneth Doyle, "Child Care Amendments on Parental Choice Backed by U.S. Catholic Conference," *United States Catholic Conference News*, 15 May 1989, 2; Reese, *Flock of Shepherds*, 212.

58. "Text of Remarks of the Vice President," 1 August 1989, attached to memorandum from Bobbie Kilberg and Jeffrey Vogt to Kerry Kollers, 23 August 1989, FOIA Files, no. 2006-1149-F, GBPL, 6, 15.

59. "Remarks by the President to the Catholic Lawyers Guild," 23 September 1989, FOIA Files, no. 2006-1149-F, GBPL, 3; George Bush, "Remarks at the Catholic University of America Anniversary Dinner," 12 December 1989, *Public Papers of the Presidents of the United States: George Bush, 1989*, vol. 2: *July 1–December 31, 1989* (Washington, D.C.: U.S. Government Printing Office, 1990), 1696.

60. Stephen McHenry, "The 'Education President' Meets with Catholic Educators," *America*, 5 August 1989, 52–53; Feuerherd, "Bush Hobnobs with Cardinals."

61. Feuerherd, "Bush Hobnobs with Cardinals."

62. Letter from Joseph Leary to George Bush, 9 January 1990, FOIA Files, no. 2006-1149-F, GBPL.

63. Letter from Douglas Wead to John Sununu, 22 March 1990, FOIA Files, no. 2006-1149-F, GBPL; letter from Thomas Melady to George Bush, 31 July 1991, FOIA Files, no. 2006-1149-F, GBPL; Dan Quayle, *Standing Firm* (New York: HarperCollins, 1994), 215; letter from John Carr to Jane Leonard, 14 January 1992, FOIA Files, no. 2006-1149-F, GBPL.

64. "Excerpts from the Pope's Encyclical: On Giving Capitalism a Human Face," *New York Times*, 3 May 1991, A10.

65. Peter Steinfels, "Papal Encyclical Urges Capitalism to Shed Injustices," *New York Times*, 3 May 1991, A10.

66. Letter from Thomas Melady to George Bush, 5 July 1991, FOIA Files, no. 2006-1149-F, GBPL; George Bush, "Remarks to American Seminarians on Community in Vatican City," 8 September 1991, *Public Papers of the Presidents of the United States: George Bush, 1991*, vol. 2: *July 1–December 31, 1991* (Washington, D.C.: U.S. Government Printing Office, 1992), 1417.

67. "Cynics at War," *Commonweal*, 25 October 1991, 595; Steve Allen, "The Lesson of Clarence Thomas," *America*, 9 November 1991, 342–343; Thomas Stahel, "Hill v. Thomas," *America*, 2 November 1991, 321.

68. White House Briefing, 14 November 1991, FOIA Files, no. 2006-1149-F, GBPL, 1–2; David Carlin, "Seizing the High Ground," *Commonweal*, 12 July 1991, 423–424; "Promises to Keep," *America*, 29 June 1991, 667;

69. Warner, 160.

70. Pope John Paul II, *Centesimus Annus*, http://www.vatican.va/holy_father/john-paul_ii/encyclicals/documents/hf_jp-iienco1051991,centesimus-annus_en.html, 13; George Bush, "Remarks at the University of Notre Dame Commencement Ceremony in South Bend, Indiana," 17 May 1992, *Public Papers, 1992–1993*, 1:787–788.

71. Letter from Rev. Roger Mahony to "Dear Pastors," 30 April 1992, ALAAC; "Days of Anguish, Nights of Flames—Moving Towards a Brighter Future, Reflections on the Days of Crisis for Los Angeles," 3 May 1992, ALAAC, 1, 3, 4.

72. "Catholic Charities of Los Angeles, Inc., Disaster Relief and Recovery Program: A Special Report to His Eminence, Roger Cardinal Mahony, Chairman of the Board

and Board of Trustees," 15 February 1993, ALAAC, 1; Roger Mahony, "A New Spirit Is Needed to Build a New Los Angeles," *Tidings*, 23 October 1992, 3; "Catholics to Offer Nine Days of Special Prayers Asking Holy Spirit to Heal Riot-Torn Los Angeles," Archdiocese of Los Angeles Press Release, 22 May 1992, ALAAC, 1.

73. Jim McKarines, "Was Dan Quayle—Gasp—Right?" *USA Today*, 18 May 2010, A11; see also James Patterson, *Freedom Is Not Enough: The Moynihan Report and America's Struggle over Black Family Life from L.B.J. to Obama* (New York: Basic, 2010).

74. William F. Buckley, "Are You Responsible?" *National Review*, 14 May 1990, 63; memorandum from Martin Gerry to Andrew Card, 7 June 1990, FOIA Files, no. 2006-1149-F, GBPL; Metzger, Leonard, and Rust to Rollins, 1.

75. Letter from Thomas Melady to Philip Brady, 14 September 1992, Office of the Chief of Staff Files, box 2, folder: Chronological File, 9/92 [1], GBPL, 1–2.

76. "President Bush's Response to the United States Catholic Conference," 30 September 1992, FOIA Files, no. 2006-1149-F, GBPL, 12.

77. Greene, *George Bush*, 168.

78. Kelly, "Data and Mystery," 345; Joseph Fichter, "The Church: Looking to the Future," *America*, 4 March 1989, 190–191.

79. Joseph McShane, "The Catholic Experience at Taming Pluralism," *Christian Century*, 26 April 1989, 445; Avery Dulles, "Catholicism and American Culture: The Uneasy Dialogue," *America*, 27 January 1990, 58, 59; Tim Unsworth, "What Does the Future Hold for U.S. Catholics?" *U.S. Catholic*, April 1990, 8.

80. Kelly, "Data and Mystery," 350; *Flock of Shepherds: A Discussion on the National Conference of Catholic Bishops: A FADICA Symposium* (Washington, D.C.: Foundations and Donors Interested in Catholic Activities, 1992), 31; Richard Neuhaus, "Religion and Public Life: The Continuing Conversation," *Christian Century*, 11–18 July 1990, 671; *FADICA Symposium*, 8.

81. *FADICA Symposium*, 28.

82. Susan Cahill, "Challenges Facing U.S. Catholics," *Commonweal*, 27 November 1989, 621; Margaret O'Brien Steinfels, "Shifting the Center," *Commonweal*, 25 September 1992, 5.

83. Philip Berryman, "The Battle for the Catholic Church," *Christian Century*, 17 May 1989, 525.

84. Castillo qtd. in Peter Steinfels, "Beliefs," *New York Times*, 14 November 1992, A7; David O'Brien, "Join It, Work It, Fight It: American Catholics and the American Way," *Commonweal*, 17 November 1989, 624.

85. Kathleen Himmenmeyer, "Helen Alvare," *St. Anthony Messenger*, January 1992, 33; "Catholics and their Church," in *The Gallup Poll: Public Opinion, 1993*, ed. George Gallup (Wilmington, Del.: Scholarly Resources, 1994), 145.

86. William Barry, "Should Religion Concern Itself with Political and Social Questions?" *America*, 5 August 1989, 69; Kelly, "Data and Mystery," 350; Unsworth, 9.

87. *FADICA Symposium*, 15.

88. George Hunt, "Of Many Things," *America*, 4 February 1989, 74; Reese, *Flock of Shepherds*, 212, 306.

89. Reese, *Flock of Shepherds*, 318; letter from Rev. Daniel Pilarczyk to George Bush, 17 September 1992, FOIA Files, no. 2006-1149-F, GBPL, 1–2; Jones.

90. Reese, *Flock of Shepherds*, 318.

91. Greene, *George Bush*, 64.

92. Letter from Rev. Bernard Law to George Bush, 5 January 1989, FOIA Files, no. 2006-1149-F, GBPL.

93. George Bush, "Remarks to Participants in the March for Life Rally," 23 January 1989, *Public Papers of the Presidents of the United States: George Bush, 1989*, vol. 1: *January 20–June 30, 1989* (Washington, D.C.: U.S. Government Printing Office, 1990), 12; Fred Barnes, "Tar Baby," *New Republic*, 13 February 1989, 12–13.

94. George Bush, "The President's News Conference," 27 January 1989, *Public Papers, 1989*, 1:29.

95. "Law Briefs," USCC, February 1989, 1; "U.S.C.C. Friend-of-the-Court Brief in Missouri Case before U.S. Supreme Court," *Origins Online*, 9 March 1989, 1.

96. "U.S.C.C. Friend-of-the-Court Brief," 8–11.

97. Ibid., 20.

98. "Justice Attorneys Petition Thornburgh on Abortion," Associated Press, 5 April 1989, FOIA Files, no. 2996-1149-F, GBPL; memorandum from George Bush to John Sununu, 5 April 1989, FOIA Files, no. 2006-1149-F, GBPL.

99. "U.S.C.C. Friend-of-the-Court Brief," 1; James Kelly, "The Koop Report and a Better Politics of Abortion," *America*, 2 June 1990, 542–543; "The Longer March," *Commonweal*, 5 May 1989, 259–260.

100. "Meeting with Key Catholic Lay Leaders Talking Points," 27 March 1989, FOIA Files, no. 2006-1149-F, GBPL; William F. Buckley, "The First March," *National Review*, 5 May 1989, 9

101. Maurice de G. Ford, "Rocking the *Roe* Boat," *Commonweal*, 2 June 1989, 327.

102. Ibid., 327.

103. Steven Valentine, "Opportunity of a Generation Lost," in *Politics over Principle? The Domestic Policy of the George H. W. Bush Presidency*, ed. Richard Himelfarb and Rosanna Perolti (Westport, Conn.: Praeger, 2004), 256, 260.

104. Greene, *George Bush*, 65.

105. "Law Briefs," USCC, July 1989, 2–3.

106. George Bush, "Statement on Supreme Court's Decision on Abortion," 3 July 1989, *Public Papers, 1989*, 2:889; "Law Briefs," USCC, July 1989, 1.

107. Burke Balch, "Abortion: What Does 'Webster' Mean?," *Commonweal*, 11 August 1989, 428; James Kelly, "Winning *Webster v. Reproductive Health Services*," *America*, 19 August 1989, 80.

108. "Abortion Ruling," *Christian Century*, 15–22 July 1989, 675; "Too Many Abortions," *Commonweal*, 11 August 1989, 419.

109. "Abortion Ruling," 675; Mary Segers, "Abortion: What Does 'Webster' Mean?" *Commonweal*, 11 August 1989, 427.

110. "Abortion," in *The Gallup Poll: Public Opinion, 1989*, ed. George Gallup (Wilmington, Del.: Scholarly Resources, 1990), 162, 164.

111. "Bush's No-No on Abortion," *Time*, 6 November 1989, 3; Kelly, "Winning *Webster v. Reproductive Health Services*," 80–81.

112. Peter Steinfels, "Bishops Map Strategy in Abortion Battle," *New York Times*, 12 August 1989, C6.

113. George Bush, "The President's News Conference," 23 August 1989, *Public Papers, 1989*, 2:1104.

114. *Congressional Quarterly* qtd. in *"Abortion," Congress and the Nation,* 8:594; memorandum from Douglas Johnson to John Sununu, 5 October 1989, Office of the Chief of Staff Files, John Sununu Series, box 2, folder: Abortion/Fetal Tissue Research (1989) [1], GBPL.

115. Letter from Rev. James Hickey to George Bush, 13 October 1989, FOIA Files, no. 2006-1149-F, GBPL.

116. Memorandum from Douglas Johnson to John Sununu, 27 October 1989, and memorandum from Johnson to Sununu, 15 November 1989, Office of the Chief of Staff Files, John Sununu Series, no box, folder: Abortion/Fetal Tissue Research (1989) [1], GBPL.

117. "Abortion," *Congress and the Nation,* 8:594; letter from George Bush to Robert Byrd, 17 October 1989, FOIA Files, no. 2006-1149-F, GBPL, 2.

118. "After Webster: An Uphill Struggle," *America,* 14 October 1989, 227; Thomas Stahel, "Abortion, Lies, and Videotape," *America,* 4 November 1989, 289.

119. "National Conference of Catholic Bishops Resolution on Abortion," FOIA Files, no. 2006-1149-F, GBPL, 1–2; Peter Steinfels, "Bishops Warn Politicians on Abortion," *New York Times,* 8 November 1989, A18.

120. Steinfels, "Bishops Warn Politicians," 18; Peter Steinfels, "Bishops Intensify Fight on Abortion," *New York Times,* 7 November 1989, A16.

121. "National Conference of Catholic Bishops Resolution on Abortion," 2; George Bush," The President's News Conference," 7 November 1989, *Public Papers, 1989,* 1:1468–1469; Herbert Parmet, *George Bush: The Life of a Lone Star Yankee (New York: Scribner, 1997), 134.*

122. Fred Barnes, "Abortive Issue," *New Republic,* 4 December 1989, 11; "Remarks by the President to the Catholic Lawyers Guild," 23 September 1989, FOIA Files, no. 2006-1149-F, GBPL, 1242–1243; "Remarks by the President at American Cardinals Dinner," 12 December 1989, FOIA Files, no. 2006-1149-F, GBPL, 2.

123. George Bush, "Remarks to Participants in the March for Life Rally," 22 January 1990, *Public Papers of the Presidents of the United States: George Bush, 1990,* vol. 1: *January 1–June 30, 1990* (Washington, D.C.: U.S. Government Printing Office, 1991), 67; memorandum from Darla St. Martin and Douglas Johnson to John Sununu, 8 February 1990, no box, Office of the Chief of Staff Files, John Sununu Series, folder: 1990 Abortion/Fetal Tissue Research, GBPL, 1.

124. "Appendix A—Digest of Other White House Announcements," 22 March 1990, *Public Papers, 1990,* 1:906; letter from Joseph Leary to George Bush, 2 April 199, FOIA Files, no. 2006-1149-F.

125. "Re: Attack on Anti-Abortion Foreign Aid Authorization Bill," 6 April 1990, Office of Chief of Staff Files, John Sununu Series, no box, folder: 1990 Abortion/Fetal Tissue Research, GBPL, 1–2; "Abortion," *Congress and the Nation,* 8:594.

126. "Law Briefs," USCC, July 1990, 1–2.

127. Joseph Bernardin, "The Consistent Ethic after 'Webster,'" *Commonweal,* 20 April 1990, 247.

128. Ari Goldman, "Catholic Bishops Hire Firms to Market Fight on Abortion," *New York Times,* 6 April 1990, A1, 16; Peter Steinfels, "O'Connor Defends Anti-Abortion Aid," *New York Times,* 22 April 1990, 30.

129. John Garvey, "Persuasion Preferred," *Commonweal,* 15 June 1990, 377; "The

Bishops and the P.R. Campaign," *America*, 19 May 1990, 491; James Baker and Eleanor Clift, "The Bishops under Fire," *Newsweek*, 23 April 1990, 24; Tamar Lewin, "Abortion Divides Firm Hired to Help It," *New York Times*, 18 April 1990, A14.

130. "Law Briefs," USCC, May 1990, 1–2.

131. Jeffrey Sheler, "Cardinal O'Connor," *U.S. News and World Report*, 31 December 1990, 78; George Bush, "Remarks to Participants in Rally for Life," 28 April 1990, *Public Papers, 1990*, 1:583.

132. Ari Goldman, "O'Connor Warns Politicians Risk Excommunication over Abortion," *New York Times*, 15 June 1990, A1, B2.

133. Ari Goldman, "O'Connor Denies Plan to Excommunicate Anyone," *New York Times*, 18 June 1990, B4.

134. "Many Catholics Object to Excommunication Threat," *New York Times*, 23 October 1990, A26.

135. Ari Goldman, "Bishops' Meeting Likely to Focus on Abortion Issue," *New York Times*, 20 June 1990, A26; Peter Steinfels, "Vatican Bars Honor for Archbishop of Milwaukee," *New York Times*, 11 November 1990, A20.

136. "Abortion," *Congress and the Nation*, 8:595; Valentine, 257.

137. Peter Steinfels, "New Voice, Same Words on Abortion," *New York Times*, 20 November 1990, A16.

138. Ibid.

139. Valentine, 257.

140. Ibid., 258.

141. George Bush, "Remarks to Participants in the March for Life Rally," 22 January 1991, *Public Papers of the Presidents of the United States: George Bush, 1991*, vol. 1: *January 1–June 30, 1991* (Washington, D.C.: U.S. Government Printing Office, 1992), 55.

142. Memorandum from Leigh Ann Metzger to John Sununu, 18 January 1991, FOIA Files, no. 2006-1149-F, GBPL.

143. "Law Briefs," USCC, May 1991, 1–3.

144. Gabrielle Glasser, "Pope Delivers Angry Sermon on Abortion to Poles," *New York Times*, 4 June 1991, A1; memorandum from Brian Waidmann to John Sununu, 19 June 1991, Office of the Chief of Staff Files, John Sununu Series, no box, folder: Right to Life/Abortion 1991 [4], Title X, GBPL; memorandum from Sue Auther to Jackie Kennedy, 3 July 1991, FOIA Files, no. 2006-1149-F, GBPL.

145. Stahel, 321; David Carlin, "You Ain't Seen Nothin' Yet," *Commonweal*, 8 November 1991, 633.

146. Memorandum from Gary Andres to John Sununu, 8 November 1991, FOIA Files, no. 2006-1149-F, GBPL; "Abortion," *Congress and the Nation*, 8:598.

147. James Kelly, "Abortion: What Americans *Really* Think and the Catholic Challenge," *America*, 2 November 1991, 312.

148. Ibid.; "Abortion," *The Gallup Poll: Public Opinion, 1992*, ed. George Gallup (Wilmington, Del.: Scholarly Resources, 1993), 2.

149. Robert Casey, "The Democratic Party: The Politics of Abortion," *Vital Speeches of the Day*, 2 April 1992, 522–524.

150. James Kelly, "Abortive Politics: The Last Two Decades, the Next Three Decades, and the 1992 Elections," *America*, 11 July 1992, 10; George Bush, "Remarks at the University of Notre Dame Commencement Ceremony in South Bend, Indiana,"

17 May 1992, *Public Papers, 1992–1993*, 1:785–788; Thomas Reese, "Bishops Meet at Notre Dame," *America*, 11 July 1992, 4.

151. George Bush, "Statement on Supreme Court Decision on Abortion," 29 June 1992, *Public Papers, 1992–1993*, 1:1032; "Talking Candidly about Abortion," *America*, 9 May 1992, 399.

152. "Liberty for Some," *Commonweal*, 17 July 1992, 3.

153. "Abortion," *Congress and the Nation*, 8:600; George Bush, "Message to the House of Representatives Returning without Approval the National Institutes of Health Revitalization Amendment of 1992," 23 June 1992, *Public Papers, 1992–1993*, 1:1005; George Bush, "Remarks to the Knights of Columbus Supreme Council Convention, New York City," 5 August 1992, *Public Papers, 1992–1993*, 2:1306.

154. "Abortion," *Congress and the Nation*, 8:600; George Bush, "Message to the Senate Returning without Approval the Family Planning Amendments Act of 1992," 25 September 1992, and "Memorandum of Disapproval for the Military Health Care Initiatives Act of 1992," 30 October 1992, *Public Papers, 1992–1993*, 2:1655, 2101; David Mervin, *George Bush and the Guardianship Presidency* (New York: St. Martin's, 1996), 118.

155. Mark Cunningham, "The Abortion War," *National Review*, 2 November 1992, 43.

156. USA *Today* qtd. ibid., 42.

157. Kelly, "Abortion: What Americans *Really* Think," 312; Cunningham, 43–44.

158. Alan Riding, "New Catechism for Catholics Defines Sins of Modern World," *New York Times*, 17 November 1992, A14.

159. Andrew Greeley, "The Abortion Debate and the Catholic Subculture," *America*, 11 July 1992, 13–14.

160. Valentine, 261; Garvey, 378.

161. Letter from George Bush to Robert Byrd," 17 October 1989, and "Draft, President Bush's Response to USCC," 30 September 1992, FOIA Files, no. 2006-1149F, GBPL, 1; "Abortion Rhetoric and Political Justice," *America*, 17 February 1990, 139.

162. Donald Burrill, "Abortion Moderates on Shaky Ground," *Christian Century*, 25 April 1990, 421.

163. Greene, *George Bush*, 66; "New Civil War," *America*, 17 November 1990, 364; Bernardin, 244.

164. Ari Goldman, "Newark Clerics Battle over Role of Women," *New York Times*, 31 January 1991, B1; William McGurn, "Rum, Romanism, and Doug Wilder," *National Review*, 12 August 1991, 39.

165. Ari Goldman, "War of Words," *New York Times*, 4 April 1992, A11.

166. Peter Steinfels, "Bishops Intensify Fight on Abortion," *New York Times*, 7 November 1989, A16; David Carlin, "The New/Old Abortion Battle," *Commonweal*, 13 September 1991, 505.

167. "Too Many Abortions," *Commonweal*, 11 August 1989, 420; Michael Kinsley, "The New Politics of Abortion," *Time*, 17 July 1989, 96.

168. R. E. B., "Bishops Should Do More to Threaten about Abortion," *U.S. Catholic*, October 1990, 2.

169. Daniel Callahan, "An Ethical Challenge to Pro-Choice Advocates," *Commonweal*, 23 November 1990, 683.

170. Memorandum from Douglas Johnson to John Sununu, 17 April 1990, Office of the Chief of Staff Files, John Sununu Series, no box, folder: 1990 Abortion/Fetal

Tissue Research, GBPL, 2; "Confidential" memorandum, 29 May 1991, FOIA Files, no. 2006-1149-F, GBPL, 1.

171. Cunningham, 43.

172. "Issue Brief: Rape and Incest Abortions," attached to letter from Bobbie Kilberg to John Sununu, 16 October 1989, Office of the Chief of Staff Files, John Sununu Series, no box, folder: Abortion/Fetal Tissue Research (1989) [2], GBPL, 3.

173. St. Martin and Johnson to Sununu, 8 February 1990, 2; letter from David Packard to George Bush, 18 June 1992; letter from Bush to Packard, 20 June 1992, and "Highlights of AID's Population Program," attached to memorandum from Jim Murr to George Bush, 22 June 1992, FOIA Files, no. 2006-1149-F, GBPL.

174. Thomas Reese, "Bishops Meet in Baltimore," *America*, 25 November 1989.

175. "New Civil War," 364; David Carlin, "Lighten Up, Guys," *Commonweal*, 1 June 1991, 359; James Kelly, "The Political Challenge to the Prolife Movement," *Commonweal*, 23 November 1990, 693.

176. William F. Buckley, "Where We Stand," *National Review*, 22 December 1989, 27.

177. "Strategy Time," *Commonweal*, 9 February 1990, 36; John Donahue, "Abortion Tests for Catholic Politicians," *America*, 21 July 1990, 28; Richard Ostling, "To Hell with Choice," *Time*, 25 June 1990, 52.

178. Walter Burnham, "The Legacy of George Bush: Travails of an Understudy," in *The Election of 1992: Reports and Interpretations*, ed. Gerald Pomper (Chatham, N.J.: Chatham House, 1993), 15.

CHAPTER EIGHT. Catholics and Bill Clinton

1. William Perry, "Bosnia: We Must Stay the Course," *Vital Speeches of the Day*, 15 April 1995, 386; "Options in Bosnia," *United States Department of State Dispatches*, 1–8 July 1995, 3.

2. "U.S. Armed Forces Abroad: Selected Congressional Roll Call Voters since 1982," *Congressional Research Service*, 27 January 2006, http://www.fas.org/sgp/ers/natsec/RC31693.pdf, 1.

3. "Bosnian Policy," *Congress and the Nation*, vol. 9: *1993–1996* (Washington, D.C.: Congressional Quarterly, 1998), 197.

4. Pope John Paul II, "Address to the Diplomatic Corps," *Origins*, 4 February 1993, 587.

5. "Margin Notes," *Origins Online*, 8 April 1993, 5; and USCC Administrative Board, "Humanitarian Nightmare in the Balkans," *Origins Online*, 8 April 1993, 3–4, http://originsplus catholicnews.com.

6. John Roach, "On U.S. Intervention in Bosnia: Letter to Secretary of State and Clarification," *Origins Online*, 27 May 1993, 2–4.

7. Ibid., 4.

8. Bernardin, 10; Bill Clinton, *My Life* (New York: Knopf, 2004), 538.

9. United States Catholic Bishops, "The Harvest of Justice Is Sown in Peace," November 1993, in *Pastoral Letters and Statements of the United States Catholic Bishops*, vol. 6: *1989–1997*, ed. Patrick Carey (Washington, D.C.: United States Catholic Conference, 1998), 563, 565.

10. "When There Is No Peace," *Christian Century*, 23 February 1994, http://www.questia.com/library, 1–2.

11. Ibid., 2.

12. "Bosnia," *The Gallup Poll: Public Opinion, 1995* (Wilmington, Del.: Scholarly Resources, 1996), 30; "Bosnian Policy," 198; Thomas Stahel, "The Folly in Bosnia," *America*, 5 March 1994, 3–4.

13. Thomas Stahel, "Interview with the Archbishop of Sarajevo," *America*, 9 April 1994, 3.

14. Letter from Rev. Anthony Petrusic to Bill Clinton, 20 April 1994, FOIA Files, no. 2007-0088-F, WHORM Subject Files, box 1, folder: CO 23-0088656, WJCPL; Stahel, "Interview with the Archbishop of Sarajevo," 1.

15. Madeleine Albright, "Bosnia in Light of the Holocaust: War Crimes Tribunals," *United States Department of State Dispatch*, 18 April 1994, http://heinonline.org.

16. Taylor Branch, *The Clinton Tapes* (New York: Simon and Schuster, 2009), 120; "Bosnian Policy," 198; Robert Dole, "Bosnia: Talking Points for CNN Newsmaker Sunday," n.d., Dole Leadership Papers, box 1, Press Clippings, Bosnia—1993–94, Robert J. Dole Archive and Special Collections, Robert J. Dole Institute, Lawrence, Kans., http://www.dole.institute.org/archives/history-bosnian.shtml.

17. Branch, *The Clinton Tapes*, 139–145.

18. "Bosnian Policy," 128.

19. Robert Woodward, *The Choice* (New York: Simon and Schuster, 1996), 260–261.

20. Scott O'Grady, "My Own Marian Visitation," *Deacon John's Posterous*, 12 July 2009, http://deaconjohn.posterous.com/my-own-marian-apparition-by-scott-ogrady; Daniel Wackerman, "Mind's Eye," *America*, 12 August 1995, 7.

21. Woodward, *The Choice*, 269; Nigel Hamilton, *American Caesars* (London: Bodley Head, 2010), 448; Bill Clinton, "Letter to Congressional Leaders Reporting on the Deployment of United States Aircraft to Bosnia-Herzegovina," 1 September 1995, *Public Papers of the Presidents of the United States: Bill Clinton, 1995*, vol. 2: *July 1–December 31, 1995* (Washington, D.C.: U.S. Government Printing Office, 1996), 1279–1280.

22. United States Catholic Bishops, "Proclaiming the Gospel of Life: Protecting the Least among Us and Pursuing the Common Good," September 1995, in Carey, *Pastoral Letters and Statements*, 735.

23. Bill Clinton, "Why Bosnia Matters to America," *Newsweek*, 13 November 1995, 55.

24. Raymond Flynn, "Letter from the Vatican: Common Objectives for Peace," *SAIS Review* 16 (Summer–Fall 1996): 4, http://muse.jhu.edu/journals/sais_review/v016/16.2flynn/html.

25. Ibid., 143.

26. United States Catholic Bishops, "America Must Lead to Preserve Peace in Bosnia," 27 November 1995, FOIA Files, no. 2006-0466-F, Jonathan Prince Files, box 7, folder: Dec. 1995 Bosnia Talking Points and Message Development, WJCPL, 2; memorandum from John Hart to Kimberly Marteau, 27 November 1995, 2–3, and "Support for Bosnia Agreement Needed," USCC, 4 December 1995, FOIA Files, no. 2007-0088-F, WHORM Subject Files, box 4, folder: Clinton Presidential Records, Intergovernmental Affairs—Hart, John, Bosnia-Catholic-State and Local [2], OAID 9730, WJCPL; email record from Richard Schifter to Jill Schuker, 21 November 1995, FOIA Files, no.

2007-0088-F, box 7, folder: Clinton Presidential Records, National Security Council Emails, Catholic and Bishops, [10/02/1996–12/07/1995], OAID 605000, WJCPL.

27. United States Catholic Bishops, "1996 Presidential Candidate Questionnaire," *Origins Online*, 26 September 1996, 4.

28. "Rob 1," "Stolen Balkan Religious Artifacts Reported 'On Sale' in Britain," *National Catholic Register*, 7 July 1996, http://www.ncregister.com/site/article/stolen _balkan_religious_artifacts_reported_on_sale_in_britain, 1; Celestine Bohlen, "Weary of War, a Divided City Now Prays," *New York Times*, 14 April 1997, A1, 6.

29. "History of the War in Kosovo," *Center for Balkan Development*, April 1999, http://www.balkandevelopment.org/edu_kos.html.

30. "Kosovo War Crimes Chronology," *Human Rights Watch*, n.d., http://hrw.org /legacy/campaign/kosovo98/timeline.shtml; David Binder, "Kosovo Violence, Past and Present," *Washington Times*, 31 March 1998, A21; Theodore McCarrick, "U.S. Bishops Issue Statement on Kosovo," 26 March 1998, and "Statement on Returning from Kosovo," 31 August 1998, USCCB, http://www.usccb.org/comm/archives/1998/98-184a .shtml.

31. Richard Holbrooke, *To End a War* (New York: Random House, 1998), 21; Douglas Waller and Massimo Calabresi, "Holbrooke's Next Mission," *Time*, 26 October 1998, http://www.time.com/time/magazine/article/0.9171.989413.00.html, 1–2; Theodore McCarrick, "Statement on Kosovo," 21 January 1999, USCCB.

32. "Statements from the Holy See Regarding Kosovo," 31 March 1999, USCCB, Department of Social Development and World Peace, http://www.nccbuscc.org/sdwp /international/vatican.shtml, 4.

33. "Mission: Uncertain," *Newsweek*, 5 April 1999, http://www.newsweek.com/1999 /04/04/mission-uncertain.html; "Statements from the Holy See Regarding Kosovo," 5; "Stick to Your Guns," *Commonweal*, 9 April 1999, 5–6.

34. Branch, *The Clinton Tapes*, 542–243; John Tagliabue, "Pope Appeals for Refugee Relief 'Corridor,'" *New York Times*, 5 April 1999, A10.

35. Tagliabue, "Pope Appeals for Refugee Relief," 10; "Catholic Leaders Urge Cease-Fire and Aid to Refugees," *America*, 17 April 1999.

36. "Stick to Your Guns," 5; Thomas Reese, "Of Many Things," *America*, 10 April 1999, 2; Joseph Fiorenza, "Statement on Kosovo," 31 March 1999, USCCB.

37. "Church Calls for a Dialogue on Kosovo, Aid Agencies Scramble," *America*, 10 April 1999, http://business.highbeam.com/410107.

38. "Stick to Your Guns," 5.

39. Adam Wolfson, "Humanitarian Hawks," *Current*, September 2000, 32.

40. Reese, "Of Many Things," 2; J. Bryan Hehir, "Kosovo: A War of Values and the Values of War," *America*, 15 May 1999, 7–12.

41. Bruce Russett, "Is NATO's War Just?" *Commonweal*, 21 May 1999, 13–14.

42. Drew Christiansen, "What We Must Learn from Kosovo," *America*, 28 August 1999, 10; John Kavanaugh, "Outcasts in the Crowd," *America*, 20.

43. Robert Reilly, "Yugoslavia: What Next?" *National Catholic Register*, n.d., http:// www.ncregister.com/site/archives, 1; Tom Hoopes, "An Albanian Meets America," *National Catholic Register*, 18 April 1999, http://www.ncregister.com/site/article/an_albanian _meets_america, 2.

44. "Excerpted from Pope John Paul II's Easter et Orbi Message," 4 April 1999;

"Pope Receives U.N. High Commissioner for Refugees," 7 April 1999; "Holy Father's Message to U.N. Secretary General Annan," 29 April 1999; and "Statements from the Holy See Regarding Kosovo," 4, 1; "The Kosovo Dilemma," *America*, 15 May 1999, 3; "Assault on Serbs Stirs Catholic Blitz," *National Catholic Register*, 11 April 1999, http://www.ncregister.com/site/archives, 1.

45. "G-8 Approves Seven-Point Peace Plan," *Express News Service*, 7 May 1999, http://www.expressindia.com/ie/daily/19990507/ige07077.html, 1–2.

46. Joseph Fiorenza, "Statement on Kosovo," 7 May 1999, USCCB.

47. Hillary Clinton, "Globalization Into the Next Millennium," 17 June 1999, FOIA Files, no. 20060505-F, Clinton Presidential Records, First Lady Office, box 1, no folder, WJCPL, 7.

48. Joseph Fiorenza, "Statement on Kosovo," 10 June 1999, USCCB.

49. Romesh Ratsenar and Douglas Waller, "Who Really Won?" *Time*, 21 June 1999, http://ww.time.com/time/magazine/0,9171,991290,00.html, 1–3.

50. "Assessing Bill Clinton's Legacy: How Will History Remember Him?" *Brookings Institution*, 9 January 2001, http://www.brookings.edu/events/2001/0109election.aspx; Michael O'Hanlon, "Clinton's Strong Defense Legacy," *Foreign Affairs* (November–December 2003): 123.

51. Gerard Powers, Colman McCarthy, and John Roach, "Bosnian Brouhaha," *National Catholic Reporter*, 18 June 1993, http://findarticles.com/p/articles/mi_m1141/is_n32_v29/ai_13979186, 1–4; "Church Calls for a Dialogue on Kosovo"; letter from Bernard Cardinal Law, James Cardinal Hickey, John Cardinal O'Connor, Anthony Cardinal Bevilacqua, Roger Cardinal Mahony, Adam Cardinal Maida, William Cardinal Keeler, and Francis Cardinal George to Bill Clinton, 31 March 1999, USCCB.

52. Michael Warner, *Changing Witness: Catholic Bishops and Public Policy, 1917–1994* (Grand Rapids, Mich.: Eerdmans, 1995), 155; "Kosovo Update," June 1999, USCCB.

53. Franjo Kuharic and Vinko Puljic, "An Appeal to the World Community," *Origins Online*, 15 December 1994, 1, 3; Vinko Puljic, "Address at the Center for Strategic and International Studies," *Catholic News Service*, 3 April 1995, 7.

54. "Vatican Daily Criticizes Verbal Diplomacy in B-H," 25 July 1995, 3, and Cable from Raymond Flynn to the Secretary of State, June 1995, 3–4, FOIA Files, no. 2007-0088-F, WHORM Subject Files, box 6, folder: Clinton Presidential Records, National Security Council Cables, Catholic and Bishops, 01/03/1995–10/13/1995, OAID 510,000, WJCPL; Cable from Raymond Flynn to the Secretary of State, November 1995, FOIA Files, no. 2007-0088-F, WHORM Subject Files, box 6, folder: Clinton Presidential Records, National Security Council Cables, Catholic and Bishops, 10/17/1995–12/23/96, OAID510000, WJCPL, 3; Flynn, "Letter from the Vatican," 4.

55. "On File," *Origins Online*, 24 February 1994, 1–2; "Margin Notes," *Origins Online*, 15 December 1994, 3–4; Hehir, 7; Robert Shellady, "The Vatican's Role in Global Politics," *SAIS Review* 24 (Summer–Fall 2004): 159.

56. Peter Steinfels, "Madeleine Albright the Cardinal?" *New York Times*, 6 May 2006, http://www.nytimes.com/2006/05/06/US/06beliefs.html; Madeleine Albright, *The Mighty and the Almighty* (New York: HarperCollins, 2006), 66; Kris Millegen, "Pope Buys Cease-Fire; Italy, Other NATO Members Waver," *ctrl*, 7 April 1999, http://www.mail-archive.com/msg09573.html, 1–2; Jonathan Luxmoore, "Holbrooke's Role

in Bosnia Hailed, Chided," *National Catholic Reporter*, 15 December 2010, http://ncronline.org/news/global/holbrooke-role-bosnia-hailed-chided.

57. Roach, "On U.S. Intervention in Bosnia," 4; Theodore McCarrick, "Religion in Foreign Affairs," *Origins Online*, 13 February 1997, 2.

58. "Margin Notes," *Origins Online*, 27 May 1993, 5.

59. "Holbrooke Says Policy Needs Moral Basis," *Christian Century*, 22–29 September 1999, 890; Kati Marton, "Waging Peace with Justice," *International Herald Tribune*, 19 April 2011, 6; memorandum from Lisa Misol and Eric Schwartz to Samuel Berger, 30 July 1997, FOIA Files, no. 2007-0088-F, WHORM Subject Files, box 5, folder: Clinton Presidential Records, National Security Council, Multicultural and Humanitarian Affairs—Wippman, David, Catholic Issues: Catholic, OAID 1570, WJCPL; email record from Maureen Shea to Heather Hurlbut, 5 December 2000, FOIA Files, no. 2007-0088-F, WHORM Subject Files, box 6, folder: Clinton Presidential Records, Automated Records, Management System (Email) WHO, Catholics, Bishops, Bosnia, 09/06/1995–12/05/2000, OAID 500,000, WJCPL; Bill Clinton, "Remarks on Presenting the Eleanor Roosevelt Award for Human Rights and Presidential Medal of Freedom," 6 December 2000, *Public Papers of the Presidents of the United States: Bill Clinton, 2000–2001*, vol. 3: *October 12, 2001–January 20, 2001* (U.S. Government Printing Office, 2001), 2018.

60. Carl Bernstein, *His Holiness* (Garden City, N.Y.: Doubleday, 1996), 535; "The Kosovo Dilemma," 3.

61. Flynn, "Letter from the Vatican," 4; Bernstein, 535; John Tagliabue, "For Vatican, Diplomacy Boston-Style," *New York Times*, 28 May 1994, 4.

62. Daniel Reilly, "The Role of Bishops' Conferences in International Affairs," *Origins Online*, 29 February 1996, 7;"Bosnia/United Nations," in *The Gallup Poll: Public Opinion, 1995*, ed. George Gallup (Wilmington, Del.: Scholarly Resources, 1996), 158; George Stephanopolous, *All Too Human* (New York: Little, Brown, 1999), 383.

63. James MacGregor Burns and Georgia Sorenson, *Dead Center* (New York: Scribner, 1999), 78.

64. James Mongan, "Health Care: Why We Failed the Last Time," *Washington Post*, 9 November 1993, A19.

65. Robert Woodward, *The Agenda* (New York: Simon and Schuster, 1994), 120.

66. Gil Troy, *Hillary Rodham Clinton* (Lawrence: University of Kansas Press, 2006), 77–78.

67. Memorandum from Mike Lux to Melanie Verveer, 20 February 1993, FOIA Files, no. 2006-0810-F, Pam Cicetti Health Care Subject Files, H–N, box 15, folder: Health-Interest Groups [3], WJCPL; letter from Mrs. Thomas Foley to Hillary Clinton, 1 March 1993, FOIA Files, no.2006-0810-F, Pam Cicetti, Health Care Subject Files, H–N, box 15, folder: Health-Interest Groups [5], WJCPL.

68. "Areas of Possible Common Ground," n.d., and William Ryan, "Catholic Bishops Meet with President Clinton, Vice President Gore," USCC, 5 March 1993, 2, FOIA Files, no. 2007-0088-F, WHORM Subject Files, box 2, folder: Verveer, Melanne, Catholic [2], OAID 20024, WJCPL, 1; letter from Rev. John Ricard to Hillary Clinton, 16 April 1993, FOIA Files, no. 2006-0810-F, Pam Cicetti Health Care Subject Files, box 11, folder: Health Care—Catholics [2], WJCPL, 1–2.

69. Clinton and Kammer were in Boys Nation together when they met President Kennedy, and Clinton would recall that he and Mrs. Clinton "wept" when he received a letter from Father Kammer commemorating his forty years of priesthood. See memorandum from Joseph Ratner to Eileen McGaughey, 5 September 2000, FOIA Files, no. 2007-0088-F, WHORM Subject Files, box 5, folder: Clinton Presidential Records, Public Liaison, Shea, Maureen—Catholic Charities [1], OAID20946, WJCPL, and National Catholic News Service interview of Bill Clinton by Patricia Zapor, 26 October 1992, FOIA Files, no. 2007-0088-F, WHORM Subject Files, box 3, folder: Verveer, Melanne—Catholic [1], OAID 20024, WJCPL, 21; letter from Rev. Fred Kammer to Hillary Clinton, 14 April 1993, FOIA Files, no. 2006-0810-F, Pam Cicetti Health Care Subject Files, box 11, folder: Health Care—Catholic [2], WJCPL, 1–2; Rev. Edward Hughes, "Letter to CHA Criticizing White House Address on Health Care Reform by Sister Coreil," *Origins Online*, 28 April 1994, 3.

70. Allen Dobson and Robert Mechanic, "Controlling Expenditures under National Healthcare Reform," *Catholic Health Association*, 5 May 1993, White House Health Care Interdepartmental Working Group, Ira Magaziner Working Papers, box 376, folder: Catholic Health Association Paper, WJCPL, preface; "Setting Relationships Right: A Working Proposal for Systematic Health Care Reform," 20 February 1992, in FOIA Files, no. 2006-0810-F, Pam Cicetti Health Care Subject Files, H–N, box 15, folder: Health—Interest Groups [4], WJCPL.

71. Hughes, 3.

72. *Our Sunday Visitor* qtd. in memorandum from Carol Rasco to Mack McLarty, 10 May 1993, Carol Rasco Domestic Policy Files, box 35, folder: Health Care, WJCPL; Peter Steinfels, "Bishops Plot Stance if Health Plan Covers Abortion," *New York Times*, 12 May 1993, A14.

73. Bill Clinton, "Remarks in the 'CBS This Morning' Town Meeting," 27 May 1993, *Public Papers of the United States: Bill Clinton, 1993*, vol. 1: *January 20–July 31, 1993* (Washington, D.C.: U.S. Government Printing Office, 1994), 749.

74. Suzy Farren, "President's Plan, CHA's Amazingly Similar," *Catholic Health World*, 15 June 1993, FOIA Files, no. 2006-0810-F, Pam Cicetti Health Care Subject Files, box 11, folder: Catholics [2], WJCPL, 1–2.

75. United States Catholic Bishops, "A Framework for Comprehensive Health Care Reform: Protecting Human Life, Promoting Human Dignity, Pursuing the Common Good," June 1993, in Carey, *Pastoral Letters and Statements*, 519, 523–525.

76. Robert Lynch, Joan Campbell, and Henri Michelman, "The Common Good: Old Idea, New Urgency," *Origins Online*, 24 June 1993, 8–9.

77. Bill Clinton, "Interview with Tabitha Soren of MTV," 21 September 1993, *Public Papers of the Presidents of the United States: Bill Clinton, 1993*, vol. 2: *August 1–December 31, 1993* (Washington, D.C.: U.S. Government Printing Office, 1994), 1547.

78. Troy, 78; "Health Care Reform," *Congress and the Nation*, 9:513, 518.

79. "As History Is Made, CHA Is There," *Catholic Health World*, 1 October 1993, 1, 8; and "It's Here!" *Catholic Health World*, 1 October 1993, 1, in FOIA Files, no. 2006-0810-F, Pam Cicetti Health Care Subject Files, box 11, folder: Catholic [2], WJCPL.

80. "CHA Pledges Support for President in Making Reform Happen," *Catholic Health World*, 1 October 1993, FOIA Files, no. 2006-0810-F, Pam Cicetti Health Care Subject Files, box 11, folder: Catholics [2], WJCPL, 5.

81. "Curley Praises Clinton's Initiative, but Voices Concerns about Specifics," *Catholic Health World*, 1 October 1993, FOIA Files, no. 2006-0810-F, Pam Cicetti Health Care Subject Files, box 11, folder: Catholic [2], WJCPL, 5, 8.

82. "White House Meetings Involve Physicians," *Catholic Health World*, 15 October 1993, 9, and "What Hillary Said," *Catholic Health World*, 15 October 1993, 1, FOIA Files, no. 2006-0810-F, Pam Cicetti Health Care Subject Files, box 11, folder: Catholics [2], WJCPL.

83. Paul Kengor, *God and Hillary Clinton* (New York: HarperCollins, 2007), 124.

84. "President Clinton's Proposal for Health Care Reform, Presented to Senate Committee on Labor and Human Resources by Sister Maryanna Coyle, S.C.," 5 October 1993, FOIA Files, no.2006-0810-F, Pam Cicetti Health Care Subject Files, box 11, folder: Catholics [2], WJCPL, 2–17.

85. John Ricard, "Reaction to Health Care Reform Plan," *Origins Online*, 7 October 1993, 1–2; Naftali Bendavid, "Health Care Reform: The Clash of Interests and Agendas," *Legal Times*, 11 October 1993, S93; Hildegarde Marie Mahoney, "National Health Care Legislation and the Funding of Abortion," *America*, 16 October 1993, 8–9.

86. Memorandum from Mike Lux to Hillary Clinton and Ira Magaziner, 30 September 1993, FOIA Files, no. 2006-0810-F, Pam Cicetti Health Care Subject Files, H–N, box 15, folder: Health—Interest Groups [2], WJCPL.

87. Memorandum from Mike Lux to Hillary Clinton and Senior White House Staff, 6 October 1993, FOIA Files, no. 2006-0810-F, Pam Cicetti Health Care Subject Files, H–N, folder: Health—Interest Groups [2], WJCPL, 1–2.

88. "Health Care Reform," *Congress and the Nation*, 9:516.

89. Memorandum from Mike Lux to Bill Clinton, 15 December 1993, FOIA Files, no. 2006-0810-F, box 9, folder: Cicetti, Pam, Health Care Materials, 1993–1994, Passing Health Reform [2], WJCPL, 1, 3, 4.

90. David Gergen, "Clinton's Abortion Problem," *U.S. News and World Report*, 19 April 1993, 74; John Ricard, "Goals for Health Care Reform," *Origins Online*, 24 February 1994, 3–4.

91. "Sister Bernice Coreil's White House Visit Incites Praise and Predictions," *Catholic Health World*, Spring 1994, FOIA Files, no. 2006-0810-F, Pam Cicetti Health Care Subject Files, box 11, folder: Catholics [2], WJCPL, 1–2.

92. Richard Szczepanowski, "Health Workers Told Reform Is Likely This Legislative Session," *Catholic Standard*, n.d., n.p., in FOIA Files, no. 2006-0810-F, Pam Cicetti Health Care Subject Files, H–N, folder: Health—Catholics [1], WJCPL.

93. "Medical Paupers," *Commonweal*, 19 August 1994, 3–4; Burns and Sorenson, 129, 133.

94. Michael Angrosino, "The Catholic Church and U.S. Health Care Reform," *Medical Anthropological Quarterly* 10.1 (1996): 1; "Health Care: Seeing Stars," *America*, 24 September 1994, 3.

95. Letter from John Curley to Bill Clinton, 12 September 1994, FOIA Files, no.2007-0088-F, WHORM Subject Files, box 1, folder: HE 036306 AID 10792, WJCPL; David Gergen, *Eyewitness to Power* (New York: Touchstone, 2000), 300; "Shalala: Government to Scale Back Health Care Reform Plans in 1995," Associated Press, 20 October 1994, in Chris Jennings Domestic Policy Council Files, box 44, folder: Health Care Reform Memos HAS, WJCPL, 1.

96. Branch, *The Clinton Tapes*, 157.

97. Robin Toner, "The Catholic Hierarchy and Clinton: Already a Complicated Relationship," *New York Times*, 3 February 1993, n.p., FOIA Files, no. 2007-0088-F, WHORM Subject Files, box 3, folder: Verveer, Melanne, Catholic, folder 3[2], OAID20024, WJCPL; "Remarks by the President in Catholic Roundtable," 15 September 1995, FOIA Files, no. 2007-0088-F, WHORM Subject Files, folder: Verveer, Melanne, Catholic, folder 2[2], OAID20024, WJCPL, 8.

98. Angrosino, 14.

99. "Avanti! Health Care Reform," *America*, 2–9 July 1994, 3; John Ricard, "The Church and the Future of Health Care Reform," *Origins Online*, 2 March 1995, 3.

100. "Feedback," *U.S. Catholic*, November 1994, 22.

101. Ricard, "The Church and the Future of Health Care Reform," 3.

102. "Phyllis Schlafly Supports Bishops, Opposes Catholic Health Association's Support of Pro-Abortion Health Care Bills," 18 August 1994, FOIA Files, no. 2007-0088-F, WHORM Subject Files, box 5, folder: Clinton Presidential Records, Public Liaison, Woolley, Barbara—Catholic Health Association, 1993–94 [1], OAID, WJCPL, 1–2; Angrosino, 12.

103. Ricard, "The Church and the Future of Health Care Reform," 3.

104. Memorandum from Linda Bergthold to Chris Jennings, 8 March 1993, 2, and handwritten notes, 1, White House Health Care Interdepartmental Working Group, Robert Valdez Working Papers, box 570, no folder, WJCPL, 2, 3.

105. Bill Clinton, "Remarks in the ABC News 'Nightline' Town Meeting," 23 September 1993, *Public Papers, 1993*, 2:1583; Szczepanowski.

106. Letter from Rev. William Keeler, Rev. Roger Mahony, and Rev. John Ricard to Melanie Verveer, and attached survey, 13 July 1994, FOIA Files, no. 2006-0810-F, Pam Cicetti Health Care Subject Files, box 11, folder: Health Care—Catholics [2], WJCPL, 1–4.

107. "Health Care and Abortion," *America*, 13–20, August 1994, 3; Gustav Niebuhr, "Catholic Leaders' Dilemma: Abortion vs. Universal Care," *New York Times*, 25 August 1994, A1.

108. Angrosino, 1; "Phyllis Schlafly Supports Bishops," 1; "Abortion Issue and CHA," and "Talking Points," attached to "Drop-By Meeting with the Catholic Health Association," 12 August 1994, FOIA Files, no. 2007-0088-F, WHORM Subject Files, box 6, folder: Clinton Presidential Records, Public Liaison, Woolley, Barbara—Catholic Health Association 1996, OAID 18048, WJCPL, 5, 7.

109. "President Clinton's Proposal for Health Care Reform," 14; Joseph Cardinal Bernardin, "A Consistent Ethic of Life Approach to Health Care Reform," *Origins Online*, 9 June 1994, 10; "White House Health Care Briefing," 17 May 1994, FOIA Files, no. 2007-0088-F, WHORM Subject Files, box 1, folder: FI 004-317093, OAID 17038, WJCPL, 2.

110. "Health-Care Reform," in *The Gallup Poll: Public Opinion, 1994*, ed. George Gallup (Wilmington, Del.: Scholarly Resources, 1995), 110; United States Catholic Bishops, "Ethical and Religious Directives for Catholic Health Care Services," November 1994, in Carey, *Pastoral Letters and Statements*, 635.

111. Gustav Niebuhr, "Public Supports Political Voice for Churches," *New York Times*, 25 June 1996, A1, 18.

112. "Remarks by Governor Bill Clinton, University of Notre Dame, South Bend, Ind.," 11 September 1992, 3, and Catholic News Service interview with Bill Clinton by Patricia Zapor, 26 October 1992, 21, FOIA Files, no. 2007-0088-F, WHORM Subject Files, box 3, folder: Verveer, Melanne—Catholic [1], OAID 20024, WJCPL; Timothy Morgan, "Clinton Urges 'Spiritual Change,'" *Time*, 7 February 1994, 43.

113. Bishop Anthony Pilla, "The Bishops' Nonpartisan Election-Year Agenda," *Origins Online*, 18 July 1996, 6; Joseph Cardinal Bernardin, "Address on the Common Ground Project," *Origins Online*, 24 November 1996, 1–12; Eugene Kennedy, *Bernardin: Life to the Full* (Chicago: Bonus, 1997), 334; Thomas Reese, "Bishops Meet in Washington," *America*, 27 November 1997, 3–4.

114. Clinton, *My Life*, 229.

115. James Kelly, "Pro-Life and Pro-Choice after Reagan-Bush," *America*, 30 January 1993, 11.

116. John Tagliabue, "Clinton Is Warned by Vatican Paper," *New York Times*, 8 November 1992, A4.

117. Kelly, "Pro-Life and Pro-Choice," 13.

118. "Abortion," *Congress and the Nation*, 9:536.

119. Archbishop Joseph Dimino, "The Rights of Military Hospital Personnel Who Oppose Abortion," *Origins Online*, 18 February 1993, 1; Gail Quinn, "Weakening of Research Protections for Unborn Children Opposed," *Origins Online*, 18 February 1993, 1.

120. "On File," *Origins Online*, 4 February 1993, 2, 1.

121. William Booth, "Doctor Killed during Abortion Protest," *New York Times*, 11 March 1993, A1.

122. "Abortion," *Congress and the Nation*, 9:537; "Unreasonable Ambitions," *Commonweal*, 23 April 1993, 4; Donald Critchlow, *Intended Consequences* (New York: Oxford University Press, 1999), 222–223.

123. "Changing Course on Abortion," *Time*, 12 April 1993, 22; Gergen, "Clinton's Abortion Problem," 74.

124. "Oh, Goodness," *Nation*, 26 July–2 August 1993, 124.

125. Peter Steinfels, "Papal Birth-Control Letter Retains Its Grip," *New York Times*, 1 August 1993, A1; Alan Cowell, "Pope Challenges President's Stance on Abortion," *New York Times*, 13 August 1993, A1; Kengor, *God and Hillary Clinton*, 122.

126. Fred Barnes, "Bush II," *New Republic*, 11 October 1993, 12; James Guth, "Clinton, Impeachment, and the Culture Wars," in *The Postmodern Presidency*, ed. Stephen Schier (Pittsburgh, Pa.: University of Pittsburgh Press, 2000), 207; "Catholic Outreach Steering Committee Working Group Meeting," 17 August 1994, FOIA Files, no. 2007-0088-F, WHORM Subject Files, box 3, folder: Verveer, Melanne, Catholic, folder 2[2], OAID20024, WJCPL.

127. Memorandums from Reta Lewis to Bruce Reed, 31 August 1993, 1, and Bob Hessey to Reta Lewis, 30 August 1993, 1, Bruce Reed Domestic Policy Council Files, box 97, folder: Abortion, WJCPL.

128. Bill Clinton, "Remarks in a Town Meeting in Sacramento," 3 October 1993, *Public Papers, 1993*, 2:1663.

129. "Abortion," *Congress and the Nation*, 9:537–538.

130. Kengor, *God and Hillary Clinton*, 126–128, 130–131.

131. Pope John Paul II, "Cairo Population Conference Draft Document Criticized," *Origins Online*, 31 March 1994, 4.

132. Pope John Paul II, "Letter to President Clinton: The Cairo International Conference on Population and Development," *Origins Online*, 14 April 1994, 3.

133. Raymond Flynn, *Pope John Paul II* (New York: St. Martin's, 2001), 106–113; "Population and the Pope," *America*, 7 May 1994, 3; "On File," *Origins Online*, 5 May 1994, 1.

134. Six Active U.S. Cardinals and Archbishop William Keeler, "Letter to President Clinton," *Origins Online*, 9 June 1994, 2; "Population and the Pope," 3.

135. Alan Cowell, "An Embrace for Berlusconi but Friction with the Pope," *New York Times*, 3 June 1994, A10.

136. Ibid.; James Franklin, "Flynn Sees Bias against Catholics, Defends Letter Criticizing Officials for Statements," *Boston Globe*, 20 July 1994, http://www.highbeam.com/doc/1P2-8288607html.

137. Alan Cowell, "Scientists Linked to the Vatican Call for Population Curbs," *New York Times*, 16 June 1994, A6; Archbishop William Keeler, "Critique of Cairo Draft Plan," *Origins Online*, 21 July 1994, 3.

138. Letter from Bill Clinton to Rev. James Hickey, 28 June 1994, FOIA 2007-0088-F, WHORM Subject Files, box 7, folder: Clinton Presidential Records, National Security Council Records Management, Catholic and Bishops, 9404264, OAID 198, WJCPL, 2; "Vatican Hits Gore on Abortion Rights," *Christian Century*, 7–14 September 1994, 808–809.

139. "Vatican Hits Gore," 808; Alan Cowell, "Vatican Says Gore Is Misrepresenting Population Talks," *New York Times*, 1 September 1994, A1, 8; "Catholic Group Releases Signature Ad to Challenge the Vatican on Contraception," *Quixote Center*, 22 August 1994, FOIA Files, no. 2007-0088-F, WHORM Subject Files, box 5, folder: Clinton Presidential Records, Public Liaison, Woolley, Barbara—Catholics Speak Out, OAID 8238, WJCPL, 1–2.

140. David Toolan, "Hijacked in Cairo," *America*, 1 October 1994, 3–4; Barbara Crossette, "Vatican Holds Up Abortion Debate at Talks in Cairo," *New York Times*, 8 September 1994, A1, 8.

141. Barbara Crossette, "Vatican Drops Fight against U.N. Population Document," *New York Times*, 10 September 1994, A5.

142. Kenneth Woodward and Daniela Deane, "Hot under the Roman Collar," *Newsweek*, 12 September 1994, 24; Toolan, 4.

143. Toolan, 4.

144. Bill Clinton, "Interview with Religious Affairs Journalists," 2 February 1995, *Public Papers of the Presidents of the United States: William J. Clinton, 1995*, vol. 1: *January 1–June 30, 1995* (Washington, D.C.: U.S. Government Printing Office, 1996), 147; Christopher Caldwell, "Pro-Lifestyle," *New Republic*, 5 April 1999, 14.

145. Caldwell, 14; United States Catholic Bishops, "Faithful for Life: A Moral Reflection," in Carey, *Pastoral Letters and Statements*, 684, 691–692.

146. Charles Morris, *American Catholic* (New York: Times Books, 1997), 414; George Weigel, *Witness to Hope: The Biography of Pope John Paul II* (New York: HarperCollins, 2001), 740, 776–777.

147. Bill Clinton, "Interview with Tabitha Soren of MTV," 11 August 1995, *Public*

Papers of the Presidents of the United States: William J. Clinton, 1995, vol. 2: *July 1–December 31, 1995* (Washington, D.C.: U.S. Government Printing Office, 1996), 1250.

148. Mark Stricherz, "Blood on Their Hands: Exposing Pro-Abortion Catholic Politicians," *Crisis*, 2 May 2003, http://www.crisismagazine.com/may2003, 1; "On File," *Origins Online*, 4 April 1996.

149. "On File," 4 April 1996.

150. Ibid.; letter from Rev. James Hickey to Bill Clinton, 1 April 1996, and memorandum from John Hart to Bill Clinton, 1 April 1996, FOIA File, no. 2007-0088-F, WHORM Subject Files, box 2, folder: WE 003-15938355, OAID 14117, WJCPL; Joseph Cardinal Bernardin, "Letter to President Clinton," *Origins Online*, 25 April 1996, 1.

151. President Bill Clinton, "President Clinton's Letter to Cardinals James Hickey and Joseph Bernardin," *Origins Online*, 25 April 1996, 2.

152. Bill Clinton, "Remarks on Vetoing Partial Birth Abortion Legislation," 10 April 1996, *Public Papers, 1996*, vol. 1: *January 1–June 30, 1996* (Washington, D.C.: U.S. Government Printing Office, 1997), 566–567.

153. "Margin Notes to the Partial-Birth Abortion Veto," *Origins Online*, 25 April 1996, 2.

154. Memorandum from Kyle Baker to Todd Stern, 17 April 1996, FOIA Files, no. 2007-0088-F, WHORM Subject Files, box 2, folder: WE 003-161942, OAID 14117, WJCPL; Margaret Ross Sammon, "The Politics of the U.S. Catholic Bishops," in *Catholics and Politics*, ed. Kristin Heyer, Mark Rozell, and Michael Genovese (Washington, D.C.: Georgetown University Press, 2008), 21; United States Cardinals and the Bishops' Conference President, "Letter to President Clinton on Veto of Partial-Birth Abortion Ban Act," *Origins Online*, 25 April 1996, 1–2; letter from Joan McGrath to Bill Clinton, 23 April 1996, FOIA File, no. 2007-0088-F, WHORM Subject Files, folder: WE 003-108457, OAID 14116, WJCPL; "Vatican Condemns Veto of H.R. 1833," April 1996, FOIA File, no. 2007-0088-F, WHORM Subject Files, box 6, folder: Clinton Presidential Records, National Security Council Cables, Catholic and Bishops, 03/06/1997–07/20/1997, OAID 520,000, WJCPL, 1–2; memorandum from John Hart to Bill Clinton, 1 July 1996, FOIA Files, no. 2007-0088-F, WHORM Subject Files, box 2, folder: WE 003-17426255, OAID 14117, WJCPL.

155. Mary Dorothy Line, "The Veto Was Right," and "The Editors Reply," *Commonweal*, 14 June 1996, 2–4.

156. Email record from John Hart, Emily Bromberg, and Suzanne Dale to Alison Bracewell, 7 February 1997, FOIA Files, no. 2007-0088-F, WHORM Subject Files, box 6, folder: Clinton Presidential Records, Automated Records, Management System (Email), WHO 9, Catholics, Bishops, Abortion, 08/08/1994–11/16/2000, OAID500,000, WJCPL, 2; Diane Gianelli, "Medicine Adds to Debate on Late-Term Abortion," *Medical News*, 3 March 1997, 54.

157. Melanie Conklin, "So I Lied: Whatever Happened to the Abortion Lobbyist Who Repented?" *Progressive*, September 1997, http://www.thefreelibrary.com; Gianelli, 54.

158. Gianelli, 54.

159. United States Cardinals and National Conference of Catholic Bishops President, "Letter to President Clinton on Partial-Birth Abortion," *Origins Online*, 20 March 1997, 1–2.

160. Email record from John Hart to Sylvia Matthews, 23 April 1997, FOIA Files, no. 2007-0088-F, WHORM Subject Files, box 6, folder: Clinton Presidential Records, Automated Records, Management System (Email), WHO, Catholics, Bishops, Abortion, 08/08/1994–11/16/2000, OAID 500,000, WJCPL, 2; "Talking Points on Fitzsimmons Story," attached to memorandum from Elena Kagan to Erskine Bowles et al., 27 February 1997, Elena Kagan Domestic Policy Council Files, box 1, folder: Abortion, Partial-Birth, Fitzsimmons, WJCPL.

161. Bill Clinton, "The President's News Conference," 7 March 1997, *Public Papers of the Presidents of the United States: Bill Clinton, 1997*, vol. 1: *January 1–June 30, 1997* (Washington, D.C.: U.S. Government Printing Office, 1998), 259–260.

162. Memorandum from Bruce Reed to Elena Kagan, 26 March 1997, Elena Kagan Domestic Policy Council Files, box 5, folder: Notes and Memos, WJCPL.

163. Memorandum from John Hilley, Elena Kagan, and Tracey Thornton to the President, n.d., Elena Kagan Domestic Policy Council Files, box 5, folder: Notes and Memos, WJCPL, 6.

164. Cardinal Bernard Law, "Letter to the Senate: Partial Birth Abortion," *Origins Online*, 29 May 1997, 2.

165. "Legislative Efforts in the United States to Prohibit Partial-Birth Abortion," *Catholic News Service*, n.d., http://www.catholicnewsagency.com.resourcephp&n=845; Bishop Robert Carlson, "Senate Minority Leader and His Bishop," *Origins Online*, 29 May 1997, 2–3.

166. Bill Clinton, "Message to the House of Representatives Returning without Approval Partial Birth Abortion Legislation," 10 October 1997, *Public Papers of the Presidents of the United States: William J. Clinton, 1997*, vol. 2: *July 1–December 31, 1997* (Washington, D.C.: U.S. Government Printing Office, 1999), 1340; "Legislative Efforts."

167. Memorandum from Rahm Emanuel to Geoffrey Garin, 22 July 1998, Elena Kagan Domestic Policy Council Files, box 5, folder: Notes and Memos, WJCPL.

168. Bill Clinton, "Message to the House of Representatives Returning without Approval the Foreign Affairs and Restructuring Legislation," 21 October 1998, *Public Papers of the Presidents of the United States: William J. Clinton, 1998*, vol. 2: *July 1–December 31, 1998* (Washington, D.C.: U.S. Government Printing Office, 2000), 1830.

169. Bill Clinton, "Remarks at the Welcoming Center for Pope John Paul II," *Public Papers of the Presidents of the United States: William J. Clinton, 1999*, vol. 1: *January 1–June 30, 1999* (Washington, D.C.: U.S. Government Printing Office, 2000), 106.

170. "Law Briefs," USCC, July–August 2000, 11; John Leo, "Partial-Sense Decision," *U.S. News and World Report*, 10 July 2000, 16.

171. USCC, "Nebraska's Partial-Birth Ban Supported in USCC Friend-of-the-Court Brief before Supreme Court," *Origins Online*, 9 March 2000, 1–8.

172. George Hunt, "Of Many Things," *America*, 31 January–7 February 1998, 2; Patricia Zapor, "Clinton Says Laws on Parental Notice for Abortion Would Be OK," *Catholic News Service*, 26 October 1992, FOIA Files, no. 2007-0088-F, WHORM Subject Files, box 3, folder: Verveer, Melanne, Catholic [2], OAID 20024, WJCPL, 1–2.

173. Annette Tomal, "Parental Involvement Laws and Abortion Rates," *Gender Issues* 18 (Fall 2000): 45; Annette Tomal, "The Effect of Religious Membership on Teen Abortion Rates," *Journal of Youth and Adolescence* 30.1 (2001): 113; James Kelly and Christopher Kudlac, "Pro-Life, Anti-Death Penalty?," *America*, 1 April 2000, http://

www.americamagazine.org/content/article.cfm?article_id=650; Paul Perl and James McClintock, "The Catholic 'Consistent Life Ethic' and Attitudes toward Capital Punishment and Welfare Reform," *Sociology of Religion* 62.3 (2001): 289, 294–295.

174. Deal Hudson, *Onward, Christian Soldiers* (New York: Simon and Schuster, 2008), 180; Helen Alvare, "Partial-Birth Abortion Debate Prepares Way for Horrible Facts," *National Catholic Register*, 13 September 1998, http://www.ncregister.com /site/article/partial_birth_abortion_debate_prepares_way_for_horrible_facts, 1; Valerie Schmalz, "These Challenges Are Not a Time to Despair," *Our Sunday Visitor*, n.d., http://www.osv.com/tabid/7621/itemid/4196/These-challenges-are-not-a-time -to-despair.as, 2; Guth, "Clinton, Impeachment, and the Culture Wars," 245; Bill Clinton, "Statement on Signing the National Defense Authorization Act for FY 1996," 10 February 1996, *Public Papers, 1996*, 1:22.

175. Dorothy McBride Stetson, "The Women's Movement Agenda and the Record of the Clinton Administration," in *The Clinton Riddle*, ed. Todd Shields, Jeannie Whayne, and Donald Kelley (Fayetteville: University of Arkansas Press, 2004), 143; Caldwell, 14; Mark Stricherz, "Playing Politics: Inside the Bishops' Conference, Part II," *Crisis*, 11 February 2004, http://crisismagazine.com/february2004, 4.

176. Clinton, *My Life*, 229.

177. Michael Sean Winters, "Stand by Them: A New Strategy for the Pro-Life Movement," *America*, 19 April 1997, 16; Adam Nagourney, "Cardinal Has Praise for Dole on Abortion," *New York Times*, 26 June 1996, A14; James McHugh, "Catholics and the 1996 Election," *First Things*, February 1997, http://www.firstthings.com/article /2007/12/002/catholics-and-the-1996-election-22, 1; "Catholic Outreach," 24 May 1996, FOIA File, no. 2007-0088-F, WHORM Subject Files, box 2, folder: WE 003-17426255, OAID14117, WJCPL, 1.

178. Bill Clinton, "Videotaped Remarks Commemorating the 25th Anniversary of the Supreme Court's *Roe v. Wade* Decision," 22 January 1998, *Public Papers of the Presidents of the United States: William J. Clinton, 1998*, vol. 1: *January 1–June 30, 1998* (Washington, D.C.: U.S. Government Printing Office, 1999), 108; United States Bishops Meeting, "The Nation Twenty-Five Years after *Roe v. Wade*," *Origins Online*, 27 November 1997, 1.

179. McGrory qtd. in Richard Neuhaus, "Forgetting the Source and Summit," *First Things*, February 1997, http://www.firstthings.com/article/2007/12/forgetting-the -source-and-summit-23, 11; Cable from Raymond Flynn to Secretary of State, June 1995, FOIA Files, no. 2007-0088-F, WHORM Subject Files, box 6, folder: Clinton Presidential Records, National Security Council Cables, Catholic and Bishops, 01/03/1995– 10/13/1995, OAID510000, WJCPL, 7; electronic interview of Donna Shalala by author, 29 June 2011.

180. Email record from Gordon Bendick to Wendy Gray, 10 January 1997, FOIA Files, no. 2007-0088-F, WHORM Subject Files, box 6, folder: Clinton Presidential Records, Automated Records, Management System (Email) WHO, Catholics, Bishops, Abortion, 08/08/1994–11/16/2000, OAID500,000, WJCPL; Hunt, 2.

181. Bishop James McHugh, "A Year That Promises to Be Politically Hyperactive," *Origins Online*, 14 December 1995, 1; Cardinal Bernard Law, "Letter to Priests on the Christian Coalition's Catholic Alliance," *Origins Online*, 15 February 1996, 1–2.

182. Peter Steinfels, "Bishops Assail Press on Sex Charges," *New York Times*, 16 No-

vember 1993, A24; Alan Cowell, "Pope Rules Out Debate on Making Women Priests," *New York Times*, 31 May 1994, A8; John Tagliabue, "Vatican Seeks Islamic Allies in U.N. Population Dispute," *New York Times*, 18 August 1994, A1.

183. "Population and the Pope"; Woodward and Deane, 24.

184. "The Pope's Gospel of Life," *America*, 15 April 1995, 3; Celestine Bolden, "Pope Calls for End to Discrimination against Women," *New York Times*, 11 July 1995, A11; Alan Cowell, "Catholic Bishops Offer Nuns Wider yet Unspecified Role," *New York Times*, 29 October 1994, A5.

185. Barbara Crossette, "Vatican Picks U.S. Woman as Delegate to U.N. Parley," *New York Times*, 25 August 1995, A3; John Tagliabue, "Vatican Attacks U.S.-Backed Draft for Women's Conference," *New York Times*, 29 August 1995, A3.

186. Fox Butterfield, "U.N. Women's Forum Is a Test for Pope's Advocate," *New York Times*, 29 August 1995, http://www.nytimes.com/1995/08/29/world/un-women-s-forum-is-a-test-for-pope-s-advocate.html; "On File," *Origins Online*, 14 September 1995, 1–2; Mary Ann Glendon, "Perspectives of the Vatican Delegation in Beijing," *Origins Online*, 14 September 1995, 1–7; Kengor, *God and Hillary Clinton*, 147–148.

187. "On File," 14 September 1995, 1; Cable from Raymond Flynn to Secretary of State, November 1995, FOIA Files, no. 2007-0088-F, WHORM Subject Files, box 6, folder: Clinton Presidential Records, National Security Council Cables, Catholic and Bishops, 10/17/1995–12/23/1996, OAID 510,000, WJCPL, 5.

188. United States Catholic Bishops, "Faithful for Life," 690; "Margin Notes," *Origins Online*, 6 June 1996, 9; "United States Bishops' Meeting: The Nation Twenty-Five Years after *Roe v. Wade*," *Origins Online*, 27 November 1997, 3.

189. Gustav Niebuhr, "Getting Below Surface of U.S. Catholics' Beliefs," *New York Times*, 13 April 1996, A11.

CHAPTER NINE. Catholics and George W. Bush

1. George W. Bush, "Address to the Nation from Ellis Island, New York, on the First Anniversary of the Terrorist Attacks of September 11," 11 September 2002, *Public Papers of the Presidents of the United States: George W. Bush, 2002*, vol. 2: *July 1–December 31, 2002* (Washington, D.C.: U.S. Government Printing Office, 2005), 1571; George W. Bush, "Address to the United Nations General Assembly in New York City," 12 September 2002, *Public Papers, 2002*, 2:1575; Donald Rumsfeld, handwritten notes, 26 September 2002, Donald Rumsfeld Papers, http://www.rumsfeld.com/librarylist.asp?page=4, 3; Neta Crawford, "The Justice of Preemption and Preventive War Doctrines," in *Just War Theory*, ed. Mark Evans (New York: Palgrave Macmillan, 2005), 39.

2. Wilton Gregory, "Letter to President Bush on the Iraq Situation," *Origins Online*, 26 September 2002, http://originsplus.cathnews.com, 1; James Nicholson, "The History of Diplomatic Relations between the United States of America and the Holy See," *30 Giorni*, n.d., http://www.30giorni.it.

3. Laurie Goodstein, "Bishops Turn to Writing Antiwar Policy," *New York Times*, 13 November 2002, A27.

4. United States Catholic Bishops, "Statement on Iraq," *Origins Online*, 21 November 2002, 1–3.

5. Frank Bruni, "Pope Voices Opposition, His Strongest, to Iraq War," *New York*

Times, 14 January 2003, A12; United States Catholic Bishops, "Serious Ethical Questions on War with Iraq," *Origins Online*, 13 March 2003, 1–2.

6. John Allen, "The Word from Rome," *National Catholic Reporter*, 2 April 2004, http://nationalcatholicreporter.org/word/word040204.htm, 3; Bruni, "Pope Voices Opposition," B33; Michael Novak, "An Argument That War against Iraq Is Just," *Orgins Online*, 20 February 2003, 4.

7. Laurie Goodstein, "Conservative Catholics' Wrenching Debate over Whether to Back President or Pope," *New York Times*, 6 March 2003, A14.

8. "Margin Notes," *Origins Online*, 13 March 2003, 4; Celestino Migliore, "Preventing a Possible War in Iraq," *Origins Online*, 6 March 2003, 2; Frank Bruni, "Pope Sending Envoy to Baghdad in Effort to Avert a War," *New York Times*, 10 February 2003, A11.

9. "Margin Notes," *Origins Online*, 13 March 2003, 4.

10. "On File," *Origins Online*, 13 March 2003, 1–2.

11. George W. Bush, *Decision Points* (New York: Random House, 2010), 243.

12. Ibid., 253.

13. George W. Bush, "Address to the Nation on Iraq," 17 March 2003, *Public Papers of the Presidents of the United States, 2003*, vol. 1: *January 1–June 30, 2003* (Washington, D.C.: U.S. Government Printing Office, 2005), 278.

14. "On File," *Origins Online*, 13 March 2013, 1–2; On File," *Origins Online*, 27 March 2003, 1; Deal Hudson, "Catholic Opinion by the Numbers: A Revealing New Crisis Poll," *Crisis*, 1 March 2003, http://crisismagazine.com/march2003, 3; Bush, *Decision Points*, 247.

15. Bush, *Decision Points*, 256–257.

16. George W. Bush, "Address to the Nation on Iraq from the U.S.S. *Abraham Lincoln*," 1 May 2003, *Public Papers, 2003*, 1:411.

17. John Allen, "Analysis: The American-Vatican Divide," *National Catholic Reporter*, 30 May 2003, http://natcath.org/NCR_Online/archives2/2003b/053003.0530033.htm, 1–2; Frank Bruni, "Pope, in Spain, Emphasizes Need for Peace," *New York Times*, 4 May 2003, A18.

18. Michael Griffin, "The Soldiers Came Asking," *America*, 23 June 2003, http://www.americamagazine.org/content/article.cfm?article_id=3029.

19. Andrew Walther, "Church Helps Troops Feed Millions," *National Catholic Register*, 13 April 2003, http://www.ncregister.com/site/article/church_helps_troops_feed_iraqi_millions, 1; Garry Wills, "A Country Ruled by Faith," *New York Review of Books*, 16 November 2006, http://www.nybooks.com/articles/archives/2006/nov/16, 12; Jack Miles, "The Iraqi Dead," *Commonweal*, 18 July 2003, 10.

20. "Rob 1," "Reconsidering Iraq," *National Catholic Register*, 22 June 2003, http://www.ncregister.com/site/article/reconsidering_iraq, 1; Gregory Foster, "Just-War Doctrine: Lessons from Iraq," *Commonweal*, 15 August 2003, 11–12.

21. William F. Buckley, "Captured," *National Review*, 31 December 2003, 12.

22. Bush, *Decision Points*, 267.

23. Jason Horowitz, "The Struggle for Iraq: Pity at the Vatican for a Captive," *New York Times*, 17 December 2003, A24.

24. John Thavis, "Has the Vatican Changed Its Position on Iraq?" *America*, 22–29 December 2003, 14.

25. Eric Schmidt and Frank Bruni, "Cheney Sees Pope, Who Makes Plea for Peace,"

New York Times, 28 January 2004, http://www.nytimes.com/2004/01/28/world/cheney-sees-pope-who-makes-plea-for-peace.html, 1.

26. George Tenet, "Iraq and Weapons of Mass Destruction," *Vital Speeches of the Day*, 15 February 2004, 262.

27. "Vatican Asks Bishops to Focus on Wider Issues," *America*, 12 April 2004, http://americamagazine.org/content/article_id=3537, 1.

28. John Ricard, "The Abuse of Iraqi Prisoners at Abu Ghraib," *Origins Online*, 3 June 2004, 1.

29. David Kuo, *Tempting Faith* (New York: Free Press, 2006), 145; "Catholics, Protestants Urge New Iraq Policy," *Christian Century*, 1 June 2004, 13–14.

30. "Pope John Paul II and President George W. Bush," *Origins Online*, 17 June 2004, 1, 3; "Pope Tells Bush of Deep Concern about Iraq," *America*, 21–28 June 2004, 4.

31. Wilton Gregory, "Statement on the United States and Iraq," *Origins Online*, 1 July 2004, 1, 3.

32. Hutchinson qtd. in Patrick Novecosky, "Campaign 2004: Iraq and the Catholic Voter," *National Catholic Register*, 25 July 2004, http://www.ncregister.com/site/article/campaign_2004_iraq_and_the_catholic_voter, 1; Mary Jony, "My Son the Soldier," *Commonweal*, 7 July 2004, 39.

33. Ian Brumberger, "Poll Shows Catholics Ignoring Church on Election Issues," *Humanist*, 10 September 2004, 5; "Catholics Rank Abortion below War, Economy," *America*, 13 September 2004, http://www.americamagazine.org/content/article.cmf/article_id=3734, 1; Matt Malone, "Catholics and Candidates," *America*, 17 May 2004, http://www.americamagazine.org/content/article/cmf?_id=3597, 1; Peter Beinart, "Blowback," *New Republic*, 5–12 July 2004, 6.

34. "Social Doctrine Compendium Promotes Human Dignity, Common Good," *America*, 8 November 2004, 4.

35. Allen qtd. in Douglas Todd, "GOP and Vatican Divided by Iraq War," *Christian Century*, 16 November 2004, 14; Jeffrey Jones, "The Protestant and Catholic Vote," 2004, http://gallup.poll//Protestant-Catholic-vote.aspx.

36. Thomas Carty, "White House Outreach to Catholics," in *Catholics and Politics*, ed. Kristin Heyer, Mark Rozell, and Michael Genovese (Washington, D.C.: Georgetown University Press, 2008), 191; "Iraq War Support," *The Gallup Poll: Public Opinion, 2003*, ed. George Gallup (Wilmington, Del.: Scholarly Resources, 2004), 384; Caspar Weinberger, "A Self-Fulfilling Prophecy," *Forbes*, 15 March 2004, 39.

37. Cindy Sheehan, *Not One More Mother's Child* (Kihei, Hawaii: Koa, 2005).

38. Nancy Gibbs, "Person of the Year 2003: The American Soldier," *Time*, 23 December 2003, http://www.time/magazine/article/0,9171,1006533,00.html; Heather Grennan Gray, "Ain't Gonna Study War No More," *U.S. Catholic*, August 2003, 49; Deann Alford, "Faith, War, Peace," *Christianity Today*, December 2004, 46.

39. Art Laffin, "Bishops Called to Speak Out against Iraq War," *National Catholic Reporter*, 24 December 2004, http://natcath.org/NCR_Oline/archives2/2004d/122404r.htm, 1; Sebastian Junger, "Why Would Anyone Miss War?" *International Herald Tribune*, 18 July 2011, 8.

40. "Margin Notes," *Origins Online*, 13 March 2003, 4; "Vatican Meeting of Pope John Paul II and President George W. Bush," *Origins Online*, 17 June 2004, 1; Gregory, "Statement on the United States and Iraq," 1; John Allen, "Interview with Cardi-

nal Theodore McCarrick," *National Catholic Reporter*, 28 April 2004, http://national catholicreporter.org/update/mccarrick.htm, 3.

41. Irwin Stelzer, "All Hat and No Cattle," *Weekly Standard*, 17 May 2004, http://www.lexisnexis.com, 1.

42. Robert Woodward, *Plan of Attack* (New York: Simon and Schuster, 2004), 261; George Tenet, *At the Center of the Storm* (New York: HarperCollins, 2007), 359–360; James Pfiffner, "Decision-Making in the Bush White House," *Presidential Studies Quarterly* 39 (June 2009): 374.

43. John Allen, "Analysis: The American-Vatican Divide," *National Catholic Reporter*, 30 May 2003, http://natchath.org/NCROnline/archives2/2003b/053003htm, 3.

44. Electronic interview of Douglas Wead by author, 25 June 2011.

45. "Vatican Meeting of Pope John Paul II and President George W. Bush," 2–5; Schmidt and Bruni; "On File," 13 March 2003, 2.

46. Bush, *Decision Points*, 116; *The Gallup Poll: Public Opinion, 2002*, ed. George Gallup (Wilmington, Del.: Scholarly Resources, 2003), 207; Alessandra Stanley, "John Paul, Hemmed In at the Twilight of His Papacy," *New York Times*, 26 May 2002, A4.

47. Laurie Goodstein, "The Bishops and Urgency," *New York Times*, 16 April 2002, A24; Janet Elder, "Many Critical of Hierarchy, but Few Say Faith Is Shaken," *New York Times*, 21 April 2002, A35.

48. Beinart, "Blowback," 6.

49. Nicholson, 33; "Vatican Meeting of Pope John Paul II and President George W. Bush," 1; Gregory, "Statement on the United States and Iraq," 2.

50. Bush, *Decision Points*, 116.

51. Ibid., 363–365.

52. Nicholson, 31; George Weigel, *The End and the Beginning* (Garden City, N.Y.: Doubleday, 2010), 328.

53. Franklin Foer, "Spin Doctrine," *New Republic*, 5 June 2000, 18.

54. June Hopkins and Anthony Cupaluolo, "For Better or Worse?" *Policy and Practice of Public Human Services* 59 (June 2001): 24–25; Foer, 3; Jo Renee Formicola and Mary Segers, "The Bush Faith-Based Initiative: The Catholic Response," *Journal of Church and State* 44 (Autumn 2002): 694; Leslie Lenkowsky, "Funding the Faithful: Why Bush Is Right," *Commentary*, June 2001, 19; Gwendolyn Mink, "Faith in Government," *Social Justice* 28 (Spring 2001): 6.

55. Wagner qtd. in Foer, 4.

56. John DiIulio, "A View from Within," in *The George W. Bush Presidency: An Early Assessment*, ed. Fred Greenstein (Baltimore, Md.: Johns Hopkins University Press, 2003), 248–249.

57. Foer, 2–3.

58. Kuo, 136.

59. Jones.

60. Kuo, 137; Formicola and Segers, 694.

61. Richard Oppel and Gustav Niebuhr, "Bush Meeting Focuses on Role of Religion," *New York Times*, 21 December 2000, A37.

62. George W. Bush, "Inaugural Address," 20 January 2001, *Public Papers of the Presidents of the United States: George W. Bush, 2001*, vol. 1: *January 20–June 30, 2001* (Washington, D.C.: U.S. Government Printing Office, 2003), 2–3.

63. Formicola and Segers, 703–704; George W. Bush, "Remarks prior to a Meeting with Congressional Leaders and an Exchange with Reporters," 25 January 2001, *Public Papers, 2001*, 1:20.

64. George W. Bush, "Remarks on Signing Executive Orders with Respect to Faith-Based and Community Initiatives," 29 January 2001, *Public Papers, 2001*, 1:25–26; DiIulio, 245–246.

65. George W. Bush, "Remarks following a Meeting with Congressional Leaders and an Exchange with Reporters," 29 January 2001, *Public Papers, 2001*, 1:31.

66. Formicola and Segers, 704–705.

67. "On File," *Origins Online*, 15 February 2001, 1–2.

68. George W. Bush, "Remarks in a Meeting with Catholic Charities Leaders," 31 January 2001, *Public Papers, 2001*, 1:39.

69. "On File," 15 February 2001, 1–2; Formicola and Segers, 705–706.

70. George W. Bush, "Address before a Joint Session of Congress on Administration Goals," 27 February 2001, *Public Papers, 2001*, 1:142–143.

71. Eyal Press, "Lead Us Not into Temptation," *American Prospect*, 9 April 2001, http://www.lexisnexis.com, 1; "Faith-Based Programs Still Popular," *Pew Research Center*, 16 November 2009, http://pewresearch.org/pubs/1412/faithbased-programs-popular-church-state-concerns, 2.

72. Ram Cnaan and Stephanie Boddie, "Charitable Choice and Faith-Based Welfare: A Call for Social Work," *Social Work* 47 (July 2002): 233; Press, 1; Kuo, 142.

73. Formicola and Segers, 697–698.

74. "Margin Notes," *Origins Online*, 12 April 2001, 4; George W. Bush, "Commencement Address at the University of Notre Dame in Notre Dame, Indiana," 20 May 2001, *Public Papers, 2001*, 1:552–553.

75. George W. Bush, "Remarks to the United States Conference of Mayors," 25 June 2001, *Public Papers, 2001*, 1:721; Formicola and Segers, 707; George W. Bush, "Statement on the Church of God in Christ's Endorsement of the Faith-Based and Community Initiative," 5 July 2001, *Public Papers of the Presidents of the United States: George W. Bush, 2001*, vol. 2: *July 1–December 31, 2001* (Washington, D.C.: U.S. Government Printing Office, 2003), 828.

76. George W. Bush, "Remarks to America's Promise Participants," 9 July 2001, *Public Papers, 2001*, 2:834; Amy Black, Douglas Koopman, and David Ryden, *Of Little Faith* (Washington, D.C.: Georgetown University Press, 2004), 142; George W. Bush, "Statement on House of Representatives Action on the Faith-Based and Community Initiative," 19 July 2001, *Public Papers, 2001*, 2:872; Formicola and Segers, 707.

77. Kuo, 124.

78. DiIulio, 254; Jo Renee Formicola, Mary Segers, and Paul Weber, *Faith-Based Initiatives and the Bush Administration* (New York: Rowman and Littlefield, 2003), 135.

79. Black et al., 147.

80. Ibid., 172, 175.

81. United States Catholic Bishops, "A Place at the Table: A Catholic Recommitment to Overcome Poverty and to Respect the Dignity of All God's Children," *Origins Online*, 28 November 2002, 1, 8.

82. George W. Bush, "Remarks at the White House Conference on Faith-Based

and Community Initiatives in Philadelphia, Pennsylvania," 12 December 2002, *Public Papers, 2002*, 2:2185–2188.

83. Kevin Kruse, "Compassionate Conservatism," in *The Presidency of George W. Bush*, ed. Julian Zeliger (Princeton, N.J.: Princeton University Press, 2010), 238; George W. Bush, "Remarks at the White House Conference on Faith-Based and Community Initiatives," 1 June 2004, *Public Papers of the Presidents: George W. Bush 2004*, vol. 1: *January 1–June 30, 2004* (Washington, D.C.: U.S. Government Printing Office, 2007), 951.

84. Elizabeth Bumiller, "Bush Talks to an Appreciative Catholic Crowd," *New York Times*, 4 August 2004, http://www.nytimes.com/2004/08/04/bush-talks-to-an-appreciative-catholic-crowd,html?19&sq=Catholics&st=ny&pagewanted=print, 1.

85. "Presidential Debate in St. Louis, Missouri," 8 October 2004, *Public Papers of the Presidents of the United States, 2004*, vol. 3: *October 1, 2004–January 20, 2005* (Washington, D.C.: U.S. Government Printing Office, 2007) 2487; "Presidential Debate in Tempe, Arizona," 14 October 2004, *Public Papers, 2004*, 3:2417.

86. Joe Feuerherd, "Respectful Disagreement Could Be Key to Kerry Catholic Vote," *National Catholic Reporter*, 26 October 2004, http://www.nationalcatholicreporter.org/washington/wnb102604.htm, 1; John Dart, "The Faith Factor," *Christian Century*, 5 October 2004, 8.

87. Paul Kengor, *God and George W. Bush* (New York: Harper 2005), 220; Dart, 8.

88. "Faith-Based Programs Still Popular," 1; "Religion and Public Life: A Faith-Based Partisan Divide," 2005, *Pew Research Center*, http://pewresearch.org/pubs/1412/faith-based-programs-popular-church-state-concerns, 33–35.

89. Bush, *Decision Points*, 279.

90. Joseph Bottum, "The Leadership of George W. Bush: Con and Pro," *First Things*, March 2007, http://www.firstthings.com/article/2009/01/the-leadership-of-george-w-bush-con-pro-32, 2.

91. Kuo, 219–220, 239–240.

92. George W. Bush, "Remarks to Leaders of Hispanic Faith-Based Organizations," 22 May 2001, *Public Papers, 2001*, 1:561; Formicola and Segers, 715; Wilton Gregory, "The Federal Budget and the Needs of the Poor," *Origins Online*, 10 April 2003, 1; "Religion and Public Life," 38–39.

93. Telephone interview of Timothy Goeglein by author, 4 August 2011; "Compassionate Conservatism Takes a Bow," *Economist*, 3 February 2001, 2, http://economist.com; Black et al., 133; Formicola and Segers, 709; Deal Hudson, "*Crisis* Interview with Jim Towey," *Crisis*, 1 June 2002, http://www.crisismagazine.com/June2002, 5.

94. Charles E. Degeneffe, "What Is Catholic about Catholic Charities?" *Social Work* 48 (July 2003): 381, 379.

95. Daniel Rigney, Jerome Matz, and Armando Abney, "Is There a Catholic Sharing Ethic?" *Sociology of Religion* 65 (2004): 163; Richard Parker, "On God and Democrats," *American Prospect*, March 2004, http://www.lexis.nexis.com/Inacui2api/delivery/PrintDoc.do?jobHan, 4.

96. Bret Schulte, "Struggling to Keep the Faith," *U.S. News and World Report*, 19 December 2004, http://www.usnews/news/articles/041227; Brumberger, 5.

97. George W. Bush, "The President's News Conference," 13 March 2002, *Public*

Papers of the Presidents of the United States: George W. Bush, 2002, vol. 1: *January 1–June 30, 2002* (Washington, D.C.: U.S. Government Printing Office, 2004), 396–397.

98. Laurie Goodstein, "Vatican Accepts Resignation of Milwaukee's Archbishop," *New York Times*, 25 May 2002, A1, 12; George W. Bush, "Remarks on the Faith-Based Welfare Initiative in Milwaukee," 2 July 2002, *Public Papers, 2002*, 2:1167.

99. Heidi Schumpf, "Stop Talking about My Generation," *U.S. Catholic*, February 2004, 50; James Guth, "George W. Bush and Religious Politics," in *Ambition and Division: Legacies of the George W. Bush Presidency*, ed. Steven Schier (Pittsburgh, Pa.: University of Pittsburgh Press, 2009), 128; Robert Vitillo, "After September 11: Changing Attitudes toward the Poor," *Origins Online*, 31 January 2002, 4; Gerda Gallop-Goodman, "The Answer to Our Prayers," *American Demographics* 23 (March 2001): 20.

100. United States Catholic Bishops, "A Place at the Table," 8; Elizabeth Wells, "Our Two Cents Worth," *U.S. Catholic*, April 2004, 13.

101. Brian Simboli, "Conservatism and Catholicism," *American Spectator*, June–July 2003, 28; Roger Mahony, "Key Questions for Catholic Social Teaching Today," *Origins Online*, 2 October 2003, 1; USCCB Administrative Committee, "Faithful Citizenship: A Call to Political Responsibility," *Origins Online*, 23 October 2003, 13.

102. Mark Stricherz, "Playing Politics: Inside the Bishops' Conference, Part II," *Crisis*, 11 February 2004, http://crisismagazine.com/february2004, 4; Daniel Burke, "A Catholic Wind in the White House," *Washington Post*, 13 April 2008, http://www.washingtonpost.com/wp-dyn/content/article/2008/04/11/AR2008041103327.html, 1; Kevin Clarke, "Wilderness Training," *U.S. Catholic*, January 2005, 33; DiIulio, 249.

103. George W. Bush, "Remarks at the White House Conference on Faith-Based and Community Initiatives in Los Angeles, California," 3 March 2004, *Public Papers, 2004*, vol. 1: *January 1–June 30, 2004* (Washington, D.C.: U.S. Government Printing Office, 2007), 297; "Taking Stock: The Bush Faith-Based Initiative and What Lies Ahead," *Roundtable of Religion and Social Welfare Policy*, 11 June 2009, http://www.religionandsocialpolicy.org/final_report, 82.

104. "Faith-Based Programs Still Popular," 1; Joseph LoConte, "Keeping the Faith," *First Things*, May 2002, http://www.firstthings.com/article/207/01/keeping-the-faith-17, 1.

105. John Wells and David Cohen, "Keeping the Charge: George W. Bush, the Christian Right, and the New Vital Center of American Politics," in Rozell and Whitney, 146; Bush, "Remarks on the Faith-Based Welfare Initiative in Milwaukee," 1167.

106. "Taking Stock," 3; Paul Hughes and Madison Trammel, "Question and Answer: John DiIulio," *Christianity Today*, March 2008, http://www.christianitytoday.com/2008/march/8.23html; "Faith-Based Programs Still Popular," 10.

107. George W. Bush, "Remarks in a Discussion in Portsmouth, Ohio," 10 September 2004, *Public Papers, 2004*, vol. 2: *July 1–September 30, 2004* (Washington, D.C.: U.S. Government Printing Office, 2007), 2004; "The Tempest around 'Tempting Faith,'" *Beliefnet*, n.d., http://www.beliefnet.com/News/2006/10/The-Tempest-Around-Tempting-Faith.aspx?p=2, 1; "Taking Stock," 85.

108. Telephone interview of Goeglein.

109. Bush, *Decision Points*, 33–34.

110. "Address by President Bush at Opening of Pope John Paul II Cultural Center," *Origins Online*, 12 April 2001, 1.

111. George W. Bush, "Statement to the Participants in the March for Life," 22 January 2001, *Public Papers, 2001*, 1:9.

112. "Trench Warfare," *Economist*, 27 January 2001, 30–31; "Bush Restricts RU-486 Funding and Closes White House Feminist Office," *LifeSite News*, http://lifesitenews.com/news/archive/ldn/2001/apr/01040303.

113. "Address by President Bush at Opening of Pope John Paul II Cultural Center," 1.

114. "Margin Notes," *Origins Online*, 12 April 2001, 3.

115. George W. Bush, "Remarks on Presenting the Congressional Gold Medal Posthumously to John Cardinal O'Connor of New York in New York City," 10 July 2001, *Public Papers, 2001*, 2:839.

116. David Frum, *The Right Man* (New York: Random House, 2003), 107.

117. "Pope John Paul II Address to President Bush at Castel Gandolfo," *Origins Online*, 2 August 2001, 3; "Reaction to President George W. Bush's Embryonic Stem Cell Research Announcement," *Origins Online*, 30 August 2001, 14.

118. Mark Johnson and Kathleen Gallagher, "Thompson Pushes for Adult Stem Cells," *Milwaukee Journal Sentinel*, 10 November 2011, B1, 5; George W. Bush, "The President's News Conference with Prime Minister Silvio Berlusconi of Italy in Rome, Italy," 23 July 2001, *Public Papers, 2001*, 2:900–901.

119. "President George W. Bush, Address to the Nation on Embryonic Stem-Cell Research Funding," *Origins Online*, 30 August 2001, 2–4; "Religion and Public Life," 30.

120. "Reaction to President George W. Bush's Embryonic Stem Cell Research Announcement," 1–17.

121. "President George W. Bush, Statement to Annual March for Life," *Origins Online*, 31 January 2002, 1–2.

122. Russell Shorto, "Slowly, Painfully Breaking Apart 'Irish Catholic,'" *International Herald Tribune*, 12–13 February 2011, 5; "A Letter to Priests from American Cardinals after Their Vatican Meeting on Pedophilia," *New York Times*, 25 April 2002, A28.

123. USCCB, "Law Briefs," June 2002, 11; Valerie Gutman, "Prenatal Care: Revisions to SCHIP Extend Health Care to 'Unborn Children,'" *Journal of Law, Medicine and Ethics* (1 April 2003), http://www.allbusiness.com/legal/3586986-1html, 1–2.

124. Frank Bruni, "For Many, Pope's Frailties Now Define Papacy," *New York Times*, 28 July 2002, A9.

125. Frank Bruni, "Pope Says Modern Mankind Is Usurping 'God's Place,'" *New York Times*, 19 August 2002, A2.

126. Poll cited in Robert J. McClory, "Irreconcilable Differences?" *U.S. Catholic*, October 2004, 20.

127. Letters to Congress from Gail Quinn, 26 September 2000 and 25 July 2000, USCCB, http://www.nccbuscc.org/profile/issues/abortion/bornalive.shtml; "Born-Alive Infants Protection Act," *National Right to Life*, 5 August 2002, http://www.nlrc.org/federal/born_alive_infants/index.html; George W. Bush, "Telephone Remarks to the March for Life," 22 January 2003, *Public Papers, 2003*, 1:372–373.

128. Deal Hudson, "Catholic Opinion by the Numbers: A Revealing New *Crisis* Poll," *Crisis*, 1 March 2003, http://crisismagazine.com, 2; "President Bush and *Roe v. Wade*," in *The Gallup Poll: Public Opinion, 2004*, ed. George Gallup (Wilmington, Del.: Scholarly Resources, 2005), 474.

129. Steven Ertfelt, "Bush Signs Partial-Birth Abortion Ban," *LifeNews*, 5 November 2003, http://www.lifenews.com/2003/11/05/nat-189; George W. Bush, "Remarks on Signing the Partial-Birth Abortion Ban Act of 2003," 5 November 2003, *Public Papers of the Presidents of the United States: George W. Bush, 2003*, vol. 2: *July 1–December 31, 2003* (Washington, D.C.: U.S. Government Printing Office, 2005), 1467.

130. Letter to the Senate, 10 March 2003, and letter to the Congress, 20 March 2003, from Rev. William Keeler, USCCB, http://www.usccb.org/prolife/issues/pla/index.shtml, 6; "Harkin Amendment to Endorse *Roe v. Wade*," National Right to Life Committee, 12 March 2003, http://ssi.capwoz.com/nrlcIissues/votes/votenum=48&chamber=s&Congress=1081; Ertfelt.

131. Daniel J. Wakin, "Bishops Open a New Drive Opposing Contraception," *New York Times*, 13 November 2003, http://www.nytimes.com/2003/11/13.

132. Karen Tumulty and Percy Bacon, "A Test of Kerry's Faith," *Time*, 5 April 2004, http://www.time.com/time/printout/0,8816,993729,00html.

133. George W. Bush, "Telephone Remarks to the March for Life," 22 January 2004, *Public Papers of the Presidents of the United States: George W. Bush, 2004*, vol. 1: *January 1–June 30, 2004* (Washington, D.C.: U.S. Government Printing Office, 2007), 102–103.

134. "Two Archbishops Challenge Lawmakers on Abortion," *America*, 2 February 2004, 4.

135. "Communion Wars," *U.S. Catholic*, March 2004, 11.

136. George Neumayr, "Kerry Catholicism," *American Spectator*, April 2004, 33.

137. Ted Jelen, "Life Issues: Abortion, Stem-Cell Research, and the Case of Terry Schiavo," in *Religion and the Bush Presidency*, ed. Mark Rozell and Gleaves Whitney (New York: Palgrave Macmillan, 2007), 148; Joe Feuerherd, "Catholic for Kerry Ousted at Bishops' Conference," *National Catholic Reporter*, 24 March 2004, http://www.nationalcatholicreporter.org/washington/wrib032404.html, 1; Tumulty and Bacon; "News Briefs," *America*, 12 April 2004, http://www.americamagazine.org/content/article.cfm?article_id=481, 3; letter to Congress, 19 February 2004, and letter to the Senate, 1 March 2004, USCCB, http://www.usccb.org/prolife/issues/abortion/victims/senate3014.shtml/and/congress021904.shtml.

138. "President Bush Signs Unborn Victims of Violence Act of 2004," 1 April 2004, http://georgewbush-whitehousearchives.gov/news/releases/2004/04/20040401-3.html.

139. Paul Kengor, *God and Hillary Clinton* (New York: HarperCollins, 2007), 223; Laurie Goodstein, "Kerry, Candidate and Catholic, Creates Uneasiness for Church," *New York Times*, 2 April 2004, http://www.nytimes.com/2004/04/02/politics/campaign/02KERR.html?pagewanted=all.

140. Laurie Goodstein, "The 2004 Campaign: The Abortion Issue; Vatican Cardinal Signals Backing for Sanctions on Kerry," *New York Times*, 24 April 2004, http://www.nytimes.com/2004/04/24; Julia Duin, "More Bishops Inject Faith into Catholic Political Life," *Catholics for Choice*, 15 May 2004, http://www.catholicsforchoice.org/news/2004/20040515morebishopsinjectfaithintocatholicpoliticallife.asp.

141. John Allen, "Interview with Cardinal Theodore McCarrick," *National Catholic Reporter*, 28 April 2004, http://nationalcatholicreporter.org/update/mccarrick.htm, 1; Laurie Goodstein, "Bishop Would Deny Rite to Deficient Catholic Voters," *New York Times*, 14 May 2004, http://www.nytimes.com/2004/05/14, 1; Joe Feuerherd, "Kerry-

as-Catholic Story Stays Alive," *National Catholic Reporter*, 5 May 2004, http://www.nationalcatholicreporter.org/washington/wnb050504.htm, 3.

142. Cathy Lynn Grossman, "Pope Names New Archbishop for Philadelphia," *USA Today*, 21 July 2011, A5; Matt Malone, "Catholics and Candidates," *America*, http://americamagazine.org/content/article.cfm?article_id=3957, 4.

143. Goodstein, "Bishop Would Deny Rite," 1.

144. "Cardinal Willing to Meet Democrats on Ban," *America*, 7 June 2004, http://www.americamagazine.org/content/article.cfm?article_id=3624, 2; John Nichols, "Kerry and Communion," *Nation*, 14 June 2004, 6.

145. "Ratzinger Advises Bishops on Principles of Denying Communion and Voting," *America*, 19–26 July 2004, 4; Peter Steinfels, "The Bishops' Debate on Roman Catholic Politicians Who Back Abortion Rights Was More Nuanced than Statement Suggests," *New York Times*, 26 June 2004, http://www.nytimes.com/2004/06/26, 1; "Bishops Warn Politicians Who Back Legal Abortion," *America*, 5 July 2004, http://www.americamagazine.org/content/article.cfm?article_id=3652; Task Force on Catholic Bishops and Catholic Politicians, "Report by Cardinal Theodore McCarrick," 17 November 2004, USCCB, http://www.usccb.org/bishops/mccarrick1104.shtml.

146. "Vatican Dismayed over Memo on Communion," *America*, 4 October 2004, 4.

147. Karen Tumulty and Percy Bacon, "Battling the Bishops," *Time*, 21 June 2004, http://www.time.com/time/printout/0,8816,994454,00.html, 2.

148. David Kirkpatrick, "Bush Sought Vatican Official's Help on Issue, Report Says," *New York Times*, 13 June 2004, http://www.nytimes.com/2004/06/13, 1; "Meeting of the Pope and President Bush," *Origins Online*, 17 June 2004, 1, 4.

149. "Hardline Bishops Threaten to Deny Kerry Sacrament," *Taipei Times*, 22 May 2004, http://www.taipeitimes.com/News/world/archives/2004/05/22/2003156518/2.

150. Joe Feuerherd, "Pro-Life Dems Meet in State House," *National Catholic Reporter*, 28 July 2004, http://www.nationalcatholicreporter.org/washington/wnb072804.htm, 5.

151. George W. Bush, "Remarks to the Knights of Columbus Convention in Dallas, Texas," 3 August 2004, *Public Papers of the Presidents of the United States, 2004*, vol. 2: *July 1–September 3, 2004* (Washington, D.C.: U.S. Government Printing Office, 2007), 1469; "Bush Courts Knights of Columbus," *America*, 16 August 2004, 2; "Text: President Bush's Acceptance Speech to the Republican National Convention," *Washington Post*, 2 September 2004, http://www.washingtonpost.com/wp-dyn/articles/A57466-2004Sep2.html.

152. David Ricken, "Letter to Catholic Politicians and Public Officeholders," *Origins Online*, 2 September 2004, 3–4.

153. "Casey '55 Meets Holy Father and Receives Medal," *Holy Cross Magazine*, Fall 1999, http://www.holycross.edu/departments/publicaffairs/hcm/hcmfall99/class_notes/1980.html; *National Abortion Federation v. Ashcroft*, Findlaw, 26 August 2004, http://files.findlaw.com/news.findlaw.com/nytimes/docs/abortion/nafash82604opn.pdf, 91.

154. "Catholics Go for Bush," *America*, 15 November 2004, http://www.americamagazine.org/content/article.cfm?article_id=3864, 1–2; Carty, 191.

155. Linda Greenhouse, "Justices Back Ban on Method of Abortion," *New York*

Times, 18 April 2007, http://www.nytimes.com/2057/04/19/washington/19scotus.html; USCCB, "Law Briefs," November 2002, 2.

156. "New Zogby Poll on Abortion: America Is Pro-Life," National Right to Life Committee, 20 April 2004, http://nrlc.org/zogby%20april%202004%20%20PPT%20slides.pdf; "The Bishops' Election Intervention," *Progressive*, September 2004, 26–27; "LeMoyne College/Zogby International Contemporary Catholic Trends Poll," 7 July 2004, http://zogby.com/news/2004/07, 1; Katherine Q. Seelye, "Moral Values Cited as a Defining Issue of Election," *New York Times*, 4 November 2004, http://nytimes.com/2004/11/04/politics/campaign/04poll.html, 1; Sharon Jayson, "Abortion Rates Fall Except among Poor Women," *USA Today*, 24 May 2011, A3.

157. Scott McClellan, *What Happened* (New York: Public Affairs, 2008), 19; Kuo, 124.

158. Karl Rove, *Courage and Consequence* (New York: Simon and Schuster, 2010), 246; Frum, 109–110.

159. Feuerherd, "Respectful Disagreement Could Be Key," 2; John Langan, "Observations on Abortion and Politics," *America*, 25 October 2004, 10–12; Thomas Kofensteiner, "The Man with a Ladder," *America*, 1 November 2004, 11.

160. "Presidential Debate in Tempe, Arizona," 2486–2487.

161. Jill Stanek, "I Oppose Abortion, Personally," *Catholic Citizen*, 6 July 2004, http://www.catholiccitizens.org/platform/platformview.asp?c=17349; George W. Bush, "The President's Radio Address," 16 October 2004, *Public Papers, 2004*, 3:2543; "Presidential Debate in Tempe, Arizona," 2487.

162. George W. Bush, "The President's News Conference," 28 October 2003, *Public Papers, 2003*, 2:1402.

163. Bush, "Telephone Remarks to the March for Life," 22 January 2004, 103.

164. "President Bush and *Roe v. Wade*," in Gallup, *The Gallup Poll: Public Opinion, 2004*, 473–474; Christopher Muste, "Hidden in Plain Sight," *Washington Post*, 12 December 2004, B4.

165. "Presidential Debate in Tempe, Arizona," 2487.

166. "Kerry, Bush Both Missed Questionnaire Deadline," *Catholic News Service*, 27 October 2004, http://www.catholicnews.com/data/stories/cns/040532.htm.

167. William Addams Reitwiesner, "Ancestry of George W. Bush," http://www.wargs.com/political/bush.html.

CONCLUSION

1. "Sacraments Today: Belief and Practice among U.S. Catholics," Executive Summary, Center for Applied Research in the Apostolate, February 2008, http://cara.georgetown.edu/sacramentshtml, 20.

2. Harry Kreisler, "Conversations with History: Father Bryan J. Hehir," University of California at Berkeley Institute of International Studies, 2 April 1987, http://www.youtube.com/watch?√=YC/woyVnoyw; interview of Rev. Theodore Hesburgh by author, 17 August 2011.

3. Kreisler; telephone interview of Rev. Bryan Hehir by author, 15 August 2011.

4. Interview of Hesburgh.

5. Electronic interview of Patrick Buchanan by author, 23 July 2011; electronic interview of Douglas Wead by author, 25 June 2011.

6. Electronic interview of Wead; Deal Hudson, *Onward, Christian Soldiers* (New York: Simon and Schuster, 2008), 190–191; Joe Feuerherd, "The American Catholic Church in Neverland," *National Catholic Reporter*, 21 January 2004, http://www.nationalcatholicreporter.org/washington/wnb012104.htm, 2; John Coleman, "American Catholicism, Catholic Charities USA and Welfare Reform," in *Religion Returns to the Public Square*, ed. Hugh Heclo and Wilfred McClay (Baltimore, Md.: Johns Hopkins University Press, 2003), 249; Peter Boyer, "The Party Faithful," *New Yorker*, 8 September 2008, http://www.newyorker.com/reporting/2008/09/08/080908fa_fact_boyer?currentPage=2, 2; Mark Stricherz, "Playing Politics: Inside the Bishops' Conference Part II," *Crisis*, 11 February 2004, http://crisismagazine.com/february2004, 1; interview of Hesburgh.

7. Telephone interview of Hehir; Coleman, 249.

8. Stricherz, 1; Ted Jelen, "Life Issues," in *Religion and the Bush Presidency*, ed. Mark Rozell and Gleaves Whitney (New York: Palgrave Macmillan, 2007), 206; Feuerherd, 3.

9. Stricherz, 1; interview of Hesburgh.

10. Mary Segers, "The Strengths and Weaknesses of the Pro-Life Agenda," in *American Catholics, American Culture*, ed. Margaret O'Brien Steinfels (Lanham, Md.: Rowman and Littlefield, 2004), 63.

11. Margaret Ross Sammon, "The Politics of the U.S. Catholic Bishops," in *Catholics and Politics*, ed. Kristin Heyer, Mark Rozell, and Michael Genovese (Washington, D.C.: Georgetown University Press, 2008), 11; Michele Dillon, "The Abortion Debate: Good for the Church and Good for American Society," in Steinfels, 73; Stricherz, 4.

12. "Sacraments Today," Executive Summary, 127; Andrew Greeley, "An Ugly Little Secret Revisited," in Steinfels, 165.

13. E. J. Dionne, "There Is No 'Catholic Vote,'" *Brookings Institution*, 18 June 2000, http://www.brookings.edu/opinions/2000/0618elections-jr.aspx, 1.

INDEX

Abernathy, Ralph, 68
Abney, Armando, 358
abortion: apprehension about, 109–110; bishops and national policy on, 280–281; George H. W. Bush and, 12, 13, 249, 272–292, 319, 381–382; George W. Bush and, 12, 13, 362–376, 381–382; Cairo Conference and, 323–325; Jimmy Carter and, 11, 13, 159, 167, 184–197, 382; Catholics as target in debate, 287–288; Bill Clinton and, 12, 13, 311–312, 316–317, 319–334, 382; College of Obstetricians and Gynecologists and, 327, 328; comparison to slavery, 236–237, 329–330; Congressional attack on, 325–326; debate over legalized, 291; decline in rate of, 331; Gerald R. Ford and, 11, 13, 133, 152–168, 272, 381–382; Hyde Amendment and, 309–310; importance to voters, 285–286; incest and, 282; legalization of, 9, 291; as life-and-death issue, 11, 12; at military hospitals, 320; Mel Miller and, 288–289; Richard M. Nixon and, 10, 13, 123–132, 381–382; number of annual, 282, 325; parental notification and, 281–282; partial-birth, 12, 325–332, 365, 366, 374–375, 381; predicting views on, 291; public awareness of alternatives to, 286; public funding of, 275–276; public opinion polls on, 128, 167–168, 187, 247, 274, 276, 280, 284, 286, 289, 327, 330, 331, 332, 366, 373, 375; rape and, 282; Ronald Reagan and, 11, 13, 230–248, 381–382; right to privacy and, 123–124; third-trimester and, 326–327; women's freedom and, 282
abortion clinics, 191–192, 321
"Abortion Eve" (booklet), 192–193
Abortion Rights Mobilization, 191–192, 280
Abramowitz, Elizabeth, 187
Abu Ghraib facility, 342
Abzug, Bella, 325
Acton Institute for the Study of Religion and Liberty, 351

Ad Hoc Committee for Population and Pro-Life Affairs, 125
Ad Hoc Committee for Respect Life Week, 124
Ad Hoc Committee on Catholic Social Teaching and the American Economy, 222
Ad Hoc Committee on Christianity and Capitalism, 219
Ad Hoc Committee on the Moral Evaluation of Deterrence, 214, 215
Advisory Committee on Refugees, 136
Afghanistan: just-war criteria and, 6; Al Qaeda in, 336; Soviet invasion of, 11, 12, 169, 378; Taliban in, 336; U.S. war in, 336
African-Americans: Catholic concerns of, 263; Mary Hanna and, 182; increase in, 262; support for John F. Kennedy, 40
Agency for International Development, 22, 44; abortion and, 238; faith-based initiatives and, 356; Fulbright Amendment and, 77; population concerns and, 48–49, 290
aggiornamento (modernization), 24, 77
Agriculture, U.S., Department of, 356
Ahmann, Mathew, 28, 38, 40, 66, 69; civil rights and, 29–30, 32, 67, 74; National Catholic Conference for Interracial Justice and, 27, 41
Aid to Families with Dependent Children, 260, 268
Aiello, Stephen, 183–184
air power, 293
Akron v. Akron Center for Reproductive Health, 235, 281, 289
Albert, Carl, 116
Albright, Madeleine, 297, 300, 305, 333
Alexander VI, *Inter Caetera* of, 1
Allen, John, 343–344
Allen, Steve, 266
all-volunteer military, 344
Alvare, Helen, 276, 331, 334
America, editorials in, 251

{485}

American Baptist Churches USA, 130–131
American Baptists' Friends for Life, 290
American Century, 293
American Citizens Concerned for Life, 164
American Civil Liberties Union, 244
American College of Obstetricians and Gynecologists, 244
American Federation of Labor – Congress of Industrial Organizations (AFL-CIO), 33, 50, 72, 226
American Jewish Congress, 223
American Life League, 241, 243, 381
American Medical Association, 77, 177, 331
Americans for Community and Faith-Centered Enterprise, 355
Americans for SALT, 171, 175
Americans United for Separation of Church and State, 210–211
Anderson, Carl, 240, 241–242, 364–365, 367
Andover conference, 18
Angrosino, Michael, 315, 317
Anti-Ballistic Missile (ABM) and SALT II Treaties, 213
anti-Catholicism, 13, 245
anti-nuclearism, 23
anti-poverty programs, 78
anti–Vietnam war movement, 95
Arinze, Francis, 369
arms race, 198
Ave Maria, 75

Baker, Donald, 81–83, 87, 92
Baker, James, 206–207, 251
Balkan Peninsula, 378–379
Ball, William, 81, 82–83, 87, 161; of Committee on Law and Public Policy, 126; family planning and, 89; states' rights initiative and, 126
Baptists, abortion and, 131
Barnes, Fred, 321–322
Baroni, Geno, 68, 73, 181; Richard M. Nixon and, 115; parish assignment of, 123; SALT II and, 175; United States Catholic Conference and, 119–120; Washington Archdiocese Office of Urban Affairs and, 118
Barr, William, 236
Barrett, Donald, 91
Barry, William, 271
Baton Rouge, 39
Bauer, Gary, 231, 234, 235

Bayh, Birch, 162–163
Bay of Pigs, 16, 18
Beal v. Doe, 157, 188–189
Beard, Edward, 187
Bennett, John, 58
Berger, Samuel, 306
Bergthold, Linda, 316
Berlin crisis, 16
Berliner, Robert, 125, 125
Bernardin, Joseph, 8, 114, 204, 212, 214, 263; on abortion, 153, 156, 159–160, 165, 166, 174, 184, 185–186, 287, 326; Jimmy Carter and, 175, 186, 195; "consistent ethic of life" and, 290, 381; ethnic cleansing in Bosnia and, 295–296; Fordham lecture of, 247; foreign policy and, 170; as great communicator, 245–246; health care reform and, 180, 318; John Paul II and, 207–208; legislative strategy of, 279–280; liberal leadership of, 140; Richard M. Nixon and, 115; Presidential Medal of Freedom and, 319; Ronald Reagan and, 202, 204; states' rights amendment and, 161; *Time* magazine, 217; as United States Catholic Conference and 134, 145; on war and peace, 199, 200, 211, 251, 254, 255, 333; world hunger and, 150
Berrigan, Daniel, 58, 60, 105–106, 109; antiwar movement and, 61, 63, 104, 140, 344; exile to Mexico of, 61; prison sentence of, 101; resurfacing of, 100–101
Berrigan, Philip, 42, 60, 61, 109; antiwar campaign of, 63, 101, 140, 344; resurfacing of, 100–101; trial of, 103
Berryman, Philip, 270
Bethell, Tom, 226
Bevilacqua, Anthony, 266, 304, 327, 352, 355–356, 364–365
Biden, Joseph, 234, 237
bilateral SALT framework, 171
Birmingham crisis, 30
birth control: Catholic Church on, 7, 145, 380–381; distribution of devices, 49; Lyndon Baines Johnson and, 76–93; John F. Kennedy and, 43–50; rhythm method of, 7; right of privacy and, 84
bishops: on abortion, 11, 280–281; "The Challenge of Peace" and, 6, 11; on communist nations, 16–17; and education, 2, 26; on Iraq war, 251–252; Lyndon Baines Johnson and, 57–60; *La Civilta Cattolica*

(1990) and, 6; procrastination of, 105–108; "Resolution on Southeast Asia" and, 102; "Resolution on the Pastoral Concern of the Church for People on the Move" and, 138–139; role in shaping political dialogue, 9; on social justice, 7–8, 11, 88; on U.S. policy in the Balkans, 306; Vatican Council II and, 24; SALT II and, 172–173; September 11, 2001, terrorist attacks and, 6; Vietnam War and, 104–105, 249
Blackmun, Harry, 123, 248
Blackwell, Morton, 98, 231, 234, 236
Blankenbaker, Ronald, 311
Blix, Hans, 339
Blum, Virgil, 168
Body and Soul, 315
"Bonds of Union" statement, 41
B-1 bomber, 173
Bookbinder, Hyman, 91
Bordelon, Marvin, 100, 101
Bork, Robert, 157, 243
Born-Alive Infants Protection Act (2002), 366, 373
Bosnia, 294–300, 378–379
Bosnia-Herzegovina, 295
Bottum, Joseph, 357
Bowen, Otis, 241
Bowles, Chester, 48
Bowman, Carl, 286
Boxer, Barbara, 277
Boyer, Peter, 380
Boynton v. Virginia, 27
Brennan, William, 184, 282
Breyer, Stephen, 330
Brezhnev, Leonid, 173, 200; SALT II and, 169, 171–172
Brown, John, 118–119
Brown, Judie, 243
Brown, Paul, 235
Brown, Robert McAfee, 64
Brown v. Board of Education of Topeka, 25–26; analogy to abortion, 275
Brunini, Joseph, 112
Bruskewitz, Fabian, 369
Bryce, Edward, 234, 235
Brzezinski, Zbigniew, 172, 174
Buchanan, Patrick, 96, 121, 123, 176, 232, 268, 285; as White House aide, 95, 106, 121, 379; as White House communications director, 226–227
Buchen, Philip, 155, 154

Buckley, Francis, 97
Buckley, James, 120, 126, 238
Buckley, William F., 212, 238, 264, 266, 274–275, 341, 379
Budget Reconciliation Act (1982), 219
Burdick, Quentin, 161
Burdick Amendment, 162
Burke, Raymond, 367–368
Burnham, Walter, 291
Burns, Harmon, 45, 46, 57, 78
Burrill, Donald, 287
Burtchaell, James, 241
Bury, Harry, 105
Bush, George Herbert Walker, 11–12, 249–292, 320, 335; on abortion, 12, 13, 249, 272–292, 319, 381–382; Catholics for, 263; election of 1988, 259, 263; election of 1992, 259, 285, 286; family and community values and, 264, 265–266, 272; family planning and, 268; foreign policy of, 249, 250, 257–258; implications in deaths of Bosnian civilians, 296; John Paul II and, 243, 348; Rodney King riots and, 260–261; Bernard Law and, 277; legislative strategy of, 279–280; March for Life and, 273; Slobodan Milošević and, 300; John O'Connor and, 258; Persian Gulf War and, 249–259; as president for Catholics, 292; at Red Mass for Catholic lawyers, 264; taxes and, 257, 269; Clarence Thomas and, 266; "thousand points of light" and, 266–267; urban crisis and, 249, 259–272; on war and peace, 11–12, 249; on War on Poverty, 354
Bush, George Walker, 335–376; abortion and, 12, 13, 362–376, 381–382; Catholic support for, 350–351; dualistic worldview of, 346; election of 2000, 335; election of 2004, 9, 335, 373, 376; embryonic stem cell research and, 363–365; faith-based initiative of, 12, 14, 335, 349–362; faith in God and, 338–339, 349; Iraq and, 335–349; John Paul II and, 336–337, 342, 348, 371–372; on leadership of Catholic Church, 353–354; as Methodist, 362; National Security strategy of, 336; Pio Laghi and, 338; post-9/11 foreign policy, 347; presidency of, 12; in redefining Christian conservatism, 360–361; on social justice, 12; Supreme Court appointments by, 372–373; terrorism and, 344; as Texas governor, 350; on war and peace, 6, 9–10, 12
Bush, Laura, 348

Butler, Francis, 149
Butterfield, Alexander, 96
Byrd, Robert, 135, 277–278

Cabirac, Henry, 28–29, 33, 39
Caddell, Patrick, 185
Cahill, Susan, 270
Cairo Conference, 323–325, 331, 333
Califano, Joseph, 60, 73, 85, 86, 88–89; abortion and, 188; Jimmy Carter and, 181–182; Hyde Amendment and, 189; national health insurance and, 176–177, 178, 180
Callahan, Daniel, 59
Calley, William, 105
Cambodia, 100–101, 134
Cannon, James, 155
Cantwell, Daniel, 31
Caput, Charles, 366, 369–370
Caputo, Philip, 254
Carberry, John, 105, 108, 186
Carmody, Bill, 370
Carr, John, 264, 271, 308–309
Carter, James Earl, Jr., "Jimmy," 169–197; on abortion, 11, 13, 159, 167, 184–197, 321, 382; arms race and, 169, 171–172, 200, 201; as Baptist, 169, 176; Joseph Bernardin and, 186; Catholic appointments of, 182; Catholic support for, 169–170; defense budget of, 219; diary of, 173, 189; election of 1976, 138, 148, 168, 186, 188; election of 1980, 190, 195; foreign policy and, 169–171; as governor of Georgia, 185; health care and, 176–184, 307; on human rights, 169, 170; Hyde Amendment and, 194, 197; inflation and, 177; John Paul II and, 172; as liberal, 230; National Catholic News Service interview of, 195; Notre Dame address of, 173, 175; nuclear war and, 169–176; opposition to anti-abortion amendment, 158; postponement of neutron bomb, 173; Pregnancy Disability Benefits Act (1978) and, 187; Religious Right and, 196; Soviets and, 173; Sarah Weddington and, 193; White House Conference on Families and, 190, 193–194
Casaroli, Agostino, 202–203, 204, 208, 209
Casey, Richard, 372
Casey, Robert, 284
Cashen, Henry, 158
Castel Gandolfo, 363–364, 365

Castelli, Jim, 138, 150, 176, 182, 183; abortion and, 165, 167, 196; *The American Catholic People*, 8
Casti Connubi ("Of Chaste Marriage," encyclical of Pius XI), 7, 77
Castillo, Dennis, 270
Catholic Alliance, 332
Catholic Association for International Peace, 18, 100; World Order Committee of, 58
Catholic bishops of South Vietnam, 52–53
Catholic Campaign for Human Development, 355, 359
Catholic Catechism, 337
Catholic Charities, 266, 267, 308–309, 355; Jimmy Carter and, 173; 1979 convention of, 183; on H.R. 7, 358; public awareness of, 286; refugee crisis and, 378
Catholic Church: arms control in division of, 173–174; George W. Bush and, 353–354; closing of schools by, 261–262; Hispanic ministry, and, 262; hunger and, 359; Islam and, 257; racism and, 262–263; sexual abuse scandal and, 358–359, 365; social justice and, 6; urban crisis of, 261–263; on war and peace, 170, 295, 296, 336, 377
Catholic Daughters of the Americas, 220, 266, 279
Catholic Digest, 109
Catholic Golden Age, 265, 266, 279
Catholic Health Association (CHA), 266, 317, 365; annual assembly of, 313–314; "Controlling Expenditures under National Healthcare Reform," 309; Jack Curley and, 310–311; health care plan of, 308, 311
Catholic health care campaign, 315–316
Catholic Hospital Association, 179
Catholic Interracial Council, 25, 29, 31, 41, 68, 70
Catholic Lawyers Guild, 279
Catholic League for Religious and Civil Rights, 245, 353
Catholic Left, 95, 105–106, 109, 378
Catholic Peace Fellowship, 60, 61, 102
Catholic Publishing Center of the College of St. Thomas, 109
Catholic Relief Services, 134, 301
Catholics for a Free Choice, 276
Catholics for Christian Political Action, 182
Catholic social teaching, 90, 166, 190, 218, 222–227, 269–271, 315, 318, 356, 360, 380, 382

Catholic Voter Project, 331
Catholic War Veterans, 98
Catholic Women's Club, 40
Celebrezze, Anthony, 83
Centesimus Annus (encyclical) of John Paul II, 265, 266
central cities, poverty in, 259–260
Chabot, Steve, 366
"The Challenge of Peace," 215, 302; as antinuclear pastoral, 305–306; arms race and, 213, 214–215, 295; legacy of, 217; Persian Gulf conflict and, 254; second draft of, 6, 204–206, 210
Chaput, Charles, 352
Charity, Aid, Recovery, and Empowerment (CARE) Act, 355, 361
Cheney, Dick, 341, 346, 363
Chief Administrators of Catholic Education, 220
child care legislation, 264
China, 104, 108
Chopko, Mark, 274
Chou Lee, 138
Christian Coalition, 332
"Christianity and Communism," 221–222
Christiansen, Drew, 302
Christi Matri ("To the Mother of Christ") (encyclical), 59, 62
Christopher, Warren, 295
church attendance and donations, 269, 358–360
Cicognani, Amleto, 22, 24
civil rights: Lyndon Baines Johnson and, 10, 64–76; John F. Kennedy and, 10, 25–43
Civil Rights Act (1964), 10, 64, 67, 70, 73
Civil Rights Act (1991), 266
Clark, Joe, 230
Clark, William, 200, 203, 206, 210
Clarke, Kevin, 360
Clausen, A. W., 238
Clergy and Laymen Concerned about Vietnam, 61, 64
Clinton, Hillary Rodham, 307–308, 309–311, 314, 315, 333
Clinton, William Jefferson "Bill," 293–334; on abortion, 12, 13, 311–312, 316–317, 319–334, 382; Balkans and, 13–14, 294–300, 303–304, 378–379; conscience clause and, 316; in election of 1992, 259, 319; in election of 1996, 299, 314–315; health care and, 307–319; Jesuit education and, 315; John Paul II and, 296, 297–299, 306, 323–324, 348; Mother Teresa and, 322–323; presidency of, 12; on social justice, 12; Supreme Court appointments of, 322, 330; on war and peace, 12; welfare reform and, 349, 350
Clinton-Magaziner task force, 308, 310, 316
Coats, Dan, 311
Cody, John, 29, 33, 144; on abortion, 125; Ad Hoc Committee on Pro-Life Activities of, 126; Congressional testimony, 126, 130; on racial issues, 38, 71
Cohen, David, 361
Cohen, Wilbur, 81, 86, 87, 91
Cold War, 9, 10, 11, 105–106, 355
Cole, Ken, 152
Coleman, John, 269, 380
College of Obstetricians and Gynecologists, 328
Colombo, Furio, 257
Colson, Charles, 101, 104, 106, 109, 120, 121
Committee for a Just and Legitimate Peace, 55
Committee for a Sane Nuclear Policy, 18
Commonweal (Catholic journal), 17, 95, 96, 97, 107, 109, 139
communism, 17, 105
Community Solutions Act (2001), 353
Conference of Catholic Bishops' Committee for Pro-Life Activities, 8, 329, 366–367, 370
Conference of Major Superiors of Men, 99, 257
Conference on Religion and Race, 30, 32, 33, 36
Congress, U.S., 67, 133, 135–136, 250–251. *See also* House of Representatives, U.S.; Senate, U.S.
Conkin, Paul, 76
Connally, John, 123
Connor, James, 154
conscience clause in Clinton's health care plan, 316, 317–318
Consedine, William, 23, 82–84, 91, 101
Consultation on Christian Concern for Peace, 97
contraception. *See* birth control
Cooke, Terence: Bayh subcommittee and, 162–163; as cardinal-elect, 95–96; Jimmy Carter and, 186, 190; Catholic Relief Services and, 143; Catholic schools and, 109; fair housing legislation and, 72; Richard M. Nixon and, 107, 121, 123, 158;

Cooke, Terence (*continued*)
    pro-life and, 124, 153–154, 155, 165, 168, 188, 196; Reagan's quoting of, 242–243; war and, 96, 100, 102, 103, 104, 107, 211
Corcoran, Lawrence, 146, 182
Cordes, Paul, 301
Coreil, Bernice, 308–309, 313, 315, 317
Cornell, Thomas, 102, 140
Corsa, Leslie, 82
Cosgrove, John, 113–114, 115, 116, 125
Cosgrove, Thomas, 114
Coston, Carol, 143
Cousins, Norman, 18–20, 23
Cousins, William, 23
Cowan, James, 154
Cox, William, 164–165, 166
Coyle, Maryanna, 311–312, 317–318
Coyne, Christopher, 368
Craven, Marie, 232, 233
Critchlow, Donald, 9
Croatia, 294, 295
Croatian National Union of the United States and Canada, 297
Cronin, John: civil rights and, 41, 67, 69, 70, 74; Congressional testimony, 33; interreligious cooperation and, 37; National Catholic Conference for Interracial Justice and, 66; Social Action Department of National Catholic Welfare Conference and, 28, 65; violence and, 39–40; writings of, 23, 26, 34
Cronkite, Walter, 156–157
Cropp, Dwight, 277
Cuban Missile Crisis, 10, 18–19, 38
Cuomo, Mario, 247, 281
Curley, Jack, 310–311, 313–314, 317
Curtis, Walter, 84, 126
Cushing, Richard, 21, 24, 32, 47, 80, 85; Cold War and, 16, 17, 18, 22; John F. Kennedy and, 24, 50

Daley, Joseph, 158
Dalgiewicz, Irene, 100
Daly, Mary, 129
Danforth, John, 313–314
Dang Sy, 57
Daschle, Tom, 313–314, 329, 361
Davis, Cyprian, 41, 263
Day, Dorothy, 61, 140, 345
Dayton Accords, 299
Dearden, John, 39, 73–74, 110–111, 128, 196

Dechant, Virgil, 240
"Declaration of Conscience," 60–61
Dee, John, 105
Deedy, John, 261–262
Defense, U.S. Department of, 159
Defense Authorization Act, 331
defense spending, Catholics and, 176
Degeneffe, Charles, 358
Delaney, James, 72
Delmolino, Deno, 98–99
Democratic Party: abortion planks of, 194–195; Catholics and, 94, 270
détente, 108
Dickinson, William, 75
DiIulio, John, 350, 351, 352, 353, 357, 359, 361
Dillon, Michele, 382
Dimino, Joseph, 320
Dingman, Maurice, 179
Dionne, E. J., 382
Dirksen, Everett, 65
distributive justice, 6
Doar, John, 71
"Doctrinal Note on Some Questions Regarding the Participation of Catholics in Political Life," 370
Doerflinger, Richard, 236, 381
Doe v. Bolton, 123, 274
Doherty, Edward, 170–171, 213, 215
Dole, Elizabeth, 206–207, 220–221
Dole, Robert, 297, 299, 314–315
Donnellan, Thomas, 149, 154, 174, 185–186, 223
Donnelly, Dorothy, 195
Donnelly, Robert, 270
Donahue, William, 353
Donohue, Thomas, 223
Dornan, Robert, 182, 239, 241–242
Douay Bible, 2
Dougherty, John, 59, 86, 108, 140
Douglas, William, 155
Douglass, Bruce, 229
Douglass, James, 60
Down syndrome, 326
Draper, William, 85, 86
Draper Report, 43
Dred Scott, 36, 329
Drinan, Robert, 16, 98, 101, 128
D'Souza, Dinesh, 242, 244
Dugan, George, 163
Dukakis, Michael, 263, 264
Dulles, Avery, 269

Dungan, Ralph, 23, 29, 31–33, 42, 45–46, 49, 67
Dunne, Jo, 12, 131
Durbin, Richard, 239

Eagleburger, Lawrence, 202
Eagleton, Thomas, 186
East, John, 232
"Economic Justice for All," 7, 228, 359
Economic Opportunity, Office of, 73, 78, 85, 87, 114
Economic Opportunity Act (1964), 82–83, 90
economic pastoral, 225–228
Economic Recovery Tax Act (1981), 219
Ecumenical Council, 37
Ecumenical Witness, 102–103
Edstrom, Eve, 49
Edwards, John, 371
Egan, Edward, 338, 352, 356, 364–366
Egan, Eileen, 100
Egan, John, 112
Ehrlichman, John, 112–113, 117
Eisenhower, Dwight D., 15, 16; birth control policy of, 46, 49; Draper Report and, 43; John XXIII and, 21
Eizenstat, Stuart, 177, 181, 185, 186
Ekeh, Ono, 368
Elliot, Roland, 136–137, 147
Elliott, Peter, 325
Ellis, John Tracy, 195, 261
Emanuel, Rahm, 329
embryonic stem cell research, 363–365
Engle, Randy, 155
Equal Employment Opportunity Commission, 187
Equal Rights Amendment, 237
Espy, R. H., 114
Etchegarry, Roger, 338
"Ethical Reflections on the Cultural Crisis" (pastoral), 225
ethnic cleansing, 12, 295–296, 302
Ethnic Heritage Studies Act, 220
Evangelium Vitae ("Gospel of Life") (encyclical), 325–326, 333
Evans, Rowland, 83
excommunication of pro-choice politicians, 281

Fahey, Joseph, 175
Fahrenkopf, Frank, 246
Fair Housing Act (1968), 10, 64, 72–73
"Fair Housing Sunday," 70
faith-based initiatives, 335, 349–362
Falwell, Jerry, 196, 246
Family Assistance Plan, 112, 113, 114–115, 117, 121, 132
family planning, 232, 268, 289–290
Family Planning Services and Population Research Act, 127, 129
Family Security System, 112
Farmer, James, 27
Favarola, John, 352
federal aid to Catholic schools, 23
Feinstein, Dianne, 329
Ferkiss, Victor, 20
fetal research, 289
Fetterhoff, Howard, 149–150
Fifteenth Amendment, 68
Findlay, James, 38
Fink, Judith, 164
Fiorenza, Joseph, 301, 303, 304, 305, 351, 364
First Amendment, 77
First Things, 265, 357, 360–361
Fiske, Edward, 103
Fitzpatrick, Joseph, 269
Fitzsimmons, Ron, 327
Flanagan, Bernard, 109
Flanigan, Peter, 102, 103, 107, 120
Flock of Shepherds, A (Reese), 270, 271–272
Flynn, Raymond, 305, 321–323, 325, 332–333
Foley, Heather Strachan, 308
Foley, William, 308
Fong, Hiram, 161–162, 163
Food for Peace, 82, 142, 144, 145, 147, 150
food security, 142
food stamps, 149
Ford, Betty, 152
Ford, Gerald R., 133–168; on abortion, 11, 13, 133, 152–168, 272, 381–382; as commander-in-chief, 134; in election of 1976, 138, 148, 151–152, 188; at Eucharistic Congress in Philadelphia, 159; on foreign aid, 153; on hunger, 11, 140–152; Hyde Amendment and, 168; Paul VI and, 144; presidency of, 10–11, 133–134, 141; at Red Mass, 145; refugees and, 133–141; on social justice, 11; at University of Notre Dame, 150; on war and peace, 10–11, 200, 378
Ford, John, 78
Foreign Affairs and Restructuring Act, 329
Foreign Assistance Act, 84
foreign policy, 109, 140, 170, 259

Forest, James, 60, 61
Forrest, John, 101
Forrestal, Michael, 57
Forty-First International Eucharistic Congress, 150
Foster, Gregory, 340–341
Fourteenth Amendment, 77, 157
Fourth Amendment, 77
Francis, Dale, 193
Frank, Stephen, 344
Frantz, Wanda, 320
Freedom of Access to Clinic Entrances Act, 321, 323–324
Freedom of Choice Act, 284, 320, 322, 331
Freedom Riders, 27–28, 30, 42
Fried, Charles, 275
Friedman, Thomas, 344
Friends for Life, 192
Friendship House, 34
Fulbright Amendment, 77

Gage Park, 71
Gag rule, 322
Gaillot, B. J., 26, 28
Galante, Joseph, 369
Gallup, George, 8, 183
Gammill, James, 193
Gardner, John, 83, 91
Gardner, Richard, 44, 45, 46, 90–91
Garton, Jean, 130
Gaud, William, 87
Gaudium et Spes ("Of Hope and Joy"), 170, 172
general justice, 6
Geneva Convention prisoner rules, 56
George, Francis, 369
Gephardt, Richard, 178
Gerety, Peter, 170
Gerster, Carolyn, 232
Gibbs, Susan, 369
G.I. Bill, 3
Giglio, James, 37, 41
Ginsburg, Ruth Bader, 322
Glendon, Mary Ann, 286, 333
"God's Hope in a Time of Fear," 203–204
Goeglein, Timothy, 358, 362
Goldberg, Arthur, 33, 54, 58
Goldwater, Barry, 52, 67
Goodstein, Laurie, 347
Gorbachev, Mikhail, 213, 214, 216, 252–253, 257

Gore, Al, 311, 313, 324, 350
Gore, Tipper, 311, 313
Gould, William, 229
Graham, Billy, 22, 253–254
Graham, John, 244
Grant, Murray, 78–79, 81
Gray, Nellie, 155, 239, 241, 243
Greater Unity Force, 53
Great Society, 64, 111, 260–261
Greeley, Andrew, 61–62, 88, 92, 99, 106, 216, 245, 286, 343, 370
Gregory, Wilton, 336–337, 343, 358, 369
Greuning, Ernest, 80, 84
Gribbin, William, 231, 236
Griffin, Michael, 321, 340
Griffin, Richard, 105
Grimm, Angela, 242
Griscom, Tom, 243
Griswold v. Connecticut, 77
Gumbleton, Thomas, 109, 252; political views of, 107, 108, 140–141, 174; Ronald Reagan and, 201, 203, 207
Gunn, David, 321
Guth, James, 322

Haig, Alexander, 103, 201–202, 224
Haldeman, H. R., 103, 132
Hall, Tony, 353
Hallinan, Paul, 26, 59, 86
Hamill, Pete, 111, 121
Hanify, Edward, 129, 161
Hanna, Mary, 8, 109, 182, 183
Hannan, Philip, 23, 27, 86, 105, 207, 210–211, 239; Ronald Reagan and, 203–204; on war, 108, 173–174, 337
Harding, Patricia, 104
Harkin, Tom, 367
Harris, Patricia Roberts, 174, 190
Harrisburg Seven, 103
Harris v. McRae, 189–190
Hart, Jeffrey, 107
Hart, John, 299, 328
Hartman, Robert, 145
"Harvest of Justice Is Sown in Peace, The" (pastoral), 296
Harvey, Thomas, 229
Hatch, Orrin, 233, 314
Hatch amendment, 233, 234, 236, 240–241
Hatcher, Robert, 185
Hathaway, Edward, 337–338
Hauser, Rita, 132

Havel, Vaclav, 301
Hays, Brooks, 24
Head Start, 260, 261
Health, Education, and Welfare, U.S. Department of, 85, 159
"Health and Health Care" (pastoral), 308
health care, 176–184, 307–319
Health Care Extension Act, 127
Health Insurance Portability and Accountability Act (1996), 314
Health Security Act, 311, 312, 317
Hehir, Bryan: "The Challenge of Peace" and, 302, 379; Congressional testimony, 229; Democratic Party and, 174; human rights and, 140; radical Catholic left and, 140; social justice and, 380; war and, 143, 201, 216, 255, 305, 378; world hunger and, 145, 146
Hellegers, Andres, 87, 88
Helms, Jesse, 157–158, 231, 232, 235–236, 246
Henican, Ellis, 38
Henry, Carl, 63–64
Herman, Edward, 139
Hesburgh, Theodore, 11, 22, 28, 175, 304, 354, 378; Carter administration and, 174–175; nuclear weapons and, 171, 379; recommendations of, 174; University of Notre Dame and, 98, 100, 150; U.S. Civil Rights Commission and, 123
Hessey, Bob, 322
Hickey, James, 207, 254, 263, 277, 279, 308–309; Bill Clinton and, 324; faith-based initiatives and, 351; "partial-birth" abortion ban and, 326
Higgins, George, 23–24, 33, 52, 67–69, 222; abortion and, 166; antiwar vigil and, 57–58; of National Catholic Welfare Conference Social Action Department, 37, 68–69; Richard M. Nixon and, 115
Hill and Knowlton (public relations firm), 280
Hilley, John, 328
Hiroshima, Japan, 199
Hispanic-Americans, 262, 269
History of Black Catholics, The (Davis), 263
Hitchcock, James, 182
Hmong people, 134
Hoang Quynh, 53
Ho Chi Minh, 55, 96, 137
Hodgson v. Minnesota, 281, 289
Hogan, Joseph, 229
Hogan, Lawrence, 125, 126

Hogan, Timothy, 340
Holbrook, Robert, 164
Holbrooke, Richard, 299, 300
Hoopes, Tom, 302
Horan, Dennis, 131
hospital industry, 177
House of Representatives, U.S., 115–116, 163, 164, 229, 252, 279
Housing and Urban Development, U.S. Department of, 71, 220
Hoye, Daniel, 207, 208, 227, 237
Hoyt, Robert, 99
H.R. 7, 357, 358
Huddleston, Barbara, 148
Hudson, Deal, 9, 350, 352, 368, 371, 380
Hughes, Edward, 313, 317
Humanae Vitae ("Of Human Life") (encyclical), 7, 128, 168, 195–196
humanitarian intervention, 148, 304, 305
Human Life Amendment, 125, 166, 191
"Human Life in Our Day," 106, 113
human rights, 140, 169, 170
Humphrey, Hubert H., 62, 104, 123, 149
Hunter, James Davis, 286
Hunthausen, Raymond, 201, 252
Hurley, Francis, 75; anti-nuclearism and, 23; birth control and, 83, 85–86, 91; civil rights and, 32, 42; foreign policy and, 48, 50; Human Life Amendment and, 166; population policy and, 46, 89; social security amendments and, 90; War on Poverty and, 80, 81
Hussein, Saddam, 253, 338, 378; capture of, 341; defiance of Resolution 1441, 339; 'despotic power' of, 337; Iran-Iraq war and, 250
Hutchinson, Tracy, 343
Hyde, Henry, 160, 206, 231, 310; as pro-life, 239, 241–242; Ronald Reagan and, 206; at University of Notre Dame, 247
Hyde Amendment, 190, 231–232, 244, 321; abortion and, 160, 309–310; administration support for, 194, 195, 197; Barbara Boxer and, 277; court attack on, 189; Medicaid funding and, 189; passage and signing of, 168, 237, 310, 322; renewing, 236

Imani Temple, 262
incest, abortion and, 282, 289–290
Indochina Migration and Refugee Assistance Act (1975), 135–136

Indochinese refugees, 133–141
inflation, 177
informed consent, 239, 240, 282
Institution of Peace and Progress, 17–18
intact dilation and evacuation (IDE), 326, 366
Intermediate Nuclear Forces Treaty (1987), 214, 251
International Conference on Population and Development (Cairo), 323–325, 331, 333
International Synod of Bishops, 170, 171
Interreligious Clearinghouse Meeting, 69
Iran-Iraq War (1980–88), 250
Iraq, 250, 335–349
Irish-Americans, 2
Islam, 257
Israel, 258

Jadot, Jean, 163
Jashari, Adem, 300
Jelen, Ted, 381
Jepsen, Roger, 237–238
Jim Crow segregation, 25
Jobs Opportunities Training and Placement programs, 147
John Paul II, 216, 225, 246, 254, 270, 378; on abortion, 189, 283, 323, 329–330; Balkan crisis and, 295, 306; Joseph Bernardin and, 207–208; Blessed Hyacinth Cormier O.P. Medal and, 372; George W. Bush and, 336–337, 342, 363–364, 371–372; *Centesimus Annus* (encyclical) of, 265, 266; Dick Cheney and, 341; Bill Clinton and, 296–299, 306, 323–324; Cold War and, 11; death of, 348; *Evangelium Vitae* ("Gospel of Life") and, 325–326; Joseph Francis and, 262; on gap between rich and poor, 227; Mikhail Gorbachev and, 252–253; humanitarian intervention and, 296; influence of, 306; invasion of Afghanistan and, 12; Iraq and, 345; on Israelis and Palestinians, 258; 1988 address to diplomatic corps, 214; Sadako Ogara and, 302–303; Parkinson's disease of, 347, 363; on Persian Gulf crisis, 256–257; plea at Newark meeting, 299; Presidential Medal of Freedom and, 342; Ronald Reagan, and, 199–200, 202–203, 204, 208, 212; sexual abuse scandal and, 365; Metropolitan Simeon and, 347; stem cell research and, 364; on terrorism, 348; travels of, 172, 183, 224–225, 299–300, 321; 2003 address to Vatican diplomatic corps, 337; on war, 253, 304–305; women's rights and, 333; on war and peace, 207, 252–253, 302, 305, 345
Johnson, Donald, 96
Johnson, Douglas, 241, 277, 289
Johnson, James, 9, 254
Johnson, Lyndon Baines, 38, 51–93, 104; birth control and, 76–93; Catholic bishops and, 57–60; civil rights and, 64–76; on Cold War, 10; death of, 10, 124; fair housing legislation under, 71–73; Great Society of, 64, 112, 149; health care system and, 181; National Day of Prayer of, 72; poverty and, 76, 229–230; on social justice, 10; State of the Union addresses of, 79, 80, 88, 91; on UN, 80; Vietnam War and, 10, 11, 51–64, 104–105, 348, 378; on war and peace, 10; War on Poverty and, 10, 90, 118, 354
John XXIII: Balzan Peace Prize and, 20; birthday of, 16; Norman Cousins on, 19–20; on Cuban missile crisis, 18, 19; death of, 21; encyclicals of, 7, 18, 20, 23, 37, 66, 170, 379; foundations laid by, 51; 1961 Easter message of, 16; on nuclear arms, 20, 106, 378–379; pontificate of, 24–25; on racism, 66
Jones, Davlyn, 165
Jones, Edith, 282
Jony, Mary (pseud.), 343
Jordan, Daniel, 255
Josephite Order, 42
Joyce, Michael, 264, 355
Justum bellum, 337
just-war theory, 4–5, 6, 139, 252, 254, 255, 304; George H. W. Bush and, 249; of Catholic Church, 295, 337; criteria for, 4, 99, 254; invasion of Afghanistan and, 6; pacifism versus, 305; Persian Gulf War and, 251–252, 259; of proportionality, 201; supreme emergency exemption in, 5

Kagan, Elena, 328
Kammer, Fred, 308–309
Kavanaugh, John, 302
Kean, Thomas, 278–279
Keeler, William, 308, 317, 323–324, 338, 364
Kelly, Bernard, 101
Kelly, James, 276, 277
Kelly, Thomas, 167, 175, 183, 193; abortion and, 186–187; on human rights, 170;

national health insurance and, 180; nuclear weapons and, 172–173, 211; Reagan budget and, 219; on Sarah Weddington, 193
Kemp, Jack, 239, 241–242, 271
Kemp-Kasten Amendment, 279
Kennedy, Anthony, 275, 285, 286
Kennedy, Edward "Teddy," 246–247, 312; abortion and, 163, 166; as Catholic liberal, 266; family planning and, 279; health care system and, 178, 181, 314; Iraq war and, 250; James McHugh and, 162
Kennedy, Jacqueline, 50
Kennedy, John F., 9, 15–50; African-Americans' support for, 40; anti-Communism of, 17; appearance before Greater Houston Ministerial Association in 1960, 42; approval rating of, 39; on arms control, 22, 50; assassination of, 36, 45, 50, 64, 65; on birth control, 43–50; on church-state questions, 22; on civil rights, 10, 25–43, 50; Bill Clinton and, 334; Cold War and, 9, 20; Conference on Religion and Race and, 32; conservative-liberal split under, 41–42; Cuba and, 10, 16, 18–19; in election of 1960, 1, 8, 12–13, 25, 94; foreign policy of, 17, 39, 77; Billy Graham and, 22; Nikita S. Khrushchev and, 16; Ku Klux Klan and, 288; New Frontier of, 64; nuclear arms and, 9–10, 15–25; *Pacem in Terris* ("Peace on Earth") (encyclical) and, 20; Paul VI and, 21–22; on population growth, 46–47; religion and, 23, 31–32; religious prejudice and, 37; social justice and, 10; State of the Union address of, 27
Kennedy, Robert, 36, 85; Mathew Ahmann and, 66; as attorney general, 24, 27, 33; death of, 60; National Conference on Catholic Charities and, 116–117
Kenny, Michael, 251–252
Kenworthy, E. W., 65–66
Kerry, John, 368; on abortion, 368–369, 370, 374–375; as antiwar, 345–346; as Catholic, 343–344, 356; in election of 2004, 1, 8, 12, 13, 356–357, 373; on faith-based social services, 355; on Iraq War, 343–344; Vietnam War and, 102
Khrushchev, Nikita S., 16, 18–19
Kilberg, Bobbie, 143, 289–290
King, Martin Luther, Jr., 34–35, 36, 38; antiwar jeremiad of, 63; assassination of, 73; Catholic Church and, 68, 70; FBI surveillance of, 74; march from Selma to Montgomery, 68–69; Nobel Peace Prize and, 68, 74; speeches of, 35, 71
King, Martin Luther, Sr., 36–37
King, Rodney, 260–261, 267, 270
Kingon, Alfred, 241
Kissinger, Henry Alfred, 103, 107, 142, 143, 144
Kissling, Frances, 276
Kistiakowsky, George, 44
Kleis, Gerald, 138
Klutznick, Philip, 47
Kmech, John, 207
Knights of Columbus, 204, 220, 228, 264, 266, 274, 280–281, 356
Knott, John, 48, 79, 80, 82, 91
Kojelis, Linas, 222
König, Franziskus, 20
Koop, C. Everett, 242, 274
Kosovo, 300, 301–303, 305, 378–379
Kou Yang, 134
Kramer, Michael, 243
Krasicky, Eugene, 153, 161
Krietemeyer, Ronald, 219
Krol, John, 121, 153, 266; on abortion, 109–110, 125, 126; Congressional testimony, 126, 130; as conservative, 108, 205; in election of 1971, 123; national health insurance and, 180; Richard Nixon and, 106, 109, 121; nuclear arms and, 171, 172, 174, 211; at Synod of Bishops in Rome, 107; United States Catholic Conference and, 124
Kromkowski, John, 220
Kuharić, Franjo, 304
Ku Klux Klan (KKK), 2, 192, 288
Kuo, David, 357, 359, 361, 374

La Civiltà Cattolica (1990), 6, 340
Ladan, Dusko, 300
Lader, Lawrence, 191–192
LaFarge, John, 25, 32, 40, 41
Laghi, Pio, 209, 225, 338, 345, 346, 348
Laird, Melvin, 95, 113, 117
Lally, Francis, 18, 146, 179
Lane Tabernacle Church (St. Louis), 31
Lao people, 134
LaPorte, Roger, 61
Law, Bernard: abortion and, 159, 264, 326, 332, 347, 368; George H. W. Bush and, 258, 263, 273, 277; Catholic Lawyers Guild and,

Law, Bernard (*continued*)
279; Committee for Pro-Life Activities and, 329; Persian Gulf conflict and, 254; resignation and, 359; SALT II Treaty and, 212

Lay Commission on Catholic Social Teaching and the U.S. Economy, 224

Leadership Conference of Women Religious, 171, 195, 196, 295

Leadership Conference on Civil Rights, 33, 42

Leary, Joseph, 265, 279

Leavitt, Milo, 84

Lee, Philip, 81, 83, 85, 90, 91

Lefevere, Patricia Scharber, 208

Lehman, John, 201

Leo XIII, *Rerum Novarum* ("Of New Things"), 6, 227, 265

Levi, Edward, 145, 155

Lewis, John, 34–35

"Liberty and Justice for All" (Simon Commission report), 227–228

Line, Mary Dorothy, 327

Lipset, Seymour Martin, 75–76

lobbying, 163, 334; for abortion, 290; for civil rights legislation, 74; for Clinton health care reform, 315–316; for funding embryonic stem cell research, 363

LoConte, Joseph, 360–361

Lofton, John, 159

Long, Russell, 117

Lucey, Robert, 56, 58

Lux, Mike, 308, 312

Lynch, Robert, 127, 161, 263

Magaziner, Ira, 308, 311, 312, 315

Maher v. Roe, 189

Mahony, Roger, 360; abortion and, 317, 320; Arinze and, 369; International Policy Committee and, 251; H.R. 7 and, 354; on King riots, 267; Persian Gulf conflict and, 254, 255, 256; on poverty, 352–353

Maida, Adam, 363

Malone, James, 148, 212, 223–224, 227, 228, 237; abortion and, 154, 165; Jimmy Carter and, 186; Pershing II missiles and, 211

Manckiewicz, Frank, 280

Manning, Timothy, 126, 130

Mansfield, Mike, 52, 53, 54, 96, 99

Mapplethorpe, Robert, 265

March for Life, 366, 375; George H. W. Bush and, 273, 279, 383; George W. Bush and, 362, 368–369; Bill Clinton and, 320; Nellie Gray and, 239; partial-birth abortion and, 365; Ronald Reagan and, 245

March on Washington for Jobs and Freedom, 34, 36

Markey, Edward, 202

Markman, Stephen, 234

Marrs, Theodore, 135, 136, 147

Marshall, Burke, 28–29, 34, 67

Martino, Renato, 341

Mason, Robert, 121

Mass for Peace at St. Patrick's Cathedral, 104

Mater et Magistra ("Mother and Teacher") (encyclical), 6, 7

Matz, Jerome, 358

Mauritania, 143

May, John, 180, 183, 187, 227, 247–248

McCarrick, Theodore, 49, 263, 296, 306, 345, 351, 356; on abortion, 367, 368, 371; on Bosnia and Kosovo, 300, 305; on George W. Bush's faith-based initiative, 351; "Catholic bashing" and, 287–288; John Kerry and, 369; Nancy Pelosi and, 370; on pre-emptive strike against Iraq, 338

McCarthy, Abigail, 257

McCarthy, Colman, 86, 195, 304

McClellan, Mark, 368

McClellan, Scott, 373–374

McConnell, Robert, 233, 234

McDermott, John, 29

McDonough, Timothy, 26

McGovern, George, 123

McGrory, Mary, 96, 332

McGuire, James, 71

McGurn, William, 266, 360

McHugh, James, 7, 84, 113–114, 126, 158, 164; on abortion, 124, 125, 155, 166, 167, 263; Family Life Division of United States Catholic Conference and, 124, 153; family planning and, 128; United States Catholic Conference Committee for Pro-Life Activities and, 162, 189, 277, 331; Women's Lobby lawsuit and, 131; on zero population growth, 130

McIntyre, James, 41, 64, 66, 177

McLaughlin, John, 99

McManus, William, 252

McNicholas, Joseph, 219

McShane, Joseph, 269

Means, Marianne, 164

Mecklenburg, Marjory, 164, 166

Medeiros, Humberto, 108, 110, 130

Medicaid, 189, 260
Meehan, Mary, 233
Meese, Edwin, 223, 231, 232
Melady, Thomas, 121, 158, 259, 263, 265; Nixon's reelection campaign and, 123; as Vatican ambassador, 265–266, 268
Menendez, Albert, 186
Mense Maio ("In the Month of May") (encyclical) of Paul VI, 53
Meredith, James, 29, 70–71
Mexico City policy, 279, 320, 329
Meyer, Albert, 26, 66
Migliore, Celestino, 338
Mikulski, Barbara, 277, 311
Miles, Jack, 340
Military Health Care Initiatives Act, 285
military hospitals, abortions at, 154, 320
Miller, Irwin, 32–33, 42
Miller, Norman, 129–130, 217
Milošević, Slobodan, 12, 294, 295, 299, 300, 302, 305
Minuteman III missiles, 212
Mitchell, George, 250, 255, 283
Monahan, Frank, 185–186, 188, 194
Mondale, Walter, 170, 178, 184, 212, 238
Mongiardo, Victoria, 181, 186
Monterisi, Francesco, 305
Montgomery March, 68–69
Moral Majority, 196, 246
moral theology of war, 99
Morey, Roy, 120–121
Morlion, Felix, 18, 19, 21
Morris, Charles, 8, 326
Morris, Dick, 318
Mother Teresa, 322–323, 350, 355
Moyers, Bill, 52, 60, 80
Moynihan, Daniel Patrick, 75, 90, 111, 112, 114, 184, 229, 284, 297; on "American Catholic hierarchy," 140; Family Assistance Plan and, 115, 117; Iraq war and, 250; racism and, 267–268; as UN ambassador, 139
Mulhauser, Karen, 192
Murnion, Philip, 182, 262
Murphy, Francis, 175, 227
Murphy Brown (CBS comedy), 267

National Abortion and Reproductive Rights Action League, 284, 312, 368
National Abortion Rights Action League, 192, 193, 233, 284
National Association of Evangelicals, 223, 224, 284
National Catholic Conference for Interracial Justice, 26, 27, 36, 67, 69, 71, 72, 74, 149
National Catholic Education Association, 123, 220, 266
National Catholic News Service, 52, 138, 150, 167, 195, 208, 238
National Catholic Welfare Conference (NCWC), 3, 17, 23, 30, 36, 50, 52, 57, 89, 139–140; birth control policies and, 80–81; Catholic Association for International Peace, 40; Catholic Charities of, 80; Catholic Relief Services of, 18, 22; civil rights message of, 23–24, 33, 34, 67, 69; Committee on International Affairs of, 47, 100; Family Life Bureau of, 7, 74, 79; family planning and, 84; Office for United Nations Affairs and, 17, 21, 45, 47, 77–78
National Coalition of American Nuns, 195, 224, 235
National Committee for a Human Life Amendment, 161–162, 164
National Conference of Catholic Bishops, 3, 134
National Conference of Catholic Charities, 115, 146, 149, 179, 182–183, 196, 224, 229
National Conference on Economic and Social Development, 45, 47
National Conference on Religion and Race, 29, 32, 33, 35, 37, 38–39, 40–41, 69, 74
National Council of Catholic Men, 67, 72
National Council of Catholic Women, 17–18, 42, 67, 72, 266, 327
National Council of Churches: on civil rights and race, 29, 30, 38, 66, 70; on First Amendment, 223, 224; interfaith conference and, 102–103; social justice and, 71, 72, 114, 116; on war and peace, 99, 252
National Council of Churches of Christ, 29, 32
National Emergency Committee of Clergy Concerned about Vietnam, 61
National Federation of Catholic College Students, 35, 67, 72
National Federation of Priests' Councils, 103, 112
National Federation of Sodality, 35
national health insurance, 176–177, 178
National Institutes of Health (NIH), 44, 48, 284

National Organization for Women (NOW), 165, 192, 194, 233, 367
National Right to Life Committee, 131, 237, 241, 277; George H. W. Bush and, 289; Kemp-Kasten Amendment and, 279; John Kerry and, 374–375; national health care reform and, 312; officers of, 7, 276, 320; pro-choice groups and, 290, 365
National School Lunch and Child Nutrition Amendments (1975), 146
National Students Association, 96–97
Nativism, 2–3
Navarro-Walls, Joaquin, 301, 323, 324–325
Negro Family, The: The Case for National Action, 75
Neighborhood Self-Development and National Consumer Cooperative Bank Acts, 182
Nelson, Jerome, 154
Nessen, Ron, 156
Neuhaus, Richard, 265, 270, 350
Neusse, Joseph, 41, 80
New Orleans, 26–27, 38
New World Order, 362
Ngo Dinh Diem, 57
Nguyen Khanh, 57
Nguyen Van Thieu, 53, 55
Nicholson, James, 337, 341, 345, 348
Niebuhr, Reinhold, 7, 39
Nineteenth Amendment, 68
Ninth Amendment, 77
Nixon, Richard M., 94–132, 149, 230; on abortion, 10, 13, 123–132, 381–82; Catholics' support for, 104; on Communism, 17; Terence Cooke and, 106; in election of 1960, 94; in election of 1968, 95, 104, 123; in election of 1972, 103, 120, 123; Family Assistance Plan of, 10, 112, 115; foreign policy of, 11, 104, 108, 109; Paul VI and, 95, 101; poverty and, 229–230; resignation of, 133; SALT I and, 108–109, 169, 201; on social justice, 10, 111–123; Vietnam War and, 94–111, 133, 348, 378; on war and peace, 10; Watergate scandal and, 104, 133; on welfare reform, 13, 149, 380
North Atlantic Treaty Organization (NATO), 200, 303
North Vietnam, 52, 104
Notre Dame, University of: abortion and, 284–285; George H. W. Bush and, 266, 267, 284; George W. Bush and, 354; Jimmy Carter and, 169, 173, 175; Bill Clinton and, 318; Gerald Ford and, 150; Ronald Reagan and, 199
Novak, Michael, 96, 105, 224, 337
Novak, Robert, 83
nuclear arms race, 9–10
nuclear freeze, 202, 211–212, 255
Nuclear Nonproliferation Treaty (1968), 63
Nuclear testing, 10, 19, 20
nuclear war: Jimmy Carter and, 169–176; John F. Kennedy and, 15–25; Ronald Reagan and, 198–217

Obama, Barack, 361
Oberdorfer, Louis, 33, 42
O'Boyle, Patrick, 65, 70, 78, 81; Catholic Interracial Council of Washington and, 68; civil rights movement and, 25–26, 27, 30, 32, 34, 39, 42, 64, 68, 71; freedom of clergy to demonstrate and, 69; on *Humanae Vitae*, 128; King assassination and, 73; March on Washington and, 34, 35; National Catholic Welfare Conference and, 34, 66; Resurrection City and, 71–72; social justice and, 112; Washington Peace Mass and, 54–55
O'Brien, David, 254, 270
O'Brien, William, 18, 97
O'Byrne, Brendan, 345
O'Connor, John, 209, 212, 263, 278, 280–281; George H. W. Bush and, 258, 264; on Cairo Conference, 324; Congressional Gold Medal and, 363; excommunication threat against, 288; war and peace pastoral, 237; war spending and, 251
O'Connor, Sandra Day, 232–233, 275, 286
Odle, Robert, 101
O'Donnell, Charles, 58
O'Donnell, Edward, 185, 288
Oettinger, Katherine, 85
O'Gara, James, 60, 171
O'Grady, Scott, 297–298
O'Hare, Joseph, 171, 223–224
O'Keefe, Charles, 175–176, 183
Olasky, Marvin, 349–350
O'Malley, Sean, 368
Onek, Joe, 181
"On Racial Harmony" (pastoral letter), 34, 69
Operation Desert Storm, 254–255
O'Rourke, John, 174

Pacem in Terris ("Peace on Earth")
  (encyclical), 21, 23, 24, 25, 37
Packard, David, 290
Paris, Treaty of (1973), 104, 133
Parker, David, 127
parochial schools, 2, 23, 26–27, 39, 109, 261
partial-birth abortion, 12, 325–332, 365–366, 374–375, 381
Partial-Birth Abortion Ban Act (2003), 367, 372, 373
Pastoral Constitution on the Church in the Modern World, 5–6, 63
"Pastoral Plan for Pro-Life Activities," 163–164, 165
Pastore, John, 70, 99
Paul VI, 246; on abortion, 167; on birth control, 84, 87, 145; Christmas message of, 53–54; Easter message of, 95; encyclicals of, 10, 53, 54, 59, 62, 87–88, 89, 170; feeding of world's population and, 81; Gerald R. Ford and, 134, 135, 137; on Indochinese refugees, 134; Lyndon Baines Johnson and, 52, 87, 89–90; John F. Kennedy and, 21–22; on liberalism, 99; Richard M. Nixon and, 95, 101; Ronald Reagan and, 203; on Vietnam War, 51, 55, 96, 101, 104, 110; on war and peace, 21–22, 102, 106–107, 170, 256, 377–378; on War on Poverty, 51
Pax Christi, 175, 215, 251, 254
Peace Pastoral, 203–212
Pearson, Drew, 22
Pelosi, Nancy, 370
Perez, Leander, 26, 28, 33
Persian Gulf War, 249–259
Pfaff, William, 95, 139
Phu Quoc refugees, 136–137
Pilarczyk, Daniel, 252, 253, 255, 256, 257–258, 272
Pilla, Anthony, 228, 306, 319, 327, 328
Pilot (newspaper), 18
Pius XI, 6–7, 17, 77
Pius XII, 7, 45, 106, 254, 301
Planned Parenthood, 83, 192–193, 279
Planned Parenthood v. Casey, 284, 289, 330
Podgorny, Nikolai, 55
Poelker v. Doe, 189
Poland, 109
"Political Responsibility" document, 165–166
Pol Pot, 140
Pontifical Council for Justice and Peace, 8, 296, 338, 343

population explosion, 43–44, 46
Populorum Progressio ("The Progress of People") (encyclical), 89, 170, 195–196
Powers, Thomas, 216
President's Commission on the Causes and Prevention of Violence, 98
Preston, Tommy, 344–345
privacy, 77, 130, 194–195
pro-choice movement, 194, 276–277, 278, 281
Project Bridge, 74
Project Commitment, 73–74
Project Equality, 69
pro-life movement: Bush, George H. W., and, 286–291; Catholics in, 276; priorities of, 240–241; retreat for, 286–287; strength of, 321
proportionality, criterion of, 201, 251
Public Works Employment Act (1975), 147
Puljic, Vinko, 296–297, 304
Purdy, William, 20

Al Qaeda, 6, 335, 336
Quartel, Rob, 151
Quayle, Dan, 267; March for Life and, 273; on UN embargo against Iraq, 265; as vice president, 261, 264
Quinn, Donna, 235
Quinn, Gail, 320
Quinn, John, 187, 192–193; address to Slovenian and Croat parishes, 295; arms control and, 201; "just war" and, 255; national health insurance and, 180; SALT II and, 171, 172; United States Catholic Conference and, 171

racism, 262–263, 267–268
Raimondi, Luigi, 102, 128–129
Rambouillet, France, 300–301, 304
Ramparts (Catholic magazine), 98
rape: abortion and, 282, 289–290; mass, in Bosnia, 295
Ratzinger, Joseph, 208, 209, 367, 370
Rausch, James, 134, 135, 145, 165; on abortion, 153, 156, 157, 161, 163, 166, 195; Jimmy Carter and, 186; Gerald R. Ford and, 135, 153; leadership of, 140; United States Catholic Conference and, 134, 143–144, 147, 184
Reagan, Ronald Wilson, 198–248; on abortion, 11, 13, 230–248, 272, 381–382; arms control and, 13, 176, 198, 214,

Reagan, Ronald Wilson (*continued*)
199–200, 209, 249, 295–296; Catholic
support for, 184; economy and, 217–230;
in election of 1980, 173; in election of
1984, 238; fall of Soviet Union and, 198;
Mikhail Gorbachev and, 213; John Paul II
and, 199–200, 202–204, 208; judicial
appointments of, 270; Mexico City policy
of, 363; nuclear arms and, 198–217, 379;
Paul VI and, 203; Peace Pastoral and,
203–212; population policy of, 239; Joseph
Ratzinger and, 208; support for Catholics
and, 199; Supreme Court appointments
of, 232–233; tax reform policy of, 226;
televangelism and, 217–218
Reaganomics, 218–222, 225
Reed, Bruce, 328
Reed, Victor, 30, 59, 86
Reese, Thomas, 9, 216, 270, 271–272, 302
Reeves, Richard, 139
Refugees, 133–141
Rehnquist, William, 275
Reilly, Daniel, 296, 306
Reilly, Robert, 211, 302
Religion and Society Report, 226
Religion at the Polls (Menendez), 186
reproductive freedom as fundamental human
right, 194–195
Republican Party: Catholics in, 271, 379; 1994
Congressional elections and, 314
Rerum Novarum (encyclical), 6, 227, 265
Resolution 770, 294
"Resolution on Peace," 59–60
"Resolution on the Pastoral Concern of the
Church for People on the Move," 138–139
Ricard, John, 308, 312, 315, 317, 342, 369;
Congressional testimony, 313; lobbying for
Clinton health care reform plan, 315–316
Ricau, Jackson, 26, 28
Rice, Charles, 233, 242
Rice, Condoleezza, 336, 338, 346–347
Ricken, David, 372
Right-to-life movement, 130, 195, 233–234
Rigney, Daniel, 358
Rigney, James, 104
Riley, Martin, 54
Ritter, Joseph, 25, 30, 41, 86
Rivlin, Alice, 313–314, 317
Roach, John, 183, 205, 207, 218, 233; Bosnia
and Kosovo and, 298, 304, 305; defense
budget and, 219; disarmament and, 257;
International Justice and Peace Committee
and, 256, 295; Ronald Reagan and, 221
Roach, Peggy, 33, 42, 72
Robbins, Richard, 98
Roberts, John, 283, 373
Roberts, William, 61
Robertson, Pat, 196, 253–254
Robinson, Aubrey, 131
Robinson, James, 114, 116, 129, 155–156, 158,
165, 184
Rock, John, 45, 47
Rockefeller, John D., 85, 86, 87
Rockefeller, Nelson, 361
Roe v. Wade, 8, 123, 124, 128, 154, 185, 274,
289; American Catholic hierarchy and,
128; anniversaries of, 155, 233–234, 236, 238,
239–240, 241, 244, 289, 320, 330, 332, 362,
366; Harry Blackmun and, 248; William F.
Buckley on, 274–275; George H. W. Bush
on, 249, 272–273, 362, 367–368; Jimmy
Carter and, 197; Catholic supporters
of, 233, 381; efforts to overturn, 153, 186,
187, 198, 231, 273–275, 284, 285; Betty
Ford's support for, 152; Tom Harkin's
endorsement of, 367; modifications of,
230–231; partial-birth abortion and, 372
Rogers, William, 78, 104
Rose, Cathy Cleaver, 368
Rosenblatt, Roger, 290
Rosow, Jerome, 119
Rostow, Eugene, 60, 201–202
Rothschild, Emma, 147–148
Rove, Karl, 350, 357, 371, 374
Rowny, Edward, 204, 212
RU-486, 320, 363, 373
Rummel, Joseph, 26, 27, 28, 38
Rumsfeld, Donald, 336, 342, 346, 348
Rusiti, Sanha, 303
Rusk, Dean, 53, 55
Russett, Bruce, 302
Rustin, Bayard, 35
Rust v. Sullivan, 283, 289
Ryan, Joseph, 254
Ryce, Amos, 31

Saigon, fall of, 53–59, 105, 139, 141
SALT I, 108–109, 199
SALT II, 11, 169, 171–172, 176, 199
Santorum, Rick, 329, 355, 366
Sarajevo, 299–300
Scalia, Antonin, 240, 275, 285

Schaefer, Catherine, 21, 45–46, 47, 78
Schlesinger, James, 200, 201
Secretariat for Pro-Life Activities, 320, 331, 334, 368, 381
Senate, U.S.: Ad Hoc Committee on the World Food Conference, 145; Banking, Housing, and Urban Affairs Committee, 229; Budget Committee, 229; Committee on Banking and Currency, 71; Committee on Human Resources, 186; Finance Committee, 116, 229; Foreign Relations Committee, 170, 174; Foreign Relations Committee Subcommittee on Arms Control, Oceans, and International Environment, 170–171; Judiciary Committee Subcommittee on Constitutional Amendments, 126, 161; Judiciary Committee Subcommittee on Constitutional Rights, 153; Judiciary Committee Subcommittee on Separation of Powers, 232; Subcommittee on Health, 179
September 11, 2001, terrorist attacks, 335, 354–355
Shalala, Donna, 309, 312–314, 332
Shannon, James, 64
Shaw, Russell, 107, 115, 155–156; on abortion, 124, 125, 131, 157, 166; Ad Hoc Committee on Pro-Life Activities and, 126; appointment of special committee for study of war and peace by, 199, 200; on Planned Parenthood, 193; Ronald Reagan and, 208–209; on women's rights, 129, 130
Shea, Donald, 222, 246, 364–365
Sheerin, John, 59, 61, 63, 98
Shehan, Lawrence, 23, 30, 39, 58, 66, 110
Shriver, Sargent, 10, 80, 81, 82, 90, 166; Carter's defeat of, 188; Congressional testimony of, 91; family planning and, 81, 83; on War on Poverty, 92
Shultz, George, 119, 206, 213
silent majority, 95, 103, 118–119
Simeon, Metropolitan, 347
Simon, William, 224
Simon Commission, 224–225, 226–228
slavery, abortion and, 236–237, 329–330
Smeal, Eleanor, 192, 194, 233
Smith, Christopher, 239, 241–242
Social Security Amendments (1967), 87, 90
Soldano, Angelo, 301, 305, 341, 346, 371
Sorensen, Theodore, 30, 34, 43, 50

Souter, David, 282, 285, 286
South Vietnam, 52, 56–57, 137
Soviet Union, 11, 169, 198, 295–296
Spellman, Francis, 25, 32, 69; death of, 60; March on Washington and, 34; Vietnam War and, 58, 59
State Children's Health Insurance Program (SCHIP), 314, 365
Steinfels, Margaret O'Brien, 8, 255, 270
Steinfels, Peter, 101–102, 105, 305
stem cell research, 363–365
Stenberg v. Carhart, 330, 372
St. Patrick's Cathedral (New York), 16, 104
Strategic Arms Reduction Talks (START), 199, 251
Strategic Defense Initiative, 209, 213, 379
Student Nonviolent Coordinating Committee (SNCC), 34, 75
Sullivan, Joseph, 220, 224, 281
Sundy, Terry, 181, 186, 188
Sununu, John, 263, 273, 274, 279, 282
Supreme Court cases: *Akron v. Akron Center for Reproductive Health*, 235, 281, 289; *Beal v. Doe*, 157, 188–189; *Boynton v. Virginia*, 27; *Brown v. Board of Education of Topeka*, 25–26, 275; *Doe v. Bolton*, 123, 274; *Griswold v. Connecticut*, 77; *Harris v. McRae*, 189–190; *Hodgson v. Minnesota*, 281, 289; *Maher v. Roe*, 189; *Poelker v. Doe*, 189; *Roe v. Wade*, 8, 10, 123, 124, 128, 152, 153, 154, 155, 185, 186, 187, 193, 197, 198, 230–231, 233–234, 236, 238, 239–240, 241, 244, 248, 249, 272–275, 284, 285, 289, 320, 330, 332, 362, 366, 367–368, 372, 381; *Rust v. Sullivan*, 283, 289; *Stenberg v. Carhart*, 330, 372; *Webster v. Reproductive Health Services*, 12, 273–276, 289, 290–291
Supreme Court justices, U.S. *See* individual justices
Susman, Frank, 275
Sweeney, John, 161–162, 163
Synagogue Council of America, 29, 30, 33, 66, 70, 71, 114, 116
Synod of Bishops, 107, 110, 170–171
Szoka, Edmund, 219–220, 263

Takaki, Ronald, 138
Talmadge, Herman, 67
Tanner, Paul, 18, 36, 23, 49, 50, 75, 78, 84, 89
Tauran, Jean-Louis, 301, 303, 306

INDEX {501}

Taylor, Michael, 331
Tenet, George, 341–342, 346
Terry, Randall, 278, 321
test-ban treaty, 22
Thao, Christopher, 138
Thomas, Clarence, 265, 283–285, 288
Thomas Aquinas, St., 6
Thornton, Tracey, 328
Title X, 239, 241, 279, 283
Tobin, William, 96
Tomal, Annette, 330–331
Toolen, Thomas, 33, 38, 68, 75
Towey, James, 355, 357
Tracy, Robert, 37, 39
Tragedy of American Compassion, The (Olasky), 349–350
Tri-Faith Statement on Welfare Reform, 116
Trudeau, Pierre, 225, 230
True Selma Story, The (booklet), 75
Truman, Harry S., 176, 335
Tuttle, Robert, 360

Unborn Victims of Violence Act, 368
United Nations (UN), 17–18, 79, 80, 171, 174, 213; Bosnia and, 294; George W. Bush and, 336; Fourth World Conference on Women, 333; hunger and, 142, 147; Indochina and, 136; Middle East and, 258; Vietnam War and, 52, 53
United States: refugee resettlement in, 135; surrender in Vietnam, 134; urban crisis in, 259–261
United States Catholic Conference (USCC), 3, 101, 119–120, 136, 173, 179, 190, 196, 210, 283; abortion and, 8, 166–167, 190–191, 196, 221, 236, 243, 273–275, 277, 288, 311, 329, 331, 366–367, 370; George W. Bush and, 352–353; Committee on Law and Public Policy of, 125, 161, 183; Terence Cooke and, 242–243; elderly and, 266; Family Life Division of, 114; family planning and, 89; Gerald R. Ford and, 135; health care and, 308; on international relations, 99, 100, 256, 296, 342; nuclear arms and, 170–171, 172; on war and peace, 71, 97, 143, 146, 210, 256, 295; Aloysius Welsh and, 113; Women's Lobby and, 131; world hunger and, 143
United States Civil Rights Commission, 28, 123

United States Conference of Catholic Bishops (USCCB), 3–4, 336, 342–343, 356, 358, 364, 382
Unlevel Playing Field (DiIulio), 354–355
urban crisis, 112, 259–272

Vagnozzi, Egidio, 23, 52, 69, 75, 77–78, 90
Valenti, Jack, 52, 58
Vance, Cyrus, 172, 174
Vatican Council II (1962–1965), 19, 24, 37, 110; *Gaudium et Spes* ("Of Hope and Joy") of, 170, 172; *Pastoral Constitution on the Church in the Modern World*, 58, 106
Versailles, Treaty of, 293–294
Vietnam War, 13, 53, 95, 96, 103, 110, 133; antiwar movement and, 95; Cambodianization of, 98–103; Catholic bishops of South Vietnam and, 52–53; end of, 103–104, 133, 134; Lyndon Johnson and, 10, 11, 51–64, 104–105; as moral issue, 61, 63–64, 100, 107; Richard M. Nixon and, 94–111; Paul VI on, 51; refugees and, 133–141; United States Catholic Bishops on, 104–105; Vietnamization of, 95–98
Voting Rights Act (1965), 10, 64, 69–70

Wackerman, Daniel, 298
Wagner, John, 36
Wagner, Steve, 350
Waidmann, Brian, 283
Walinsky, Adam, 183
Wallace, George, 39, 68
Warner, Michael, 9, 139–140, 175, 304
War on Poverty, 51, 88, 90, 91, 92, 118
Washington, D.C.: antiwar protests in, 102; November 15 march on, 96–97
Washington, Walter, 73
Watergate scandal, 10, 133, 168
Watkins, James, 211, 217
Wattleton, Faye, 192, 193
Wead, Douglas, 263–265, 346, 379
Weakland, Rembert, 174, 218–219, 221–224, 226, 228, 229, 230, 265, 272, 281, 359
weapons of mass destruction (WMDs), 340–342
Weaver, Robert, 71
Weber, Paul, 129
Weber, Vin, 239, 241–242
Webster v. Reproductive Health Services, 273–276, 289, 290–291

Weddington, Sarah, 193
Weigel, George, 9, 216, 254, 255
Weinberger, Caspar, 145, 154, 201–202, 204
Weisskopf, Victor, 200
welfare reform: Bill Clinton and, 349, 350; Richard M. Nixon and, 111–123, 149
Wells, John, 361
Welsh, Aloysius, 113
Westmoreland, William, 54
Whealon, John, 163, 171
Wheatcroft, G. R., 64
While America Watched: The Bosnian Tragedy (Jennings), 296
White, Lee, 28, 42
white ethnic Catholics, 120–121
White House Conference on Faith-Based and Community Initiatives, 355–356, 360
White House Conference on Families, 190
White House Conference on Health, 82
White House Office for Women's Initiatives and Outreach, 363
White House Office of Faith-Based and Community Initiatives, 351–352
White House's National Goals Research Staff, 119
Whittlesey, Faith, 222, 226
Wiesel, Elie, 303
Wilder, Douglas, 287–288
Wilson, Woodrow, 21, 293
Winters, Francis, 139, 199, 255, 257
Wofford, Harris, 28, 39, 307
World Food Conference, 142, 143, 150–151
world hunger, 11, 140–152
World Justice and Peace, Division of, 60, 97

Yugoslavia, 293, 294

Zablocki, Clement, 84, 210
Zahn, Gordon, 107, 215, 257

www.ingramcontent.com/pod-product-compliance
Lightning Source LLC
Chambersburg PA
CBHW012333230426
43664CB00044B/2889